CHRISTOPHER LEE

The Loneliness of Evil

CHRISTOPHER LEE

The Loneliness of Evil

Stephen Mosley

Midnight Marquee Press, Inc.
Baltimore, Maryland, USA

Stephen's writing and drawings are superb.
His imagination is fantastic,
but he must learn to move away from vampires and werewolves.
—The author's school report, 1988

Copyright © 2022 Stephen Mosley
Interior Layout: Gary J. Svehla
Cover Design: Susan Svehla
Copy Editor: Janet Atkinson

Without limiting the rights under copyright reserved above, no part of this publication may be reproduced, stored in or introduced into a retrieval system, or transmitted, in any form, or by any means (electronic, mechanical, photocopying, recording or otherwise), without the prior written permission of the copyright owner or the publishers of the book.

ISBN 978-1-64430-128-9
Library of Congress Catalog Card Number 2022938074
Manufactured in the United States of America
First Printing May 2022

For my parents—
who set the video for *Dracula: Prince of Darkness* all those years ago.
—and—
For my beautiful Ellie,
with Love.

And finally in Memory of Ted Newsom (1952-2020)

Table of Contents

9	Introduction: A Secret World of Fears and Dreams
13	Fallen Among Barbarians: The Early Years (1922-1955)
18	Alias John Preston (1955)
20	The Curse of Frankenstein (1956)
29	Dracula aka Horror of Dracula (1957)
37	Corridors of Blood (1958)
39	The Hound of the Baskervilles (1958)
43	The Man Who Could Cheat Death (1958)
48	The Mummy (1959)
52	Uncle Was a Vampire (1959)
54	The City of the Dead (1959)
58	The Two Faces of Dr. Jekyll (1959)
62	The Terror of the Tongs (1960)
65	The Hands of Orlac (1960)
67	One Step Beyond: "The Sorcerer" (1960)
68	Taste of Fear aka Scream of Fear (1960)
70	Hercules in the Haunted World (1961)
72	The Whip and the Body (1963)
74	Katarsis (1963)
75	The Virgin of Nuremberg (1963)
76	Crypt of Horror (1963)
77	The Gorgon (1963)
81	The Alfred Hitchcock Hour: "The Sign of Satan" (1964)
82	The Castle of the Living Dead (1964)
84	Dr. Terror's House of Horrors (1964)
87	She (1964)
90	The Skull (1965)
94	The Face of Fu Manchu Films (1965)/The Brides of Fu Manchu (1966)/The Vengeance of Fu Manchu (1966)/The Blood of Fu Manchu (1967)/The Castle of Fu Manchu (1968)
98	Dracula: Prince of Darkness (1965)
104	Rasputin: The Mad Monk (1965)
106	Theatre of Death (1965)
108	Circus of Fear (1965)
110	The Avengers: "Never, Never Say Die"/"The Interrogators" (1967/1968)
112	Night of the Big Heat (1967)
114	Blood Demon (1967)
116	The Devil Rides Out (1967)
122	Curse of the Crimson Altar (1968)/Whicker's World: " I Don't Like My Monsters to Have Oedipus Complexes" (1968)
127	Dracula Has Risen from the Grave (1968)
132	The Oblong Box (1968)
134	Eugenie ... The Story of Her Journey into Perversion (1969)
135	Scream and Scream Again (1969)
137	The Bloody Judge (1969)

138	Count Dracula (1969)/The Magic Christian (1969)/One More Time (1969)/Cuadecuc Vampir (1969)/Umbracle (1970)
143	Taste the Blood of Dracula (1969)
149	Scars of Dracula (1970)
155	The House That Dripped Blood (1970)
157	I, Monster (1970)
160	In Search of Dracula (1971)/Theatre Macabre (1971)
163	Dracula A.D. 1972 (1971)
168	Horror Express (1971)
171	The Creeping Flesh (1972)
174	Death Line (1972)
178	Nothing But the Night (1972)
182	The Wicker Man (1972)/A Feast at Midnight (1994)/Strictly Supernatural (1996)/The Wicker Tree (2009)/Season of the Witch (2010)
188	Poor Devil (1972)
189	The Hollywood Meatcleaver Massacre (1972/1975)/The Occult: Mysteries of the Supernatural (1977)/Tales of the Haunted: Evil Stalks this House (1981)
191	Dark Places (1972)
192	The Satanic Rites of Dracula (1972)
196	Orson Welles Great Mysteries: "The Leather Funnel" (1973)/Space 1999: "Earthbound" (1974)
198	To the Devil a Daughter (1975)
203	The Keeper (1975)
204	Dracula and Son (1976)
205	Starship Invasions (1976)
207	End of the World (1977)
209	House of the Long Shadows (1982)
213	Faerie Tale Theatre: "The Boy Who Left Home to Find Out About the Shivers" (1983)/New Magic (1983)/Mio in the Land of Faraway (1986)
215	Howling II (1984)
217	Panga (1989)
218	Gremlins 2: The New Batch (1989)/The Rainbow Thief (1990)
222	Funny Man (1993)
222	Edgar Allan Poe's Tales of Mystery and Imagination (1994)
224	Flesh and Blood: The Ted Newsom Productions (1994-1996)
233	Talos the Mummy (1997)
235	Ghost Stories for Christmas (2000)
237	Multi-Media Macabre: Books, Audio Recordings and Video Games
245	The Tim Burton Films
248	Final Fantasies (2000-2015)
254	Sources and Acknowledgements
255	Select Bibliography
256	Author's Biography
257	Index of Film & TV Titles

INTRODUCTION

A Secret World of Fears and Dreams

Anything that's different, anything that's unconventional, anything where I can surprise somebody is always interesting …—Christopher Lee, to Jane Killick, *Shivers* #13 (December 1994)

When Sir Christopher Lee passed away at the age of 93 on Sunday June 7, 2015, it was truly the end of an era. He was the last of the great horror stars, a hallowed lineage that began with Lon Chaney, Bela Lugosi and Boris Karloff in the 1920s and '30s, and continued with Lee's contemporaries Peter Cushing and Vincent Price in the latter half of the 20th century.

Given that they make the unbelievable believable, the stars of horror films deserve wider recognition for their art, especially as even good actors can fail to convince in genre roles. Compare Robert De Niro's Monster in *Mary Shelley's Frankenstein* (1993) and Richard Roxburgh's Dracula in *Van Helsing* (2003) to Lee's performances of the same parts and you'll see what I mean. Moreover, contrast Laurence Olivier's Van Helsing in the 1978 *Dracula* with Peter Cushing's interpretation of the character, and you'll find yourself wishing to see what Cushing could have made of *King Lear*.

"*Dracula*—the shame of it!" Olivier complained to his son on accepting the vampire hunter role. But why should he have felt that way? After all, Shakespeare was not ashamed when he used supernatural effects to enhance his plays (the witches of *Macbeth*, the ghost of *Hamlet*'s father and the monstrous Caliban of *The Tempest*, to name but three examples). The monsters of folklore

Christopher Lee, Hazel Court and Anton Diffring attending a Hammer Christmas party.

INVITE CHRISTOPHER LEE INSIDE YOUR LIVING ROOM! - with HAMMER'S DRACULA L.P.

A must for all fear-fans, this album features the voice of Christopher Lee narrating the chilling saga of Count Dracula, Lord of the Undead!

Plus... on the 'B' side, four fantastic theme tunes from FEAR IN THE NIGHT, SHE, THE VAMPIRE LOVERS and DR. JEKYLL AND SISTER HYDE.

Order now, adding 30p to cover post and packing, from:
HOUSE OF HAMMER
BARGAIN BASEMENT,
GENERAL BOOK DISTRIBUTION,
135-141 WARDOUR STREET,
LONDON, W1.

ONLY £4.20 Plus Postage

"Invite Christopher Lee inside your living room," says the ad for a record that appeared in a 1977 issue of *House of Hammer* magazine.

have provided the lifeblood of our storytelling culture since the earliest shamans donned their pelts. Despite this, a sneering critical attitude still prevails when it comes to horror cinema, as if, in the eyes of "highbrow" critics, the imagination and emotions that genre films cater to are qualities to be ashamed of, rather than explored.

To my mind, Dracula is a classical role up there with Hamlet and Richard III that any actor worth his salt would be willing to sink his teeth into. And no one sank their teeth into the part more times onscreen than Christopher Lee, whose accomplishments in the genre are far more varied than one might initially expect.

I first became acquainted with Lee in the summer of 1987, when I was a monster-fixated six-year-old. The previous year, I had fallen under the spell of Lugosi's *Dracula* (1930), Karloff's *Frankenstein* (1931) and *The Mummy* (1932), and Lon Chaney, Jr.'s *The Wolf Man* (1941) during a Channel 4 season of Universal horror films. Thanks to forbidden glances at *Fangoria* magazine on the racks of my local news agent, I was also aware of Freddy Krueger's gruesome visage from *A Nightmare on Elm Street* (1984) and sequels. Until I saw Christopher Lee, however, I'd never realized that there was an Eastman Color bridge between the quaint, black-and-white horrors of the Universal era and those grisly *Elm Street* pictures.

I'll never forget creeping downstairs that fateful Friday night and catching the closing moments of Hammer's *Dracula* (1957) on television. Unused to seeing the vampire character in color, at first I thought I was watching a commercial (I recall Dracula being used to advertise cigars at this time). When I saw the Count crumble into dust, however, I knew this was the real deal.

The program was *Hammer: The Studio That Dripped Blood!*—an excellent BBC documentary, which I sat down to watch in full the following morning, my parents having videotaped it. I was especially shocked by a clip from *The Curse of Frankenstein* (1956) which showed Lee's Creature throttling Peter Cushing. What alarmed me most was that the monster's head wasn't square (as Boris Karloff's had been), but rounded, giving the Creature a more pathetically human look. Hammer's sense of realism brought the horror closer, made it more direct. To my young eyes, Karloff's Monster was a misunderstood, child-like being, whereas Lee's creation, with its lightning-fast lunges, was far more visceral and frightening.

Lee and Cushing could also be seen in the documentary, but while Cushing was interviewed at home, with a porcelain figure of Winston Churchill looking on from the windowsill, Lee was filmed in a gloomy, candlelit studio, which lent his face the shadowy look of Dracula. Nevertheless, he was able to discuss his work with typical insight: "What we did was to create a morality play. It was a fairy story. It really was fantasy, it was magic …"

The documentary preceded a season of Hammer films on BBC 2 which included *Dracula: Prince of Darkness* (1965), *Rasputin: The Mad Monk* (1965), *Dracula Has Risen from the Grave* (1968) and *The Devil Rides Out* (1967). As well as seeing Lee in the aforementioned horrors, I also thrilled to his performances in more family-oriented fare such as *The Three Musketeers* (1973), *The Man with the Golden Gun* (1974) and *Return from Witch Mountain* (1977). I would sit through any film he appeared in, collecting them on video. At the age of 19, I plucked up the courage to write to the great man. I didn't expect a response, I just wanted to let him know how much his work meant to me. Over a year later, I was pleasantly surprised to receive a photo in response to my gushy letter, complete with printed signature ("Warmest regards, Christopher Lee").

This book, then, is my tribute to those treasured years of imagination. My aim is for a comprehensive overview of Lee's work in the horror genre, including books, audio recordings and video games (most of which have never been examined in detail before). For the main part, dates given are those of production rather than release and, due to the tiresome preponderance of alternative monikers, I have decided to call the films by their most familiar English-language titles. I have also conducted new interviews with Lee's co-workers, some of them speaking here for the first time, which shed fresh light upon the man and his work. (Unless otherwise stated, quotes from Lee himself are taken from his autobiography, *Tall, Dark and Gruesome*, published by Midnight Marquee Press.)

But, before we go on, let us first define "horror." Lee famously hated the word, preferring "terror." *The Mummy* (1959) "certainly wasn't a horror film," he told John Brosnan, and: "You can't call [Lon Chaney's] *The Hunchback of Notre Dame* a horror film." ("I can," was Brosnan's blithe response.)

As this exchange illustrates, horror can be a subjective term. Lee would most likely be unimpressed by *The Wicker Man* (1972) being described as a horror film, but I am happy to call it just that—for not only does this movie horrify us, it also appeals to our sense of wonder and imagination.

An element of the otherworldly is, I believe, essential to a good horror film. The best, and even worst, of the genre can be experienced with the same feeling of magic and awe that one finds in, say, *The Wizard of Oz* (1939) or *The 5,000 Fingers of Dr. T* (1952). As well as presenting scenes of great creative beauty, the allegories of horror films can reveal far more about life than so-called "naturalistic" dramas designed specifically to depict "reality" (which often forget that imagination is a fundamental part of the human condition anyway). In fact, far from being merely escapist, horror allows us to confront the more searching questions of existence: Who are we? Where do we come from? Where are we going?

In addition, the words "horror film," for me at least, conjure up the cozy thrill of being huddled in the darkness before a glowing screen, an equivalent to the reading of ghost stories round the fire in more distant times. A further appeal lies within the genre's romantic imagery, derived mainly from Gothic literature—a world of haunted castles, mist-shrouded cemeteries and lurching monsters, in which our own inner lives are explored, our secret world of fears and dreams.

"The best horror films are adult fairy tales, no more and no less," director Terence Fisher wrote in his Foreword to Alan Frank's 1977 book *Horror Films*, before pointing out that film, with all of its trickery, is the ideal medium for imaginative expression. After all, it was Georges Méliès (1861-1938) who, at the turn of the 20th century, first realized that cinema could show us more than trains arriving at stations. By presenting such wondrous visions as giant snow-beasts, expanding heads and a rocket in the eye of the Moon, Méliès gave filmmakers the key to let loose their internal worlds, and cinemagoers were all the richer.

The "adult fairy tales" Lee made with Terence Fisher are a vital part of British cinema. Not only were they the first versions of *Dracula* and *Frankenstein* to be made in color, but Hammer were also the first to film these classic works in the country that they were written. As David Pirie points out, in his seminal tome *A Heritage of Horror* (1973), the Gothic horror film is as indigenous to Britain as the Western is to America.

In addition, the range of the Horror Film seems far broader than any other genre. As well as the traditional elements mentioned above, secular shockers like *Psycho* (1959), or even Stanley Kubrick's *Dr. Strangelove* (1963), can fall within the horror category, what with their imaginative staging of frightening possibilities. This book, however, will focus on films in the supernatural vein, and/or those that were clearly packaged as terror ventures, even if their content was less horrific than the advertising suggested (e.g., the Fu Manchu series).

Also included are horror-science fiction hybrids like *Night of the Big Heat* (1967) and projects in which the actor's renown as a "horror star" was clearly part of the deal (e.g., his guest-villain spots on cult TV shows like *The Avengers* [1961-1969]). Regrettably, Lee's out-and-out fantasy sagas, such as *Arabian Adventure* (1978) or *The Lord of the Rings* (2000), will not be covered in any depth as they were marketed outside of the Horror Film's usual target audience. They will, however, be mentioned within the text, along with the actor's other notable work.

While all of Lee's Hammer horrors are, of course, explored in depth, there is no room, alas, for similar treatment to be accorded the two swashbucklers he made for the company, *The Pirates of Blood River* (1961) and *The Devil-Ship Pirates* (1963).

Alan Frank, who appeared as an extra in *Corridors of Blood*, then turned to authoring books—many covers featuring the likeness of Christopher Lee (the artist here is Les Edwards).

Although the latter was issued by Warner Home Video in 1999 with "Horror Classic" daubed across its blood-red packaging, it is no such thing. While this serves as a good example of how synonymous Lee's name is with the genre, it's worth noting that his work in other fields earned him the record for most onscreen sword fights and made him an honorary member of at least three stunt unions. According to the *Guinness Book of World Records*, Lee made more films than any other actor.

With such accomplishments, would Lee have welcomed an in-depth exploration of his horror legacy? After all, it's been broadly reported that he wished to distance himself from his Dracula portrayals, especially in later years. While answering questions at the 2013 Locarno Film Festival, for example, the actor felt compelled to say: "I made very few [horror films]. I counted them the other day … maybe 12?"—a conservative estimate that would make this present volume very slim indeed.

Are we to take from this that the actor was ashamed of his horror association?

In actual fact, of all the stars connected to the genre, Lee was the one who loved it the most. From an early age, his reading habits embraced the macabre; this healthy regard for fantastic literature is evidenced by a judicious selection of tales, and enlightened editorial comments, within several anthologies. One such book, *The Great Villains* (1978), saw Lee expound upon his

The Loneliness of Evil

A smiling Dracula played by Christopher Lee.

approach to screen villainy: "Villains … are very often tragic, desperately unhappy creatures who have been pushed into their wicked ways by sheer force of circumstances. As an actor, it is above all this aspect of villainy, 'the loneliness of evil' as I call it, which most fascinates me."

Furthermore, in his Introduction to *Vampire Stories* (Michael O'Mara Books, 1992), Peter Cushing recalled that his "very dear" friend's party piece was a recitation of the Dylan Thomas poem "Welsh Vampire." Cushing described the "bloodcurdling relish" which Lee brought to the rhyme, adding that it "always went down extremely well." This is hardly the behavior of a man who felt ashamed of his bloodsucking past. He even named his pet cat Renfield (because it ate flies).

Lee also kept up with scary films at the cinema, often citing *The Night of the Hunter* (1954) and *Rosemary's Baby* (1967) as favorites. When the opportunity to produce his own movie came about in 1972, he didn't make a historical romance or screwball comedy, but *chose* to make a horror film (*Nothing But the Night*).

It was around then that Lee, ironically, became disenchanted with the way the genre was presented onscreen: His own tasteful effort found itself upstaged at the box office by an ever-increasing display of cheap, exploitative devices, such as misogyny and gratuitous brutality, which left little to the imagination. As a result, one doesn't have to dig very far to find opinions of the kind Lee expressed to Craig Cabell and Howard Maxford in *Shivers* #50 (February 1998): "I've often been quoted as saying that I would *never* do another horror movie, and that's totally untrue. What I *did* say was: 'I'm not going to make any more poorly-made horror movies.'"

By 2009, the actor was telling CNN: "I find it quite nauseating what they do [today] … The blood is all over the screen like an avalanche—the mutilation—dreadful things, and I just don't enjoy that." Lee was referencing such modern franchises as *Friday the 13th* (1979-2008), *Saw* (2003-2019) and *Hostel* (2005-2011), which forsake the ghost-train chills of his own output and emphasize special effects above acting. By contrast, Lee's philosophy was always: "What you don't see is far more frightening than what you do see."

What he objected to, therefore, was not imagination, but *lack of imagination*—particularly in the way his persona was reflected by the media.

For instance, when Lee was knighted in 2009, even the respectable newspapers carried headlines like *ARISE, SIR DRACULA* and *KNIGHT OF THE LIVING DEAD*—all of which were accompanied by blood-smeared portraits of the actor as Dracula. BBC News actually emblazoned their footage of Lee outside Buckingham Palace with the words *DRACULA KNIGHTED*. While I had previously been baffled by Lee's reported reluctance to discuss Dracula, when I saw all of this, I had sympathy.

Nonetheless, few actors have spanned the generations with such lasting appeal. One of the secrets to Lee's longevity was an ability to keep with the times. From his ventures with Hammer—whose swift gradation of flesh and blood into a staid 1950s cinema broke new ground—to his work, in the next century, on numerous video games and interactive formats, Lee was constantly abreast of advancements in his industry. Consequently, this book can be read not only as an alternative history of the horror film, but also of the myriad developments within cinema itself.

So, without further ado, in the words of Bram Stoker's immortal Count: "Enter freely. Go safely and leave something of the happiness you bring." It is time for the lights to go down.

Prince Charles bestows a knighthood on Christopher Lee.

Fallen Among Barbarians:

The Early Years
1922-1955

Just think of all the appalling people you'll meet!
—Christopher Lee's mother, on learning that
her son wanted to be an actor.

Christopher Frank Carandini Lee seemed predestined for a life in horror. At the time of his conception, the great German filmmaker, F.W. Murnau, was creating *Nosferatu*—the first screen adaptation of Bram Stoker's *Dracula* and, in Lee's opinion, "the greatest vampire film ever made" (*The Monster Times*, May 1972). In addition, Lee's birth in London, on Saturday May 27, 1922, was not only preceded by a thunderstorm, but also coincided with the 11th birthday of Vincent Price (Peter Cushing had turned nine the day before).

The son of Geoffrey Lee (1879-1941), an ex-colonel of the King's Royal Rifle Corps, and Estelle Marie (1889-1981), an Italian contessa, Christopher joined a sister, Xandra (1917-2002), who later became the mother of famed classical actress Dame Harriet Walter (b. 1950).

In a 2002 *Sunday Times* interview with Ann McFerran, Harriet—who eventually followed her uncle into the *Star Wars* franchise—recalls being inspired to take up acting after visiting the Hammer *Dracula* sets as a girl. She also remembered stuffing her bra with socks and donning high heels and dark glasses in order to get into a showing of *Dracula: Prince of Darkness*. "To me as a child, my uncle was a roving, exotic bachelor figure ... The heart rate went up when he walked in the door." It certainly did when she was nine years old, as Harriet told McFerran: "Soon after [*The Mummy*] came out, [Christopher] had supper with my parents, and came up to my bedroom to kiss me goodnight. He knocked on my door and his silhouette in the lighted corridor appeared in the doorway. Then he lurched into the dark bedroom and did his mummy's walk towards me. I was absolutely terrified." Nevertheless: "He was a great raconteur and a flamboyant dresser ... so very handsome and very gentle."

As well as being the great-grandson of opera singer Marie Carandini ("the Tasmanian Nightingale," 1826-1894), Lee could trace his ancestry back, on his mother's side, to the Holy Roman Emperor, Charlemagne (ca. 742-814). According to *The Ingrid Pitt Bedside Companion for Vampire Lovers* (Batsford, 1998), one of Charlemagne's proclamations was "that anyone burning alleged vampires without good proof would themselves be executed." Long after his own onscreen executions as a vampire, Lee himself discovered a personal lineage that stretched back to the 15th century (as he told Lee Bury in 1980): "I took part in a psychic regression session with Kebrina Kinkade and saw myself as a man of 70 lying on my deathbed. I didn't see my burial, but I saw a plain stone with a coat of arms on it and the inscription, 'He Served God and Man.' I saw my name: Francesco di Sarsanio, Duke. This is extraordinary because my grandfather's name—in this present life—was Francesco and he was the Marquis of Sarsanio." Most amazingly, author

Lee's great-grandmother, Marie Carandini

Mark A. Miller notes that Lee was a distant relative (through his grandmother) of Percy Bysshe Shelley (1792-1822)—a fact confirmed by the actor when he introduced Karloff's *Frankenstein* on the Sci-Fi Channel in October 1993.

Not only was Shelley one of England's most celebrated Romantic poets, but the only two novels he authored, *Zastrozzi* and *St. Irvyne* (both published in 1810), are works of Gothic horror involving vengeful passions and devilish pacts. Shelley was also the partner of Mary Wollstonecraft Godwin (1797-1851), whom he married in December 1816. Earlier that year, on May 27 (the future birthdate of Christopher Lee), they joined Lord Byron and Dr. John Polidori at the Villa Diodati in Geneva, Switzerland—an event which led to the birth of the vampire and Frankenstein in literature.

Over 140 years later, Shelley's descendant found fame in films based on those very concepts. In his 1974 book *Christopher Lee's New Chamber of Horrors*, the actor revealed that when he later lived in Switzerland, he "took a house very close to the Villa Diodati" and visited the surroundings where Shelley and company "told their ghost stories that wet summer of 1816."

Although growing up in auspicious surroundings, Lee's half-Italian background incited racist taunts from peers (Boris Karloff, himself of Anglo-Indian heritage, had also suffered xenophobia when young; both actors would first earn success by portraying characters deemed as outsiders). When he was only six, Lee's parents divorced, but, on a happier note, his mother's second marriage brought a step-cousin in the shape of future James Bond creator, Ian Fleming (1908-1964). Around this time, Lee made a prescient acting debut in the name part of *Rumpelstiltskin* for a school production (Peter Cushing's first kindergarten role was as a goblin, Vincent Price's was as a sprite, and Boris Karloff was the Demon King in *Cinderella*). As Lee wrote in his autobiography: "I learned at the outset that the best lines are given to the baddies and that these make the most impact on the audience—especially if there is some pathos in their situation."

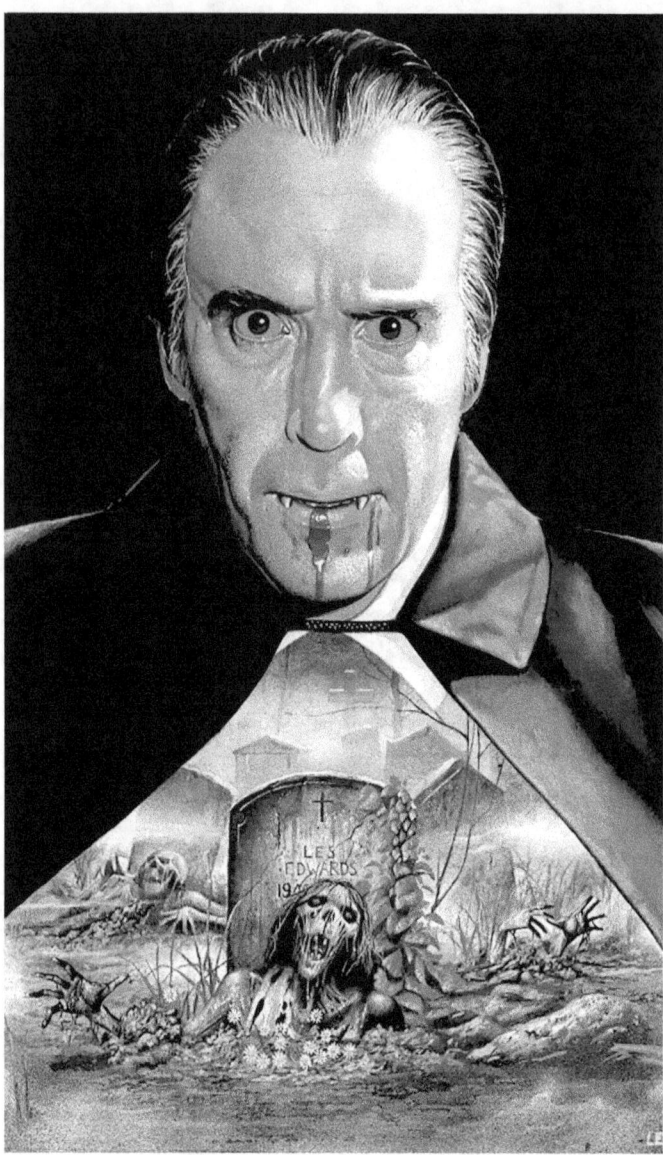

The artwork for one edition of *Christopher Lee's New Chambers of Horrors*.

Aside from this pearl of wisdom, Lee seemed disinterested in anything else the education system had to offer. At the age of 14, he just missed out on the desired Eton scholarship—the interview for which had been conducted by ghost story writer extraordinaire M.R. James—and attended, instead, the more military-minded Wellington College. Discipline here was harsh, with canings meted out for the mildest offences: "It seemed I had fallen among barbarians," Lee recorded in his memoirs, "with nothing to be done about that but grit it out for the next four years."

The adolescent sought escape in fantasy: "I was a solitary by nature and spent much of my time reading books in trees." Lee's tastes in literature already ran to the fantastic as he absorbed works by Bram Stoker, Edgar Allan Poe and Sir Arthur Conan Doyle, along with the supernatural tales of E.F. Benson and Algernon Blackwood, little appreciating that adaptations of the first three authors would loom large in his later career. A personal acquaintance with E.F. Benson came even earlier when the writer, a former Wellington pupil, revisited his old school to give a reading. In *Christopher Lee's New Chamber of Horrors*, Lee recalled: "I can still hear his quiet voice chilling the blood of every single person in that room—I don't think anyone, masters or pupils, slept a wink that night!"

The teenage Lee reached his final height of six feet four inches ("at night dreams came to me in which I was stretched out on the rack"). Towering above his classmates, he couldn't help but feel further adrift ("I am surrounded by midgets. Their midgetry is enviable"). While holidaying in Paris, in the summer of 1939, he was taken to see the last public execution in France by a journalist friend of his stepfather's, who could have been describing Lee's future audiences when he said: "You'll never forget how people behave. How people like to see blood." The sight of the blade severing the murderer's head left Lee "afflicted (as I would be ever more) by nightmares of the guillotine."

That same year, along with the outbreak of World War II, Lee's stepfather went bankrupt. To keep the wolves from the door, the 17-year-old was forced to abandon his education. Finding employment in a London office, he cast aside the drudgery of licking stamps and making tea by becoming a frequent attendee of the cinema. To author Jonathan Rigby, Lee confessed that he was "scared witless" by Bela Lugosi's nasty British shocker *The Dark Eyes of London* (1939), little dreaming that he would one day be billed above that film's leading lady, Greta Gynt, in the 1956 thriller *Fortune is a Woman*. "I saw almost everything that [Boris Karloff] did with Bela Lugosi," Lee told Marcus Hearn of his cinema-going days, while describing the impact *Frankenstein* had on him as a youngster: "I was appropriately petrified, expecting [the Monster] to come up out of the floor and wake me up when I was in bed …" Despite this, *Son of Frankenstein* (1938) was Lee's personal favorite of the Universal series, on accord of its cast. He also recalled enjoying the gruesome melodramas of Tod Slaughter.

Born Norman Carter Slaughter, in Newcastle upon Tyne, 1885, Tod brought his raised eyebrows and loping gait to a handful of films in the 1930s, perhaps the most effective being *The Face at the Window* (1939), with its galvanized corpse and drooling "wolf man." Lee's screen idol, however, was Conrad Veidt (1893-1943), whom historian Denis Gifford would call "the first great figure of fright" for his roles in *The Cabinet of Dr. Caligari* (1919), *Waxworks* (1923) and *The Student of Prague* (1926). (He had also been Universal's first choice to play *Dracula* before Bela Lugosi claimed the role; Lugosi had dubbed Veidt's voice for the Hungarian-language sound version of *The Last Performance* [1927]). A mere two days after seeing him as *The Spy in Black* (1938), a gobsmacked Lee encountered Veidt on a golf course, and was further awed when the German star deigned to chat to his young fan for a good half hour, before departing to Hollywood and films like *Casablanca* (1942).

After the death of his father in 1941, Lee joined the RAF, but his enthusiasm to aid the war effort as a pilot was hampered by a defective optic nerve. His initial disappointment was countered shortly thereafter by successful application into Intelligence work, firstly as a prison warder for the Rhodesian Police Force. Here, Lee experienced the first of many wartime horrors (including two wounded buttocks, seven bouts of malaria and various concentration camp visits), which instilled in him a staggering emotional breadth to put to use as an actor. While filming *The Lord of the Rings* some 60 years later, director Peter Jackson instructed Lee to cry out when his character was stabbed in the back. The actor, recalling his own experience, questioned this decision and emitted instead a more truthful noise. "All wars are terrible," Lee told an audience at the Rome Film Festival in 2009, "and most of the time they're political. I've seen things done in wartime which I've tried to forget …"

After the war, Lee felt somewhat aimless on his return to London. While regaling his mother's cousin, Niccolo Carandini, with his exploits over lunch one afternoon, the older man took note of Lee's story-telling skills and suggested: "Have you ever thought of being an actor?"

Christopher Lee and Edana Romney in his first film *Corridor of Mirrors* (1947)

Against his mother's wishes, Lee acquired an introduction to Josef Somlo of Two Cities Films. Somlo took one look at the novice thespian and declared: "I don't know why people waste my time sending me people like you. You are much too tall to be an actor, and you are far too foreign-looking." These were words that Lee would hear repeatedly during the formative years of his career, but they only served to make him more determined.

Lee secured dramatic training at the J. Arthur Rank Company of Youth (better known today as the "Rank Charm School") where his fellow students included Diana Dors (*Nothing But the Night*), Hazel Court (*The Curse of Frankenstein*), Carol Marsh (*Dracula*), and Patricia Owens (future leading lady of *The Fly*). From here, he embarked to Paris in February 1947 for his first film: Produced by Rudolph Cartier (who would go on to direct the BBC's *Quatermass* serials, as well as *Nineteen Eighty-Four* with Peter Cushing), *Corridor of Mirrors* is a twee but visually resplendent fairy tale, which concerns an age-spanning romance between Edana Romney—who also wrote and co-produced—and Eric Portman—star of Tod Slaughter's *Maria Marten* (1935) and *The Crimes of Stephen Hawke* (1936). The film's opulent shadows, courtesy of cinematographer André Thomas, are invested with a Cocteau-like sensibility, and, in a portent of things to come, the story is conveyed from a Chamber of Horrors wax exhibit. While Lee can make little impact with his single onscreen line ("Take a look, standing in the entrance: Lord Byron"), *Corridor of Mirrors* does mark an impressive debut for director Terence Young (1915-1994). Not only did Young go on to establish the cinematic character of James Bond with *Dr. No* (1962), *From Russia with Love* (1963) and *Thunderball* (1965) but he also directed *Wait Until Dark* (1967), a film which Stephen King cites, in *Danse Macabre*, as one of the scariest ever made.

Corridor of Mirrors would go on to become one of the movies introduced by Maila Nurmi's iconic horror host on *The Vampira Show* (1954-1955), where it nestled alongside cheapies like *King of the Zombies* (1941), *The Flying Serpent* (1945) and *Strangler of the Swamp* (1945). It also features Lois Maxwell (1927-2007), to whom Lee became briefly engaged. The romance broke off, however, when Lois was summoned by Warner Bros. to Hollywood, where her attendant publicity wondered whether her fiancé "will come here to make movies or she will go to England." As it was, Lee remained at home (Maxwell would later be spooked by *The Haunting* [1962] and immortalized as Miss Moneypenny in the James Bond films, including Lee's *The Man with the Golden Gun*).

It was while filming his second movie, *One Night with You* (1947), at Denham Studios that Lee slipped into his third: Hearing that Laurence Olivier was both directing and starring as *Hamlet* on the soundstage next door, Lee snuck onto the set, garbed in a stray spear carrier's outfit. The Player King scene was being shot (with future Hammer regular Patrick Troughton) and at its dramatic denouement, Lee heaved out a great cry of "Lights!" Despite his efforts, Lee can neither be heard nor seen in the finished film. Peter Cushing, on the other hand, is quite visible as the King's messenger, Osric.

"If I played Hamlet, they'd call it a horror film," Cushing once said. A tale of ghosts, madness and murder, which takes place within a gloomy, mist-wreathed castle, *Hamlet* can't be described as anything but. Especially effective is Olivier's realization of the ghost. In a decade when Hollywood preferred to render its supernatural aspects unseen, the phantom's nightly visitations atop the battlements are as terrifying as anything in a legitimate horror film—something which late '40s audiences were starved of.

Deeming their gruesome imagery a threat to wartime morale, the British Board of Film Classification (BBFC) had banned the importation of horror films altogether between 1942 and 1945. With the embargo lifted after the war, Ealing Studios, soon to be famed for their comedies, created the classic portmanteau chiller *Dead of Night* (1945). Considering this film's commercial and critical success, the non-emergence of further supernatural efforts is quite surprising, with British filmmakers erring on the side of caution in fear of upsetting the censors. By this stage, Hollywood Gothics were also on hiatus, their cut-off point marked by the Christmas Day 1946 premiere of *The Beast with Five Fingers* (distributed in the UK by Hammer's subsidiary company Exclusive). Robert Florey's delirious tale co-stars Peter

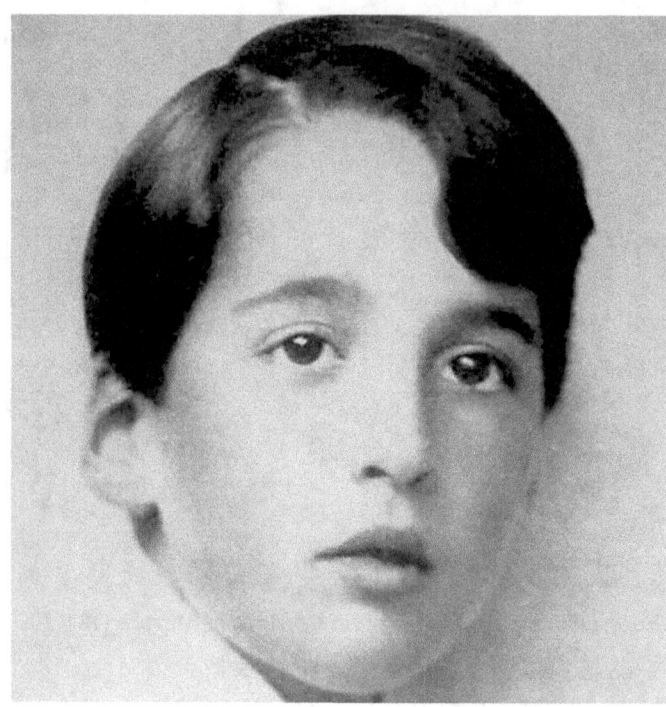

Christopher Lee as a child

Lorre with a disembodied hand and ends with some unnecessary comic mugging from J. Carroll Naish. Presumably because wartime audiences had supped full of real-life horrors, the genre next descended into complete parody with titles like *Abbott and Costello Meet Frankenstein* (1948), *Mother Riley Meets the Vampire* (1951), and *Bela Lugosi Meets a Brooklyn Gorilla* (1952). Although there were odd exceptions, like *House of Wax* (1953), it wasn't until Hammer released its Christopher Lee-starrers *The Curse of Frankenstein* and *Dracula* that Gothic horror would flourish once more.

Akin to *Hamlet*, in the dearth of bona fide fright films, post-war British cinema abounds with images that capture a succinct mood of terror. For example, David Lean's *Great Expectations* (1946), with its glowering skies, clutching trees and Miss Havisham in her cobwebbed room, or the staring dead eyes of Edith Evans in *The Queen of Spades* (1948), the Draculean manifestations of Robert Helpmann for *The Tales of Hoffmann* (1950) and the black-shrouded Ghost of Christmas Yet to Come in *Scrooge* (1951).

On Christmas Eve, 1947, exactly 10 years prior to shooting the climax of *Dracula*, Lee filmed a single scene for another quasi-Gothic, Basil Dearden's *Saraband for Dead Lovers*. Unfortunately, Lee's sequence was cut, as it was felt that, even in blonde wig and on horseback, he resembled the film's star, Stewart Granger, too closely.

Lee was very much evident, however, as murderous artist Jonathan Blair in the airy thriller *Penny and the Pownall Case* (1947). Speaking with a slightly lighter voice than one is used to, and gracing his early appearances with a wide, boyish smile, Lee is quite impressive in his first leading role, even if it's evident from his later scenes that he had yet to learn how to fully relax in front of the cameras. Nonetheless, this 47-minute film is of historical importance for being the first ever British feature to be scored by a female composer: Elisabeth Lutyens (1906-1983). She would go on to write music for *Dr. Terror's House of Horrors*, *The Skull* and *Theatre of Death*. Furthermore, *Penny and the Pownall Case* marks the first of Lee's many onscreen deaths; the actor even had the same altercation with director, H.E. "Slim" Hand, on how it should be done, as he did with Peter Jackson over half a century later ("I felt I knew about people dying …").

The director of his next film proved far more amenable. *A Song for Tomorrow* (1948), in which Lee has a bit part as a nightclub compère, is notable for being his first for Terence Fisher. It's somewhat incredible that within his foremost year as a professional actor, Lee had appeared, albeit briefly, in films with Gothic touches and with artists who would be so vital to his later, full-blown ventures in that genre. Even more incredibly, Lee would next work with several people who had played an important hand in horror's glorious past.

After a failed audition for *Blithe Spirit* author Noël Coward ("Looks like an undertaker," the Maestro muttered from the stalls), Lee performed his first onscreen duel (against Gregory Peck) in *Captain Horatio Hornblower R.N.* (1950). This led to similar swashbuckling duties with Burt Lancaster on *The Crimson Pirate* (1951). Although ostensibly an actioner, the film includes such fantasy interpolations as makeshift submarines, anachronistic hot air balloons and flame-throwing tanks made from barrels. Despite having only two lines of dialogue as henchman to the villainous Baron Gruda (*Attack of the Crab Monsters'* Leslie Bradley), Lee is a glowering, bearded presence in green velvet, clasping Eva Bartok (c. 1927-1998) against a Mediterranean backdrop.

A concentration camp survivor, the Hungarian-born Bartok would go on to star in *Spaceways* (1952)—a forerunner to Hammer's *Quatermass* series—and another British sci-fi piece, *The Gamma People* (1955). She is best remembered by horror fans, however, for her role in Mario Bava's *Blood and Black Lace* (1963).

The Crimson Pirate's rich cinematography was the first Technicolor assignment for Otto Heller (1896-1970), the renowned cameraman who had brought chiaroscuro depth to *The Queen of Spades* and would later lens Michael Powell's *Peeping Tom* (1959), as well as *The Curse of the Mummy's Tomb* (1964) for Hammer.

Direction came courtesy of Robert Siodmak (1900-1973)—the man behind genre classics *Son of Dracula* (1943), *Cobra Woman* (1943), and *The Spiral Staircase* (1945).

But Siodmak wasn't the only connection to Universal horror that Lee encountered during this period. In late 1951, he featured as a slave trader in Edgar G. Ulmer's *Babes in Bagdad*. Purveyor of the perverse Karloff and Lugosi masterpiece *The Black Cat* (1934), Ulmer's career ranged from scenic artist duties on 1920's *The Golem*, to helming cult favorites *Bluebeard* (1944), *The Man from Planet X* (1950) and *Daughter of Dr. Jekyll* (1956).

While filming *Babes in Bagdad* in Spain, Lee would attend the opera with his director. Ulmer "was a little strange, slightly inward," he told Tom Johnson and Mark A. Miller, and "found it difficult to express himself." Further up the *Babes in Bagdad* cast list was John Boles—the romantic lead of James Whale's *Frankenstein*. In a 2004 interview with Marcus Hearn, Lee recalled Boles regaling him with tales of the "rather strange" Colin Clive, who'd played the equally tormented Henry Frankenstein. Two years later, however, Lee came face to face with the Monster.

Based upon the fiction of John Dickinson Carr, *Colonel March of Scotland Yard* (1952-1953) was a tailor-made TV vehicle for Boris Karloff, who, in fetching eye patch, heads the "Department of Queer Complaints," some of which border on the supernatural. In the series' fifth episode, "At Night All Cats Are Grey," Lee plays a French fashion designer suspected of murdering one of his models. "I liked him from the first," Lee wrote of Boris, although, on this occasion, he was much too awestruck to talk to the screen legend. Nevertheless, the younger actor is able to hold his own against Karloff onscreen, even if he rather gives himself away with some overly shifty acting during the Colonel's investigation.

In the summer of 1952, Lee made his second film with future Frankenstein, Peter Cushing. *Moulin Rouge* is John Huston's zestful biopic of artist Toulouse-Lautrec (an Oscar-nominated José Ferrer). In one brief scene, Lee plays the pipe-smoking founder of pointillism, Georges Seurat, seated at a sidewalk café in Paris, discussing Lautrec's state of mind with friends. Huston's sole line of direction to Lee, "Just be yourself, kid," may seem glib, but it is actually good advice for screen acting and the results can be seen in the natural warmth that comes across in Lee's reactions. While Cushing can be spotted as one of Lautrec's romantic rivals, a further horror connection comes via Freddie Francis, who served as the film's camera operator. Parenthetically, at the outset of his illustrious career, John Huston had been employed as a staff writer at Universal where his duties included providing additional dialogue for *Murders in the Rue Morgue* (1931).

Although Lee and Cushing never actually met until their first Hammer film, *The Curse of Frankenstein*, in 1956, it has only recently come to light that, before then, they featured in a third movie together. While Cushing has the showier part of General Memnon in *Alexander the Great* (1955), Lee provides the voice of the Egyptian soothsayer Nectenabus (Helmut Dantine). As he foretells the omens of Alexander's birth to the boy's father (Fredric March), we witness a future Jekyll and Hyde addressing a former enactor of those archetypal characters.

And it was in an adaptation of Jekyll and Hyde author Robert Louis Stevenson's *The Mirror and Markheim* (1953) that some feel Lee made his true horror debut. This half-hour film features Lee as a ghostly figure in a mirror, appealing to the conscience of Markheim (Philip Saville), whose mind is bent on murdering an antiques shop owner (Arthur Lowe) on Christmas Day. By showing Markheim the consequences of such an action, Lee is more of an avenging angel than a demonic entity in this alternative exploration of human duality from Stevenson. Lee's co-star Philip Saville (1930-2016), who had last appeared with him in *Penny and the Pownall Case*, went on to a distinguished career as a television director whose works include a 1956 version of *Dr. Jekyll and Mr. Hyde* with Dennis Price, and *Count Dracula* (1977), the closest screen adaptation of Bram Stoker's novel. *The Mirror and Markheim* is further notable for being Lee's first association with Hammer Films, as the short was issued theatrically by the company's distribution arm, Exclusive.

Having profitably distributed *Rocketship X-M* (1950) in the UK, Hammer decided to make their own science fiction entries, *Four Sided Triangle* and the aforementioned *Spaceways* (both directed by Terence Fisher in 1952). The advances of science *fact* also played its part in the company's burgeoning success. When

Christopher Lee celebrates his joint birthday with Vincent Price at Madame Tussaud's, along with Utka Levka, during the shooting of Scream and Scream Again.

the coronation of Queen Elizabeth II was televised in June 1953, most homeowners in Britain equipped themselves with a set. Hammer hit upon the novel idea of luring viewers back into cinemas by adapting TV plays. Thus, Nigel Kneale's extremely popular sci-fi serial *The Quatermass Experiment*—which aired in the summer of 1953—was a more than desirable property for the company to film. Retitled *The Quatermass Xperiment*, to capitalize on the nascent "adults only" "X" certificate, the result was Hammer's first international horror success, paving the way for *The Curse of Frankenstein*.

The advent of television also proved crucial in the career of Christopher Lee. Hollywood legend Douglas Fairbanks, Jr. (1909-2000) offered the young actor a broad spectrum of roles in *Douglas Fairbanks Presents*. Made in Britain between 1952 and 1955, Lee essayed everything from a Russian circus performer to a Moroccan pimp over 16 of the series' episodes. Of these, "The Awakening," filmed in 1954, was an adaptation of Nikolai Gogol's quirky tale of horror "The Overcoat." Although Lee's voice only features at the outset, blaring over an address system as a factory foreman, the show is notable for giving Buster Keaton his first non-comedy role. Credited simply as "the Man," Keaton's sad-eyed demeanor is well suited to embodying the lonely civil servants of Gogol's fiction, and the Kafkaesque world he inhabits is watched over by a sinister "Regiment"— represented, so aptly, by Lee's commanding tones.

The Loneliness of Evil

A relatively young Christopher Lee

Nightingale," Lee was even introduced to the King and Queen of Sweden when they visited the set.

The following year, Lee's fencing skills were again put to good use. While dueling with broadswords for *The Dark Avenger* (released in the US as *The Warriors*), his opponent, a tipsy Errol Flynn, mistimed his lunges and consequently sliced into the little finger of Lee's right hand. The wounded digit was crooked ever after and Lee would take great delight in holding it up to interviewers and proclaiming: "Errol Flynn did this!" One good thing came of the accident, however; as Jonathan Rigby rightly states, the bent finger "would lend a peculiarly spidery quality to many future scenes of Lee's hand groping its way out of coffins."

Before almost losing his finger, Lee was top-billed for the first time in *Cross-Roads* (1954)—a 20-minute short that has more than a whiff of the grave. The only reason Lee remembered its making in later life was because he had been reported to the actors' union Equity for corpsing at co-star Ferdy Mayne's jokes. Such levity is at odds with this neat little supernatural tale, which is quite unworthy of being forgotten. Lee stars as a mysterious young man out to avenge himself on Mayne's seedy impresa-

Christopher Lee in *Cross-Roads*

A similar training ground for versatility was provided by *Tales of Hans Andersen* (1953). Lee's participation in these made-for-television fairy stories came as a result of his desperate bid to find work in Scandinavia, where he had hopes of becoming a singer (an opportunity cut short by penury). Nevertheless, the Hans Andersen series enabled Lee to further stretch his range, playing an old man in "The Old House," a peasant in "The Cripple Boy" and a young student in "Wee Willie Winkit." While starring as the bald-domed Emperor of China in "The

Lee is featured on this poster for *The Warriors*.

rio. Most of the action takes place on lonely country roads with tangled trees stretching towards a whitewashed sky. There is also a startling close-up of Lee's eyes as he corners Mayne in the latter's office, a shot that cinemagoers would soon grow familiar with in the Dracula sequels (Mayne would make a memorable bloodsucker himself in *Dance of the Vampires* [1966]). Sadly, the writer, director and (uncredited) composer of *Cross-Roads*, John Fitchen, would commit suicide not long after filming, with only an episode of *Armstrong Circle Theatre* and a documentary photographed by Freddie Francis, *Dream of Home* (1954), as his other directorial credits.

With efforts like this, it seemed that Lee was beginning to grow familiar with hints of the supernatural, but those hints were about to become far more pronounced.

Alias John Preston
1955

Is this man a devil in the flesh?

The above question, posed by Christopher Lee's first full-length horror film, *Alias John Preston*, is a prescient one, given the actor's future incarnation as the Prince of Darkness. Equally appropriate, considering Lee's later obsession with the game, *Alias John Preston* opens on stock footage of golfers in idyllic surroundings. One of which, we assume, is Bob (Peter Grant), who has just won the championship. Despite this, his girlfriend Sally (played by Peter Grant's real-life wife Betta St. John) prefers the company of stranger-in-town John Preston (C. Lee). Despite the romance being encouraged by Sally's banker father Richard (John Longden), Preston is disturbed by murderous dreams and goes to see psychoanalyst Dr. Walton (Alexander Knox).

Filmed at MGM-British Studios in early 1955, *Alias John Preston* marked Lee's fifth association with the New York-born producers, Edward and Harry Danziger. "Any film they made that lasted more than three days began to run over budget," was Lee's telling assessment of the brothers' working methods; third-billed, but above the title, he remembered being paid just £75 to star as John Preston.

Fresh from their success with camp sci-fi outing *Devil Girl from Mars* (1954), the Danzigers now turned their attentions to psychological horror, bringing on board the same director. Scottish-born David MacDonald (1904-1983) was responsible for two of Lee's earlier Danziger shorts (*Final Column* and *The Price of Vanity*, both 1954) and had even directed Tod Slaughter in *It's Never Too Late to Mend* (1937) and *Crimes at the Dark House* (1939). Although Tod's regular producer George King is usually attributed with direction of the latter (which bears no onscreen credit), contemporary advertisements list MacDonald as sole director. Remembered chiefly for its opening scene of Slaughter merrily hammering a tent peg into someone's head, *Crimes at the Dark House* is one of the actor's best. In 1958, MacDonald helmed "Jack the Ripper," the only episode of unaired anthology series *The Veil* not to feature its host Boris Karloff.

Alias John Preston also enlists two other *Devil Girl from Mars* technicians in cinematographer Jack E. Cox (1896-1960) and composer Edwin Astley (1922-1998).

Cox had lensed 12 of Alfred Hitchcock's pre-Hollywood movies, including *Murder!* (1930), *Rich and Strange* (1931) and *The Lady Vanishes* (1937). He also lent a suitably dingy look to *The Man Who Changed His Mind* (1936), *Doctor Syn* (1937) and *The Ghost Train* (1941).

Best known for scoring such ITC shows as *Danger Man* (1960-1966), *The Saint* (1962-1969) and *Randall and Hopkirk (Deceased)* (1968-1969), Edwin Astley's other credits include *Gilbert Harding Speaking of Murder* (1953), *Womaneater* (1957), *Behemoth the Sea Monster* (1959) and Hammer's *The Phantom of the Opera* (1961). One of the first film composers to use synthesizers in his work, he was also father-in-law to another synth pioneer, the Who's Pete Townshend (Astley's final project was a symphonic album of his son-in-law's tunes for the London Philharmonic).

The story credit for *Alias John Preston* goes to Hungarian writer Paul Tabori (1908-1974), who had penned the Hammer sci-fiers *Four Sided Triangle* and *Spaceways*. Tabori was better known, however, for his psychical research, most notably a 1950 biography of ghost hunter Harry Price, for whom he was literary executor. He was also vice-president, alongside Karloff biographer Peter Underwood, of the Ghost Club—a British paranormal research group, whose members included Dennis Wheatley and Peter Cushing.

Despite such talent behind the cameras, *Alias John Preston* lacks the all-round panache of *Devil Girl from Mars*. With its Jekyll and Hyde theme of split personality muted by stodgy scenes, the film's small-town setting is of equal ambiguity; while both Lee and Peter Grant speak with American accents, everyone else enunciates in the clipped tones ubiquitous to British films of the time (even the California-born Betta St. John sounds as though she hails from Borehamwood).

Overall, *Alias John Preston* has the feel of a creaky stage play on which a camera has been trained. The stench of amateur dramatics wafts its way to the smears of white greasepaint at Lee's temples. Nevertheless, it is a treat to see the burgeoning actor as an earnestly romantic young man, something audiences would be deprived of in his later career (John Preston is a mere gangling youth compared to the doomed lovers Lee enacts in *The Hound of the Baskervilles* and *The Whip and the Body*). Looking good in a tuxedo, he treats Betta St. John to a theater performance, smiling at her as strings swell in rapture from the stage. Later, they enjoy a passionate embrace in one of many drawing room scenes. If we're not in a lounge, we're in the psychoanalyst's study. Here, after much finger twitching, Lee deserves credit for saying, with utter conviction, "Tell me, doctor ... Can [dreams] mix reality and fantasy in a kind of poisonous hodgepodge?" A moist-eyed close-up precedes the dream he then relates—the midnight strangling of a blackmailing mistress, played by Sandra Dorne (1924-1992).

A contemporary of Lee's from the Rank Charm School (she had just appeared with him in *Police Dog*), Dorne would star in two eerie and underrated British horrors: *The House in Marsh Road* (1960), wherein she finds herself besieged by phantoms, and *Devil Doll* (1963), in which she is the put-upon assistant of Bryant Halliday's mad ventriloquist. Her real-life husband (and fellow Rank Charm School graduate), Patrick Holt (1912-1993),

plays her screen spouse in *Alias John Preston*, complete with dodgy French accent. Arriving shortly after his wife's murder, instead of being upset, he conspires with Preston to bury her outside. While doing so, the two men *shout* their nefarious, secret plans to each other so that they can be heard above the wind. Holt's later genre roles include Broderick Crawford's butler in *The Vulture* (1966), the police sergeant mown down by zombie bikers in *Psychomania* (1971) and a brothel frequenter in *Legend of the Werewolf* (1974).

Strangled blondes and howling gales aside, *Alias John Preston* fails to drum up much excitement. One startling close-up provides exception: Hunched and wide-eyed over his victim's grave, the wind whips through Preston's hair as he brings

Alias John Preston gave viewers the rare opportunity to see Christopher Lee as an earnestly romantic young man (with Betta St. John).

those twitching fingers to his lips. When remembering the film to Jonathan Rigby, Lee referenced this scene: "That's the one with me going mad on a grave, clawing at tufts of grass. God! When I think what a terrible actor I was in those days …" Far from being overplayed, the moment delivers some welcome energy to the film's dull unravelling, with its stylized madness no doubt taking influence from the silent thrillers of Conrad Veidt.

Lee later externalizes the character's inner turmoil with a short peal of manic laughter—then raises his hand in a seeming effort to cram the offending sound back inside. Here, the actor is again unhinged to an Expressionistic level that we would never see him reach in subsequent horrors. When he is eventually led away by the men in white coats, whatever the preceding hour is supposed to have meant is dully explained away by the doctor as he hands Sally back to Bob. This is unsettling, not only because it affirms the film's stuffy 1950s attitude that women are useless without men, but also because Bob seems to be as unstable as Preston, having earlier confronted the latter with a gun, simply for earning Sally's love.

Although Lee seems to be the only actor trying to bring some vigor to the proceedings, his co-stars are not without status.

A former matinee idol of the silent era, John Longden (1900-1971) had appeared in five early Hitchcock films (*Blackmail* [1929], *Juno and the Paycock* [1929], *The Skin Game* [1930], *Young and Innocent* [1937] and *Jamaica Inn* [1938]), before essaying Sherlock Holmes for a failed TV pilot, *The Man Who Disappeared* (1951). The year after starring in *Alias John Preston*, he would play Inspector Lomax in Hammer's *Quatermass 2*—made, on a rare excursion from Bray, at the Danzigers' New Elstree Studios.

Bill Fraser (1908-1987), who can be seen as Bob's father, gave Peter Cushing his first professional stage work in 1936 when he was director of the Connaught Theatre (scene of Lee's first on-stage attempts a decade later). Fraser would star as undertaker Basil Bulstrode in the Hammer comedy *That's Your Funeral* (1972), before creating a memorable impression as General Grugger—the grizzled space pirate of *Doctor Who* adventure "Meglos" (1980).

Canadian actor Alexander Knox (1907-1995) had enjoyed an auspicious start in Hollywood, with an Oscar-nominated turn as Woodrow Wilson (opposite Vincent Price) in 20th Century Fox's all-star biopic *Wilson* (1944). Not long after starring as Dr. Lanyon in *The Son of Dr. Jekyll* (1951), Knox was blacklisted by the House Un-American Activities Committee for supposed Communist affinities. Forced to find work in England, his later roles included a weak-hearted victim of *The Psychopath* (1965), the US President in *You Only Live Twice* (1966) and, most memorably, the cold cultivator of radioactive children in Hammer's *The Damned* (1961), directed by another blacklisted talent, Joseph Losey. For a brief period in 1979, Knox was also father-in-law to Imogen Hassall, the tragic star of *When Dinosaurs Ruled the Earth* (1968) and *Incense for the Damned* (1969), who committed suicide in 1980.

Alias John Preston was British actor Peter Grant's first and only film. He married Betta St. John in 1952 and the pair remained together until his death in 1992. A former child actress, Betta met her husband when she starred alongside him in the first West End showing of *South Pacific* (she had been cast as Liat by Rodgers and Hammerstein in their original 1949 Broadway production). Despite the occasional Hollywood role, such as a Native American who's sweet on Vincent Price in RKO's *Dangerous Mission* (1953),

Betta chose to live in England where she played the lead in a better-than-average Hammer thriller, *The Snorkel* (1957). She was reunited with Lee (and his American accent) in *The City of the Dead* (1959). "[I] liked him very much and always enjoyed working with him," she told Tom Weaver. "*Very* intellectual, very with-it, a very interesting person."

Released in the US on Wednesday December 14, 1955, *Alias John Preston* didn't see the light of day in the UK until the following June. Unanimously panned by the few critics who bothered to review it, the lone voice of assent came from *Today's Cinema* who called *Alias John Preston* "a lively little heebee jeebee," before adding: "Christopher Lee roams around town convincingly as a psycho."

The only other horror project in the Danzigers' future was *The Tell-Tale Heart* (1960), a minor gem scripted by Brian Clemens. Lee's last role for the producers was as a red herring in *The Traitor* (1956). This murder mystery would not be released stateside until September 1958 (after Lee's newfound horror fame) under the catchpenny title *The Accursed*.

Shortly after *Alias John Preston*, Lee went on to small roles in John Boulting's *Private's Progress* (1955) and two Powell and Pressburger films, *The Battle of the River Plate* (1955) and *Ill Met By Moonlight* (1956). Despite the prestige of the filmmakers involved, none of these parts would give the actor much in the way of either dialogue or billing. It was, however, a mute portrayal for director Terence Fisher that really changed everything.

The Curse of Frankenstein 1956

The creature created by man and forgotten by nature!

> Have you seen my Fanny?
> Blimey! I saw *The Curse of Frankenstein*—that was enough!—Rita Webb and Robin Askwith in *Confessions of a Pop Performer* (1975)

> There was no conscious policy of creating a Hammer team of actors. It just happened, [Peter] Cushing at that time was a big catch for us because he had just won the Best Television Actor of the Year Award. Christopher Lee just happened to be six-foot four-inches tall.—Michael Carreras, *The Horror People*

By 1956, Christopher Lee felt he had made little impact in his chosen profession. After 10 years and over 30 movies, the actor signed on to play the Creature in *The Curse of Frankenstein* oblivious as to how important it would be, not just for his own career, but to the history of British cinema. As Lee explained to Mark A. Miller: "I decided if people weren't going to pay much attention to me as I was and as I looked … I would make myself so unrecognizable that people would then say, 'I wonder what the actor who is playing this part really looks like?'"

In the spring of 1956, Hammer Films received a script, eventually titled *Frankenstein and the Monster*, from New York-born writer-producer Milton Subotsky (1921-1991). Originally intended for a three-week schedule, *Frankenstein and the Monster* would have been a black-and-white cheapie with Boris Karloff as the Baron. However, when Hammer were made aware of the legal difficulties that would ensue if they borrowed any ideas from the Universal canon, Karloff, by association, was dropped. It was felt, also, that Subotsky's screenplay included too many visual references to the earlier films, such as the scientist's inadvertent use of a criminal brain, and, à la *Bride of Frankenstein* (1935), a prologue in which Mary Shelley, Lord Byron, et al. set up the action at the Villa Diodati.

Milton's business partner, Max J. Rosenberg (1914-2004), revealed to Tom Weaver that Hammer offered them $5,000 and 20% of any profits for providing the idea. Producer Anthony Hinds (1922-2013) then retained Subotsky's wraparound notion that Frankenstein should narrate his story from a prison cell—as well as the enlarged participation of a minor Shelley character called Krempe—and set Jimmy Sangster (1927-2011) to work on a new script.

At 29, Sangster was closer in age to the young audience that Hammer wished to attract. A former production manager, he had previously written only one full-length screenplay, *X the Unknown* (1956), a promotion he'd secured by having the most ideas at a story conference, not least that the monster should come from "inner" rather than "outer" space. With such innovations, Sangster would become one of the key architects of Hammer horror (someone at the BBFC once referred to his scripts as the work of "an insane but very precocious schoolboy").

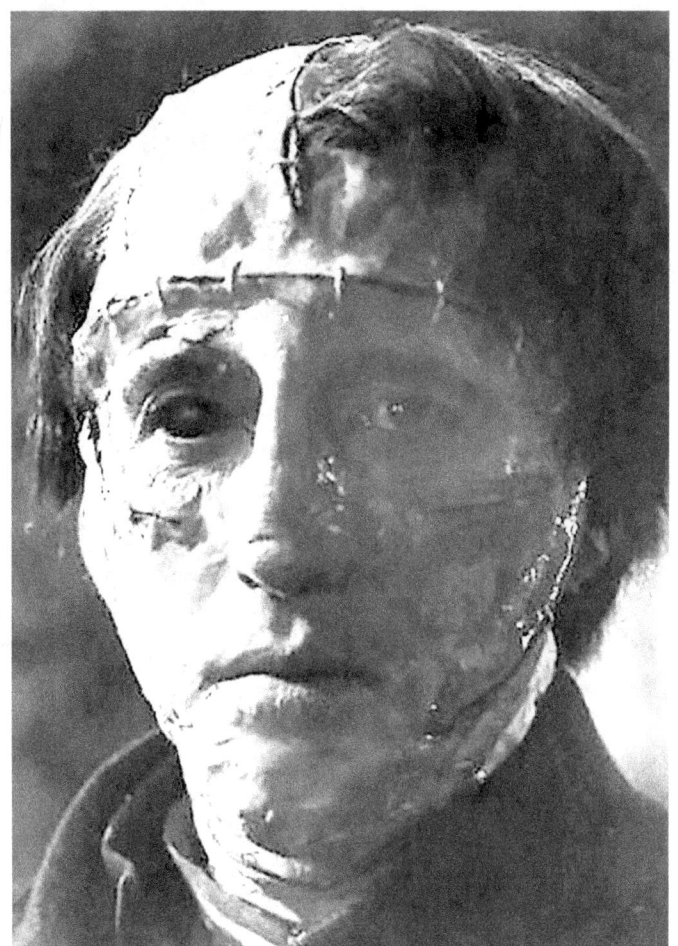

Christopher Lee as the Creature

Sangster remained unaware of Subotsky's earlier screenplay and, instead, gleaned ideas from Mary Shelley's original novel, largely because it was in the public domain. As such, Hammer's version feels closer to the book than the Universal classic, which took its inspiration, instead, from Peggy Webling's 1927 stage play. Sangster restored the novel's Swiss locale and the character names of Victor Frankenstein and the family servant Justine who is, in both novel and film, a victim of the monster's crimes. Indeed, so nervous were Hammer about a lawsuit from Universal that they changed the name of the "Monster" (as he was known in Karloff's film) to the "Creature." Hinds also viewed prints of Universal's first three Frankenstein films to ensure that his own product was completely original.

Sangster claimed that he wrote his Gothic horrors as "elaborate fairy tales," which was entirely in line with the philosophy of director Terence Fisher (1904-1980). After losing his father at the age of four, Fisher was raised by a faith healer mother, whose Christian Scientist beliefs instilled spiritual notions of Good and Evil that would inform his later work. Fisher entered the film industry in 1933 as "the oldest clapper-boy in the business," working his way up into the cutting rooms with *Tudor Rose*—a 1936 historical drama written by Miles Malleson and starring Cedric Hardwicke (of Universal's *The Ghost of Frankenstein* [1941]). It was this background in editing which gave Fisher his work ethic when he eventually graduated to direction: Assembling the film in his mind as he shot, he never wasted a frame of celluloid, keeping the action moving at all times. As such, he ranks as one of British cinema's most efficient visual storytellers.

The Creature's make-up premiered at the Brooks Wharf reception.

After making his directorial debut with the supernatural comedy *Colonel Bogey* (1947), Fisher made two Hammer films that—in their shared theme of doomed obsession—provided a dry run for Frankenstein: *Stolen Face* (1951) stars Paul Henreid as a surgeon who gives a disfigured criminal the face of his unrequited love (Lizabeth Scott); and *Four Sided Triangle* (1952) has scientist Bill (Stephen Murray) replicating the wife of his best friend, in a noisy, light-filled sequence which looks back to *Metropolis* (1926) and forward to *The Fly* (1958). Fisher had also worked with Boris Karloff on "The Invisible Knife," a *Colonel March of Scotland Yard* episode.

The Curse of Frankenstein was Fisher's 12th film for Hammer, and with it, he would emerge as the most effective British horror director since James Whale (as if to underline the fact, Whale was found dead in his swimming pool in the month of *The Curse of Frankenstein*'s release). On being asked at the start of production if he wanted to see Whale's original, Fisher retorted: "Certainly not. If one is going to make this film, I think that one has got to start from a personal concept and what you yourself think."

Fisher's "personal concept" was one he termed "the attraction of evil": By presenting the Devil's face as handsome (all the better for luring the innocent), Fisher showed that appearances are deceptive—it is inner values which truly count. Cushing's Byronic Frankenstein was the first of Fisher's attractive villains, but it was Christopher Lee's *Dracula*, made the following year, which realized the notion to its best effect.

Recalling his brief appearance in Fisher's second film, *A Song for Tomorrow*, Lee countered that the director must have "thought I'd been so grotesque as the MC that I'd be just right for the Creature." The course of British horror could have been very different indeed, however, if Hammer had cast their first choice for the monster role. Requiring a tall actor with experience in mime, the studio approached the six-foot seven-inch Bernard Bresslaw, who would later make a name for himself as the affable giant of the *Carry On* team (one of whose films, *Carry On Screaming!* [1966], is a Hammer horror spoof with Bernard as a zombie butler). According to Melvyn Hayes: "Bresslaw's agent said his going rate was £10 a day, Christopher Lee's agent wanted £8. Guess who got the job?"

As the monster's creator, Hammer cast an actor whose affecting performance as Winston Smith, in a controversial TV adaptation of *Nineteen Eighty-Four* (1954), had labeled him "The Horror Man of the BBC." In his autobiography, Peter Cushing recalled the first time he met Christopher Lee: "He was wearing the grotesque make-up conceived by Phil Leakey, and a story was put about by the publicity department that when it was removed at the end of the day's work, he and I came face to face in the corridor, and *then* I screamed!"

Lee remembered their first encounter differently, with him bursting into Cushing's dressing room and complaining that he had no dialogue. "Consider yourself lucky," said Cushing, "I've read the script." Lee was immediately won over by his co-star's "gentle humor which made it quite impossible for anybody to be pompous in his company." There was no disparity in another of Lee's memories, either: "From the first time we met on the set of *The Curse of Frankenstein*, Peter Cushing and I were friends."

The British Quad poster

Born in Kenley, Surrey, on Monday, May 26, 1913, Peter Cushing's connections to Frankenstein came early in his career. Arriving in Hollywood with just $16 to his name, the struggling actor miraculously talked his way into his first film *The Man in the Iron Mask* (1939)—directed by James Whale (also in the cast was Dwight Frye, the hunchbacked Fritz of *Frankenstein*). Following this debut, Cushing went swiftly into the Laurel and Hardy comedy *A Chump at Oxford* (1939), with art direction from *Frankenstein*'s Charles D. Hall), before going uncredited in Whale's last film, *They Dare Not Love* (1940). Two further links to *Frankenstein* came that year when Peter played the part of Colin Clive's illustrious forebear, Clive of India, in the MGM short *Your Hidden Master*, and then featured with Mae Clarke (Elizabeth in Whale's 1931 film) for *Women in War*. Cushing also found time during his Hollywood sojourn to play cricket for C. Aubrey Smith's famed team, whose members included Boris Karloff.

Returning to England, Peter married his soulmate, Helen Beck, on April 10, 1943, but suffered a nervous breakdown in 1950. "I went through a low period in my career when I almost gave up acting," he told John Brosnan, adding: "I was in such desperate straits … I had nothing." Thanks to the steadfast love and support of his wife, however, Cushing rallied and successfully broke into the nerve-wracking arena of live television which brought him to Hammer's attention. An admirer of Whale's *Frankenstein*, Cushing was keen to lend his talents to the latest version of Shelley's novel. In yet another fateful twist, he had just finished a West End run of *The Silver Whistle*, alongside Ernest Thesiger—Dr. Pretorius of Whale's *Bride of Frankenstein*. Hammer enticed Cushing into the fold with a screening of *X the Unknown*, which he thought "splendid."

The Curse of Frankenstein began production at Bray Studios on Monday November 19, 1956—the same day that filming started at Elstree on another British horror classic, *Night of the Demon* (coincidentally, Universal's *Frankenstein* had begun filming on the same day [August 24, 1931] as another Hollywood horror classic, Paramount's *Dr. Jekyll and Mr. Hyde*). While Peter Cushing climbed a gibbet in the cold night air, Christopher Lee was in the small bathroom of Down Place (a dilapidated old house which Hammer had transformed into a studio). The bathroom served as Phil Leakey's make-up room. Fresh from transform-

ing Richard Wordsworth into a human cactus for *The Quatermass Xperiment*, Leakey (1908-1992) dumped his supplies on the closed toilet lid, stuck a tiny mirror on the opposite wall and cursed the inadequate light by which he was forced to work. Shooting was already underway, and he had still yet to develop a suitable make-up for the Creature. Working against the clock, he experimented by applying greasepaint and mortician's wax directly onto Lee's face. Recalling these unsuccessful first attempts, Lee wrote: "I wound up looking like a madman's picture of a circus freak …"

Leakey elaborated in *Little Shoppe of Horrors* (hereafter abbreviated to *LSoH*) #6: "One [make-up] which we tried was with a completely bald head, but nobody liked it, least of all Christopher who had a fine head of hair … Then we tried something that looked like a cross between a man and a gorilla that had had an argument with a truck …"

"Finally, Lee said to Phil desperately, 'I ought to look more like a human being, but I should look a mess.'" On reflection, the actor felt that, in their haste, they "overdid the mess" and, grudgingly, had to agree with the subsequent review which compared his face to "a road accident" (another critic, amusingly if unfairly, wrote that Lee's Creature resembled "Jerry Lewis with acne"). Terence Fisher, in a July 1964 *Films and Filming* interview, further expounded on the Creature's look, saying: "We wanted the Monster to fit Chris Lee's melancholy personality. We wanted a thing which looked like some wandering, forlorn minstrel of monstrosity, a thing of shreds and patches, but in flesh and blood and organs …"

Topped by what looks like the world's first Beatle wig (to evoke Shelley's description of "lustrous black" hair), the make-up was finalized on the evening of Wednesday November 21— only moments before Lee was required to showcase his monster at a London press reception, an occasion which displayed Hammer chairman James Carreras' flair for showmanship: The Brooks Wharf cellar location was adorned with a coffin, candles and bubbling apparatus, while bright red cocktails ("the Blood of Frankenstein") were handed out to the 200 guests. Suddenly, Lee's Creature burst through the doors with Hazel Court in his arms. Said one newsman present: "I can vouch that monster Lee makes monster Karloff look almost like a benevolent uncle who has dressed up to make the children laugh at Christmas." (*My Night Out-With Frankenstein*. Peter Evans, *Kinematograph Weekly*, November 29, 1956.)

Early the following morning, Lee was required on-set to shoot his first scenes. Because the make-up had been assembled in such a rush the night before, Leakey recalled wondering aloud (in *LSoH* #5): "What the heck did I do?"

"I know what you did," said Lee. "My face is coming off where you did it!"

Without the use of prosthetic molds, Leakey had to work from scratch every day, leading to subtly different looks for the Creature throughout the film. "A bit of a cock-up," was the make-up artist's summation.

Taking up to three hours to apply, Lee would have to be in the make-up chair at six o'clock each morning to be ready for the shoot. "This is the last horror picture I'll ever do," Leakey remembers the actor complaining (in *LSoH* #5): "Nobody is going to mess my face up like this again." "Well, it might lead to something," came the make-up man's astute reply.

The torturous application was eased somewhat by the two men listening to early morning radio broadcasts of the Melbourne Olympics. According to Leakey, whenever Lee became excited at a particular sporting triumph, he would leap from his chair, causing a freshly applied piece of make-up to fall from his face. Despite endless re-gluing, Leakey surmised that the actor "always remained good-tempered and we became good friends."

Lee was left to his own devices when it came to the conceptualization of the Creature's character. According to the actor, Fisher's mode of direction was very much: "Show me what you're going to do, and I'll tell you if it's right or wrong." Absorbed by the challenge, Lee was "never so content … It was a case of inventing a being who was neither oneself nor anybody else, but a composite of pieces of other people, mostly dead … I decided that my hands must have an independent life, and that my movements must be sudden and unbalanced."

For the Creature's first appearance, Lee remembered having hot water poured over his bandages to produce the required steam. As filming took place in wintry conditions (there was snow on the ground outside), it didn't take long for the water to freeze against the actor's skin. "It would have broken

Mary Shelley's heart to see how the poor old Creature's teeth chattered," he later wrote. To ease Lee's discomfort, associate producer Anthony Nelson Keys (1911-1985) brought forth a bottle of brandy. "I drank most of it," said Lee, although it did little to ease his shivers. ("I might as well have poured it on with the water for all the good it did.")

Nevertheless, the moment when the Baron first comes face to face with his creation is the stuff of classic Hammer horror. The jerking, under-cranked tracking shot into the Creature's scarred, green face still lends a peculiar frisson. With a baleful glare from its single dark eye, the monster bares broken teeth and lunges forward. (Apart from a single shadowy glimpse, Lee's Creature was kept out of the trailers to further exacerbate the impact of this moment.) So impressive is the scene that Stanley Kubrick chose it to aid a key moment in *Lolita* (1960), albeit adding a surfeit of shrieks and growls to the soundtrack. (It turned up again, without the silly noises, in Michael Carreras' musical *What a Crazy World* [1963].)

With its birth, the Creature becomes a shadowy doppelganger of its father—an extension of Frankenstein's id so indivisible that the latter must eventually pay for the former's crimes. (Poking high above the studio walls, Hammer's prop guillotine was a grim diversion to motorists passing through Bray's quiet country roads.) Escaping to the nearby woods, the monster attacks a child (Claude Kingston) and his blind grandfather (Fred Johnson). While Jimmy Sangster's brisk screenplay doesn't allow time for explanation, Lee, through his confused gestures, attempts to express the motive at the heart of Shelley's novel (namely that the monster resorts to violence as a consequence of being shunned by humanity). "I played him … as a kind of bewildered child," Lee told Marcus Hearn—and nowhere is that more apparent than here (these woodland scenes were shot in Black Park, December 1956).

When the Baron and his unwilling assistant arrive, Krempe shoots the Creature through the eye. For this effect, Lee slapped a palm full of fake blood into his face. Unfortunately, some of the "Kensington Gore" seeped beneath the actor's contact lens. "It was excruciating," wrote Lee: "For an hour, I thought I'd lost my sight, until with bathing the pain subsided." Nevertheless, the likes of this shocking sequence had never been observed in the cinema before. Hammer were at the vanguard when it came to the depiction of onscreen gore (*X the Unknown* contains a still surprising close-up of a melting face). As such, subsequent filmmakers, from Sam Peckinpah (*The Wild Bunch* [1968]) to Quentin Tarantino (*Reservoir Dogs* [1991]), owe them a great debt for daring to push the envelope.

After Frankenstein revives the Creature with crude brain surgery, Lee totters about on unsteady legs like a new-born calf. But it isn't long before he's up to no good again. Such is the Baron's revolt against nature, that when he creates life in the traditional way, by impregnating Justine (Valerie Gaunt), he has the poor girl killed by his pet monster. Later, in a haunting image, the Creature peers down, *Nosferatu*-like, through a broken skylight at Frankenstein's fiancée Elizabeth (Hazel Court)—a moment which leads to a fiery rooftop climax. The monster's demise was filmed on New Year's Day 1957. Despite being hungover, Lee's stunt double Jock Easton (1912-1980) had no qualms about plunging through a window in flames, but, according to the film's publicist, Leslie Frewin, Lee offered to perform the stunt himself.

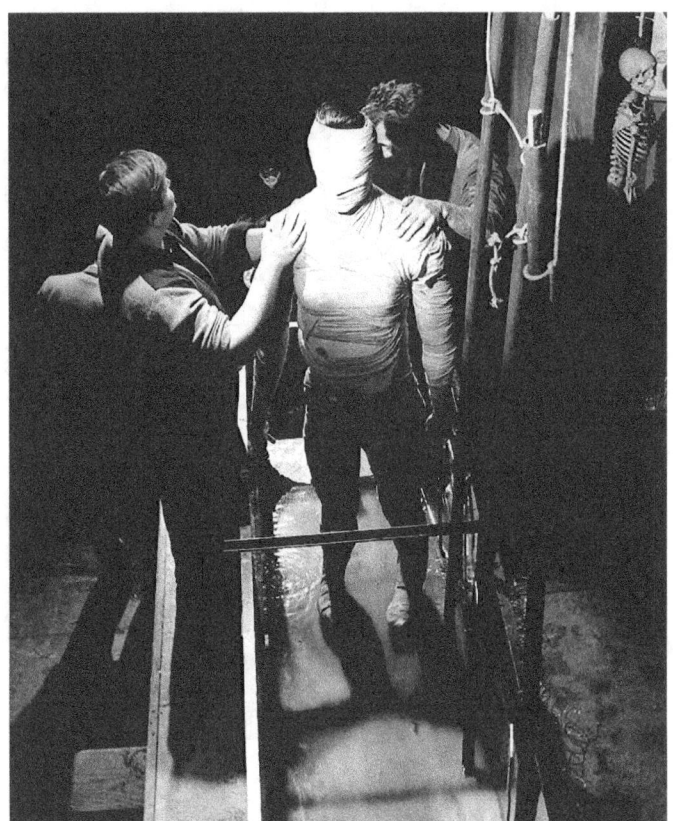

As Frewin reports: "Terence Fisher stared hard at him. 'My dear fellow, I want to finish the picture with my Creature intact, not in hospital with broken ribs. We'll use a double.'" Captain Jock Easton was no stranger to Christopher Lee, having served with the actor during the war. As well as being the founder of Britain's first agency for stunt performers, Easton would go on to play one of the briefly glimpsed Yetis in Hammer's *The Abominable Snowman* (1957).

Krempe is played by Scots-born Robert Urquhart ("by permission of A.B.P.C."), who, along with Christopher Lee, had been a prime suspect in the 1952 mystery *Paul Temple Returns*. In *Hammer Horror* #1, Urquhart spoke about *The Curse of Frankenstein* to Alan Barnes: "I was horrified when I saw what it did, how an audience took it … or *could* take it." Indeed, so disgusted was the actor that he allegedly stalked out of the movie halfway through its premiere. On a happier note, Robert was allowed to keep the dog that he and Peter Cushing revive in the film; the new pet was named Frankie. In 1980, Urquhart played Christopher Cazenove's father in the *Hammer House of Horror* TV episode "Children of the Full Moon," and later that year was reunited with Peter Cushing for the well-regarded Hallmark Hall of Fame presentation, *A Tale of Two Cities*. By 1994, Urquhart's feelings toward *The Curse of Frankenstein* had softened: "I watched it this year and got great pleasure from seeing the dog. And great pleasure from seeing Peter, too." He died not long after saying those words, at the age of 72, on March 21, 1995.

Melvyn Hayes had just appeared in the original television play of *Quatermass II* (1955) when Hammer cast the 21-year-old actor as the young Victor Frankenstein. "It was 60 years ago!" Hayes protests when I ask him to share his memories (on what would have been Peter Cushing's 103rd birthday). "Peter was wonderful to me," Hayes recalls. "On our first meeting, he said: 'This ring I'm wearing, I think it would be a good idea for you to

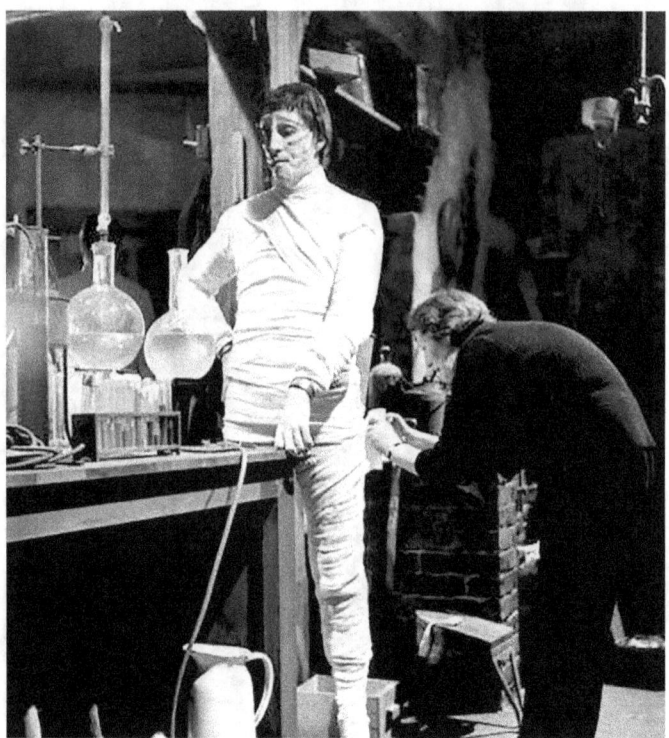

wear it in your scenes.'" This is a good indication of the attention to detail which Cushing brought not just to his own performance, but to the production as a whole. Hayes remembers him fondly: "On my first day on the set, I saw him looking at an eye through a magnifying glass. It was a sheep's eye. I worked on four films with him." The others were *Violent Playground* (1957), *The Flesh and the Fiends* (1959) and the disastrous *A Touch of the Sun* (1978), wherein one wishes the comedic repartee between the two actors could have found its way into a better film (preferably one that wasn't released only in Africa). "As for Christopher Lee," Hayes continues, "I didn't meet him for another 25 years …" This was at the bar in Pinewood Studios, where Lee, now a big star, was standing with his "cronies." Melvyn crept up behind him and said: "Hello. I made you." To which Lee replied, "I beg your pardon?"

"I … I made you," Hayes stammered.

"What are you talking about?" said Lee.

An embarrassed Hayes then tried to clarify: "Well, you were my monster. I made you …"

The reference was lost on Lee. "I didn't meet him [again] for another 25 years to try and explain to him 'my joke,'" says Melvyn. "He still didn't find it amusing."

Hayes' feelings toward *The Curse of Frankenstein* are far more positive: "I felt very honored to be connected with the film that put Hammer Films on the map. Every time it appears on television, I think to myself: It really stands the test of time, the acting, the cinematography, its Eastman Color … it all makes up for an exciting movie. Even though I'm only on the screen for about three minutes!"

Lee's fellow Rank signee Hazel Court (1926-2008), who had been an angelic Earth girl in *Devil Girl from Mars*, stated in her memoirs: "I loved every moment of making [*The Curse of Frankenstein*] … I remember [Christopher Lee] as an excellent storyteller. He was always great fun, very funny, and really not scary at all. It was a delight to listen to these stories coming out of him when he was in his monster makeup. He was a wonderful monster …"

Hazel Court's previous genre work includes Vernon Sewell's *Ghost Ship* (1952), in which she starred with her first husband Dermot Walsh. Their daughter, Sally (then aged six), plays the young Elizabeth in *The Curse of Frankenstein*. In conversation with Matt Gemmell Robertson (for *We Belong Dead* #12), Walsh recalled her first day on-set where she saw "a terrifying monster thing that waved at me." Sally had no idea that it was "the man I used to endearingly refer to as 'Uncle.'" Although Christopher Lee tried to assure her that it was only "Uncle" in make-up, Sally was still "petrified."

To avoid ruining his make-up, Lee was forced to subsist on a diet of mashed potatoes and minced meat, which Hazel witnessed "dribbling down his front." It's no wonder, then, that Lee recollected "nobody was keen to eat with me." Nevertheless, as assistant director Derek Whitehurst (1928-2005) revealed to David Miller, Lee amused his fellow actors at mealtimes, by examining his plate and proclaiming: "Bird theed! I'll *thtarve*!!" It must have been quite something to hear the voice of Sylvester the Cat emerging from the Creature's withered lips.

The Curse of Frankenstein also showcases the talents of those who worked behind the cameras at Hammer. The impressive matte paintings of Swiss mountains are the work of Les Bowie (1913-1979), who learned his craft as a prisoner of war: To affect escapes, Bowie would forge passports, using his skills to paint "photographs." Bowie contributed to nearly all the major Hammer horror films and died while working on the Frank Langella version of *Dracula*, little realizing that he would be awarded a Special Achievement Oscar for his effects work on *Superman* just over two months later.

The opulent production design of Bernard Robinson (1912-1970) utilizes every inch of Bray's cramped sound stages. With Lee likening the laboratory set to "a tiny grotto," the early Hammer horrors possess a more intimate feel than the vast, and thus more distancing, scenery of their higher-budgeted equivalents. The interiors of Down Place were also used as studio space. In *Flesh and Blood: The Hammer Heritage of Horror* (1994), Hazel Court recalled the house being in such a decrepit condition that rain slashed down through holes in the roof as they tried to film. Meanwhile, an unfazed Terence Fisher cheerily informed cast and crew to "Carry on."

The suitably forbidding façade of Frankenstein's habitat is provided by Oakley Court—a reportedly haunted Victorian manor house situated a little further along the Thames from Down Place. The building would become familiar in many films over the years, especially as "the Frankenstein Place" of *The Rocky Horror Picture Show* (1974), in which the whole edifice eventually blasts off into space. (According to Bruce Hallenbeck, Lee's bandaged dummy prop from *The Curse of Frankenstein* can also be seen in the film.) Oakley Court has evidently returned from the planet Transsexual and is today a five-star hotel.

The Curse of Frankenstein was the first British horror film to be made in color and, prior to it, only nine Hollywood horrors had not been filmed in black-and-white. (Excluding the Technicolor sequences of *The Phantom of the Opera* [1924] and *The Picture of Dorian Gray* [1944], these were: *Doctor X* [1932], *Mystery of the Wax*

Museum [1932], *Dr. Cyclops* [1939], *Phantom of the Opera* [1943], *The Climax* [1944], *Scared to Death* [1946], *House of Wax* [1953], *Phantom of the Rue Morgue* [1953] and *Gorilla at Large* [1954].) Cinematographer Jack Asher (1916-1991) makes full use of his Eastman Color stock, contrasting autumnal browns with splashes of bright crimson blood. "It was said that he 'painted with light,'" Peter Cushing wrote of Jack, "which was not a bad summing up of his masterly contribution."

The Curse of Frankenstein wrapped on Thursday January 3, 1957. In April, James and Michael Carreras, along with Anthony Hinds, flew to New York where they successfully sold the worldwide distribution rights to Warner Bros. Prior to that, the only way Hammer could ensure visibility in the US was by casting American stars in leading roles, such as Brian Donlevy in *The Quatermass Xperiment* or Dean Jagger in *X the Unknown*. The credible approach of the Frankenstein film's all-British cast would be key to its overseas success.

Premiering at Leicester Square's Warner Theatre on Thursday May 2 (when Lonnie Donegan was at No. 1 in the UK pop charts with "Cumberland Gap"), *The Curse of Frankenstein* was double billed with *X the Unknown* for its US release on Monday June 25, 1957 (when America's favorite sound was Pat Boone singing "Love Letters in the Sand"). Whereas the reviews for *The Quatermass Xperiment* had been, in the main, quite respectable, *The Curse of Frankenstein* was treated with less kindness by the press.

"*Depressing, degrading*—for all lovers of the cinema only two words describe this film," the *Tribune* raved, while C.A. Lejeune of the *Observer* opined: "I should rank *The Curse of Frankenstein* among the half dozen most repulsive films I have encountered … I could not discern one moment of art or poetry." The *Daily Sketch*, on the other hand, cited more "highbrow" material in their review: "Makes Shakespeare's *Titus Andronicus* … seem positively anemic by deadweight comparison." This is a noteworthy allusion, given that there is more gore and violence, not to mention bawdy humor, in the celebrated Bard's plays than there is in the worst excesses of Hammer horror. As nostalgia has the power to make once-offensive material respectable, by 1957, even Mary Shelley's original novel was accepted as a classic of literature. Consider, however, the critical reception that greeted the book on its original publication in 1818: John Wilson Croker's critique of *Frankenstein* in *The Quarterly Review*, for instance, reads: "What a tissue of horrible and disgusting absurdity this work presents," then goes on to describe "passages which appall the mind and make the flesh creep … Our taste and judgement alike revolt at this kind of writing …" Substitute "writing" for "filmmaking" and the above could easily be mistaken for a 1950s Hammer review. Furthermore, by 1971, *The Curse of Frankenstein* was considered worthy enough to be shown at London's National Film Theatre, something which "horrified" Michael Carreras, as he admitted to John Brosnan: "I thought if they made us respectable it would ruin our whole image."

Unfazed by negative assessments on its initial release, the public flocked to view the (mainly imagined) salacious details mentioned by the critics and Hammer's first color Gothic became one of the most profitable British films to be made up to that point. Prior to its production, the closest thing to a UK horror film in the 1950s, outside of Hammer, was the rib-tickling *Mother Riley Meets the Vampire* (1951) and even Hollywood had

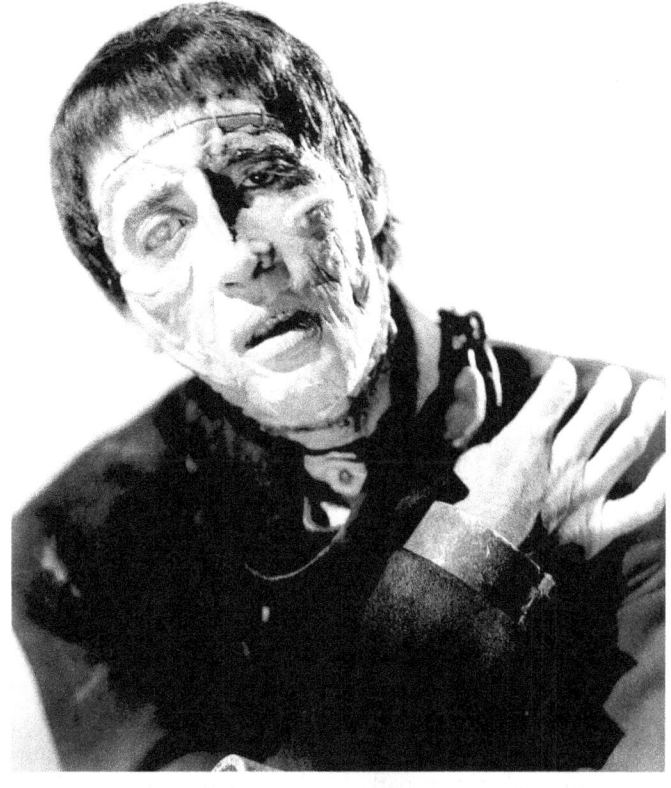

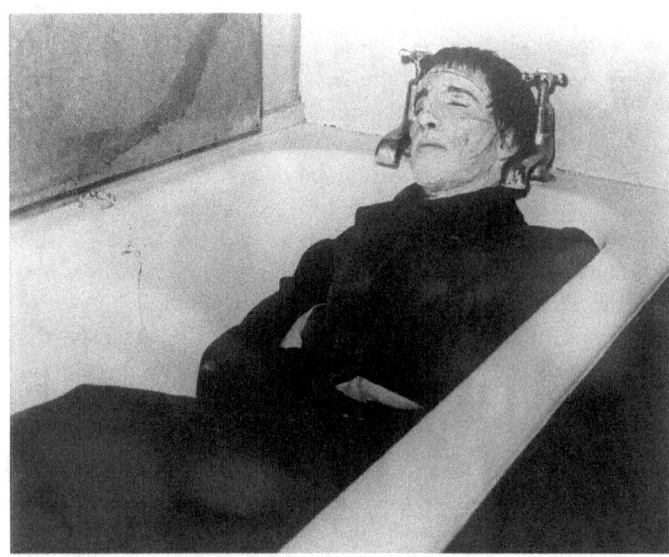

Lee relaxes between takes.

chosen to eschew the Gothic in favor of giant bugs and threats from outer space (*Them!* [1953], *The War of the Worlds* [1952], *Invaders from Mars* [1952], etc.).

While breaking new ground, *The Curse of Frankenstein* does owe more to the oeuvre of Tod Slaughter than has previously been acknowledged. Jimmy Sangster's script, for example, often verges into knowing black humor, and lines like: "I'm harming nobody, just robbing a few graves" are tailor-made for Slaughter's tongue. In addition, the debut assignment of Bernard Robinson was *Crimes at the Dark House* (1939), wherein we get our first look at the Baronial dwellings which make up Hammer's world. In the same film, Slaughter's fiendish Squire seduces the maid, and her outspoken disappointment of his upcoming marriage to someone of higher class echoes Frankenstein's callous treatment of Justine. Likewise, the heroine of *Maria Marten* (1935) meets a sticky end when she confronts Slaughter's caddish nobleman about the part he played in her pregnancy. At the close of this, Tod's debut film, his prison cell histrionics and subsequent execution mirror equivalent moments in *The Curse of Frankenstein*. Arranged marriages, such as the one between Victor and Elizabeth, are another preoccupation of Slaughter's work; witness his aged and lecherous *Sweeney Todd* (1935) bargaining for the hand of young Johanna with the ingénue's cash-strapped father. Further antecedents can be found in the rooftop finale of *The Crimes of Stephen Hawke* (1936), or the same film's opening, in which a child strays too far from his guardian and finds Slaughter's spine-breaker waiting for him in the foliage, à la Lee's Creature. Additionally, the whirling electrical apparatus which seemingly revives a murder victim in *The Face at the Window* (1939) is identical to that in Baron Frankenstein's laboratory.

Slaughter's world of corrupt aristocrats and bawdy taverns was occupied by Hammer and redecorated with broad strokes. What sets the Hammer films aside, however, is the acting of their main players. As we already know, Lee had been reared on Slaughter's horrors as a teenage cinemagoer, but both he and Cushing dispel Tod's ripe theatrics (which reduce his dark acts to the hissable frolics of pantomime), for a more measured approach, eschewing exaggeration to exude a quieter menace. It is the artistry of Lee and Cushing which lifts Hammer's material into an altogether darker realm. The death of Slaughter in February 1956, while appearing on-stage in yet another revival of *Maria Marten*, left the way open for this new breed of horror acting to come forth. To add a further twist, Christopher Lee's next acting assignment directly after *The Curse of Frankenstein* saw him working for Slaughter's producer George King, as a dueling Roundhead in an episode of *The Gay Cavalier*. Peter Cushing, on the other hand, starred with Slaughter himself in a 1951 tour of *The Gay Invalid*.

The Curse of Frankenstein's success in 1957 led Hollywood to rush out copycat releases, such as the disappointing *Frankenstein 1970* (1958)—with Karloff as the Baron—and *Frankenstein's Daughter* (1958), in which Sandra Knight turns into a monster with ping-pong ball eyes. Unlike Hammer's comparatively glossy work, these are cheap films that *look* cheap. The most enjoyable of these catchpenny inspirations, however, went into production in October 1957 at AIP under the guidance of producer Herman Cohen: *I Was a Teenage Frankenstein* grafts *Curse*'s plot onto a 1950s American milieu and features the in-joke of Frankenstein addressing a crate to 113 Wardour Street, London—the location of Hammer's offices. Jimmy Sangster responded with a jest of his own when he has Cushing say of his family lineage in *The Revenge of Frankenstein* (1958): "There are offshoots everywhere—even in America, I'm told."

The Curse of Frankenstein did more than revive the Gothic horror genre, it *revitalized* the British film industry. In the afterglow of Ealing comedies, English filmmakers tended to serve up largely bland amusements, like *Doctor in the House* (1953), which may make for pleasantly nostalgic viewing today, but, at the time, held limited appeal to the all-important American market. Additionally, these films found little room for Christopher Lee, whose dark, exotic looks failed to meet their requirements. One can only wonder what direction his career may have taken had he not accepted the role of the Creature. Would he have persevered with cameos for the "tall and foreign-looking"? Or could he have become, like Bernard Bresslaw, an amiable beanpole in slapstick farces? Uncertainties aside, *The Curse of Frankenstein* would prove such a landmark in Lee's career that it was one of three films screened by the BBC to commemorate his death; the others were *The Mummy* and …

Dracula aka Horror of Dracula 1957

Who will be his bride tonight?

I'd say the most effective part I've ever played is Dracula; there's no question of that, in terms of impact upon the audiences all over the world.
—Christopher Lee, "Dracula L.A. 1972," *Famous Monsters of Filmland* #105.

Since their literary conception in the summer of 1816, Frankenstein and the vampire have often appeared in tandem. The dramatic interrelation of the Villa Diodati's gruesome stablemates began with the very first theatrical presentation of Mary Shelley's novel, *Presumption; or, the Fate of Frankenstein* (1823), in which the part of the monster was played by Thomas Potter Cooke—an actor who had previously essayed Lord Ruthven in an adaptation of John Polidori's *The Vampyre*. Hamilton Deane, the actor-playwright who successfully adapted *Dracula* for the stage in the 1920s, would eventually play both roles, a tradition which was upheld by Hollywood's Dracula, Bela Lugosi, when he donned the Monster make-up for *Frankenstein Meets the Wolf Man* (1942).

History goes in cycles, and just as Universal's one-two punch of *Dracula* and *Frankenstein* in 1931 had created the first horror boom, Hammer naturally turned to Bram Stoker's vampire as a follow up to *The Curse of Frankenstein*. (The studio had been toying with the idea of filming *Dracula* as a seven-part live TV serial as early as Halloween 1956.) With equal logic, they considered no other actor could play the monster in their new film than the one who had been so effective in their prior effort. According to Christopher Lee, *Dracula* "was the one that made the difference. It bought me a name, a fan club and a second-hand car …"

Hammer paid Lee £750 to portray the vampire Count, 10 times that which he had earned for *Alias John Preston* just two years previously, but still far off Peter Cushing's salary of £2,500 for starring as Dracula's arch-nemesis Van Helsing. With *The Curse of Frankenstein* a proven success, copyright holders Universal allowed Hammer to make *Dracula*, providing just over half of the budget in return for US distribution rights—while Stoker's novel would not enter the public domain in the UK until 1962, due to an oversight on the author's behalf the book was never copyrighted in the US. This is why two 1957 B-movies, *Blood of Dracula* and *The Return of Dracula*, could be released in America without threat from Universal, but had to be retitled, respectively, *Blood Is My Heritage* and *The Fantastic Disappearing Man* for the British market.

After writing *The Curse of Frankenstein*, Jimmy Sangster worked for producers Robert S. Baker and Monty Berman on *The Trollenberg Terror* and *Blood of the Vampire* (for which he was billed as Jimmy "Frankenstein" Sangster on all publicity). Although produced in October 1957,

"Never did I imagine such wrath and fury even in the demons of the pit ..."

Blood of the Vampire would not be released until August 1958, over two months after *Dracula*, when the success of the latter could be referenced with the tagline: "He begins where Dracula left off!"

Rather than being a dry run for *Dracula*, as its title might suggest, *Blood of the Vampire* owes more to *The Curse of Frankenstein*: Donald Wolfit's Doctor Callistratus conducts nefarious experiments in a blood-splattered smock with a reluctant bearded assistant, a housekeeper who "knows too much," and a wonky-eyed hunchback whom the mad doctor shoots through the face with callous indifference. (Mary Marshall, who played a female prisoner in *Blood of the Vampire*'s Continental version, recalled Christopher Lee visiting the set.) As well as aping Sangster's previous hit, *Blood of the Vampire* still owes a certain debt to Tod Slaughter with its sadistic prison setting being similar to *It's Never Too Late to Mend*.

With *Dracula*, however, Sangster comes into his own. Written over four weeks in the summer of 1957, the film possesses a brash confidence on all fronts, dragging the viewer through the action at a rollicking pace. "We were finding our way [with *The Curse of Frankenstein*]," said Terence Fisher (in *LSoH*), and the successful elements introduced by that entry are firmly established with *Dracula*, making it, in my opinion, not only the greatest Hammer horror film but, along with Whale's *Bride of Frankenstein*, the greatest horror film ever made. (When Caroline Munro and Martine Beswick were both asked in my presence what their favorite Hammer film is, they both answered simultaneously and without missing a beat: "*Dracula*.")

Sangster expertly streamlines Stoker's novel to accommodate the movie's low budget (his background as a production manager stood him in excellent stead to this aim); hence, Dracula's three brides become one, the action takes place, more or less, within a single locale, and Dracula himself is spared his supernatural transformations into bats, mists, and wolves ("a common fallacy" in Van Hels-

ing's words), making him a more human figure, albeit a tortured one. Aged between 500 and 600 years old and cursed to a living death, Dracula best befits Lee's perception of "the loneliness of evil." In *Hammer: The Studio That Dripped Blood!*, he described the character as: "A romantic, erotic, heroic, fascinating figure. Highly dangerous, savage, but, above all, which I think is the most important thing when you're playing characters of this kind: Tormented, agonized, *sad*; what a ghastly fate to be immortal." The Count is also the perfect culmination of Terence Fisher's "attraction of evil" concept (Fisher's widow, Morag, recalled the director being troubled by terrifying nightmares during the film's shoot).

When filming began at Bray on Monday November 11, 1957, Bela Lugosi still embodied vampirism in the world's cultural consciousness. Lugosi had, in fact, starred in Hammer's first thriller, *The Mystery of the Mary Celeste* (1935), for which he earned his highest ever salary of $10,000 (by contrast, MGM paid him just $3,000 for starring in *Mark of the Vampire* that same year). In addition, the Hungarian's Hollywood shockers *Scared to Death* (1946) and *Bride of the Monster* (1954) were distributed in the UK by Exclusive. Fortuitously, Christopher Lee hadn't seen Bela's classic *Dracula* portrayal and, instead, restudied the book, which he had first read at the age of 14. Building his own personal interpretation from Stoker's words, Lee gave the demon lover a new guise and voice. Lugosi's oratorical introduction in the 1930 film is so far removed from the British actor's clipped tones that the overall effect defied the expectations of 1950s cinemagoers.

Remembering *Dracula*'s midnight premiere in New York, Lee recorded in his memoirs that, as the film began, the rowdy audience were clearly prepared to laugh at what they thought would be another cheesy horror film (some drunken wag in the crowd even fired a gun). The disheartened actor was about to leave the theater when Peter Cushing grabbed his arm, persuading him to stay. "When [Dracula's] silhouette showed at the top of the stairs," Lee wrote, "the roof was like to have been lifted off. But the ordinary conversational tone of the Count switched them off like a knob being turned on the radio. From then on there was only one direct reaction. The Count tamed them."

To give the vampire a more ethereal presence, producer Anthony Hinds instructed editors James Needs (1919-2003) and Bill Lenny (1924-2002) to remove the sound of Lee's footsteps. Although it's not something that many viewers notice today, this is a good example of the attention to detail which Hammer's skilled craftsmen brought to their work, despite limits on time and budget. What no one can fail to be aware of, conversely, is the tremendous close-up of Lee's snarling face as his vampire mistress is about to sink her fangs into Jonathan Harker's neck. Unlike *The Curse of Frankenstein*, wherein the horror scenes are carefully built up as the film goes along, *Dracula* hits the ground running. Against a blue-lit background, Lee's blood-smeared mouth is crammed full of teeth, and his eyes are bloodshot and wild, giving the viewer a marvelous jolt. This startling image of the Count illustrates perfectly Stoker's description: "Never did I imagine such wrath and fury even in the demons of the pit. His eyes were positively blazing. The red light in them was lurid, as if the flames of hell-fired blazed behind them. His face was deathly pale, and the lines of it were hard like drawn wires …"

While, famously, Lugosi never wore fangs, Lee was not quite the first vampire to bare his canines onscreen. That honor goes to Atif Kaptan in the little-seen Turkish adaptation *Drakula Istanbul'da* (*Dracula in Istanbul*, 1952). Although it's certain that no one at Hammer was even aware of it, *Drakula Istanbul'da* looks back, in all other particulars, to *Nosferatu* (in which we only see Max Schreck's incisors) and the Lugosi version for visual inspiration. Lee's approach, on the other hand, is vastly unique. He invests Dracula with a feral, beast-like energy when he bounds over the table, cloak flailing around him, and swoops upon his misbehaving Bride (Lee's athleticism here is rendered even more impressive when one considers how occluded his eyesight was by the bloodshot contact lenses he wore; on the first take, he, not surprisingly, missed Valerie Gaunt altogether and lunged at thin air). This animal ferocity contrasts alarmingly with his earlier suave stillness. As Lee often said of his acting technique: "I always try to do something unconventional which will surprise the audience … something unexpected." Another unexpected element is Dracula's turning of Jonathan Harker into a vampire, not only because we have been led to believe that Harker is the film's main protagonist, but also because cinemagoers were unused to the idea of Dracula biting a man (he later tries to sink his teeth into Van Helsing), a quality which lends Lee's vampire a liberated air.

Balking at Hammer's suggestion that Dracula should be clad in evening dress (Lee found it "very unlikely" that such a creature would be found in the wilds of Transylvania), the actor did consent to a cloak, which was created specially by the London costumiers, Angels. Once filming was over, the long black garment was believed lost, but in the run-up to Halloween 2007, it was rediscovered on the racks of Angels' fancy dress department, along with Van Helsing's overcoat (which they had also supplied for the film). After Lee confirmed the cloak's authenticity, the store's manager, Emma Angel revealed to BBC News: "We certainly won't be hiring this one out again in the near future." The mind boggles at the number of parties attended by fancy dress Draculas oblivious to being garbed in the bona fide attire of the Prince of Darkness. The cloak was sold at auction in 2009 for £26,400—just under a third of Hammer's original budget for the whole film, every penny of which is on the screen.

Never better were the ornate sets of Bernard Robinson ("the real star of the picture," according to Lee). Having designed Lugosi's lair for *Mother Riley Meets the Vampire* (1951), Robinson brings a similar decor to the interiors of Christopher Lee's castle with shields, crossed spears and antlers adorning the walls, and suits of armor upon the checked floors. One surprising innovation is how clean Lee's abode looks, with its archways and twisting pillars so different from Lugosi's vast, cobwebbed dwelling (despite initial misgivings from Hammer over Robinson's spotless designs, it's worth noting that Stoker's Castle Dracula is largely devoid of dust and cobwebs). Also impressive is the gloom-speckled crypt where Dracula lies at one with the darkness. When the vampire's eyes snap open, it still electrifies the viewer. (It's my belief that Lee borrowed this trick from Dame Edith Evans in *The Queen of Spades*—the look of sly triumph, which fills his blood-lined face, is also the stuff of nightmares.)

Bernard Robinson does such a good job that it's hard to believe Bray's newly constructed 90 by 80 foot soundstage (which contained the Count's elegant dining room) was redressed to become the mist-wreathed graveyard, with Dracula's staircase transformed, as if by magic, into the stone steps leading down to Lucy's tomb. (Visitors to the *Dracula* set included Bram Stoker's granddaughter and her son.)

Upon the movie's release, *Films and Filming* concluded their complaint about the amount of blood on display with the words: "No wonder the make-up man's name is Phil Leakey." Although the slip-on vampire fangs were made specially by dentists, Leakey originally fitted a pump against the roof of Christopher Lee's mouth which, when squeezed with his tongue, would allow Kensington Gore to drip through the canines. This idea was soon jettisoned when Lee kept gagging on the fake blood. Leakey's assistant was Roy Ashton (1909-1995), who would go on to become the greatest creator of film monsters since Universal's Jack Pierce. As well as designing the most gorgeous lycanthrope and zombie in horror history (for *The Curse of the Werewolf* [1960] and *Tales from the Crypt* [1971] respectively), Ashton was responsible for the acid-scarred visage of *The Phantom of the Opera* (1961) and the scaly, fanged menace of *The Reptile* (1965), among many others. After entering the movie business with *Tudor Rose* (which was also Terence Fisher's debut credit as editor), Roy did everything from creating Boris Karloff's wig in *The Man Who Changed His Mind* (1936) to supplying Orson Welles with false noses for *Mr. Arkadin* (1954). His first monster make-up, however, was on *Fire Maidens from Outer Space* (1956), in which the lumpen-faced menace is played by Richard Walter, son of Wilfred Walter, who had so terrified the young Christopher Lee as Lugosi's monstrous henchman in *The Dark Eyes of London*. On *Dracula*, it was Ashton who suggested having Lee's eyebrows meet over his nose to accentuate the vampire's feral nature.

Before working for Hammer, Ashton had been a singer with Benjamin Britten's English Opera Group where he originated the role of Mr. Upfold, the Mayor, in the very first production of *Albert Herring* (1947). A further Hammer-Britten connection comes via James Bernard (1925-2001), who was a protégé of the celebrated composer. The pair first met when James was a student at Christopher Lee's old school Wellington College. A fan of macabre stories, Bernard first read *Dracula* during World War II when he helped to decipher the German Enigma machine, a part of history retold in the Oscar-winning film *The Imitation Game* (2013). Bernard himself had won an Oscar for co-writing, with his partner Paul Dehn, the intelligent anti-war thriller *Seven Days to Noon* (1949), but the swelling, spiked strings and pounding percussion of his music scores could first be heard in *The Quatermass Xperiment*. (James usually had about four weeks in which to write his Hammer scores—or, in the case of *The Legend of the 7 Golden Vampires*, two weeks—which were then recorded in one or two takes with a small orchestra of up to 36 players.) After supplying an appropriately brooding soundtrack for *The Curse of Frankenstein*, Bernard excelled himself with *Dracula*. Among the most recognizable pieces of music in horror history, Bernard's *Dracula* theme does more than merely evoke the syllables of the character's name; its strident bursts of brass are the very essence of Lee's vampire translated into sound.

To a sweeter refrain, Jonathan Harker arrives at Castle Dracula to act as the Count's librarian ("as if he were delivering

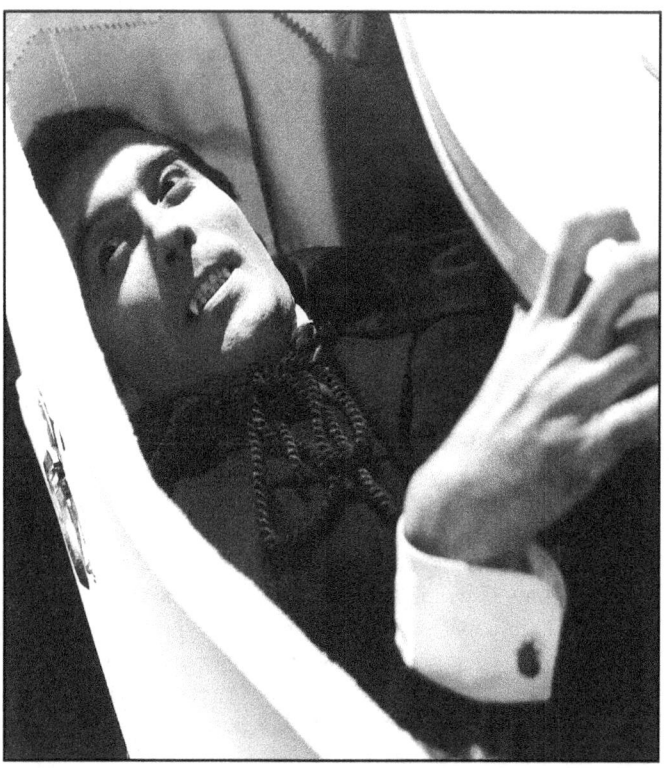

the peas," in one critic's opinion). As Harker, the South African actor John Van Eyssen (1922-1995) had recently dueled with Christopher Lee in "Love Token," an episode of *The Errol Flynn Theatre* filmed at Bray; figuratively speaking, they were about to cross swords again on the very same grounds. Van Eyssen's other credits include Will Scarlet in Hammer's first color production *Men of Sherwood Forest* (1954) and the sinister P.R.O. in *Quatermass 2* (1956). In 1969, he gave up acting to become head of Columbia Pictures' British division, although his efforts as a thespian were not entirely forgotten: While out dining around this time, Van Eyssen was startled to hear the gleeful voice of Sammy Davis, Jr. calling out across the restaurant: "Jonathan Harker! Jonathan Harker!"

Fresh from her stint as Justine the maid in *The Curse of Frankenstein*, Valerie Gaunt (1932-2016) returns as the vampire woman. *Dracula* was her second and final film. She retired from acting after her marriage in 1958 and shunned the limelight from then on, much to the consternation of Hammer fanatics. Her plea to Harker, "You're my only hope," must have been ringing through the head of Hammer fan, and 1950s teenage moviegoer, George Lucas when he gave Princess Leia's holographic image the same dialogue with similar intonation in *Star Wars* (1976).

When Jonathan makes the mistake of staking Dracula's bride, the vampire exacts revenge by going after Harker's fiancée, Lucy (Carol Marsh). Lying back upon her bed, exposing the wounds on her neck, Lucy looks to the open French windows with romantic yearning as a drift of autumn leaves falls outside. Soon the empty space is filled with the silhouette of Dracula. He glides into the chamber, to the sound of James Bernard's nerve-shredding strings (backed, conversely, by dreamlike chimes) and, looming over her bed, conceals the bite (and fills the screen) with the blackness of his cloak.

This scene is intercut with Van Helsing making notes on vampires. His use of a phonograph for this purpose is in authentic accord with the novel, in which Dr. Seward likewise records his thoughts. Interestingly, Van Helsing refers to the thrall Dracula has over his victims as being "similar to addiction to drugs." But rather than the death-like state that suggests, we see new life infused in those who feel the vampire's kiss. When Lucy's prospective sister-in-law Mina falls under Dracula's spell, her prim exterior melts away. She becomes smiling and playful; her eyes radiate sly mischief. Famously, for this moment, Fisher directed actress Melissa Stribling (1926-1992) to imagine she'd just returned from "one whale of a sexual night." The results are written all over her face, so to speak.

Lending fine support as Mina's husband, Arthur Holmwood, is Michael Gough (1916-2011). Born on Boris Karloff's birthday, November 23, Gough made his film debut in *Blanche Fury* (1947)—a colorful melodrama with Gothic undertones, which sees him married to *Bride of Frankenstein*'s Valerie Hobson. After appearing with Ernest Thesiger in Ealing's comic fantasy *The Man in the White Suit* (1951), Gough played one of the two murderers, along with Michael Ripper, in Olivier's *Richard III* (1954)—a most prescient piece of casting. Describing him as "the cheaper version of Vincent Price," Herman Cohen (the American producer of *I Was a Teenage Frankenstein*) cast Gough as the murderous crime writer in *Horrors of the Black Museum* (1958), the bonkers botanist in *Konga* (1960) and the demented keeper of *Black Zoo* (1962). But the actor's next role for Hammer proved more satisfying—as swinish music publisher, Lord Ambrose D'Arcy, he is the real villain of *The Phantom of the Opera*.

Melissa Stribling's next appearance for Hammer was in "The New People," an episode of their 1968 TV series *Journey to the Unknown*. Although she didn't appear in another genre feature until 1971's tatty Mike Raven vehicle *Crucible of Terror*, Melissa locked lips with future Dracula Udo Kier for *Road to St. Tropez* (1966)—the debut of *Myra Breckinridge* director Michael Sarne—and later made a surprising appearance as a suburban dominatrix (along with *Taste the Blood of Dracula*'s Linda Hayden) in Val Guest's *Confessions of a Window Cleaner* (1974). Prior to playing Mina, Stribling can be seen (alongside *The Fly*'s Patricia Owens) as a guest at the launch of Hazel Court's *Ghost Ship*.

Like Owens and Court, Carol Marsh (1926-2010) was another of Christopher Lee's fellow trainees at Rank. Following her sweet portrayal of the deceived waitress in *Brighton Rock* (1947), Carol starred as *Alice in Wonderland* (1949) and the sister of *Scrooge* (1951). As well as featuring Hammer regulars Francis De Wolff and Fred Johnson, this definitive Christmas classic also boasts Miles Malleson (1888-1969) as the disheveled pawnbroker, Old Joe. In *Dracula*, Malleson plays doddery undertaker, J. Marx, who, along with the wheezy border guard played by George Benson (1911-1983), leavens the horrors with comic relief.

Responsible for writing—as well as acting in—one of the greatest British fantasy films, *The Thief of Bagdad* (1940), Malleson was also the hearse driver in *Dead of Night*, a segment directed by Melissa Stribling's husband Basil Dearden (their son, James Dearden, wrote *Fatal Attraction* [1986]). Malleson can also be seen to droll effect as the professor who creates *The Perfect Woman* (1949), the hangman in *Kind Hearts and Coronets* (1949) and the hypochondriac doctor in *The Brides of Dracula* (1960).

George Benson, who had been a bumbling police sergeant in *Mother Riley Meets the Vampire*, went on to play vicars in *Journey to the Unknown*: "Paper Dolls" (1968), the Amicus thriller *What Became of Jack and Jill?* (1971) and the 1972 offering of *A Ghost Story for Christmas*, "A Warning to the Curious." He would be reunited with Lee and Cushing for *The Creeping Flesh* (1972).

The remainder of the cast is filled by superb character actors from Hammer's repertory company. The keeper of the garlic-festooned inn is George Woodbridge (1907-1973), whose gravel-voiced inflections brought life to landlords, policemen and even a Spanish goatherd (in *The Curse of the Werewolf*). His last genre appearance was as the boatman taking Ian Bannen to the mutant-infested island in *Doomwatch* (1971).

Van Helsing's hotel porter is played by Geoffrey Bayldon (1924-2017), who would become familiar to British TV viewers as the wild-eyed wizard *Catweazle* (1969-1970) and the mysterious Crowman, creator of living scarecrows, in *Worzel Gummidge* (1979-1981). While *Dracula: Prince of Darkness*' Charles Tingwell appears in the former, the latter series—which could be downright creepy at times—features Hammer luminaries Michael Ripper and Thorley Walters in recurring roles. Bayldon appeared with Walters in *Frankenstein Must Be Destroyed* (1969), before essaying memorable eccentrics in *The House That Dripped Blood* (1970), *Tales from the Crypt* (1971), *Asylum* (1972) and *Doctor Who*: "The Creature from the Pit" (1979).

As Dr. Seward, Charles Lloyd Pack (1902-1983) was another refugee from *Quatermass 2*, who would go on to play an altogether creepier doctor in *The Terror of the Tongs* (1960). Pack's other genre credits include the chief of police in *Mother Riley Meets the Vampire*, a chemist in *Night of the Demon* (1956), a vicar in *The Reptile* and an asylum inmate in *Frankenstein and the Monster from Hell* (1972). His most satisfying role in the fantasy field, though, is the villainous Makovan in *The 3 Worlds of Gulliver* (1959).

The Holmwoods' housekeeper, Gerda, is portrayed by Olga Dickie (1900-1992), who performs similar duties in *The Curse of the Mummy's Tomb* and can be seen in the graveyard opening of *The Kiss of the Vampire* (1962).

Gerda's daughter, Tania, is played by nine-year-old Janina Faye, who turns up again in *The Two Faces of Dr. Jekyll* (1959) and, more substantially, in a film which Christopher Lee considered Hammer's best (although he wasn't in it): Cyril Frankel's *Never Take Sweets from a Stranger* (1959) is an astonishing work with Faye as a pedophile's victim. Following her turn as a schoolgirl on the run from meat-eating plants in *The Day of the Triffids* (1961), she went on to some prestigious work as the youngest member of the National Theatre Company. Kept away from Lee's vampire during filming, Janina gave a reading from Stoker's novel at the 2012 Vault Festival screening of *Dracula*.

In the late 1800s, Peter Cushing's grandfather, Henry William, was a member of Sir Henry Irving's theatrical troupe and, as such, would have been more than familiar with Irving's manager, Bram Stoker; the author first encountered the actor in an 1867 production of Sheridan's *The Rivals*—the very play in which Cushing starred with Michael Gough 78 years later. Of Christopher Lee, Cushing wrote in his autobiography: "He is a man of so many attributes, among them a most marvelous sense of humor plus the ability to laugh at himself, and uncanny skill as an impersonator, which helped to lighten the darkness hanging over Count Dracula's entombed habitat, when we were not shooting."

One light-hearted moment took place while filming Dracula's burial of Mina: An over-enthusiastic Lee fell into the grave on top of Melissa Stribling's stunt double, Daphne Baker, to which Peter allegedly responded: "We're not making that kind of film, dear boy."

Quips aside, Cushing presents Van Helsing as the flipside of Dracula; both are predatory loners whose obsessive stalking of prey sets them apart from a customary life. Whereas the vampire takes blood, by penetrating the living with fangs, his opponent gives it back, via transfusions, and penetrates the undead with stakes. As Cushing told Bill Kelley in *Video Watchdog* #25: "Any man who leaves home in the morning with a doctor's bag filled with crucifixes and sharpened stakes … he's got a few problems of his own!" After Dracula makes Lucy a vampire, Van Helsing places a crucifix on her head and we see, for the first time on film, the flesh beneath it sizzle and burn—an effect which has been copied in every vampire film since. Also unparalleled is Lucy's graphic staking; brief close-up shots of blood welling around the stake and Lucy's resultant scream were originally cut from British prints but have since been restored. Terence Fisher felt it was important to show this scene in detail, as the consequent look of calm on Lucy's face illustrated her "release" from Dracula's hold. "Even now," Cushing recorded in his second volume of memoirs (1988), "the knuckles of my left hand, which held the wooden spike in place, still bear the scars of many a miss."

In *LSoH* #23, Michael Gough revealed a stronger version of this staking to historian David Del Valle. For the Japanese market,

Gough endured a mouthful of oatmeal and "each time Peter would bring down his hammer into the coffin, I would turn and hurl my oatmeal against the wall; by the third take I was feeling ill myself …" Nowhere else but in David's interview have I found reference to this, and if it was ever filmed, the footage has (thankfully?) not survived.

Hammer added more to horror than just color and gore. The innovation of Dracula using the Holmwoods' home as a hideout foreshadows the "killer-in-the-house" trope of slasher outings *Black Christmas* (1974), *When a Stranger Calls* (1978) and *Scream* (1996), while the Count's raptorial drives introduce an extra component. Whereas the most passion Mina receives from Arthur is a restrained peck on the forehead, Dracula is ready and waiting with his open, blood-smeared kiss. When Lee climbs the stairs to Mina's room and

The Loneliness of Evil

shuts the door behind him, we expect the scene to finish here, as previous films would have done, but Hammer instead take us even further, into the very bridal chamber, in fact. To Mark A. Miller, editor Bill Lenny recalled sitting with Lee as they viewed the dailies in the Bray screening room. Not expecting the sudden cut to a screeching owl when the Count approaches Mina's throat, Lee jumped out of his seat in terror. "I frightened Dracula!" Lenny stated with pride.

Although the vampire's seduction of Mina seems tame now, its mingling of sex and death proved too much for the censor, who complained on reviewing it: "There is still a strong sex element in this scene. This is due to Mina's anticipating expression in close-up and Dracula's face (and expression) as it 'hovers' over Mina's before he applies himself to her neck …" At this stage, Hammer would cheekily submit black-and-white prints of their movies to the BBFC in hopes that the horror scenes would appear more innocuous. Nevertheless, the film's erotic aspects were consolidated by taglines like: "The TERRIFYING Lover—who died—yet lived!"

The Dracula myth is one of the most enduring in our culture, having transcended all media from comic books and video games to theater. Ballet, in particular, allows for a powerful (and literal) expression of the story's dance between sex and death (see *Dracula: Pages from a Virgin's Diary* [2001] and *Dracula by Northern Ballet* [2019]), while, onscreen, there has been a version for every generation. Although set in a distant past, each retelling has reflected the fears and tribulations of the time in which it was made, from Lugosi ushering in the Great Depression, to AIDS allusions in *Bram Stoker's Dracula* (1991). Christopher Lee's stimulating vampire enhanced the more liberated world of the rock 'n' roll era; from the hip-swiveling gestures of Elvis Presley and the emergence of the teenager as an economic force, to the advent of wily seducers onscreen, such as Laurence Harvey in *Room at the Top* (1958) and Sean Connery's James Bond (from *Dr. No* [1962] to *Never Say Never Again* [1982]). As critic Raymond Durgnat confirmed in a 1961 piece, as Dracula, Lee was "the sexiest male in English pictures since James Mason in *The Seventh Veil*." Mason had starred as cruel, brooding lovers in such '40s "bodice-rippers" as *The Man in Grey* and *The Wicked Lady*. These semi-Gothic melodramas would have been fresh in the memories of Hammer's creative team, especially as some of whom (including Terence Fisher, Jack Asher and Roy Ashton) had cut their teeth at the Gainsborough studios which produced them.

Lee had a dry run in this line of work when he starred as the corrupt aristocrat, the Marquis St. Evrémonde, in *A Tale of Two Cities* (made just prior to *Dracula* in July 1957). In a part previously essayed by Basil Rathbone, Lee's Marquis preys on women in his peacock-infested pile—a more palatial Castle Dracula—until a lone villager stalks the decadent nobleman back to his lair and stabs him through the heart. (The local innkeeper is, of course, played by George Woodbridge.)

With a total of 13 lines in *Dracula*, Lee is onscreen for only seven minutes and yet, such is his presence, we feel the threat of his shadow loom throughout the film. Especially effective is the dynamic climax wherein all the technical and artistic elements of cinema combine to their best advantage; James Bernard's score reaches fever pitch, Jack Asher's lighting dazzles, and the astounding physicality of Lee and Cushing brings further innovation to the art of horror film acting.

The sequence is all the more magical for being filmed on Christmas Eve, 1957—the actors' final day of filming. Between takes, Cushing sucked pear drops so that his tongue would be a nice shade of red for when Lee throttles him. The script called for the actor to whip out a crucifix from his pocket and use it to force Dracula into the sunlight. Cushing hesitated, however, at the handy amount of crucifixes Van Helsing seemed to have about his person,"as if he were a travelling salesman in these relics" and suggested the crossing of the candlesticks as an alternative. The actor further proposed the idea of leaping from the refectory table to tear down the curtains in a thrilling piece of derring-do. The resultant scene of Lee writhing in sunrays, clawing at his face as he crumbles to dust, is absolutely first-rate. (In Stoker's novel, daylight merely reduces the vampire's supernatural powers; the lore that sunlight is fatal to them stems, instead, from Murnau's *Nosferatu*.)

After Christmas, Syd Pearson and his special effects team regrouped to photograph the disintegration of Dracula (Lee handed Pearson a photo of himself in character which he signed: "To Syd—who dissolved all my problems"). As the vampire's ashes blow away with the wind, like a fairy tale, his curse is lifted and the mortal lovers are restored, stronger and wiser from their experience. Cushing, however, communicates a weariness, through his gestures, of the vampire hunter's own deep sense of loneliness, which mirrors Dracula's. Now that Van Helsing's purpose is achieved (he earlier describes the pursuit of Dracula as his "life's work"), he seems at a loss, uncertain of his future.

Dracula is the best example of Hammer's morality plays, exemplifying Terence Fisher's wish to show the powers of light stifling those of darkness, as he told Allan Eyles in 1973: "If my films reflect my own personal view of the world in any way, it is in their showing of the ultimate victory of good over evil, in which I do believe. It may take human beings a long time to achieve this, but I do believe that this is how events work out ..."

With the effects work over, the 25-day shoot officially wrapped on Friday January 3, 1958. (To evidence the breakneck pace of Hammer's production schedule, Peter Cushing was rushed into *The Revenge of Frankenstein* only three days later on redressed *Dracula* sets—learning his lines over the Christmas break.) *Dracula* received its world premiere at the Warner Theatre, Milwaukee, Wisconsin, on Thursday May 8, 1958. For the film's UK opening at the Gaumont Haymarket on Thursday May 22 (Connie Francis was at No. 1 with "Who's Sorry Now?"), the façade of the theater featured a gigantic hoarding of Christopher Lee's Count looming over Mina. Red neon blood dripped across her throat as, below, nervous Londoners formed lines around the block. The lobby was adorned with cobweb-strewn coffins, long candles and skulls. One young man, when asked by a TV interviewer how he had enjoyed the screening, said simply: "I love to see the blood spurt!" On hearing this, Lee must have been taken back to the 1939 execution he witnessed in Versailles, where members of the baying crowd dipped their scarves in the murderer's blood to keep as souvenirs.

Blood, too, played a part in the film's UK promotion, especially in Birmingham (the birthplace of Valerie Gaunt) where the Midland Regional Blood Transfusion Service approved a worthy gimmick to enlist prospective donors. According to film critic (and former member of Hamilton Deane's *Dracula* troupe) Ivan Butler, 41 people signed up "before shocked complaints put an end to the scheme." Butler added: "Some person's life may since have been saved by the gift of one of those 41 volunteers."

On Sunday May 25, Lee and Cushing were flown out for the New York premiere. Celebrations were held for the actors' birthdays; Cushing's took place atop the Empire State Building on the 26th, and, the following day, Lee gleefully stabbed his cake for the photographers at a Universal press luncheon. It was Christopher's first visit to the US. For the occasion, he had managed to get time off from *Corridors of Blood*, albeit with a badly wounded knee after attacking Boris Karloff (for the purposes of the film). The premiere took place at Loew's Mayfair Theatre in Times Square on the night of Lee's 36th birthday (the Everly Brothers were topping the *Billboard* charts with "All I Have to Do Is Dream"). A 50-foot depiction of Lee's vampire graced the building next door to the theater and two actors, dressed as Dracula and his Bride, arrived in a hearse-like carriage to greet the stars of the film. After patrons filled out their last will and testament in the lobby (should they die of fright), they were

The Loneliness of Evil

handed complimentary paperbacks of Stoker's novel. Also on offer was free "first aid" for those who "chicken out" and "courage cocktails if you lack the nerve to see the picture." Further rewards came after the screening when Lee and Cushing signed autographs in the foyer.

While the film was issued through Rank on the British circuit, Universal retitled it *Horror of Dracula* in the US, so as to distinguish it from their 1930 classic, and paired it with *The Thing That Couldn't Die* (1958). On numerous occasions, from his autobiography to an onscreen interview in *Flesh and Blood*, Lee swore that Universal's president, Al Daff, personally told him that *Horror of Dracula* had single-handedly rescued the studio from bankruptcy. This isn't too surprising. In the 1930s and 1940s, Universal knew that their monster movies could be relied upon to lift them out of the red and they now took the unprecedented step of giving Hammer free reign to plunder their vaults for future ideas (no more fear of lawsuits à la *The Curse of Frankenstein*).

Dracula's New York premiere coincided with the US release of Hitchcock's *Vertigo*, which, to the surprise of many, was out-performed at the box office by Hammer's low-budget opus. The success of *Dracula* inspired a wave of vampire movies, with increased eroticism and gore, to be made in every corner of the globe by such revered filmmakers as Roger Vadim (*Blood and Roses* [1960]), Mario Bava (*Black Sunday* [1960]) and Jean Rollin (*Requiem for a Vampire* [1971]).

Whereas the Hammer progenitor was appraised respectfully by most of the American reviewers (with the *New York Daily News* saying, for example, "some of the photography is good enough to frame"), the English critics lay in wait with sharpened claws.

Nina Hibbin, of the *Daily Worker*, went to see *Dracula* "prepared to enjoy a nervous giggle" but found herself instead "revolted and outraged," concluding that "this film disgusts the mind and repels the senses … a degradation of cinema entertainment." Elsewhere, the *Jewish Chronicle* found it "a dreadfully unhealthy picture," while Leonard Mosley at the *Daily Express* called *Dracula* "one of the most revolting pictures I have seen for years," suggesting further that James Carreras should be dubbed the "King of Nausea." As with Shelley's *Frankenstein*, these reviews echo contemporary opinions of Stoker's novel when it was first published on May 26 (Peter Cushing's birthdate) 1897. By August 1996, however, during a season of Hammer films at London's Barbican Centre, the *Evening Standard* critic was moved to describe *Dracula* as: "Romantic cinema that transcends genre. Unimpeachable and unsurpassed."

Director Richard Lester also paid tribute by incorporating the film's climax into his 1978 thriller, *Cuba*. A tantalizing still of Lee in disfiguring make-up from *Dracula*'s finale, which went unseen in extant prints, led to rumors of a Japanese version including scenes disallowed by the British censor. Long dismissed as a myth, it wasn't until 2011 when Hammer fan Simon Rowson actually made the effort to locate the missing (and badly water-damaged) Japanese reels at the National Film Center in Tokyo, that extended shots of Dracula nuzzling Mina and his subsequent dissolution were reinstated by the BFI. Although we can now enjoy Hammer's greatest horror in its fullest version possible, current Blu-ray and DVD prints are a far cry from the film's earliest home viewing release. In 1966, Americom issued 10-minute digests of *Dracula*, *The Curse of Frankenstein* and *The Face of Fu Manchu* which could be projected on 8mm reels with the soundtrack available as a separate flexi-disc. As such, the synching of sound and vision was completely at odds, especially when the film and disc ran at varying speeds.

In 1958, Christopher Lee was in perfect synch with his vampire portrayal, although it wouldn't be long before he'd observe: "Count Dracula might escape, but not the actors who play him."

Corridors of Blood
1958

Tops in Terror!

In August 1957, Boris Karloff approached British producer Richard Gordon (1925-2011) with a Jan Read story he owned the rights to called *Stranglehold*. An enthusiastic Gordon (whose brother Alex had provided Bela Lugosi with his last great role in *Bride of the Monster*) set up a two-picture deal for the 70-year-old Karloff and, with his business partner John Croydon, formed Producers Associates. Shot back-to-back with *Fiend Without a Face*, the company's first film, *Grip of the Strangler* (as the Read property was retitled) features Boris as a Jekyll and Hyde-type killer married to Elizabeth Allan, the actress who had been menaced by Lugosi in 1935's *Mark of the Vampire*.

Having brought Lugosi to England for an ill-conceived tour of the *Dracula* stage play in 1951, Gordon next proposed a widescreen, Technicolor remake of Stoker's novel with Karloff as the Count ("Just so long as I don't have to imitate Bela"). This idea fell through, however, when Hammer announced their version which had the blessing of copyright holders Universal. Gordon instead settled on an original script from Jean Scott Rogers (1908-2000) entitled *The Doctor from Seven Dials* and James Carreras recommended his Dracula, Christopher Lee, for the production.

With Hammer's *Dracula* yet to see release, Gordon told authors Tom Johnson and Deborah Del Vecchio: "Jim tipped me off that Lee would soon be a big horror star too big for me to afford!" The minor character of Resurrection Joe was thus expanded to accommodate Lee's nascent horror stardom.

Providing her first feature-length screenplay, Rogers had previously worked, uncredited, as a production assistant on *Trottie True*—a 1948 melodrama which features Christopher Lee. Despite devoting the rest of her short career to television dramas like *Emergency-Ward 10* (1957-1967), Rogers is remarkable for being one of the few women writing horror films in the late 1950s (an American equivalent would be Pat Fielder [1929-2018], who penned *The Vampire* [1956], *The Monster That Challenged the World* [1956] and *The Return of Dracula* [1957]). For her sole genre credit, Rogers drew on historical research to tell the story of Dr. Thomas Bolton (Karloff), who, after becoming addicted to the anesthetic drugs he's developing, finds himself embroiled with

Boris Karloff and Christopher Lee, two of the horror greats

Black Ben (Francis De Wolff) and his warped family of villains—including Christopher Lee's Resurrection Joe.

While the screenwriter was certainly inspired by history's most famous "resurrection men," Burke and Hare, her main motivation was American dentist Horace Wells (1815-1848), whose pioneering use of laughing gas (nitrous oxide) resulted in him being the first person to be operated on under anesthesia. Rogers, however, was far more interested in the less successful elements of Wells' career. After a patient cried out with pain during a public demonstration (the anesthetic had been insufficiently supplied), Wells was discredited from the medical profession. He never got over the humiliation, spending the rest of his days hopelessly addicted to chloroform. After splashing acid in the faces of two prostitutes, he committed suicide with a razor blade at the age of 33.

The Doctor from Seven Dials began production at MGM-British Studios on Monday, May 12, 1958, with a four-week shooting schedule. The director was *Grip of the Strangler*'s Robert Day (1922-2017), who would work again with Lee on *She* (1964), and with his *Dracula: Prince of Darkness* co-stars Barbara Shelley and Charles Tingwell on the clever comic fantasy *Bobbikins* (1959). Tingwell also starred in Day's action-packed *Tarzan the Magnificent* (1960) alongside Betta St. John and John Carradine.

After playing the Creature in *The Curse of Frankenstein*, Lee found fresh empathy for the man he had last appeared with in *Colonel March of Scotland Yard*. Karloff, however, would discuss anything *but* his horror roles with the younger actor. Even when Lee had to leave the production for 10 days in order to attend the New York premiere of *Dracula*, the subject never came up. Lee told Marcus Hearn: "When I came back [from New York], he just took up the conversation as if nothing had happened. I was so anxious to talk to him about *Frankenstein*. I never admitted that I'd played it. I didn't *dare*. I was really scared of mentioning it to him, in case he said: 'Oh, really, I'd like to see it …'"

Lee needn't have worried. In a 1965 interview with Peter J. Jarman on the set of *Die, Monster, Die!*, Karloff admitted that while he thought both Lee and Peter Cushing were "very good actors," he'd never seen any of their Frankenstein or Dracula films. "I'm sure they're done quite well," Karloff conceded, "but there is a modern tendency with the so-called horror film … to introduce shocks just for their own sake. This I believe to be wrong. Shocks should evolve naturally

Christopher Lee looks like the Creature from *The Curse of Frankenstein*, with less facial make-up.

from the situation and story. They should not be forced into a film without excuse."

Nevertheless, as Lee revealed to Marcus Hearn, Karloff did share his thoughts on typecasting: "It's better to be cast as a type which becomes known and popular than not to be cast at all." The older actor also imparted the priceless advice he had been given by Lon Chaney in 1926: "Find something that you do that other people can't or won't do, and if it's successful, you'll never be forgotten." Lee, of course, took those words to heart. Another invaluable bit of Karloff counsel was unveiled by Lee at L.A.'s first Science Fiction and Fantasy Film Convention, November 1972 (transcribed in *Famous Monsters of Filmland* #105): "He always said, 'Leave it to the audience, Christopher ... Always leave it to them. They will think of something 50 times worse than anything we can do.'" To Marcus Hearn, Lee recalled that whenever he was questioned about Bela Lugosi, Boris "always gave the same answer. He looked into the distance and just said two words: 'Poor Bela.'" What little Karloff did reveal to Lee about his own genre career was that his casting as "the dear old Monster" in *Frankenstein* came about as a result of being spotted by James Whale in the Universal studio canteen, and that his role in *The Mummy* had been a rather arduous one (although Lee had yet to play that part).

But it wasn't just the characters of Frankenstein's Creature, the Mummy, Fu Manchu, Dr. Jekyll and Rasputin that the two actors had in common: Boris Karloff's daughter, Sara, was born on his 51st birthday, November 23, 1938, and Christopher Lee's daughter Christina was born on November 23, 1963. "Make of that what you want," as Lee himself put it.

In the 1960s, they were also next-door neighbors, as Lee told Hearn: "People used to say that the dustmen collected the bodies every morning." In the same interview, Lee expounded on his friendship with Boris: "We used to go and watch cricket together at Lord's, which gave rise to a certain amount of comment on occasions, as you can imagine."

He also remembered that, during the *Corridors of Blood* shoot, a newspaper reporter cornered Karloff and said: "Your [real] name is rather a funny one, really, isn't it? William Henry Pratt!" As Lee told the story: "I saw Boris' face set like stone. It was the only time I ever saw him lose his cool ... He didn't shout ... he just said: 'I don't think it's any funnier, or more amusing, than *yours*.' The devastated journalist made a quick exit."

Far superior to its Producers Associates stablemates, *Corridors of Blood* emerges as a powerful treatise on the evils of addiction—the Jekyll and Hyde story presented as documentary, if you will. Karloff gives one of his most three-dimensional performances as Dr. Bolton, showing both the determination and humility of a man determined to prove that pain and the knife are separable.

Lee's Resurrection Joe, garbed from head to toe in black, seems a living extension of the shadows from which he creeps. With this portrayal, Lee fully realizes the arresting power of stillness; his sly and sinewy character barely moves among the tavern's roving bodies, and yet we cannot keep our eyes off him, worrying what dangerous act he will perform next (he has a nasty habit of smothering folks with pillows). From his scarred face, a low Cockney accent unfurls slowly like poison gas.

When describing his new character to *Picturegoer* magazine in November 1958, Lee referenced the heartthrob status that *Dracula* had recently conferred upon him: "He's a grotesque, pock-marked chap. The girls won't like me at all." The girls certainly wouldn't like the lurid, slow-motion close-up of Joe's screaming, acid-flecked face. During the filming of this climactic scene, Lee "crashed blindly into an iron stove," causing the knee injury that blighted his first trip to America.

Although evoking another of Karloff's finest works, *The Body Snatcher* (1944), *Corridors of Blood* also looks ahead to John Gilling's *The Flesh and the Fiends* (1959) and Terence Fisher's *Frankenstein Must Be Destroyed*. (Lee and Karloff's stabbing of a night-watchman, while raiding medical supplies, is identical to a pivotal moment restaged by Peter Cushing and Simon Ward for the latter.)

The Dickensian squalor of 1840s London is perfectly realized in the monochrome photography of Geoffrey Faithfull (1893-1979), who also lent his black-and-silver tones to *Village of the Damned* (1959). In a further echo of Dickens' world, Finlay Currie (1878-1968), the hulking Magwitch of David Lean's *Great Expectations* (1946), appears as Superintendent Matheson. The actor could later be seen as the eccentric doll maker in Otto Preminger's *Bunny Lake is Missing* (1965), which also features Adrienne Corri (1930-2016), whose feisty performance as Rachel, the lover of Black Ben in *Corridors of Blood*, conveys that she is really the brains behind their criminal operation.

One of the finest actresses to grace the horror genre, Corri was an occupant of the Scottish pub invaded by the *Devil Girl from Mars*, the object of Laurence Payne's obsessive desire in *The Tell-Tale Heart* and "the woman with the ugliest face in the world" in *A Study in Terror* (1965). She later enacted four parts for Hammer: Beatrice, the fierce sister of *The Viking Queen* (1966), a neighbor from Hell in *Journey to the Unknown*: "The New People," the groovy Liz of *Moon Zero Two* (1969) and the top-billed flamboyant ringmaster of *Vampire Circus* (1971). Although best remembered as the unfortunate Mrs. Alexander in *A Clockwork Orange* (1971), her tormented spider lady in the undervalued *Madhouse* (1973) also deserves note. Four years after starring in a 1980 *Doctor Who* serial as Mena, the green-skinned controller of "The Leisure Hive," Corri authored a well-received book on the painter Thomas Gainsborough. Remembering Karloff as "the gentlest of Monsters," Corri was quoted, in Favius Friedman's 1974 book *Great Horror Movies*, as saying that, "Boris was the first actor I'd ever heard of for whom all the cast and crew clubbed together to buy a farewell gift …" Indeed, once shooting was completed, they handed Boris a broom. According to Lee, this was because, throughout production, Karloff was always meekly complaining, in his self-effacing way, that he was good for nothing but to "thweep the thtage."

In accordance with the censor's demands for all bedroom scenes of that time, Lee also recalled having to attack Yvonne Warren's Rosa with one foot planted firmly on the floor. As Yvonne Romain (b. 1938), the actress would next appear as the acid-scarred lion tamer in *Circus of Horrors* (1959), before playing Oliver Reed's mother in *The Curse of the Werewolf*, his lover in *Captain Clegg* (1961), and his sister in *The Brigand of Kandahar* (1964). She worked again for Richard Gordon in *Devil Doll* (1963), in which the Great Vorelli hypnotizes her into doing the Twist, and she was also Elvis Presley's leading lady in *Double Trouble* (1966). After turning down a seven-year contract with Federico Fellini, Yvonne chose to focus on her happily married family life with Leslie Bricusse, who composed the Oscar-nominated scores for *Doctor Dolittle* (1966), *Scrooge* (1970) and *Willy Wonka & the Chocolate Factory* (1970). Yvonne stayed in contact with Christopher Lee. When I met her in November 2014, she told me that she had dined with the great man only the previous week. Pointing to the image of Dracula on my shirt, she then said, reassuringly: "He didn't look like that, though."

Fresh from playing Peter Cushing's faithful assistant in *The Revenge of Frankenstein*, Francis Matthews (1927-2014) stars as Karloff's son, Jonathan, who is in love with Lee's old friend from *Alias John Preston*, Betta St. John. The couple play their goody-two-shoes roles well, serving to provide a requisite light to all the gloom. Matthews would be reunited with both Adrienne Corri and Cushing in Jimmy Sangster's *The Hellfire Club* (1960). Also returning from *Dracula* is Charles Lloyd Pack, who had just starred with Matthews as the reproachful head of the Medical Council in Hammer's first Frankenstein sequel.

Inspector Donovan is played by South African-born Nigel Green (1924-1972), who would do some of his best work as Christopher Lee's adversary in *The Face of Fu Manchu* (1965). The two actors had also endured the grueling Libyan Desert shoot of *Bitter Victory* (1957) and would later be in cahoots as the proprietors of a sleazy nightclub in *Beat Girl* (1959). Following cameos in *Stranger from Venus* (1954) and *Gorgo* (1959), Green essayed Hercules in *Jason and the Argonauts* (1961), Color-Sergeant Bourne in *Zulu* (1963) and Vincent Price's prisoner in *The Masque of the Red Death* (1963). His other credits include Major Dalby in *The Ipcress File* (1964), the eponymous kinsman of William Castle's *Let's Kill Uncle* (1966), the arch nemesis of Bulldog Drummond in *Deadlier than the Male* (1966), the Captain devoted to *Countess Dracula* (1970) and the "Electric Messiah" of *The Ruling Class* (1971).

Another familiar face in *Corridors of Blood* is Francis De Wolff (1913-1984), whom no one can describe without using the words "beetle-browed." The Hammer regular enjoys one of his most substantial horror roles as Black Ben, although his finest turn is as the Spirit of Christmas Present in *Scrooge* (1951). De Wolff's last film appearance would be as the Sea Captain preparing to ferry Lee's villainous Rochefort across the English Channel in *The Three Musketeers*.

Looking on at Karloff's grisly operations is Desmond Llewelyn (1914-1999), an actor who seemed fated for uncredited walk-ons, in everything from *Hamlet* to *The Pirates of Blood River*, until he landed the fortuitous role of Q, James Bond's gadget inventor, in 17 films, beginning with *From Russia with Love* (1963) and ending with *The World is Not Enough* (1999). Cinemagoers worldwide mourned this endearing actor's death in a car crash shortly after the latter film's release. Also among the medical students is future horror historian Alan Frank, whose richly illustrated books on the genre inspired a whole new wave of fans in the 1970s.

Originally intended to support another Producers Associates opus, Robert Day's *Quatermass* clone *First Man into Space* (1958), distributors MGM sat on *The Doctor from Seven Dials* for four years before releasing it in the UK as *Corridors of Blood* on Monday, September 24, 1962. The film was paired with *The Nights of Rasputin* (1960)—a French biopic of a character already played by Karloff, but yet to loom in Lee's career. *Corridors of Blood* didn't see a US release until Wednesday, June 5, 1963, when it formed the lower half of a "NERVO-RAMA" double bill with Italian shocker *Werewolf in a Girls' Dormitory* (1961). According to the *New York Times*, anyone who went to see the latter "deserves exactly what he gets," while *Corridors of Blood* was merely "a plodding, shuddersome exercise in blood and pain."

Receiving fairly good reviews (despite a dubious claim in the US press book that Karloff "actually smoked his first pipeful of opium as a research gesture for his role"), *Corridors of Blood*'s limited distribution inevitably led to poor box office takings and spelled the end of Producers Associates (their only other film is a 1958 Brian Clemens-penned spy thriller, *The Secret Man*).

Nonetheless, in a 1959 *Picturegoer* article entitled "What Horror Means to Me," Lee was enthused enough by the production to write of Karloff: "If I can have as successful a career as this noted 'pioneer' into horror fantasy, I shall be well content …"

The Loneliness of Evil

The Hound of the Baskervilles 1958

Sherlock Holmes and the Deadly Necklace (1962)
The Private Life of Sherlock Holmes (1969)
Sherlock Holmes: The Golden Years (1990)

Never has the night known a beast like this!

It gives me a curious feeling to reflect that on [the day of my birth], the list of attractions offered by London's picture palaces was headed by *The Adventures of Sherlock Holmes*. Had my mother known that one day I would myself be playing Sherlock ... she would certainly have felt that she had wasted her weekend!"—Christopher Lee, *Tall, Dark and Gruesome*

Shortly after *The Curse of Frankenstein*, renowned film critic Leslie Halliwell remembered attending a Hammer press conference at which James Carreras (1909-1990) announced his intention of making a "sexy Dracula." Peter Cushing, at his side, looked aghast. "Not you, Peter," Carreras assured him. "We'll leave that to Chris Lee. *You* can be a sexy Sherlock Holmes ..."

One of the unexpected consequences of *Dracula* for Christopher Lee was his newfound image as a sex symbol, illustrated by an August 1958 *Picturegoer* column headed: "Scream Boy? No—Dream Boy." Writer Gordon Campbell began his piece by calling Lee "filmdom's most fantastic heart-throb," and ended it, "His biggest beef? That he'll be saddled with that monster tag for good.

"'I'm really loveable,' he pleads.

"I'm not arguing," Campbell responded. "A bumper female postbag can't be wrong."

Certainly, at the height of his horror fame, Lee was receiving over 18,000 fan letters a year from around the world. To John Brosnan, he recalled one such missive from Romania which read: "We have decided, after careful thought and consideration, that you are, without any doubt, the most terrible actor in the world."

"A great compliment," said Lee.

In accord with his darkly romantic screen persona, "the most terrible actor in the world" arrived at Bray Studios on Monday, September 8, 1958, to play Sir Henry Baskerville in *The Hound of the Baskervilles*. Not only was this the first Sherlock Holmes film to be made in color, but also the first since Basil Rathbone's 14th enactment of the character in *Dressed to Kill* (Universal, 1946). Basil's debut outing as Holmes had been the previous filmed version of *The Hound of the Baskervilles* in 1939 (that same year, Peter Cushing met Rathbone and his Dr. Watson, Nigel Bruce, in Hollywood). As well as featuring such genre stalwarts as John Carradine and Lionel Atwill, this 20th Century Fox production had, as Sir Henry, a top-billed Richard Greene—who would later play Nayland Smith to Lee's Fu Manchu.

The rights to Sir Arthur Conan Doyle's stories were held by his son, Adrian, whom Hammer flew over from New York to serve as a consultant. In *Christopher Lee's New Chamber of Horrors*, Lee wrote: "I have been an admirer of Sir Arthur Conan Doyle and his work ever since I was a youngster," and revealed that Adrian "helped me with a lot of background information on his father and on Holmes"—information that the actor would put to good use when he later played the character.

First serialized in the *Strand Magazine* from August 1901 to April 1902, *The Hound of the Baskervilles* was referred to by its author as "a real creeper." A devotee of the paranormal, Conan Doyle had been inspired by legends of the spectral "black dog" of Dartmoor told to him by his friend Fletcher Robinson, whose valet, Harry Baskerville, lent his name to the resultant opus. In 1959, Hammer found Harry, then aged 88, and quoted him in their press book: "According to the legend, the dog once belonged to a girl who was murdered on the moor in the early 18th century by a jealous-crazed husband who suspected her of infidelity." A scenario which, although not mentioned in Conan Doyle's story, matches Hammer's sensational origin of the Baskerville curse.

Related to Holmes by Francis De Wolff's Dr. Mortimer, the stormy prologue sees Sir Hugo Baskerville forcing a man's head into a roaring fire, before chasing his daughter across the moors. The foregoing action takes place on Bernard Robinson's Castle Dracula set to recycled snatches from that film's soundtrack; although James Bernard had composed original music for this scene, against his knowledge, it was never used. Nevertheless, with the flashback's finale of a bloodied dagger on fallen leaves, and the crinoline hem of the heroine's dress at the edge of the frame, Terence Fisher perfectly encapsulates the ingredients of Hammer horror in a single image.

This preamble also serves to incorporate the theme of depraved nobility which saturates Hammer's work. Indeed, it could be argued that Sir Hugo represents the wickedest character in the company's oeuvre. The actor who plays him, David Oxley (1920-1985), had previously starred with Christopher Lee in *Ill Met By Moonlight* and would make his last screen appearance in the South African-shot *House of the Living Dead* (1973).

The Hound of the Baskervilles also explores inherited evil, the physical manifestation of which is a Hammer horror anomaly not found in the book, i.e., the webbed hands of both Sir Hugo and his embittered descendant Stapleton. The latter character is enacted by New Zealand-born Ewen Solon (1917-1985), who would go on to be the prime suspect in *Jack the Ripper* (1958), a camel vendor in *The Stranglers of Bombay* (1959) and Oliver Reed's stern employer in *The Curse of the Werewolf*.

Stapleton's daughter, Cecile, is played by Marla Landi (b. 1933). Impressed by her performance alongside Rod Steiger in the James Bernard-scored *Across the Bridge* (1957), Peter Cushing recommended the Italian actress to Hammer. A successful ex-model, she had played the girlfriend of the *First Man into Space* and, as the virtuous Bess Standing, would reteam with Christopher Lee at Bray for *The Pirates of Blood River*. Following her retirement from acting, Marla became the fashion editor of *Harper's Bazaar*, and, in 1977, married Sir Francis Dashwood—whose namesake ancestor founded the notorious 18th century Hellfire Club, the exploits of which inspired the 1960 film of that name with Peter Cushing.

Sir Henry's clinches with the fiery Cecile propose that the ideal role for Christopher Lee at this time would have been Heathcliff in a version of *Wuthering Heights*; a suggestion confirmed by Lee's indignant defense of his doomed romance and his look of confused heartbreak when he is finally harangued by the girl. Here, contrary to popular belief, Hammer gave the 36-year-old Lee a tremendous opportunity to show his range: There is a world of difference between the Creature, the Vampire Count, and Sir Henry. As well as being a fine, upstanding figure in jodhpurs and tweeds, Lee also serves to make the character a beautifully rounded human being, not only showing his vulnerability in the face of passion, but also his fear of the family curse. In addition, the actor's natural amusement when faced with Miles Malleson's twittering bishop makes their scene together a delight to watch.

Malleson (who, in po-faced reality, had recently helped organize the Campaign for Nuclear Disarmament's first protest march) is just one of the outstanding players on view in *The Hound of the Baskervilles*.

Prior to playing Sir Henry's butler, familiar-faced John Le Mesurier (1912-1983) had been a Scotland Yard man in *Mother Riley Meets the Vampire*, the twitchy psychiatrist in *Private's Progress* and the judge in *Blood of the Vampire*. While playing a captive in *The City Under the Sea* (1964), Vincent Price took the actor aside on the first day of filming and related that he owned a totem pole on which the name "Le Mesurier" was carved. It turned out that John's great-uncle had been friendly with a group of Native Americans who'd made the engraving in his honor. In another twist, Le Mesurier picked up one of the ancient books used as props in the film, only to discover his name written on the flyleaf.

Holmes shakes hands with Sir Baskerville as Watson (Andre Morell) looks on (back row, right).

The signature was dated 1873. "I nicked it, of course," John wrote in his memoir, *A Jobbing Actor*, but after reading a few pages, decided that "insect habits in Southern Borneo did not make for compelling literature." Le Mesurier's other credits include Dr. Tranter in *Jack the Ripper* (1958), Dr. Slattery in *The Wrong Box* (1965) and Dr. Monnet in *Eye of the Devil* (1965), but he is most fondly remembered as the woolly-headed Sergeant Wilson in *Dad's Army* (1968-1977)—a favorite sitcom of Christopher Lee's (as he revealed in a 1990s *Radio Times* interview).

"Holmes is not a particularly attractive character, you know, if you really look at him closely," Lee told Marcus Hearn in 2004, before elaborating: "There's an element of Baron Frankenstein in Sherlock Holmes; that cold, calculating approach to the problem." Nevertheless, in the same interview, Lee revealed how Peter Cushing kept him amused in the role by over-pronouncing his *t*'s and wagging his finger in the air to make a point. With a manic energy that suggests the detective was ingesting something stronger than

Sherlock Holmes (Peter Cushing) prepares to knock the tarantula off Sir Baskerville's shoulder with his cane.

The Loneliness of Evil

Watson and Sir Henry Baskerville peer outside.

tobacco, Cushing has the soul of Holmes down pat. Once filming was over, the actor kept his deerstalker hat and could often be seen wearing it while painting watercolors around Whitstable. Before essaying Sir Arthur Conan Doyle, in *The Great Houdini* (1976), Cushing reprised his finely detailed characterization of *Sherlock Holmes* in 1968. This BBC series includes an altogether shakier adaptation of "The Hound of the Baskervilles" that benefits, nevertheless, from authentic Dartmoor locations and is, at least, superior to the 1972 TV version with Stewart Granger. Hammer's Sherlock, however, remains the best of them all, and *The Hound of the Baskervilles* was screened by the BBC to commemorate Peter Cushing's death in August 1994.

Playing in stark contrast to Nigel Bruce's doddery depiction of Watson is Andre Morell (1909-1978), who had enacted a very different relationship with Cushing as his po-faced torturer in both *Nineteen Eighty-Four* and Hammer's *Cash on Demand* (1961). Directly after giving us cinema's finest interpretation of Holmes' official biographer, Morell went on to play Professor Quatermass in the BBC's *Quatermass and the Pit*. Having previously worked with Terence Fisher in *So Long at the Fair* (1949) and *Stolen Face*, Morell was also the superintendent, racing against time to locate a stolen nuclear weapon, in *Seven Days to Noon* (co-written by James Bernard). As Inspector Byard, he appeared in Hitchcock's *Stage Fright* (1949) with Miles Malleson, and, as Professor James Bickford, he faced *Behemoth the Sea Monster*. Morell's other Hammer credits include the unflappable Colonel Lambert in the powerful prisoner-of-war drama *The Camp on Blood Island* (1957), the scheming Walter in *The Shadow of the Cat* (1960) and Sir Basil Walden, discoverer of *The Mummy's Shroud* (1966). His best role for the company, however, is the formidable Sir James Forbes, who battles *The Plague of the Zombies* (1965). In real life, Morell was good pals with David Lean (for whom he played Colonel Green in *The Bridge on the River Kwai* [1957]) and served as Best Man at the director's fourth wedding. Morell's own spouse, Joan Greenwood, took part in a head-spinning *Exorcist* spoof for Paul Morrissey's 1977 take on *The Hound of the Baskervilles*, scripted by Peter Cook and Dudley Moore.

Scripting duties on Hammer's *Hound* fell to Peter Bryan (1919-1972). A former camera operator, Bryan had impressed Anthony Hinds with an un-filmed treatment for Hammer's abortive *Tales of Frankenstein* TV series (the basis of Bryan's storyline would eventually be made as *The Evil of Frankenstein* [1963]). As well as contributing to *The Brides of Dracula*, Bryan also wrote *The Plague of the Zombies*, which similarly shows the horror of a corrupt aristocracy who believe that their wealth entitles them to abuse humanity. The result is one of Hammer's greatest films, so it comes as a surprise that Bryan would later be responsible for *The Blood Beast Terror* (1967), which Peter Cushing apparently considered his worst (it wasn't—that accolade must go to *Hitler's Son*, a 1977 "comedy" in which Cushing's Nazi character tries to resurrect the Third Reich). Bryan's other credits include a Richard Gordon sci-fi production, *The Projected Man* (1965), and *Trog* (1969), which he co-wrote with *Plague of the Zombies* director John Gilling.

One innovation that Bryan brings to his *Hound of the Baskervilles* script is to have Sir Henry attacked by a tarantula (in the novel, he merely receives a threatening note). A sufferer of arachnophobia, Christopher Lee was not looking forward to having the "ghastly bird-eating spider from South America" crawl up his shoulder. On being brought to the set in a plastic box, the tarantula's guardian told Lee that it wasn't deadly, it would just, at worst, give him "a nasty bite." Nevertheless, this didn't stop the entire crew from running away in terror when the creature crawled towards them. After shedding its skin on the studio floor, Lee refused to have the arachnid on his neck as Terence Fisher desired. A compromise was reached whereby it would creep only as far as Lee's shoulder. "This was enough to turn me green with nausea," the actor later wrote. "The realism of my performance was universally commended."

Indeed, the scene carries a palpable tension through Lee's sweat-dripping expression, even if the spider, when seen in mid-shot, is quite clearly a prop (all the better for Cushing to knock it to the floor with a swish of his cane).

Lee was less impressed by the realism of the hound itself, which Conan Doyle described as "a great, black beast" with "blazing eyes and dripping jaws." After a parade of canine candidates had auditioned unsuccessfully ("Even Crufts failed us," Cushing remembered in his memoirs), a Great Dane named Colonel was eventually selected. But how to transform him into the terrifying hound of Doyle's imagination? One solution was to garb three young lads in the clothing of Lee, Cushing and Morell, and then film them on miniature sets to give the dog a more gigantic, fearsome appearance. Alas, on viewing the rushes, Cushing observed: "We saw three small boys dressed up as if playing a game of charades, foggy toy scenery with a wet, hungry dog in the middle, contentedly wolfing a bone. The sequence was scrapped."

It fell, instead, to former make-up assistant Roy Ashton who, following Phil Leakey's departure from Hammer after *The Revenge of Frankenstein*, was now the company's head make-up man. Thrown in at the deep end for his first solo assignment, Ashton worked at creating a suitably terrifying mask to place over Colonel's head, only to find that the canine thespian would pull off the results and attempt to eat them. Eventually, and much to Ashton's relief, the job was passed on to Margaret Carter (1920-2016) in the special effects department, who made the finished piece from rabbit fur. Fortuitously, she also fell in love with Bernard Robinson; the pair were married in 1960.

The well-fed Colonel was prompted into action by the sound of paper being crumpled until, appropriately riled, he actually bit Christopher Lee on the arm. Despite the actor's statement that the hound was "not at all realistic" and "made a nonsense of the story," the eventual effect is, in fact, nowhere near as unconvincing as Lee and others have made out, especially as the animal is supposed to be wearing a mask, anyway. Rather, its attack on Sir Henry is appropriately feral, thanks to a winning combination of frenzied acting, punchy editing and James Bernard's intensive score. The only sour note comes when Cushing unmasks the beast—the face beneath the mask looks identical to its covering. On the other hand, Jack Asher's photography and Bernard Robinson's sets are typically flawless.

The Hound of the Baskervilles wrapped on Friday October 31, 1958 (Halloween). Distributed by United Artists, the film premiered at the London Pavilion on Saturday March 28, 1959, before going on general release in the UK on Monday, May 4 (when the late Buddy Holly was at No. 1 with "It Doesn't Matter Anymore"). Whereas some would dispute that *The Hound of the Baskervilles* is truly a horror film, with taglines like "The most horror-dripping tale ever written!" and "Sherlock Holmes' most terrifying adventure!", its publicists certainly wanted us to think that it was. After all, the 19th century detective fiction of Conan Doyle and others often called upon Gothic devices to instill a mysterious atmosphere.

Hammer's publicity also included ties with the Briar Pipe Trade Association, who placed posters of Cushing as Holmes in the windows of Britain's tobacconists declaring: "Be like Sherlock Holmes! Smoke a pipe … and see *The Hound of the Baskervilles* at your local cinema!" A Stateside release followed on Friday, July 3, 1959 (when Johnny Horton enjoyed the last of six weeks at the top of the charts with "The Battle of New Orleans"). Despite good opening business and some fairly positive reviews, the

Sir Henry Baskerville (Christopher Lee) is about to confront the hound from Hell.

eventual profits for *The Hound of the Baskervilles* were too slight for Hammer to consider making any further Holmes adventures. What a shame that they never pitted him against Lee's Count—as proven by the novels *Sherlock Holmes vs. Dracula* (Loren D. Estleman, 1978) and *The Tangled Skein* (David Stuart Davies, 1992), this would have been a more than ideal match. (The latter title actually serves as a coda to *The Hound of the Baskervilles*, with scenes and dialogue lifted straight from the Hammer canon; in his Foreword, Peter Cushing writes: "[Davies'] vivid descriptive passages of action make one long to see 'the film of the book'!")

The more family-oriented "A" certificate may have kept horror-hungry hordes away from *The Hound of the Baskervilles* in the UK, but one US patron was so impressed by the "sheer Englishness" of Christopher Lee that, as he revealed in his memoir, she offered the actor $10,000 to impersonate a lawyer; the intention being that, in such a guise, he would convince her Anglophile father that her impending marriage was worthy of approval. Although "sorry to disappoint her," Lee was sure that, unlike Sir Henry and Cecile, "love would find a way" for his young fan.

The summer of 1962 saw Lee rejoin Terence Fisher in Berlin to take his first stab at the role of the Master Detective in *Sherlock Holmes and the Deadly Necklace*. "Deadly is the word," Lee surmised to Marcus Hearn, before acknowledging that the film had "the best Baker Street set I've ever seen." Scripted by horror legend Curt Siodmak (*The Wolf Man*, *I Walked with a Zombie*), *Sherlock Holmes and the Deadly Necklace* is supposedly based on Doyle's 1915 novel *The Valley of Fear*, but the plot, instead, involves some nonsense about Cleopatra's missing necklace. Often resembling a 1940s B-production, there are creaky goings-on in an old dark house and a near-suspenseful moment with a mummy's casket, but the results are curiously unengaging for all the talent involved. Shot without live sound, as was the German practice at that time, the English-language version sees Lee revoiced by an American actor, who, at one point, speaks with the campest Cockney accent ever to grace the screen. To make matters worse, none of the voiceover artists seem capable of pronouncing the name of Holmes' arch-nemesis, Moriarty. While physically, at least, Lee and Thorley Walters make an ideal pairing as Holmes and Watson, it's regretful that they

This East German poster for *The Hound of the Baskervilles* features Christopher Lee.

didn't play the duo in a decent film together (although, in 1975, Walters played Watson alongside Douglas Wilmer in *The Adventures of Sherlock Holmes' Smarter Brother*). On the plus side, Lee affects Doyle's description of Holmes' "great hawk's-bill of a nose" and gets to don a variety of disguises. In fact, Lee is the actor who best resembles Sidney Paget's original *Strand* illustrations to Doyle's stories (from which the public gleaned their visual idea of Holmes, right down to the deerstalker hat which was never mentioned by the author).

Sherlock Holmes and the Deadly Necklace was granted a limited theatrical release in the UK, six years after it was made, and was sold directly to US television in 1964. As such, a mooted follow-up, *Sherlock Holmes Unmasks Jack the Ripper*, was never made—unless one counts *A Study in Terror* (1965) and *Murder by Decree* (1978), which share the same idea. Summing up his experience on *Sherlock Holmes and the Deadly Necklace*, Terence Fisher told historian Tony Dalton (in *LSoH*): "The only good thing about the whole sorry mess was that I got to go to Germany and I didn't much enjoy it there either."

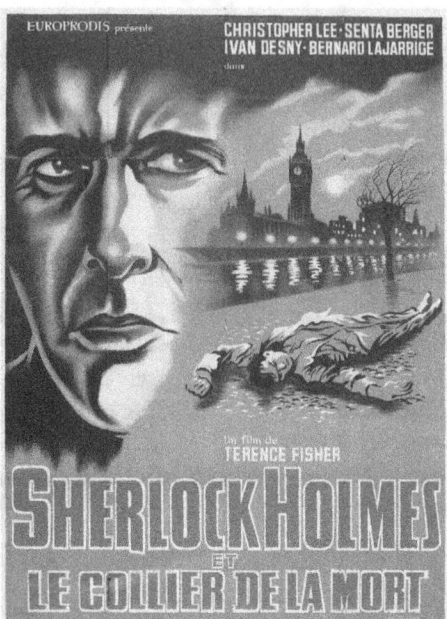

French poster for **Sherlock Holmes and the Deadly Necklace**

In May 1969, Lee was cast as Sherlock's brother Mycroft in *The Private Life of Sherlock Holmes* by Billy Wilder (1906-2002). The celebrated director had not only gifted cinema with some of its biggest comedies (*The Seven Year Itch* [1954], *Some Like It Hot* [1958]), but also with some of its most chilling visions via *The Lost Weekend* (1944) and *Sunset Blvd.* (1949, the ultimate in Hollywood Gothic). Wilder's aim with *Holmes* was to present the emotional frailties of the seemingly infallible sleuth, but for such a master filmmaker, the results are curiously un-cinematic: Everything is revealed through the literate dialogue, leaving little in the way of visual storytelling, despite a premise involving the Loch Ness Monster and an old Scottish castle. While filming at the aforesaid location, a swarm of bats soared over the actors' heads, to which Wilder, addressing Lee, quipped: "You must feel quite at home here." Originally running at over three hours, two episodes were cut from the film before release: "The Dreadful Business of the Naked Honeymooners" and "The Case of the Upside-Down Room." The sacrifice of the latter meant that *Dracula*'s George Benson saw his performance as Inspector Lestrade hit the cutting room floor. On a happier note, the 30-foot Loch Ness Monster prop, which had sunk to the bottom of the Loch during filming, was rediscovered in April 2016, disappointing Nessie hunters, who, at first, assumed it to be the real thing. Despite winning critical plaudits, *The Private Life of Sherlock Holmes* was a flop when first released in October, 1970, but is now widely regarded as a classic.

While hosting *Saturday Night Live* in March 1978, Lee filmed a sketch as Holmes alongside John Belushi's Watson, but his next serious take on the role came in 1990 for executive producer Harry Alan Towers (more of whom later). Set in 1910, *Sherlock Holmes: The Golden Years* comprises two made-for-

Lee and Patrick Macnee in **Sherlock Holmes: The Golden Years**

television features, "Incident at Victoria Falls" and "Sherlock Holmes and the Leading Lady," in which Holmes and Watson are dragged out of retirement to solve the respective mysteries. Along the way, they hop across the globe, meeting various special guest stars as real-life historical figures. In essence, the idea is a very good one, although the execution is far less impressive, with each adventure's three-hour running time being far too long to sustain interest. Nevertheless, there are some charming moments between Lee and his old school chum Patrick Macnee as Watson (both actors testified to a lot of corpsing going on behind the scenes). A few years later, Lee brought his story-telling skills to the fore when he recorded Doyle's *The Casebook of Sherlock Holmes* as an audio book.

On a final note, in 2014, 75-year-old Ian McKellen (who competed with Lee to win the roles of Gandalf in *The Lord of the Rings* and Magneto in *X-Men* [1999]) starred as a 93-year-old Sherlock in *Mr. Holmes*. As Lee would actually have been that age upon the film's release, I, for one, would have loved to have seen him play the role of the Great Detective one last time, in what could have been a most intriguing valediction.

Lee as Mycroft Holmes with Robert Stephens as Sherlock in **The Private Life of Sherlock Holmes**

The Man Who Could Cheat Death 1958

His hideous obsession led him to commit ghastly crimes of passion and violence.

In 1939, 17-year-old Christopher Lee thrilled to Barré Lyndon's play *The Man in Half Moon Street* at London's New Theatre. In the title role was Leslie Banks, the inhumane Count Zaroff of *The Most Dangerous Game* (1932). When the play was filmed by Paramount in 1943, Nils Asther topped the bill and the script was provided by Garret Fort, who'd previously worked on Universal's *Dracula* and *Frankenstein*. After Hammer's late '50s success with those characters, Paramount offered them *The Man in Half Moon Street* for the usual distribution rights. This marked an unprecedented achievement for an independent British company, as Hammer could now boast of having ties with all the major American studios (with the obvious exception of Disney).

Once again, Jimmy Sangster paid no heed to the earlier film when writing his script; in fact, as he admitted in his memoirs, he wasn't even aware there had been a prior adaptation. While the 1943 version had taken place in contemporary London, Sangster set his action in 1890s Paris.

Announced as *The Man in the Rue Noire*, an exhausted Peter Cushing pulled out of the title role only six days before production began on Monday, November 17, 1958. Given that *The Hound of the Baskervilles* had wrapped just over a fortnight before, and he had been working for the company non-stop since *Dracula*, Cushing's fatigue is more than understandable. Despite this, in his book *A New Heritage of Horror*, David Pirie uncovered a letter from Hammer's lawyers which severely reprimands their star actor for "the extremely difficult position" they felt he had placed them in.

Christopher Lee stayed on, nonetheless, in the supporting role of Dr. Pierre Gerrard. Unfortunately, the part gives him precious little to do except look dashing in evening dress and false moustaches against Bernard Robinson's busy sets. Landed with such a dull character, why wasn't Lee elevated to the title role after Cushing stepped down? The answer can be found in the film's pressbook, which doesn't even trade on the actor's recent monster roles, describing him, instead, as just one of the "attractive performers" who have been "seen on many top television shows." The publicity angle is focused mainly on leading lady Hazel Court, who "will be remembered as the heroine of *The Curse of Frankenstein*." It's clear from this that Hammer had yet to fully realize Lee's star potential, despite his triumph as *Dracula*.

The company itself had failed with a Hollywood TV project they'd embarked upon in February 1958. Entitled *Tales of Frankenstein*, only one episode, "The Face in the Tombstone Mirror," was made. Written and directed by Curt Siodmak, the Monster was played by Don Megowan (*The Creature Walks Among Us*). Although the American crew were treated to a screening of *The Curse of Frankenstein* before filming began, the results seem more inspired by Universal, with only the use of Peter Cushing's outfit from *Curse* establishing any sort of Hammer link. Garbed in said costume, as the Baron, was Anton Diffring (1918-1989); *The Man Who Could Cheat Death* would see him stepping into Cushing's place once more.

German and Jewish, Diffring, ironically, made a career playing Nazi-like characters in such films as *Fahrenheit 451* (1966) and *Where Eagles Dare* (1968). He had previously appeared with Christopher Lee as a fellow suspect in *The Traitor*, but then came to Hammer's attention when Anthony Hinds saw his performance in a June 1957 broadcast of "The Man in Half Moon Street" for ITV's *Hour of Mystery* (perhaps, too, this is where Hinds spotted *Dracula*'s Melissa Stribling, who played the female lead).

Diffring's fellow countryman Arnold Marle (1887-1970) was also plucked from the TV play to reprise his role as Dr. Ludwig Weiss (Marle had given a standout performance as the wise old Lhama in *The Abominable Snowman* and went on to essay Dr. Murton in *The Snake Woman* [1960]).

For Bonnet's former lover, Margo, Hammer cast Delphi Lawrence (1932-2002), who, after playing Lee's mistress in *Beat Girl*, would wine and dine Peter Cushing in *Cone of Silence* (1960).

Subsequent to *The Man Who Could Cheat Death*, Anton Diffring became the TV game-show host of *Win a Mink* (1959),

Italian poster for *The Man Who Could Cheat Death*

Christopher Lee as Dr. Pierre Gerrard in *The Man Who Could Cheat Death*

which must have made a nice change from Nazis and mad doctors. Or maybe not. That same year, he was immortalized as the obsessive surgeon with an eye for scarred women in *Circus of Horrors*. This was one of three graphic shockers, all released by Anglo-Amalgamated in the late 1950s, that would cause an uproar (the others were *Horrors of the Black Museum* and *Peeping Tom*). Similar controversy followed *Mark of the Devil Part II* (1972), in which Diffring's sadistic witchfinder wallows in torture and bared breasts. After going topless himself in Antonio Margheriti's *Seven Deaths in the Cat's Eye* (1972), Diffring made his second and final Hammer appearance in the Hong Kong-shot actioner *Shatter* (1973). The latter also starred Peter Cushing, with whom Anton would be reunited in Amicus' *The Beast Must Die* (1973) and Tyburn's *The Masks of Death* (1984). Diffring's last screen role was as a fascist ally of the Cybermen in the 1988 *Doctor Who* adventure "Silver Nemesis."

In her autobiography, Hazel Court remembered Anton as "charming to work with, but there was a distance in him." She attributed *The Man Who Could Cheat Death*'s eventual lack of success to Peter Cushing not being in the title role, which shows how important actors were to Hammer's fortunes. Cushing may have invested some much-needed energy to the proceedings, but it's doubtful that even he could have brought much sympathy to the thoroughly dislikeable Dr. Georges Bonnet. The 104-year-old character appears to be 35, thanks to human glands he obtains through murder. One such killing spree opens the film and its shadowy, fog-bound presentation recalls Jimmy Sangster's most recent screenplay *Jack the Ripper* (it's worth noting that the play's original author Barré Lyndon had scripted the Ripper-inspired Hollywood thrillers *The Lodger* [1943] and *Hangover Square* [1944]).

There's an additional whiff of Jekyll and Hyde as Bonnet drinks a bubbling green fluid to provide temporary relief from his ills. One of Terence Fisher's more interesting set-ups shows Diffring chugging back the potion from within the safe where he keeps it locked. Otherwise, aside from Bonnet's pop-eyed attack on Margo and a fiery climax, *The Man Who Could Cheat Death* reverts to the inert staginess of *Alias John Preston* and its ilk, with the sole difference being Jack Asher's gorgeous lighting.

As Anthony Hinds was engaged at the company's London offices, *The Man Who Could Cheat Death* saw Michael Carreras (1927-1994) produce the first of three consecutive Hammer horrors with Christopher Lee (the others were *The Mummy* and *The Two Faces of Dr. Jekyll*). Music lover Carreras was also a talented jazz trumpeter (he can be seen playing with the band in Terence Fisher's 1953 thriller *Face the Music*). As such, he thought carefully about his films' scores, bringing in outside composers, not only to give James Bernard a rest, but also to differentiate his product as much as possible from Hinds' (Carreras was so closely involved with his soundtracks that he later scrapped a perfectly good score by Benjamin Frankel for *The Lost Continent* [1967] and commissioned a new one from Gerard Schurmann, despite the expensive film being already over budget). *The Man Who Could Cheat Death* features music from the revered Richard Rodney Bennett, then aged just 22. Bennett would also work on *The Nanny* (1965) and *The Witches* (1966) at Hammer, before providing one of his final scores for the BBC's *Gormenghast* (1999), starring Christopher Lee.

Despite a hectic schedule, Carreras found time to grace European prints of *The Man Who Could Cheat Death* with a topless view of Hazel Court as she poses for a sculpture. In her autobiography, Hazel recalled the sequence as "very beautifully shot." To achieve the finished statue in the film, she also remembered being covered in plaster at Pinewood Studios by two Cockney gentlemen who remarked: "It's like slapping fish, isn't it?" as they applied the wet mixture to her skin. (Hammer's late '50s competitors Tempean Films had initiated the practice of adding nude sequences to Continental prints with *Jack the Ripper* and later *The Flesh and the Fiends*.)

"I always seem to be in horror movies about making dead men live again," Hazel Court mused in her memoirs. One such film is *Doctor Blood's Coffin* (1960), which, akin to *The Man Who Could Cheat Death*, sees Hazel being grasped at by a living, rotting corpse in the final reel. Far more interesting, however, are the three diverse characters she plays in Roger Corman's Edgar Allan Poe adaptations, *Premature Burial* (1961), *The Raven* (1962) and *The Masque of the Red Death* (whose trailer describes her as "The Devil's Own Darling").

A talented painter and sculptress, Hazel's artwork was long supported and admired by her Poe co-star Vincent Price,

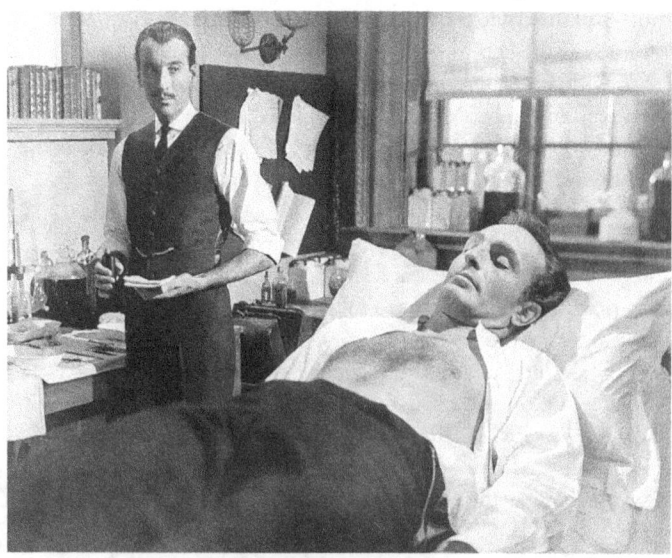

Christopher Lee and Anton Diffring

who purchased some of her pieces for his famed Sears and Roebuck Collection (in her youth, she had even been painted by the eminent artist Augustus John). In 1964, the same year that she appeared in The Twilight Zone episode "The Fear," Hazel married American actor/director Don Taylor, whom she met while filming "The Crocodile Case" (1958), the first of her four appearances on Alfred Hitchcock Presents. Taylor had starred as Robin Hood in Hammer's Men of Sherwood Forest and would later direct Escape from the Planet of the Apes (1970), The Island of Dr. Moreau (1977), and Damien: Omen II (1977). Court's last feature film was Omen III: The Final Conflict (1980), in which she can be seen handing out refreshments at a fox hunt. As well as possessing a magical aura (Olive Sturgess told Tom Weaver that Hazel went around reading everybody's palms in between takes on The Raven), Court was the only actress to have starred alongside all five of the era's major horror stars: Lee, Karloff, Price, Cushing, and Peter Lorre.

The real star of The Man Who Could Cheat Death, however, is Roy Ashton's make-up. To achieve the realistic burns on Delphi Lawrence's face, Ashton consulted medical textbooks, and when Bonnet rapidly ages at the film's climax, every disease that the character would have avoided over the years becomes visible. The collapsible veins that run down Diffring's head were just blue threads from one of Ashton's old cardigans, covered in liquid latex. As Roy remembered the actor complaining: "My God! If I had known what all of this involves, I would never have accepted the role!"

One man who was more impressed with Ashton's work on The Man Who Could Cheat Death was Oscar-winning make-up artist Dick Smith (1922-2014): While puzzling over how to transform 32-year-old Dustin Hoffman into the 121-year-old Little Big Man (1969), he contacted Ashton for advice. The older artist revealed his secrets, and Smith would further utilize them in such films as House of Dark Shadows (1970), The Hunger (1982) and Amadeus (1983).

Filming of The Man in the Rue Noire wrapped on Tuesday December 30, 1958. Renamed The Man Who Could Cheat Death during post-production, the film was trade-shown in the US on Thursday, June 4, 1959, but didn't premiere in the UK until Monday, November 30, 1959 (almost a year after shooting had finished) when Cliff Richard and the Shadows were at No. 1 with "Travelin' Light." The hoarding at London's Plaza Theatre depicted Diffring's image from the poster and hawked: "Sensational! Sexsational X Programme" of its double bill status with French melodrama The Evil That Is Eve (1957).

The critics, of course, thought differently. "Another feeble, cliché-ridden film," C.A. Lejeune sniffed in the Observer. "I feel sorry for everyone concerned; what dreary, lifeless work the concoction of these horror pictures must be…"

The Star, meanwhile, lamented: "After … the intelligent and provocative Yesterday's Enemy, and the well made The Mummy, the horror boys at Hammer films get back to ham and ketchup."

They also got back to promotional gimmicks; one of the most curious being a tie-in with the Better Driver Safety Campaign, who issued posters declaring: "The Man Who Could Cheat Death outsmarted himself. YOU could be smarter. Be a *Better* Driver. Arrive Alive."

Despite such ballyhoo, the film's small profits were not as high as hoped for, and Paramount wouldn't distribute another Hammer horror until Frankenstein and the Monster from Hell in 1974.

While, for copyright reasons, Bram Stoker's Dracula could only be reprinted as a tie-in to Hammer's film in the US, no such legislation prevented Ace Books (who had just brought out Britain's first authorized paperback edition of Lady Chatterley's Lover) from issuing a novelization of The Man Who Could Cheat Death, in 1959. Bashed out in two weeks by Jimmy Sangster under the pen name of John Sansom, the novel was copyrighted to Sangster and Barré Lyndon, who both receive credit on the cover of Avon Books' US edition. Unfortunately, a lengthy mid-section detailing Bonnet's escapades abroad fails to make the story any more interesting, even if Sangster's prose offers lurid descriptions that were not permissible on film, such as: "Margo's scream of terror was cut off as Georges whipped out his hand and clapped it across her mouth. With his other hand he grabbed her across the shoulders, ripping her dress and allowing her breasts to tumble free. For a moment they stood close together, the beautiful half naked woman and the ghastly green skeleton that held her."

Although the movie itself is far more disappointing than the above passage suggests, Dr. Bonnet's desire to remain perpetually young feels more relevant today than ever: In a media-fixated world of airbrushed flesh and cosmetic enhancement, creations far more unnatural than anything cooked up by Bonnet or Frankenstein stare back at us from newspapers, magazines and TV screens every day.

Back in the more innocent days of November 1958, though, Christopher Lee told Picturegoer: "Horror is pure escapism and rattling good entertainment if directed with the skill and polish of Dracula." Never were truer words spoken. But sadly, The Man Who Could Cheat Death is entertainment that never quite rattles, and while there is certainly great skill in evidence onscreen, the final product very much lacks the required polish.

Lee's next film for Hammer, however, would be an altogether different concern.

The Mummy
1959

Torn from the tomb to terrify the world!

In *The Mummy*, I only kill three people. And not in a ghastly way. I just break their necks."—Christopher Lee, *Picturegoer Film Annual 1959-1960*

After the resounding success of *Dracula*, Universal-International allowed Hammer the unprecedented right to remake or reuse ideas from their considerable back catalogue of horror classics. With no literary antecedent to draw upon, *The Mummy* was one instance in which an alliance with Universal was essential for production to go ahead. A number of the studio's forays with the undead Egyptian were screened for screenwriter Jimmy Sangster at Bray. As well as adopting the revivifying Scroll of Life and reincarnated love angle from *The Mummy* (1932), Sangster employed an amalgamation of ideas and character names from its sequels *The Mummy's Hand* (1940), *The Mummy's Tomb* (1942), *The Mummy's Ghost* (1943) and *The Mummy's Curse* (1944).

Production of Hammer's *The Mummy* began on Monday, February 23, 1959. Director Terence Fisher outlined his approach in an on-set interview: "We don't go in for monsters from outer space, man-devouring vegetables or killer spiders the size of locomotives. Our monsters are always human, or near-human—like Dracula, Frankenstein's Creature and the Mummy. They are believable, and for that reason far more terrifying."

Christopher Lee completed his triumvirate of classic monsters as Kharis, the Mummy. During their early morning make-up sessions, Lee and Roy Ashton would belt out opera together over Bray's intercom system. "Christopher was an excellent performer to work with," Ashton recalled (in *Greasepaint and Gore*), "a most cooperative gentleman." Of the Hammer monsters, he further revealed: "Beneath the grotesque exterior, each one struggles with a very humanizing dilemma. That's why I have never felt ashamed of the genre in which I work." Ashton certainly has nothing to be ashamed of with his work on *The Mummy*.

Beneath those suitably decayed bandages, Lee gave new meaning to the Mummy's curse when banging his knees against the network of pipes that ran beneath the studio swamp. Nevertheless, he still managed to elicit amusement from his favorite co-star, Peter Cushing, this time cast as the film's archaeologist hero, John Banning. "There was a gap in the conversation," Lee told Bruce Sachs and Russell Wall, "and I leaned towards [Peter] and said in a high-pitched voice, 'I'm just waiting for someone to say: Just don't stand there—kill someone!' Then I can go home to the wife and kids!"

Such light-heartedness was vital for Lee, as, entrapped within his make-up, he could only breathe through the mask's eyeholes; with surprising dereliction, no one had thought to ventilate his nose. This wasn't the only indignity Lee suffered during production. "I did things in that film that Arnold Schwarzenegger wouldn't do," he revealed in *100 Years of Horror* (1995), before cataloguing cuts, bruises and a dislocated shoulder from bursting through a door, as well as shards of glass from a window, which stuck into his bandages, making him look "like a hedgehog." This was in addition to powder burns inflicted by explosive squibs and torn muscles in his back from carrying Yvonne Furneaux ("120 pounds, at least, of inert womanhood").

Born in France, 1928, Furneaux first made the acquaintance of Christopher Lee as a singing barmaid who repels his advances in *The Dark Avenger*. Having made her debut, in the 1952 Noël Coward portmanteau *Meet Me Tonight*, opposite *Bride of Frankenstein*'s Valerie Hobson, Yvonne would end her career as *Frankenstein's Great-Aunt Tillie* (1983). In between, she enjoyed leading roles in Fellini's *La Dolce Vita* (1959) and *The Secret of Dr. Mabuse* (1963), before simulating British cinema's first audible onscreen orgasm in *Repulsion* (1964). When Mark A. Miller asked the actor what inspired her to accept the dual role of Kharis' lover, Ananka, and Banning's wife, Isobel, she replied: "I was bored." Nevertheless, in the same interview, she conceded: "Lee was totally involved in what he was doing. He attacked his part like an actor would attack Hamlet ... He took it so seriously. And so did Peter ... I thought to myself: 'Woman, you better start taking this part seriously. You've got good people around you here.'"

Furneaux was less endeared when Lee picked her up and said, "My God, you're heavy!"—before dropping her into the swamp (as she revealed to David Del Valle in *LSoH #24*).

Anthony Hinds was similarly unimpressed by *The Mummy*, preferring full-blooded Gothics. Hence, production chores were handed to Michael Carreras, who was typically selective when it came to the film's composer: An ex-student of Vaughan Williams, Franz Reizenstein (1911-1968) provides a bombastic score, among Hammer's best (he also scored *Circus of Horrors*).

Keen to make the movie look as glossy as it sounded, Carreras hired a large stage at Shepperton Studios to film the burial procession of Princess Ananka. The producer even employed Andrew Low, an expert on Egyptian history, to ensure that all the hieroglyphics on Margaret Carter's props were authentic (Ananka's fiberglass sarcophagus was toured to cinemas during the film's promotion and today resides in the basement of Perth Museum, Scotland). Although Hammer are often dismissed as a cheapjack production company, their attention to detail is more than commendable, even if Low's objection that Karnak was a place name and not a God, as in the script, fell on deaf ears.

As with *The Man Who Could Cheat Death*, Carreras shot additional footage for foreign export, this time of topless handmaidens. Further decoration was provided by a leopard, loaned from Southport Zoo, named Chiefy (or "Big Chief Horrible Noise" as Barbara Shelley dubbed him when he played her feline counterpart in 1957's *Cat Girl*). Lee told Marcus Hearn that, while looking "noble and sad and priestly" for the scene, he heard Chiefy's owner say behind him: "If I let go of the chain, that'll start this lot into a gallop!"

In the same interview, Lee revealed that he was reunited with Chiefy for publicity purposes—an idea which was sprung upon him as he arrived for a press interview at a Manchester hotel. Lee recalled a van pulling up outside, from which Chiefy was handed to him on a chain. Michael Carreras then asked the actor to escort the big cat indoors, to which an aghast Lee thought: "Can you imagine getting stuck in a swinging door with an angry leopard?" On finally agreeing to take Chiefy inside, but not through the swinging doors, Lee was greeted by frantic cries of: "Get that animal out of here, for God's sake!" and wasn't too surprised when "people just vanished."

A similar outcome affects Peter Cushing's head, when dwarfed within a massive pith helmet, as Banning excavates Ananka's tomb. Accompanied by his father Stephen (Felix Aylmer) and uncle Joseph Whemple (Raymond Huntley), the trio plunder on despite the warnings of George Pastell's Mehemet Bey (in Sangster's typical no-nonsense style, he pares down Universal's flowery High Priest admonitions to, simply: "He who robs the graves of Egypt, dies"). As a consequence of what he sees in the green-lit tomb, Stephen suffers a mental breakdown and Terence Fisher makes excellent use of tilted angles to suggest his disordered mind.

Felix Aylmer (1889-1979) had last been directed by Fisher as the British Consul in *So Long at the Fair* (1949). He was also Polonius in Olivier's *Hamlet*, one of *The Ghosts of Berkeley Square* (1947), and both Carol Marsh's father and the Cheshire Cat in 1949's *Alice in Wonderland*. His next Hammer assignment was as the seamy child molester in *Never Take Sweets from a Stranger*.

Raymond Huntley (1904-1990) had previously worked with Fisher on the director's Hammer debut *The Last Page* (1951), but is most renowned to horror fans for playing Dracula in Hamilton Deane's legendary West End stage production of 1927. When the play came to Broadway in October of that year, Huntley turned down the role, paving the way for a little-known Hungarian actor named Bela Lugosi to step into his shoes. This fateful decision led, of course, to Bela's immortal film performance which, in turn, kick-started the Horror Film proper into being. Nevertheless, Huntley holds the record for most on-stage appearances as the Count. To honor this achievement, Dacre Stoker—Bram's great grand-nephew—named a character Inspector Huntley in his 2009 "official sequel," *Dracula the Un-dead*. Another of the book's main protagonists—a tall, ex-military man—was called Sergeant Lee in "homage to the actor Christopher Lee."

"It was all rather like working for Hamilton Deane," Huntley recollected of Hammer to David J. Skal, and the actor later told David Williams, in *LSoH* #32, that Christopher Lee ("a very respectful gentleman") was interested in his experiences playing Dracula. Huntley would be reunited with Cushing in the Boulting Brothers' thriller *Suspect* (1959) and would next work for Hammer in *That's Your Funeral*—an entertaining farce about undertakers. He was also a stranded passenger in *The Ghost Train* (1941), Colonel Wentworth in *The Black Torment* (1964), and the village shop owner in *Symptoms* (1973).

A Cypriot actor who played everything but Cypriots, George Pastell (1923-1976) had not only replaced Herbert Lom in the original London stage production of *The King and I*, but was also a Parisian bar dweller in *Moulin Rouge*, an Indian professor throttled by *Konga*, Inspector Etienne in *Maniac* (1962), the conductor of the Orient Express in *From Russia with Love* and, in an about-turn, he desecrated "The Tomb of the Cybermen" (1967)—one of the best *Doctor Who* adventures. The latter also features Jamaican-born Roy Stewart (1925-2008), who goes uncredited in *The Mummy* (and *She*) but went on to play Count Karnstein's manservant in *Twins of Evil* (1971) and James Bond's ally Quarrel, Jr. in *Live and Let Die* (1972). Pastell reteamed with Terence Fisher at Bray in July 1959 to portray the High Priest of Kali in *The Stranglers of Bombay*.

After supping some suspiciously watery pints at the local pub, Pat (Harold Goodwin) and Mike (Denis Shaw) transport the Mummy into England, but their ineptitude sees it sink to the bottom of a swamp. Both actors would return as somewhat bungling characters in other horror movies: Denis Shaw (1921-1971), who also played tavern dwellers in *Jack the Ripper*, *The Man Who Could Cheat Death*, and *The Two Faces of Dr. Jekyll*, was, in real life, a drinking accomplice of the actor Oliver Reed. When playing the latter's jailor in *The Curse of the Werewolf*, Shaw was reportedly so frightened by Reed's lupine form that he lost control of his bowels (or so Reed told Denis Meikle). Christopher Lee revealed, in Robert Sellers' biography of Reed (*What Fresh Lunacy Is This?*), that he would sometimes give both actors a lift to Bray in his car, until the chain-smoking Denis almost set the vehicle on fire. Harold Goodwin (1917-2004) likewise refuses to take Nick Adams to Boris Karloff's house in *Die, Monster, Die!* (1965), and would later be traumatized after trying to burgle the Baron's laboratory in *Frankenstein Must Be Destroyed*.

The swamp set of *The Mummy* is another fantastic creation from Bernard Robinson, mounted at Shepperton, and lit supremely by Jack Asher. Indeed, Leslie Halliwell wrote of Asher's lighting on this film: "Color so thick that one would like to scrape off some of it with a palette knife."

Beneath scudding skies and thin, twisted trees, Mehemet Bey revives Kharis from the mist-wreathed swamp. When the Mummy's head first rises, we see not Lee, but Eddie Powell (1927-2000), who, at the suggestion of Roy Ashton, was making his first appearance as Lee's long-time stunt double, a position he would retain all the way up to *The Care of Time* (1989). "He was marvelous," Powell said of Lee, to Tim Greaves in *LSoH* #13: "You could sit down

Dr. John Banning (Peter Cushing) vs. Kharis, the Mummy (Christopher Lee)

and chat to him like the fellow next door, no problem." Eddie would also play a Mummy in Ridley Scott's *Legend* (1984), as well as the title creature in the same director's *Alien* (1978).

After a close-up of eyes snapping open in a muddy face, the Mummy staggers forth to wreak vengeance. Lee told Marcus Hearn that, for this scene, Terence Fisher gleefully called for "more mud, more mud" to be poured over the actor: "Which I didn't appreciate at all."

Still, there is something unsettling about Lee's slick, otherworldly Mummy stalking gas-lit country lanes. His vicious mangling of the asylum's barred windows, before sliding down the padded walls to throttle Felix Aylmer, is properly terrifying. Many jokes have been made about the plodding movements of earlier screen Mummies, but what sets Lee aside is the speed and athleticism he brings to the role (42 years before the fast-moving zombies of *28 Days Later*). Indeed, Kharis' limping gait in the Universal series has, instead, been transferred to John Banning and, as they are both determined achievers, in love with the same woman, *The Mummy* presents the third Lee and Cushing pairing (after *The Curse of Frankenstein* and *Dracula*) in which their characters appear to be murky transpositions of one another.

During the flashback scene related by Cushing, Lee looks regal in priestly robes as he intones the sacred words that will guide his departed sweetheart into the afterlife. Yet, beneath the nobility, Lee's eyes betray a secret sadness. By night, he breaks into the Princess' sealed tomb and attempts to revive her with the Scroll of Life. Caught in the act, he is sentenced to have his tongue cut out "so that the cries he would utter ... should not offend the ears of the gods."

In a contemporary American piece on *The Mummy*, it was reported that, "Nobody loves Hammer more than a Windsor butcher who has grown fat on selling the studio his offal: Lamb tongues, entrails, eyeballs ..." Regardless, Fisher tastefully shoots the tongue removal from behind, and although a shot of the severed organ was snipped by the British censor, the sound of Lee's wrenching cry is far more horrific than if we were to actually see all the gruesome details.

As further punishment, Kharis is encased in bandages and entombed alive; from the shadow of the closing sarcophagus, Lee's terrified eyes stare out. "Film acting is basically done with your mind and with your eyes," Lee told Mark A. Miller. "If it doesn't show in your eyes, it doesn't convince anybody." Indeed, Lee's soulful dark orbs were adept at expressing the most complex of emotions, and nowhere were they put to better use than in *The Mummy*: Blazing with vengeance as he strangles Raymond Huntley, Lee tempers the savagery with tenderness when faced with the reincarnation of his love. Acres of feeling shine forth through the muddy bandages as he raises his arms in a pleading gesture. The look of horror Yvonne Furneaux gives him in return causes Lee to lower his head and slowly slump away. With such gestures, the actor brings an element of the lovelorn teenager to Kharis, especially when he also bows his head in sulky deference to George Pastell's autocratic father figure.

Lee's gift for mime additionally conveys the determination of the character through his purposeful flight. It is this energy that makes Hammer's the greatest of the *Mummy* movies (even Karloff's original has a soporific quality at times).

During his nocturnal strolls, the Mummy startles a drunken poacher in the person of Michael Ripper (1913-2000), here making his first appearance in a Christopher Lee horror movie (although cast as a morgue attendant for *The Man Who Could Cheat Death*, his scene was never filmed). During his DVD commentary for *Scars of Dracula*, Lee called Ripper "the man who, as far as I'm personally concerned—and I've said this many times—represents Hammer more than any one individual, more than myself and Peter." Indeed, like George Woodbridge (who appears as the police constable in *The Mummy*), Ripper was a much-loved mainstay of the company (for whom he made a total of 32 features), essaying policemen, landlords and even a Japanese soldier. My personal favorite of his performances, though, is his benign barman, Tom Bailey, who helps to defeat *The Reptile*. Ripper told Denis Meikle: "In any business, there are artists and there are craftsmen. There were more artists at Hammer than in any other film production company I worked for."

One such artist makes a particularly fine contribution to *The Mummy*. "Cushing was the one that really directed the film," Yvonne Furneaux told David Del Valle in *LSoH* #24. "He was the brains behind it." After adding so much to the thrilling climax of *Dracula*, Peter Cushing provides *The Mummy* with one of its most exciting and unforgettable moments, as he recalled in his memoirs: On seeing an early mock-up of the poster, which depicted a flashlight beam shining through a hole in Lee's chest, Peter enquired of the publicity department how it had got there. "Oh," came the response, "that's just to help sell the picture."

Never one to short-change his audience, Cushing consequently devised the action of grabbing a harpoon from the wall and driving it through Kharis' body. Accordingly, Lee said that the weapon "made a nice change from stakes." In Don Fearney's 2013 documentary *Legend of Hammer Mummies*, third assistant director Hugh Harlow (b. 1939) remembered giggling at the sight of Lee enjoying a cup of tea, during a break, with the harpoon still protruding from his chest. "What are you laughing at?" said the Mummy, which only served to amuse Harlow further (Hugh went on to a successful career as a production manager; his credits include the 1978 *Dracula*, *Octopussy* [1982], *Legend* and *Aliens* [1985]).

Along with Lee, George Pastell makes his villainous character a sympathetic one, especially when Banning smugly trashes his personal beliefs. In fact, *The Mummy* is full of rational men whose practical ideals are exploded by the supernatural. Most notable among these is Inspector Mulrooney, who blurts: "I deal in facts, Mr. Banning ... not fantasies straight out of Edgar Allan Poe!" The doubting lawman is played by Irish actor Eddie Byrne

(1911-1981), who essayed similarly investigative characters in *Jack the Ripper* (1958) and *Island of Terror* (1965). After going uncredited as the Ship's Captain in *The Vengeance of Fu Manchu* (1966), his final film role was as General Willard in *Star Wars*.

Pursued by Byrne and Cushing, Lee takes Yvonne Furneaux in his arms and heads for the swamp. Given that he has earlier shown himself to be impervious to bullets, his subsequent destruction by gunfire doesn't quite make sense. Neil Barrow, however, provides food for thought when he states (in *LSoH* #19): "Releasing [Isobel] as she requests, it is perhaps this rejection, rather than the accumulated gunfire of a posse, which ultimately defeats the seemingly indestructible mummy."

Production of *The Mummy* wrapped on Thursday, April 16, 1959. The film's premiere took place at the London Pavilion on Friday, September 25 (when Craig Douglas topped the charts with his cover of "Only Sixteen"). The impressive Pavilion hoarding for *The Mummy* can be glimpsed in *Gorgo*, when the supine title creature is paraded around England's capital on the back of a flatbed truck.

The Mummy's US release came on Wednesday, December 16, 1959 (when Guy Mitchell was at No. 1 with "Heartaches by the Number"). Double billed with Universal's vampire Western *Curse of the Undead* (or, for some New York showings, with Vincent Price's *The Bat*), *The Mummy* was a record-breaking success in America, out-grossing even Hammer's *Dracula*.

But not everyone was pleased. Following a preview in *Time* magazine, Nina Wilcox Putnam, author of the 1932 Karloff *Mummy*, wrote to the editor. "Thank you for the April 6th exposé of the horror motion pictures being made in England at the Hammer studios. Without this review, I might not have known that my story, *The Mummy*, was being remade in a debased form. This story, as originally written by me, was a perfectly clean and decent archaeological 'chiller' which I wrote expressly for Boris Karloff. This disgusting English remake was done without my knowledge or consent, and it has been a terrible shock, at the age of 75, to find such a work attributed to me, however wrongly, and by indirection."

Putnam would surely be shocked to learn that the poster image for Hammer's *The Mummy* was featured on a UK postage stamp in 2008. The film also inspired one of the scariest *Doctor Who* fantasies, "Pyramids of Mars" (1975), and was adapted as a comic strip for *Halls of Horror* #22 (1978). Perhaps the strangest homage to *The Mummy* came via "an unusual rock 'n' roll song" (to quote the pressbook) of the same name by American humorist Bob McFadden. The sleeve of the record features a photo of Lee in character, grasping towards the buyer.

Hammer followed *The Mummy* with *The Curse of the Mummy's Tomb* (1964)—an underrated sequel, writ-

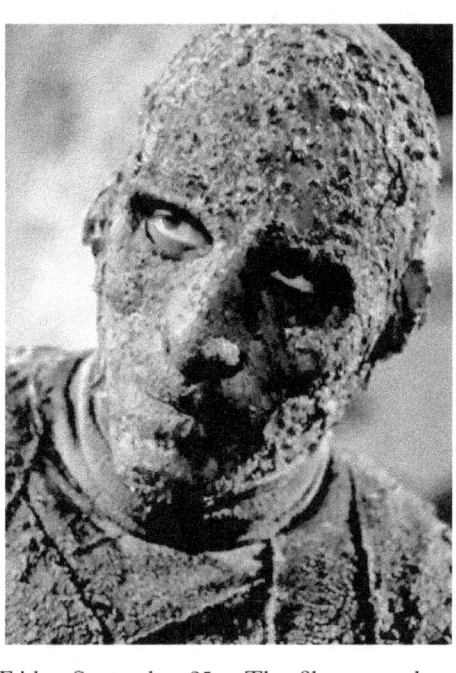

Yvonne Furneaux is dragged into the swamp by Kharis.

ten, produced and directed by Michael Carreras (who scripted under the pseudonym of Henry Younger—a pun on Anthony Hinds' alias John Elder). The film is highlighted by an atmospheric sewer-set climax, and fine turns from American actor Fred Clark (of *Sunset Blvd.* fame) and Terence Morgan (Laertes of Olivier's *Hamlet*) as the human villain. Both George Pastell and Harold Goodwin return from *The Mummy*, along with a portion of Franz Reizenstein's score.

Scripted and directed by John Gilling, *The Mummy's Shroud* was the last Hammer film to be mounted at Bray (in October 1966). Despite some moments of tedium, all of the scenes involving the Mummy are very effectively staged, and Michael Ripper delivers one of his most beautiful performances as the subservient Longbarrow. The film was released on a double bill with *Frankenstein Created Woman* in June 1967, with the tagline: "Beware the beat of the cloth-wrapped feet!"

In both sequels, Christopher Lee was succeeded in the part of the Mummy by stuntmen Dickie Owen and Eddie Powell respectively. Their performances only serve to illuminate how vital Lee was. Without his soulful animation, the monster becomes merely a pile of lumbering bandages.

Hammer's final entry in the bandaged undead series was far more interesting than its immediate predecessor. Despite a splash or two of gore, *Blood from the Mummy's Tomb* (1971) comes closest, out of all the studio's horrors, to evoking the spirit of Val Lewton's shadowy, suggestive productions of the 1940s (*Cat People*, *The Seventh Victim*, *Isle of the Dead*). Based on Bram Stoker's 1903 novel *The Jewel of Seven Stars*, Valerie Leon stars in the dual roles of Queen Tera and her modern-day reincarnation, Margaret. Originally cast as her father, Peter Cushing had to bow out after one day's filming to care for his dying wife. He was replaced by Andrew Keir. Nevertheless, it is tempting to imagine Cushing in the finished movie playing alongside Christopher Lee as James Villiers' sly Corbeck.

Fantasy casting aside, Lee was present at the film's premiere, which opened a three-week season of Hammer horrors at the National Film Theatre in October 1971. Among the classics screened were *The Curse of Frankenstein*, *Dracula*, and *The Mummy*, of which Paul Willemen's program notes state: "Terence Fisher's surrealistic use of color is at its most unforgettable ..."—a far cry from the *News of the World* likening the movie to a "piece of mummified corn" in their 1959 review.

The most valid critique, however, comes from Kharis himself: In a 1980 TV interview with Ben Hunter, Christopher Lee claimed: "*The Mummy* ... I think was probably the best picture of its kind that Hammer ever did."

Uncle Was a Vampire
1959

In his article, "What Horror Means to Me," printed in *Picturegoer Film Annual 1959-1960*, Christopher Lee outlined some career objectives: "It is of the greatest importance to me nowadays that I should be known internationally. I am in the process of furthering this aim by working all over Europe." In the same piece, he wrote of the effect *Dracula* was having on his life: "My appearance in the title role in this film has done more than anything to establish my name with picturegoers. The number of letters I still receive from people of *all* ages who saw this film is quite considerable." It made sense, therefore, for Lee to capitalize on his vampiric renown by traveling to Italy, where *Dracula* had been especially popular. The country's dictator, Benito Mussolini (who came to power in 1922), had previously banned horror films, deeming them unhealthy (unlike Fascism). Following Mussolini's execution at the end of World War II, the once-forbidden Universal monster movies would creep on to Italian television by the early 1950s and, in 1956, Riccardo Freda and Mario Bava produced *I vampiri*—the first Gothic chiller to be made in Italy since 1920's *Il mostro di Frankenstein*.

Although initially reluctant to play the vampire in a serious horror film so soon after *Dracula*'s success, Lee was quite happy to do so in a parody. "The result was fairly jolly," he wrote later. "It went down very well, in Italy."

Directed by comedy specialist Stefano Vanzina (1915-1988), who signs himself Steno, *Uncle Was a Vampire* went before the cameras as *Tempi duri per i vampiri* (literal translation: *Hard Times for Vampires*) in the late spring of 1959, with Lee joining the production on Thursday July 30. The Rome location was Castle Odescalchi, overlooking Lake Bracciano, which Jonathan Rigby calls "Italy's equivalent of Oakley Court." Indeed, the 15th century fortress would play host to further horrors, not only as Lee's dwelling in *Katarsis* (1963) and *The Castle of the Living Dead* (1964), but also as a wedding venue for Tom Cruise and Katie Holmes.

Unlike the aforementioned couple, horror and comedy are not such strange bedfellows, for both genres have at their basis the intrusion of incongruous events upon normalcy. James Whale's *The Old Dark House* (1932), *The Invisible Man* (1933) and *Bride of Frankenstein* are significantly rich in humor, while George Romero's *Martin* (1976) and *Dawn of the Dead* (1977) operate on a satirical level. Other effective blends of horror and hilarity include Douglas Hickox's *Theatre of Blood* (1972), John Landis' *An American Werewolf in London* (1981) and Sam Raimi's *Evil Dead* trilogy (1979-1991). *Uncle Was a Vampire*, however, is a far cry from any of the above.

Once the credits have played out to the strains of a colorful song, "Dracula Cha Cha Cha," the color and music continue with hotel gardener Lilina (Susanne Loret) singing a wistful ballad beneath sapphire skies. Watching over is love-lorn bellhop Oswaldo (Renato Rascel), who soon receives a visit from his bloodsucking uncle Baron Roderigo (Christopher Lee).

A publicity shot with Christopher Lee and Renato Rascel

Rising from his coffin at the stroke of midnight, Lee looks amazing in red-lined cloak, pale face and black wig, although the echo effect applied to the character's voice is an unnecessary intrusion. Unfortunately, as with most of the actor's Euro-horrors, Lee's voice is dubbed by someone else in the English-language print. The usual Italian practice at the time was to shoot silent, with the various actors speaking in their own tongue, and dub the dialogue for export in post-production, when the ever-busy Lee was usually otherwise engaged. Nevertheless, towering above the pint-sized Rascel (a lot of the humor derives from their contrasting heights), Lee invests his part with alacrity. Whether looking with wicked longing from a window at the carefree female guests who gather below, or charging across the castle ramparts, cloak billowing out behind, the actor understood that the only way to play the vampire in a comedy was to do it absolutely straight (just as Lugosi had done in *Abbott and Costello Meet Frankenstein*).

The only downside is that *Uncle Was a Vampire* isn't funny at all. Rascel's line, "I wonder if I need a rabies shot," after being bitten by Roderigo, represents the height of wit on display. It's hard to believe that the script combines the work of at least *seven* different writers, including Rascel, director Steno and, maybe, Lucio Fulci: The future architect of *The House by the Cemetery* was an assistant to Steno throughout the 1950s and, in an interview with Robert Schlockoff for *L'ecran Fantastique*, alluded that he had worked, uncredited, as a writer on *Uncle Was a Vampire*.

Fulci *was* credited as writer and director of the 1975 farce *Dracula in the Provinces*, which, as well as displaying a similar style to *Uncle Was a Vampire*, shares its leading lady Sylva Koscina (1933-1994). After playing Steve Reeves' beloved in *Hercules* (1957) and *Hercules Unchained* (1958), the Yugoslav-born Koscina tempered starring roles in spy capers *Hot Enough for June* (1963) and *Deadlier than the Male* with work for such diverse filmmakers as Georges Franju (*Judex* [1963]), Federico Fellini (*Juliet of the Spirits* [1964]), Jess Franco (*Justine* [1968]) and Mario Bava (*Lisa and the Devil* [1972]).

Making her debut in *Uncle Was a Vampire* is Susanne Loret, who would next play the heroines of *Atom Age Vampire* and *The Minotaur* (both 1960), before retiring from movies a few years later.

German actress Kai Fischer (b. 1934) rounds out the cast. She would appear again with Lee in *Too Hot to Handle* (1959), and with Peter Cushing in *The Hellfire Club*.

As for Renato Rascel (1912-1991), he was not only one of Italy's leading comedians, but also a popular singer who represented his country in the 1960 Eurovision Song Contest. After making a comic role of *Napoleon* (1951), he gave an award-winning lead performance in the 1952 Gogol adaptation *The Overcoat* and was among the all-star cast of Vittorio De Sica's *The Last Judgement* (1961). Rascel also starred with De Sica in *Marriage* (1954), *The Monte Carlo Story* (1956) and *The Orderly* (1961), before making his final screen appearance as the blind man healed by *Jesus of Nazareth* (1975).

An Italian lobby card from *Uncle Was a Vampire*

Akin to Richard Gordon's contemporaneous Italian presentation *The Playgirls and the Vampire* (1960), the European sensibility of *Uncle Was a Vampire* lends a heightened, untethered air, which makes the progressive productions of Hammer seem rather strait-laced by comparison: Witness the display of scantily clad vampire victims, or the extra-large fangs which stretch Lee's face into a caricature.

Unfortunately, once he turns Oswaldo into a vampire halfway through the picture, Lee is barely onscreen, and we have to endure seemingly endless shots of Rascel bumbling about the castle to a "humorous" saxophone leitmotif. There are also some uninteresting antics with pop singer Victor, played by an uncredited Rik Van Nutter (Felix Leiter in *Thunderball*), whose hits include "The Okey-Dokey Calypso."

Lee returns towards the film's close, springing from his grave to menace Lilli, before exiting the scene, arm in arm with two women (a charming touch).

Released in Italy under its original title on Wednesday October 28, 1959, the film was renamed *Uncle Was a Vampire* and sold directly to US television in 1964 (where it also became known as *Dracula Is My Uncle*).

In 1960, fresh from his *Mummy*-inspired record, Bob McFadden issued a cover version of *Uncle Was a Vampire*'s theme tune, "Dracula Cha Cha Cha," with sleeve art containing images from Hammer's *The Brides of Dracula*. The song was composed by Renato Rascel and Bruno Martino. The latter also performed it for Vincente Minelli's *Two Weeks in Another Town* (1962), which stars Lee's future leading lady from *The Whip and the Body*, Daliah Lavi. In further tribute, *Dracula Cha Cha Cha* became the title of the third novel in Kim Newman's *Anno Dracula* series (Newman gives thanks to Lee in the books' acknowledgements).

While *Uncle Was a Vampire* works neither as a horror, nor a comedy film, it is never less than beautiful to look at thanks to Lee's awesome presence and the stunningly vibrant cinematography of Marco Scarpelli (1918-1995). What's more, it is, at least, superior to Steno's next attempt to spoof the genre, *Dr. Jekyll Likes Them Hot* (1978). Crumbs.

The City of the Dead
1959

Scream with guests from the 'Other World when you ring for doom service!

They don't like strangers in Whitewood.—Garage attendant (Jimmy Dyrenforth) in *The City of the Dead*.

"Milton came from a home in which his parents spoke exclusively in Yiddish. He was a quiet, shy young boy who loved the movies and found the darkness and solitude of the movie theater more conducive to peace of mind than the often raucous atmosphere of life at home."—Producer Max J. Rosenberg on his business partner Milton Subotsky (quoted in *Amicus: The Friendly Face of Fear* by Allan Bryce)

Since having his script rejected for *The Curse of Frankenstein*, Milton Subotsky had scored with two rock 'n' roll musicals, *Rock Rock Rock!* (1956)—for which he co-wrote a song ("Baby, Baby")—and *Jamboree* (1957), featuring Count Basie, Fats Domino and Jerry Lee Lewis. After making one last film in his native New York (1958's *The Last Mile* with Mickey Rooney), Milton embarked for England with a story he'd written in 1957 as a possible TV hour for Boris Karloff. Based upon the real-life 1692 Salem witch trials, *Witchcraft* would instead provide a more than worthy vehicle for the actor who was fast becoming Karloff's successor, Christopher Lee.

Retitled *The City of the Dead*, Milton's treatment was expanded into a screenplay by fellow New Yorker George Baxt (1923-2003), whose main strength as a writer was in the field of mystery novels (one of which, *A Queer Kind of Death* [1966], is progressive in its depiction of homosexuality, including fiction's first gay black detective, Pharaoh Love). In addition to providing additional dialogue for *The Revenge of Frankenstein* and *Night of the Eagle* (1961), Baxt penned the racy *Circus of Horrors* and *The Shadow of the Cat*, before furnishing original stories for two 1971 productions: *Vampire Circus*, a minor Hammer gem, and *Tower of Evil*, an altogether grubbier affair produced by Richard Gordon.

For *The City of the Dead*, Subotsky and business partner Max J. Rosenberg were joined by British producer Donald Taylor (1911-1966)—who would also handle the Christopher Lee films *The Hands of Orlac* (1960) and *The Devil's Daffodil* (1961)—and Vulcan Films was formed. Nothing to do with the alien race later created by Gene Roddenberry for *Star Trek*, Vulcan is the Latin name for the God of Fire; Milton would call his next movie enterprise by another Latin word—Amicus.

Some of the imagery in *City of the Dead* is worthy of Ingmar Bergman.

The City of the Dead began shooting on Monday, October 12, 1959, at Shepperton. During the film's 14-day-schedule, Christopher Lee received a letter "from a cinema manager in the north of England" who claimed that one of his usherettes had been impregnated by *Dracula* purely from running the film every day of the week. Said Lee: "That one, I felt, I could safely ignore."

Less influenced by Hammer horror was the man whom Subotsky chose to direct. "One thing we *didn't* want was to make a Hammer film," John Moxey (1925-2019) told Tom Weaver (in *Fangoria* #167): "We wanted to make something *better*, we wanted to make something with a little class."

Moxey came to *The City of the Dead* (his debut feature) fresh from television work, where, through his duties as an assistant director, he'd already become familiar with Christopher Lee. "With his knowledge of horror films and horror film acting, [Lee] did everything he could to help me, and made [*The City of the Dead*] a very pleasant experience," Moxey told Weaver, before revealing that his star held no qualms about having his arm set alight for the film's climax: "He was an experienced guy and we had good special effects people." The two were reunited for *Circus of Fear* (1965), following which Moxey relocated to Hollywood where he helmed *The House That Would Not Die* (1970), two Jimmy Sangster scripts (*A Taste of Evil* [1971], *No Place to Hide* [1981]), and the highest rated TV film of its day, *The Night Stalker* (1971). Further dips into small-screen terror include the pilot of William Castle's short-lived series *Ghost Story* (1972), *The Strange and Deadly Occurrence* (1974) and *I, Desire* (1982), in which *An American Werewolf in London*'s David Naughton falls in love with a vampire prostitute.

Moxey wasn't the only director who owed their first big break to Subotsky and Rosenberg: As well as putting a young William Friedkin in charge of Harold Pinter's *The Birthday Party* (1968), the producers hired Richard Lester to exercise his madcap visual style on *It's Trad, Dad!* (1961).

Stylish visuals also define *The City of the Dead*: An arresting flashback opening shows the burning of a witch, Elizabeth Selwyn (Patricia Jessel), in Salem, 1692. For this, Moxey makes eerie use of reversed film (a technique which Brian De Palma also deployed effectively for the climax of *Carrie* [1976]) and the cries of the gurning spectators segue into the present-day declamations of Lee's anthropology professor, Alan Driscoll. Framed before a wall of grotesque voodoo masks, Lee recounts his history lesson with the American accent last heard in *Alias John Preston*. Once class is dismissed, he sends apt pupil Nan Barlow (Venetia Stevenson) to further her witchcraft researches at the Raven's Inn, Whitewood, much to the disapproval of her brother Richard (Dennis Lotis).

When Richard decries black magic as "fairy tale mumbo-jumbo," Driscoll responds: "The basis of fairy tales is reality; the basis of reality is fairy tales"—a key line which provides a neat summary of Lee's horror output, wherein folklore and superstition meld with the veracity of human emotion to provide uniquely stylized morality plays. As ever, the actor brings great conviction to his character, persuading not only Nan, but also we in the audience, that witchcraft is very real indeed.

Despite this, top billing in *The City of the Dead* is awarded to crooner Dennis Lotis (b. 1925), who would go on to play Alan A'Dale in Hammer's *Sword of Sherwood Forest* (1960). "Christopher Lee and I shared a dressing room," Lotis remembered, in Derek Pykett's 2012 documentary *Amicus: House of Horrors*, "and he said to me, 'You know, Dennis, I really should have been an opera singer, because I studied opera singing …' He was such a tall guy, I felt like a midget standing next to him … Nice man, though … because he knew that I was sort of 'new to the game' and he gave me one or two tips … Not to blink too much …"

The casting of Lotis (*Melody Maker*'s Top Male Singer of 1957) is an indication of both Subotsky's background in pop musicals and the newfound recognition of teenagers' spending power: Films of the late 1950s were now catering to younger audiences and *The City of the Dead* marks the first instance of a pop star appearing in a British horror venture, a trend which would continue with Jess Conrad in *Konga* (1960), Adam Faith in *What a Carve Up!* (1961), Pat Boone in *The Horror of it All* (1963), Frankie Avalon in *The Haunted House of Horror* (1968), Paul Jones in *Demons of the Mind* (1971), Jack Jones in *The Comeback* (1977), David Bowie in *The Hunger* (1982) and Sting in *The Bride* (1984).

Although given an introductory credit on *The City of the Dead*, American actress Venetia Stevenson (b. 1938) had already starred in 1958's *Island of Lost Women*, *Day of the Outlaw* and *The Big Night* before venturing to England, where, alongside Subotsky, she reviewed the latest pop discs on two episodes of BBC TV's *Juke Box Jury*. Stevenson is the daughter of actress Anna Lee, who had been a sassy foil to Boris Karloff in both *Bedlam* (1945) and *The Man Who Changed His Mind*. The latter was helmed by Venetia's father, Robert Stevenson, who, as well as directing Vincent Price in *The Las Vegas Story* (1951), was responsible for many Disney classics, including *Mary Poppins* (1963), *The Love Bug* (1968) and *Bedknobs and Broomsticks* (1970). Venetia went on to appear with a young Burt Reynolds in the *Alfred Hitchcock Presents* episode "Escape to Sonoita" (1960), before retiring from acting to become a producer, notably on the Dean Koontz adaptation *Servants of Twilight* (1990).

When Nan arrives in Whitewood, she finds it peopled by the mysterious Jethro Keane (Valentine Dyall), the witchy hotel owner Mrs. Newless (Patricia Jessel) and her mute, nervous servant Lottie (Ann Beach).

Christopher Lee as Professor Driscoll

Making her debut here, Beach (1938-2017) would go on to play Hugh Grant's mother in *Notting Hill* (1998), but in real life was the parent of Charlotte Coleman—the tragic child star of *Worzel Gummidge*, who died from an asthma attack at the age of 33.

Also fated for an early death was Tony Award-winning stage actress Patricia Jessel, who, aged just 47, suffered a fatal heart attack in 1968. While filming *The City of the Dead* with Christopher Lee, Jessel would dash off in the evenings to star opposite Peter Cushing in *The Sound of Murder* at the Aldwych Theatre in London's West End. Her last film role was as Domina in *A Funny Thing Happened on the Way to the Forum* (1965).

Valentine Dyall (1908-1985), whom no one can describe without using the word "sepulchral," had last featured with Lee in *Paul Temple Returns*, but was best known for narrating BBC Radio's *Appointment With Fear* (1943-1955). After playing the *very* enigmatic psychic investigator of *The Ghost of Rashmon Hall* (1947), Dyall made three Hammer films, firstly as the Sherlock Holmes-like detective *Dr. Morelle* (1948). The actor's next two assignments for the company, both in 1949, were not only primary exercises in Gothic horror, but also Hammer's first to be filmed at Oakley Court: As *The Man in Black* ("The BBC Sensation"), Dyall introduces a tale of yogic trances, ghostly tappings, and femme fatales, while, in the Jack the Ripper-inspired *Room to Let*, his sinister lodger gradually exerts control over a household—a plot mirrored 20 years later by *Frankenstein Must Be Destroyed*.

Dyall went on to portray the caretaker of Hill House in *The Haunting* (1962), the sinister head of an old dark house in Terence Fish-

Elizabeth Selwyn (Patricia Jessel) gets burned at the stake in Salem, 1692.

The Loneliness of Evil

City of the Dead was released in the US as *Horror Hotel*

er's *The Horror of it All* and a 1,000-year-old mummy who narrates the *Secrets of Sex* (1969). As well as announcing the "Werewolf Break" in *The Beast Must Die*, he lent his velvet tones to the voice of God (in *Bedazzled* [1967]), Dr. Noah (in *Casino Royale* [1966]), Count Karnstein (in *Lust for a Vampire* [1970]) and the genie (in *Arabian Adventure*). His spooky reputation also saw him author various anthologies of strange but true tales. In his Introduction to the first of these, *Unsolved Mysteries* (1954), Dyall writes: "Here is my chance to put down a rumor which started with my weekly broadcasts as 'The Man In Black'—that my appetite for mystery and horror was acquired at six years of age, when Christmas parcels got mixed up and I received *The Works of Edgar Allan Poe* instead of *Mother Goose*. It is absolutely untrue. I was only five …" In the early 1980s, Dyall would terrify youngsters of a similar age as the evil Black Guardian in *Doctor Who*.

The frightened forces of Good in *The City of the Dead* are represented by the blind Reverend Russell (Norman MacOwan) and his granddaughter Patricia (Betta St. John, from *Alias John Preston* and *Corridors of Blood*). The 82-year-old MacOwan was appearing in his final feature film; a playwright as well as an actor, his screen roles ranged from Captain MacPhee in Ealing's *Whisky Galore!* (1948) to Old Tom in Hammer's *X the Unknown*.

His pale face shining from the darkness of a ruined church, the helpless priest describes Whitewood as a place over which the Devil hovers, where "evil has triumphed over good," and the town certainly lives up to that depiction, thanks to art director John Blezard (b. 1927). Built upon Shepperton's Stage H, Whitewood is a fantastic, mist-wreathed set of rotting timbers and skewed bricks, while Driscoll's classroom is similarly detailed, with its old books, tribal relics and Hogarth engravings. Blezard's other credits include *The Hands of Orlac*, *First Men in the Moon* (1963) and *When Dinosaurs Ruled the Earth*, and his work on *The City of the Dead* really brings to life Lee's description of the film as "an American Gothic with a Lovecraftian flavor." Indeed, with its shadowy denizens and their dark, arcane practices, *The City of the Dead* is, in fact, truer to the spirit of H.P. Lovecraft than the first official adaptations of the author's work, which would emerge in the following decade.

The City of the Dead also anticipates another horror classic: Alfred Hitchcock's *Psycho*. Not only does a seemingly main protagonist meet a surprisingly early death in a strange residence (an idea that was actually first presented in Hammer's *Dracula*), but the heroine is seen wearing black underwear shortly before her death, and, in another detail not found in Robert Bloch's 1959 source novel, a disfigured female corpse is turned over in a chair for the closing shot (Betta St. John's consequent scream is mirrored by Vera Miles in *Psycho*).

While Hitchcock's Hollywood opus didn't begin filming until Monday, November 30, 1959 (just under a month after *The City of the Dead* had wrapped), there is no way that the celebrated director could have been aware of the British movie's content. Any graphic similarities between the two are merely the kind of bizarre coincidences that frequently occur in the creative industries. To cite further examples, along with the fog and cowled figures, Mario Bava's Italian *Black Sunday* (filmed in March/April 1960) also resembles *The City of the Dead* by opening with the rain-dampened execution of a witch. Furthermore, a number of shots in the Subotsky film prefigure Kan-

sas-based filmmaker Herk Harvey's dreamlike *Carnival of Souls* (1961), such as the devil worshippers approaching the camera, fingers flexed, or dancing in quick, tight circles (although the latter is, perhaps, a nod to *The Devil and Daniel Webster* [1941]). Either way, it's highly unlikely that either Bava or Harvey could have seen *The City of the Dead* ahead of its release in their respective countries.

What *can* be acknowledged is that the film was a big influence on *Buffy the Vampire Slayer* creator Joss Whedon, who, in the spring of 2014, shot parts of *Avengers: Age of Ultron* on the same Shepperton soundstage. Calling *The City of the Dead* "the seminal movie that scared the shit out of me," in *The Monster Book* (Pocket Books, 2000), Whedon added: "It's just people in cowls and foggy old graveyards, chanting. For me, that's just the scariest anything needs to be. People are scarier than creatures … Creatures are fun."

Indeed, *The City of the Dead* is full of nightmarish images: The hooded devil worshippers skulking through the fog-shrouded graveyard, with its slanted crosses, is a tableau worthy of Ingmar Bergman's *The Seventh Seal* (1956), and an almost surreal juxtaposition of horror and ordinariness reaches its peak when a cloaked Driscoll is caught unawares sacrificing a white dove. Lee hurriedly washes his hands in a gargoyle font before greeting his unwanted guest with complete normalcy. Also unforgettable is the heavy stone slab that drops abruptly, cutting off Venetia Stevenson's scream, while the cobwebbed cellar which entraps her showcases one of *The City of the Dead*'s major assets: The sharply defined black-and-white cinematography of Desmond Dickinson (1902-1986). The lighting cameraman of Olivier's *Hamlet*, Dickinson would work on Herman Cohen's British productions, *Horrors of the Black Museum*, *Berserk* (1966) and *Trog*, as well as *The Hands of Orlac*, *Incense for the Damned* and *Tower of Evil*.

In another echo of *Psycho*, Nan's disappearance in *The City of the Dead* is investigated by her sibling and a boyfriend, Bill Maitland (Tom Naylor). The latter marks the first instance of Milton Subotsky naming a character Maitland, a trick he would repeat in seven further films. While genre fans have long wondered over the deep, arcane reasons behind this, Subotsky told Philip Nutman: "I just liked the name." The heroes arrive in Whitewood just in time for the movie's second sacrifice (at the hour of 13 on Candlemass Eve). Any slight tedium that arises from this recycling of events is more than made up for with a suspenseful climax, employing tilted camera angles, tight editing, and more mist and shadows than one film can contain. (Moxey reported that many among his cast and crew fell sick when subjected to the paraffin-based fog effect.)

Making an important contribution to this finale is Australian composer Douglas Gamley (1924-1998), who had just scored Hammer's Jekyll and Hyde comedy *The Ugly Duckling* (1959). The latter incorporates James Bernard's *Dracula* motif for its transformation sequences, and Gamley would become something of an Amicus equivalent to Bernard, with such titles as *Tales from the Crypt*, *Asylum* and *The Beast Must Die*. While his only other full score for Hammer belongs to the rib-tickling *Watch It, Sailor!* (1961), Gamley did orchestrate Bernard's waltzes and play the solo piano pieces for *The Kiss of the Vampire*. His appropriately mournful soundtrack for *The City of the Dead* foreshadows Jerry Goldsmith's Oscar-winning work on *The Omen* in its use of choral chants. Gamley even precedes the closing credits with the medieval hymn *Dies Irae* ("Day of Wrath"). This doom-laden melody, quoted in Requiem Mass, would recur in horror movies as diverse as *The Return of Dracula* and *The Shining* (1979). Gamley himself would reuse the theme several times, most notably for the opening titles of *From Beyond the Grave* (1973) and *The Vault of Horror* (1972).

Joining Gamley on *The City of the Dead* is jazz specialist Ken Jones (1927-1988), who provides for the action sequences a whirling, glitzy piece reminiscent of Nelson Riddle's later work on the 1960s *Batman* TV series (Gamley and Jones had previously collaborated on *Tom Thumb* [1957] starring Venetia Stevenson's athletic ex-husband Russ Tamblyn). Jones would next score *Two Way Stretch* (1959) and *Tarzan the Magnificent* (for *Corridors of Blood* director Robert Day), as well as the Donald Pleasence starrer *Dr. Crippen* (1962).

Given a UK release in September 1960 (the same month as *Psycho*), *The City of the Dead* didn't arrive in America until Wednesday September 12, 1962, where, paired with *The Head* (1959), it was renamed *Horror Hotel* and shorn of two minutes' worth of dialogue. Distributed in the US by Trans-Lux (whom Max J. Rosenberg described, to Tom Weaver, as "fascist cocksuckers"), the film was met with the usual disdainful reviews reserved for horror subjects, but has since shown its influence in other media. For example, scenes from *The City of the Dead* were incorporated into the 1990 music video for Iron Maiden's "Bring Your Daughter to the Slaughter" and one of Christopher Lee's lines from the film ("Superstition, fear, and jealousy") introduces Rob Zombie's 1998 song "Dragula." In addition, a clip of Elizabeth Selwyn's execution was inserted into the Sci-Fi Channel mockumentary *Curse of the Blair Witch* in 1999—a promotion for that year's phenomenal horror hit *The Blair Witch Project*, which, for all its clever trickery, cannot hold a sacrificial candle to *The City of the Dead*.

The Two Faces of Dr. Jekyll 1959

Sometimes, terror has a handsome face.

I don't really think I ever tried to love that film very much.—Terence Fisher (on *The Two Faces of Dr. Jekyll*), *Midi-Minuit Fantastique #10-11*, 1964

I'm not giving you bullshit; they were made by people who cared.—Michael Carreras on Hammer films (*Flesh and Blood: The Hammer Heritage of Horror*).

Robert Louis Stevenson's 1886 novella *Strange Case of Dr. Jekyll and Mr. Hyde* had been filmed more times than any other horror story by the time Hammer turned their attentions to it in 1959. Taking their cue from Richard Mansfield's 1887 stage version, by way of Oscar Wilde's *The Picture of Dorian Gray*, the three most significant of these earlier adaptations (starring John Barrymore [1919], Fredric March [1931], and Spencer Tracy [1941]) had enlarged upon Stevenson's treatise on human duality by becoming parables of sexual desire, an area which Hammer further explored, albeit with a new twist. Whereas previous Jekylls were handsome chaps who transform themselves into physically monstrous beings, Hammer's Hyde, a young and depraved sensualist, would emerge, instead, from a grizzled, unfeeling scientist.

The company first examined this concept in May 1959 with *The Ugly Duckling*—a comedy starring Bernard Bresslaw as nerdy pharmacist Henry Jekyll, who changes into slick gangster Teddy Hyde. Although little seen today, this enjoyable film is clearly a forerunner to Jerry Lewis' better known *The Nutty Professor* (1962). (A tiny role in *The Ugly Duckling* is filled by Norma Marla, who helped to promote *The Mummy* by touring US theaters with Princess Ananka's sarcophagus. In *The Two Faces of Dr. Jekyll*, she would be handed more substantial acting duties as Hyde's snake dancer lover, Maria.)

The idea for reversing the accepted notions of Jekyll and Hyde came from Michael Carreras. Not long after producing *The Ugly Duckling*, he was introduced to Wolf Mankowitz (1924-1998), whose West End Musical *Expresso Bongo* had just been filmed by Hammer regular Val Guest. Carreras had a proposition for the writer (quoted in *LSoH*): "What about doing a Jekyll and Hyde where the guy's good looking and the other guy's a bit of a donkey?" Thus armed, Mankowitz wrote his script in the summer of 1959 under the original title *The Three Faces of Dr. Jekyll*.

Mankowitz envisioned Laurence Harvey in the title roles. Indeed, the seductive young Hyde of Wolf's script bears more than a passing resemblance to Harvey's Joe Lampton in *Room at the Top*. The British posters for *The Two Faces of Dr. Jekyll*, showing Hyde abed with his mistress, even mimicked those for Harvey's film—just as certain lustful clinches between he and Simone Signoret had imitated those of Christopher Lee and Melissa Stribling in *Dracula*. (*Room at the Top*, incidentally, had been sneak-previewed by its nervous producers during a double bill of *The Curse of Frankenstein* and *Dracula* at the Bruce Grove Cinema, Tottenham; Hammer would continue Lampton's adventures in *Man at the Top* [1973], with Kenneth Haigh.)

Although Harvey, who had already turned down the lead role in *Peeping Tom*, was keen to do the Jekyll and Hyde picture, his agent, *Moulin Rouge* producer James Woolf, warned that appearing in a horror film would be bad for his career. In a sense, Woolf was right: Harvey both directed and starred in the cannibalistic thriller *Welcome to Arrow Beach* (1973), which not only proved to be his final film, but was also pretty shoddy to boot.

With Laurence Harvey out of the running, the title roles were filled, instead, by Canadian actor Paul Massie (1932-2011), who had just won a Most Promising Newcomer BAFTA for his debut lead in Anthony Asquith's *Orders to Kill* (1958). Although Massie is effective as Jekyll and Hyde, it remains something of a mystery as to why Christopher Lee wasn't cast, especially as he had scored so heavily as the title monsters of Hammer's previous Gothic triumphs.

What does seem apparent is that, by hiring a respected writer like Mankowitz in place of Jimmy Sangster, Michael Carreras was trying to prevent the Hammer formula from going stale (Mankowitz was paid a whopping £5,000 for his efforts—compare this to the £750 earned by Sangster for writing *Dracula*). In a further move to keep things fresh, Carreras enlisted the songwriters of *Expresso Bongo*, Monty Norman (b. 1928) and David Heneker (1906-2001), to score his latest Hammer horror. Norman would soon become famous for writing the ubiquitous "James Bond Theme," while Heneker created the music and lyrics for *Half a Sixpence* (based on

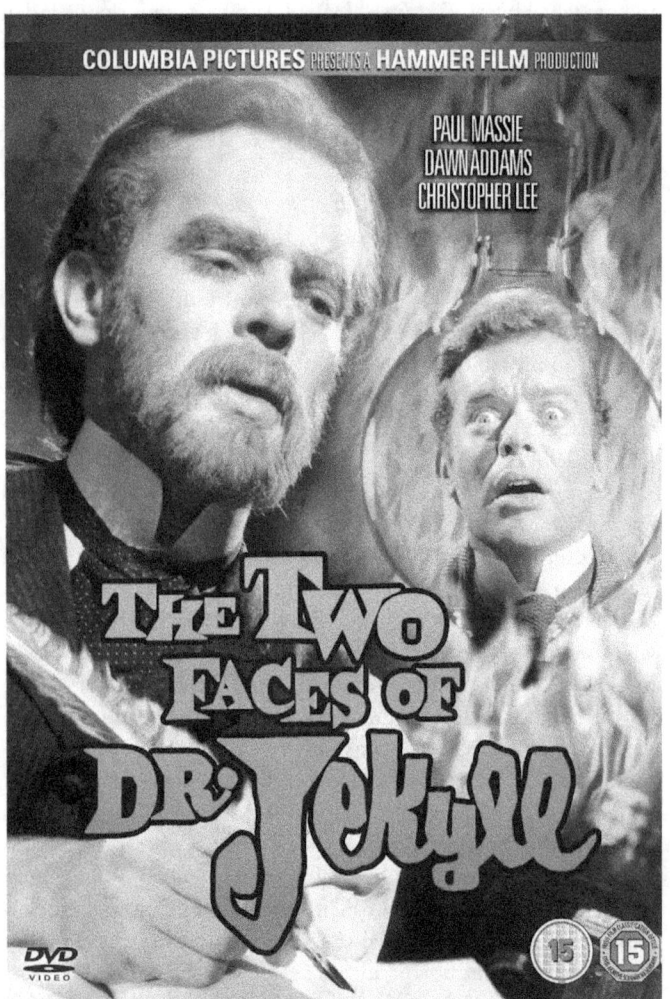

In this British DVD cover, we can see Mr. Hyde's youthful handsomeness and Dr. Jekyll's age and wisdom.

H.G. Wells' *Kipps* and filmed in 1967 with Tommy Steele). Both men provide excellent orchestration on *The Two Faces of Dr. Jekyll*, with galumphing brass and freewheeling strings echoing the changes between Jekyll and Hyde.

Lee was cast as Jekyll's unlikely friend, the caddish Paul Allen. In a 2004 interview with Marcus Hearn, the actor described Allen as "possibly the best performance" he ever gave for Hammer, going on to say: "I wanted to play Jekyll and Hyde, but Hammer shot that one down. I also wanted to play *The Phantom of the Opera*, and they shot that one down. I suppose they thought: 'We can't have the same man all the time.'" Perhaps inspired by feelings of disappointment that he was not cast in the title roles, Lee manages to make Paul a far more interesting character. (He would, of course, finally portray Jekyll and Hyde in 1970's *I, Monster* for Amicus.)

Production of *The Two Faces of Dr. Jekyll* began at Bray on Monday, November 23, 1959, and, by all accounts, filming didn't go as smoothly as planned. On his few visits to the set, Mankowitz made no secret of the fact that he disliked Terence Fisher's approach to shooting his script. With a certain degree of snobbery, perhaps, the writer felt that his intelligent material, which exposed Victorian hypocrisy and "the evil of scientific pride," was being treated as though it were some run-of-the-mill monster picture by Hammer's Gothic maestro.

And it wasn't just Mankowitz giving Fisher a headache. Jack Asher related, in *LSoH*, that, for reasons not divulged, leading lady Dawn Addams (1930-1985) simply did not get on with her director—to the extent that they refused to even speak to each other during filming. As such, Fisher relayed his directions to Addams through Asher, and she, in turn, gave her responses via Jack. "This had its farcical moments," said Asher, unsurprisingly. Nevertheless, Addams, who had starred with Christopher Lee at the beginning of 1959 in Alvin Rakoff's thriller *The Treasure of San Teresa*, would make a welcome return to Hammer horror as Countess Karnstein in *The Vampire Lovers* (1970), before falling afoul of an Indian rope trick in her final feature *The Vault of Horror*.

With such a lack of faith from the film's writer and female lead, it's not surprising that Terence Fisher lost enthusiasm for *The Two Faces of Dr. Jekyll*. In Michael Carreras' words, "the picture got bogged down," but the producer was still dedicated to making his movie look as good as it could. As he had on *The Mummy*, Carreras sought a bigger studio, aside from Bray, to lend a more expansive feel. Thus, Bernard Robinson built Jekyll's laboratory set at Elstree. It was here that Christopher Lee was interviewed by Sarah Stoddart for a *Picturegoer* piece eventually published, in January 1960, as "Horror Heart-Throb." "My fans aren't horror-struck morons," the actor explained. "They're sensitive to romantic loneliness and it's this quality I try to get across in even my most melodramatic roles."

Nattily dressed, with a fine pair of sideburns, Paul Allen is described as "a useless waster" even by Kitty, the woman who desires him (she also happens to be Jekyll's wife). We first see Paul pacing in Jekyll's parlor. Once he has successfully weaseled another loan from the good doctor, Paul enjoys a romantic clinch with Kitty, who purrs, "I deserve nothing better than you." The couple are next seen waltzing at the Sphinx nightclub, taking relish in poisonous barbs, which only seem to ignite their passions

Christopher Lee and Dawn Addams

further. "You're the most utterly shameless man I've ever met," says Kitty.

"I do hope so," Paul spits back, "because if you ever meet a more shameless man, I might lose you to him."

Mankowitz's script is peppered with such satisfying one-liners, not least the croaky old coachman's description of the Sphinx to Hyde as "very nearly halfway respectable." Slouched in his chair, puffing a cheroot, Lee gives a very convincing act of insobriety as the drunken Paul, followed by a suitably wounded look when Hyde takes Kitty away from him. Indeed, the role is given full shading by the actor and allows us glimpses into his range that he wouldn't get the chance to perform in other movies—he even delivers a swift blow to the back of Oliver Reed's head and, with an easy-going charm, actually makes his reprehensible character quite likeable at times.

Paul later takes Hyde on a tour of London's most debauched nightspots, including an opium den, where Lee lies strung out on a top bunk. Another such shady place is a bare-knuckle boxing ring, in which the opponents are played by brothers Joe and Douglas Robinson, who, in real life, owned a West End gym

The Loneliness of Evil

which counted Christopher Lee among its members ("Tiger" Joe Robinson could later be seen grappling with Sean Connery's James Bond in *Diamonds Are Forever* [1971]). This underworld montage was originally longer: Scenes of Lee and Massie attending a Black Mass, a cock fight and something to do with dwarves, were cut by the censor before release.

Paul meets a worthy end when Hyde entraps him with the snake dancer's python. Despite Margaret Robinson (née Carter) going to the trouble of creating a mechanical snake, only the real thing was used in the end (Michael Carreras casually picked the reptile up one day before he realized, to his horror, that it wasn't a prop). "We had a python crawl across Christopher Lee," Len Harris confirmed to Al Taylor, in *LSoH* #9. "I don't know how he did it. He was a very patient man."

Incidentally, the wallpaper on the snake dancer's boudoir wall was Bernard Robinson's own from home, much to the shock of his wife, who told *LSoH*: "How is it that these papers are absolutely ideal for this tart's flat and right for our sitting room?" When faced with this accusation, her husband swiftly changed the subject.

Unfortunately, Hyde's own denouement in the film is weak. What a shame that there was no time to film the brilliantly visual climax from Mankowitz's script, which would have shown Jekyll hanging for his crimes: As his body turns on the gibbet, we see the face of Hyde.

"I suppose in all of us, in small measure, there is the will to wickedness," Paul Massie told a contemporary reporter, before reflecting on the "glazed, staring look" he adopted as Hyde. "One night, hardly realizing it, I found myself solidly staring at my wife and it upset her so much she rushed from the room. I think she was very relieved when I finished the part." In the same interview, Massie revealed that Hammer originally wanted to cast him only as Hyde, until the actor convinced them that he was capable of essaying both roles.

In *LSoH* #9, camera operator Len Harris confessed that Massie added a third part to the film: Bored one morning when not needed, the actor donned a dress and powdered wig and joined the women in the bordello scene. Much to his consternation, no one recognized him. "I guess it must be somewhere in the film," said Len, "but it'd be very hard to tell."

Before retiring from acting in the mid-1960s to become a drama teacher in America, Massie starred as the struggling

One of Christopher Lee's most interesting roles was that of Paul Allen.

young painter who shares his studio with Tony Hancock in *The Rebel* (1960). One of Massie's fellow artists in this Robert Day-helmed comedy classic is played, with great gusto, by Oliver Reed (1938-1999), who makes the first of nine Hammer film appearances in *The Two Faces of Dr. Jekyll*.

A grandson of the famed Victorian actor-manager Sir Herbert Beerbohm Tree (whose Shakespearean recitals had entranced a teenage Boris Karloff), Reed was struggling to make a name for himself when he signed on to play a nightclub brawler in the Jekyll and Hyde film. Perhaps recognizing in the younger actor his own early hardships, Christopher Lee would give Reed a lift to and from the studio in the second-hand Mercedes he had acquired with his *Dracula* wages. Lee remembered those journeys with Reed for Stuart Basinger (in *Monster Bash Special* #2): "He was very young and very thin and very unsure of what his future was going to be … whether he ought to continue as an actor and so on. And I used to try to calm him down and cheer him up and say: 'You will be all right …'"

Reed had rather different memories of the early morning drives: "We'd have to listen to [Lee] sing opera all the way down. *German* opera—all the time!" The actor further told Denis Meikle: "I've never forgotten Christopher Lee. He was very sweet … I've got a lot of time for Christopher—a lot of time; he's a very clever actor."

The same could also be said for Reed: Although he never stepped on a stage in his life, he had the art of screen acting down pat, with his intense, almost whispered delivery put to excellent use alongside Lee in *Treasure Island* (1989) and the *Musketeers* films. The two actors first appeared together in *Beat Girl*—made three months prior to *The Two Faces of Dr. Jekyll*—and, in 1990, Reed narrated a series of film clips, *The World of*

Hammer, which dedicates an episode to Lee. Before lampooning the handsome Hyde twist himself in the oddball *Dr. Heckyl and Mr. Hype* (1980), Reed gave his greatest genre performances in *The Curse of the Werewolf*, *The Devils* (1970), and *The Brood* (1978). His other credits include the haunted tenant of *Burnt Offerings* (1975); the Russian villain of *Condorman* (1980); the crippled telepath in *Spasms* (1981); the Devil in *Two of a Kind* (1983); Vulcan in *The Adventures of Baron Munchausen* (1987); and the immured Cardinal of Stuart Gordon's *The Pit and the Pendulum* (1990). Despite achieving international stardom with breakout roles in *Oliver!* (1967) and *Women in Love* (1968), Reed always acknowledged his debt to Hammer, where he stabbed Peter Cushing in *Sword of Sherwood Forest*, played the sociopathic gang leader of *The Damned* and was one of Lee's cut-throat gang in *The Pirates of Blood River*. Elsewhere, the drunken, glowering psychopath he presents for *Paranoiac* (1962) is both amusing and tragic, given the actor's real-life exploits as a hellraiser. In fact, the phrase most often employed to describe Oliver by those closest to him is that he was "a Jekyll and Hyde"—a charming gentleman who could turn uncouth when in his cups (Robert Louis Stevenson, who also liked his tipple, had partly written his story as an allegory on the transformative effects of alcohol). True to form, Reed died of a heart attack while arm-wrestling sailors in a Maltese pub, leaving his unfinished role in Ridley Scott's *Gladiator* (1999) to earn him a posthumous BAFTA nomination.

Prior to writing *The Two Faces of Dr. Jekyll*, Wolf Mankovitz was responsible for a BAFTA-winning Gogol adaptation, *The Bespoke Overcoat* (1955). The star of this supernatural short was David Kossoff (1919-2005), who can be seen as Jekyll's confidant, Dr. Litauer. Kossoff would portray a less level-headed professor in *The Mouse That Roared* (1958) and its 1962 sequel *The Mouse on the Moon*, as well as Donald Wolfit's assistant in *Svengali* (1954), the owner of a flea circus in *The Woman for Joe* (1954) and Montgomery Clift's dad in *Freud* (1961). In real life, Kossoff was the father of Free guitarist Paul Kossoff, whose untimely death in 1976 inspired David to become a fervid anti-drugs campaigner. He was also a well-known Christian advocate, speaking out against the commercialization of sex and violence—in movies like *The Two Faces of Dr. Jekyll*.

The film wrapped, a fortnight behind schedule, on Friday, January 22, 1960; just four days later, Fisher began shooting *The Brides of Dracula*. As for Mankowitz, he next scripted the Peter Sellers-Sophia Loren vehicle *The Millionairess* (1960), Val Guest's vérité-style sci-fi *The Day the Earth Caught Fire* (1961) and the chaotic Bond parody *Casino Royale* (1966), before writing a biography of Edgar Allan Poe, *The Extraordinary Mr. Poe*, in 1978.

Columbia, the distributor of *The Two Faces of Dr. Jekyll* in the UK, demanded all dialogue containing the words "Hell," "bitch," and "damn" be changed to "Hades," "witch," and "darn," respectively. Expenses were incurred by rehiring the actors involved to dub in the appropriate phrases. Even when further cuts were made to the US print, Columbia's American executives were so disappointed with the film that they sold it to AIP, who initially retitled it *Jekyll's Inferno*. Before release, they cut eight minutes from the running time and then rechristened it *House of Fright*, unleashing it on a double bill with the 1958 "Psychorama" cheapie *Terror in the Haunted House* on Wednesday, May 3, 1961 (when Del Shannon topped the *Billboard* Hot 100 with "Runaway"). As the *Jekyll's Inferno* posters had already been printed, AIP just slapped a sticker of the new title over the old.

The Two Faces of Dr. Jekyll opened at the London Pavilion in Piccadilly Circus on Friday, October 7, 1960 (when Ricky Valance was at No. 1 with "Tell Laura I Love Her"). That same day, *Spartacus* was released over the pond. The Stanley Kubrick epic may have enjoyed more success than Terence Fisher's opus, but Dave Prowse, who worked with both directors, was quoted in *LSoH* as saying: "I learned more about filmmaking from Terry Fisher than Stanley Kubrick."

Despite being paired with an X-rated French comedy, *The Green Mare's Nest* (1959), for general UK release, *The Two Faces of Dr. Jekyll* failed to set the box office on fire and actually made a loss for Hammer (as had *The Ugly Duckling*). When the company next approached Robert Louis Stevenson's work, 12 years later, it was, again, with a novel twist, but *Dr. Jekyll and Sister Hyde* was only marginally profitable. Nevertheless, the influence of Hammer's first serious attempt at the subject can be felt in the BBC's well-regarded *Dr. Jekyll and Mr. Hyde* (1980), wherein David Hemmings' grubby, bewhiskered Jekyll becomes a clean-shaven rake and seduces his own fiancée.

While *The Two Faces of Dr. Jekyll* is not the best version of Stevenson's tale, it is still, in the words of *Daily Cinema*: "A stylish variation on an old theme," and the lush cinematography of Jack Asher (in "Megascope"), along with one of Christopher Lee's most beautifully mounted performances, make it more than worthwhile.

The Terror of the Tongs
1960

See … the dreaded Chinese needle torture! See … the throbbing dance of the Manchu maidens!

It will be seen that this is basically Boy's Own Paper stuff, transformed into criminal Lunatic's Own Paper stuff by the addition of some recherché brutalities … I suspect that the fertile imagination of Jimmy Sangster has been at work in details of how [the Tong] carried on, though I am told that they really did carry and use hatchets for their killings …—BBFC reader Audrey Field comments on *The Terror of the Tongs* screenplay, March 1960.

One of those Hammer grislies that makes you check the backdoor lock 23 times before you go to bed and leaves the armrests of your chair deformed …—*Evening Mail* review

Christopher Lee receives top billing as Chung King.

The success of Hammer's *The Stranglers of Bombay* (1959), with its sadistic look at tribe violence (including lopped off hands and cobra attacks), paved the way for *The Terror of the Tongs*, which focuses, instead, on the antics of criminal gangs in turn-of-the-century China

Announced as *Terror of the Hatchet Men*, Jimmy Sangster was asked to write a script around Bernard Robinson's Chinese dockside set, which had been built for *Visa to Canton*—a Cold War thriller with Richard Basehart. As Sangster had recently bought a house, which, in his own words, he "couldn't afford," he agreed to the project. "I should have kept my mouth shut," the writer reflected in his autobiography: "*The Terror of the Tongs* was probably the second or third worst piece of writing I ever did."

Cast as Chung King, head of the Red Dragon Tong, Christopher Lee would receive top billing in a feature film for the first time. Six days before production began on Tuesday, April 19, 1960, he arrived at Bray for make-up tests, having just returned from an Italian holiday with a robust tan. As such, Roy Ashton had to work extra hard to make him appear paler for the film. False rubber eyelids were created from a mold and, in a process that took about an hour, were applied and blended over the actor's own. The inflexibility of this uncomfortable make-up created problems that would inform the stillness of Lee's ethnic roles. As he explained to Wayne Kinsey, once the eyelids were on: "You cannot look up, or all you see is a white eyeball, and [if you] look down … your own eyelid comes down from underneath, which is why you have to play the whole thing with your head horizontally."

Although the casting of Caucasian actors in Asian parts is seen as an unfortunate trend of less enlightened times, it still goes on today—witness the debates surrounding Tilda Swinton's Ancient One in *Doctor Strange* (2016), or Scarlet Johansson's Motoko Kusanagi for *Ghost in the Shell* (2016). Almost 100 years previously, Lon Chaney had brought a heroic dignity to the Chinese gentlemen he enacted in *Outside the Law* (1920), *Shadows* (1922) and *Mr. Wu* (1927) that was sadly lacking in Hollywood's usual depiction of Asian characters at that time. Subsequently, Boris Karloff added a triumvirate of Chinese characters to his own oeuvre with *The Mask of Fu Manchu* (1932), *West of Shanghai* (1937) and *Mr. Wong, Detective* (1938), a role he reprised in four sequels. Bela Lugosi, on the other hand, was an unrelated villain known as *The Mysterious Mr. Wong* (1934), while, in the same decade, Lugosi's fellow Hungarian, Peter Lorre, starred as the Japanese detective *Mr. Moto* for a series of popular mysteries at 20th Century Fox. Following in these footsteps, Christopher Lee was always careful to bring a respectful poise to his Asian roles, despite the murderous acts he is required to carry out.

Akin to his later Fu Manchu ventures, Lee lounges in an ornate lair as Chung King, flanked by henchmen and dealing out torture to those who betray him. "Have you ever had your bones scraped, Captain?" he leans forward to enquire of Captain Jackson Sale (Geoffrey Toone) in a way that only Christopher Lee could make sound entirely natural: "It is painful in the extreme, I can assure you." ("Heaven only knows where I came up with that one," Jimmy Sangster remarked.) Other actors would have been tempted to play such lines to the hilt, making them all the less effective because of it. Indeed, Lee seemed to foretell Chung King when he wrote in his 1959 *Picturegoer* article: "Working in horror films has been a fascinating experience, since they call for complete sincerity in one's acting. I have always felt the dividing line between conviction and absurdity to be very slight. I

think that all of us who have been connected with these films at Bray Studios have managed to achieve that conviction."

Of the Bray regulars working on *The Terror of the Tongs*, Bernard Robinson has clearly done his homework: The Eastern designs displayed on his sets are immaculately detailed. Likewise, James Bernard's score expertly mixes Oriental themes and instrumentation with his traditional Hammer horror strings. In the director's chair, however, is a man entirely new to the Hammer formula: Anthony Bushell (1904-1997) had been Laurence Olivier's associate on *Hamlet* and *Richard III*—as well as being responsible for casting Peter Cushing in the former, he joined Christopher Lee among the extras. As an actor, Bushell also starred with Lee in Nicholas Ray's war drama *Bitter Victory* (1957), and with Cushing in *The Black Knight* (1953), before portraying Colonel Breen for the BBC's *Quatermass and the Pit* (1958). Earlier in his career, he had played in James Whale's *Journey's End* (1929), appeared with Boris Karloff in *Five Star Final* (1931) and *The Ghoul* (1933) and starred in *Forbidden Territory* (1934), the first film to be adapted from a Dennis Wheatley novel.

Bushell sets the ball rolling on his only Hammer credit with a typically alarming pre-titles sequence (in which a man has his hand slashed at with a hatchet) and refuses to slacken the pace from there. He also draws fine performances from a typically adept cast.

Lee's main henchmen are personified by Roger Delgado and Milton Reid. Delgado (1918-1973) had last appeared onscreen with Lee in *The Battle of the River Plate* but, for a 1953 radio broadcast of Somerset Maugham's *The Noble Spaniard*, the two actors had enhanced the play's realism by actually dueling, with swords, in the studio. Immortalized as the evil Master in *Doctor Who* from 1970 until his death in a car accident, Delgado was also one of *The Stranglers of Bombay*, the Mexican Consul in *First Man into Space*, Hasmid in *The Mummy's Shroud* and a member of Oliver Reed's *Assassination Bureau* (1968).

Milton Reid (1917-c. 1987), who wrestled under the alias of "The Mighty Chang" (which was also the name of his character in *Deadlier than the Male*), played executioners in both *The Camp on Blood Island* and *Blood of the Vampire*, before essaying a particularly villainous role in *Ferry to Hong Kong* (1958). Reunited with that film's star and director—Curt Jurgens and Lewis Gilbert respectively—for *The Spy Who Loved Me* (1976), Reid also portrayed a James Bond henchman in *Dr. No*. His other credits include the vengeful mulatto of *Captain Clegg*; a musical strongman in *Berserk*; Patrick Wymark's dog handler in *Blood on Satan's Claw* (1970); a victim of *Dr. Phibes Rises Again* (1971); Sabbala in *The People That Time Forgot* (1977); a nightclub bouncer in *Terror* (1978) and the saucer-eyed Jinnee of *Arabian Adventure*. By all accounts a gentle

giant, Reid's death in India, the country of his birth, is shrouded in mystery.

Geoffrey Toone (1910-2005), who enjoyed one of his few leading roles as Captain Jackson Sale, can also be seen in *The King and I* (1955, as Sir Edward Ramsay), *Captain Sinbad* (1962, as Mohar), *Dr. Crippen* (as the defense lawyer) and *Dr. Who and the Daleks* (1965, as a Thal). Sale's daughter, Helena, who dies at the hands of the Tong, is played by Barbara Brown (b. 1940). Her next, and final, feature film appearance was as the romantic lead of Robert Hartford-Davis' incredible sci-fi musical *Gonks Go Beat* (1965).

The Terror of the Tongs' main leading lady, however, is Yvonne Monlaur (1939-2017), who was fresh from starring as the winsome Marianne in *The Brides of Dracula*. Her *Tongs* heroine, conversely, displays far more gumption. After making the acquaintance of Captain Sale by smashing a jug over Ewen Solon's head, she again comes to the Captain's rescue by stabbing Charles Lloyd Pack in the neck with a syringe, before giving her life entirely to save the ineffectual hero. Having earlier played a death-defying performer at the *Circus of Horrors*, it's no surprise that Monlaur was in the running to play Domino Derval in *Thunderball* (the part eventually went to Claudine Auger). After Christopher Lee's death, Yvonne paid tribute to the actor in *Monster Bash* magazine: "Truly he was larger than life! During the breaks [on *The Terror of the Tongs*] we chatted, and had laughs together. We joked around in our Asian costumes. He was very warm, cultivated and had such a dry sense of humor. He had seen me in Paris cinema and paid me wonderful compliments. I will treasure our movie memories of happy days."

One of the few genuinely Chinese actors in *The Terror of the Tongs* is, unfortunately, killed off rather early in the proceedings. Although born in Warrington, England, Burt Kwouk (1930-2016) was raised in Shanghai until the age of 16. Opposed to the villains in *Tongs*, Kwouk crossed over to the dark side for both *The Brides of Fu Manchu* (a performance that was repeated, via stock footage, in *The Castle of Fu Manchu*) and *The Fiendish Plot of Dr. Fu Manchu* (1980). Immortalized as Cato in the *Pink Panther* series, Burt also appeared in three James Bond films, *Goldfinger* (1964), *Casino Royale* (1966) and *You Only Live Twice*, as well as *Curse of the Fly* (1964) and *I Bought a Vampire Motorcycle* (1989). His other Hammer roles include the Japanese sergeant of their hard-hitting war film *Yesterday's Enemy* (1959) and the sinister tattooist in the *Hammer House of Mystery and Suspense* episode "Mark of the Devil" (1983). A regular on Britain's longest-running sitcom *Last of the Summer Wine* from 2002 to 2010, Burt's assuring voice also became familiar to TV viewers as the narrator of the English-language versions of Japanese imports *The Water Margin* (1976-1978) and *Monkey* (1978-1979).

The Loneliness of Evil

Spanish herald promoting *Terror of the Tongs*

Another Hammer stalwart in *The Terror of the Tongs* is Anglo-Indian actor Marne Maitland (1920-1992), who would go on to supply ammunition for Christopher Lee's *Man with the Golden Gun*. Maitland was also Captain Sakamura in *The Camp on Blood Island*, Xavier in *The Phantom of the Opera* and the sinister servant of *The Reptile*.

Aside from the actors, *The Terror of the Tongs*' main attraction is the photography of Arthur Grant (1915-1972), whose exquisite color epitomized Hammer's 1960s mien with such classics as *The Curse of the Werewolf*, *The Phantom of the Opera* and *The Plague of the Zombies* (in addition, he helped make *The Tomb of Ligeia* [1964] the best-looking of Roger Corman's Poe adaptations). Grant's work at Hammer, which spread from *The Abominable Snowman* (1957) to (his last film) *Fear in the Night* (1971), made him a more than worthy successor to Jack Asher. (Despite having just done some of his greatest work on *The Brides of Dracula*, Asher was regrettably let go, as his painstaking methods were taking too long to meet the company's increasingly breakneck schedules.)

Completing his work on *The Terror of the Tongs* within the first 10 days of its schedule, Christopher Lee returned to promote the film, while it was still in production, on Wednesday, May 18, 1960. The occasion was a riverside Chinese barbecue at Bray, where he was joined by the cast of the hit West End musical *The World of Suzie Wong*—the show's star, Tsai Chin, would go on to play Lee's daughter in the *Fu Manchu* series.

Once finished, *The Terror of the Tongs* fell below the expectations of its distributor, Columbia, and a UK release was delayed. After US showings in March 1961 proved fruitful, however, the film finally opened at the London Pavilion on Friday, September 29, 1961 (the most fancifully attired of those arriving at the premiere in costume were promised parts in Hammer's upcoming *The Phantom of the Opera*).

Double-billed with William Castle's *Homicidal* ("The Horror Kings of Britain and America Combine to Thrill You!"), *The Terror of the Tongs*' Pavilion hoarding—which can be spotted in *The Day of the Triffids*—boasted a giant depiction of Lee's brooding face, besides which a neon-lit clock signified the gimmicky "Fright break" of Castle's thriller (incidentally, Harry Alan Towers would append a similar "whodunit break" to his 1965 *Ten Little Indians*, for which Christopher Lee lent his voice, before the idea was seen again as "the werewolf break" in *The Beast Must Die*). In 2016, the London Transport Museum organized a tour of Underground tunnels beneath Euston Station, which had been closed off since 1962. A *Terror of the Tongs* poster was discovered upon the walls, alongside heralds for contemporaneous releases, *Psycho*, *The Naked Edge* and *West Side Story*.

As with *The Man Who Could Cheat Death*, a Jimmy Sangster novelization was issued, this time by Digit Books, and, like the earlier Hammer tie-in, proffered salacious details that couldn't be seen on film, i.e., "He stared up at the woman, his mutilated hand pumping blood in throbbing spurts ... "

Lee's performance as Chung King most probably inspired his step-cousin Ian Fleming to suggest that he be cast as the Chinese villain *Dr. No* in the first James Bond film. Although Joseph Wiseman, who ultimately played the role, is excellent, it would have been wonderful to behold Lee crushing statuettes with his steel hands. Of course, Lee finally got to play a Bond villain (one of the best, in fact) in *The Man with the Golden Gun*.

Although far from being one of Hammer's greatest films, *The Terror of the Tongs* rattles along like an old-fashioned serial with never a wasted moment and plenty of action to commend it. In 1976, the story was melded with *The Phantom of the Opera* to produce one of the greatest *Doctor Who* adventures, "The Talons of Weng-Chiang" (made when the sci-fi series was at its Hammer-inspired height).

The Terror of the Tongs was also spoofed, along with the Fu Manchu films, in "Frenzy of Tongs," an episode of Steve Coogan's 2001 series *Dr. Terrible's House of Horrible*, with Mark Gatiss doing his best Christopher Lee impersonation as Hang Man Chang. A member of *The League of Gentlemen* comedy troupe—whose debt to classic horror films is lovingly apparent—Gatiss (b. 1966) would pay further homage to Lee with his Mycroft Holmes in *Sherlock* (2009-2016), an essential documentary (*A History of Horror with Mark Gatiss* [2010]) and a 2019 reinvention of *Dracula*.

Such tributes notwithstanding, Lee and Hammer would have to wait until 1965 to reach the apogee of their historical horrors with *Rasputin: The Mad Monk*.

The Hands of Orlac
1960

The frightening nightmare of a man who finds himself with hands which he can't control!

"Some people took exception to my knife throwing," Christopher Lee wrote in his memoirs. This teenage occupation got him into especially hot water when he stood a young girl named Penelope against a door and "threw knives all around her." Fortunately, although Lee soon outgrew this interest, it stood him in good stead for the blade-wielding magician he would play in *The Hands of Orlac*. The actor, who consequently became a member of the illustrious Magic Circle, was coached in his screen illusions by Belfast-born magician Billy McComb (1922-2006). Sometimes billed as "The World's Largest Leprechaun," McComb later appeared in Clive Barker's *Lord of Illusions* (1994).

The Hands of Orlac marks the third attempt to film Maurice Renard's 1920 source novel. The first, *Orlacs Hände*, was released in 1924. Despite a great physical performance from Conrad Veidt, this Austrian silent is a slow-moving affair with few of the visual flourishes that director Robert Wiene brought to his previous collaboration with Veidt, *The Cabinet of Dr. Caligari*. The second screen adaptation is far livelier: With Peter Lorre in his Hollywood debut as the obsessive Dr. Gogol, and innovative direction from Karl Freund, *Mad Love* (1935) is, quite simply, one of the greatest horror movies ever made.

The same cannot be said for the interpretation starring Christopher Lee. Director Edmond T. Gréville (1906-1966) adapted Renard's story with the help of John Baines (1909-1962)—a writer who had formerly contributed to both *Dead of Night* and Terence Fisher's *Colonel Bogey*. Having last worked with Lee in August 1959 on the extraordinary *Beat Girl*, Gréville's career began 30 years previously, when E.A. Dupont invited him over to England to assist on *Piccadilly*—a classic Anna May Wong showcase, which also includes Charles Laughton in his feature debut. Gréville went on to direct another screen legend, Erich Von Stroheim, in three movies (*Under Secret Orders* [1937], *Menaces* [1938] and *The Other Side of Paradise* [1953]), before co-writing *The Virgin of Nuremberg* (1963) for Lee. The French filmmaker, whose middle initial stood for "Thonger," died in a car crash in May 1966; his last movie was titled, ironically, *The Accident* (1963).

Filmed in both French and English-language versions (with Lee retaining his own voice in both), *The Hands of Orlac* began shooting at the Studios de la Victorine, Nice, in late May 1960. Following an excursion to Shepperton, production wrapped on Sunday, July 17. Lee wrote that he made the picture under the weight of heartbreak, after he had been stood up by a certain Danish model, Birgit Kroencke ("I did what I had never done for any woman—I gave up my golf that Sunday …"). The actor found consolation, not only in what he called "a marvelous part" in "quite a good picture," but by playing golf (when not required at the studio in Nice) with his *Corridors of Blood* chum Nigel Green. As for Birgit, or Gitte as she is more frequently known, on Friday, March 17, 1961, she married Christopher Lee.

The title role in *The Hands of Orlac* went to Mel Ferrer (1917-2008), who, at the time, was the husband of Audrey Hepburn. Ferrer had just escaped the exquisite environs of Roger Vadim's *Blood and Roses* (1960), where he played another piano-playing character, Leopoldo Karnstein. Ten years later, in Sweden, he produced *The Night Visitor*, for which Christopher Lee was asked to play the leading role of Salem, a vengeful asylum escapee. Despite Lee investing some of his own money into the project, he was unduly replaced by Max Von Sydow (given that the majority of his screen time would have been spent running through the snow in his underwear, Lee may have had a lucky escape; the film does find room, nonetheless, for two of his *Dracula* sequel co-stars, Andrew Keir and Rupert Davies). Ferrer went on to star in *The Girl from the Red Cabaret* (1973), an obscure feature from *Horror Express* director Eugenio Martin, before staggering about with a scythe in his neck for Tobe Hooper's unpleasant *Death Trap* (1976). The remainder of his genre credits consist of cheap Italian knockoffs, such as *The Antichrist* (1974), *The Great Alligator* (1979) and *City of the Walking Dead* (1980).

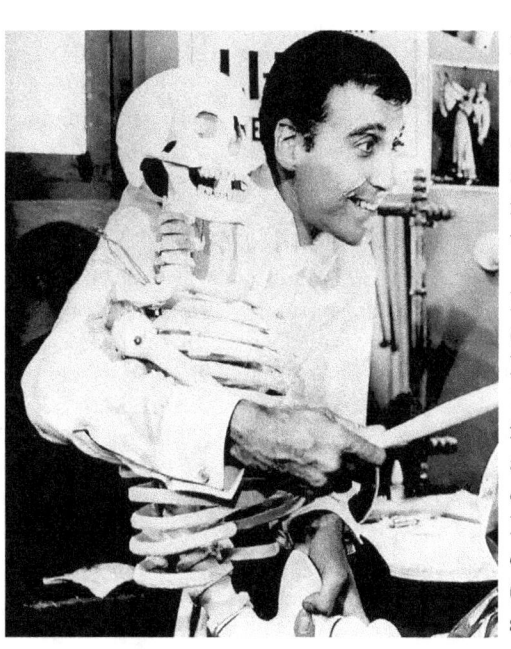

In a gag publicity shot, Christopher Lee mugs with a prop skeleton.

As concert pianist Stephen Orlac, Ferrer injures his hands in a plane crash. The pilot is David Peel (1920-1981), who had just delivered an excellent performance as Baron Meinster, Hammer's vampiric substitute for Lee, in *The Brides of Dracula*. Peel, whose film career stretched back to *We Dive at Dawn* (1942) and the Miles Malleson-penned *Squadron Leader X* (1943), became a neighbor of both Lee and Boris Karloff in the mid-1960s. By that time, he was retired from acting and had gone into the antiques business, where the bemused ex-thespian would find the occasional Hammer fan traipsing to his place of work in search of Baron Meinster (Peel's cinematic past was a well-kept secret from colleagues).

Awaking from the accident with the largest plaster casts in film history,

Orlac finds it difficult to tickle the ivories and, believing his hands to be no longer his own, occasionally attempts to strangle his fiancée, Louise (Lucile Saint-Simon, [b. 1932]; she would play a less substantial role in *The Virgin of Nuremberg*).

Escaping to a seedy hotel, Orlac encounters Lee's dark-lidded magician Nero and his assistant, Li Lang (Dany Carrel, [b. 1932], fresh from *Mill of the Stone Women* [1960]). A dapper dresser with a mysterious air and Jerry Lewis haircut, Lee presents an unpredictable character. One is always aware of a simmering violence beneath the outward charm, as evidenced by his treatment of Carrel: Purring persuasive demands while playfully addressing grotesque effigies, including a skeleton (which he keeps in his dressing room), Nero could either erupt with hysterical laughter or lash out in any given situation. It's this unpredictability which makes him both dangerous and intriguing.

Leech-like, Nero clings to Orlac, goading and tormenting, listening in at windows with blackmail on his mind. He even appears at the foot of the pianist's bed in the middle of the night wearing a fright mask with hooks for hands and a scar across his throat. Unfortunately, what could have been the creepiest scene in the whole of Lee's horror oeuvre is totally wasted by Gréville. Despite the gruff voice applied by the actor, he unmasks himself all too soon and the deflated atmosphere just can't compete with the corresponding vignette enacted by Peter Lorre in *Mad Love* (Lee told Tom Johnson and Mark A. Miller that *Mad Love* was "one of the most terrifying films I've ever seen"). Indeed, the major failing of *The Hands of Orlac* is that it ultimately eschews any hints of the supernatural to become a rather standard crime drama, despite the weirdness of Lee's character, who even laughs as he is carted away by the police.

While disappointed not to be playing Orlac himself, Lee again makes his secondary lead more interesting than the title character (as he had in *The Two Faces of Dr. Jekyll*) and seems to enjoy playing the unusual Nero. A heavy with a light touch, his performance is the highlight of an otherwise quite unremarkable film.

Aside from Mel Ferrer, Lee is joined by a distinguished cast who are, unfortunately, given little to do. Orlac's old friends are played by *The Mummy*'s Felix Aylmer and Basil Sydney (1894-1968). Recently seen as the Emperor of Lilliput in *The 3 Worlds of Gulliver*, stage veteran Sydney had played *Hamlet* on Broadway in 1923 and Claudius in Laurence Olivier's 1947 film version.

Two "guest star" Donalds also put in appearances: Donald Pleasence (1919-1995), an actor who would amass four Tony Award nominations for his theater work, is best known for his sinister screen presence in roles such as the grave-robbing Hare in *The Flesh and the Fiends*, the drunken former owner of the *Circus of Horrors* and the dodgy priest in *Eye of the Devil*. Despite this, his only Hammer appearance is, surprisingly, in a non-horror film—as a runny-nosed accountant in Val Guest's gritty police drama *Hell is a City* (1959). A former prisoner of war, which no doubt influenced his performance in *The Great Escape* (1962), Pleasence was also the sinister lawyer of *What a Carve Up!*, "The Man with the Power" on *The Outer Limits* (1963-1965) and the shrunken scientist of *Fantastic Voyage* (1965). His scar-faced Blofeld of *You Only Live Twice* (which became the inspiration for Dr. Evil in *Austin Powers*) ties with Lee's Scaramanga as the most memorable villain of the James Bond franchise. The two actors would next work together in *Death Line* (1972).

In 1962, Donald Pleasence gave a sympathetic rendering of real-life poisoner *Dr. Crippen*, whose drink-besotted wife is played by the future Mrs. Vincent Price, Coral Browne. The film was helmed by Robert Lynn, assistant director of Lee's *Dracula*, and features Sir Donald Wolfit (1902-1968) as Crippen's prosecutor, R.D. Muir. In *The Hands of Orlac*, Wolfit can be glimpsed as the surgeon who saves the titular organs—a surprisingly negligible role for such a famed Shakespearean. As well as being the model for Albert Finney's "Sir" in *The Dresser* (1983), Wolfit was the Draculean mesmerist *Svengali* (1954); the host of ITV's *Hour of Mystery* (1957) and the fiendish Dr. Callistratus in *Blood of the Vampire*. He was also Christopher Lee's one-armed accuser in *The Traitor*, on the set of which, Lee introduced the grateful older actor to the works of J.R.R. Tolkien.

A far more prominent contribution to *The Hands of Orlac* is provided by renowned jazz pianist Claude Bolling (b. 1930), whose score is full of jaunty xylophones that sound, at times, as if they've seeped in from a Jacques Tati comedy. A brief six-track soundtrack album was issued in France on the Philips label (under its French title *Les Mains d'Orlac*), which includes a puckish little number, "C'est Parti," sung by Dany Carrel. In 1979, Bolling would compose the music for *The Awakening*—a big-budget, *Omen*-inspired variant of Bram Stoker's *The Jewel of Seven Stars*.

Following a December 1960 UK preview, *The Hands of Orlac* didn't see general release in the US until Wednesday May 13, 1964. Three years earlier, Four Square Books in England brought out a novelization by Robert Bateman, which follows the action of the film fairly closely; even if descriptions like "the stream of blood pouring down her stomach and thighs" were a far cry from the author's usual writings, such as *Horse and Pony Stories for Girls* and *Thematic Stamp Collecting*. (Bateman was also responsible for a racial sci-fi novel, *When the Whites Went*.)

The Hands of Orlac was parodied as "Voodoo Feet of Death" for *Dr. Terrible's House of Horrible* (2001). The following year, the story was again referenced in another BBC comedy, "The One-Armed Man is King," from *The League of Gentlemen*.

Back in 1960, Lee's thoughts on the genre could be found in *Picturegoer Film Annual*: "I can honestly say that, from every angle, horror films have been a considerable asset in my screen career ... I have never believed horror films to be bad for people's minds. I would prefer to call them films of fantasy, particularly the ones I have made. If a horror film is convincingly directed with good production value and sincere performances, it becomes more in the nature of a fairy story ... To my mind, they don't do any mental harm ... As long as the public wants to see me in horror films, I shall continue to make them ..."

One Step Beyond: The Sorcerer 1960

One of the most interesting by-products of the late 1950s horror boom was the supernatural TV anthology format, including Hammer's own failed foray into the field, *Tales of Frankenstein*. Considerably more successful was Rod Serling's classic series of morality plays, *The Twilight Zone*, first televised by CBS in October 1959. Ten months prior to this, ABC broadcast *One Step Beyond*—a series which took its inspiration from supposedly true accounts of the paranormal. The format broke tradition, just once, for an unprecedented experiment in which John Newland (1917-2000), the show's host and director, ate hallucinogenic mushrooms on camera to see if they could induce extrasensory perception. They couldn't.

No stranger to the horror genre, Newland starred as Dr. Frankenstein in *Tales of Tomorrow* (1952, with Lon Chaney, Jr. unaware that his inebriated performance as the Monster was being broadcast live), and went on to direct episodes of *Thriller*, *The Man from U.N.C.L.E.*, *Star Trek* and *Night Gallery*, before reviving the *One Step Beyond* format, as *The Next Step Beyond*, for a single season in 1978. His finest works, however, are two unsettling TV-movies: *Crawlspace* (1971), in which a childless couple allow a strange young man to live under their house, and *Don't Be Afraid of the Dark* (1973), wherein tiny, prune-faced demons terrorize Kim Darby. Of working with Christopher Lee, Newland told John Kenneth Muir (at *Retro TV Files*): "Oh, he was funny and charming. He makes his living being spooky but he's really got a great sense of humor."

One Step Beyond had a total of 96 episodes, the last 13 of which were shot in the UK for economic reasons. "The Sorcerer"—the 31st episode of season three—was originally broadcast on Tuesday May 23, 1961. Despite shakier production values than the altogether slicker *Twilight Zone*, the caliber of actors hired by Newland was often impressive. Lee's recent co-stars Andre Morell and Anton Diffring had both guested in preceding stories and, like them, Lee was cast as a German military man.

As Wilhelm Reitlinger, an officer during the First World War, Lee is careful to present the vulnerability of his character. Employing a convincing accent, his stiff exterior belies a hangdog expression reminiscent of Peter Lorre's gallery of maligned losers. Lee admitted that he based his characterization of Reitlinger on "the Butcher of Czechoslovakia, Reinhardt Heydrich," a real-life monster whom the actor had personal knowledge of through his war work. In an interview with Calum Waddell, for *The Dark Side* #168, director Philippe Mora recalled that when Lee arrived in Prague to film *Howling II* in 1984, there was a military welcome at the airport. On wondering aloud who it was for, a stunned Mora was told by Lee: "That's for me, dear boy. I'm a war hero here … I was involved in the assassination of SS Chief Reinhardt Heydrich." (This historical slaying is depicted in *Hitler's Madman* [1942] starring Lee's fellow Dracula, John Carradine, as Heydrich.)

The sorcerer is a clairvoyant farmer Klaus Karnak, played by Martin Benson (1918-2010), who also worked as story supervisor on this, and 13 other *One Step Beyond* entries. Best known for originating Kralahome in *The King and I* (a part he recreated for the 1955 film), Benson was also the alien visitor in *The Strange World of Planet X* (1957), the circus owner who exploits *Gorgo*, the fiendish innkeeper of *Captain Clegg*, Mr. Solo in *Goldfinger* and Father Spiletto in *The Omen* (1975). Karnak—who seems to be patterned after Bela Lugosi's character in *The Wolf Man*—is rumored to converse with animals and start fires with his mind. He also has the power to see beyond the façade of Wilhelm Reitlinger, to the "much troubled man" who hides within.

Lee shows us Reitlinger's true state of mind during a tavern scene: Slurring drunkenly, a strand of hair falls from an otherwise well-coiffed head. Suspecting his lover, Elsa, of being unfaithful, he pays a visit to the sorcerer, who uses his magic to transport the officer to the lady's home. Once there, Wilhelm looks on watery-eyed as she slinks into the arms of another man. Facing her with grim resolve, like *The Mummy* without his covering, her taunts prove too much and Reitlinger shoots her dead with a shaking hand. Fading back to the sorcerer's hovel, the event leaves the officer wracked with guilt, although not entirely a changed man.

Making her debut as Elsa is Gabriella Licudi (b. 1941)—the alien lead of *Unearthly Stranger* (1963). She can also be seen as Beryl Stapleton opposite Peter Cushing in the 1968 BBC version of "The Hound of the Baskervilles." Elsewhere in the cast is a young Frederick Jaeger (1928-2004), who would go on to play an intergalactic Jekyll and Hyde in *Doctor Who*: "Planet of Evil" (1975), as well as *Dracula* in a 1991 BBC Radio dramatization.

At the close of "The Sorcerer," Newland is on hand to remind us that we have witnessed an allegedly true event from 1915, the records of which were "discovered among the files of the German War Ministry"—although I have been unable to trace any evidence of this.

Nevertheless, within the episode's scant 24-minute running time, Christopher Lee gives feeling to a character purported to lack emotion. Whether clutching at the sorcerer with heartbroken desperation, or laughing in disbelief at his tricks, the actor presents a well-rounded human being throughout. On awaking in his barracks, he even treats us to one of Peter Cushing's favorite tricks—the weary neck rub. That Lee can make us feel sympathy for a fascist like Reitlinger is a tribute to his skills. "I don't play villains; I play people," he often stated, attributing the quote to Anthony Hopkins, whose cannibalistic Hannibal Lecter (of *The Silence of the Lambs* [1990], *Hannibal* [2000], and *Red Dragon* [2002]) is both alarming and affable. This philosophy is given full application here, in one of Lee's best, and least-known, performances.

Christopher Lee in "The Sorcerer" episode of *One Step Beyond*

Taste of Fear aka Scream of Fear 1960

For maximum thrill ... we earnestly urge you to see this motion picture from the start!

Hammer going posh ... Christopher Lee ... has very credible accent. I kept a wary eye on him [and] he did not revert to his old Dracula trick ... There should be an Oscar for such good behavior.—*Evening News* review for *Taste of Fear*

In 2004, Christopher Lee described *Taste of Fear* to Marcus Hearn as "the best film I was in for Hammer." It was also the personal favorite of Jimmy Sangster. Enchanted by the French thriller *Les diaboliques* (1954), which he had seen when double billed with his own *X the Unknown*, Sangster sought to emulate its cleverly staged shock sequences and byzantine twists. "My wife was highly pregnant when we saw that," the writer revealed in *Flesh and Blood*, "I thought we'd nearly lost the baby there, because she was so frightened. I thought I'd love to do a movie like that."

Sangster's resultant script—the first of what he dubbed his "mini Hitchcocks"—was originally sold to Sydney Box, producer and co-writer of *The Seventh Veil* (1945). When Box suffered a heart attack, Michael Carreras optioned the film (titled tentatively *See No Evil*, then *Hell Hath No Fury*) and allowed Sangster to make his debut as a producer. Because "he was the perfect red herring" (as Sangster recorded in his memoirs), Christopher Lee was cast as Dr. Pierre Gerrard, who shares his name with the character he'd played earlier in *The Man Who Could Cheat Death*. Although it's pleasing to think that the two are related, Jimmy Sangster admitted to Jonathan Rigby, in *Shivers* #34: "It was probably the only French name I could come up with ..."

Lee joined the production (which had begun on Monday, October 24, 1960, in Nice, France) when the team regrouped at Elstree on Tuesday, November 8. "It was an unforgettable experience," he told Stuart Basinger in *Monster Bash*, "because when I was doing a rehearsal of a scene one day in the studio after lunch, I looked up and I saw Gary Cooper standing by the camera. As you can imagine, I forgot my lines." Cooper was at Elstree working on what turned out to be his final film, *The Naked Edge*, which co-starred Peter Cushing.

While Dr. Gerrard is hardly Lee's best part for Hammer (he is, as Sangster intended, merely a red herring, lending a sinister presence and handing out sedatives), I would agree that *Taste of Fear* is among his best films. Much of the credit for this must go to Seth Holt (1923-1971), whom Lee called, in his autobiography, "one of the best British directors ever." Like Terence Fisher, Holt had entered the film industry as an editor. His work in this capacity included such classics as *Dead of Night* (1945), *The Lavender Hill Mob* (1951) and *Saturday Night and Sunday Morning* (1960). Sangster and Michael Carreras were both impressed by Holt's first film as a director, *Nowhere to Go* (1958), and, on its strength, hired him to helm *Taste of Fear*. His next film for Hammer, *The Nanny* (1965), scripted and produced by Sangster, is another jewel in the company's crown. After being replaced by Mario Bava on *Danger: Diabolik*, Holt followed on with *Danger Route* (1967), a non-horror film for Amicus.

Screenwriter Christopher Wicking told *Fangoria* in 1988: "Seth ... understood the idea of a particular form of English madness and took the idea of the genre very seriously." Five weeks into filming Wicking's *Blood from the Mummy's Tomb*, on Valentine's Day 1971, Holt died from a heart attack and Michael Carreras had to finish what many involved considered to be a cursed production. Although some have stated that Hammer provided the horse-driven hearse that transported Seth's body to its final resting place, it was actually the one used in Ealing's *Kind Hearts and Coronets*—a film directed by Holt's brother-in-law, Robert Hamer, and lensed by *Taste of Fear*'s Douglas Slocombe (1913-2016).

Slocombe gives a chiaroscuro look to *Taste of Fear*, his camera floating through Bernard Robinson's old dark house sets, taking in the bric-a-brac and banging shutters. One of Britain's finest cinematographers, Slocombe's impressive CV also boasts *Dead of Night*, *Circus of Horrors*, *Dance of the Vampires*, *Never Say Never Again* and the first three *Indiana Jones* movies (his final credit was *Indiana Jones and the Last Crusade* [1988]). He worked again for Hammer on *The Lady Vanishes* (1978).

Starting as it means to go on, *Taste of Fear* opens with a body being dredged from a Swiss lake (actually Black Park). When crippled heiress Penny Appleby (Susan Strasberg) goes to stay with her stepmother Jane (Ann Todd), she finds her dead father (Fred Johnson) popping up in the most unexpected of places. Penny first spots the corpse propped up in a chair (looking very much like Bela Lugosi in *Glen or Glenda*), with glassy eyes staring out from baggy sockets.

Scream of Fear was the US title of *Taste of Fear*

Since playing the grandfather killed by Lee's Creature in *The Curse of Frankenstein*, Irish actor Fred Johnson (1899-1971) had fallen afoul of *Doctor Blood's Coffin* and appeared as the priest in *The Brides of Dracula*. His noble eyes also gazed out from the face of *The Abominable Snowman*, as well as the witch-burning village elder in *The City of the Dead*.

Johnson's most startling appearance in *Taste of Fear* finds him upright at the bottom of a disused swimming pool, a ghoulish vision comparable to Shelley Winters' watery grave in *The Night of the Hunter*. (A similarly submerged cadaver serves as the centerpiece of Francis Ford Coppola's "legitimate" debut, *Dementia 13* [1963], a shocker which seems to have been blueprinted from *Taste of Fear*; the sinister doctor part in Coppola's film is played by Lee's co-star from *The Skull*, Patrick Magee.) *Taste of Fear*'s suspenseful underwater photography is carried out by Egil Woxholt (1926-1991) and John Jordan (1925-1969); their drift through murky, weed-strewn depths (where we know something nasty will lurk) anticipates similar moments in Steven Spielberg's *Jaws* (1974). Both cameramen would go on to capture some of the most dangerous action shots of the James Bond series. (Tragically, after having a foot amputated following an accident on *You Only Live Twice*, Jordan fell to his death from a plane shooting *Catch-22*.)

Another film which mirrors the Hammer thriller is Roger Corman's *Pit and the Pendulum* (1961), wherein Barbara Steele affects to render Vincent Price senseless with, among other things, a ghostly harpsichord—a device first seen in *Taste of Fear*, via eerie piano notes in the dead of night. These were provided by composer Clifton Parker (1905-1989), whose score ratchets up the tension throughout. (Parker also wrote the music for Disney's *Treasure Island* [1949], as well as *Night of the Demon* and *The Hellfire Club*.)

The aforementioned correspondences with subsequent horrors are of interest given that *Taste of Fear* is often described as a derivative film. In fact, while the influence of *Les diaboliques* is acknowledged, *Taste of Fear*'s true antecedent seems to be Hammer's own *The Man in Black*, made as early as 1949, which involves a similar plot to drive a young heiress insane.

Much has been made also of the influence that Alfred Hitchcock's *Psycho* had on *Taste of Fear*, but it should be noted that Sangster drafted his screenplay before *Psycho*'s September 1960 release. It is worth considering, however, Hammer's influence on Hitchcock; after all, it's acknowledged (in Stephen Rebello's *Alfred Hitchcock & The Making of Psycho*) that Hitch's masterpiece came into being as a result of the director keeping a watchful eye on Hammer's profits. The small British company was also foremost when it came to pushing the boundaries of onscreen violence, creating a climate which made it possible for *Psycho* to be made in the first place. Finally, in casting youthful matinee idol Anthony Perkins in the role of madman Norman Bates (who, in the novel, is a balding, overweight pervert), Hitchcock gave further leeway to Hammer's "attraction of evil" philosophy, best personified by Christopher Lee's Dracula.

Taste of Fear's Ann Todd (1909-1993) had actually played a major role for Hitchcock, as Gregory Peck's self-sacrificing wife in *The Paradine Case* (1947). Her film career stretched back to a 1931 production of *The Ghost Train* and H.G. Wells' prophetic science fiction classic *Things to Come* (1935), before she rose to fame as the romantic lead of *The Seventh Veil*. After starring with Peter Cushing in Joseph Losey's excellent thriller *Time Without Pity* (photographed by Freddie Francis in 1956), Ann played the title role of "Sylvia" in a 1958 episode of *Alfred Hitchcock Presents* and was a very nervous murder suspect in "Letter to a Lover" (1961) for Boris Karloff's *Thriller*. Following a six-year break from the big screen, Todd made a surprising comeback as the fanatical mother of *The Fiend* (1970), one of whose victims is picked up in a cinema lobby festooned with posters for *Scars of Dracula*.

Todd's strong performance in *Taste of Fear* is matched by the actress portraying her stepdaughter. Susan Strasberg (1938-1999) was, in real life, the offspring of famed New York acting guru Lee Strasberg, whose Method Acting classes had furthered the careers of James Dean, Montgomery Clift and Dustin Hoffman, to name but three. During his fortnight in New York promoting *Dracula* in May 1958, Christopher Lee had seen Susan perform with Richard Burton in the Broadway play *Time Remembered*. Her mother Paula (a mentor and coach to Marilyn Monroe) visited the *Taste of Fear* set and kept a watchful eye over her daughter's performance. According to Jimmy Sangster's memoirs, this made the actress ill at ease, to say the least (Sangster further revealed that it was he who had to politely remove the older woman from the studio). After her psychedelic love scene with Peter Fonda in *The Trip* (1967), Susan starred with that film's writer, Jack Nicholson, in another AIP drug venture *Psych-Out* (1967), before making *The Name of the Game is Kill!* (1968), a bizarre mystery, and *Hauser's Memory* (1970), a TV follow-up to *Donovan's Brain* (1953). Her most memorable genre performance after *Taste of Fear*, though, came in *The Manitou* (1977), wherein an evil little shaman grows out of her back. As herself, she can be seen sharing a personal supernatural experience and extolling the virtues of *Our Town* (1939) in the John Carradine-hosted *Hollywood Ghost Stories* (1986).

Strasberg's chauffeur in *Taste of Fear*, Robert, is played by Ronald Lewis (1928-1982), who had just starred in another Hammer thriller set in France, *The Full Treatment*. Two decades after playing the doctor hero of William Castle's *Mr. Sardonicus* (1961), and the vengeful lead in Hammer's *The Brigand of Kandahar*, Lewis would be found dead in his London flat from an apparent drug overdose.

Taste of Fear wrapped on Wednesday December 7, 1960. Prior to its release, only a single publicity photograph was issued, of a screaming Susan Strasberg, coupled with the legend: "This is *positively* the only photograph we are allowed to show you. Under *no* circumstances may we give away *any* of the startling secrets of this Great Screen Thriller."

The film premiered at London's Warner Theatre on Thursday March 30, 1961 (when Elvis Presley was at No. 1 with Britain's biggest-selling single of the year, "Wooden Heart"), before going on general UK release from June 5. The first New York showing, as *Scream of Fear*, took place on Tuesday August 22, 1961 (when Bobby Lewis was at No. 1 with America's biggest-selling single of the year, "Tossin' and Turnin'"). At initial screenings in the Big Apple, tickets were handed out which bore a missive inspired by Hitchcock's *Psycho* publicity: "To guarantee to my friends the same measure of excitement and enjoyment that I had when I saw SCREAM OF FEAR, I hereby pledge not to reveal any of the plot or the unusual ending of this motion picture. I urge everybody to see it." Additionally, the US poster for *Scream of Fear*, showing a tower of screaming Strasbergs in pastel shades, was voted the Best of 1961 by the Motion Picture Association of America.

Dr. Gerrard (Christopher Lee) from *Taste of Fear*

Although box office receipts in both the UK and US were not as high as hoped, the film was a huge hit on the Continent, prompting a return to France for *Maniac* (1962): With its offbeat love triangle and blowtorch-wielding villain, Sangster's second "mini Hitchcock" allows director Michael Carreras to indulge his preference for more expansive set-ups, especially during a climax that takes place at the ruins of Les Baux-de-Provence.

While, subsequently, it could be argued that the company's thriller formula was stretched a little thin by Freddie Francis' *Paranoiac* (1962), *Nightmare* (1962) and *Hysteria* (1964), each is not without merit; *Paranoiac*, in particular, ranks among Hammer's scariest films—an accolade it shares with *Taste of Fear*.

The Loneliness of Evil

Hercules in the Haunted World 1961

An all new height in fright and might!

Don't trust the shadows of Hades!
—Hercules (Reg Park)

In December 1956, while Hammer were hard at work on *The Curse of Frankenstein*, ex-art critic turned filmmaker Riccardo Freda (1909-1999) attempted a Gothic revival in Italy. His movie, *I vampiri*, released in the US as *The Devil's Commandment*, appends skull-laden crypts, billowing curtains and mad science to a fast-paced crime thriller in the tradition of Fritz Lang's *M* (1931). One of *vampiri*'s most stunning moments comes when Gianna Maria Canale, as the Elizabeth Bathory-inspired Duchess, ages before our very eyes—a special effect courtesy of Freda's cinematographer, Mario Bava (1914-1980). When Freda walked off the production, Bava completed the second half of the picture in two days. Once this formula had been repeated for the *Quatermass*-influenced *Caltiki, the Immortal Monster* (1959), Mario struck out on his own with *Black Sunday* (1960)—an atmospheric feast for the eyes and honest-to-God contender for Greatest Horror Movie Ever Made. When distributed in the US by AIP, *Black Sunday* became the fledgling company's biggest hit, out-grossing even their own Hammer-inspired smash *House of Usher*. Having already worked uncredited on two of Italy's biggest *peplum* (or "sword and sandal") blockbusters, *Hercules* (1957) and *Hercules Unchained* (1958), Bava's second film as director would blend the tropes of that field with the Gothic horrors of *Black Sunday*. While the latter had introduced the world to a new Horror Queen in Barbara Steele, Mario's next outing makes use of the genre's reigning Prince, Christopher Lee.

The actor's three-week shooting schedule for *Ercole al centro della terra* (*Hercules in the Centre of the Earth*) began at Cinecittà Studios, Rome, on Monday May 29, 1961. First seen slouched in his throne and barking: "You dog!" at some unworthy minion, Lee cuts a striking figure in black wig and cloak as Lico, King of the Underworld. Lee's rocky dwelling, with its boiling pits, was

realized, beneath the streets of Rome, in the Castellana caves. These bat-filled grottoes would also serve as a location for both Bava's *Danger: Diabolik* (1967) and Luigi Cozzi's *Starcrash* (1978).

After leading the aforementioned lackey to a slyly nefarious death, Lico stands before seven stone coffins, from one of which he summons his niece Deianira (Leonora Ruffo), who also happens to be the lover of Hercules (Reg Park). Accompanied by a blonde Theseus (Giorgio Ardisson) and comedy relief Telemachus (Franco Giacobini), Hercules journeys through the Underworld to rescue Deianira from Lee's clutches. On the way, they face such delightful horrors as a rock monster. "You should be longer," it intones in a robotic voice, while stretching Theseus on a makeshift rack: "You will be as thin as the ropes that bind you, then I will tie you into a knot!"

Acknowledging his *Dracula* reputation, to attain everlasting life, Lee has to drink the blood of Deianira during a lunar eclipse. His attempts to do so are thwarted by Hercules, but not before an attack from some amazing grey zombies who rise, cobweb-strewn from blue crypts. Soaring through the air, their ragged shrouds trail in the wind. Despite such somber goings-on, Lee admitted to Tom Johnson and Mark A. Miller that the absurdity of he and Parks' disparate sizes would cause the two actors to collapse with laughter as they fought, inciting an icy glare from the usually cheerful Bava. (Indeed, in his autobiography, Lee recalled that Italy's Master of Horror "mugged before the camera before saying 'Cut!'" and resembled the lean-faced native comedian Toto, several of whose films, including *Toto in the Moon* [1958], were directed by *Uncle Was a Vampire*'s Steno and written by Lucio Fulci.) A rather effective climax was eventually concocted and, as he revealed to Tim Lucas, Lee so enjoyed working with Bava that he convinced Boris Karloff to accept his one and only vampire role for the director's *Black Sabbath* (1963).

Born in Leeds, West Yorkshire, Reg Park (1928-2007) was a three-time recipient of the Mr. Universe title (1951, '58 and '65), who made his movie debut in Vittorio Cottafavi's *Hercules and the Captive Women* (1961) for which Bava supplied special effects. Park would reprise his bearded hero in two further features, *Hercules, Prisoner of Evil* (1964, directed by Antonio Margheriti) and *Hercules the Avenger* (1965). His only other starring role is as Maciste in *Samson in King Solomon's Mines* (1964).

Leonora Ruffo (1935-2007) was fresh from playing the same character Deianira in another Italian fantasy *Goliath and the Dragon* (1960) and would follow on with *Goliath and the Vampires* (1961).

Lico, King of the Underworld, played by Christopher Lee.

Gaia Germani (b. 1942), who plays the mystic Medea in a mask filched from Federico Fellini's *La Dolce Vita*, would later star alongside Christopher Lee in *The Castle of the Living Dead*, while Giorgio Ardisson (1931-2014) next encountered the actor in *Katarsis* (as well as starring opposite Barbara Steele in *The Long Hair of Death* [1964], he can be seen as a model in Fellini's *Juliet of the Spirits* [1964]). Comedic actor Franco Giacaboni (1926-2015), whose main purpose in *Hercules in the Haunted World* is to get tangled in nets and cause no end of unwarranted mirth for his macho companions, would later appear in Vittorio de Sica's *The Orderly* alongside *Uncle Was a Vampire*'s Renato Rascel.

Also on view in an early role is Rosalba Neri (b. 1939, a.k.a. Sara Bay). After reteaming with Lee for *The Castle of Fu Manchu* (1968), she became a fixture of the Italian horror scene in such features as *Lady Frankenstein* (1971), *The Devil's Lover* (1971) and *The Devil's Wedding Night* (1972).

Hercules in the Haunted World is Mario Bava's first color production, and he brings a masterful, painterly eye to the rich tapestry of hues filling the screen. The contrast of blazing reds against cold blues, often in the same tableau, enhances the fire and ice, good and evil, dichotomy at the film's heart. Especially sumptuous are the scenes of our heroes sailing towards Hades, where a thick black apparition curls its way through flaming skies above bright, azure waters; or the deep dark blue of the storm-lit forest against which Hercules seems to emit a golden glow.

If all Bava had ever done in his life was the cinematography on this film, he would still be a figure worthy of celebration. But, in addition to writing and directing such masterpieces as *Black Sunday* and *Black Sabbath*, he also introduced giallo to the screen with *The Girl Who Knew Too Much* (1962) and *Blood and Black Lace* (1963).

In fact, Bava's innovations would be woven into better-known films by more widely celebrated filmmakers. For example, his presentation of the Devil as a seemingly innocent child in the crepuscular *Kill, Baby … Kill!* (1966) was an idea filched by both Fellini for *Spirits of the Dead* (1967) and Martin Scorsese for *The Last Temptation of Christ* (1987). Moreover, the stylish visuals and overall pacing of his *Planet of the Vampires* (1965) informed the look and feel of *Alien*, whereas the gruesome lakeside murders of *A Bay of Blood* (1971) are replicated almost exactly for *Friday the 13th* (indeed, they proved too much for Christopher Lee, who allegedly walked out of *A Bay of Blood*'s screening at the 1973 Avoriaz Festival). Elsewhere, certain set-ups in *Danger: Diabolik* are restaged for such blockbusters as *Indecent Proposal* (1992), *For Your Eyes Only* (1980), and *A View to a Kill* (1984), not to mention a 1998 Beastie Boys music video ("Body Movin'").

Even *Hercules in the Haunted World* would find an echo in a future horror classic: Having paid tribute to Terence Fisher by allowing some leaves to drift into an early scene, Bava later introduces an image of Lee's face reflected in a pool of blood; a visual borrowed by Dario Argento for *Deep Red* (1974). The same director's *Inferno* (1979) would go a step further by allowing Bava to provide its nightmarish visual effects. (It would be the last film Bava worked on.)

Where Bava's genius truly lies is in making the most of the scant materials at his disposal. On *Hercules in the Haunted World*, he had only a single wall and four moveable columns (leftover from Riccardo Freda's *The Giants of Thessaly* [1960]) with which to construct his sets. Like the canny magician he was, Bava would make his scenery appear larger with the use of mirrors; at one stage, he even stuck a matchstick in a wad of gum and filmed it at just the right angle to create a fifth column.

Premiered in Italy on Thursday November 16, 1961, *Hercules in the Haunted World* would not see release in Britain (as *Hercules in the Centre of the Earth*) for another full year. In the US, it had to wait until April 1964 when it went out with Margheriti's *Castle of Blood* (1963). By 2010, however, the film had gained enough of a cult following to be transformed into an opera by composer Patrick Moganelli: Titled *Hercules vs. Vampires*, the work debuted in Portland and was performed by the Los Angeles Opera as recently as 2015.

Hercules vs. the Vampires is also the name the movie went under in Austria, where, on its initial release, it was seen by a weedy 14-year-old boy named Arnold Schwarzenegger. Inspired by Reg Park's appearance, the teenager decided to take up weight-lifting ("All my dreams suddenly came together and made sense," Arnie writes in his 2012 memoir *Total Recall*). An auspicious meeting with Park in the late 1960s resulted in the latter becoming a mentor to the young Arnold (the two are featured together in the 1975 documentary *Pumping Iron*). By 1970, the year that he beat Reg for the title of Mr. Universe, Schwarzenegger had already made his acting debut—as *Hercules in New York*.

Christopher Lee, meanwhile, returned to the Underworld for *The Odyssey* (1996), where, as blind prophet Tiresias, he sits before the River of Fire, guarded by flaming spirits. Francis Ford Coppola serves as executive producer on this lavish TV spectacular, which also features brilliant effects from Jim Henson's Creature Shop.

While *Hercules in the Haunted World* remains a rousing fantasy-adventure (and is easily the best of the Italian muscleman epics), most would argue that Lee and Bava's next collaboration is even greater…

The Loneliness of Evil

The Whip and the Body
1963

Horror beyond the bounds of Hell!

I am a frightened man. If I am alone at home, I turn on all the lights.—Mario Bava in *Monster and Horror Movies ... Thomas G. Aylesworth*

I didn't really understand it.—Christopher Lee, to Jonathan Rigby on *The Whip and the Body*

In the two years between his Mario Bava pictures, Christopher Lee had kept busy on non-horror assignments, the first of which, surprisingly, was for Hammer. In *The Pirates of Blood River* (filmed in July 1961), Lee impresses as the black-clad Captain LaRoche, complete with eyepatch and withered arm, while Hammer horror is alluded to with some nasty piranha attacks.

The Pirates of Blood River became one of the biggest money-spinners of 1962 when paired with Ray Harryhausen's *Mysterious Island* that summer, proving that, even at this early stage in his career, Lee could survive in leading roles outside of the genre. In fact, the actor was making so many European pictures at this time (including *Sherlock Holmes and the Deadly Necklace* and *The Devil's Agent* [1961]), that relocation seemed a wise decision. In March 1962, the Lees moved to Switzerland, where their neighbors included Robert Siodmak. (Lee would remain Swiss-based until April 1965.)

The Whip and the Body would capitalize not only on Lee's burgeoning success as a European leading man, but also on his brooding, romantic screen presence. (Revealingly, in the typical teenager's bedroom of 1963, recreated for *The Beatles Anthology*, Lee's Dracula is among the pin-ups.) Evidence for this status could also be found in the mailbag of Forrest J Ackerman's celebrated magazine *Famous Monsters of Filmland* (whose first issue went on sale in February 1958; the cover of #4 dubs Lee "the handsome horror"). Ackerman told John Brosnan: "At *Famous Monsters* I have intercepted letters to [Christopher Lee] from young girls who say, in effect: 'Look, Mr. Lee, your wife has got to be generous. After all, she's had you for many years and I'm ready, willing and able to get on the next plane and camp on your doorstep, so surely she could spare you for one week of love with me.'" Mrs. Lee was pregnant when her husband emplaned to Italy on Tuesday, May 7, 1963, for the six-week shoot of *The Whip and the Body*. In addition, as Tim Lucas reports, she was understandably uncomfortable about the impassioned scenes Christopher would enact with Daliah Lavi for the film.

Indeed, the fervent atmosphere of *The Whip and the Body* is apparent right from the opening credits which unfurl over crushed scarlet satin to Carlo Rustichelli's rapturous piano score (a portion of which can be heard in both *Kill, Baby ... Kill!* and, less obviously, *The Mummy's Revenge* [1973]). The first shot shows Lee's Kurt Menliff charging on horseback towards a silhouetted castle—his familial home (the beach he rides across, at Tor Caldara, can also be seen in *Hercules in the Haunted World*). While the setting sun paints an orange haze across deep cyan skies, storm-lit atmospherics infuse the hallway where Kurt's family await his return. (The castle interiors were standing sets from another Italian Gothic, made earlier in the year, *The Blancheville Monster*.)

The Whip and the Body contains Bava's most exquisite use of color (which is saying something), and Lee is lit in every one of them. His Kurt Menliff is a Gothic romancer whose fiery beach-side clinches with sister-in-law Nevenka (Lavi) dissolve into frantic whipping sessions. "You always loved violence," he purrs, before throwing the whip aside and embracing his lover amid the crashing waves. Unfortunately, once Kurt is stabbed behind a billowing red curtain 20 minutes in, the action reverts to Nevenka wandering round the castle at night, reacting to the sounds of ghostly whips. While such scenes are sumptuous to look at, they do become repetitive. Attention is snapped back by the sight of Lee glowering in at the rain-lashed window, a bloody bandage round his throat; or clutching for Lavi at the foot of her bed, his green-lit hand a seeming appendage of the serpent Kurt's father earlier described him as. Further images stay in the mind: Lee's boots dirtying the floors with graveyard mud; or the frequent symbolism of blooming roses, an ostensive representation of the natural urges which Nevenka fights to suppress, especially when their beauty is tempered by blood-letting thorns. (As a publicity wheeze, Lee was photographed giving blood, in full costume, at a local hospital.)

Elsewhere, there are less original echoes of Roger Corman's Poe films, most notably the Menliff family crypt, which resembles Vincent Price's in *House of Usher*; or Lavi's trepid descent into forbidden quarters, à la Barbara Steele in *Pit and the Pendulum*. Tellingly, screenwriter Ernesto Gastaldi revealed to Tim Lucas (in *Video Watchdog* #39) that, prior to filming *The Whip and the Body*, producers Ugo Guerra and Elio Scardamaglia screened a print of Corman's *Pit and the Pendulum* and told the writer: "Give us something like this."

Born in 1934, Gastaldi's first credits as a writer, *The Vampire and the Ballerina* (1959) and *The Vampire of the Opera* (1961), were similarly inspired by Hammer's *Dracula*. After scripting *Corridors of Blood*'s US co-feature, *Werewolf in a Girls' Dormitory*, he would go on to write original Gothics for both Christopher Lee (*Crypt*

Kurt Menliff (Christopher Lee) embraces Nevenka (Daliah Lavi) before dissolving into intense whipping sessions.

of Horror [1963]) and Barbara Steele (*The Horrible Dr. Hichcock* [1962]; *The Long Hair of Death*).

In fact, *The Whip and the Body* was almost another Steele vehicle, but when the actress proved too busy elsewhere, Daliah Lavi (1942-2017) fulfilled the leading role. Although made-up to resemble Steele's character in *Pit and the Pendulum*, Lavi's presence is enough to make the picture her own.

The Israeli actress and singer, who made her genre debut in *The Return of Dr. Mabuse* (1961), would respond yet again to Lee's accusatory presence in *Ten Little Indians* (1965). "He was a very nice man," she told Tim Lucas, "very well-educated, very well-read. He spoke beautifully. I could never understand why he didn't play more leading roles as a lover …" Daliah herself enjoyed a varied career: The light comic flair she displays in spy parodies *The Silencers* (1965), *Casino Royale* (1966) and *Some Girls Do* (1968) can also be seen to good advantage in *Jules Verne's Rocket to the Moon* (1967).

All of the above are a far cry from her solemn lead in *The Whip and the Body*. Three months prior to which, Lavi was flogged in bed for another horror film from producer Ugo Guerra. Based on a true account, *Il demonio* (*The Demon* [1963]) is a particularly disturbing tale of possession in which, a decade before *The Exorcist*, a lacerated Daliah affects a spider walk and growls at the cross. In an interview (recounted in Peter Haining's *The Mammoth Book of True Hauntings*), she recalled: "I played the part of a girl possessed by demons and the devil. I was completely possessed myself, in a way. At nights after filming, I couldn't sleep. I used to have terrible nightmares …" She also remembered that the crew, fascinated by the film's occult theme, began dabbling in séances between takes. As a result, Daliah witnessed "the most amazing things … Once we watched the mouthpiece of a telephone rise into the air, hang in space and then drop back. Another night we got in touch with Mussolini … I became so fascinated by all this, I started practicing things. Then I stopped because it was so frightening." Ghosts of Mussolini aside, *The Demon* contains her strongest performance.

On hand to lurk around with a lantern in *The Whip and the Body* is Luciano Pigozzi (1927-2008) as Losat, the family retainer. Nicknamed "the Italian Peter Lorre" for his resemblance to the more famous actor, Pigozzi is usually credited as "Alan Collins" on English-language versions of his films. These include *Werewolf in a Girls' Dormitory*, *Terror-Creatures from the Grave* (1965), *All the Colors of the Dark* (1971), *Seven Deaths in the Cat's Eye* and *Frankenstein's Castle of Freaks* (1973). More often than not cast as hapless lackeys, Luciano would reteam with Bava for *Blood and Black Lace* and *Baron Blood* (wherein he rises from a spiked coffin) and with Lee on *The Castle of the Living Dead*.

Ironically, Kurt's brother (and rival for Nevenko's affections), Cristiano, is played by Tony Kendall (1936-2009), a former model who resembles Lee's vampiric ancillary at Hammer, David Peel. After Bava, Kendall worked with two other Euro-horror greats: Amando de Ossorio (on *The Lorelei's Grasp* [1972] and *Return of the Blind Dead* [1973]) and Paul Naschy (in *The People Who Own the Dark* [1973]).

The actor playing Kurt's father, Gustavo De Nardo, is actually a few years younger than Lee and can also be seen in

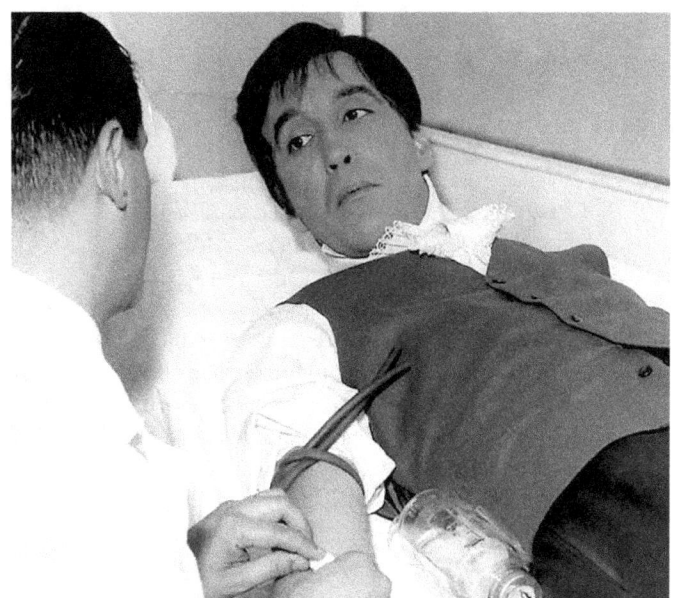

Dressed as Kurt Menliff, Christopher Lee gives blood.

Bava's *The Girl Who Knew Too Much*, *Black Sabbath* and *Baron Blood* (1971).

Credited as John M. Old on US prints, Bava kept up the playful atmosphere he had developed with Lee behind the scenes on *Hercules in the Haunted World*. Showing that he was not averse to a little tomfoolery himself, he even interrupted one of the actor's screen clinches with Lavi by enquiring: "Mind if I join you?"

Subsequently responsible for what is, arguably, Vincent Price's worst movie, *Dr. Goldfoot and the Girl Bombs* (1966), Bava redeemed himself with *Kill, Baby … Kill!*, *Baron Blood* and *Lisa and the Devil* (1972). His final film as director, the creepy *Shock* (1977), plays out like a modern-day retelling of *The Whip and the Body*, with Daria Nicolodi being haunted by a sadistic former lover who wields, not whips, but razor blades. *Shock* was co-scripted (and, by all accounts, co-directed) by Mario's son, Lamberto, who followed his father into fantasy filmmaking with *Macabre* (1980), *Demons* (1985) and *Demons 2* (1986). Lamberto would further replicate Mario by casting Christopher Lee as Azaret, the Enchanter, in his charming TV fantasy *Sorrelina* (1995).

Released in Italy on Thursday August 29, 1963, *The Whip and the Body* (*La frusta e il corpo*) wouldn't reach English-speaking territories until 1965, where, in edited form, it was retitled *Night is the Phantom* (in the UK) and *What?* (in the US). An unsuccessful obscenity charge in its native country seemed to hurt the picture's fortunes, rather than aid them. The result was, undeservedly, one of the least financially rewarding ventures of Mario Bava's career. Nevertheless, *The Whip and the Body* is, quite simply, the most beautiful-looking film in Christopher Lee's entire oeuvre. It is no exaggeration to say that every frame belongs on the walls of the Louvre. Lee's next horror film wouldn't be out of place in a museum, either—as a long-lost relic.

The Loneliness of Evil

Katarsis
1963

I've never seen it, and I don't think anyone else has, either!—Christopher Lee on *Katarsis* (to Tom Johnson and Mark A. Miller)

Immediately after making *The Whip and the Body*, Lee returned to his *Uncle Was a Vampire* haunting ground, Castle Odescalchi, to film *Katarsis*. Although production had already begun on Tuesday, May 14, 1963, the actor (top-billed as Cristopher Lee) was required for only a single week (filming ended Friday, June 7).

Initially released, only in Italy, on Monday September 9, 1963, *Katarsis* disappeared shortly thereafter, before emerging in re-edited form, with new wraparound footage, as *Sfida al diavolo* (*Challenge to the Devil*) in August 1965. With only a single Italian TV screening since then (from which available prints are sourced), *Katarsis* has become the most obscure horror film in Lee's canon. Roundly dismissed by the few who have already reviewed it, the movie is actually something of a pleasant surprise.

The first asset to strike the viewer is the jazz-fused score by Berto Pisano (1928-2002), whose well-placed acoustic guitars give way to doomful organs for the story's latter half. Indeed, *Katarsis* is a merging of two worlds: that of an early 1960s beatnik gang (the kind recently seen in Hammer's *The Damned*) and the moldering Gothic figure of Christopher Lee in his castle where "nothing is real." Lee told Jonathan Rigby that writer and director Guiseppe Vegezzi committed suicide shortly after completing this, his only movie. This is doubly sad, as *Katarsis* displays some original ideas, even if their execution confirms a novice talent. Particularly eerie is the scene wherein one gang member, Gugo, finds himself trapped and exhausted in a rocky passageway; up to this moment, the character has never stopped laughing, but he now finds himself screaming "It's the Devil!" as ominous creaking noises sound all around him …

Photographed in black-and-white by Angelo Baistrocchi (*The Vampire and the Ballerina*) and Mario Parapetti (*The Embalmer* [1965]), *Katarsis* begins with the aforementioned padding added for the film's 1965 re-release: Some gangsterish activity is followed by performances from nightclub variety acts, such as "the Argentinian star" Sonia singing "They Saw You," and a couple of dancers (all backed by a band with I Palatini written on their bass drum). We then go backstage to witness a conversation between a bearded monk and a Diana Dors lookalike that deserves quoting:

"A few years ago you were the worst asshole around, Pejo," the Dors wannabe tells the monk.

Pejo replies: "It's precisely because I was an asshole that I understand that you can only be happy when you're at peace with yourself."

Following this pearl of wisdom, the reformed monk reveals, in flashback, how he found religion: "It was still day and we were already tipsy," he begins. We then see the original film proper as Pejo, in his past life, goes joyriding with five freewheeling friends, including Maga, "or Scatterbrains, as she liked to be called," and Gugo, "who loved playing the cursed poet, and found alcohol to be his only source of inspiration." Gugo is played by Giorgio Ardisson (Theseus, from *Hercules in the Haunted World*).

"In the mood to do something crazy," the gang chant "Whiskey! Whiskey!" and "Drugs! Drugs!" before beating up a fellow motorist ("We were animals. We loved the taste of blood …"). As night falls, the youths arrive at a spooky castle and, once inside, indulge in a little light dancing and bongo bashing (described on-screen as "a hysterical orgy") only to be disturbed by "an ageless figure, out of this world." This is, of course, Christopher Lee, whom we first see as a hunched, cane-wielding shadow. Shuffling to his seat by the fire, in snow-white wig and ruff, Lee laments over his lost love like a hero from Poe. "I knew the Devil for her … I sold my soul to him," he warns the rapt youngsters, who applaud his theatrics.

Once alone, at midnight, Lee warms his hands over the fire and grows younger, his hair now a black crow's-nest sputtering from his face. After making an alarming, bat-like appearance, he smothers two gang members in his raised arms as they explore the candle-lit corridors. Later, Lee's ghostly lover steps forth from a painting, there's some business in a room full of mirrors; and the youngsters, confronted by spiders, go slowly insane.

Lee, meanwhile, reverts to his true age before the fire and, as the gang break free of the claustrophobic corridors, Pisano's guitars make a return to the soundtrack. (The composer's future credits would include two disparate zombie ventures, *Death Smiles on a Murderer* [1972, with Klaus Kinski] and Andrea Bianchi's *Burial Ground* [1980].) Finding Lee's dead paramour entombed within a clock, the beatniks carry her white-shrouded body outside into the light …

In short, *Katarsis* is an interesting curio in Christopher Lee's career and well worth a watch (if one can track down a print) for its dark fairy tale atmosphere and madcap dialogue.

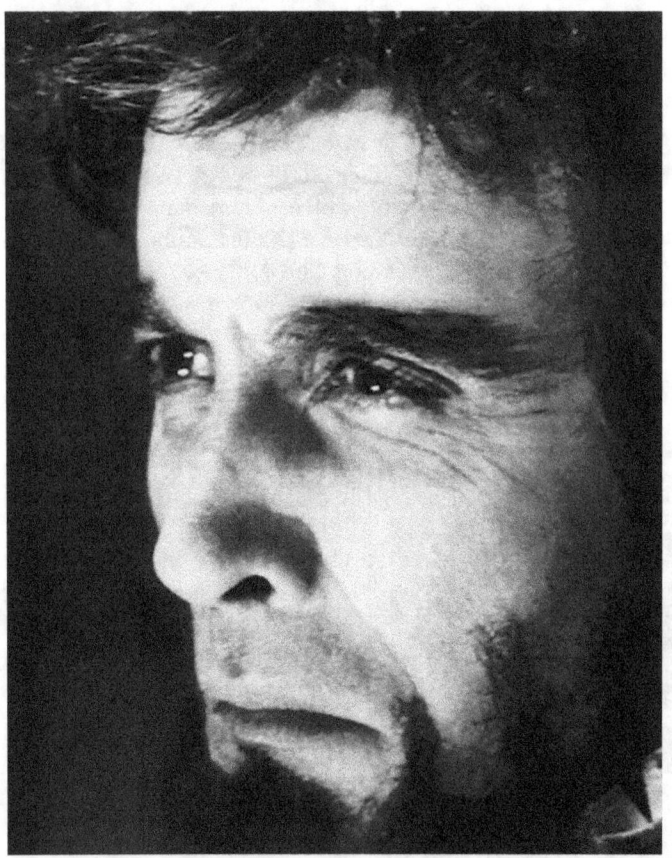

Christopher Lee in *Katarsis*

The Virgin of Nuremberg 1963

Women's virtues made him a killer!

Christopher Lee's protracted Italian sojourn in the spring and summer of 1963 continued with his next film *La vergine di Norimberga* (*The Virgin of Nuremberg*), which wrapped after a three-week shoot on Saturday, July 13. Filming took place at Rome's Villa Sciarra, which had already served as a location for director Antonio Margheriti's *Castle of Blood* and would later play host to Mario Bava's *Blood and Black Lace*.

The Virgin of Nuremberg was adapted by Margheriti and Edmond T. Gréville, Lee's *Hands of Orlac* director, from a novella by Frank Bogart. The publisher of the original story, Marco Vicario, became the film's producer and cast his wife Rossana Podestà (1934-2013) in the lead. This was no act of nepotism, as Podestà had already starred with Kirk Douglas in *Ulysses* (1954) and played the title role of Robert Wise's *Helen of Troy* (1955). She would end her career as Hera, Queen of the Gods, in Luigi Cozzi's *Hercules* (1982).

The Virgin of Nuremberg begins with a remarkable lightning-suffused pre-credits sequence, which sees Podestà's Mary in a pure white nightgown prowling the German *Schloss* she inhabits with her new husband Max (Georges Rivière). Stumbling upon the castle's torture chamber, Mary looks within the titular Virgin of Nuremberg (a spike-lined sarcophagus) and finds a blonde with her eyes gorged out. (The corpse, surprisingly, is personified by Lee's co-star from *The Hands of Orlac*, Lucile Saint-Simon.)

This atmospheric start is cut off abruptly, and rather cleverly, as the titles kick in, by Riz Ortolani's giddy jazz score. Ortolani (1926-2014), whose catchy theme is the best thing about

Christopher Lee in *The Virgin of Nuremberg* released as *Horror Castle* in the US.

Cannibal Holocaust (1979), also scored Margheriti's *Seven Deaths in the Cat's Eye*, as well as *Madhouse* (1980) and *Revenge of the Dead* (1982). Towards *The Virgin of Nuremberg*'s close, he even provides some splendidly tension-filled strings, reminiscent of James Bernard's work on *Dracula*.

Second-billed behind Podestà is Christopher Lee as Erich, a war-wounded custodian of the torture chamber (or museum, as Max likes to call it). With impressive scarring down the left side of his face, Lee possesses a stiff bearing in reference to his character's military background. His main purpose, though, is to pop out of shadows at opportune moments and frighten the heroine.

Things are not made any easier for her when the scarlet-robed, black-hooded Punisher (Mirko Valentin) gets up and about ("You thought I wanted to abuse your body," he tells one flame-haired victim, "on the contrary, death is the fate I have in store for you! Mwahahaha!"). Mary witnesses this poor girl having a cage of rats placed over her head. (There's a truly horrible close-up of a rodent chewing on the girl's nose.)

Aside from the cobwebbed dungeon, in which the aforementioned atrocity takes place, Riccardo Dominici's production design includes such highlights as a simple but effective cruciform of skulls upon a passageway wall, and a chamber which fills with water, imperiling Rivière. As the Punisher says: "Instruments of torture are more or less the same, wherever you go!" Indeed, the character has a habit of babbling madly at his victims like Lionel Atwill in *Mystery of the Wax Museum*, and akin to that film, there is

The Loneliness of Evil

a shocking unmasking sequence, revealing the villain's skull-like head (an astonishing make-up by Franco Di Girolamo, who would later work on Umberto Lenzi's *City of the Walking Dead*, as well as Lucio Fulci films like *The Black Cat* [1980] and *Zombie 3* [1987]).

The real monster of the movie is Adolf Hitler, who appears via stock footage, as Erich outlines the reasons behind the Punisher's madness. If only Lee's own voice had been maintained for the English-language version; the actor would undoubtedly have given real feeling to this speech, especially when one considers his own experiences of war. Physically, at least, Lee is able to bring some pathos to his character. Most notably, he shows a touching devotion to the Punisher. Sinking to his knees amid the climactic flames, he tearfully cradles his old friend's perishing body, a moment which recalls similar scenes enacted by Boris Karloff for both *The Old Dark House* and *Son of Frankenstein*.

As with *The Whip and the Body*, the influence of Roger Corman's first two Poe adaptations is also heavily apparent here, with the torture devices of *Pit and the Pendulum* joined by the familial curse and final conflagration from *House of Usher*. There's even an echo of Lee's own *Taste of Fear*, with a supposedly delusional heroine deceived by those closest to her while glimpsing strange things in an old dark house. (The torture chamber setting also points the way forward to *Blood Demon* [1967], more of which later.)

The direction of Antonio Margheriti (1930-2002), however, is not quite up to the standards set by Corman, Bava, or Seth Holt, despite an occasional promising visual, such as the moonlit castle reflected in a dank tarn, and a mildly exciting climax.

Margheriti, whose onscreen credit was often anglicized to Anthony Dawson, made his debut with *Assignment Outer Space* (1960). He was subsequently responsible for Claude Rains' final fantasy film, *Battle of the Worlds* (1960), and two of Barbara Steele's best vehicles, *Castle of Blood* (which also stars Georges Rivière) and *The Long Hair of Death*. (The former was remade by its director as *Web of the Spider* [1970], with Klaus Kinski as Edgar Allan Poe.)

Antonio's other credits include *War of the Planets* and its back-to-back sequel *Wild, Wild Planet* (both 1965); the stylish thriller *Seven Deaths in the Cat's Eye*, which, akin to *The Virgin of Nuremberg*, involves murders in a Gothic pile and the Vietnam allegory *Cannibal Apocalypse* (1980), with John Saxon. In addition to second unit direction on Paul Morrissey's cult favorites *Flesh for Frankenstein* and *Blood for Dracula* (both 1973), Margheriti provided special effects for Sergio Leone's *Fistful of Dynamite* (1971) and Aldo Lado's *The Humanoid* (1979).

The Virgin of Nuremberg premiered in Italy, just over two months after it had finished production, on Thursday, August 15, 1963, while a UK release, as *The Castle of Terror*, followed on Sunday, April 19, 1964 (when the Beatles were at No. 1 with the year's best-selling single "Can't Buy Me Love"). Almost a year later, as *Horror Castle*, the film was issued in America on Sunday, January 10, 1965 (when the Beatles topped the *Billboard* charts with "I Feel Fine").

While certainly not the best of Lee's European outings, *The Virgin of Nuremberg* is of interest for the color photography of Riccardo Rallottini (who also lensed *Castle of Blood*, *The Long Hair of Death* and *Lady Frankenstein*), and as a Gothic mood-piece which decries the more modern horrors of Nazism.

Crypt of Horror
1963

How much shock can the human brain endure before it cracks?

On Wednesday, July 17, 1963, just four days after filming had wrapped on *The Virgin of Nuremberg*, Christopher Lee arrived at the Castello Piccolomino, Balsorano, to start *Crypt of Horror* (shooting title: *La cripta e l'incubo* [*The Crypt and the Nightmare*]). Helmed by 62-year-old Camillo Mastrocinque (1901-1969), who usually specialized in comedy (one of which, *Toto, Peppino e i fuorilegge* [1956] had featured Barbara Shelley), *Crypt of Horror* was adapted by *The Whip and the Body*'s Ernesto Gastaldi and Tonino Valerii from a seminal work by Joseph Sheridan Le Fanu.

Born in Dublin, 1814, Le Fanu's supernatural tales are among the finest in Victorian literature. An ex-journalist, he began writing fiction in the late 1830s. Although renowned for stories of Satanic monkeys, ghostly hands and blood-stained walls, he is perhaps most famous for his (non-supernatural) mystery novel *Uncle Silas* (1864)—filmed in 1947 with Jean Simmons. A man with a genuine interest in the bizarre, Le Fanu became a virtual recluse after his wife died in 1858. Until his own death in 1873, he wrote from his bed in the early hours and was haunted by recurring dreams. Only two adaptations of the author's macabre fiction had made it onto the screen by 1963, and, like *Crypt of Horror*, they were both based upon his 1871 novella *Carmilla*. A major influence on Bram Stoker's *Dracula*, Le Fanu's eponymous female vampire also inspired Carl Dreyer's dream-like *Vampyr* (1930) and Roger Vadim's elegant *Blood and Roses*. (The cinematographer of Dreyer's film, Rudolph Maté, would direct Christopher Lee in *Port Afrique* [1955].)

Looking very much as he would in *I, Monster* seven years later, *Crypt of Horror* stars Lee as Count Ludwig Karnstein. Fearing that his daughter Laura (Adriana Ambesi) may be the reincarnation of an evil sorceress ancestor named Sheena, Ludwig's suspicions are not entirely put at ease by the arrival of the mysterious Lyuba (Pier Anna Quaglia).

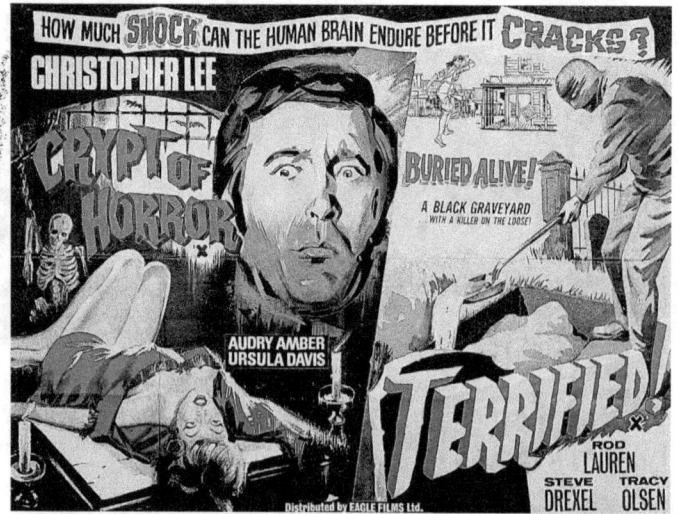

Christopher Lee's *Crypt of Horror* shares a double bill in this British quad poster.

Adriana Ambesi made her debut with Lee in *Katarsis* earlier in the year, and would later star as Dyanira, opposite Reg Park, in *Hercules the Avenger* (1965). Her last screen appearance came, as a bloodsucker, in Amando de Ossorio's *Fangs of the Living Dead* (a.k.a. *Malenka, the Vampire*, 1968)—a near retelling of Stoker's *Dracula* with Anita Ekberg taking the place of Jonathan Harker.

Pier Anna Quaglia would star alongside Barbara Steele in Mastrocinque's second, and final, horror film *An Angel for Satan* (1966), before featuring in the cheap Italian knock-off *King of Kong Island* (1968).

Happily, *Crypt of Horror* retains Christopher Lee's voice for the English-language version. Around this time, the actor had it written into his contracts that he should provide his own dubbing on foreign productions (there were, of course, exceptions, notably Lamberto Bava's *Sorrelina*). Unfortunately, Lee is given nothing of any value to do, except slink around his castle wearing a silken, monogrammed dressing gown.

Aside from some atmospheric black-and-white cinematography (by Julio Ortas and Giuseppe Aquari), all that is left to commend are two brief but disturbing scenes. In the first, a beautifully shot moonlit stroll is cut short when Laura and Lyuba find a hunchbacked beggar hanging in a hut. (The character is reminiscent of Marty Feldman's Igor from *Young Frankenstein*.)

The second moment of note sees the corpse of the witchy housemaid sit up during a flash of lightning to point an accusatory finger at Laura.

Otherwise, *Crypt of Horror* is unexceptional and slow-paced. A *Black Sunday*-inspired flashback to Sheena's execution, for example, lacks any of the power Mario Bava gave to the equivalent moment. By comparison, Mastrocinque seems to think that getting the actress involved to bare her back will provide the requisite frisson, failing to understand that far more style is required to lift the scene from mediocrity.

Premiered in Italy on Wednesday, May 27, 1964 (Lee's 42nd birthday), *Crypt of Horror* was retitled *Crypt of the Vampire* by AIP for a US double bill with Lew Landers' final movie *Terrified* (1962), before a UK release was granted on Monday, March 15, 1965 (when Tom Jones was at No. 1 with "It's Not Unusual").

In a more permissive age, it was left to Hammer to craft a blatant retelling of *Carmilla*. Their so-called Karnstein trilogy comprises the surprisingly faithful, if tackily presented, *The Vampire Lovers* (1970), the enjoyably trashy *Lust for a Vampire* (1970) and the outstanding *Twins of Evil* (1971). Lee, meanwhile, found himself back at Bray in August 1963 for *The Devil-Ship Pirates*, before making a triumphant return to Hammer horror …

The Gorgon
1963

She had a face only a mummy could love !

Do I believe in the supernatural? Oh yes, certainly … I can't accept that you die and that's the end … there's something about the mind that's more than that. It goes on, it must go on …—Terence Fisher, "Horror is My Business," *Films and Filming*, July 1964

We're men of science. I don't believe in ghosts or evil spirits, and I don't think you do, either.

That's one of the most unscientific remarks I ever heard. I believe in the existence of everything which the human brain is unable to disprove.—(Doctor Namaroff [Peter Cushing] and Professor Jules Heitz [Michael Goodliffe]).

In 1962, while Christopher Lee was busy in Europe, Sir James Carreras invited the public to submit new ideas for Hammer to film. "The only conditions we make," he told the press, "is that subjects must fall into the action or gimmick categories; and please, gentlemen, no comedies."

One such gentleman, a Canadian by the name of J. Llewellyn Devine (whose sole foray into film writing this was),

Italian poster for *The Gorgon*

delivered a story outline which transplanted the Gorgon of Greek mythology into Hammer's Gothic milieu. Devine's idea was handed over to John Gilling (1912-1984), who turned it into a professional script.

An assistant director for Hammer as early as *The Mystery of the Mary Celeste* (1935), Gilling went on to write their late 1940s Gothics *The Man in Black* and *Room to Let*, before making his directorial debut for the company with *The Shadow of the Cat* (1960). (He also provided the screenplay for Tod Slaughter's Burke and Hare picture, *The Greed of William Hart* [1947], which he subsequently dusted off for one of Peter Cushing's finest non-Hammer horrors, *The Flesh and the Fiends* [1959].)

Although a tough, war-scarred veteran, whose preference was for writing and directing actioners (such as *Fury at Smugglers' Bay* [1961], with Cushing; *The Scarlet Blade* [1963], with Oliver Reed and *The Pirates of Blood River*, with Lee), Gilling would prove himself to be Hammer's second most effective genre director, after Terence Fisher, with two of the company's best middle-period horrors *The Plague of the Zombies* and *The Reptile*. When he saw what they had done with his script for *The Gorgon*, though, he demanded that his name be removed from the credits.

It "made me vomit," Gilling revealed in an audio interview (included as a special feature on Don Fearney's DVD documentary *Legend of Hammer Vampires*): "I thought [the Gorgon] was more like Old Mother Riley" (something Gilling should know, having produced and directed *Mother Riley Meets the Vampire*). The writer's main objection was what he saw as Anthony Hinds' "interference." Apparently, Hinds, in keeping with the fairy tale element of Hammer horror, was keen on reducing shades in characterization, so that heroes and villains were clearly marked as polar exemplifications of Good and Evil. He also inserted an explanatory intertitle at the beginning and a matte shot from *The Evil of Frankenstein*, before writing to producer Anthony Nelson Keys: "Once Peter Cushing appears, the picture comes to life … Congratulations!"

Rather than being "interference," Hinds' suggestions were, more often than not, thoughtful, effective and beneficial to Hammer's productions as a whole. After all, it was he who suggested to Nigel Kneale that the London Underground would make a more effective setting for the discovery of Martians in *Quatermass and the Pit* than Kneale's original building site location (as confirmed in Andy Murray's *Into the Unknown: The Fantastic Life of Nigel Kneale*). Indeed, the fact that Hinds expressed the most interest in pursuing Gothic subjects in the first place, and hired the relevant creative personnel to do so, makes him more responsible than anyone for Hammer's success.

Describing Bray as "a parochial village," Hammer's regular continuity girl Renée Glynne confirms to me that: "In terms of business, the driving force behind Hammer was the Colonel (James Carreras), but Anthony Hinds was in charge of artistic decisions. [Hinds] was a shy man with an attractive persona. He used to come down from his office at five o'clock every day to collect the day's shoot—cans of 35mm negative for the labs and my accompanying continuity sheets for the film editor at Hammer House in Wardour Street. We had an in-joke that we were just fantasizing this in our asylum!"

The Gorgon would be the first female monster to stalk from Hammer's "asylum," a trend that would continue with *The Reptile*, *Dr. Jekyll and Sister Hyde*, and various vampiresses. "I need hardly say that I am not portraying the good lady herself," Christopher Lee assured his fan club before arriving at Bray, eight days into production on Tuesday, December 17, 1963, for a four-week shoot.

It was an interesting decision to cast the 41-year-old Lee as the aging hero, Professor Meister. Indeed, the actor's roles at Hammer were far more varied than is usually supposed: As well as three very different monsters, two ruthless pirates, a Chinese Tong leader and three romantic leads of varying shades, Lee now donned an Albert Einstein-style get-up for his peppery old professor. The result is as far removed from Dracula, on the one hand, or Henry Baskerville on the other, as it's possible to get. As Lee himself would say: "Where is the typecasting?"

Blunt and to the point, Meister is a refreshingly tactless force of nature who blusters his way through the film's second half. His approach is best exemplified by a response to his protégé Paul's polite complaint of illness: "Ill? You look as if you've been in your grave and dug your way out!" Such rudeness is most satisfying when aimed at ignorant villagers, or pricking the bureaucratic pomposity of Patrick Troughton's police inspector. Despite the character's age, Lee brings a brusque energy to Meister and even succeeds in squeezing his lanky frame through a tiny window at one point. The actor also allows momentary glimpses of the concern which motors the professor's personality, once after striking Paul across the face and, later, when bringing the tale to its tragic conclusion.

Interviewed on the set by Francis Wyndham, Lee expounded on his philosophy of horror: "I try to emphasize the loneliness of evil. Frankenstein's Monster and the Mummy didn't ask to be brought to life. Dracula couldn't help being like he was. I hate the word 'horror.' I prefer to call them 'adult fairy tales.'" In the same interview, Lee bemoaned the kitchen sink realism of recent films, such as *Look Back in Anger* (1958) and *A Taste of Honey* (1961), which clearly had no place for his talents: "I don't mind telling you that I resent the present trend in British movies … If I want to know about the boy and girl next door, I can knock on the door. If I want to be sick, I can go to a hospital." (In John

Cushing and Lee on the set of *The Gorgon*

Brosnan's summation: "A former secret agent, an expert swordsman, a linguist, an opera singer—Christopher Lee couldn't be ordinary if he tried …")

Peter Cushing, too, would struggle to find satisfactory roles outside of the genre at this time. *The Gorgon* marks Lee's first teaming with his old sparring partner since 1959's *The Mummy*. (Although they had both filmed separate scenes for the non-horror thriller, *The Devil's Agent* [1961], Cushing was excised from the finished print.) Doctor Namaroff (or "Baron Nasty Cough" as Lee dubbed him, owing to the nervous affliction Peter affected for his character) possesses an unrequited longing for his charge Carla (Barbara Shelley), which, when coupled with his efforts to protect her true identity, makes him one of the edgier characters in Cushing's oeuvre.

Although, due to his recent spate of Euro-horrors, Lee received top billing over his co-star on French, German and Italian prints, he told Tom Johnson and Mark A. Miller that, "I've never been too concerned about billing, except on a few occasions when I wished my name wasn't on the picture at all!" He further opined that, when it came to he and Cushing, "Audiences came to see us *both*. Peter never worried about [billing], either."

Indeed, as Barbara Shelley told Al Taylor, in *LSoH* #7, she and Cushing were far more concerned with who could sing Gilbert and Sullivan patter songs the fastest, a competition which "used to perplex Christopher Lee who was a great devotee of opera … Chris used to bring opera records to the studio, and he had a marvelous collection of Caruso and we used to spend our time analyzing them in the dressing rooms. He in fact has a marvelous operatic baritone voice … both he and Peter Cushing were wonderful actors to work with, were wonderful people to relax with …"

Elaborating further, she added: "Chris has a very dry sense of humor … Peter does a marvelous impression of Sylvester [the cat], which can always be relied upon to make Chris Lee laugh. We were all very happy working together." Shelley was less happy about two other particulars: a) that she couldn't, for reasons of time, play the monster role, and b) that her idea of grass snakes being used for the Gorgon's hair was ignored.

Syd Pearson, instead, constructed a headpiece of 12 rubber snakes (with articulated tongues). Far from allowing ex-ballerina Prudence Hyman, in the Gorgon role, to move with the balletic grace for which she was presumably hired, assistant director Bert Batt told Wayne Kinsey: "She may as well have been wearing an old deep-sea diver's helmet and his massive boots." The snakes' movements were controlled off-camera by cables and crouched technicians. Batt recalled observing the shadow this created on the studio floor: "It looked as though the Gorgon was trailing a rope to which were clinging three rather large chimpanzees." After all this, Shelley revealed that while filming *The Secret of Blood Island* in July 1964, Anthony Nelson Keys popped into her trailer and admitted it would have been much better if they had used real snakes as she'd originally suggested.

The Gorgon herself, Prudence Hyman (1914-1995), would quietly get on with her knitting between takes. She can also be seen in *The Two Faces of Dr. Jekyll*, *Rasputin: The Mad Monk* and as Kay Walsh's maid in *The Witches*. During the war, as a member of ENSA, Hyman had been piloted by a young Christopher Lee, whose flying, as he confessed in his memoirs, made her "terribly, terribly sick." It must have been the actor's destiny to somehow

Christopher Lee and Peter Cushing together again

endanger the poor woman's life as, at the close of *The Gorgon*, he almost decapitated her for real. According to Roy Ashton (in a letter to *LSoH* #12), Lee slightly misjudged the distance of his sword. Fortunately, Bert Batt pulled Prudence out of harm's way just in time. "Thank God!" wrote Ashton: "For Christopher was an expert swordsman—and surely would have severed dear old Prudence's head from her body."

Much derided is the fake head created by Syd Pearson for the decapitation scene, although it's hard to disagree with Terence Fisher when he told interviewer Jan Van Genechten (in *LSoH* #19): "It didn't look like a solid head but it didn't look like a bouncing football either." Nevertheless, the special effects' main detractor seems to be Lee himself, who revealed to Mark A. Miller that "the only thing wrong with *The Gorgon* is the gorgon."

On a happier note, the actor told Bill Kelley in *LSoH* #13 (1996): "My favorite Hammer leading lady has always been Barbara Shelley," while, in the same periodical, Shelley described Lee as: "A man of great dignity … he was a friend, a mate. We used to drive back to London together. We talked a lot; we used to tell each other personal things. He's a very vulnerable man, quite a nervous man in a certain way."

Barbara Shelley (1932-2021) made her film debut, under her real surname of Kowin, in Terence Fisher's early Hammer thriller *Mantrap* (1952). During subsequent revue work in Rome, she was rechristened by Italian comedian Walter Chiari after his favorite poet (and Christopher Lee's ancestor). On returning to England, in 1957, Shelley played the Simone Simon role in a less subtle variation of *Cat People* (*Cat Girl*), the heroine of *Blood of the Vampire* and the gutsy Kate Keiller in Hammer's controversial *The Camp on Blood Island*. Before reteaming with Lee for *Dracula: Prince of Darkness* and *Rasputin: The Mad Monk*, she mothered an alien child in *Village of the Damned* and survived having a blade thrown at her by Freda Jackson in *The Shadow of the Cat*. Post-Hammer, Barbara spent two years with the Royal Shakespeare Company (from 1976 to '77), before guesting in *Doctor Who*: "Planet of Fire" (1983), the revivifying flames of which are a direct lift from Hammer's *She*.

The Loneliness of Evil

Another *Blood Island* resident returning for *The Gorgon* is Michael Goodliffe (1914-1976), who, aided by the superbly stylized make-up of Roy Ashton, perfectly captures the horror of a man turning into stone. Goodliffe had previously appeared with Christopher Lee in *Captain Horatio Hornblower R.N.*, *The Battle of the River Plate* and *Fortune is a Woman*; and with Cushing in *The End of the Affair* (1954). He was also Nelson in Hammer's maritime comedy *Up the Creek* (1957), Don Jarvis in *Peeping Tom* and a newspaper editor in *The Day the Earth Caught Fire*, before reappearing with Lee as one of James Bond's superiors in *The Man with the Golden Gun*. Just six months after they filmed *To the Devil a Daughter* together, Michael took his own life by leaping from a hospital fire escape.

Goodliffe's son, and Shelley's love interest, in *The Gorgon*, Paul, is played by Richard Pasco (1926-2014), who, in real life, was a regular attendee of Peter Cushing's legendary games parties, during which toy soldiers and battleships were played until dawn. (The two men had previously starred in *Sword of Sherwood Forest*.) After portraying a very different character in *Rasputin: The Mad Monk*, Pasco brought gravitas to audiobook recordings of *Frankenstein*, *Classic Ghost Stories*, and *Classic Vampire Short Stories*, among others. He remembered Lee, to Mark A. Miller, as: "A very nice man, but … not an easy man to know," while describing Terence Fisher as "a gentle, always positive creator … we played [*The Gorgon*] for absolute truth and reality under Terry's guidance."

Lee had last worked with Fisher on *The Two Faces of Dr. Jekyll* in 1959. Since the disappointing performance of that effort, the director had been held responsible for two further box office flops, *The Curse of the Werewolf* and *The Phantom of the Opera*. Tellingly, neither of those films featured Lee or Cushing, which confirms how vital these actors were to Hammer's success.

Although the company had replaced him on recent Gothics (most notably with Don Sharp for *The Kiss of the Vampire*), Terence Fisher outdoes himself on *The Gorgon*, introducing not just his usual drift of falling leaves, but a whole gust of them. Presenting the title creature as an otherworldly figure, sliding in and out of shadows, or reflected in a rain-filled trough, the results are both eerie and suspenseful, especially when married to James Bernard's most ethereal score. The composer employs a Novachord (an early synthesizer) for his soundtrack, fusing the instrument's weird sound with the vocal stylings of soprano Patricia Clark (who had provided Heather Sears' singing voice on *The Phantom of the Opera*).

In addition, the ruined castle set of Megaera the Gorgon is a masterpiece of production design from Bernard Robinson and art director Don Mingaye: Littered with dust, dead leaves,

Italian poster for *The Gorgon*

billowing cobwebs, ragged hangings and broken statues, one can even see the globe from *Dracula*. A new motif is the flutter of birds; a lyrical stylization that brings to mind the kind of lavish visuals presented in 1980s music videos (or the white birds which pervade the glossy haze of Tony Scott's *The Hunger*).

In concert with the above, Michael Reed's beautiful color photography makes *The Gorgon* one of the most exquisite-looking films in horror history. Born in 1929, the cinematographer had started at Hammer as a focus puller (on *The Man in Black*) and would go on to become one of the greatest exponents in his field, not least for lensing the most visually stylish of the James Bond films, *On Her Majesty's Secret Service* (1968). His other Hammer credits include *The Devil-Ship Pirates*, *Dracula: Prince of Darkness*, *Rasputin: The Mad Monk*, and *Slave Girls* (1966).

Paired successfully with *The Curse of the Mummy's Tomb* on Sunday, October 18, 1964, in the UK (when Roy Orbison was at No. 1 with "Oh, Pretty Woman"), *The Gorgon* was also a hit in America from its release there on Thursday, December 31, 1964 (when the Beatles topped the charts with "I Feel Fine"). At US screenings, cardboard masks, with blacked-out eyes, were handed out so that viewers could shield themselves from Megaera's gaze.

Along with *The Curse of Frankenstein*, *The Revenge of Frankenstein* and *The Curse of the Mummy's Tomb*, Pan Books issued *The Gorgon* as a novella in *The Hammer Horror Film Omnibus* (1966). The films were adapted by John Burke, a former story editor for 20th Century Fox, who, as well as providing the original idea for Michael Reeves' *The Sorcerers* (1967), novelized everything from *A Hard Day's Night* (1964) to *The Entertainer* (1959). In addition to restoring the Gorgon's mythological name of Medusa, Burke's novelization provides minor background details of character and setting, while lovingly depicting any offscreen attacks, a feature it shares with the comic strip version (by Scott Goodall, Trevor Goring and Alberto Cuyas), which appeared over issues 11 and 12 of *The House of Hammer* magazine in the summer of 1977.

Poetic and romantic, *The Gorgon* is a classic that improves with every viewing. Not only does it showcase Terence Fisher's most accomplished job of direction, but it also offers further evidence that Christopher Lee could succeed in varied roles. As 1963 came to a close, however, the actor was preparing to make his first trip to Hollywood …

The Alfred Hitchcock Hour: The Sign of Satan 1964

In the winter 1958 issue of *Sight and Sound*, a disdainful Derek Hill reported that "Peter Cushing and Christopher Lee have now, apparently, joined Alec Guinness to become the only three British stars whose names attract American cinemagoers." But it wouldn't be until March 1964 that Lee would first work in the US, taking part in a show which capitalized on the suspenseful image of another genre icon.

Alfred Hitchcock Presents (1955-1962) set the precedent for TV thrills with such unforgettable sights as Tom Conway's unusual ventriloquist in "The Glass Eye," Hazel Court being ground into chicken feed by Laurence Harvey's "Arthur," and Peter Lorre raising a cleaver to Steve McQueen's pinkie in "Man from the South." (The series' producer Joan Harrison went on to oversee Hammer's *Journey to the Unknown* in 1968.) As well as being of exceptionally high quality (each entry serves as a satisfying mini-movie in itself—Hitch would use his TV crew on *Psycho*), the open cynicism to TV sponsorship espoused by Hitchcock in his darkly humorous introductions is equally refreshing.

In 1962, the series' 25-minute episode format was expanded into *The Alfred Hitchcock Hour*. The idea to do so came from CBS executive Hunt Stromberg, Jr., who, as well as creating *The Vampira Show* (1954-1955), oversaw the development of *The Twilight Zone*, *The Munsters* (1964-1966), and *Lost in Space* (1965-1968). (Stromberg later produced *Frankenstein: The True Story* [1973] and had a Bond villain named after him in *The Spy Who Loved Me*.) Also in 1962, *The Twilight Zone* had its running time bumped up to an hour for its fourth season, but both shows suffered as a result, with the snappier half-hours bearing a greater impact. Indeed, unlike the Hitchcock program, season five of *The Twilight Zone* reverted to shorter episodes the following year.

Christopher Lee was brought on board for the 27th entry of *The Alfred Hitchcock Hour*'s second season, "The Sign of Satan." Robert Bloch's 1938 source story "Return to the Sabbath" was introduced by the actor in *Christopher Lee's New Chamber of Horrors* as being "a favorite of mine for years because of its marvelous central character—a Black Magic-practicing horror film-star!"

A protégé of the legendary H.P. Lovecraft, Bloch's writing would provide many memorable moments of TV fantasy. His story "The Cheaters," for instance, about a pair of spectacles revealing hidden truths, made for a clever *Thriller* entry, as did "The Weird Tailor," in which a dummy twitches to hideous life. In addition, the *Star Trek* episode "Wolf in the Fold" (1967) is a futuristic reworking of the author's 1943 tale "Yours Truly, Jack the Ripper." The latter had previously been adapted for a 1961 *Thriller* by *The Man in Half Moon Street*'s Barré Lyndon, who would also script "The Sign of Satan."

It was with mixed feelings that Lee made his first journey to Hollywood; his daughter Christina had been born on Boris Karloff's 76th birthday (Saturday, November 23, 1963) with, in Lee's words, "her feet turned at right angles, almost backwards"—a complication that required frequent hospital visits and the wearing of splints to correct. (A major reason why Lee never turned work down in the remainder of the '60s was so that he could pay for Christina's medical treatment.) "It was horrible to leave

Christopher Lee, with puffy hair, in *The Alfred Hitchcock Hour*

The Loneliness of Evil

Gitte and the 12-week-old baby behind," the actor wrote in his autobiography, "but we both felt I should not let the opportunity slide." Once in the air, however, the nervous father "was a prey to strange imaginings, that I would never see Christina and Gitte again, that the plane would ditch with everything still to do." Consequently, "I was filled with an absolute horror of flying … which was never to leave me again…"

Once in L.A., Lee was met by a man from Universal and placed in a half-built motel (proprietor: Norman Bates?) opposite the studio; he would take all his meals at a nearby Chinese restaurant ("By the end I could have eaten Hollywood itself with soy sauce"). Further disappointment came when he learned that Alfred Hitchcock would not actually be directing "The Sign of Satan," just introducing it. (In fact, Hitchcock would only personally helm one of the hour-long shows: "I Saw the Whole Thing" [1962], an interesting piece on human perception with John Forsythe and *Cat People*'s Kent Smith.) The closest Lee actually got to the celebrated filmmaker during the shoot at Universal was seeing him pass by in "a large black Cadillac" while the actor cycled to the studio commissar. ("He was real. That was all I needed to know.")

"The Sign of Satan" was directed, instead, by British-born TV veteran Robert Douglas (1909-1999), whom Lee was already familiar with from Douglas' days as an actor (one of his roles was as Colonel Parker in *Tarzan, the Ape Man* [1959]). Filming began on Wednesday March 11, 1964, for a six-day shoot.

Following the familiar theme music (Charles Gounod's "Funeral March of a Marionette") and Hitchcock's droll, tuxedo-clad intro (this time "from the planet Mars"), the story opens on a misty graveyard set, which could well come from *The City of the Dead*, as Lee's Karl Jorla rises from a stone sarcophagus, followed by two hooded, candle-bearing figures. The Black Mass that follows is not only a television first, but also part of a forbidden movie being unspooled in a Hollywood screening office for producer Max Rubini (Gilbert Green) and actress Kitty Frazier (Gia Scala). The two bring Jorla over to America to star in their latest horror production. The film's publicity agent is played by Myron Healey (1923-2005), stalwart of such genre offerings as *The Unearthly* (1956), *Varan the Unbelievable* (1958) and *The Incredible Melting Man* (1977).

Lee was made-up at Universal by another horror veteran, Bud Westmore (1918-1973), who, since taking over the monster-making reins from Jack Pierce on *Abbott and Costello Meet Frankenstein*, had headed the team responsible for *Tarantula* (1955), *The Mole People* (1956), *Man of a Thousand Faces* (1956) and *Monster on the Campus* (1958). Mere months after working on Lee, Westmore would be busy overseeing *The Munsters*. (Although Westmore received sole screen credit for creating the monsters of *It Came from Outer Space* [1953], *Abbott and Costello Meet Dr. Jekyll and Mr. Hyde* [1953], *Creature from the Black Lagoon* [1953] and *This Island Earth* [1954], they were actually designed by the unsung Milicent Patrick [1915-1998].) In his memoirs, Lee revealed that, one day, Groucho Marx entered the make-up room, took one look at Lee in his thick black wig and quipped: "I bet you played Abe Lincoln many times," before making a swift exit. Westmore dissuaded Lee from pursuing the legendary comic for an autograph with the words: "He's not known as Groucho for nothing."

Whether cloaked, or clad in cardigan and slacks, Karl Jorla seems permanently ill at ease. Indeed, Lee presents a character seemingly from another time, another world, with twitchy mannerisms and foreign accent, respectful of preserving legends in a world that doesn't believe. One imagines that Lee, an intelligent actor, often felt the same way when faced with the brash vulgarities of Hollywood. "There are many vampires in the world today," he was once quoted as saying in the *Radio Times*, "you only have to think of the film business." And, much like the presentation of Max Schreck as a bona fide bloodsucker in *Shadow of the Vampire* (1999), it comes as no surprise that Jorla is, of course, a real-life devil worshipper, pursued by some very real demons.

While the plot may be a little obvious, the production values are uniformly high and the notion of an actor portraying an exaggerated version of his public persona is simply irresistible. Indeed, Lee was the first horror star to *play* a horror star: See also Boris Karloff in *Targets* (1967), Vincent Price in *Madhouse* (1973), Peter Cushing in *Tender Dracula* (1974), Donald Pleasence in *The Uncanny* (1976), John Carradine in "McCloud Meets Dracula" (1976), Caroline Munro in *The Last Horror Film* (1981), Robert Englund in *Wes Craven's New Nightmare* (1993) and Paul Naschy in *Rojo sangre* (2003).

Broadcast by CBS at 10pm on Friday, May 8, 1964, immediately after the latest episode of *The Twilight Zone* ("Mr. Garrity and the Graves"), "The Sign of Satan" would have to wait until Sunday, June 16, 1968, for its UK unveiling.

When *Alfred Hitchcock Presents* was revived in 1985, another highlight of the *Hitchcock Hour*'s second season, Ray Bradbury's "The Jar," was remade to showcase the talents of a young Tim Burton. The emerging director transforms Bradbury's original protagonist into an artist humiliated by an arrogant critic—a notion that takes direct inspiration from *Dr. Terror's House of Horrors*. Before making that movie, however, Christopher Lee had one more Italian commitment to perform.

The Castle of the Living Dead 1964

The story of a man who violates the forbidden frontiers of science.

The above line is taken from the trailer for *The Castle of the Living Dead*, which announces its star as "the unforgettable creator of *Dracula*" (Bram Stoker may have had something to say about that). Indeed, it was the success of Hammer's first *Dracula* that inspired New Jersey novelist Warren Kiefer (b. 1929) to write and direct *The Castle of the Living Dead* in collaboration with a man who would become one of Christopher Lee's closest friends in the industry: New York producer Paul Maslansky (b. 1933) went on to oversee *Death Line*, as well as the Blaxploitation zombies of *Sugar Hill* (1974), the country music-loving Satanists of *Race with the Devil* (1975) and the dark fantasy milieu of *Return to Oz* (1984). He is most famous, however, for the *Police Academy* movies, the seventh entry of which, *Mission to Moscow* (1993), features a chucklesome turn from Lee as Commandant Rakov.

The Castle of the Living Dead began production on Monday, April 27, 1964, for a 24-day shoot. (Lee was present for only 10 of those days.) The titular fortress is Castle Odescalchi and this would mark the third time that Lee had made a horror film there (after *Uncle Was a Vampire* and *Katarsis*).

The film's plot somewhat prefigures *Dracula: Prince of Darkness*, in that a group of people find themselves imperiled at a castle belonging to Christopher Lee. (Even the *Dracula* film's hero Francis Matthews bears a slight resemblance to *The Castle of the Living Dead*'s Philippe Leroy.) In this instance, Lee plays host to a tribe of strolling players, whose numbers include *Hercules in the Haunted World*'s Gaia Germani, *The Whip and the Body*'s Luciano Pigozzi and Antonio de Martino (who would play an elf in *The Christmas That Almost Wasn't* [1966]). Before arriving at the castle, the troupe are warned of inherent danger by an old witch played by Donald Sutherland (in a performance that has to be seen to be believed). With the latter character clearly patterned after the apple-bearing crone of Disney's *Snow White and the Seven Dwarfs* (1937), the fairy tale feel extends into Carlo Gentili's production design; the castle hallway is a veritable petrified forest, full of stuffed birds and creatures. The taxidermist himself, Lee's Count Drago, arrives to announce, "Welcome to my home," in true Draculean fashion, before explaining, "I was working in my laboratory …" (At this point, one expects him to burst into the "Monster Mash.")

With panda eyes, goatee beard and turned-up collar, Lee gives a delightfully eccentric turn as Drago. His only living companion is a sinister servant played by *The Virgin of Nuremberg*'s Mirko Valentin (who looks just as creepy without heavy makeup). Treated to a private show by his guests, Drago resembles a more somber version of Lewis Carroll's Mad Hatter, seated in a throne and applauding the grimmer aspects of the performance with the escalating glee of an unhinged child. Indeed, Lee invests the part with such childlike innocence that Drago's enthusiasm for the dead seems a perfectly natural outgrowth of this naive wonder. He even explodes with a petulant rant when one of his little dead birds is knocked over during the climactic scuffle, and there's an additionally awkward adolescent bumbling to his dealings with Gaia Germani's heroine ("You're a very beautiful woman …"). Of course, Drago is far more comfortable around people once they're dead, when he can add them to his "eternal theater" ensemble. One such corpse lies in a cobwebbed bridal chamber. As a large black spider rests upon her pillow, and a rat nibbles at her fingers, Lee addresses the lifeless woman with tender grace. ("Did they disturb you, my dear?")

Another part in Drago's collection of stuffed corpses is played by the film's assistant director Michael Reeves (1943-1969), who, owing to his subsequent filmic triumphs, is believed to have played a larger hand in the production than he actually did. While the full extent of Reeves' involvement remains unknown, Paul Maslansky recalled to David Pirie that his second unit footage was striking enough to warrant an enlarged contribution, something which Warren Kiefer refuted. Nevertheless, reward came when Maslansky allowed Reeves to direct Barbara Steele in *Revenge of the Blood Beast* (1965). Despite a jocular tone, this crude debut (enlivened by a creepy, screeching witch) led to the director's true masterpieces, *The Sorcerers* and *Witchfinder General* (both 1967).

While Reeves' involvement on *The Castle of the Living Dead* may have been exaggerated in recent years, his presence on-set was certainly strong enough to impress Christopher Lee, who was keen to star in a thriller co-written for him by the precocious filmmaker entitled *Appassionata*. (The screenplay was ultimately rewritten by Jimmy Sangster after Reeves' premature death. Re-

Italian poster for *The Castle of the Living Dead*

The Castle of the Living Dead marks the screen debut of Donald Sutherland.

titled *Crescendo*, with James Olson in the lead, Hammer issued the completed film on a double bill with *Taste the Blood of Dracula* in 1970.) *The Castle of the Living Dead* would be screened at the National Film Theatre's Michael Reeves retrospective, along with the three films he *did* direct, on Saturday January 17, 1970.

Unfortunately, so much has been made of Reeves' supposed authorship of *The Castle of the Living Dead* that Warren Kiefer's input has been sorely overlooked. The director makes brilliant use of Bomarzo's Park of the Monsters: The creation of 16th century architect Pirro Ligorio, the park's entryway, resembling a gaping mouth (the "Door of Hell"), and giant statues, including a turtle, perfectly emphasize the weird ambience. (The gardens would also serve as a location for *The Bride* [1984].)

Kiefer (credited as Luciano Ricci for quota purposes) would only work on a handful of films after this; Lee told Brad Stevens, in a filmed interview, that the director went on to manage an oil company. In the same discussion, Lee revealed that Kiefer's intention was to make the movie look like an Expressionistic German silent. Realizing this ambition, the black-and-white cinematography is from Aldo Tonti (1910-1988), whose credits include Luchino Visconti's *Ossessione* (1943), Federico Fellini's *The Nights of Cabiria* (1957), John Huston's *Reflections in a Golden Eye* (1967) and Marco Ferreri's *The Ape Woman* (1963).

While Lee was happy to record his own voice for the English-language version of *The Castle of the Living Dead*, the dubbing session itself, overseen by Mel Welles (Mr. Mushnik in Corman's *The Little Shop of Horrors* and future director of *Lady Frankenstein*), was less than happy: All continuity sheets for the film had been lost, along with the continuity girl, and the actors had to remember, or, in some cases, make up the dialogue from scratch.

Nevertheless, *The Castle of the Living Dead* benefits from a music soundtrack by Angelo Lavagnino (1909-1987), who, in addition to credits for Orson Welles (*Othello* [1951] and *Chimes at Midnight* [1965]) would score *Gorgo*, *Goliath and the Vampires*, *Queens of Evil* (1970) and *The Curse of the Vampire* (1971).

The Castle of the Living Dead is further notable as the film debut of Canadian actor Donald Sutherland (b. 1935). His dual role of the witch and a soldier (he even gets to act alongside himself) was swiftly followed by another appearance with Christopher Lee in *Dr. Terror's House of Horrors*, while his third screen credit, as a pallid handyman who reads an upside-down Bible, came in Hammer's *Fanatic* (1964). Since then, he's been the bereaved father of *Don't Look Now* (1972), the tormented Homer Simpson in *The Day of the Locust* (1974), *Fellini's Casanova* (1976), and the health inspector who uncovers an *Invasion of the Body Snatchers* (1978). After playing psychic Robert Lees in *Murder by Decree* (1978), he was the original Watcher of *Buffy the Vampire Slayer* (1992), the Old Man in Robert A. Heinlein's *The Puppet Masters* (1994) and the cursed landowner of *An American Haunting* (2005). During production of *The Castle of the Living Dead*, Donald became friendly with Warren Kiefer and, in 1966, named his first son after the director—Kiefer Sutherland launched his own career with memorable turns in Stephen King's *Stand by Me* (1985) and *The Lost Boys* (1986). (Look out for posters announcing Warner Home Video's first issues of *The Curse of Frankenstein* and *The Mummy* in the background of this vampire comedy.)

Released in Italy, as *Il castello dei morti vivi*, on Wednesday, August 5, 1964, before sinking into undeserved oblivion, *The Castle of the Living Dead* remains the most consistently entertaining of Christopher Lee's Euro-horrors, especially as he seems to be having such fun with his offbeat character.

Dr. Terror's House of Horrors 1964

Acclaimed as 'THE FEAR OF THE YEAR'

There is within each of us a twin destiny; the natural and the supernatural... —Dr. Schreck (Peter Cushing)

Officially formed by Milton Subotsky and Max J. Rosenberg in November 1961, Amicus Productions operated from a shed, Chalet #3, on the backlot of Shepperton Studios. The word Amicus is Latin for *friend*—or, if you prefer Robert Bloch's translation: *Low budget*.

Like Anthony Hinds at Hammer, Subotsky was very much the creative member of the partnership, while Max, akin to James Carreras, handled the financial side. In addition, whereas Hinds concerned himself with the ongoing battle between Good and Evil, Subotsky was more interested in presenting the karmic consequences of those who do wrong to others. The producer also admitted to John Brosnan that, while he admired the "mythic quality" of Hammer's *The Kiss of the Vampire*, he found the company's subsequent over-reliance on sex "boring." Unlike his rivals, Milton had no interest in the fleshier side of horror, telling Brosnan: "We try to make films that are imaginative and relate to an audience in a different way. We never have any blood and gore in our films."

Nevertheless, the cozier horrors of Amicus employed many of Hammer's key creative personnel, including make-up man Roy Ashton, assistant director Bert Batt and musical director Philip Martell, among others. At the forefront, Christopher Lee and Peter Cushing were both handed roles dissimilar to the Byronic anti-heroes they personified at Bray.

Since last working with Lee on *The City of the Dead*, Subotsky and Rosenberg had fallen back on their successful staple, the teen musical, with *It's Trad, Dad!* (the first official Amicus Production) and *Just for Fun* (1963), but soon decided that the time was right to return to the horror genre. Entranced by *Dead of Night*, Subotsky had long desired to emulate its portmanteau style. Indeed, he had written the five tales, which make up *Dr. Terror's House of Horrors*, as far back as 1948, for an unmade TV series he hoped to produce.

Although no one was keen on the idea then, in 1961, Roger Corman crafted a fine anthology movie from Poe's *Tales of Terror*, whose star, Vincent Price, went on to enact Hawthorne's *Twice-Told Tales* (1962). The following year, Boris Karloff introduced the Italian *Black Sabbath*, while over in Japan, production was underway on Masaki Kobayashi's slow-moving but beautiful *Kwaidan*, based on the writings of Lafcadio Hearn. But, in all of these films, the stories are presented as separate entities, whereas Subotsky linked his tales with clever wraparounds. (A twist he had learned from *Dead of Night*.)

Another difference is that the aforementioned portmanteaux all take their stories from literature, while Subotsky wrote his own material. What wasn't original was the title. Max J. Rosenberg had already released a film called *Dr. Terror's House of Horrors* in 1943, but this was merely a collection of clips the producer had cobbled together from five independent genre films, namely the Bela Lugosi starrers *White Zombie* (1932) and *The Return of Chandu* (1934), Carl Dreyer's *Vampyr* (1930), a German spoof with Paul Wegener, *The Living Dead* (1932) and the French version of *The Golem* (1936).

To direct the new *Dr. Terror's House of Horrors*, Subotsky hired Freddie Francis (1917-2007) on the strength of his work at Hammer. Along with the psychological thrillers *Paranoiac*, *Nightmare* and *Hysteria*, Francis had helmed *The Evil of Frankenstein* (1963) when Terence Fisher proved unavailable (he was busy directing Pat Boone in *The Horror of it All*). To all of the above, Francis brought a pictorial élan, thanks in no small part to his background as a cinematographer (in which capacity he won Oscars for *Sons and Lovers* [1959] and *Glory* [1989]). Freddie also photographed Hammer's *Never Takes Sweets from a Stranger* and the classic ghost story *The Innocents* (1961), but his debut as a genre director came via *The Day of the Triffids*: When Steve Sekely's original cut proved unsatisfactory, Francis was hired to film, uncredited, the additional scenes of Janette Scott and Kieron Moore being menaced by the title creatures in a deserted lighthouse. Ironically, these became

Peter Cushing deals the cards of fate in the British artwork for *Dr. Terror's House of Horrors*.

the movie's best moments and, the following spring, he directed *Vengeance* (1962), another variation on *Donovan's Brain*.

Dr. Terror's House of Horrors began filming at Shepperton on Monday, May 25, 1964, with the opening train station footage being shot at London King's Cross (later the site of another fantasy journey: Platform 9 ¾ in the *Harry Potter* franchise). The film's wraparound premise involves five men sharing a train carriage with the mysterious Dr. Schreck (Peter Cushing), who, when producing his Tarot deck (his "house of horrors"), reveals frightening destinies for his fellow passengers. As well as being the German word for terror, Schreck is also a nod to Max Schreck, the skeletal actor who portrayed Count Orlok in *Nosferatu*. (After whom Tim Burton would also name Christopher Walken's narcissistic tycoon in *Batman Returns* [1991], a movie which, like *Dr. Terror's House of Horrors*, stars Michael Gough.)

First seen fixing Roy Castle with a withering look when the latter almost shuts the train door on him, Lee's snooty art critic, Franklyn Marsh, hides behind his newspaper once aboard, offering the occasional harrumph at Dr. Schreck's "nonsense." (The subtitle on the Italian print declares, "Dracula has arrived!," when Lee makes his entrance.)

The first vision foretold by Schreck concerns architect Neil McCallum (*The Lost Continent*), who travels to the Scottish home of Ursula Howells (*Mumsy, Nanny, Sonny & Girly*), only to discover a werewolf named Cosmo Waldemar. A nicely atmospheric opener, this is surely where Spain's premier horror star Paul Naschy (1934-2009) acquired the name for his own lycanthropic character Waldemar Daninsky. An openly acknowledged fan of Lee and Cushing, Naschy rampaged through 11 self-penned ventures as Waldemar until 2003's *Tomb of the Werewolf* (written and directed by Fred Olen Ray). The first in the series, *The Mark of the Wolfman* (1968), takes further inspiration from *Dr. Terror* via its eerie old house, complete with werewolf's crypt, its soundtrack of pounding voodoo drums, its episodic introduction of different monsters and its lonely train station, where vampires emerge from the mist.

Schreck's second story sees Alan Freeman (a DJ who had played himself in *It's Trad, Dad!*) attacked by a creeping vine; a ridiculous premise played commendably straight by its cast, especially Bernard Lee, who has to utter the deathless lines: "A dog strangled by a vine? I can hardly believe it ... A plant like that could take over the world." (Immortalized as M in every 007 picture from *Dr. No* [1962] to *Moonraker* [1978], Bernard graces *Frankenstein and the Monster from Hell* with a mute cameo.)

Next, musician Roy Castle (*Dr. Who and the Daleks*) gets into hot water when he steals the sacred music of a voodoo tribe. Despite some politically incorrect leanings in its depiction of West Indian characters, this segment is raised considerably by the multi-talented Castle and his charismatic co-star Kenny Lynch (who, as well as writing hits for the Small Faces ["Sha-La-La-La-Lee"], was the first artist to cover a Beatles tune, "Misery," in 1963—10 years later, Lynch would appear with Christopher Lee on the cover of Paul McCartney's *Band On the Run* LP). Another interesting feature of this story is the movie poster for *Dr. Terror's House of Horrors* which can be seen adorning an alleyway wall—in a neat merging of worlds, the characters' names are listed as actors (i.e., Starring Franklyn Marsh and Sandor Schreck). Subotsky created a similar inversion for his final anthology *The Monster Club* (1980), in which the film's author, R. Chetwynd-Hayes, is introduced as a major character. The part was played by John Carradine after Christopher Lee turned it down.

Dr. Terror's closing tale has Lee's recent co-star from *The Castle of the Living Dead*, Donald Sutherland, wondering if his new bride (Jennifer Jayne) is a vampire. A movie-going chum of writer Denis Gifford, Jennifer Jayne (1931-2006) is a figure worthy of mention. Having starred in an early Hammer thriller directed by Vernon Sewell, *The Black Widow* (1950), she went on to play the besieged heroine of *The Trollenberg Terror* (1957) before appearing in Freddie Francis' *Hysteria*, *They Came from Beyond Space* (1966) and *The Doctor and the Devils* (1985). In 1972, she even wrote her own Amicus-style compendium, *Tales That Witness Madness*, as well as "the first rock-and-roll Dracula movie," *Son of Dracula* (1972), for the same director.

Squeezed between the "Voodoo" and "Vampire" segments, the starkly titled "Disembodied Hand" sees Lee's Franklyn Marsh publicly humiliated by artist Eric Landor (Michael Gough) with the help of Isla Blair and a chimpanzee. (Concurrently, over at AIP, Boris Karloff could also be seen admiring a chimp's artwork in *Bikini Beach*: "I must tell Vincent Price about this place," he enthuses.)

Born in 1944, Isla Blair's big scene with Beatle Paul McCartney in *A Hard Day's Night* had unfortunately been cut from the finished film (and is not likely to have survived), making *Dr. Terror's House of Horrors* her debut. She remembered her simian co-star to Oscar Martinez in *LSoH* #13: "It was very temperamental ... just as you were about to go on ... the chimp would put its nappy down." (Blair would have more substantial [ape-free] screen time with Christopher Lee in *Taste the Blood of Dracula* [1969]).

As ever, Lee brings the inner vulnerability of his pompous character to the surface. Driven to faltering madness by the memory of Landor's prank, Marsh, with tight-lipped determination and saddened eyes, runs down the artist, severing his hand. Lee then shows the critic's growing distress, first while studying the news of his crime when he should be typing reviews. Through the actor's stiffened body language and detached communication with others, one can feel the palpable flutters of guilt that must be assailing his body.

Gough, too, delivers a marvelous performance; witness his tear-streaked face as he turns from a gallery window looking down at his bandaged stump. Unable to paint, Landor blows his brains out, but his disembodied hand survives ...

Recognizable by the seam running along its side, the crawl-

Freddie Francis, Christopher Lee and Milton Subotsky on the set

ing hand became, after Lee and Cushing, Amicus' third major star, reappearing in both *And Now the Screaming Starts!* (1972) and *Tales from the Crypt*.

Refusing to be upstaged by the special effects, Lee's performance lifts the film into a whole new realm. The shuddering terror he communicates hits the viewer straight in the gut—a visceral level that the surrounding stories, although charming, fail to reach. Perhaps inspired by Franklyn Marsh, Vincent Price requested that Lee play one of the arrogant critics he kills off in *Theatre of Blood*, but the producers vetoed the suggestion, believing that their film was really a black comedy and Lee's involvement would make people think it was a horror film, which it certainly is!

A ragbag of pleasing chills, *Dr. Terror's House of Horrors* is further enhanced by some good ideas, particularly the deserted train station that serves as a purgatorial afterlife, and an eerily atonal score from Elisabeth Lutyens. Since *Penny and the Pownall Case*, the composer had scored *Never Take Sweets from a Stranger*, *Paranoiac* and *The Earth Dies Screaming* (1964). Her music would also play a great part in evoking the off-kilter worlds of *The Psychopath*, *The Terrornauts* (1966) and *Theatre of Death*.

Another feather in the cap is the color lighting of one of Britain's finest cinematographers, Alan Hume (1924-2010), whose other credits include *The Kiss of the Vampire*, *The Legend of Hell House* (1972), *From Beyond the Grave*, *The Watcher in the Woods* (1979) and *The Hunchback of Notre Dame* (1981), as well as *Return of the Jedi* (1982), three James Bond films (*For Your Eyes Only*, *Octopussy* and *A View to a Kill*), and 20 *Carry Ons* (including *Carry On Screaming!*).

After six weeks of shooting, *Dr. Terror's House of Horrors* wrapped on Friday, July 3, 1964, and was a big hit when released in the UK on Tuesday, February 23, 1965 (when the Seekers were at No. 1 with "I'll Never Find Another You") and in the US five days later (when "This Diamond Ring" by Gary Lewis and the Playboys topped the charts).

With some additional musings on the nature of fate, John Burke's tie-in novelization, published by Pan Books, makes for a satisfying read, not least because it manages to make the "Creeping Vine" a little more exciting ("His fingers dug madly into the coil of pulsating, living green …"). Burke also provides an intriguing reason for Franklyn Marsh's scathing attitude towards

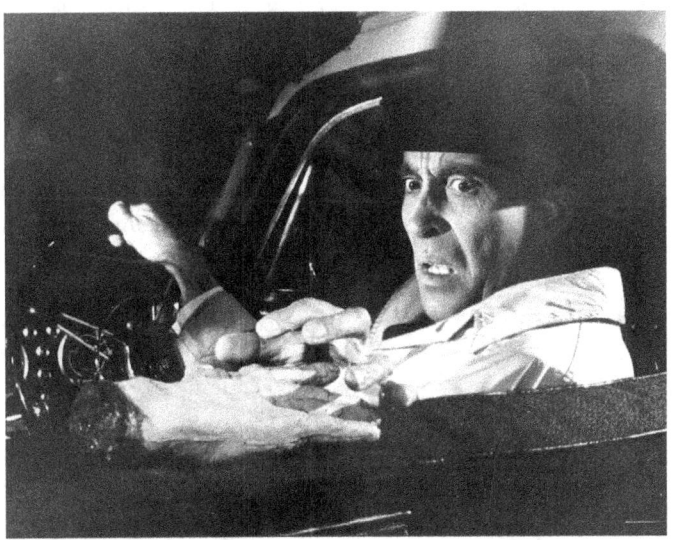

Mr. Marsh the art critic is paralyzed by the hand that appears on his shoulder.

modern art in that the critic is a failed painter himself. One wonders if this tidbit of knowledge guided Lee's performance, especially as his character appears more fully fleshed than his companions. Ranging from hateful to sympathetic, Marsh incites a conflict of feelings from the viewer, something which Lee, with his love of the unexpected, must have relished. Parenthetically, in the book, Marsh's critical faculties are undone, not by a chimpanzee, but by a little boy. Given that Burke was working from Subotsky's original screenplay, this shows that the ape must have been a late addition, perhaps suggested by Freddie Francis during pre-production.

In October 1966, John Burke completed a horror screenplay, *The Devil's Discord*, which would have teamed Christopher Lee with Raquel Welch under the direction of Michael Reeves. The project, alas, was ultimately rejected by Tigon and never made. One (very) pale Hollywood imitation of *Dr. Terror's House of Horrors*, though, *was* completed that year: In *Dr. Terror's Gallery of Horrors*, John Carradine introduces five ineptly put-together tales from the pen of *Famous Monsters of Filmland* artist Russ Jones, including Lon Chaney, Jr. as a Frankenstein-like scientist with an accomplice named Dr. Cushing.

On a happier note, Dr. Terror also lent his name to a BBC horror host, played by Guy Henry (in great prosthetics from *Hellraiser*'s Geoff Portass). Broadcast on Friday nights, *Dr. Terror's Vault of Horror* (1992-1996) offered such Lee and Cushing starrers as *The Curse of Frankenstein*, *Horror Express*, *The Mummy*—and *Dr. Terror's House of Horrors*. Bringing things full circle, in 2016, Guy Henry gave voice to a digitized Peter Cushing for *Rogue One: A Star Wars Story*.

Back in 1964, however, Lee and Cushing would join forces with Hammer once more …

She
1964

The greatest adventure story of them all …

> The fact is that it was written at white heat, almost without rest, and that is the best way to compose … it came faster than my poor aching hand could set it down.—Sir Henry Rider Haggard on the creation of *She*

While Michael Carreras had proven his taste for exotic fare with *The Mummy*, he was also keen to break away from Gothic subjects. In *She*, the producer found a lavish fantasy that could be targeted at family audiences *and* provide a showcase for the Swiss-born leading lady of *Dr. No*, Ursula Andress. As the immortal Ayesha, Andress would be joined by two other actors whose parts in Hammer's most expensive production to date were immediately assured. "I personally cast many of the roles," director Robert Day told Tom Johnson and Deborah Del Vecchio, "but not Peter [Cushing] or Christopher [Lee]. They were part of Hammer's package and the film was planned round them."

H. Rider Haggard's 1886 source novel had been filmed at least five times (beginning with Georges Méliès' 1899 short, *La Danse du Feu*) before the first full-length feature version emerged in 1925. A German-British co-production, this silent adaptation, shot in Berlin with Betty Blythe in the title role, was followed 10 years later by an RKO presentation from *King Kong* producer Merian C. Cooper. Employing many of *Kong*'s creative personnel, including writer Ruth Rose and composer Max Steiner, the 1935 *She* is a thrillsome adventure, co-directed by Irving Pichel (the ghoulish manservant of *Dracula's Daughter*), which stars future Congresswoman Helen Gahagan, in her only movie, amid some fantastic Arctic sets. The Christopher Lee role of Billali is played by Gustav von Seyffertitz, the hatchet-faced actor of *The Bells* (1926), *Sparrows* (1926) and *The Bat Whispers* (1930). (Incidentally, Rider Haggard's great grandnephew is Piers Haggard, director of *Blood on Satan's Claw* and *Quatermass* [1978].)

On an exceptional outing from Bray, and to accommodate the fabulous settings required by the script, Hammer's version began filming at Elstree on Monday, August 24, 1964. Lee completed all of his scenes in the studio, before the remaining leads embarked for location shooting in Southern Israel on Monday, October 5. (The film wrapped on the 17th of that month.)

An exotic bit of eye tinsel for a rainy afternoon, *She* is at its best when expressing the travails faced by lovers. With its theme of romance spanning the ages, the story is, in fact, a reversed-gender equivalent to *The Mummy*. As the intrepid Major Holly, Peter Cushing provides the most interesting lines on the subject: "A deep, sincere love will last most people a lifetime," he tells his young charge, Leo Vincey, "but even that changes, from the frantic yearnings of its beginnings, to a quiet, unspoken understanding at its end. The physical side of human love wasn't designed to last forever." Cushing had actually written these words himself in deference to his beloved wife Helen, a relationship which endured more than its own fair share of struggles.

Christopher Lee was not having an easy time of it, either, during the filming of *She*. "I was going through a form of nervous breakdown," he later wrote, elaborating further: "I brooded savagely. I tried to write, and found myself producing an account of an execution with a guillotine …" Perhaps Lee had used this growing sense of panic to enhance his nervy characterization of Franklyn Marsh in *Dr. Terror's House of Horrors*? Whatever, the feeling certainly carried over into his next production. While shooting the scene in which Ayesha hurls her captives into a lava pit, Lee "felt totally hemmed in" and ran from the set. Once in his dressing room, "the walls started closing in," so, still wearing the priestly robes of Billali, he escaped into a freezing rain until "the hideous threat dissolved in the downpour and I returned, drenched, to the set." Happier times were spent when Lee brought his baby Christina to Elstree to be photographed with Cushing and Andress (whom Lee found "charming").

Subservient to Ayesha, the part of Billali may be a waste of Lee's talents, but it is, at least, a departure from anything he'd played at Hammer before, especially when one considers that his last role for the company was the aging Professor Meister. Although the Billali of Haggard's novel is also an old man (bearing close physical resemblance to the bearded wizard later essayed by Lee in *The Lord of the Rings*), the actor's interpretation is far younger. Sporting a short black goatee, he matches Haggard's description of "a deep and low voice" and "eyes as keen as a snake's," while looking very good in costume. As Robert Day told Mark A. Miller: "You don't think just anyone could dress like Billali, do you?"

Christopher Lee and Ursula Andress in costume

Billali's most interesting scene comes when Holly catches him worshipping among the mummified corpses of former high priests. Despite having his beliefs challenged, Lee maintains his dignity: "Each one of us has his own destiny to fulfill." Ironically, Billali only comes fully to life for his death scene, when all of his repressed desires spill forth. Thrashing savagely at Leo with his sword, the High Priest receives a flaming torch in the face ("causing me to look like Al Jolson," Lee mused). This is not enough to dim his once-concealed determination, though, and even after Ayesha spears him in the back, he still reaches for "The Flame of Eternal Life," before expiring at its edge. This fiery resolve is recurrent in Lee's characterizations, stemming no doubt from his own will to succeed against the odds. ("You are far too tall and foreign-looking to be an actor …")

Lee rallied against further disappointment when a chance to showcase his musical skills fell by the wayside. James Bernard, whose superlative score for *She* is among his greatest, told Bruce Hallenbeck and John McCarty in *LSoH* #6: "[Christopher had] always wanted to be able to sing in a film. He has a very good voice … We wrote a chant for him. He wrote some marvelous nonsense words that were supposed to be in this archaic language, and they were totally good. I wrote a little tune and I rehearsed it with him. He was going to appear in front of this great crowd and they were all going to sing this chant. He was delighted with it and so was I. And then they got behind in the shooting and they had to cut the whole thing out. So it was never done. I've never heard him sing except for this *She* thing, and he's really got a very good voice and his words were very convincing."

Conviction is also the word for Robert Day's direction. Lee's former *Corridors of Blood* collaborator never allows the action to hit the heights of camp it could so easily have reached (by comparison, witness Michael Carreras' handling of *Slave Girls*). Day revealed to Mark A. Miller that Lee and Cushing "actually spoke to each other in cartoon characters' voices. It was really something." (The director would next work with both actors on their respective 1967 entries of *The Avengers*.)

After earlier drafts from *Captain Clegg*'s John Temple-Smith, *Dr. No*'s Berkely Mather and Day himself, scripting duties on *She* eventually went to American writer David T. Chantler (1925-2012), who, having cut his teeth on the 1950s *Adventures of Superman* series, ramped up the action and diluted the horror. Chantler also co-scripted one of Cushing's most interesting (and least seen) films, *Cash on Demand*, as well as another of the actor's more obscure works, *Some May Live* (1966).

Another Hammer newcomer is cinematographer Harry Waxman (1912-1984), whose color lighting brings ambience to *She*, as it would to *The Wicker Man*, *Blue Blood* (1973) and *Vampyres* (1974). His best work remains the glacial monochrome he supplied for *Brighton Rock*, *The Day the Earth Caught Fire* and *The Nanny*.

With Bernard Robinson engaged on *The Secret of Blood Island* (filmed concurrently at Pinewood), production design on *She* fell to Robert Jones and Don Mingaye. While their sets are certainly admirable, the extra space at Elstree only serves to expose their deficiencies, unlike the more intimate confines of Bray, which, conversely, had given Hammer's productions a more polished look. (The prop shields glimpsed in the film are hand-me-downs from Elizabeth Taylor's *Cleopatra* [1962]; they can also be viewed in *The Viking Queen* and *Monty Python's Life of Brian* [1978].)

Undeniably impressive, on the other hand, are *She*'s desert locations, even if the shoot there was not without incident. Peter Cushing recalled in his memoirs that John Richardson (as Leo) was laid low after drinking some contaminated water, and Bernard Cribbins (as affable batman Job) suffered a wound "dangerously near his anus" when an explosive charge detonated beneath him. Despite valiantly soldiering on to complete the rest of the film, Bernard later showed Cushing a review of *She*, which stated: "What a pity Mr. Cribbins tried to get laughs by adopting a funny walk …" Worst of all, one of the special effects men had a finger blown off after handling the wired explosive; Robert Day told Tom Johnson and Deborah Del Vecchio that the injured technician merely "stuck [the finger] in his pocket, and yelled 'Get me to the hospital!,'" before apologizing "for his rudeness."

Born in 1934, John Richardson's most notable role was as the young hero of *Black Sunday* (1960). Both he and his co-star from that horror classic, Barbara Steele, were among the last of the Rank Charm School graduates, whose number had included Christopher Lee. (Richardson and Steele would actually appear together four times prior to *Black Sunday* in the non-fantasy films: *Bachelor of Hearts* [1958], *The 39 Steps* [1958], *Sapphire* [1959] and *The Heart of a Man* [1959].) While filming *One Million Years B.C.* (1965), John began a romance with Hammer favorite Martine Beswick, before returning for *The Vengeance of She* (1967)— one of the worst films in Hammer's canon.

Christopher Lee and Ursula Andress are reunited at the Royal premiere of *Born Free* (March 1966).

John Richardson and Lee in *She*

Not much better are his Italian genre outings *Frankenstein '80* (1972), *Eyeball* (1974) and *War of the Planets* (1977). After cameoing as the Architect of *The Church* (1988), Richardson retired from acting to concentrate on photography. He died in January 2021 of COVID-19.

Bernard Cribbins (b. 1928) had previously worked for Hammer in *Visa to Canton* (1960), and with Robert Day on the Peter Sellers prison caper *Two Way Stretch*. Reteamed with Sellers for *The Wrong Arm of the Law* (1962), Cribbins also appeared in the James Bond spoofs *Carry On Spying* (1964) and *Casino Royale* (1966), *Daleks Invasion Earth 2150 A.D.* (1966), *The Railway Children* (1970), Alfred Hitchcock's *Frenzy* (1971) and *The Water Babies* (1976). On television, he gave voice to *The Wombles* (1973-1975), beat up John Cleese in *Fawlty Towers* (1975) and endeared a whole new generation of fans as UFO-spotter Wilfred Mott in *Doctor Who* (2007-2010).

The real star of *She*, is, of course, Ursula Andress (b. 1936). Trumpeted by Hammer as "the world's most beautiful woman," Andress is dubbed in the film by German actress Nikki Van der Zyl, who would later lend her vocal talents to Susan Denberg in *Frankenstein Created Woman*, Jenny Hanley in *Scars of Dracula* and Jane Seymour in *Live and Let Die*. Nikki had previously revoiced Andress for *Dr. No* (1962), in which Ursula's sea-rising entrance, as Honey Ryder, became a key image of 1960s cinema. The night before filming began on that first James Bond epic, NBC broadcast "La Strega," a particularly creepy episode of Boris Karloff's *Thriller*, in which Andress gives one of her best performances as a suspected witch. The following year, she had *Fun in Acapulco* with Elvis Presley, before starring as Dean Martin's love interest in *4 for Texas* (1963) and the snuff TV huntress of *The Tenth Victim* (1965). After making two zany Burt Bacharach-scored comedies with Peter Sellers, *What's New, Pussycat?* (1965) and *Casino Royale* (1966), Ursula was Aphrodite in *Clash of the Titans* (1979) and a guest star in the TV pilot of *Manimal* (1983). (The less said about *The Mountain of the Cannibal God* [1978], the better.) Appearing on Peter Cushing's *This Is Your Life* in 1990, Andress reminded the audience that she'd starred with him as "She-Who-Must-Be-Obeyed," to which Cushing quipped: "Yes, darling, and you still are; what would you like me to do?"

Frippery aside, Ursula provides *She* with its one true moment of horror: Bathing in "The Flame of Eternal Life," her character ages to a wizened husk, then shambles after a horrified Leo. As well as portending the most nightmarish moment of Kubrick's *The Shining*, this scene is a testament to the skills of Roy Ashton—especially when one considers he was called in at the last minute (from *The Secret of Blood Island*) and forced to complete his work in a single day. Rivalling the disintegration of *Dracula*, *She*'s chilling climax lends purpose to the preceding 100 minutes of interminable voyaging, despite Andress being reduced to tears on seeing her beauty submerged.

Ayesha's mortal rival for Leo's affections, Ustane, is played by Rosenda Monteros (b. 1935), whose distinguished credits include Luis Bunuel's *Nazarin* (1959) and *The Magnificent Seven* (1960). After her refreshingly self-assured lead in the Spanish-shot Boris Karloff chiller *Cauldron of Blood* (1967), Rosenda would pretend to be Christopher Lee's granddaughter in *The Face of Eve* (1967).

Elsewhere in the cast, Ustane's father is portrayed by a bare-chested Andre Morell (whose voice belongs to *The Mummy*'s George Pastell), while Lee's stunt double Eddie Powell can be seen as one of Billali's henchmen at the outset.

Despite the usual bad reviews, *She* was released to great success on Sunday, April 18, 1965 (when Cliff Richard was at No. 1 with "The Minute You're Gone"). In the UK, the film was paired with *Pop Gear*—a compilation of performances from such British acts as the Animals, Herman's Hermits and the Beatles, all introduced by disgraced DJ Jimmy Savile. Receiving its first US screening on Wednesday, June 9 (when the Beach Boys topped the charts with "Help Me, Rhonda"), *She* scored again, in August 1969, when re-issued as a double bill with *One Million Years B.C.* ("Hammer Glamour! Hammer Spectacular!"—the studio had originally considered Ursula Andress for their dinosaur epic until Raquel Welch stepped to the fore). On initial release, H. Rider Haggard's novel was reissued as a tie-in with a photograph of Andress on the cover, and a vocalized version of James Bernard's theme tune, performed by Michael Allen, was issued on 45.

Hammer's next attempt to launch a film around a dominant female character met with far less success, when they cast newcomer Carita as *The Viking Queen* (1966). Surprisingly, Christopher Lee turned down the romantic lead in this, allowing American star Don Murray to take his place.

Although 1964 had been something of an *annus horribilis* for Lee (personally if not professionally), 1965 would prove a golden year for the actor, beginning with a return to Amicus Productions.

The Skull
1965

When the Skull strikes you'll scream!

Milton Subotsky had a genuine love for horror. The walls of his apartment were literally lined with genre books, and the obsessive nature of collecting, so close to the heart of every horror fan, is the underlying theme of Robert Bloch's 1945 story "The Skull of the Marquis de Sade." From here Subotsky plucked not only his favorite character name of Maitland, but also the basis for his second Amicus fantasy, *The Skull*. (Milton dropped the last part of Bloch's original title, so as not to offend de Sade's living descendants. Indeed, they took legal action when the film was announced in Paris as *The Dreadful Crimes of the Marquis de Sade*.)

Both *The Skull* and *I, Monster* were written by Subotsky over five days in early 1964 (or so he claimed to Philip Nutman). While *I, Monster* would emerge as a Christopher Lee vehicle in 1970, *The Skull* hit the floor at Shepperton on Monday, January 18, 1965, with Peter Cushing top-billed as Christopher Maitland, a demonology author, and Lee in "Guest Star" mode as a collector of bizarre artefacts, Sir Matthew Phillips (wisely renamed from Bloch's Sir Fitzhugh Kissroy). The two actors were reunited with their director from *Dr. Terror's House of Horrors*, Freddie Francis.

The Skull begins with a pre-credits flashback. In an atmospheric 19th century graveyard, complete with creaking gate and howling wolf, we witness a grave robber sever the skull of the Marquis de Sade. In a nod to Dreyer's *Vampyr*, Francis employs the first of numerous subjective views, this time from inside de Sade's coffin. We are even treated to some stock footage of a flustered owl—previously seen in Hammer's *Dracula*.

Also familiar from that film is Michael Gough, who, following the credits, presides over a modern-day auction at which Phillips and Maitland compete for the sale of some demonic stone figures. Establishing the story's theme of possession, Sir Matthew places the winning bid while seemingly under the statues' spell. ("Why did you want them so badly?" asks Maitland. "I don't know," Phillips responds. "I really don't know …")

Later, grimy dealer Marco (Patrick Wymark) visits the home of Maitland and successfully sells him a biography of the Marquis de Sade bound in human skin. Maitland is less sure about Marco's second offer of de Sade's skull, and confers with Sir Matthew over a game of billiards.

Lee and Cushing admitted they knew absolutely nothing about the game and had to learn quickly in order to shoot the scene (an aghast Freddie Francis remembered: "The only two actors in Britain who couldn't play snooker!"). Nevertheless, they certainly knew how to act. When Maitland questions the authenticity of the skull, Phillips responds: "It's genuine enough."

"Well, how could you possibly know that?"

"Because, my dear fellow, it was stolen from me. Brandy?"

While advising Cushing against the skull, Lee brings great credibility to lines like: "[De Sade] was possessed by an evil spirit, a spirit that still inhabits the skull …" He goes on to describe "those who use its power" as: "Invisible beings, spirits from a strange, evil world. Sometimes I used to hear them calling me …" The temptation for an actor here would be to get carried away by the lines, declaiming and gesticulating wildly, as Lee himself had done exactly 10 years earlier in *Alias John Preston*. But he had learned a lot since then. Lee, instead, fights against his character's words. Forcing down his fear with perfectly applied control, he brings an authentic sense of terror to his scenes.

The centerpiece of *The Skull* is a Kafkaesque dream sequence which, while recalling Orson Welles' *The Trial* (1962), also points the way forward to the surreal approach taken by Roger Corman's *The Trip* (1967), or cult TV shows like *The Avengers* and *The Prisoner* (1966-1967). Both Maitland's nightmare and the mostly wordless action that follows was improvised by Freddie Francis on-set when Subotsky's shooting script came in at a scant 53 pages (the rule of thumb for screenplays is that one page equals one minute of screen time). Consequently, Milton told John Brosnan that the "final 25 minutes" of *The Skull* were assembled in the editing room from "teeny trims and bits and pieces of film." While there is, perhaps, some exaggeration to this statement, post-production *was* tangled enough to preclude Francis from joining Cushing on Amicus' next production, *Dr. Who and the Daleks*—which went before the cameras on Friday, March 12, 1965, under the guidance of Gordon Flemyng.

Although a terrific showcase for the expressive range of Cushing, *The Skull*'s lengthy, dialogue-free scenes do seem rather overstretched, becoming, as a result, quite soporific and tedious. In fact, the drifting camerawork and billowing curtains on display bring to mind similar dream-like passages from *The Whip and the Body*.

In essence, the second half of *The Skull* becomes an extended music video for Elisabeth Lutyens' nerve-jangling themes, while also demonstrating its director's powers of invention. Francis worked closely with his cameraman John Wilcox (they would eventually complete nine films together, including *The Evil of Frankenstein*, *Hysteria* and *Legend of the Werewolf*) and the subjective camerawork they devised involved the director shooting through a giant skull replica while being pushed about on roller skates. Prefiguring the point-of-view cinematography of slasher classics like *Black Christmas* (1974) and *Halloween* (1978), Francis would recreate the effect, to again demonstrate rampant evil, for his next Lee and Cushing opus, *The Creeping Flesh*.

Christopher Lee as Sir Matthew Phillips in *The Skull*

The Loneliness of Evil

But what of the skull itself? Roy Ashton told Richard Klemensen (in *LSoH* #4) that the titular cranium was one he had used on *Paranoiac* (over which he had built-up the decayed features of the corpse seen in the film). Freddie Francis remembered the prop and had his hairdresser pick it up from Bray. Another leftover was Maitland's study, which was a standing set from John Schlesinger's *Darling* (1964), redecorated with grotesque *objets d'art* by art director Bill Constable and set dresser Scott Slimon.

Having now starred in two Robert Bloch adaptations, Christopher Lee didn't actually meet the author until they were introduced by Forrest J Ackerman at the 23rd World Science Fiction Convention in London, late August 1965. Bloch, who was in the UK to oversee Amicus' production of his script *The Psychopath*, became a frequent visitor to "Lee's elegant and book-filled flat" during his stay. In return, the author would play host to Lee in L.A. when the latter stopped by on completing *The Vengeance of Fu Manchu* in December 1966. In his memoir (which Lee noted was "A joy to read"), Bloch wrote of Lee: "He proved to be an interesting guest, full of amusing anecdotes … His favorite American performer was W.C. Fields, whom he imitated better than [Ray] Bradbury did, and he was well versed in the artistry of Laurel and Hardy." Before we get too excited at the thought of Lee's W.C. Fields impersonations, Bloch also recalled that "Christopher chafed at the bit identifying him as a star of horror films."

Bloch wrote *The Deadly Bees* as a vehicle for Lee and Boris Karloff. The film went before the cameras in December 1965, but with Guy Doleman and Frank Finlay in the Lee and Karloff parts. By all accounts, the two actors were best off out of it as *The Deadly Bees* was another troubled Amicus production, with Freddie Francis rewriting Bloch's script as he went along. The result is 80 minutes of honey-hued tedium that wouldn't emerge until 1967 when paired with Lee's *Theatre of Death*.

Following *The Skull*'s US release on Wednesday, August 25, 1965 (when Sonny and Cher were at No. 1 with "I Got You, Babe"), a tie-in collection of Robert Bloch stories entitled *The Skull of the Marquis De Sade* was issued by Pyramid Books with a picture of Cushing as Maitland on the front cover. Despite the publication winning a Trieste Science Fiction Film Festival Award for Bloch, *The Skull* would not be released in the UK until Friday, November 4, 1966 (when the Four Tops were at No. 1 with "Reach Out, I'll Be There"). While it would later be paired with *The Psychopath*, *The Skull*'s first British issue saw it form the lower half of a double bill with Daniel Petrie's drama *The Idol* (1966). Incidentally, the skull of the Marquis de Sade *and* one of his whips also turn up in another 1965 thriller, *Bunny Lake is Missing*, this time in the possession of Noël Coward's Chihuahua-gripping landlord.

November 1966 saw Peter Cushing enact another avid collector, this time of Edgar Allan Poe, in Robert Bloch's *Torture Garden*. According to Allan Bryce, the part of Cushing's fellow Poe fanatic was earmarked for Christopher Lee, but when distributor Columbia insisted on an American star, the role went to future *Dracula*, Jack Palance.

While not the masterpiece some would claim, *The Skull* does contain the greatest cast ever assembled for a Christopher Lee horror movie.

Patrick Wymark (real name: Patrick Cheeseman, 1920-1970) was fresh from playing an army Commander in *Children of the Damned*, a Japanese Major in *The Secret of Blood Island* and the sleazy landlord of *Repulsion*. He would later essay the Inspector on the trail of *The Psychopath* and Oliver Cromwell in *Witchfinder General*. After coming face to face with the *Blood on Satan's Claw* (1970), he succumbed to a heart attack in Australia, where he was due to appear in *Sleuth*—a play from *Wicker Man* author Anthony Shaffer. Wymark was buried in Highgate Cemetery, which had just been used as a location for *Taste the Blood of Dracula*.

Wymark's landlord in *The Skull* is an equally down-at-heel character played by Peter Woodthorpe (1931-2004), an actor who enjoyed a distinguished stage career: As well as starring alongside Vincent Price in the short-lived Broadway musical *Darling of the Day* (1968), he originated the role of Estragon in the first London production of *Waiting for Godot* (1955). More importantly, he was Zoltan, the fairground hypnotist in *The Evil of Frankenstein* and Marcus Allan, the underwear model photographer in *Hysteria*. In 1966, he essayed Quasimodo for a BBC adaptation of *The Hunchback of Notre Dame*, then went up against Peter Cushing's *Sherlock Holmes* in "The Greek Interpreter" (1968). After voicing Pigsy in cult Japanese fantasy series *Monkey* and Gollum in the 1977 animated version of *The Lord of the Rings*, Woodthorpe appeared in *The Odyssey* (1996), along with Christopher Lee.

Peter Cushing's wife, Jane, is played by another classical thespian, Jill Bennett (1931-1990), who, in real life, endured a vituperative matrimonial life with playwright John Osbourne. As Calpurnia, bride to *Julius Caesar* (1969), she would be tortured by visions of Christopher Lee's Artemidorus, while her other screen credits include Aunt Pen in *The Nanny*, Mia Farrow's sister-in-law in *Full Circle* (1976), a Bond villainess in *For Your Eyes Only* and an assistant to a Frankenstein-like professor in *Britannia Hospital* (1981). The director of the latter, Lindsay Anderson, scattered Jill's ashes into the River Thames following her suicide from a barbiturate overdose.

Another victim of *The Skull*, Dr. Londe, is played by George Coulouris (1903-1989). The British actor's career had begun Stateside as a member of Orson Welles' Mercury Theatre, where he starred alongside Vincent Price in the 1938 productions *Heartbreak House* and *The Shoemaker's Holiday*. In July of the same year, Welles cast Coulouris as Jonathan Harker for his CBS radio adaptation of *Dracula* (who could forget his terrible cry: "I'm alone in the castle! I'm *alone!*"), which, in turn, led to his acclaimed performance as Walter Parks Thatcher, guardian to *Citizen Kane* (1940). After such auspicious beginnings, Coulouris returned to Britain where roles in *The Man Without a Body* (1957), *Womaneater* and *Fury at Smugglers' Bay* awaited. He later met grisly deaths in both *Blood from the Mummy's Tomb* and *Tower of Evil*. The latter also features Anna Palk (1941-1990), who can be seen as Cushing's maid in *The Skull*. She would enjoy more substantial roles in *The Earth Dies Screaming* and *The Frozen Dead* (1966).

The Skull is brought to Dr. Londe by April Olrich (1933-2014), who had kicked Christopher Lee's shin in *The Battle of the River Plate*. April's final movie was *Supergirl* (1983), in which she can be glimpsed as one of Faye Dunaway's party guests; the scene takes place in a disused ghost train festooned with glowing skulls.

After his gavel-banging turn in *The Skull*, Michael Gough reteamed with Freddie Francis at Amicus for *They Came from Be-

yond Space*, in which he played the Master of the Moon. The actor would be far better served by TV roles as "The Celestial Toymaker" (1966) in *Doctor Who*, the March Hare in Jonathan Miller's beautiful *Alice in Wonderland* and the store manager in *Journey to the Unknown*: "Eve."

Elsewhere in *The Skull*, Patrick Magee (1922-1982) can be glimpsed as a police surgeon. The Irish actor, who had just gifted *Séance on a Wet Afternoon* with a strong cameo (as the Superintendent with a part-time interest in psychical research), was a favorite of playwrights Samuel Beckett—who wrote *Krapp's Last Tape* for him—and Harold Pinter—for whom he starred as McCann in *The Birthday Party*. Resembling Boris Karloff's Mord the Executioner, from *Tower of London* (1939), with modern dress and hair, Magee reprised his sinister McCann for Amicus' 1968 movie version, directed by a pre-*Exorcist* William Friedkin. Shortly after making *The Skull*, Patrick won a Tony Award for playing the Marquis de Sade himself in *Marat/Sade*—a harrowing characterization preserved on film in 1967. Magee's genre credits include the depraved Alfredo in *The Masque of the Red Death*, the sinister Minister in *The Fiend* and two vengeful characters: Blind George Carter in *Tales from the Crypt* and the writer, Mr. Alexander, in *A Clockwork Orange*. He also seemed to specialize in dubious men of science, as Dr. Henderson in *Die, Monster, Die!*, Dr. Falkenberg in *Demons of the Mind*, Dr. Rutherford in *Asylum* and Dr. Whittle in *And Now the Screaming Starts!* (One of his most haunting performances was as the scientist who believes he's turning into a wolf for "What Big Eyes," an episode of Nigel Kneale's *Beasts* [1976].) Magee's final films, all made in 1980, were *The Monster Club* (as a ghoul), Lucio Fulci's *The Black Cat* (as a psychic Professor) and *The Strange Case of Dr. Jekyll and Miss Osbourne* (as a lecherous General).

The Skull ends with Nigel Green, as Inspector Wilson, stating that the supernatural couldn't possibly exist, "not in this day and age," while unknowingly being observed through gaping sockets. Green had previously appeared alongside Cushing in *Sword of Sherwood Forest*, as Little John, and *The Man Who Finally Died* (1962), as another policeman, but immediately after *The Skull*, he would go on to his most notable collaboration with Christopher Lee.

The Face of Fu Manchu
1965

The Brides of Fu Manchu (1966)
The Vengeance of Fu Manchu (1966)
The Blood of Fu Manchu (1967)
The Castle of Fu Manchu (1968)

The world shall hear from me again!

Imagine a person, tall, lean and feline, with a brow like Shakespeare and a face like Satan …
—Sax Rohmer's description of Fu Manchu.

In those days, Christopher was the horror star.
He was the Boris Karloff of his day.
—Harry Alan Towers (*The Dark Side #195*).

The Skull wrapped on Friday, February 19, 1965. The following day, Christopher Lee began filming *The Face of Fu Manchu* in Ireland. The actor had been unsuccessfully trying to interest Hammer in buying the rights to Sax Rohmer's Fu Manchu stories ever since his turn as Chung King in *The Terror of the Tongs*. It wasn't until the books were reprinted with great success in the early 1960s, however, that Harry Alan Towers (1920-2009), at Hallam Productions, took note.

Christopher Lee catches up on his reading.

Towers was an ex-child-actor of the London stage who switched to writing in the 1940s, firstly on radio, where he produced scripts for Old Mother Riley and had Laurence Olivier enact *Dr. Jekyll and Mr. Hyde*. Also, during his wireless days, Towers scored a coup with a *Sherlock Holmes* series for which he teamed John Gielgud (as Holmes), Ralph Richardson (Watson) and Orson Welles (Moriarty); the latter also worked on Towers' *The Black Museum* and *The Adventures of Harry Lime*—an audio prequel to *The Third Man* (1948). After progressing to television in the 1950s, Towers entered the film industry with an Edgar Wallace adaptation, *Death Drums Along the River* (1962), and it wasn't long before he turned his attention to the works of Wallace's contemporary.

Sax Rohmer was the pen name of Birmingham-born Arthur Henry Sarsfield Ward (1883-1959), who began his career with the ghost-written memoirs of English music hall comedian Little Tich (for whom he also wrote songs and monologues). Between 1913's *The Mystery of Dr. Fu-Manchu* and *Emperor Fu Manchu* (1959), Rohmer published 13 novels and various short stories detailing the exploits of his Chinese supervillain. A major influence on Ian Fleming's *Dr. No*, the character's nefarious schemes often employed such horror devices as zombies, giant spiders and man-eating plants. (Rohmer also had several supernatural works to his name, including *Brood of the Witch Queen* [1914], *The Green Eyes of Bast* [1920] and *Grey Face* [1924], as well as a nonfiction study, *The Romance of Sorcery* [1914].)

Fu Manchu was first adapted for the screen in two British silent serials, *The Mystery of Dr. Fu Manchu* (1923) and *The Further Mysteries of Dr. Fu Manchu* (1924), with Harry Agar Lyons. In Hollywood, the Swedish-born actor Warner Oland—who made a career playing Chinese characters, such as Dr. Yogami in *Werewolf of London* (1935)—starred as Fu in three features: *The Mysterious Dr. Fu Manchu* (1929), *The Return of Dr. Fu Manchu* (1930) and *Daughter of the Dragon* (1931), while Henry Brandon—the villain of Laurel and Hardy's *Babes in Toyland* (1934)—essayed the character in Republic's 15-part serial *Drums of Fu Manchu* (1940). For television, John Carradine lent his talents to an unaired pilot, *The Adventures of Dr. Fu Manchu* (1952), which became a 1956 series with Glen Gordon.

The most significant adaptation before Christopher Lee took over, though, was Boris Karloff's *The Mask of Fu Manchu*, made at MGM in 1932. Karloff brought a sadistic glee to his performance which was countered by Lee's more measured interpretation over 30 years later. While filming *The Face of Fu Manchu*, Lee revealed, in *Christopher Lee's New Chamber of Horrors*, that he befriended Sax Rohmer's widow "who was most enthusiastic about my portrayal of Fu Manchu" and "told me that she thought I looked very much as her husband had intended." This was thanks, in part, to "the most murderous make-up that any actor could possibly be asked to wear" (as Lee put it in Colin Webb's 1995 documentary *The Many Faces of Christopher Lee*). Taking some two and a half hours to apply, the Chinese make-up was created by Gerry Fletcher, who would later work with Lee on both *Count Dracula* (1969) and *Taste the Blood of Dracula*.

Having bought the rights to Sax Rohmer's stories, Harry Alan Towers then proceeded to discard them and write his own plots under his usual pseudonym of Peter Welbeck. *The Face of Fu Manchu* begins on a strident note with a lightning-infused execution backed by pounding drums. There follows the graveyard abduction of Professor Muller (Walter Rilla, *The Gamma People*) and, later, his daughter Maria (Karin Dor, who next starred with Lee in *Blood Demon*). They are taken to Fu Manchu's lair beneath the River Thames, where he drowns a girl and tuts, "Another suicide." In another instance, Fu brings relief to an exhausted, elderly Professor (Harry Grogan) by hypnotizing the poor man into killing himself. The calm collected manner with which Lee performs these callous acts makes them all the more disturbing.

Fu is aided in his efforts by daughter Lin Tang, who, in the person of Tsai Chin (b. 1933), is just as cold and deadly as her father. Tsai had previously appeared with Lee in *The Treasure of San Teresa* (1959) and played a victim of racism in Basil Dearden's powerful treatise on juvenile delinquency *Violent Playground* (1957), which also starred Peter Cushing. "Asian actors had no opportunities," she recalled of the 1960s to Mark Cerulli (in *Cinema Retro*, Vol 13, #39), "this [Lin Tang] was *my* opportunity. At least I was playing someone powerful instead of a waiter!" After portraying Nurse Lim in Alan Bridges' cozily atmospheric *Invasion* (1965), Tsai was complicit in the shooting of Sean Connery's James Bond at the outset of *You Only Live Twice* (1966) and, 40 years later, could be seen playing poker with Daniel Craig's Bond in *Casino Royale*. (Incidentally, Tsai's brother, Michael Chow—co-founder of the famous restaurant chain Mr. Chow—would play a guard in *The Brides of Fu Manchu* and also has a small role in *You Only Live Twice*.)

Fu's plans to distill the lethal fluid from a rare Tibetan poppy are thwarted by an associate of Muller's, played by Joachim Fuchsberger (veteran of German Edgar Wallace ventures), Nigel Green's Nayland Smith and Dr. Petrie (Howard Marion-Crawford—grandson of supernatural fiction author F. Marion Crawford). As an added attraction, "Guest Artiste" James Robertson Justice (unforgettable as Lord Scrumptious in *Chitty Chitty Bang Bang*) harrumphs in his patented fashion as Sir Charles someone-or-other.

Tasmanian-born director Don Sharp (1921-2011), who was responsible for *The Devil-Ship Pirates*, keeps the action rolling at a rollicking pace with car chases and fist fights galore. Indeed, one critic was moved to describe the film as "Chop-Suey Bond" and the scene in which Fu renders an entire village inert with the use of poisonous gas is lifted directly from the then-most recent Bond film *Goldfinger*. (It also echoes an eerie sequence in *Village of the Damned*, directed by Walter Rilla's son, Wolf.)

Lit in colorful tones by cinematographer Ernest Steward (1910-1990, later to lens *Circus of Fear* and *Dark Places* [1972]), *The Face of Fu Manchu* wrapped on Thursday, March 25, 1965. By all accounts, the Dublin shoot was particularly cold and unpleasant, with flu proving more ruinous than Fu: "Walter Rilla almost died," Lee wrote in his autobiography, while he himself fell prey to an ear infection, "which has given me constant nausea and loss of balance" (as Lee reported to his fan club).

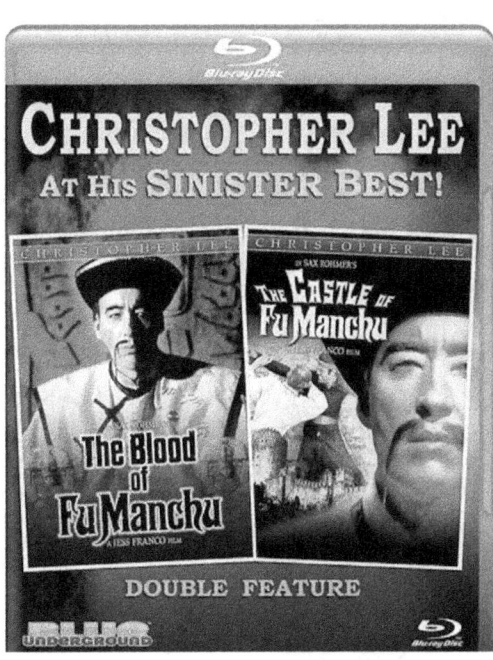

Nevertheless, *The Face of Fu Manchu* is easily the strongest of the series and was a hit when released on Sunday, October 24, 1965. The *New York Times* didn't like it, though. Calling the film "about as frightening as Whistler's Mother," critic Howard Thompson went on to write: "Christopher Lee, as the old evil one, complete with waxy moustache, looks and sounds like an overgrown Etonite." Despite this, posters of Lee in character were plastered around New York's subways during the 1965 election, declaring "Fu Manchu for Mayor" ("I think I got a few votes," Lee quipped in *The Many Faces of Christopher Lee*). In another tie-in, Boston garage band the Rockin' Ramrods released a single, "Don't Fool with Fu Manchu," which features riffs cribbed from Richard Berry's "Louie, Louie" and lyrics like: "He'll slip poison pizza in your fortune cookie."

But worse than poison pizza was to come. "*Brides of Fu Manchu* was tosh," Lee recorded in his memoirs. Actually, the inevitable sequel—although, admittedly, a lesser effort than *Face*—still has certain aspects in its favor, such as a typically arresting opening sequence wherein one of Fu's victims is suspended over a snake-pit by her hair. Another boon is the use of Bray Studios as a location; some of Bernard Robinson's leftover Hammer work seems to have been dusted off and re-used. Fu's lair, for example, looks suspiciously like the Tibetan monastery set from *The Abominable Snowman* and is decked out with Egyptian relics very much like those seen in *The Mummy*.

Filmed between Sunday, January 9 and Sunday, February 20, 1966, *The Brides of Fu Manchu* sees Fu abduct 12 young women so that their husbands or fathers (all eminent scientists) will help him build a death ray. In a publicity ploy very much of its time, Lee, accompanied by his wife, selected the European starlets that would play his "brides." The one professional actress among the throng is Carole Gray (b. 1940), who was very much the scream queen of the day, having starred in *Devils of Darkness*, *Curse of the Fly* and *Island of Terror*. A former dancer (she had played Cliff Richard's girlfriend in *The Young Ones* [1961]), Carole disappeared from the acting world at the end of the 1960s.

Don Sharp returns to helm the fast-paced comic book action, and Ernest Steward is also back with his eye-popping color. However, Nigel Green—who best befits the "lean bronzed features" described by Sax Rohmer for Nayland Smith—was busy in Hollywood (on William Castle's *Let's Kill Uncle*) and, thus, found himself replaced by Douglas Wilmer (1920-2016).

Wilmer, who had appeared with Green in *Jason and the Argonauts*, was also the golden-masked Grand Vizier in *The Golden Voyage of Sinbad* (1972), Fanning, art expert to James Bond, in *Octopussy* and *Sherlock Holmes* in the 1964-1965 BBC series. (Peter Cushing took over the role in 1968, and both actors later starred together in *The Vampire Lovers*.)

As Nayland Smith, Wilmer would continue the Holmes and Watson dynamic with Dr. Petrie: Howard Marion-Craw-

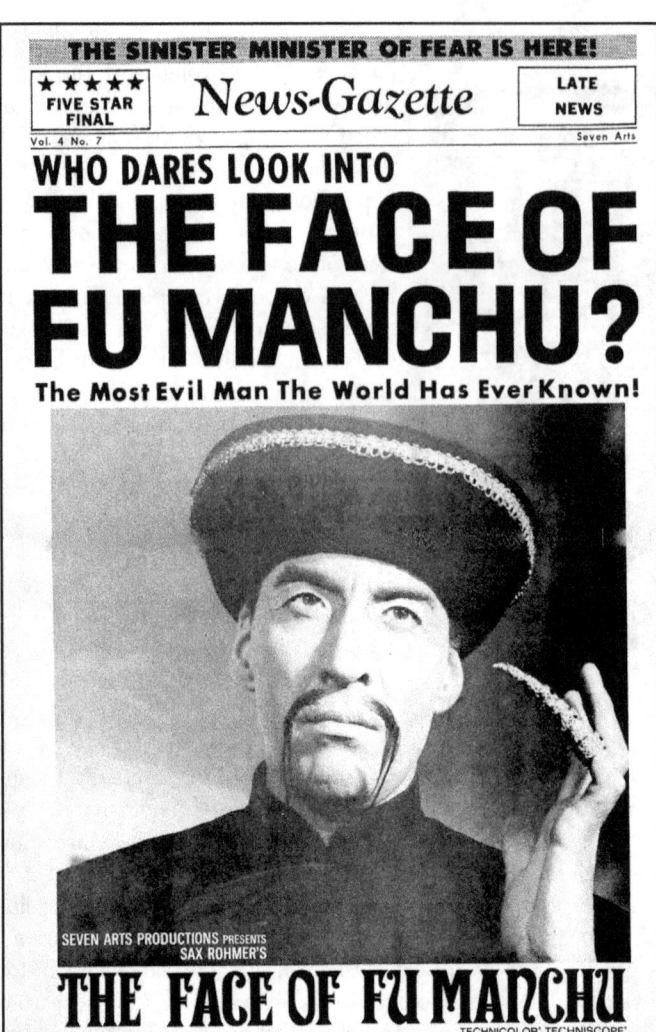

A pressbook flyer created for the first *Fu Manchu*.

ford (1914-1969), incidentally, was one of the few actors to have played both Holmes *and* Watson: He enacted the former in a 1948 radio drama and the latter to Ronald Howard's *Sherlock Holmes* in the TV series of 1954-1955—the Mill Creek Entertainment DVD release of which features brief introductions by Christopher Lee, taken from a 1985 documentary, *The Many Faces of Sherlock Holmes*.

Following its release on Friday, December 16, 1966, *The Brides of Fu Manchu* suffered the usual bad reviews, not least from Christopher Lee, who told his fan club that, after viewing the movie, he "came out of the cinema in a mood of extreme depression." Not even the *New York Times* could top that. Nevertheless, Lee agreed to sign on for three more sequels, each of lessening quality.

Playing a kidnapped scientist in *The Brides of Fu Manchu* is Rupert Davies (1916-1976), who had last appeared with Christopher Lee in *The Traitor*. The two men would become more frequent co-stars from now on, beginning with their next Harry Alan Towers collaboration: In mid-September 1966, Lee embarked to Hong Kong for his cameo in *Five Golden Dragons*, a lackluster crime adventure with a wasted all-star cast, including Klaus Kinski, George Raft and Brian Donlevy. After a cool entrance in trilby and shades, Lee is next seen seated round a table with his fellow "dragons" wearing a ludicrous mask, the removal of which upsets the flap at the back of his toupée, providing the movie with its sole frisson. Happier moments were spent backstage, where Lee chatted to Donlevy's wife, Lillian, about her former husband—Bela Lugosi.

Lee remained in Hong Kong for *The Vengeance of Fu Manchu*, which began filming in October 1966, under the guidance of *Five Golden Dragons'* director Jeremy Summers (1931-2016).

Summers (whose father, Walter, directed *The Dark Eyes of London*) had earlier infused the verisimilitude of working-class Liverpool with the breezy pop of Gerry and the Pacemakers for *Ferry Cross the Mersey* (1964), but was less successful at marrying the mysteries of the ancient Orient to the early 20th century. Actually, the most horrifying thing about *The Vengeance of Fu Manchu* occurred offscreen, when, as Lee recalled to Robert Pohle and Douglas Hart, a pushy extra at the Run Run Shaw studios was chased down the road and murdered by his colleagues.

The film itself begins on a promising note, with Lee doling out varied (*fictional*) executions, including a rather nasty beheading, but then devolves into familiar territory with the kidnapping of a scientist and his daughter. This time, in a nod to John Frankenheimer's just-released *Seconds*, Fu commands Dr. Lieberson (Wolfgang Kieling) to give one of his henchmen the likeness of Nayland Smith (Douglas Wilmer again).

There's a marvelous sequence which sees Lee bite his lower lip in suspense as he awaits the success of his experiment. Once the bandages are removed, the Smith replica, with a face crisscrossed by surgical scars, resembles Raymond Massey's Boris Karloff-clone in *Arsenic and Old Lace* (1941). What could have been an interesting plot point, however, is not exercised to its fullest potential and, aside from a fireside throttling, Smith's pasty-faced facsimile is given nothing else to do but stand trial with robotic indifference.

Much better is the cinematography of John von Kotze (1928-1986), whose vivid colors really snap from the screen. (Von Kotze had been an assistant cameraman on such varied movies as *The Third Man*, *The African Queen* [1951] and *Circus of Fear*.) Curiously, on its initial US release in January 1968, *The Vengeance of Fu Manchu* was shown in black-and-white—a bigger mystery than anything in the film.

As for the cast: One of Lee's frequent co-stars, Maria Rohm (1945-2018) is on hand to sing "Where Are the Men?" with the dubbed-in voice of Samantha Jones, while the cigar-chomping Stetson-wearing tycoon Rudy Moss is German actor Horst Frank (1925-1999)—who can also be seen in Jess Franco's *Justine*, Dario Argento's *The Cat o' Nine Tails* (1970) and as the repellent *Whispering Death* (1975), tracked down by Christopher Lee. When Rudy instigates a potential knife attack in Fu's quarters, Lee gives an expression of sly relish, but there's no disguising the fact that *The Vengeance of Fu Manchu* is, on the whole, less satisfactory, and marks the beginning of a slide in quality for the Rohmer series. The entry is notable, though, for being the first of Lee's horror films to feature art direction from Scott MacGregor (1914-1971), who would replace Bernard Robinson at Hammer in 1969.

The promise shown by Jeremy Summers in his early work, such as Tony Hancock's *The Punch and Judy Man* (1962), seemed to evaporate under the aegis of Harry Alan Towers. Further evidence for this can be found in *House of a Thousand Dolls* (1967)—a tedious tale of human trafficking which even Vincent Price can't save—and *The Face of Eve*. Filmed in Madrid, July 1967, *Eve* is a kitsch jungle adventure with Christopher Lee falling out of his wheelchair as retired explorer Colonel Stewart, and Celeste Yarnall (*The Velvet Vampire* herself) plays his granddaughter—a female Tarzan, with perfectly applied make-up.

The Vengeance of Fu Manchu was granted a general UK release on Sunday, December 3, 1967, supported by another Sax Rohmer adaptation from Harry Alan Towers, *The Million Eyes of Sumuru* (1966). This rather fun picture, from *Devil Doll* director Lindsay Shonteff, stars Shirley Eaton (*Goldfinger*) as a female Fu, who owns "disgusting" pictures of Klaus Kinski and turns men into statues. Sumuru returned in *The Girl from Rio*, a bewildering mess which Jess Franco (1930-2013) filmed concurrently with Christopher Lee's fourth series entry, *The Blood of Fu Manchu*, in December 1967. (Retitling her the Black Widow, Franco even inserted shots of Eaton into *Blood* without the actress' knowledge or consent.)

The Blood of Fu Manchu sees Lee's titular villain in Rio, instilling 10 ingénues with a literally blinding poisoned kiss. As intriguing as that sounds, the idea is inexplicably abandoned early on and the majority of the action is given over to bandit chief Sancho Lopez, whose salacious antics would be more at home in a Sergio Leone Western. Lopez is played by Ricardo Palacios (1940-2015), who reappeared with Lee in *The Return of the Musketeers* (1988) and can also be seen with Klaus Kinski in *Star Knight* (1985), with Alice Cooper in *Monster Dog* (1984); and with Paul Naschy in *The People Who Own the Dark* (1973), *Human Beasts* (1980) and *The Night of the Werewolf* (1980).

While Lee's pronouncements as Fu are drearily familiar, a new element is introduced via Richard Greene's Nayland Smith. Unfortunately, once rendered sightless near the outset, he isn't given much of interest to do except stare into the middle distance with a look of mild anguish. Greene (1918-1985) fared much better as Sir Henry Baskerville in *The Hound of the Baskervilles* (1939), and as Robin Hood in both a successful TV series and Hammer's *Sword of Sherwood Forest*. He also starred opposite Boris Karloff and Lon Chaney, Jr. in *The Black Castle* (1952) and was condemned to a painful living death in *Tales from the Crypt*.

First released in August 1968, *The Blood of Fu Manchu* went by various names, including *Kiss and Kill* and *Against All Odds*. Under any title, though, the fifth and final film of the series, *The Castle of Fu Manchu* (1968), amounts to little more than a montage of meaningless images. With Franco again at the helm, the dire tone is set from the very beginning via poor camerawork and mismatched stock footage: Blue-tinted scenes from Roy Ward Baker's black-and-white Titanic epic *A Night to Remember* (1958) are interspersed with a sequence from *The Brides of Fu Manchu*. Later, Dirk Bogarde and Stanley Baker can be glimpsed running from a bursting dam in clips pilfered from Ralph Thomas' 1957 drama *Campbell's Kingdom*.

Chief among those officially hired to appear in *The Castle of Fu Manchu* is Maria Perschy (1938-2004), star of such Paul Naschy horrors as *Hunchback of the Morgue* (1972), *Blue Eyes of the Broken Doll* (1973) and *Exorcism* (1974). Elsewhere, Franco himself turns up in a fez, and future *Lady Frankenstein* Rosalba Neri is an underworld figure with a fine line in snazzy suits. There's also a brief Holmes and Watson-style interaction between Richard Greene and Howard Marion-Crawford on a fishing trip that recalls Basil Rathbone and Nigel Bruce at the outset of *The Spider Woman* (1943).

Lee's scenes were filmed in Barcelona, and the use of Antoni Gaudí's Park Güell as a location is the most interesting thing about the movie. Although made in July '68, *The Castle of Fu Manchu* didn't see release until 1972. Five years later, Lee turned down an offer to spoof the character in John Landis' *Kentucky Fried Movie*.

Back in the 1960s, however, Christopher Lee's portrayals had suffused the cultural consciousness to such an extent that both Fu Manchu and Dracula are among the British institutions which composer Ray Davies wishes to save in his 1968 song with the Kinks, "The Village Green Preservation Society."

Few actors have revived Rohmer's criminal mastermind since then, although Peter Sellers ended his career with *The Fiendish Plot of Dr. Fu Manchu* (1980), and Paul Naschy had a stab at the role in both *Howl of the Devil* (1987) and a comedy short, *The Daughter of Fu Manchu* (1990). Bizarrely, Lee's co-star from *Season of the Witch*, Nicolas Cage, cameoed as Fu for Rob Zombie's faux-trailer *Werewolf Women of the SS*, a segment of Robert Rodriguez and Quentin Tarantino's *Grindhouse* (2006).

Today, of course, the *Fu Manchu* films are seen as a politically incorrect emblem of their times, a problem that Lee himself addressed: "Who could possibly relate Fu Manchu to real Chinese people?" he asked Tom Johnson and Mark A. Miller, before stating: "I played him as a man of great dignity and some charm. Of course, he's a villain, but it *is* only a story. I'm sure no offense was meant, but one can't please everyone. I'm lucky that Transylvanians didn't object about Dracula …"

Belgian poster for *The Brides of Fu Manchu*

Dracula: Prince of Darkness 1965

The world's most evil vampire lives again!

Continental film critics acknowledge the English as the world experts in horror. It's because we're timid. Shyness breeds shadows and shadows breed vampires.—Terence Fisher, "Horror is My Business," *Films and Filming*, July 1964.

Dracula: Prince of Darkness?
I don't even know what that is!
—the film's writer Jimmy Sangster
(to Ted Newsom, *LSoH* #8)

In December 1964, *(Horror of) Dracula* was re-released on a US double bill with *The Curse of Frankenstein* ("Frankenstein spills it! Dracula drinks it! In the screen's greatest double creature feature!"). The massive success of this pairing caused Hammer to turn their thoughts once more to reviving Dracula.

A new distribution deal from 20th Century Fox (who were more than confident that a Dracula sequel would turn a profit) saw Hammer produce four new horrors from late April to mid-October, 1965. (Kicking off with *Dracula: Prince of Darkness*, the others were *Rasputin: The Mad Monk*, *The Plague of the Zombies* and *The Reptile*.) In a bid to cut costs, the films were shot back-to-back on the same sets and designed to run as double bills. (By being responsible for both the main and supporting features, Hammer were assured greater financial reward.) Christopher Lee was lured back into the Count's cloak by the additional promise of *Rasputin*, and he was joined by some familiar faces.

Returning from *The Gorgon* is Barbara Shelley as Helen. "I didn't take a lot of persuading," she told Peter Haining, in *The Dracula Scrapbook*, "because I loved working at Bray Studios which had such a stimulating atmosphere. I also really enjoyed working with Christopher Lee because he is such a good companion and has a very rich sense of humor."

Francis Matthews, who'd last worked with Lee in *Corridors of Blood*, makes a solid hero as Charles. "Christopher Lee was fun," Matthews told Adam Jezard, in *Hammer Horror #2*, "a bit stiff, but my goodness, he was good …"

Charles' wife, Diana, is played by Lee's leading lady from *The Devil-Ship Pirates*, Suzan Farmer (1942-2017). Despite starring roles in the latter and *The Scarlet Blade* (1963), Famer was given a special introductory credit, just prior to *Dracula: Prince of Darkness*, as Boris Karloff's daughter in *Die, Monster, Die!* (1965). Her final film appearance was in Tyburn's first production, *Persecution* (1973).

Helen's husband, Alan, is portrayed by Australian actor Charles "Bud" Tingwell (1923-2009). As well as lending his voice to Gerry Anderson's cult puppet shows *Thunderbirds* (1964-1966) and *Captain Scarlet and the Mysterons* (1967; the titular hero of which was voiced by Francis Matthews), Tingwell starred with Peter Cushing in the aviation mystery *Cone of Silence* (1960), and with Barbara Shelley in *The Secret of Blood Island*. He was most familiar to cinemagoers, though, as Inspector Craddock in all four of Margaret Rutherford's Miss Marple outings. The first of which, *Murder, She Said* (1961), features Thorley Walters (1913-1991), who plays the Renfield-like Ludwig in *Dracula: Prince of Darkness*.

After starring as theater manager Lattimer in *The Phantom of the Opera*, Walters essayed a string of absent-minded characters for Terence Fisher in such favorites as *The Earth Dies Screaming*, *Frankenstein Created Woman* and *Frankenstein Must Be Destroyed*. He was a German violinist who falls prey to *The Psychopath*, a magistrate in *Trog*, the child-like Burgermeister of *Vampire Circus*, an actor working on a Hammer horror-type movie in *Beasts*: "The Dummy" and the paleontologist attacked by a pterodactyl in *The People That Time Forgot*.

Dracula's sinister manservant, Klove, is played by Philip Latham (1929-2020), another cohort from *The Devil-Ship Pirates*, who would make a less-than-assuring doctor in *Hammer House of Horror*: "The Two Faces of Evil." Latham's other credits include *The Monster of Highgate Ponds* (1960), *The Secret of Blood Island* and *Doctor Who*: "The Five Doctors" (1983). Klove would return five years later in the different guise of Patrick Troughton for *Scars of Dracula*.

Not making a comeback in *Dracula: Prince of Darkness*, however, is Van Helsing. Despite his absence, the robust Father Sandor makes for an interesting alternative. A man of the cloth who takes his "earthly pleasures" seriously ("fortunately my calling still allows me the luxury of a warm posterior …"), Sandor is brought brilliantly to life by Andrew Keir (1926-1997). Throughout the shoot, the Scottish actor (and ex-coal miner) spent his evenings taking center stage in Lionel Bart's West End musical *Maggie May* (quite a change from battling vampires by day). Since receiving his first film credit on Hammer's *The Lady Craved Excite-*

ment (1950), Keir had starred with Christopher Lee in *The Pirates of Blood River* and *The Devil-Ship Pirates*, but his most high profile role was as Agrippa in *Cleopatra*. After going on to personify an underground resistance fighter in *Daleks Invasion Earth 2150 A.D.*, he was the rebellious Roman soldier Octavian in *The Viking Queen*, Professor Fuchs in *Blood from the Mummy's Tomb* and the definitive Professor Quatermass in *Quatermass and the Pit* (1967), a role he reprised for BBC Radio's *The Quatermass Memoirs* in 1996. (*Quatermass and the Pit* not only stars Barbara Shelley as the intrepid Barbara Judd, but a *Dracula: Prince of Darkness* poster can be glimpsed on a wall of the underground railway set.)

As well as Christopher Lee, two other *Dracula* actors can be seen in the sequel: George Woodbridge, again as the innkeeper, is joined by John Maxim (1925-1990), an Australian actor who'd made his debut as one of Woodbridge's customers in the first film. This time, he's the coach driver who refuses to acknowledge the vampire's castle. Immediately after *Dracula: Prince of Darkness*, he would play alongside a Dracula robot as Frankenstein's Monster in *Doctor Who*: "The Chase" (the monster's bandaged appearance is clearly patterned after Lee's from *The Curse of Frankenstein*). Maxim also appeared in *She*, *Frankenstein Created Woman* and as a Cyberman in *Doctor Who*: "The Moonbase" (1967).

With Terence Fisher again at the helm, *Dracula: Prince of Darkness* began filming at Bray on Monday, April 26, 1965. Over the six-week shoot, Christopher Lee was required for only 10 working days (the actor was paid on a daily basis). "I did the first Dracula seven or eight years ago," Lee told *Films and Filming* at the time, "and I always mentally said to myself that I wouldn't do another one, purely and simply because I don't wish to be associated entirely with one part …"

Indeed, when Jimmy Sangster was preparing the first sequel to *Dracula*, shortly after its 1958 release, he remembered, in his memoirs, that Anthony Hinds warned him to "not go overboard with Chris Lee." Acknowledging Dracula as "a really magnificent part" to his fan club in November 1963, the actor was more than aware of the character's power; how, for instance, it had so dominated Bela Lugosi's career that the Hungarian was even

Lee puts the bite on Barbara Shelley.

buried in his Dracula cape. Not keen to tread a similar path, Lee busied himself in Europe, as we have seen. Thus, in draft screenplays entitled *The Disciple of Dracula* and then *Dracula II*, Sangster had a vampire named Baron Meinster as the chief menace. Making a brief appearance at the script's climax, Dracula was summoned by vampire hunter Latour to aid in Meinster's destruction (the latter's sins against undead law include taking the blood of his own mother). A rewrite, in November 1959, by *The Hound of the Baskervilles'* Peter Bryan, saw Latour replaced by Van Helsing and Dracula swapped for a horde of demonic bats. When Peter Cushing rejected the idea of his Godly character enlisting the aid of Satanic forces, it was re-used, to great effect, for *The Kiss of the Vampire* (even if some of the rubber bats were toys bought from Woolworths). Ultimately, although Hinds recollected in *LSoH*, that Lee was "asking too much money" to reprise the role, Dracula was out of the picture, eventually known as *The Brides of Dracula*, before the actor could even be offered the part. (Tellingly, in Dean Owen's tie-in novelization, Van Helsing's first name is given as Lee.)

As proven by *The Man Who Could Cheat Death* and *The Two Faces of Dr. Jekyll*, Hammer did not seem to value Lee's star potential at that point—and nor would they until the Dracula sequels of the mid-to-late-60s proved his bankability. As Denis Meikle put it: "Peter Cushing was Hammer's *star*—Christopher Lee was only its monster." Furthermore, in terms of horror history, having a Dracula sequel without the King Vampire was not all that unique. In 1936, Universal also chose to focus on Van Helsing for their *Dracula* sequel, *Dracula's Daughter*, in which the Count is glimpsed briefly as a dummy on a funeral pyre; therefore, it's not altogether unnatural that Hammer would follow suit.

For *Dracula: Prince of Darkness*, however, Jimmy Sangster appropriated an old script he had written as long ago as 1958: *The Revenge of Dracula* came "from an idea by John Elder" (the pseudonym of Anthony Hinds), and Sangster, too, would eventually adopt his *nom de plume*, John Sansom, on the credits. As he revealed in his book *Inside Hammer*: "I was fed up with

Gothic horror movies and felt that my career had moved well past this phase." Accordingly, *Dracula: Prince of Darkness* would be the last Christopher Lee horror film from the influential Sangster; although the two did work together again on the 1980 Hollywood Bond pastiche *Once Upon a Spy*, in which Lee's villain has a shrinking ray *and* a missile-launching wheelchair.

Of his post-Hammer days in LA, Sangster reported (in *LSoH* #8): "Christopher Lee and I see each other occasionally out here. I'll be at a party ... and he'll make a beeline for me and introduce me as the man who wrote *Dracula* and started his career." As well as illustrating Lee's generosity, this anecdote proves that the actor acknowledged his debt to the Count and wasn't afraid to do so in the company of Hollywood's bigwigs.

But back in 1965 (as Anthony Hinds told *LSoH* #10/11): "[Lee] was not very happy," on being handed Sangster's script for *Dracula: Prince of Darkness* and finding that he had no dialogue. "I pointed out that it would save him a lot of time learning lines," said Hinds, "but he was not amused!"

The actor himself told a different story in the 1995 documentary *The Many Faces of Christopher Lee*: "People all over the world who've seen that film have asked me why I didn't speak in it ... The answer's very simple: I'd read the script and the lines were literally unsayable." He goes on to provide such sample dialogue as: "I am the apocalypse!" Although this line was *never* in the *Dracula: Prince of Darkness* screenplay, Lee is not entirely exaggerating: "I am the apocalypse" comes from a speech he refused to say in *Dracula A.D. 1972*, written by Don Houghton.

The infamous "scratch and kiss" scene where Dracula opens a vein in his chest for Diana to sup.

According to Jimmy Sangster: "Vampires don't chat. So, I didn't write him any dialogue." One has to remember that Sangster wrote his original screenplay back in 1958, at a time when Lee was very much Hammer's bogeyman, and a silent monster, like *The Mummy*, would have been very much the order of the day. As Sangster verified, in *Inside Hammer*, once Dracula had established himself as a vampire in the first movie, there was no need for him to open his mouth "except to suck blood." Lee himself appeared to agree with this notion, as he told John Brosnan: "In the book, Dracula hardly ever stops talking. I think he should say something in these films, though when he does speak, it has to be something worth saying."

Such is the eloquence of Lee's movement in *Dracula: Prince of Darkness*, one never misses the dialogue and his silent scenes carry real power, especially the very first one he shot for the film, at Bray's Stage 2 on Wednesday, April 28, 1965: Stemming directly from Bram Stoker's novel, Dracula opens a vein in his torso on which Diana can sup. What could have been a gruesome and perverse sequence is raised to the level of a romantic gesture through Lee's agonized, yearning expression. Referred to in correspondence with Hammer as the "scratch-and-kiss" scene, the BBFC originally demanded that it be removed. "We fought long and hard with the censor a lot of the time," Jimmy Sangster revealed, before going on to state that the BBFC were also particularly squeamish about another set-up taking place in Father Sandor's lodgings: The staking of the vampirized Helen.

As with the destruction of Carol Marsh's Lucy in *Dracula*, Terence Fisher felt it was important to juxtapose the graphic violence of the staking with the calm and release it begets. The result is potent stuff, despite Barbara Shelley accidentally swallowing one of her fangs during the filming of it. "Never mind, darling," she recalled Terence Fisher telling her (in *Greasepaint and Gore*): "We'll do it again in a couple of days when the other fang turns up." To which Barbara replied: "If it ever does show up, I won't be putting that thing back in my mouth."

Shelley gave a more serious insight into her director's methods (to Al Taylor in *LSoH* #7): "He does a lot of psychology, not only of the victims, but of the monsters, and the marvelous thing about it was that you never catch him at it." Indeed, in Stoker's novel, Dr. Seward describes the undead Lucy as being "more radiantly beautiful than ever," which is something that really comes across in Shelley's portrayal. In fact, her transformation from prim, repressed Victorian lady to wild, uninhibited vampiress is among the greatest female performances in horror, ranking alongside Elsa Lanchester in *Bride of Frankenstein*, Simone Simon in *Cat People*, Sissy Spacek in *Carrie* and Kathy Bates in *Misery* (1990).

While Shelley told Taylor that her characterization was based upon the Furies of Greek tragedy, in *Greasepaint and Gore*, she recalled Christopher Lee "laughing to himself out of shot" at her attempts to speak through her fangs, which transformed a simple line like, "You don't need Charles," into: "Hew gon't gleed Kharlz." The aforementioned frivolity took place during scenes filmed upon the Stage 1 Castle Dracula hallway set from Wednesday, May 5. In stark contrast to his comparatively humanized behavior with Diana, Lee is on properly feral form here, providing further proof of his physical skills. Indeed, the actor says far more with his snarling demeanor than Stoker conveys via such theatrical lines as: "This man belongs to me!" Lee's subsequent bound down the stairs and snapping of a sword is an ample demonstration that, in accordance with Stoker, Dracula has the strength of 20 men. Lee's athletic prowess is all the more astounding when one learns that his cloak alone weighed eight stone (or so says the blurb outside Whitby's Dracula Experience exhibit where the garment is currently on display). When those blood-red contact lenses are also taken into account, one wonders yet again at the discomfort the actor must have endured for the role. On a lighter note, Barbara Shelley told *LSoH* that she used to pinch Lee's bottom beneath the cloak; "You terrible woman!" she remembers him purring. (Lee confirmed this in a 1997 interview with Bill Kelley for *Femme Fatales*.)

On Monday, May 17, Dracula's memorable death scene was filmed on the frozen moat surrounding his castle. This marked the first cinematic use of Stoker's notion that vampires cannot cross running water, and the outcome is inventive. The one-and-a-half story exterior set was built just to the left of the studio car park, where Kharis' sarcophagus had taken a slide into the bog for *The Mummy* (long shots of the castle re-use Les Bowie's model from *The Kiss of the Vampire*). As for the "ice," this was a wooden platform painted white and covered with salt. During his tussle with Francis Matthews, one of Lee's contact lenses popped out. When the lens was placed back in his eye, Lee felt agonizing pain as it had not been properly cleansed of salt grains. Nevertheless, as Francis Matthews revealed to Tom Johnson and Mark A. Miller: "Not one word of complaint or blame left Christopher's lips. Despite his considerable pain, he simply carried on ..."

Matthews himself was injured during rehearsals: His fall onto a discarded mallet caused back trouble that would plague him for the rest of his life. In addition, Lee's stunt double, Eddie Powell, almost drowned: Such was the rush to get these things done, no one had foreseen that once the trap door on the "ice" had closed behind him, the stuntman would be plunged into darkness; thus, he struggled to find the oxygen cylinders concealed in the water tank below. Fortunately, Powell was dragged to safety in time and would continue to perform stunts as Dracula, not just for Lee, but also for Jack Palance and Frank Langella (in their 1973 and 1978 incarnations respectively).

A new face at Hammer on *Dracula: Prince of Darkness* was future production manager Christopher Neame (1942-2011), who recalled the filming of the Count's icy demise in his 2003 book *Rungs on a Ladder*. Employed as an assistant to cinematographer Michael Reed, Neame was none too impressed by the "ghastly" screenplay, the "third-world" camera department and the "sets crammed into too little space." This was all before he encountered Christopher Lee, however. The young apprentice became aware of an "affable, large" technician nodding towards the stage door and saying with a grin: "Dad-Drac is among us." Looking over, Neame "gasped," as Christopher Lee strode towards the castle exteriors. Lee "looked nothing short of magnificent," Neame wrote: "At that instant I realized that this apparently clumsy little film company had got all of its values right, and from then on I started to learn the real truth about filming, both creatively and commercially." Neame would stay with Hammer until *Frankenstein and the Monster from Hell* (1972).

Two days after filming his death, on Wednesday, May 19, the vampire's resurrection was staged. Barbara Shelley walked onto the set that day to find Charles Tingwell hanging over Dracula's coffin with blood dripping from his slashed throat. Despite knowing that Terence Fisher was merely filming the Count's revivification, the usually unperturbable Shelley immediately headed for her dressing room to calm down. "I think Terry was rather pleased," she told Al Taylor. In the film itself, when Helen discovers Alan's body, Suzan Farmer provided the resultant scream. ("It came out more like a sea lion," Shelley said of her original noise, which can be heard in the film's trailer.)

In *Rungs on a Ladder*, Christopher Neame recalled Terry Fisher chuckling to himself as he filmed the "blood pouring from the slashed neck." Neame elaborated: "The laughter (unheard by the audience) behind the camera had the effect of taking the weight off the horror scenes, and, to the initiated, it shows in the finished film."

Despite hanging upside down with a bleeding throat, actor Charles Tingwell also enjoyed himself. "I loved doing that film," he told John Harrison, in *LSoH* #33: "It was one of the nicest experiences I've ever had. And it was all very good humored ..."

Nevertheless, most critics were appalled by Dracula's gory revival, which was even gorier in Sangster's original screenplay, detailing a complete decapitation (Klove would fling the head away with disdain). In one of the genre's first histories, *The Horror Film* (1967), Ivan Butler wrote: "One either felt sick, or found the sequence boringly incredible." In fact, Fisher suggests Alan's throat-slashing (as he had done the removal of Kharis' tongue for *The Mummy*) in a way that allows our own imaginations to enhance the horror. (By the time Butler's book reached its third revised edition in 1979, as *Horror in the Cinema*, the author excised his earlier opinion. The fact that Hammer's horrors seemed rather cozy in comparison to the excesses of 1970s genre cinema was illustrated in the same volume by Butler affectionately captioning a still of Lee and Cushing from *Horror Express* as: "Two friends together again.")

Defending the bloodletting, to John Brosnan, on the grounds that it was "a religious ritual," Fisher builds up to the moment by allowing his camera to prowl the castle interiors with ominous stealth; the director even throws in a nod to *Psycho* when Klove is shown silhouetted against the curtains, arm raised for his attack on Alan. Although the "ritual" itself looks ahead to the human

butchery of *The Texas Chainsaw Massacre* franchise (1973-) and the gooey restoration of "Frank" in *Hellraiser* (1986), it's worth remembering that Barbara Steele had been similarly trussed up for a blood sacrifice at the fiery close of *The Horrible Dr. Hichcock* (1962); a piece of business accompanied by a frantic string score recalling James Bernard's *Dracula* music. On *Dracula: Prince of Darkness*, Bernard provides a masterclass on how to score a horror movie, using both sound and silence to increase suspense.

During his mist-wreathed regeneration, as veins and sinews grow from the dust, Dracula looks like a peeled orange, before, in an interesting touch, emerging naked from his tomb. Once clothed, the vampire sires Barbara Shelley on the Stage 2 cellar set. Despite being Dracula's first appearance in the film, this was one of Christopher Lee's last scenes to be shot (on Friday May 21). Thanks to Michael Reed's shadowy lighting, Lee looks especially frightening here and, consequently, this segment reached No. 36 in *The 100 Greatest Scary Moments* (2003), as voted for by Channel 4 viewers in the UK. (*The Wicker Man* came in at No. 34—No. 1 was *The Shining*.)

From Tuesday May 24, location filming took place in Black Park while the Dracula sets were transformed into Rasputin's Russia (or, at least, Hammer's stylized take on it). Among the scenes shot here was the funereal staking which opens the film. Set to a particularly melodic passage from James Bernard, this moment actually takes its precedent from history: In the 18th century, superstitious Europeans really did stake corpses to prevent reported outbreaks of vampirism. The plotline of *Dracula: Prince of Darkness* also reaches back into the mists of time. The idea of travelers being at the mercy of a bloodsucker in a mysterious castle had first been explored by Alexandre Dumas, *pere* for his 1851 play *Le Vampire* (itself adapted from John Polidori's *The Vampyre*). But *Dracula: Prince of Darkness* also houses enough original imagery to have inspired, among others, Mexico's *The Empire of Dracula* (1966), the Spanish-shot *Count Dracula's Great Love* (1972), portions of the hit US TV show *Buffy the Vampire Slayer* (1996-2003), and Germany's *Blood Demon* (1967), with Christopher Lee.

Filming wrapped on Friday, June 4, 1965. Once edited, the movie came in at just under the contractually agreed running time, so the exciting denouement of the previous *Dracula* was tacked on to the beginning. This ingenious afterthought by Anthony Hinds was also welcome in that it reminded viewers

Christopher Lee as the silent Count Dracula

of what had gone before. In return for allowing them to re-use his performance, Hammer paid for Peter Cushing's roof to be fixed.

Dracula: Prince of Darkness was first trade-shown at a press luncheon, on Friday, December 17, 1965, which celebrated "10 Years of Hammer Horror" (marking their first true success in the genre as *The Quatermass Xperiment*). Nina Hibbin, of the *Daily Worker*, was present at the event and reported: "It was sad to look around at the bright and intelligent faces of present and former horror players—like Peter Cushing, Andre Morell, Charles Tingwell, Heather Sears and Oliver Reed—and to dwell upon that prestigious waste of talent. Saddest of all was the contemplation of Hammer's spectacular rise to power and prosperity through 10 years of trading in morbidity, putrefaction and pain …"

The following day, Christopher Lee was recalled to Bray for the filming of a special television commercial; although since lost, a transcript of its wording survives: Amid lightning flashes, Dracula explained his resurrection to the audience: "Now once more, Castle Dracula is ruled by the Prince of Darkness. Do you dare join him there? Do you?" He then flashed a toothsome smile as the film's title rolled up ("New and in Color. The Better to see the Blood … "). Such tactics obviously worked as the movie was a great success when released with *The Plague of the Zombies* on Sunday, January 9, 1966, in the UK and three days later in the US (the Beatles were at No. 1 with their double A-sided hit "Day Tripper/We Can Work It Out" on both sides of the Atlantic). According to Ted Newsom, *Dracula: Prince of Darkness* and *Rasputin: The Mad Monk* were two of only a dozen movies released by Fox in 1966 that actually made a profit. They were also, along with *The Gorgon* and *To the Devil a Daughter*, two of the few Hammer films on which Lee received a portion of the producer's net, although, as he told Bill Kelley in *LSoH* #13 (1996): "It hasn't amounted to much more than several thousand dollars, over the years since."

Publicity for the double bill declared: "From Hammer—the House of Horror," marking the first time that the studio had been identified as such. Meanwhile, the films' American trailer trumpeted, "These are the overlords of death," while reminding patrons. "Boys! Get your Dracula fangs free as you enter the theater!" The girls were handed Zombie eyes. Remembering those cardboard gimmicks, 1960s moviegoer and Waterloo, Iowa resident Ronald Fink wrote in to *LSoH* #33: "Every kid in the theater punched those teeth out and had them slobbering wet before the movie started. Most got thrown on the floor. I'm sure that was a nasty job for whoever cleaned up the theater afterward."

Novelized by John Burke (along with *Rasputin: The Mad Monk*, *The Plague of the Zombies* and *The Reptile*) for *The Second Hammer Horror Film Omnibus* (Pan Books, 1967), *Dracula: Prince of Darkness* was adapted as a comic strip for *The House of Hammer* #6 in 1977 (of which reader Stephen Kay of Lanarkshire wrote: "I thought John Bolton's artwork was … well, I can't think of any words to describe it. Maybe beautiful …"). Later that year, Father Sandor (renamed "Shandor") received his very own comic strip in the magazine. As Dez Skinn wrote in his editorial for *The House of Hammer* #8: "We were so knocked out by the unusual concept of a rifle-toting, horse-riding, vampire-slaying *priest*, that we felt we just had to develop the character further."

After Lee's death, on Thursday July 2, 2015, the Horror Channel in the UK screened *Dracula: Prince of Darkness* in tribute to the actor (on a quadruple bill with *The Devil Rides Out*, *Scars of Dracula* and *To the Devil a Daughter*).

Clips from *Dracula: Prince of Darkness* can also be seen playing on TV in *Vampires* (1978)—a BBC *Play for Today*—and "Crossing the Road and Phoning the Doctor"—an episode of 1970s sitcom *Some Mothers Do 'Ave 'Em*. The latter causes Michael Crawford's hapless Frank Spencer to wonder: "Don't [the Prime Minister's] teeth look different?" But surely the burning question that *Dracula: Prince of Darkness* raises is: Who's Horace Peabody?

French poster for *Dracula—Prince of Darkness*

The Loneliness of Evil

Rasputin: The Mad Monk
1965

Now, at last! The real, shocking story can be told!
—*Rasputin: The Mad Monk* trailer

I hope she hasn't seen the movie.
—Christopher Lee, on being told that Rasputin's daughter, Maria, wanted to meet him (*The Many Faces of Christopher Lee*).

It is the usual nasty Hammer stuff with the emphasis on bleeding stumps.—BBFC reader Frank Crofts comments on the *Rasputin* script (May 21, 1965)

If *Dracula: Prince of Darkness* offered Christopher Lee no dialogue aside from the occasional hiss, *Rasputin: The Mad Monk* more than makes up for this with its baroque script by Anthony Hinds (again, using the pseudonym John Elder). Hinds told *LSoH* that the idea to make *Rasputin* came from actor George Woodbridge, who had just read a book on the subject which he recommended to the screenwriter.

The mysterious and flamboyant character of Rasputin is an actor's dream, having previously been played by Conrad Veidt in the German *Rasputin, Dämon dur Frauen* (1931), Lionel Barrymore in *Rasputin and the Empress* (1932) and Boris Karloff in a TV episode of *Suspense*, "The Black Prophet" (1953). As such, Lee was in good company when donning his wig and false beard for the first day's filming on Tuesday, June 8, 1965 (just four days after *Dracula: Prince of Darkness* had wrapped).

Bernard Robinson's *Dracula* sets were efficiently revamped: The exterior of Castle Dracula, with its frozen moat, became the Tsarina's palace; the interior was used as Rasputin's lodgings and the vampire's crypt was transformed into the Café Tzigane. Also familiar from the *Dracula* film were Lee's co-stars Francis Matthews, Suzan Farmer and Barbara Shelley. Interviewed by Tony Earnshaw in *We Belong Dead* #9, Shelley remembered: "If *Rasputin* hadn't been a Hammer film he [Lee] would have got far more critical acclaim ... he was magnificent." In the same interview, she added that her leading man "used to almost mesmerize me and terrify the Jesus out of me on that film." Also in the cast was Richard Pasco, showing his versatility by playing the disgraced, drunken Doctor Zargo. (Pasco

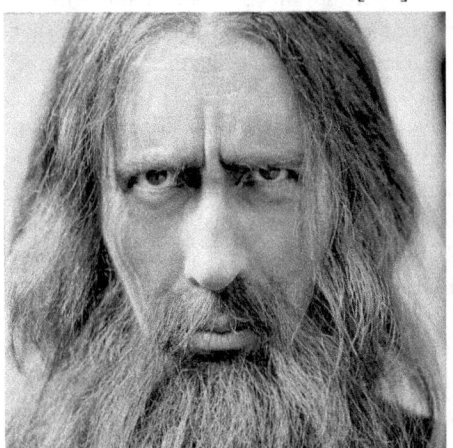

had, of course, previously played the romantic hero of *The Gorgon*, alongside Lee and Shelley.)

As ever, when approaching the playing of a historical character, Lee steeped himself in research. Francis Matthews remembered (to Adam Jezard in *Hammer Horror* #2) that, having completed his role as Dracula, Lee "kept popping into the studios," as the remaining cast finished *Prince of Darkness*, loaded with books. "You'd better read that," he'd say, handing one over to Matthews, "if we're going to do it properly."

Despite this, Hinds' script, for reasons of litigation, had to distort the facts. In real life, Grigori Yefimovich Rasputin was neither mad, nor a monk. Born in 1869, he was a deeply religious Russian peasant, supposedly gifted with prophecy and healing powers. He allied himself with the Tsar and Tsarina, Nicholas II and Alexandra, offering advice to the Royals and healing their hemophiliac son Alexei when the medical profession couldn't. In his 1972 biography *Rasputin*, author R.J. Minney paints a portrait of a gentle man with a wife and three children, whose reputation was sullied by tales of drunkenness and orgies. These legends were reportedly spread by those who were jealous of Rasputin's influence over the Tsar and his wife.

As Christopher Lee pointed out in *The Many Faces of Christopher Lee*, Rasputin "antagonized all the religious fraternity of Russia because of the power he had, which took theirs away. Naturally, he antagonized all the politicians and all the military people ... because through Tsarina ... he ruled Russia. No question about that ... He had these powers that have never been explained." Rasputin himself (quoted in Minney's book) gave a simple explanation as to the source of his powers: "It is not a miracle. All that is necessary is to ask God's help. Prayer can do anything."

Nevertheless, the idea of a debauched holy man in league with the Devil was just the stuff for Hammer horror. Hence, we have the requisite gore (a rather nasty hand dismemberment) and eroticism (the bared back of Barbara Shelley). Hinds' script has Rasputin using his hypnotic powers to further himself and gain access to the Tsarina, even purposefully causing harm to young Alexei so that he can impress the aristocracy by healing him. Hinds does, however, add one interesting element to Rasputin's character, that his sins are a means of feeling closer to God, and Lee brings great force and meaning to lines such as: "I offer Him sins worth forgiving."

During production, Lee told his fan club that Rasputin "is without doubt the most demanding role I have ever undertaken," before complaining of his wig and beard: "I am festooned in hair from morning till night ... as far as I am concerned the Rolling Stones can have it all!"

The film's director was Don Sharp, with whom Lee had previously worked on *The Devil-Ship Pirates* and *The Face of Fu Manchu*. Throughout his career, Sharp was capable of staging unforgettable images: The climactic bat attack of *The Kiss of the Vampire*, the creepy sorceress in *Witchcraft* (1964), and *Curse of the*

Fly's shadowy mutants being just three examples. In *Rasputin*, one haunting moment sees Lee opening frost-strewn windows to cast a searing gaze over the rooftops, his mesmeric influence reaching Barbara Shelley in her bed. (The sequence is none the worse for being a direct lift from Archie Mayo's 1931 *Svengali*.)

Sharp executes a suspenseful game of cat and mouse between Lee and Dinsdale Landen, culminating in a virulent acid attack. (Landen [1932-2003] was the husband of Jennifer Daniel [*The Kiss of the Vampire, The Reptile*]; he would later portray Colonel Masters in *Digby: The Biggest Dog in the World* [1972], Commander Grenville Matteson in *Morons from Outer Space* [1984] and the possessed Dr. Judson in *Doctor Who*: "The Curse of Fenric" [1989].)

Also effective is the staging of Rasputin's protracted murder which, more or less, follows the account of lead assassin Prince Felix Yusupov, who swore that Rasputin refused to die (despite being loaded with poisoned cakes and bullets). Whether true or not, it makes for a suitably thrilling climax, with Lee dragging himself across the floor, wild-eyed, towards Richard Pasco, who cries: "He *is* the Devil! I've tried to kill him. But he won't die!" This action points the way forward to films like *Halloween* and *The Terminator* (1984), whose antagonists also refuse to stay down once "killed." What Hammer don't show is the dumping of Rasputin's body into the frozen River Neva. (They opt for Francis Matthews pushing him out of a window instead, where his body forms a cross on the ice below.) According to R.J. Minney, when the real-life Rasputin's body had been exhumed from its icy tomb, his lungs were found to be full of water, "indicating that he was still alive when thrown into the river."

Francis Matthews, meanwhile, had his own interpretation of the finale. "I made Ivan camp in that scene," he told Adam Jezard. "I said to Don: 'Can I make him look a bit as though he fancies Rasputin?' and Don agreed." Nevertheless, Matthews' big regret was that a titanic fight scene, which took three days to shoot, was cut from the finished movie. ("I was falling over, the sofa collapsed, something fell on me and I was slamming him and he was slamming me. It was wonderful …")

Filming wrapped on Tuesday, July 20, 1965, six weeks after it began, and the movie was graced with a typically adventuresome score from Australian composer Don Banks (1923-1980), who also provided music for *Captain Clegg*, *The Evil of Frankenstein* and *The Reptile*. Paired with the latter, *Rasputin: The Mad Monk* was released by 20th Century Fox on Sunday, March 6, 1966 (a month later in the US). Originally, to "disguise" American cinemagoers "from the forces of evil," free Rasputin beards were "given to guys and gals alike" (blue beards for guys and red ones for gals), inspiring Michael Weldon's droll observation: "I can imagine a matinee audience of bearded kids throwing candy at the screen." Predictably, the critics wanted to hurl things at the screen, too. Typical of their opinions was the one-line critique Leslie Halliwell accorded the movie in his popular *Film Guide*: "Dreary excuse for Christopher Lee to go berserk."

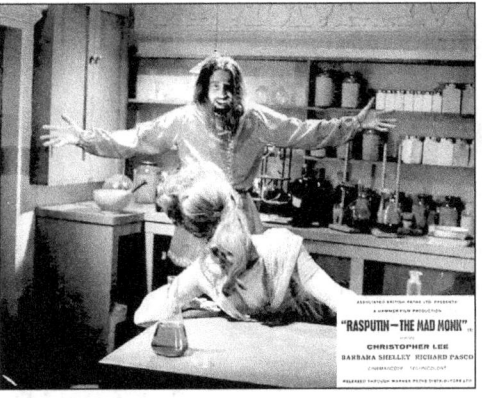

Rasputin terrorizes Sonia (Barbara Shelley).

It is easy for critics to snipe at Hammer, but the company did not have the artistic freedom of today's filmmakers; every splash of blood or glimpse of flesh was observed with distaste by the censor and his scissors, dictating what should go forth on the screen. It is amazing that, despite such opposition, Hammer films stand up so well. But it was not just the shadow of the censor that haunted the *Rasputin* sets. Creative limits were also enforced by Yusupov himself. The surviving assassin had famously sued MGM over their Rasputin picture in 1932. To avoid a similar lawsuit, Hammer allowed Yusupov (and his lawyers) to scrutinize the script and sign every page once it was to their satisfaction. Though some commentators like to carp about the weakness of Anthony Hinds' writing, with such limitations in place, it's a wonder that the final screenplay was filmable at all.

Critics have also sneered at Hammer's presentation of early 20th century Russia. The film, rather, takes place in a convincing fantasy land; that mythical World of Hammer, a milieu once chilling, now cozy, in which the nefarious exploits of Baron Frankenstein and Count Dracula co-exist among various mummies, zombies, and a werewolf played by Oliver Reed. As such, we have the usual Cockney wenches haunting the Café and a coach driver who speaks with the dubbed-in rasp of Michael Ripper.

In his autobiography, Lee described Rasputin as "one of the best [parts] I'd had" and admitted to an "eerie sense of contact" with the film through a childhood meeting with Yusupov, and another of Rasputin's assassins, the Grand Duke Dmitri Pavlovich. The actor recalls being "hauled out of bed" for the event by his well-connected mother. Indeed, Lee acts with every fiber of his being in the role, making great use of his voice and presence. He is just as convincing when bounding into a tavern and roaring appraisals of the landlord's daughter as he is when issuing husky murmurs during the seductive hypnotism scenes. He also uses his hands to tremendous effect, whether placing them on feverish foreheads to cure the ill, or holding them up to his accusers while explaining his power. Similar to the real-life Rasputin, Lee also had a fine pair of eyes, which are in mesmerizing form here. Indeed, he invests the part with such ferocious energy that one fears he may burst through the celluloid at any moment.

After Tom Baker's excellent portrayal of the character in *Nicholas and Alexandra* (1971), *Rasputin* returned in the capable hands of Alan Rickman for the 1995 HBO movie of the same name. Working on the latter was production supervisor Hugh Harlow and first assistant director Bert Batt, both of whom had provided similar duties for Hammer's movie 30 years earlier.

While it may not be a truthful retelling of its subject's life and exploits, *Rasputin: The Mad Monk* succeeds as a richly colored melodrama and contains a first-rate performance from its star.

Theatre of Death
1965

Where acting can be murder.

This building, located in a back street, far from the conventional Paris of the tourists, once housed a church. For the past 60 years, it has sheltered a unique theatrical company, whose stock-in-trade is horror. Together with avarice, murder and mayhem, these are the principal ingredients of le *Théâtre* de la Mort—the *Theatre of Death*.—Christopher Lee's offscreen narration for *Theatre of Death* (in some prints, this is spoken by Julian Glover)

Between 1897 and 1962, Paris' Théâtre de Grand Guignol staged "a nightly round of vile murders, manglings and assorted acts of torturing, fang-baring, acid-throwing …" [in the words of a visiting reporter from *Time*, March 10, 1947]. Although the onstage action would find its truest cinematic equivalent in the splatter fare of Herschell Gordon Lewis (*Blood Feast* [1963], *Color Me Blood Red* [1964] and *A Taste of Blood* [1967]), the French theater also inspired the settings of *Mad Love* (1935), *Murders in the Rue Morgue* (1970) and *Interview with the Vampire* (1993), while Rafaela Ottiano, an actress who had actually performed there, made a startling contribution to Hollywood horror when she starred as the wide-eyed miniaturizer of *The Devil-Doll* (1936).

Christopher Lee brought his own brand of genre acting to the Grand Guignol with *Theatre of Death*. Filmed from Monday, September 27 to Wednesday, November 10, 1965, at Elstree, with London's Lyric Hammersmith standing in for the titular playhouse, the film opens on an alarming title sequence: To the staccato rhythms of Elisabeth Lutyens' score, a bewigged skull with glassy eyeball snaps toward the viewers, before we segue immediately to an onstage beheading. The actress beneath the guillotine is Nicole Chapelle (Jenny Till), protégé of the theater's writer and director, Philippe Darvas (Christopher Lee). We catch up with both at an after-show party, where, in an echo of *Mad Love*, Darvas previews a new play involving witchcraft.

What differentiates *Theatre of Death* from its 1930s predecessor is the color camera work of cinematographer Gil Taylor (1914-2013), who, in concert with first-time feature director Samuel Gallu (1918-1991), employs some interesting angles. A Tarot card reading is viewed through a glass table, for example, and we are treated to a corpse-eye-view from a mortuary trolley. Taylor also brings the hand-held techniques he had developed on *A Hard Day's Night* and uses them to capture similar backstage moments. As well as his influential work on the Beatles opus, the cameraman's other credits include *Dr. Strangelove*, *Repulsion*, *Frenzy*, *The Omen*, *Star Wars* and the 1978 *Dracula*. The New Jersey-born Gallu, on the other hand, was a former opera singer (which particularly endeared him to Christopher Lee), who would go on to helm only a handful of movies, culminating with *Arthur? Arthur!* (1969), a comedy starring Donald Pleasence and Shelley Winters.

While *Theatre of Death* is quite hoary in terms of plot, what with its vampire-like killings and the peephole painting used by Darvas as a spying device, the film does contain some of the juiciest dialogue that Christopher Lee ever had to utter. During a voodoo scene rehearsal, for instance, he roars at the spear-wielding actors, "That's about as frightening as an old lady spearing a cocktail cherry," before rounding on the star of the skit, Heidi (Dilys Watling): "You look about as frightened as a baby with a rattle! Just what the hell are you thinking about?" When Heidi responds that she was thinking of her missed lunch, the tension can be cut with a knife. Darvas takes the spear and hisses: "I suppose you realize that I could *ram* this right through your delicious little stomach!" With his point made, the director sneers: "Don't feel quite so hungry now." This is Lee at his barnstorming best; the actor relishes the unsavory dialogue and makes the scene an unpleasant delight. (Writer Ellis Kadison [1928-1998], who was married to *Invasion of the Saucer Men* ingénue Gloria Castillo, went on to script the Disney fantasy *The Gnome-Mobile* [1966], as well as eight episodes of *The Banana Splits Adventure Hour* [1968-1969].)

Although he disappears from the film after 45 minutes, Lee dominates the movie's first half. Cutting an extremely dashing figure, the actor presents a man who lives and breathes for the theater. His obsessive nature even evokes *Rasputin*, whether he be hypnotizing Nicole, or snarling at "broken-down ballerina" Dani Gireaux (Lelia Goldoni) before a mirror: "I think I'd better tell you just why you're so *unattractive*, both as a woman and as an actress … *Take a look at yourself!* Look at that makeup! It's *ridiculous*! That eye shadow is *grotesque*!" He then smears it across her face: "We're actors and actresses here, you know, not dying swans!" He also tells Dani: "You're only happy in the presence of deformity"—a line which should be addressed to himself. Indeed, Darvas only seems content when sitting down in his shadowy hideaway to look at horrific images, like Fredric March leering at Miriam Hopkins (from *Dr. Jekyll and Mr. Hyde*), the spirit of Astaroth from *The Golem*, or, in a nicely self-reflexive move, a *Dracula* still of Valerie Gaunt pressing her fangs against John Van Eyssen's throat. Although the intention of this scene is to place suspicion in the viewer's mind that the theater director must indeed be the killer, the effect is, rather, akin to watching an enthusiastic monster fan flicking through the pages of his favorite reference tomes. While the aforementioned isn't enough to redeem the arrogant and misanthropic Darvas, he *does* grow tender towards his pet cat, a nice little detail wherein Lee shows, yet again, that his character is not *all* bad.

Clearly on the side of good, Julian Glover (b. 1935) brings a likeable quality to his police surgeon protagonist, Charles Marquis, whose personal quirks, such as a yen for writing fiction, make him far more nuanced than the usual horror heroes. Surprisingly, his relationship with Christopher Lee was just as frosty offscreen. "We took an instant dislike to each other," Glover told Stephen Laws (in *LSoH* #12): "I found him arrogant. It was very unpleasant." Happily, though, in the same interview, he further revealed: "I've worked with [Lee] since and find him charming now, so the fault must have lain with me!" The actor's opinions on the film itself are rather more succinct: "Bit silly, isn't it?"

Christopher Lee as Philippe Darvas in *Theatre of Death*

Writer/director Christopher Lee shows them how to do it in *Theatre of Death* (US title *Blood Fiend*).

Glover went on to play the officious Colonel Breen in Hammer's *Quatermass and the Pit*, as well as icy villains in *The Empire Strikes Back* (1979), *For Your Eyes Only* and *Indiana Jones and the Last Crusade*. In the latter film, Julian's screen wife is played by his real-life spouse, Isla Blair, whom he married in 1968, prior to her performance as Lucy in *Taste the Blood of Dracula*. Glover is also well regarded in cult circles for playing Scaroth, the alien art thief of *Doctor Who*: "City of Death" (1979).

Fresh from playing a less sympathetic lead in Hammer's *Hysteria*, American Lelia Goldoni (b. 1936) would star alongside Donald Sutherland in both *The Day of the Locust* and the remake of *Invasion of the Body Snatchers*. As well as harboring *The Unseen* (1980), she cameos in two disparate exorcism shockers: Jimmy Sangster's *Good Against Evil* (1977) and *The Devil Inside* (2011).

Despite receiving an introductory credit on *Theatre of Death*, Jenny Till (b. 1940) had already done uncredited bits for *The Masque of the Red Death* and *Help!* (1965). She would go on to play Lady Marian in Hammer's *A Challenge for Robin Hood* (1967).

Inspector Micheaud is portrayed by Ivor Dean (1917-1974), who would also essay jaded policemen in *The Sorcerers*, *The Saint*, and *Randall and Hopkirk (Deceased)*. After reappearing with Lee in *The Oblong Box* (1968), Dean was cast as the bodysnatching Burke of *Dr. Jekyll and Sister Hyde* (1971).

Briefly glimpsed in *Theatre of Death* is belly dancer Julie Mendez (1938-2013), who performed similar duties in *She*, *Devils of Darkness*, *The Abominable Dr. Phibes* (1970) and throughout the opening credits of *From Russia with Love*. She had also choreographed Norma Marla's snake dance for *The Two Faces of Dr. Jekyll*.

Paired with *The Deadly Bees*, *Theatre of Death* went on general release in the UK on Sunday, December 10, 1967 (its first US screening, as *Blood Fiend*, came at some point in the preceding month). A stylish and underrated murder-mystery with horror overtones, the film is further notable for housing one of Christopher Lee's most enjoyable performances.

The Loneliness of Evil

Circus of Fear
1965

The most horrifying syndicate of evil in history!

After such splendid fare as *The Skull*, *The Face of Fu Manchu* and *Dracula: Prince of Darkness*, 1965 ended on a damp squib for Christopher Lee with *Circus of Fear*. Supposedly based on an Edgar Wallace story (though bearing no relation to any that I've read), the film was shot back-to-back at Bray Studios with *The Brides of Fu Manchu*. (Both ventures also share leading man Heinz Drache—a veteran interpreter of Wallace.)

Originally announced as *The Man Without a Face*, *Circus of Fear* began its five-week shoot on Monday, December 6, 1965, under the auspices of writer-producer Harry Alan Towers and director John Moxey (whom Lee had last worked with on *The City of the Dead*).

Although the movie starts promisingly with a pre-credits robbery at London's Tower Bridge, once Johnny Douglas' snazzy theme tune has played out, its downhill all the way. The action shifts to the circus, where there is a killer at large. Chief among the suspects, of course, is Christopher Lee's lion tamer, Gregor, who speaks with a gruff Russian accent and wears a black mask to hide his supposedly scarred features. In his autobiography, Lee recalled that his double for the film, a real lion tamer, "gained my great respect when he told me he was terrified of lions." The

actor also revealed that, as the double was "half my height," he had to be shot in close-up, so as to not make him look as though "he'd shrunk through sheer terror."

The circus location was actually Billy Smart's in Berkshire, which had previously played host to the far more entertaining *Circus of Horrors*. Indeed, there is little to say about *Circus of Fear*, other than it is a very dull whodunit, with some awkward shots of Lee's hairy arms grasping for Margaret Lee (no relation). Things pick up only slightly for the climax, which sees Lee running through the same woodland sites he had haunted in *The Curse of Frankenstein*, before plunging to an outlandish death.

There's a lovely performance from Victor Maddern (1926-1993) as the runt of the criminal gang—the kind of role usually essayed by Elisha Cook, Jr. in such Hollywood noir classics as *Stranger on the Third Floor* (1940) and *The Maltese Falcon* (1941). Maddern, who had previously been Donald Wolfit's hunchbacked assistant in *Blood of the Vampire*, is more often seen in comedies, like *I'm All Right Jack* (1959) and five *Carry On*s.

Leo Genn (1905-1978), who turns up as Scotland Yard detective Elliott, was a qualified barrister, who laid down his gavel for a successful acting career. As well as being the leading man of Hammer's wartime drama *The Steel Bayonet* (1956), Genn gave electro-shock treatment to Olivia de Havilland in *The Snake Pit* (1948), then earned a Best Supporting Actor Oscar-nomination for playing Petronius in *Quo Vadis* (1951). Interviewed on Gary Svehla's *A Legacy of Horror and Terror* DVD, Christopher Lee claimed to have completed some uncredited stunt work as a chariot driver on this Roman epic. Lee also went unbilled as the voice of the mysterious Mr. U.N. Owen in Harry Alan Towers' *Ten Little Indians* (made the same year as *Circus of Fear*), in which Genn was General Mandrake, one of the movie's all-star victims. Between those assignments, Genn's Johnny Solo owned the Pink Flamingo nightclub in *Too Hot to Handle* (1959), where Lee's shady emcee introduces Jayne Mansfield. The two men would next appear together in *The Bloody Judge* (1969).

Elliott's supervisor is portrayed by Cecil Parker (1897-1971), who'd been Dr. Gratton to Karloff's *The Man Who Changed His Mind*, the adulterous Mr. Todhunter in Hitchcock's *The Lady Vanishes* and the British Prime Minster of *A Study in Terror*.

Cast at the very last minute as Gregor's "niece" was Suzy Kendall (b. 1937), who would later star in such thrillers as Peter

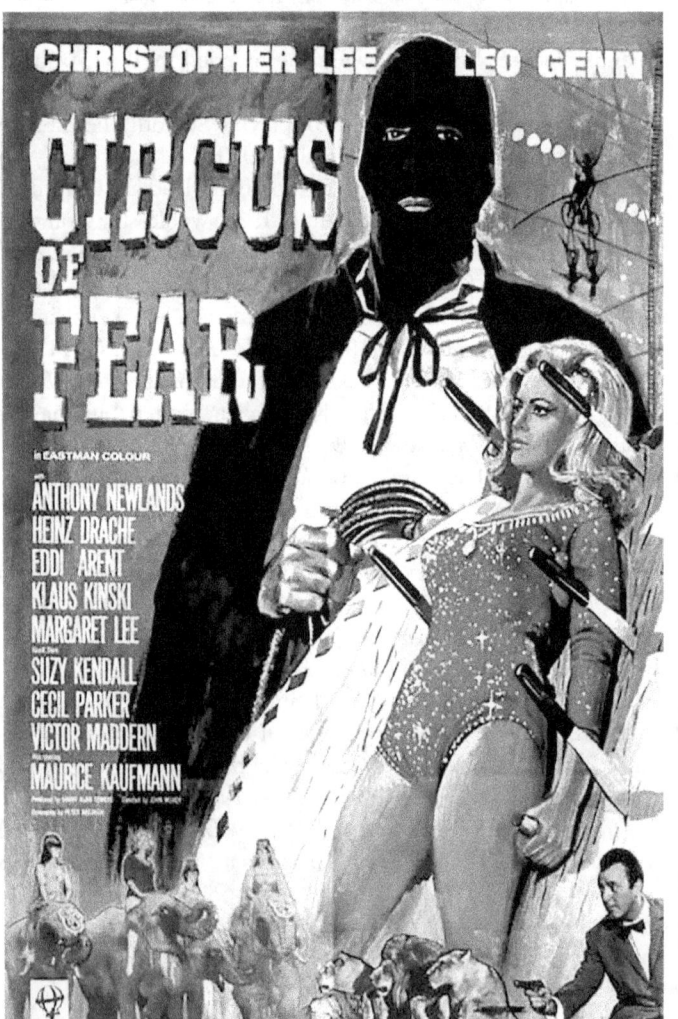

Collinson's *The Penthouse* (1967), Dario Argento's *The Bird with the Crystal Plumage* (1969) and Sergio Martino's *Torso* (1972). The circus' tempestuous knife thrower, Mario, is Maurice Kaufmann (1927-1997), veteran of *Gorgo, Fanatic* and *The Abominable Dr. Phibes*. At the time he made *Circus of Fear*, Kaufmann was married to *Avengers* (and future *To the Devil a Daughter*) star Honor Blackman.

Another familiar face is that of Skip Martin (1928-1984) as the blackmailing dwarf, Mr. Big. Following an uncredited bit in *Corridors of Blood*, Skip's more substantial genre credits include the vengeful Hop Toad in *The Masque of the Red Death*, the creepy, clown-faced compere of *Vampire Circus* and Michael Gough's malicious sidekick in *Horror Hospital* (1972).

Also on hand to skulk about, with proverbial cigarette in mouth, is Klaus Kinski (1926-1991), who had previously starred with Christopher Lee in two 1961 Edgar Wallace adaptations. Shot in Hamburg, *The Devil's Daffodil* and *The Secret of the Red Orchid* saw Lee enact, respectively, a Chinese detective and an American FBI agent, both in German. As well as appearing in borderline Wallace horrors *The Avenger* (1960), *Dead Eyes of London* (1961), *Creature with the Blue Hand* (1967) and *Double Face* (1969), Kinski was a mainstay of Spaghetti Westerns, most memorably as the Hunchback of Sergio Leone's *For a Few Dollars More* (1965), wherein Lee Van Cleef strikes a match off his hump, *A Bullet for the General* (1966, with Martine Beswick) and Sergio Corbucci's *The Great Silence* (1967). According to his colorful memoir, *Kinski Uncut*, the Polish-born actor grew up in poverty, before becoming a prisoner of war and, later, a psychiatric patient. While the former stood him in good stead for his scene as a belligerent anarchist in *Doctor Zhivago* (1965), the latter would inform his next contribution to a Christopher Lee horror outing—Renfield in *Count Dracula*.

Although first issued in truncated black-and-white form as *Psycho-Circus* for a May 1967 US release, *Circus of*

German poster for *Circus of Fear*

Fear formed the lower half of a double bill with Hammer's superior *Quatermass and the Pit* in the UK from Sunday, November 19, 1967. By Christmas, no fewer than four of Lee's horror movies were vying for attention in London's West End (the others being *Theatre of Death, The Vengeance of Fu Manchu* and *Night of the Big Heat*). Also on release at that time was *Berserk*, the Big Top murders of which were again staged at Billy Smart's, but handled with a little more pizzazz. The film's star, Joan Crawford, had initiated her career, 40 years previously, with another circus melodrama, *The Unknown* (1927), one of Lon Chaney's greatest vehicles. The same cannot be said, alas, for Christopher Lee and *Circus of Fear*—a film which succeeds only in proving that a decent cast and director cannot make a good movie from a bad script.

The Avengers: Never, Never Say Die 1967

"The Interrogators" (1968)

In 1967, Christopher Lee was in the running to play a guest villain in ABC's popular *Batman* series, but the opportunity never came to pass. Perhaps the producers felt that Lee's surly screen persona would be at odds with the show's camp style; although George Sanders, one of Lee's role models, acquitted himself brilliantly as Mr. Freeze, and Vincent Price was an absolute hoot as Egghead. While we can only wonder at how Lee might have fared in Gotham City, we can, at least, treasure his two guest appearances on another show broadcast by ABC in the US.

In his autobiography, Lee called *The Avengers*, "the best of all television series." Another fan was Jack Torrance, from Stephen King's 1977 novel *The Shining*, who "would skip a party to stay home and watch" it—if only it had been playing the night Jack decided to pursue his family with a mallet. The brainchild of *Doctor Who* creator Sydney Newman (1917-1997), *The Avengers* began life as a gritty black-and-white ITV crime drama in 1961. Under producers Brian Clemens (1931-2015) and Albert Fennell (1920-1988), however, it soon evolved into a fantastic and surreally inventive show, whose villains' nefarious plots borrowed heavily from the iconography of horror and science fiction cinema. As, too, did the choice of guest stars.

By February 1967, when Christopher Lee arrived at Elstree to film his appearance in "Never, Never Say Die" (the 10th episode of season five), *The Avengers* was shot on color film (in a successful bid for US ratings) and had already featured Barbara Shelley, Andrew Keir, Nigel Green and Julian Glover. The name of Lee's character, Dr. Frank N. Stone (creator of human duplicates) is a good indicator of both the show's waggish humor and its reliance on horror references. Indeed, the series' dapper crime-fighter, John Steed, even refers to Stone and his robotic doppelganger as "Jekyll and Hyde."

The actor beneath Steed's familiar bowler hat is Patrick Macnee (1922-2015), whom Lee had first met when they were both boarders at Summer Fields prep school (Christopher had to concede that Patrick was the best thespian on campus, playing the title role in *Henry V*, while he looked on as the Dauphin). Like Lee, Macnee would go on to small roles in *Hamlet* and *The Battle of the River Plate*. He even worked for Hammer, on *Dick Barton at Bay* (1948), and with Boris Karloff in an episode of *The Veil*. Despite appearances in *Scrooge* (1951), *Alfred Hitchcock Presents* and *The Twilight Zone*, it wouldn't be until *The Avengers* came along that Patrick received the recognition he'd long deserved.

When the series wrapped in 1969, Macnee indulged in some very *Avengers*-style action as Major Longbow in the scrappy but interesting *Incense for the Damned*, then faced further vampiric shenanigans for Dan Curtis' *Dead of Night* (1976). He was also Dr. George Waggner, patron of lycanthropes, in *The Howling* (1980); Dr. Stark in *Alien* spoof *The Creature Wasn't Nice* (1981); band manager, Sir Denis Eton-Hogg, in *This Is Spinal Tap* (1983); supernatural expert, Sir Wilfred, in *Waxwork* (1987) and *Waxwork II: Lost in Time* (1991); Professor Plocostomos, in *Lobster Man from Mars* (1988) and the Red Death in Roger Corman's 1989 remake, *Masque of the Red Death*. In addition to hosting *Patrick Macnee's Ghost Stories* (1997), he played Watson to both Christopher Lee (in *Sherlock Holmes: The Golden Years*) and Roger Moore (for *Sherlock Holmes in New York* [1975])—the pair would re-enact a Holmes and Watson-style relationship in Moore's final James Bond outing, *A View to a Kill*.

On *The Avengers*, Macnee was partnered most adeptly by Diana Rigg (1938-2020). At a time when actresses were poorly served by dramatic screen roles, Rigg's self-assured and witty Emma Peel emerges as one of the greatest female characters in '60s TV. Just as her predecessor, Honor Blackman, had been plucked from *The Avengers* to play the feisty Pussy Galore in *Goldfinger*, the James Bond producers also took note of Diana, casting her as headstrong Teresa di Vicenzo in *On Her Majesty's Secret Service* (she had previously starred with the film's villain, Telly Savalas, in *The Assassination Bureau*). After essaying Helena in *A Midsummer Night's Dream* (1968), Rigg was Portia in *Julius Caesar* (1969)—but doesn't appear in Christopher Lee's one brief scene. She does, however, play Vincent Price's daughter in *Theatre of Blood* (1972); following which, Hammer considered her for the role of 18th century pirate Anne Bonny in *Mistress of the Seas*, but this proposed biopic was never made. Instead, Diana enjoyed a Tony Award-winning stage career, while taking time out to star as Lady Holiday in *The Great Muppet Caper* (1980), Miss Hardbroom in *The Worst Witch* (1986), and the Evil Queen in *Snow White* (1987). Honored with a Damehood in 1994, Rigg unleashed "The Crimson Horror" on *Doctor Who* (2012), before earning a whole new legion of fans with her Emmy-nominated turn as the Queen of Thorns in *Game of Thrones* (2013-2017).

Written by series regular Philip Levene (1926-1973), who would later provide the story for Lee's *Diagnosis: Murder* (1974), "Never, Never Say Die" was directed by Robert Day (of *She* and *Corridors of Blood*). The episode opens on Dr. Stone's silver-wigged and black-coated replicate stomping through muddy fields, only to be knocked down by a car. After being pronounced dead, he gets up and storms off, only to be mowed down once more. The driver of the vehicle, on both occasions, is actor Christopher Benjamin (b. 1934), who is best remembered by sci-fi fans for his contributions to *Doctor Who*, most notably as Jago, the musical hall proprietor in "The Talons of Weng-Chiang."

Lee brings great power to these early scenes. With strong, stiff movement and fierce, determined expression, his performance resembles a less vulnerable, more mechanical version of his Creature from *The Curse of*

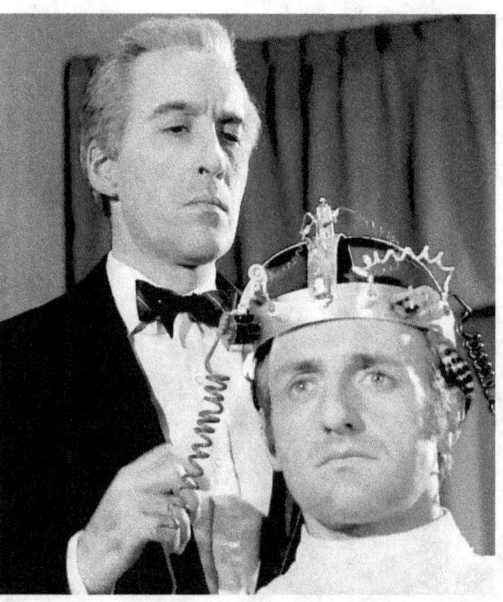

"Never, Never Say Die"

Frankenstein. Smashing any radios that cross his path, he even shoves a banana into one chap's mouth. In another bit of patent *Avengers* eccentricity, grandfatherly actor Arnold Ridley (1896-1984) can be seen, complete with admiral's hat, piloting his remote-control boat across a tarn. While trying to deliver a karate chop to the old geezer's head, Lee finds himself responding to the toy boat's controls and marching off in other directions. Lee plays the scene perfectly po-faced and it is all the funnier for it. Although best known for starring as Private Godfrey in *Dad's Army*, alongside *The Hound of the Baskervilles*' John Le Mesurier, Ridley was also the author of *The Ghost Train*, filmed in both 1931 and 1941—and enacted by Peter Cushing on the New York stage. (Arnold's great-niece is Daisy Ridley, currently making a splash in *Star Wars* movies.)

Christopher Lee in "Never, Never Say Die"

While the old man escapes his intentions, Lee *is* successful in knocking out a soldier played by comic actor and TV scriptwriter John Junkin (1930-2006), whose credits include *A Hard Day's Night, How I Won the War* (1966) and "Matakitas is Coming," an episode of Hammer's *Journey to the Unknown*.

After punching his way through doors and smashing windows, Lee roughs up Macnee in a sequence which echoes his grapples with Francis Matthews for *Dracula: Prince of Darkness* (only, this time, Christopher has a chair smashed over him, before being put in a net and carried away by the men in white coats). In contrast to his replicate, Lee plays the human Stone as a smooth, bow-tied figure. The doctor's assistant, Penrose, is portrayed by TV regular, Jeremy Young (b. 1934), who had an uncredited bit as a court messenger in *Rasputin: The Mad Monk* and would later make an impression as Count de Ricordeau in the BBC sci-fi series *The Tripods* (1984).

"Never, Never Say Die" is *The Avengers* at its best: A fantastic cast enacting colorful adventures, the tilted camera angles of the final fist-on-fist action even recall the cartoon violence of *Batman* (all that is missing are the "Kapows!"). The high production values are further enhanced by the photography of Ernest Steward (*Circus of Fear*) and the puckish music themes of Laurie Johnson (b. 1927), whose other scores include *Dr. Strangelove, First Men in the Moon* and *Captain Kronos: Vampire Hunter* (1972).

First broadcast in the UK on Saturday, March 18, 1967 (at 9.10pm), "Never, Never Say Die" premiered in the US on Friday, March 31 (at 10pm). Clips of Lee from the episode were featured in a 1969 entry "Homicide and Old Lace" and, in October of that year, "Never, Never Say Die" was paired with "The Superlative Seven" to form an *Avengers* movie for Portuguese release.

Later, in the same series, Peter Cushing starred in "Return of the Cybernauts"—itself a sequel to a 1965 episode with Michael Gough (moments from which can be seen in "Never, Never Say Die"). The final *Avengers* entry of 1967, "Mission … Highly Improbable," cast Francis Matthews against type as a villain with a shrinking ray opposite *Night of the Big Heat*'s Jane Merrow, who very nearly took over from Diana Rigg as Steed's new accomplice, Tara King.

Instead, the role was taken by Linda Thorson (b. 1947), who would turn down a contractual offer from Hammer in the early 1970s and later played a witch in the 1986 *Tales from the Darkside* entry "Auld Acquaintances." (When George Romero's anthology series was issued on VHS in the UK, the episodes had specially recorded introductions by Patrick Macnee.)

Linda wasn't the only change in place by the time of Lee's second *Avengers* appearance; Macnee had equipped himself with a groovy pair of sideburns *and* a new credit: "Mr. Macnee's suits designed by *himself*."

Filmed in October 1968 (between *The Castle of Fu Manchu* and *The Oblong Box*), "The Interrogators" (1968) sees Lee as the mustachioed Colonel Mannering, extracting information from British agents via nefarious means. Although the episode owes less to classic horror than "Never, Never Say Die," Lee is on top form. Whether offering a captive a cup of tea in the midst of torturing him, or rubbing his sore knuckles after socking another man in the jaw, the actor veers smoothly from stern to amusing. The 14th entry of the *Avengers*' sixth and final season, "The Interrogators" was first broadcast on New Year's Day 1969 in the UK and was directed by Ealing regular Charles Crichton (1910-1999), who'd earlier helmed the light-hearted "Golfing Story" in *Dead of Night*. This was based on H.G. Wells' "The Inexperienced Ghost," which Lee "several times considered filming," according to author Peter Haining (in *The Mammoth Book of Haunted House Stories*).

While borrowing from genre cinema's past, *The Avengers* also helped set the tone for its future: The show's delightfully offbeat style is at play in such horrors as *The Satanic Rites of Dracula, Theatre of Blood* and *The Abominable Dr. Phibes*. Bearing in mind the latter's 1920s décor and baroque sense of fun, it's no coincidence that *Phibes*' director Robert Fuest (1927-2012) had not only served as production designer on *The Avengers*, but also helmed several of its later episodes. He would work again with Brian Clemens on the modish thriller *And Soon the Darkness* (1969).

Clemens went on to pen two of Hammer's most inventive 1970s horrors, *Dr. Jekyll and Sister Hyde* and *Captain Kronos: Vampire Hunter* (which he also directed), as well as two feature-length entries for *Hammer House of Mystery and Suspense*. In addition, he created the exemplary series *Thriller* (1973-1976), which features many of Christopher Lee's horror co-stars, such as Ingrid Pitt, Ralph Bates, Anton Diffring and Suzan Farmer, among others.

Lee remained a lifelong friend to Patrick Macnee (the two can be seen playing card games together in the 1988 TV-film *Around the World in 80 Days*). Sadly, they both died in June 2015 at the same age of 93 (Patrick passed away just over a fortnight after Christopher). In *The Dark Side* #168, the magazine's editor, Allan Bryce, recalled a funny story told to him by the *Avengers* star. When *The Skull*'s Patrick Magee died in 1982, a well-meaning British friend rang Macnee's daughter, who lived in Palm Springs, to offer their condolences: "'But [my father's] not dead!" said the daughter. 'In fact, I was only just talking to him on the phone.'

"'A ha,' sighed the friend. 'That'll be the time difference …'"

The Loneliness of Evil

Night of the Big Heat
1967

See mysterious invaders from outer space create their scorching heat rays that consume the people and an island!

While *Night of the Big Heat* marks Christopher Lee's science fiction movie debut, it was the fifth and final entry in the genre for Terence Fisher. *Four Sided Triangle* and *Spaceways* had been followed by *The Earth Dies Screaming* (1964) and *Island of Terror* (1965). The former is a tale of marauding robots and blank-eyed zombies, whereas the latter pits Peter Cushing against bone-sucking tentacles.

Although Fisher admitted that the sci-fi genre was not one for which he held any affinity, his preoccupation with human emotion and the tension it creates under extraordinary circumstances is given full rein in *Night of the Big Heat*. As the characters take precedence over bug-eyed monsters, the director is on firmer ground, especially as the frustrated romances of his Hammer Gothics find a modern-dress equivalent in the love triangle that takes place between rugged author Jeff Callum (Patrick Allen), his publican wife Frankie (Sarah Lawson) and Callum's conniving new secretary Angela Roberts (Jane Merrow).

Amid this small island community, Christopher Lee's Godfrey Hanson arrives to investigate the wildly soaring temperatures. Hanson is a mysterious scientist with an abrupt manner and a fine line in NHS spectacles. À la Claude Rains' *Invisible Man*, he holes himself away in a poky room above Frankie's pub, and sets all the locals wondering about his strange experiments. Seemingly impolite, he cuts through all the niceties with great urgency, because only he knows the true nature of the outside threat, and time is of the essence.

John Lymington's 1959 source novel had first been adapted as an *ITV Play of the Week* in June 1960, with Bernard Cribbins (*She*), Patrick Holt (*Alias John Preston*) and Melissa Stribling (*Dracula*). The movie version was the final project of Tom Blakely's Planet Film Productions, the company behind *Island of Terror* and a low-budget vampire yarn, *Devils of Darkness* (1964). Filmed at Pinewood Studios, from Monday, February 20 to Friday, March 31, 1967, the script had gone through several rewrites before landing in the hands of Pip and Jane Baker.

The husband-and-wife team were making their first contribution to a genre in which they would find their niche, especially as writers on *Doctor Who* from 1984-1987 (wherein they created the villainous Rani character enacted by former Hammer star Kate O'Mara). *Night of the Big Heat* is, in fact, pleasingly reminiscent of the earthbound escapades of 1970s *Doctor Who*. Malcom Lockyer's adventuresome score supports this comparison, being similar to his work on both *Dr. Who and the Daleks* and *Island of Terror*.

Another appealing factor is the immediacy of the action, which takes place over a single night, much like '50s favorite *The Blob*. The cozy colloquial setting lends the film most of its charm. As aliens invade, the protagonists take refuge in the local pub—a natural sanctuary in British genre outings (see *Devil Girl from Mars*, *The Earth Dies Screaming* or *Shaun of the Dead*).

The aliens' talent for inducing great heat also affects the island's livestock. Indeed, Hanson's discovery of maimed sheep anticipates real-life accounts of cattle mutilation by supposed extra-terrestrials, the first reported case of which came within six months of *Night of the Big Heat*'s production. In his book *The Andreasson Affair*, investigative author Raymond E. Fowler writes that 1967 was "a vintage year for UFOs," with numerous sightings of "glowing egg-shaped object[s]" in the sky—an apt description given Lee's later comment, in his autobiography, that the monsters in *Night of the Big Heat* look "like fried eggs."

In the novel, Lymington has a character refer to the aliens as "spiders" with "eyes like brandy balls," but the film's briefly glimpsed glowing jellies are only partly to blame for a disappointing climax. Although it does seem inspired by the similarly abrupt conclusion to *The War of the Worlds*, the *deus ex machina* ending (a flaw imported from the novel) is even more of a letdown after such a careful build up. One visitor to the set during the final week of production was Charlton Heston, who was working on a neighboring stage at Pinewood. In her DVD commentary for *Night of the Big Heat*, Jane Baker remembered Heston looking at the aliens. "I don't think he actually laughed," she said, "he just was very surprised."

"Guest star" Peter Cushing gives an exquisite expression of surprise when succumbing to the monsters as Dr. Vernon Stone, although his usual meticulous standards are conspicuously absent when, no matter how insufferably hot it's supposed to be, he refuses to remove his tie or even his jacket. The frigid hues of Reg Wyer's photography also do little to evoke the alien heat. (Wyer had lensed the similarly pallid *Island of Terror*, but the crisp monochrome he engendered for *Night of the Eagle* is impeccable.)

Lee and Cushing are supported by a strong cast. Whether flicking the sweat from his brow with a pen, or rattling Hanson's parcel to gauge what's inside, Patrick Allen (1927-2006) gives a nicely detailed performance as Jeff. An early contender for the role of James Bond, Allen's first screen credit was as Detective Pearson in Hitchcock's *Dial M for Murder* (1953). His subsequent roles include Captain Collier in *Captain Clegg*, Kingsor—the tribal chief of *When Dinosaurs Ruled the Earth*, and another philandering sci-fi hero in *The Body Stealers* (1968). (He also lent his distinctive voice to various narrations and announcements, from *The Viking Queen* to *The Smell of Reeves and Mortimer* [1993-1995].)

Christopher Lee and Peter Cushing (as Dr. Vernon Stone) together again

Allen's screen wife is played by his real-life spouse Sarah Lawson (b. 1928). The couple would reteam with Lee and Fisher for *The Devil Rides Out* later in the year.

Kenneth Cope (b. 1931), who plays the heat-maddened Tinker Mason, had been a soldier in Hammer's *X the Unknown* and one of Oliver Reed's motley crew in *The Damned*. He would find lasting cult TV fame, though, as the white-clad shade of Marty Hopkirk in *Randall and Hopkirk (Deceased)*.

The aliens' first victim is a cave-dwelling tramp played by Sydney Bromley (1909-1987). Wild-eyed and bearded, Bromley played drunks and vagrants in everything from *Dance of the Vampires* to *An American Werewolf in London*, but his greatest characterization came as the gnome-like scientist of *The NeverEnding Story* (1983).

Acting honors in *Night of the Big Heat*, however, belong to Jane Merrow (b. 1941). A chorus girl in Hammer's *The Phantom of the Opera* and Oliver Reed's leading lady in *The System* (1963), Jane was fresh from playing Le Fanu's "Carmilla" in a 1966 episode of *Mystery and Imagination* when she was cast as Angela. In October 2016, she kindly took the time to share her memories with me while preparing to play Lady Macbeth ("a real horror role") at the Groundlings Theatre, Portsmouth (the show opened, appropriately enough, on Halloween). "I admired Christopher Lee and Peter Cushing greatly," Jane says. "Christopher was very charming. At first, I found him slightly imposing and thought he might be a little bit humorless, but this wasn't the case. He had a great sense of humor. His first words to me were, 'Do you play golf?'" Jane laughs. "He had no interest in me as an actor, just whether I could play golf or not! He talked a lot about his lovely wife and daughter. He was clearly a family man and clearly professional."

While speaking highly of Tom Blakely ("We had good producers in those days") and Terence Fisher ("A lovely man"), mention of Peter Cushing causes her voice to lift: "Oh, Peter! A dream! One of the most charming, most delightful men. He was so generous and a bloody good actor. I got to know him a bit better than Christopher, who was quite a private man. Peter talked a lot about his wife, Helen, to whom he was devoted; living by the sea in Whitstable. I really liked him a lot."

She also has fond memories of Patrick Allen and Sarah Lawson: "They were a very happy couple. Delightful. I got to know them well and would chit-chat with Sarah on-set." Of her character, Angela, Jane reveals: "She was so much fun to play. It's nice to play sad and put-upon women, but it's much more fun to play a naughty girl!"

The sports car Jane drives in the film, an Austin Healey Sprite, was her own. "My favorite car of all time! Lots of happy memories." Less happy are memories of the glycerin which was constantly sprayed on cast members to make them appear hot and sweaty in the cold February air. I ask if the film had a premiere. "If there was one," she replies, "I didn't go to it." By the time of the film's release, Jane was busy playing Princess Alais in *The Lion in Winter* (1967), a role which earned her a Best Supporting Actress Golden Globe nomination (the winner that year was Ruth Gordon for *Rosemary's Baby*). I'd read that it was her performance in *Night of the Big Heat* that won her the part of the Princess, but Jane denies this. "That's the first time I've heard that," she says. "Peter O'Toole had seen me in the play *Country Dance*—one of the best things I've ever done—and that's how I came to be tested for *The Lion in Winter*."

Christopher Lee plays a mysterious scientist trying to save the planet.

After guesting as mind-reading photographer "Number 24" on *The Prisoner*, Jane went on to play the blind Laura in Hammer's most poignant horror film, *Hands of the Ripper* (1971). The following year, she starred with William Shatner in two TV mysteries: *The Hound of the Baskervilles* and *The Horror at 37,000 Feet*. Another made-for-television thriller, 1974's *Diagnosis: Murder*, was eventually released theatrically, and although Jane shared no dialogue with its villain Christopher Lee ("He'd gone beyond Dracula by that point"), she did work with Lee's *Wicker Man* co-star Edward Woodward on a little-seen chiller, *The Appointment* (1981).

"There was a feeling at the time: 'Oh, you're doing a horror movie?' People could be very snooty about it," Jane remembers of the late 1960s, although this is not a view she shares, having recently returned to the genre as a producer with *New Chilling Tales*—a series of atmospheric shorts based on classic stories, such as Poe's "The Tell-Tale Heart" and Charlotte Perkins Gilman's "The Yellow Wallpaper." "I thought if young people saw them, they might read the books," Jane explains, while voicing an appreciation of the genre, particularly the writings of Ambrose Bierce and John Wyndham. "There is so much outside of our world that we should open our minds to and think about. Nothing is impossible. The films I like to make, including the horror films, have some kind of social comment"—a philosophy which spurs her current desire to make a feature film of John Caine's ethical stage play *Reunion*.

Night of the Big Heat was paired with *The Tenth Victim* for its UK release on Sunday December 10, 1967. (The same day that soul singer Otis Redding died in a plane crash—the Beatles were at No. 1 with "Hello Goodbye.") The film wasn't released until June 1971 in the US, where, as *Island of the Burning Damned*, it played with *Godzilla's Revenge* (1969)—the title was later toned down to *Island of the Burning Doomed* for American television.

But the last words on *Night of the Big Heat* must go to Jane Merrow: "I liked working with both Christopher and Peter enormously. I felt privileged to be appearing with these icons of the British film industry. The whole film was a happy one."

The Loneliness of Evil

Blood Demon
1967

A mature person's trip through the ultimate in horrific wickedness.

In 1967, the first major book-length studies of horror cinema arrived via Carlos Clarens' *An Illustrated History of the Horror Film* and Ivan Butler's *The Horror Film*. Although neither writer was enamored of the then-current product from Hammer, both had good things to say about Christopher Lee. While Clarens called Lee a "better actor" than Bela Lugosi, Butler wrote: "Lee is an actor of considerable presence, who brings to all his roles a strong personality and impressive appearance—the straighter roles showing that he need not depend on a grotesque make-up for results …"

With the genre's history being treated on a non-superficial level by critics, Lee arrived in Munich, on Monday June 19, 1967, to enact his part in a veritable cocktail of the horror film's recent past. Filmed under the title *Die Schlangengrube und das Pendel* (the literal English translation of which is *The Snake Pit and the Pendulum*), *Blood Demon* is currently available on DVD as *Castle of the Walking Dead* (not to be mistaken for Lee's earlier venture *The Castle of the Living Dead*). It is also known as *The Torture Chamber of Dr. Sadism* and *The Snake Pit*. (Definitely not to be confused with Anatole Litvak's harrowing 1948 treatise on mental illness.)

Scripted by Manfred R. Köhler (1927-1991), who would work uncredited on *The Blood of Fu Manchu* and *Daughters of Darkness* (1970), *Blood Demon* was the first Gothic horror film to be made in Germany since 1935's *The Student of Prague* and *Fährmann Maria*. This is surprising, not only because the country was slow in joining the Gothic revival sparked by Hammer, but also, having housed such influential silents as *The Cabinet of Dr. Caligari*, *The Golem* and *Nosferatu*, Germany is arguably the birthplace of horror cinema.

Austrian director Harald Reinl (1908-1986) was fresh from recreating one landmark *Schauerroman*, Fritz Lang's *Die Nibelungen* (and would go on to helm the Oscar-nominated ancient aliens documentary *Chariots of the Gods* [1970]). Under Reinl's guidance, Lee must have been experiencing a terrible sense of déjà vu. For not only is he, as Count Regula, draining virgins and muttering lines like, "The blood is the life," but the film itself plays like a virtual remake of *Dracula: Prince of Darkness* (with splashes of Mario Bava's *Black Sunday* and Roger Corman's *Pit and the Pendulum* thrown in for good measure).

Blood Demon opens on Regula awaiting judgement in a dank cell for killing 12 virgins. (More than one commentator has mentioned that the character's name evokes some kind of grim suppository aid, so I'll refrain from doing that here.) When the Judge (Lex Barker) decrees that the Count will be drawn and quartered in the village square, Regula spits out a curse: He will take revenge, from beyond the grave, on the families of his prosecutor and 13th would-be victim (Karin Dor).

Carl Lange, Christopher Lee and Karin Dor in *The Torture Chamber of Dr. Sadism* aka *Blood Demon*

Once the Count has said his piece, he has a spike-lined mask slammed onto his face (just like Barbara Steele at the outset of *Black Sunday*) and then the titles roll. Pumping from the soundtrack is a delirious organ dirge full of pounding drums and scratchy brass, courtesy of Peter Thomas (b. 1925), who would provide similarly inappropriate music for *Chariots of the Gods*. While the credits inform us that what follows is based on Edgar Allan Poe's "novel [*sic*] 'The Pit and the Pendulum,'" we are, instead, treated to a smattering of borrowings from classic horror films. Thirty-five years after Count Regula's public execution, a group of travelers find themselves en route to his castle. Among the protagonists are the descendants of Regula's prosecutors (again enacted by Barker and Dor) and a bearded priest (Vladimir Mebar). The *Dracula: Prince of Darkness* parallels grow even deeper on arrival at the *Schloss*, where they find themselves greeted by the Count's candelabra-clutching manservant Anatol (Carl Lange). The waxen-faced aide proceeds to revive his master by slitting his wrist with a mangy-looking blade. Thick green blood

Count Regula (Christopher Lee) in the sinister lab

drips onto the sarcophagus where Regula lies. *Et voilà:* instant Vampire.

The remainder apes the work of Terence Fisher's American counterpart, Roger Corman, especially torture sequences that bear more than a passing resemblance to *Pit and the Pendulum*, and a crashing finale, which recalls *House of Usher*. In his autobiography, Lee himself called *Blood Demon*, "a perfectly dreadful composite," but far from being "dreadful," this overlooked film is, rather, a florid, offbeat fairy tale that holds several points of interest. Foremost is the sumptuous production design of Gabriel Pellon

Blood Demon with Christopher Lee (holding axe) and Lex Barker

(1900-1975) and Rolf Zehetbauer (b. 1929), which constantly reminds us that we are in a dark and elegant fantasy land (Zehetbauer later designed *The NeverEnding Story*). Their work is best exhibited during the voyage to the castle, where corpses hang from the trees like strange decorations; the effect is gruesome yet oddly beautiful.

The castle makes for a convincingly macabre world in itself. Full of creaking gates and slamming shutters, the gloomy chambers are more like caves and the walls are festooned with paintings, depicting oddly beaked figures doing horrible things. (One of the slightly more normal accoutrements of Count Regula's home is a skeleton in a suit of armor.)

Visual delights aside, *Blood Demon* is also worth watching for its cast. German actress Karin Dor (1938-2017) is best remembered as Helga Brandt, the red-headed she-villain of *You Only Live Twice*. In one unforgettable scene, she straps Sean Connery's James Bond to a chair and holds a surgical blade to his throat, before, finally, seducing her prey. This alluring display of villainy perfectly illustrates Terence Fisher's "attraction of evil" philosophy. As such, it's a shame that Karin graced no further Gothics.

Blood Demon was a reunion of sorts for the actress. She had previously starred alongside Christopher Lee in *The Face of Fu Manchu* and collaborated with Barker and (her husband) Reinl on *The Invisible Dr. Mabuse* (1961). After divorcing Harald in 1968, her poetic death scene formed the visual highlight of Alfred Hitchcock's otherwise dull *Topaz* (1969). From Hitchcock, she next worked with Paul Naschy, as an extra-terrestrial scientist in *Assignment Terror* (1969).

Lex Barker (1919-1973) had made two 1947 appearances with Boris Karloff (in *Unconquered* and *Dick Tracy Meets Gruesome*), before succeeding Johnny Weissmuller in the role of Tarzan. Barker not only played the yodeling vine-swinger five times (from *Tarzan's Magic Fountain* [1948] to *Tarzan and the She-Devil* [1952]), but also had five wives (the third of whom was Lana Turner). Lex's final screen credit was "The Waiting Room," a 1972 segment of *Night Gallery*.

Another point in *Blood Demon*'s favor is that Christopher Lee's own voice is retained on the English-language soundtrack. As such, he is able to try out new inflections on over-familiar dialogue, such as the impressive rasp he deploys for the line: "Destroy the cross! Throw it away; *throw it away!*" Other moments that look forward rather than back include Babette (Christiane Rucker) plunging towards a spike-lined floor—a spectacle reminiscent of a would-be witch falling head-first into roaring flames for the yet-to-be-filmed *Witchfinder General*. Additionally, the stunning skull-studded walls of Count Regula's subterranean dwelling anticipate the similarly effective blue-lit crypt of *Vampire Circus* (Regula's bone-filled enclosure would thrill again when seen beneath the opening credits montage of TV's *This Is Horror* [1989]).

The most charming aspect of *Blood Demon*, however, is the pervading influence of fairy tales. We see it in the haunted forests, ghoulish castle, stoic hero and distressed maiden; it's also in the cobbled Bavarian streets (where Robert Helpmann's terrifying Child Catcher would caper in *Chitty Chitty Bang Bang*) and the Count's grey woolen tights, buckled shoes and glass coffin (though Regula is no *Snow White*—more a purplish gray). The uniquely Germanic quality is what ultimately sets *Blood Demon* aside from the raft of Hammer-inspired chillers of the mid-1960s. Sadly, this fairy tale feel was seeping away.

On its eventual release in May 1969 (UK viewers saw it double billed with Barbara Steele's equally lurid *Nightmare Castle* [1965]), the horrors of *Blood Demon* would seem very tame indeed when compared to *Rosemary's Baby* and *Night of the Living Dead* (both issued in 1968). The horror film was losing its innocence. The genre was "growing up." In hindsight, *Blood Demon* seems a crystallization of that fading innocence, the last vestige of a changing field.

Nevertheless, Christopher Lee's next horror assignment saw him happily re-ensconced at Hammer with Terence Fisher, for what would become one of the most defining movies of both men's careers.

The Loneliness of Evil

The Devil Rides Out
1967

The beauty of woman—the demon of darkness—the unholy union of "The Devil's Bride"!

Many people who represent ... various religious faiths all over the world when they've met me have talked about [*The Devil Rides Out*] ... and they've all said the same thing: 'We have no problems with this kind of picture, none whatsoever. We do not consider it blasphemous. On the contrary, because Light destroys and vanquishes Darkness—it is exactly what we teach. —Christopher Lee, *The Many Faces of Christopher Lee.*

What is the cinema? It's the place where the lights are put out. Enjoyment of horror is one of the deepest things ... And do you know what the worst horror is? It's when you switch on the electric light and the ghost is still there.—Terence Fisher, "Horror is My Business," *Films and Filming*, July 1964

First published, in serialized form, on Halloween 1934, Dennis Wheatley's *The Devil Rides Out* became the biggest-selling horror novel in the UK since Stoker's *Dracula*. One enthusiastic reader later wrote in his own tome, *Christopher Lee's New Chamber of Horrors*: "Dennis Wheatley [1897-1977] is a writer whose work has given me pleasure for years, and as we now live in the same London square, we have become very good friends." The two men first met in November 1957, when Lee was filming *Dracula*. (The occasion was a lecture on "Magic and the Supernatural" given by the author at Harrods.)

In 2004, the actor told Marcus Hearn: "It was [thanks to] my association with Dennis Wheatley, and my knowledge of his work, and the fact that he was also a neighbor of mine, that I managed to get his permission to approach Hammer to make *The Devil Rides Out*." Indeed, Lee initially proposed the idea to Anthony Hinds in 1963. At that time, there was no way the censors would pass the story's taboo subject of black magic. Just four years later, however, and the so-called "Age of Aquarius" brought forth a resurgence of spiritual interest, which was expressed through popular media. Consequently, the Devil was riding out in more film genres than horror in 1967, appearing not only via Peter Cook's clever anthropological satire *Bedazzled*, but also Richard Burton's version of the Christopher Marlowe play *Doctor Faustus*. The music world, too, felt the lure of Beelzebub that year, with the Rolling Stones releasing *Their Satanic Majesties Request*, an LP which came complete with a psychedelic 3-D cover showing the band garbed as medieval wizards. (The following year, the recording of their song "Sympathy for the Devil"—in which Mick Jagger recounts the horrors of history from the perspective of Lucifer [or is it God?]—was documented by Jean-Luc Godard as *One Plus One*, which features *The Devil Rides Out*'s Nike Arrighi.)

By the time *The Devil Rides Out* went into production at Elstree on Monday, August 7, 1967, the Beatles were also bringing spirituality to the masses, courtesy of their well-publicized meetings with Maharishi Mahesh Yogi. Ever at the forefront of '60s culture, the Fab Four gave further indication of their newfound interest in magical, mystical matters when, earlier in the summer, they included Aleister Crowley (1875-1947) among the notables on their *Sgt. Pepper's Lonely Hearts Club Band* album cover.

Dubbed "The Wickedest Man in the World" by the British press, Crowley informed the creation of Mocata, the villainous Satanist of *The Devil Rides Out*, after lunching with Dennis Wheatley in May 1934. A one-time member of the infamous occult society, the Hermetic Order of the Golden Dawn (of which Bram Stoker, Sir Arthur Conan Doyle, Algernon Blackwood and Sax Rohmer were all rumored to have joined, however briefly), Crowley went on to practice "magick" rituals involving hedonistic sex and drugs. He also had some influence on the horror film genre: In 1920s Germany, for example, Crowley attended a conference with Albin Grau, the producer of *Nosferatu*, an affirmed occultist. Grau peppered his vampire classic with hermetic symbols, most notably in Count Orlok's cryptic correspondence with the deranged estate agent, Knock. Elsewhere, Crowley inspired Somerset Maugham's 1908 novel *The Magician* (filmed in 1926

Christopher Lee meets author Dennis Wheatley, who wrote *The Devil Rides Out*.

with Paul Wegener), as well as Boris Karloff's sly Satanist in *The Black Cat*, and Karswell, the practitioner of "appalling rites" in M.R. James' story "Casting the Runes" (filmed as *Night of the Demon* with Niall MacGinnis). Furthermore, in May 1941, Christopher Lee's step-cousin, Ian Fleming, was working in Naval Intelligence and, knowing of the Nazis' predilection for the Occult, enlisted Crowley to offer his guidance (as documented in John Pearson's 1966 biography *The Life of Ian Fleming*). Although there's no evidence that the Black Magician did more than confirm he was at Britain's disposal, Fleming did import a number of Crowley's characteristics into Le Chiffre, the villain of his first James Bond novel, *Casino Royale*, written in 1952. Twenty years later, at L.A.'s first Science Fiction and Fantasy Film Convention, Lee himself revealed: "I have been asked to play Aleister Crowley. I don't know whether it will come off." It didn't. Nor did Hammer's original casting of him in *The Devil Rides Out*:

"I was actually asked to play Mocata," Lee told *LSoH* #4, "but I said no." The actor, instead, persuaded his employers that he should portray the gallant Duc de Richleau. Wheatley, too, was insistent that his friend and neighbor be cast against type; although the writer initially showed some reservations about the film company itself, fearing that Hammer, with their penchant for blood and gore, would sensationalize his material. It wasn't until Terence Fisher met with him personally that Wheatley's fears were allayed, with both men agreeing that such a story should be told with the utmost respect. After all, Wheatley himself took the subject of black magic rather earnestly, basing the rituals he described in his books on actual practices and warning his readers not to get involved as "my own observations have led me to an absolute conviction that to do so would bring them into dangers of a very real and concrete nature." Anthony Hinds (quoted in *LSoH*) concurred: "Dennis Wheatley … took Satanism very seriously, without, I must add, practicing it himself. I remember Terry [Fisher] being a bit spooked. I thought it was rubbish!" Christopher Lee, on the other hand, gave an on-set interview to Derek Todd from *Kinematograph Weekly* in which he cautioned: "Satanism is rampant in London today. It's generally acknowledged in certain circles that the so-called swinging city is a hotbed of devil worship and such practices—just ask the police." Todd made a note to do so.

To adapt Wheatley's novel for the screen, Anthony Hinds chose the man whom Stephen King would call (on thousands of book covers) "the author who influenced me the most": Richard Matheson (1926-2013) had already explored the evils of black magic onscreen by co-writing the classic *Night of the Eagle* (1961), but he was also no stranger to Hammer. Fresh from the success of his first screenplay *The Incredible Shrinking Man* (1956), Matheson arrived in England in September of 1957 to adapt his significant novel *I Am Legend* for the company. The resultant script, entitled *Night Creatures*, was prohibited outright by the censors and eventually made in Italy with Vincent Price as *The Last Man on Earth* (1963; although revised from Matheson's original, the film's bleak visuals were an obvious influence on George Romero's *Night of the Living Dead*, while *Night Creatures* would become the US title for *Captain Clegg*). Matheson would eventually write *Fanatic* (1964) for Hammer, but this disappointing thriller, which served as Tallulah Bankhead's swansong, found the writer's comic touch unusually misplaced. Matheson found his talents better served at AIP as a lyrical interpreter of Edgar Allan Poe with *House of Usher*, *Pit and the Pendulum*, *Tales of Terror*, and *The Raven*, while also allowing Price, Karloff, Lorre and Rathbone to flex their considerable comic skills for *The Comedy of Terrors* (1963). As well as penning 17 *Twilight Zone* episodes, a popular *Star Trek* entry ("The Enemy Within") and the Jack Palance *Dracula* (1973), Matheson was responsible for such terror classics as *Duel* (1971), *The Night Stalker*, *The Night Strangler* (1972), *The Legend of Hell House*, *Scream of the Wolf* (1973), *The Stranger Within* (1974), *Trilogy of Terror* (1975) and *Dead of Night* (1976).

With *The Devil Rides Out*, the writer provides a masterclass on how to effectively adapt a novel for the screen; its strength lies in his decision to follow Wheatley's original storyline closely, leaving just enough out to maintain energy and pace, without sacrificing the author's intent or ideas. Despite this, two of the film's most celebrated lines originate with Matheson himself. Firstly,

Charles Gray as the evil Mocata

when the Duc is asked by his friend, Rex, if he can borrow a car, Lee responds, with brilliant weariness: "Yes, take any of them." This line never fails to raise a laugh from an audience, while, conversely, the icy warning delivered by Charles Gray's Mocata ("I shall not be back … but something will") never fails to induce a shiver. These two very different pieces of dialogue reveal much about the characters who speak them; simple yet effective, they illustrate both the horror and humor of Matheson's oeuvre.

The Devil Rides Out wrapped on Friday, September 29, 1967, as Lee later told his fan club, "after five extremely unpleasant nights in the rain and the damp in the woods near Pinewood Studios." He went on: "I have high hopes for this film, and it will prove once and for all that I can be accepted in a completely normal role." While it's debatable whether a Satan-busting aristocrat could be described as "completely normal," Lee does bring perfect naturalism to the role; note the way he calmly lights his cheroot from a candle then eavesdrops among the Satanists, all the while maintaining a cool composure. The charm then explodes with concerned fury as he warns his charge Simon: "I'd rather see you dead than meddling with black magic!" Fiercely loyal, he even shows, by punching Simon's lights out, that he is not above using physical violence to protect those closest to him. Indeed, the Duc will do all that is necessary to ensure moral rightness is restored. Lee's characterization forms a strong, heroic backbone to the film and the authority he brings to the part enforces the story's verisimilitude. In Lee's hands, for example, no one could fail to believe such assertions as: "The power of

The Duc and his friends (Patrick Mower and Paul Eddington) undergoing some sort of dark ritual of protection.

Darkness is more than just a superstition. It is a living Force, which can be tapped at any given moment of the night." Indeed, the actor took his role so seriously that, like de Richleau, he spent hours researching in the British Museum, from where he plucked an authentic prayer of exorcism for the movie's finale. In all, I would argue that *The Devil Rides Out* contains Lee's greatest ever screen performance, because the merging of character and actor is so absolute (one cannot see where de Richleau ends and Lee begins). The film itself is Hammer's strongest horror after *Dracula*.

The Devil Rides Out succeeds, not only as a supernatural parable, but also as a rip-roaring adventure with derring-do aplenty. We are even treated to a car chase on country roads familiar from the cult TV show that Lee had recently guested in. "*The Avengers* was being filmed right next door," Rosalyn Landor confirmed to Bruce Hallenbeck (in *LSoH* #12): "I remember eating lunch one day [at Elstree] and seeing Diana Rigg in her full Emma Peel costume sitting at the table with her two poodles. I was very impressed." Cast as seven-year-old Peggy in *The Devil Rides Out*, Landor (b. 1958) also revealed in the same interview that Christopher Lee seemed to be embracing the "Age of Aquarius," by practicing something which his character in *Horror Express* would denounce, bafflingly, as a supernatural art: "[Lee] was always doing yoga a lot between takes," Rosalyn told Hallenbeck: "I remember that he was into yoga at that time and he taught me how to do it, how to meditate … It was the first time I ever smelled incense. I still think that smell is quite disgusting." Concurrent to *The Devil Rides Out*, Landor was offered the young lead in *Chitty Chitty Bang Bang* (eventually played by Heather Ripley), but chose, instead, to make her debut for Hammer ("I was afraid of Dick Van Dyke!" Rosalyn told Hallenbeck: "But, obviously, I was not afraid of the Angel of Death!"). Thirteen years later, Landor fell afoul of Satanists once more at the *Hammer House of Horror* in "Guardian of the Abyss"—the plot of which bears more than a passing similarity to *The Devil Rides Out*. Her other credits include *The Amazing Mr. Blunden* (1971; as a ghost), *Arthur the King* (1982; as Guinevere) and *Star Trek: The Next Generation*: "Up the Long Ladder" (1989; as the fiery Brenna Odell).

In her discussion with Hallenbeck, Rosalyn also refuted any notion that Christopher Lee was aloof (as is sometimes reported): "He was very charming and kind. All the people on the set were kind to me." She was especially fond of Terence Fisher, whom she likened to "a big teddy bear": "He was a very kind man, even though he did have water thrown on me." This was to elicit her response to the demonic spider, part of an unforgettable set-piece where de Richleau guards his friends against the visiting Forces of Evil from within a hand-drawn pentacle. This powerful, suspenseful scene is let down only by its special effects, which fall far below Hammer's usual standards. The Angel of Death optic, for instance, was never even completed; hence, the blue screen is still visible in the background of its close-up. The reason for this is that the man responsible for them, a certain Michael Stainer-Hutchins, owned the rights to Wheatley's novel and wouldn't give them up unless he could at least attempt the effects, a field in which he had little prior experience. Remarkably, and feeling that they had no choice, Hammer let him have a go.

Much better is the music of James Bernard, who often cited that *The Devil Rides Out* was a personal favorite among his own scores. He was also a fan of Dennis Wheatley's book. "I'd always loved ghost stories and horror stories from when I was a teenager," the composer told Wayne Kinsey. "Some of the earliest books that I remember loving were ones for which I later wrote music …"

Shooting simultaneously with *The Devil Rides Out* at Elstree was another Wheatley adaptation, *The Lost Continent* (from the author's novel *Uncharted Seas*). Although it doesn't look it, this goofy adventure was Hammer's most expensive production yet, with special effects courtesy of Robert A. Mattey, who'd won an Oscar for his giant squid in *20,000 Leagues Under the Sea* (1954) and would later create the monstrous shark in *Jaws*. Wheatley posed for photos with Mattey's rubber creatures while visiting the sets of both *The Devil Rides Out* and *The Lost Continent*. For the latter, Lee was tentatively tempted to conceal his famous features beneath a pointy-headed mask as the disfigured Inquisitor, "a non-speaking part," as he described to his fan club, "with no billing or mention of any kind. At least this will give the audience something to think about." Ultimately, *The Lost Continent* gives its viewers nothing to think about and the role went to Eddie Powell, who receives both billing *and* dialogue. (The latter was reportedly dubbed in by the film's star, Eric Porter, who, in a duologue with himself, imitates Lee's clipped Fu Manchu tones.)

Powell also appears in *The Devil Rides Out* as the Goat of Mendes, beneath a Roy Ashton-designed make-up. The Satanic orgies, which surround the Goat, were staged by choreographer David Toguri (1933-1997), who would later teach Mocata himself, Charles Gray (1928-2000), how to do "The Time Warp" on *The Rocky Horror Picture Show*.

Christopher Lee would voice *The Rocky Horror Show*'s narrator on record in the mid-1990s, but this wasn't the only role he had in common with Gray: The latter was also a Bond villain (an icily suave Blofeld in *Diamonds Are Forever*) and played Mycroft Holmes in both *The Seven-Per-Cent Solution* (1975) and the acclaimed Jeremy Brett TV series, *Sherlock Holmes* (1984-1994). When Jack Hawkins sadly lost his larynx to cancer in 1966, Gray regularly dubbed the actor's voice for his subsequent film appearances, including *Theatre of Blood* and *Tales That Witness Madness*. On television, he also lent his dulcet tones to an atmospheric rendering of Le Fanu's *Schalcken the Painter* (1979) and the 1987 documentary *Hammer: The Studio That Dripped Blood!* A suspected werewolf in *The Beast Must Die*, Gray's other genre credits include *The Legacy* (1978; in which he becomes a human inferno); Judge Oliver Wright in the 1980 *Rocky Horror* follow-up, *Shock Treatment*; and the world-weary gastronome who sets out to eat a ghost in *The Gourmet* (1986).

Cast as Tanith, the young girl whose soul is endangered by Mocata, is Nike Arrighi (b. 1947), who had just had a small role as a Portuguese waitress in the Jerry Lewis comedy *Don't Raise the Bridge, Lower the River* (the female lead of which was another Hammer favorite, Jacqueline Pearce). Nike can also be glimpsed as a Contessa in *Women in Love* (1968), before her more prominent role as the fortune teller who fails to foresee being stabbed in the neck by Ingrid Pitt's *Countess Dracula*.

Tanith's love interest, Rex Van Ryn, is played by Australian actor and opera singer Leon Greene (b. 1931) but voiced by Lee's *Night of the Big Heat* co-star, Patrick Allen (Leon's own voice can be heard in the film's trailer—which Allen narrates; Greene's other credits include *A Funny Thing Happened on the Way to the Forum*, *The Four Musketeers* and *Flash Gordon* [1979]).

While Patrick Allen's wife Sarah Lawson, also familiar from *Night of the Big Heat*, plays Marie Eaton in *The Devil Rides Out*, her screen husband, Richard, is portrayed by Paul Eddington (1927-1995). Eddington had acted Shakespeare alongside Christopher Lee during their Connaught Theatre days, 20 years previously, and would go on to become a familiar face on British TV for his role in *Yes, Minister/Yes, Prime Minister* (1980-1988), one of Lee's favorite comedies (as he revealed in a 1990s *Radio Times* interview).

The Duc's misguided young friend, Simon Aron, is essayed by Patrick Mower (b. 1938). As well as playing a professor of the paranormal in the lost TV series *Haunted* (1967-1968), Mower is one of the few actors to have starred alongside all three of the 1960s horror greats. Unfortunately, the two films he made in 1969 with Peter Cushing and Vincent Price are not of the caliber of *The Devil Rides Out*. As Cushing's prospective son-in-law in *Incense for the Damned*, Mower succumbs to a Greek vampire cult. While both his stirring diatribe against academia and Cushing's tearful denouement belong to a stronger movie, at least *Incense for the Damned* has some thought-provoking ideas, Johnny Sekka's black hero and a catchy theme tune in its favor. *Cry of the Banshee*, on the other hand, has only the animated titles of Terry Gilliam to commend it, with Mower's demon-werewolf, ironically, being the most dignified character on display. After appearing alongside Isobel Black in the final instalment of *Mystery and Imagination*, "Curse of the Mummy" (broadcast Monday February 23, 1970), Mower starred in "Czech Mate"—the first episode to be filmed for *Hammer House of Mystery and Suspense* (1983).

The most distinguished of the Satanists is personified by Gwen Ffrangcon-Davies (1891-1992), who had previously been one of Hammer's *The Witches*. Gwen's theater roles include Mrs. Manningham in the first production of Patrick Hamilton's *Gas Light* (1938), and Ophelia in a 1930 Command Performance of *Hamlet*, alongside Colin Clive (*Frankenstein*), Ernest Thesiger (*Bride of Frankenstein*) and Cedric Hardwicke (*The Ghost of Frankenstein*). Reunited with Hardwicke for her screen debut as Mary Tudor in *Tudor Rose* (1936; edited by Terence Fisher), Gwen's final appearance, aged 100, was as a dowager in *Sherlock Holmes*: "The Master Blackmailer" (1991), which also starred Cedric's son, Edward, as Dr. Watson.

Paired with Hammer's preposterous jungle fantasy *Slave Girls*, *The Devil Rides Out* went into general release on Sunday July 21, 1968, in the UK and December of the same year in America. Wheatley's novel was reissued as a tie-in edition ("NOW A GREAT FILM"), with a lurid publicity still of Charles Gray menacing Nike Arrighi on the cover. In addition, a psychedelic slice of garage rock entitled "The Devil Rides Out," by Icarus, was released as a single in June 1968 ("You better watch out when the Devil rides out!"). Although the song was unrelated to James Bernard's themes, the band were invited to the film's premiere as a result of their effort.

While *The Devil Rides Out* did good business in England, Stateside, it fared even worse than Hammer's recent flops *The Viking Queen* and *The Vengeance of She*. Whereas those two ventures deserved such a fate, *The Devil Rides Out* did not. Despite best-selling status all over Europe, Wheatley never really broke the US market, and things were not helped by the American distributor's decision to foist a more generic title, *The Devil's Bride*, upon the movie. Lee revealed, in *The Many Faces of Christopher Lee*, that 20th Century Fox demanded *The Devil Rides Out* be renamed "because everybody in America will think it's a Western."

Christopher Lee as the Duc de Richleau

Although Fisher long desired to film Wheatley's 1948 novel *The Haunting of Toby Jugg* (a pre-production poster was even drawn up with green-tinged artwork of Christopher Lee's leering face), only *To the Devil a Daughter* would be made by Hammer. Fisher's much-needed presence was sadly absent from the latter. Indeed, *The Devil Rides Out* marks his final collaboration with Lee. The director made only two more horrors (*Frankenstein Must Be Destroyed* and *Frankenstein and the Monster from Hell*), before dying, aged 76, on Wednesday, June 18, 1980, of emphysema and lung cancer. He was buried the following Monday to the strains of Louis Armstrong singing "When the Saints Go Marching In" ("I went to the funeral. Only a few turned up … It was all very sad," Anthony Hinds lamented in *LSoH* #6). Nevertheless, Terence Fisher's vital contribution to Gothic cinema will never be forgotten.

The film's poor showing in the US put the kibosh on Hammer's plans to follow on with further Wheatley adaptations, such as *The Ka of Gifford Hillary* and *They Used Dark Forces*. Nevertheless, the author was pleased with the finished feature and sent a telegram to Terence Fisher, which read: "Saw film yesterday. Heartiest congratulations and grateful thanks for splendid direction." To give thanks to Lee, Wheatley presented him with a first edition of the novel and, according to the actor, the film rights to all his black magic books, free of charge.

Terence Fisher and Lee on the set

Remaking *The Devil Rides Out*

Christopher Lee long desired to star in a remake of *The Devil Rides Out*, something which almost came to prominence in the late 1990s, as Ted Newsom now explains, exclusively for this book:

"Lee liked the idea of a *Devil Rides Out* remake: 'With what they can do with effects now, it could be marvelous.' With the aid of writer Bill Kelley, I thought that'd be a pip. Employed as a movie critic for the Fort Lauderdale *Sun-Times* and frequent contributor to *Cinefantastique*, Bill was also a friend of Lee's, far closer than I was. It was Bill who kept encouraging Lee to be part of the Hammer documentary [Ted's *Flesh and Blood: The Hammer Heritage of Horror*, 1994]. We sketched out the plot along Wheatley's original lines, [which were] obviously similar to Hammer's.

"Since we weren't necessarily doing it under Hammer's aegis, I didn't let them know yet. I didn't yet want to wrestle with the complex issues of adaptation rights. For protection, we pushed the time of the story ahead 10 years to the eve of World War II, with Mocata in league with the Nazis; assorted capitalists, foreign and domestic and international creeps in general, all of whom deferred to Mocata's authority. Wheatley's later black magic novels used the same characters in further adventures with different villains, including Nazis in *Strange Conflict*, and the SS had strong occult beliefs, so that could hike the odds. Instead of only a little girl's life and soul at stake, there was also the entire world. And on the side of good, MI5 pulls the Duc and his friends into the fray. I figured, worst case, the rights to the first book were tied up, fine, we'd write an original script based on the later books. I spoke with Wheatley's son, who assured me that rights to the later books were indeed available.

"Kelley and I would discuss the project at length on the phone, but there were often peculiarities. We toyed with incorporating the feeling of *Night of the Demon* and riffed on Duc de Richleau visiting the British Museum for research, implied but unseen in the book and film. When he comes out, I suggested, the busy area is absolutely devoid of people. Not a soul anywhere. And this thick, gray fog starts appearing. De Richleau walks through the streets and becomes aware that he's not alone. A couple of weeks later, Bill called and said, 'I just told the old man about this great sequence I thought of. The Duc goes to the British Museum to research occult stuff, but when he comes out, there's nobody, anywhere! And as he starts walking away, there's this fog—' Yeah, that, uh … that sounds … great.

"Bill and I both thought Joe Dante would be a cool choice to direct. 'I've got the paperback right here on my desk,' he said. Joe also was far closer to Lee than I was. Any smart crack that all he could make is comedies ought to be negated by the scary stuff in *The Howling*, and the sensitive handling of the kids in the first half of *Explorers*.

"Lee fixated on an odd choice for the heavy. 'Brian Dennehy would be just right,' he said. 'He's an immensely powerful screen presence. Excellent actor. Love his work. He should be Mocata, he's absolutely perfect.' I countered that Dennehy would be great if Mocata was a head-busting chief of a crooked labor union but was a bit too rough-edged to play the suave high priest of a sophisticated international Satanic cult. Lee remained convinced he was right.

"Lee's old friend Paul Maslansky became involved. Bored with retirement, he liked the idea of plunging once more into the breech; he'd started in low-budget films like *The Castle of the Living Dead* (when he and Lee became pals) … [Maslansky] began the intricate job of nailing down all rights and pitching the project. Paul certainly had more credibility than I did as a major producer. Within a couple months, he had secured financing from Canal+. Roy Skeggs of Hammer was willing to throw in the Hammer name, along with any remake rights Hammer might have. Paul then spent a much longer time trying to get various distributors to sign off. The film's distribution rights were scattered, and any one of the companies might conceivably have a claim that they owned remake rights, not Hammer.

"I wrote and shot a promo with Lee to help with the pitch, dovetailing it onto my shoot for *A Century of Science Fiction* [1996], which Lee hosted. Bearded and in a tux, Lee addressed the camera, blue-screened into an ornate English drawing room. These shots were intercut with period footage from films like *The Night of the Generals*, *The Ninth Gate*, *Mephisto*, *Subspecies*, *Eye of the Needle* and the older Lee in *Talos the Mummy*. 'I am Nicholas, Duc de Richleau. Thirteen years ago, in the company of trusted friends, we stood on the edge of the abyss and gazed into the pit—of Hell.' Then follows a truncated clip from the first film ("Back to back, quickly! Join hands!"), with the phantom attack of the spider-demon on the little girl.

"'Those dark forces were vanquished,' the Duc explains, 'but *not* destroyed. Now, a group of dangerous men seek to use those forces for their own sinister ends.' Following this, footage from *End of Days* with looming demonic shadows. 'Make no mistake. These are not young dabblers, but ruthless adversaries to whom power means everything—and life … means nothing.' A knifing and a car crash from *Eye of the Needle* over shots of Nazis arriving at a mansion and young Klaus Brandauer being feted, Lee warns, 'My godson Simon Aron has fallen in with these people.' Sexy shots from *Bram Stoker's Dracula* and other films: 'The temptations will be sensuous … intoxicating. But you must resist. Fight it.' Stronger sexy stuff. 'Fight it!' Then a huge close-up of Lee's face: '*Fight it!*'

"Some biplane action from *Raiders of the Lost Ark* and a nighttime punch-out in a European hotel. 'My American friend Rex Van Ryn has joined our fight. We will need his courage—and his bravery.' Moody shots from *Subspecies*, a girl stalked through cobblestone streets by a giant looming shadow. 'There is a girl—Tanith. She may be one of them—or may be our only hope.' The montage accelerates, with seductive females, horrified faces, Nazis, Gothic interiors and finally a shot from *Talos the Mummy*, with an older Lee reaching for a dynamite plunger and pressing down. An explosion—and a shot of a lightning bolt streaking through the night sky and blasting a tree in half. A quick cut back to the Duc in the manor house. He stares into camera and intones ominously, 'It begins.' I kept the entire mini movie down to a tight six minutes.

"Maslansky often found himself explaining who he was and what he'd done to college-age studio executives who'd never

heard of *Police Academy*, much less *Race with the Devil*. After a year of legal wrangling, he managed to get all the possibly interested companies to sign quit claims. I'd become supernumerary at that point, which I'd expected.

"Then, Hammer changed hands. Roy Skeggs retired. Former Warners exec Terry Iliot became the new CEO and Ric Senat became his managing director. They stepped into a situation where they had a fully funded exploitable movie with a name actor, a bankable director and producer and they would get the company name back on the screen without spending a dime or lifting a finger. They pulled the plug. Over and done with. Finis.

"In L.A., a couple months later, Ric Senat and I met about *Flesh and Blood*, and he explained. 'Terry and I are both film makers. That's why we got involved with reviving the company and the franchise. *The Devil Rides Out* is one of the jewels in the Hammer crown. To give it away, to have only passive involvement with the company name on a movie we didn't make, even if we owned a piece of it, we felt it didn't benefit the company's credibility. If anybody's going to remake it, we want to do it.' It was understandable, and I might have made the same decision.

"But what a bummer. Imagine what could have been."

The Loneliness of Evil

Curse of the Crimson Altar
1968

Whicker's World: "I Don't Like My Monsters to Have Oedipus Complexes" (1968)

The King, Crown Prince and Queen of Suspense!

On October 18, 1963, *The Hollywood Reporter* announced that H.P. Lovecraft's "The Dunwich Horror" was to be filmed by AIP as *Scarlet Friday* in Italy with Mario Bava directing. The project would reteam Christopher Lee with Boris Karloff for the first time since *Corridors of Blood*. Sadly, *Scarlet Friday* was never made, and when AIP did get around to filming *The Dunwich Horror* in 1969, it failed to live up to such tantalizing credentials.

Largely ignored in his lifetime, H.P. Lovecraft (1890-1937) is today regarded as one of the most influential writers of fantasy. His "Great Old Ones"—a tribe of demonic elder Gods who ruled the earth before humanity's arrival—spawned a whole mythology (the "Cthulhu Mythos"), which has led to numerous spin-off books, movies and video games.

In *Christopher Lee's New Chamber of Horrors*, Lee wrote: "I have come to know the work of the American H.P. Lovecraft from A to Z and admire it greatly." After describing the writer as "a strange, reclusive figure living his life by night and carrying out his contact with the outside world solely by correspondence," Lee reveals: "I have some of his letters in my possession and they are brilliantly written in a most meticulous hand, covering a variety of subjects, not the least of these being the craft of terror. It is interesting to see how he addressed his mail from 'The Cave of the Crumbling Bones' at the 'Hour of the Rustling and the Slithering' and signed himself, 'Yours, by the Sunken Pylon—Ech-Pi-El.'" (The actor shows off a facsimile of one such missive in *100 Years of Horror*: "Demons.") He goes on: "My only regret is that so much of what he wrote is so full of weird creations that it would be impossible to film without brilliant and extremely expensive special effects."

When Christopher penned those words, there had been some attempts to film Lovecraft's work. The first of which, *The Haunted Palace* (1963), is erroneously accredited to Poe, but benefits, nevertheless, from some atmospheric sequences and Vincent Price in a dual performance. This Roger Corman-directed effort later went out on a UK double bill with AIP's second stab at Lovecraft, *Die, Monster, Die!* (1965), in which Boris Karloff keeps shrieking green mutants in his conservatory. Warner Bros. then entered the fray with *The Shuttered Room* (1966). Here, despite stylish direction and a sullen turn from Oliver Reed, Lovecraftian horrors play second fiddle to tedious gang violence.

In February 1968, Lee finally joined with Karloff and Barbara Steele for *Curse of the Crimson Altar*. Based on one of Lovecraft's greatest tales, "The Dreams in the Witch-House" (1932), the film was a collaboration between AIP and a new company, Tigon British, headed by Tony Tenser (1920-2007).

Dubbed the "Irving Thalberg of the exploitation movie" by screenwriter David McGillivray, Tenser began his career producing nudie shorts such as *Naked as Nature Intended* (1961) under the Compton Films banner. Realizing that horror could be as profitable as sexploitation, he followed up with *The Black Torment* and *A Study in Terror*, while backing Roman Polanski's first English-language films, *Repulsion* and *Cul-de-Sac* (1965). When Compton dissolved in 1966, shortly after the release of *The Projected Man*, Tony formed Tigon British Film Productions (with offices based at Hammer House on Wardour Street). Initially a distribution company, Tigon entered the field by re-releasing two early 1960s horrors, *Tower of London* and *Carnival of Souls*, but their first original productions were Michael Reeves' *The Sorcerers* and *The Blood Beast Terror*, with Peter Cushing. Tenser next bought the rights to Ronald Bassett's novel *Witchfinder General* and hired Reeves as director, resulting in one of the most revered horror films of the decade. Less admired is Tigon's next production.

"A rather dreadful film," was Lee's summation of *Curse of the Crimson Altar* (to Marcus Hearn in 2004), although he did enjoy working with Boris Karloff again. Despite rejecting a starring role in Hammer's new version of *The Old Dark House* (1962), Karloff's career was undergoing something of an Indian summer with such lasting classics as *How the Grinch Stole Christmas!* (1966), *Mad Monster Party?* (1966), *The Sorcerers* (1967) and *Targets* (1967). Although *Curse of the Crimson Altar* is often mistakenly cited as the actor's swansong (as is *Targets*), Boris made four more movies in the spring of 1968. These Mexican American co-productions (*The Fear Chamber*, *Snake People*, *House of Evil* and *The Incredible Invasion*) were shot over five weeks on a small Hollywood soundstage. Seated in his wheelchair with only half a lung, Karloff sucked oxygen from an ever-ready tank, before giving his all for the cameras.

"He [Karloff] was very sick," Lee confirmed to Marcus Hearn. "He couldn't walk. He had braces on his legs. He had emphysema, but tremendous courage and humor." Lee himself was somewhat infirm throughout *Curse of the Crimson Altar*, having slipped a disc in December 1967 following production on *The Blood of Fu Manchu*. After spending the Christmas period "flat on my back," Lee told his fan club that *Curse of the Crimson Altar*, "was one of the very few occasions in my career when I can honestly say I did not enjoy my work. This was not due to any individual, or to the film itself, but rather because I was in a state of constant apprehension about my wretched back. It is not easy to go through life suffering from any form of disability, still less so when this can affect one's professional career and work. And I was constantly worrying about whether I would be able to perform adequately and complete the picture without any disasters."

Lee does well to hide his discomfort, but the tweedy, mustachioed Squire Morley is not one of his most memorable characterizations, serving only to provide hospitality to antiques dealer Robert Manning (Mark Eden), who is looking for his lost brother (we know he has been sacrificed at the house, even if Lee denies all knowledge). More satisfactory are the film's self-reflexive moments: Firstly, the witch-detecting blade exhibited by Eden is the very one that pricks Rupert Davies' back in *Witchfinder General*—a neat in-joke, which not only serves as a nifty re-use of a prop, but also helps to establish a self-contained world of horror for Tigon. This is further enhanced by Davies guest-starring in *Curse of the Crimson Altar* as Vicar Radford. (He would next work alongside Lee on *Dracula Has Risen from the Grave*; was there a British horror film released in 1968 that Davies didn't appear in?)

Later, when Morley's niece, Eve (Virginia Wetherell), is showing Mark Eden around the family manor, she says, "It's a bit like one of those old houses in horror films," to which Eden responds, "I know what you mean: As though Boris Karloff's going to pop up at any moment." Naturally enough, he does.

As Professor Marsh, Karloff is nothing short of a delight. Note the look of distaste on his face as Eden chugs down the Professor's finest brandy and calls it "Good stuff," or the sweet way he looks into the camera and intones, "Instruments of torture." Unfortunately, the 80-year-old actor caught pneumonia during a night-shoot detailing a witch-burning simulation. (Karloff is actually hit by a firework in this scene, which he hurriedly brushes away.)

The film's impressive location is Grim's Dyke Hall, one of England's foremost haunted houses and the former residence of W.S. Gilbert, whose lyrics evoked a world of "Topsy-Turvydom" when set to the music of Arthur Sullivan (Lee was a great admirer of their operettas, as was H.P. Lovecraft). As well as being a one-time neighbor of Bram Stoker (who was a regular visitor to Grim's Dyke), Gilbert was not above penning the occasional strange tale himself, as evidenced by Peter Haining's 1982 collection *The Lost Stories of W.S. Gilbert*. In 1911, the lyricist died of a heart attack, aged 75, while rescuing a drowning girl in the lake at Grim's Dyke. Vincent Price would later haunt the location for *Cry of the Banshee*, while Vernon Sewell (1903-2011), director of *Crimson Altar*, had earlier shot *The Blood Beast Terror* there.

Lee had last worked for Sewell in 1957, playing the cruel SS officer, Brunner, in *Battle of the V-1*, and Nazi submarines had been the subject of the director's first film, *Morgenrot*, which he made in 1932 for the legendary German studio UFA. Continuing the maritime theme, 20 years later, Sewell wrote and directed *Ghost Ship*, purely because he owned the vessel on which it was filmed. The faux-supernatural plot of *Ghost Ship* was one that Sewell had introduced in 1934 with his first British film *The Medium*, and, with art studios and haunted houses in place of boats, would come to again with *Latin Quarter* (1945) and *House*

Barbara Steele plays the iconic Lavinia.

of Mystery (1960). Elsewhere, he directed two early thrillers for Hammer in 1950 (*The Black Widow* and *The Dark Light*), *The Ghosts of Berkeley Square* with Robert Morley and *Some May Live* with Peter Cushing. When David Pirie interviewed Sewell for his book *A Heritage of Horror* in the early 1970s, the young author was amazed to encounter "a weather-beaten old seadog with a commanding style and a very nautical line in expletives." After the woeful *Burke and Hare* (1970), Sewell grew "f****ed off with films" (as he put it to Pirie) and retired at sea on the very boat seen in *Ghost Ship*. He died in South Africa just a few weeks shy of his 98th birthday.

Sewell is aided on *Curse of the Crimson Altar* by Dutch cameraman John Coquillon (1930-1987), whose background filming wild animals for nature documentaries stood him in good stead when capturing the human savagery of *Witchfinder General*, *Cry of the Banshee* and Sam Peckinpah's *Straw Dogs* (1970). Coquillon would light *The Oblong Box*, *Scream and Scream Again* and *The Body Stealers*, as well as *The Changeling* (1979), a superior ghost story.

The script for *Crimson Altar* is by Mervyn Haisman (1928-2010) and Henry Lincoln (b. 1930), who were responsible for some of *Doctor Who*'s most memorable 1960s adventures, including "The Abominable Snowmen" (1967; for which they created the titular robotic monsters) and "The Web of Fear" (1968; wherein they introduced the popular recurring character of Lethbridge-Stewart).

Doctor Who, and his monstrous Daleks, also appear on a special edition of the BBC current affairs program *Whicker's World*, for which Christopher Lee is interviewed at home: Made in January 1968, shortly before filming commenced on *Curse of*

The Loneliness of Evil

Squire Morley (Christopher Lee)

the *Crimson Altar*, "I Don't Like My Monsters to Have Oedipus Complexes" (a quote from theater director, Peter Dowell, who is shown working on a ballet of Le Fanu's *Carmilla*), explores the manifestation of horror across 1960s pop culture.

Following a clip from *Dr. Terror's House of Horrors*, host Alan Whicker asks Lee to explain the appeal of horror films: "Principally, I suppose, escapism," the actor responds, "because it's utterly unlike our real lives, which, I suppose, today are inclined to be, perhaps, humdrum. I think that this particular kind of film gives you a jolt—an emotional jolt; it can help you to blow off steam: An emotional safety valve. But, principally, escapism into a world of fantasy and unreality and the weird ... I think, we harbor, within all of us, a basic, perhaps, subconscious love for things that we don't understand and don't know." Whicker then mentions those who regard "all horror movies as decadent and unwholesome and dangerous." Taking a puff on his cigarette, Lee rejoins: "Well, I think that's absolute nonsense ..."

Whicker is next seen in a gym, talking to a couple of actors who'd played henchmen in Lee's *Fu Manchu* films, one of whom is performing a handstand on two iron bars. When asked what he had to do in *The Brides of Fu Manchu*, the upside-down gentleman wheezes: "I was thrown into a snake pit."

There follows a discussion with Elisabeth Lutyens ("My contribution is to make this film what it is with knobs on") accompanied by a clip from *The Skull*, while, elsewhere, Milton Subotsky extolls the virtues of killer pianos. As a sign of the times, we also witness the dubious staging of a black magic ceremony and comments from youths, who equate the burgeoning world of horror with sex. The latter angle is exploited in *Curse of the Crimson Altar*, which opens on an "extract from Medical Journal," detailing the effects of hallucinogenic drugs, before plunging into a psychedelic gathering, complete with body painting and a writhing dancer, pouring not one, but two bottles of champagne down her breasts.

Barbara Steele (b. 1937) can be seen in the *Whicker's World* special, chatting upon a sofa. "I have a really spooky feeling that I've just made the same film over nine times," she says of her work, before wondering about fan mail: "I can't imagine why [men] propose to me, because I'm such a castration symbol."

To coincide with *Curse of the Crimson Altar*'s shoot, Tigon's distribution arm paired Lee's *The Castle of the Living Dead* with Steele's *Terror-Creatures from the Grave*, accompanied by the slogan "Lee & Steele!—Names That Spell Terror!" Green-skinned in wild head-dress, Steele looks incredible in *Curse of the Crimson Altar* as the witch Lavinia, but the role gives her little to do but oversee lame rituals surrounded by half-naked minions, her voice slathered in echo, although some animal-headed attendants during one session do prefigure similar sights in *The Wicker Man*.

Once described as "the illegitimate daughter of Christopher Lee and Cyd Charisse," Steele had been signed to the Rank Charm School by Olive Dodds, the very same woman who'd put Lee under contract a decade earlier. Steele's subsequent Hollywood career was cut short when a disagreement with *Invasion of the Body Snatchers* director Don Siegel caused her to abandon her starring role opposite Elvis Presley in *Flaming Star* (1960). Instead, she headed to Italy where Mario Bava cast her as the vengeful witch in *Black Sunday*. Reviewing the latter upon its 1960 release, R. Michael Johnson wrote: "Miss Steele ... gives one of the most chilling portrayals of a vampire seen on the screen, ranking in my opinion with Christopher Lee's new interpretation of Dracula." A star cameo as Vincent Price's deceitful wife in *Pit and the Pendulum* was followed, in 1962, by a brief appearance in Fellini's *8 ½* and a more substantial role as the haunted bride of *The Horrible Dr. Hichcock* and its sequel, *The Ghost*. Her renown as the Queen of Horror was further consolidated by leads in *Castle of Blood* (1963), *The Long Hair of Death* (1964), *Terror-Creatures from the Grave* (1965), *Nightmare Castle* (1965), *Revenge of the Blood Beast* (1965) and *An Angel for Satan* (1966).

Steele told an interviewer that she accepted the part of Lavinia "to pay the rent," but she, nonetheless, got on well with her leading man. "Barbara has a special affection for Christopher Lee," wrote Peter Haining, in *The Dracula Scrapbook*, who quoted the actress as saying: "Christopher has often called me up and said, 'I've had enough of seeing the producers get all the money—why don't we produce a film ourselves?' Then we've had a drunken lunch and laid plans to make a really gorgeous horror movie, with lots of sincerity and not another of those cheap, write-as-we-shoot efforts." Lee would eventually produce a horror film in 1972, *Nothing But the Night*, but the results could hardly be called "gorgeous" and Miss Steele was nowhere to be seen.

In the wake of *Crimson Altar*, Barbara's screen credits diminished somewhat until her "comeback" as the crippled prison warden in Jonathan Demme's *Caged Heat* (1974), a role she followed with such cult items as David Cronenberg's *Shivers* (1974, as a bathtub victim); Joe Dante's *Piranha* (1978, as the skeptical Dr. Mengers) and *Silent Scream* (1979, as a madwoman in an attic). Long wearied by her recognition as a "horror icon," Barbara has, in recent years, returned to the genre with two anthologies, *The Boneyard Collection* (2008) and *Minutes Past Midnight* (2016).

Steele, Karloff and Lee are joined, in *Curse of the Crimson Altar*, by a fourth Master of the Macabre. "The reason I'm not in the phone book is because I do these horror films," Michael Gough explained to Dr. David Soren in 1971. "You get crank calls and they really like it if they can get at your wife." In the same interview, Gough confessed: "You know, I never really made it like Chris Lee and Peter Cushing, but I wouldn't trade places with them for anything. I'm doing what I like." The actor, whose last horror film appearance had been as Joan Crawford's ill-fated business partner in *Berserk* (1966), is seen here as Lee's guilt-riddled butler, a role even more unrewarding than his cameo as a dead body in *The Legend of Hell House*. Gough would be awarded juicier parts in *The Corpse* (1969, as a controlling father), *Trog* (1969, a grouchy businessman), *Horror Hospital* (1972, the maniacal Dr. Storm), *Satan's Slave* (1976, a mustachioed warlock), *Top Secret!* (1982, a captured scientist), *The Little Vampire* (1985, Uncle Ludwig) and *Batman* (1988, as Alfred the butler; a character he reprised in *Batman Returns*, *Batman Forever* [1994] and *Batman & Robin* [1996]).

Far better served by his role in *Curse of the Crimson Altar* is Mark Eden (1928-2021; real name: Douglas Malin), who brings an appealing naturalism to his not altogether saintly protagonist. Best known to UK viewers as the dastardly Alan Bradley in Britain's longest-running soap opera *Coronation Street*, Eden had made his debut as "second journalist" in *Quatermass and the Pit* (1958), before starring as the father of the kidnapped child in *Séance on a Wet Afternoon* (1964) and, that same year, as "Marco Polo" in *Doctor Who*.

Eden's leading lady in *Curse of the Crimson Altar*, Virginia Wetherell (b. 1943), had also made an early appearance in *Doctor Who* (as a Thal in "The Daleks" [1963]), before being stabbed to death by her future spouse, Ralph Bates, in *Dr. Jekyll and Sister Hyde*. As well as essaying one of Jack Palance's vampire brides in the 1973 *Dracula*, Wetherell is throttled by Shane Briant for *Demons of the Mind*, provides a nude temptation for Malcolm McDowell in *A Clockwork Orange* and quite literally loses her heart to Mike Raven's *Disciple of Death* (1972). Today, she runs a London antiques shop and does much charitable work for *The Ralph Bates Pancreatic Cancer Research Fund*, in honor of her late husband. While calling Boris Karloff "the most wonderful person," Virginia told Bruce Hallenbeck (in *LSoH* #31) that she found Christopher Lee "aloof," stating that he would spend time between takes reading the newspaper: "He has a cold way about him. I wouldn't call him in the middle of the night if I was in trouble."

In Lee's defense, there was the aforementioned back trouble, ensuring he wasn't his usual self throughout production, and, furthermore, he was well aware that co-workers sometimes found him "aloof"—a point he addressed with Wayne Kinsey, in *The House That Hammer Built* (#16): "A lot of people have said I was rather aloof and kept very much to myself … When I'm making a movie, I am concentrating very hard. I may not appear to be, but I am, so that when we shoot the shot, I can deliver to the best of my ability." Therefore, when not required for a scene, he would "sit down, read a paper, read a book, or say nothing." As he explained: "Now, that's not being aloof and unapproachable. It's simply because I'm saving my energy and I'm not getting involved in conversations which would make me lose my concentration. I mean, we had a lot of laughs, we had a lot of fun. Everybody was cracking jokes all the time and I joined in, too—but, when it mattered, I would go and sit somewhere and not speak to anyone, and if people think that's me being aloof, grand and distant, I can't do anything about that."

Lee has a point. As the star of the show, a lot was riding on him to deliver a smooth performance, so that production would run on time, budgets wouldn't overflow and cast and crew (and their families) could eat. As Peter Cushing said of filmmaking in his second volume of memoirs, *Past Forgetting*: "There is too much at stake, and too little time, to have 'fun' in the true sense of the word." Both Lee and Cushing were artists who took their craft seriously, as was Boris Karloff.

During the filming of *Curse of the Crimson Altar*, Boris presented Lee with a photo of himself, inscribed: "Dear Christopher. Many, many more together, I hope." The picture would remain on Lee's drawing room wall for the rest of his days. "I can never look at that photograph without feeling really rather sad," he told Marcus Hearn. "I was very fond of him."

Michael Gough confirmed this to David Del Valle (in *LSoH* #23): "Christopher was devoted to Boris, and that was quite moving to observe, since I had never seen Christopher defer to anyone as he did to Karloff." Barbara Steele backed this up by stating that Lee tended to Boris like "a guardian angel."

On the film's completion, Lee told his fan club: "I really felt I had no cause to complain when I looked at Boris Karloff, with

Christopher Lee and Boris Karloff on the set rehearsing a scene.

The Loneliness of Evil

and devoted to the field and above all serious about their work. The scripts were written with taste, integrity and style—and the directors were men of the highest attainments and considerable knowledge of their craft. Alas, I cannot say the same today. I frequently spoke about this to Boris, and we were fully in agreement over this matter. He, like me, deplored the flood of garbage spattering the screen today—not only in our field, but in most of the major productions …"

Although, after an intriguing beginning, *Curse of the Crimson Altar* descends into a confusing muddle, the film is not complete "garbage": There is a wintry charm to its settings that feels almost cozy at times, while Barbara Steele's Lavinia alone provides one of the most iconic images in 1960s horror cinema. But the story bears scant resemblance to its literary source.

Indeed, it wouldn't be until 1984, and Stuart Gordon's *Re-Animator*, that a satisfying adaptation of Lovecraft would reach the screen. (Though it's doubtful that the author would have approved of Gordon's subsequent liaisons with his work [*From Beyond*, 1986; *Castle Freak*, 1994], he would certainly have accepted two exquisite films from the H.P. Lovecraft Historical Society, *The Call of Cthulhu* [2005] and *The Whisperer in Darkness* [2011].)

A Lovecraftian feel also suffuses such diverse blockbusters as John Carpenter's *The Thing* (1981), Ivan Reitman's *Ghostbusters* (1983) and Jordan Vogt-Roberts' *Kong: Skull Island* (2015), even if, sadly, it can't be found in *Curse of the Crimson Altar*.

whom it was a joy to work again … With all [his infirmities], he remains indomitably cheerful and full of good spirits. A lesson to us all."

Immediately following *Curse of the Crimson Altar*, Karloff was all set to star alongside a young David Bowie in Tigon's *The Haunted House of Horror* (also shot at Grim's Dyke), but Bowie was rejected by co-producers AIP, and Karloff proved too ill (his part was taken by Dennis Price, while Julian Barnes replaced the future music icon). Retitled *Horror House*, the film would serve as *Curse of the Crimson Altar*'s co-feature in the US. (Until November 1970, when it was replaced by *Count Yorga Vampire*.)

Curse of the Crimson Altar was first issued in the UK on Sunday, December 8, 1968, but wouldn't see release in America until Friday, May 1, 1970, where, retitled *The Crimson Cult*, its advertising made reference to Karloff with the tagline: "The Master of Evil in his last and most shocking role." Boris passed away, at the age of 81, on Sunday, February 2, 1969. Shortly afterwards, Lee communicated his feelings in Forrest J Ackerman's paperback tribute, *The Frankenscience Monster*: "I always found him a wise and understanding friend, with a fund of warmth and humor and above all, of indomitable courage and cheerfulness in the face of great adversity. He truly loved his fellow men …"

Lee also paid tribute to Karloff in his fan club bulletin, and this allowed him to make some interesting comments on the genre in which they both toiled: "The impact that [Boris] made on the history of the cinema will last as long as films are made. I can only hope that when my time comes, it may be possible in some measure to say the same about my contribution to the world of the fantastic and the strange. In one respect I envy him greatly. He made his name at a time when the 'horror' film was not in any way a gimmick. Performers were talented

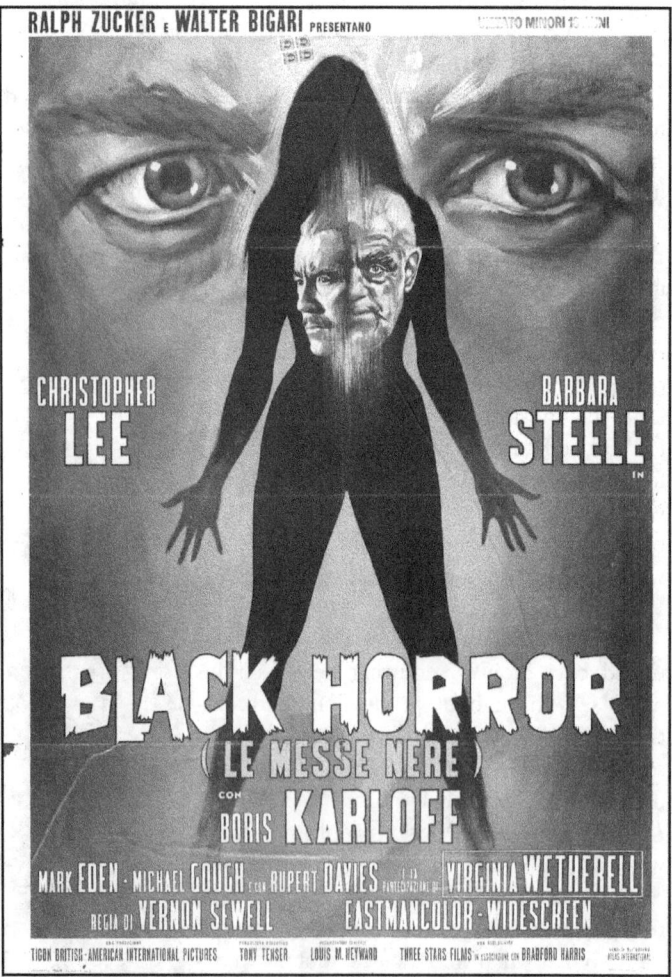

The Crimson Altar was released under various titles including The Crimson Cult and Black Horror. Top poster is French and bottom poster is Italian.

Dracula Has Risen from the Grave 1968

You just can't keep a good man down.

The third Dracula, which I have not dared to look at, as I am convinced it is a very indifferent film, is making fantastic sums of money on the London circuit. I have got past understanding any of this now.—Christopher Lee, in the January/February 1969 edition of his *Club Bulletin*

Whereas they used to do it very well 20 years ago—you know, Bela Lugosis and the Boris Karloffs—I don't think they're as frightening as old Christopher Lee. I think he scares people more than anybody else.—James Carreras, *The World This Weekend*, BBC Radio 4, April 1968

The first Hammer film to be made as part of a new US distribution deal with Warner Bros.-Seven Arts, *Dracula Has Risen from the Grave*, began production at Pinewood Studios on Monday, April 22, 1968. The script was by Anthony Hinds and the director's chair was filled, at short notice, by Freddie Francis. (Terence Fisher had originally been set to direct but was out of action with a broken leg after being hit by a motorcycle; he would be knocked down again, on the same stretch of road, two years later.)

"Get [Christopher Lee] in a horror film and you're half-way there," Francis told Marcelle Perks, in *The Dark Side* #51, but that was easier said than done. The actor initially rejected *Dracula Has Risen from the Grave*, as he revealed to Marcus Hearn in 2004: "I got *frantic* telephone calls from Hammer," one of which came from James Carreras. Although Lee admitted to being "very fond" of Hammer's managing director, he was less pleased with Sir James' inveigling approach. According to the actor, Carreras said: "I'm 61 years of age, the strain is too much for me, I can't stand this; I'm on my knees begging you. You've got to do it; you've got to do it!" Unmoved, Lee turned the offer down again. More frantic phone calls ensued. "And then the truth came out," said Lee, Sir James "had sold the picture to the American distributor on the condition that I play the part." And then Carreras said: "Think of the people you'll put out of work." "A monstrous thing to say," in Lee's opinion, but nevertheless, "I can't be held responsible for putting loads of people out of work. That is the *only* reason I did those extra films beyond the first two."

Freddie Francis gave a different perspective to Lee's relationship with the Count (in *The Dark Side* #51): "Chris, like any artist, likes to be admired and recognized. He and Tony Hinds had to go to the East End once for a premiere for one of the Dracula films. Chris was made up as Dracula and they went all through the East End and nobody recognized him. Chris was absolutely livid!"

The actor was not much happier with *Dracula Has Risen from the Grave*, as he revealed to his fan club: "The film was made with complete absence of style, taste or production quality. The critics tore it to bits, as they always do with a Hammer Film Production, and yet, according to Seven Arts and Hammer, it is probably the most successful picture they have made. In its first day, on general release in the Southern area of London, it grossed over £25,000."

While Lee's tone is certainly refreshing (can you imagine any of today's stars promoting their movies with such candor?), nothing could be further from the mark when it comes to his criticism of style—*Dracula Has Risen from the Grave* is loaded with visual flair, courtesy of Freddie Francis (whose last Hammer film this was). At the suggestion of cinematographer Arthur Grant, the director even brought along the amber camera filters he had used on *The Innocents*, which give Dracula's scenes an eerie tint. Consequently, Lee is especially sepulchral in this one: Waiting alone in shadows, he looks as though he has been carved from stone. (*Dracula Has Risen from the Grave* was one of Tim Burton's favorite films growing up, and shots of Dracula standing sentinel atop the rooftops, cloak billowing in the wind, are echoed by the director's caped crusader in *Batman*.)

Also effective is the look of gentle pleading in the vampire's bloodshot eyes when he first approaches Maria (Veronica Carlson), while the intimacy of his bite is presented with fresh explicitness. After the obligatory nuzzling established by Hammer's first *Dracula*, Francis zooms into Carlson's jugular vein and adds the rather loaded symbolism of her hand pushing away a childhood doll from beneath the vampire's cloak. (As Carlson remembered, in *LSoH*, the doll was actually a valuable antique, and a prop man lay beside the bed to catch it as it fell.) Lee spits out his few lines with ferocious energy but, as in *Dracula: Prince of Darkness*, speaks a thousand words via his presence alone.

After a startling credits sequence, which looks to be set against a montage of pulsating veins (Tobe Hooper would employ a similar effect for the opening titles of *The Texas Chain Saw Massacre*), *Dracula Has Risen from the Grave* begins with the discovery of a victim inside a church bell. A year after the vampire's death, and the villagers still live in fear. As George A. Cooper's landlord explains, the shadow of Dracula's castle "touches the church." (The dark fairy tale look of the castle is courtesy of matte artist Peter Melrose, who had previously worked on Polanski's *Dance of the Vampires*.) When the Monsignor (Rupert Da-

Peter Cushing visits the set of *Dracula Has Risen from the Grave* with Veronica Carlson, Christopher Lee and Barbara Ewing to accept the Queen's Award for Industry, awarded May 29, 1968.

vies) arrives to exorcise the offending edifice with a priest (Ewan Hooper), they succeed only in freeing the Count from his icy tomb. (The way Lee suckles at the blood spilling from the priest's head is a particularly unpleasant detail.)

Ewan Hooper (b. 1935) had met a similarly bloody and watery death in his previous feature, *How I Won the War*, and would later appear with Lee in Stuart Burge's *Julius Caesar* (1969). As well as being splendidly creepy when under Dracula's dark enchantment, Hooper marvelously conveys the priest's torn feelings between Light and Darkness. (Fittingly, the Scots-born actor had earlier written a musical based on the life of Christ entitled *A Man Dies*, which was filmed as a Belgian TV-movie in 1969.) "The thing I remember most ... was having lunches with Christopher Lee," Hooper told Adam Jezard in *Hammer Horror* #6: "He was fascinating ... we were amazed to find out he had been an intelligence officer and had interviewed the leading Nazis at the end of the war."

For *Dracula Has Risen from the Grave*, Lee wears a copy of the ring worn by Bela Lugosi in *Abbott and Costello Meet Frankenstein*. Similar to that movie, his vampire also casts a reflection on being resurrected. Freddie Francis excused this misappropriation of Bram Stoker lore to Marcelle Perks (in *The Dark Side* #51): "If I did [give Dracula a reflection] it's because I didn't know the true legend! Anyway, it would be boring if all films just repeated the same old stuff."

Also controversial is the scene where Dracula rips the stake from his heart because the atheist hero, Paul (Barry Andrews), cannot bring himself to utter the requisite prayers. Shortly after the film's release, Lee told journalist Tim Stout: "It was all wrong that Dracula should have been able to remove the stake. Everyone knows a stake through the heart is the very end of a vampire. I objected at the time, but it was overruled. It is an extremely gruesome sequence; the blood comes pouring out ..."

Critics and viewers have long carped about this moment, but as well as being a powerful image, it is not without credence: Christian folklore dictates that not only should a vampire's staking be carried out by a priest in a ritualistic fashion (including prayers), but that, if the stake is not delivered with a single blow, the vampire would have the power to free itself of his impalement.

Furthermore, Paul's atheistic stance brings an interesting dynamic to the drama, especially when matched against the Monsignor's spiritual beliefs. The Hammer horrors, after all, deal compellingly with the greatest conflicts at the heart of existence: Love and Hate, Good and Evil, Science and Superstition. As such, it's significant that Hammer's Dracula films were banned outright in then-Communist countries such as Poland (whose authorities, like Paul, denied the existence of God), because they promoted the power of the cross, whereas, in Catholic countries like Italy, they were a huge success. (Hammer's attention to the spiritual aspects of their horror films even extended to hiring a religious adviser, Reverend Charles Sinnickson, for *Taste the Blood of Dracula*.)

The scene of Dracula removing the stake from his body was shot on Lee's 46th birthday, Monday, May 27, 1968. Barry Andrews told Tom Johnson and Deborah Del Vecchio that, during its filming, "the lights went out and suddenly two beautiful maidens appeared bearing a cake ... 'Happy Birthday' was sung by everyone on the set and, slowly, Mr. Lee began to rise from his coffin, 'blood' dripping from his hands and chest." Lee plunged the stake into the center of the cake and hissed "Suck off!" through gleaming fangs. "Everyone roared," said Andrews, "before breaking into uncontrollable laughter."

Two days later, there was an on-set celebration of a different kind, when Hammer were presented with the Queen's Award to Industry—the first and only time a movie company had been so honored, although ITC, the TV production outfit behind *Thunderbirds*, had won the award in 1966. Tellingly, Alix Palmer of the *Daily Express* added: "It is really Mr. Lee, [Hammer's] monster king, who should collect [the award]."

Mr. Lee described the award itself as "a sort of plastic block with these crossed whatever-they-are, cogs, in the middle," while Michael Carreras told John Brosnan: "It was a marvelous thing for us, because the majority of the British film industry, up to that time, regarded us as a bit of a joke." (A cartoon in London's *Daily Mirror*, headlined "'Dracula' star to be honored by the Queen," showed a likeness of Lee's vampire floating into Buckingham Palace, as one guard says to another, "I bet she won't ask him to stay to dinner.")

The award ceremony was held at Pinewood on Wednesday, May 29, 1968. After a salmon luncheon with wine, Sir Henry Floyd, Lord Lieutenant of Buckinghamshire, addressed the cast and crew: "I know you have had great success with what are termed 'horror films,' but I was glad to learn from your chairman that the word 'horror' does not include scenes of actual personal violence." The speech was delivered only moments before the Lord Lieutenant witnessed Lee writhing around impaled on a giant golden crucifix, blood weeping from his eyes. ("I gave extra thought to highly visual ways to do in the Count," Anthony Hinds told *LSoH*.) According to Lee, Sir Henry watched the scene with a blank expression, then turned to his wife and said: "You know, my dear, that man is a member of my club." Aside from this minor embarrassment, the impalement was also difficult for Lee to film as he was still recovering from a slipped disc. Nevertheless, the actor brings a powerful sadness to the vampire's expiration, evoking a release from damnation that is pitiful to behold. (Remembering this scene, Peter Jackson had Lee re-enact it for his denouement in the final *Lord of the Rings* entry, *The Return of the King*.)

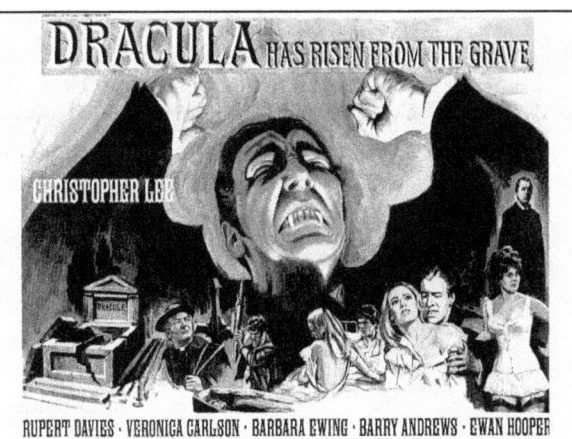

Dracula Has Risen from the Grave further benefits from some fantastic sets, courtesy of Bernard Robinson, who was working on his last Christopher Lee movie. (Robinson would die in 1970, not long after designing *Frankenstein Must Be Destroyed*.) The rooftops, by which the lovers make secret rendezvous, betray an almost *Caligari*-like angularity and add immeasurably to the film's fairy tale feel, as do scenes of Veronica Carlson, in her white nightdress, traipsing after Dracula through Black Park.

Trumpeted in the film's trailer as "Hammer's new star discovery; Dracula's most beautiful victim," Veronica Carlson (b. 1944) would skip college classes to enjoy the latest escapades of Lee and Cushing at the cinema, as she told LSoH: "I must have been Hammer's biggest film fan." Although her movie career had begun with a small role in *Casino Royale* (1966, which also features Caroline Munro), Veronica revealed to Bruce Hallenbeck (in *LSoH* #13): "For the first time, I felt a real contact with an actor when I worked with [Christopher Lee] … He always gave me an eye-line. Some actors wouldn't … I felt the impact of acting opposite a fine actor. It was the most wonderful moment, and I've savored it many times since." In the same interview, she said of Lee: "He's the most helpful man … I really had no acting experience. And here's this very highly thought-of actor with a wonderful reputation … And I expected him to make me afraid, but he doesn't do that at all. He helps you, he's gentle, he's respectful of your feelings … He was very warm to me, very kind."

A talented artist, Veronica drew a fine rendering of Christopher backstage, telling *LSoH*: "He was as good as gold, he hardly blinked." The actor would have good reason to blink on other occasions during the shoot, as Veronica remembered, to Al Taylor, in *LSoH* #8: "His eyes would often tear from [the red contact lenses]. I can remember times when he would remove them, and his own eyes would be as red as the contacts were intended to make them look. But he never complained."

Carlson next appeared with Lee on his *This is Your Life* in April 1974, along with Joanna Lumley and Valerie Van Ost ("the most attractive blood group in pictures"). Following her bravura turn as the beleaguered heroine of *Frankenstein Must Be Destroyed*, Veronica's talents were somewhat underused in subsequent horror films, *The Horror of Frankenstein* (1970, as Elizabeth), *Vampira* (1973, as a *Playboy* Playmate), and *The Ghoul* (1974, as a 1920s flapper). Nevertheless, her stand-out performances for Hammer ensure that she remains one of the genre's most popular actresses.

Veronica's love interest in *Dracula Has Risen from the Grave*, Barry Andrews (b. 1944), would later star with her in a Freddie Francis-directed episode of *The Saint*, "The Man Who Gambled with Life" (1968). Reunited with Roger Moore for *The Spy Who Loved Me* and *North Sea Hijack* (1979), Barry can also be seen as the discoverer of ancient evil in *Blood on Satan's Claw*, the glowering police sergeant in *Revenge* (1971), and the Mandrel-zapping Stott in *Doctor Who*: "Nightmare of Eden" (1979).

Freddie Francis, meanwhile, would next approach the *Dracula* legend in 1970—with very different results. Filmed in the same Austrian castle where Mario Bava would stage *Baron Blood*, *The Vampire Happening* is a bizarre sex comedy, in which Ferdy Mayne's Count arrives at a party via helicopter and, after being tickled on a bed by four nude blondes, proceeds to flounce about with his pants round his ankles. Amid all this, Mayne pays tribute to an old friend by having his Dracula announce: "Call me Christopher. I'm sure he won't mind."

Dracula Has Risen from the Grave wrapped two days behind schedule on Tuesday June 4, 1968, and was released in the UK on Sunday November 24, 1968 (when the Hugo Montenegro Orchestra were at No. 1 with the theme tune from *The Good, the Bad and the Ugly*), and on Thursday February 6, 1969, in the US (when Tommy James and the Shondells topped the charts with "Crimson and Clover"). Aided by a campy ad campaign, with slogans like, "Boy does he give a hickey," *Dracula Has Risen from the Grave* did excellent business on both sides of the Atlantic, becoming one of Hammer's highest grossing movies (certainly the most financially successful of their *Dracula* ventures), despite the usual sneers from the press. Heading his column, "Monster Disappointment," Dick Richards complained in the *Sun*: "Isn't it time that dear old Dracula was pensioned off?", before concluding: "Fangs ain't what they used ter be."

Things were certainly not what they used to be, as the film's producer, Aida Young (1920-2007), was one of the first women

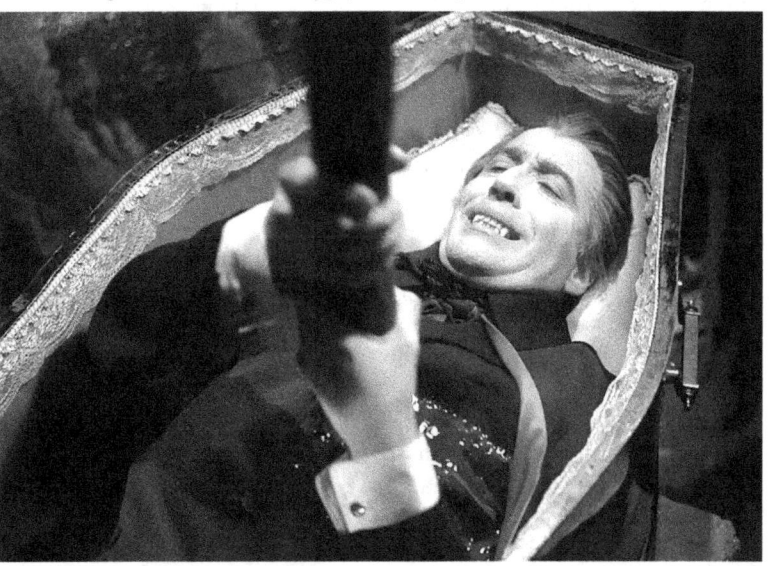

Barbara Ewing and Christopher Lee on location at Black Park

to succeed in a very male-dominated field. As Young herself said of that era (quoted in Sinclair McKay's *A Thing of Unspeakable Horror*): "If you were a woman, you had to do continuity, or you were a secretary, or you were wardrobe, make-up and hair—that was it."

A second assistant director for Hammer as early as *The Quatermass Xperiment*, Young had served as associate producer on *She*, *One Million Years B.C.* and *Slave Girls*, before becoming a full-blown producer with *The Vengeance of She*. "Aida was extraordinary," Jane Merrow tells me. "One of the best producers I've ever worked with."

To prepare for *Dracula Has Risen from the Grave*, Young watched five Hammer horror films in a row, with very low expectations; but, as she told Tom Paans, in *LSoH* #13: "I remember staggering out of the theater, feeling very high on these films and very impressed by the quality of them." This belief was reinforced on *Dracula Has Risen from the Grave*: "When anybody knocked the Hammer horror films, which a lot of snooty people did, as I had done before I made any, I got very indignant because I knew the work that had gone into it and that it was done by wonderful technicians ... This wasn't like a violent film ... This was pure fantasy ... There was nothing there to upset anybody and it was a good story. How times have changed!"

The producer also told Paans that, prior to filming, she dined with Lee ("because I felt I ought to know him ... It was quite an interesting lunch") and found that he was "a unique character," who "probably wouldn't get a leading role elsewhere ... whatever part he got in a film [outside of the genre] would have to be a secondary or tertiary part. With Dracula, he was king." Backhanded compliments aside, she had "a whale of a time" on her first vampire movie, surmising: "I have nothing but good thoughts and feelings about the time I worked for [Hammer]."

Indeed, throughout the late 1960s, at least, it could be argued that Hammer were providing stronger roles for women in front of the camera, too; the feisty Zena in *Dracula Has Risen from the Grave* being one example. Zena is brought brilliantly to life by Barbara Ewing (born in New Zealand, 1944), who tells me: "The whole thing was a very weird experience for someone who had recently graduated from RADA with the gold medal for best student and had hopes of working for the Royal Shakespeare Company. (I did briefly, just before, or just after, *Dracula*!)"

Fresh from her RADA triumph, Freddie Francis gave Barbara a special introductory credit for *Torture Garden*, in which she is menaced by a killer piano. Her other genre credits include the vengeful witch of *A Ghost Story for Christmas*: "The Ash Tree" (1975), the owner of a demonic mirror in *Hammer House of Horror*: "Guardian of the Abyss," and the mysterious lollipop lady of *Chiller*: "Number Six" (1994). After appearing in *Eye of the Needle* (1981) with Donald Sutherland, and *Haunters of the Deep* (1984), with Andrew Keir, Barbara established herself as a novelist. (Of her books, Hammer fans should particularly enjoy *The Mesmerist* for its Victorian backdrop of mesmerism and murder.) In July 2017, she very graciously took time out from working on her latest manuscript to answer my questions:

SM: *Having recently been awarded the Gold Medal for best student at RADA, how did you feel about doing a Hammer horror film? I've heard that people in the industry could be quite snooty about them at the time.*

BE: Of course, I was snooty about doing "horror films" at that time! I was aiming rather for the Royal Shakespeare Company! But by the time I did *Dracula Has Risen from the Grave*, I had already been in *Torture Garden*, directed by Freddie Francis, and I had liked working for him, and appreciated that he was teaching me about working in front of a camera—of which I had no experience whatsoever, and not much training for that at RADA, either, in those days. I have a memory that I was paid £400 for *Dracula* (my pay in my first repertory companies playing leads was £14 per week), but I am not certain. Who was to know that I'd still be getting fan mail, etc. for that film in 2017!

James and Michael Carreras, who ran Hammer at that time, wanted to fire me as soon as they saw me because they thought I wasn't "sexy" enough (I was very thin). Freddie and Aida Young weren't having that. They took me away, found me that red wig, and Aida taught me to make that stuffed-bra bosom, dressed me in low cut blouses and took me back. The bosses were very happy. I have *no idea* whether they knew it was still me or thought I was someone else. Freddie and Aida were both absolutely and totally supportive of me. Freddie knew I was shy of appearing in corsets, etc. so when I had to do that scene with Barry Andrews, he cleared the set. Aida took me one night to my very first opera ever, *Don Giovanni*, I think, at the Royal Opera House. I liked them both very much indeed.

Freddie's wife asked me to go to his funeral and I was working and couldn't, and I regret that so much, to this day.

SM: *What were your impressions of Christopher Lee? How did it feel to be bitten by him?*

BE: Christopher Lee was very tall and upright and quite self-contained, but pleasant and professional. There's always something reassuring about working with someone who always knows the lines and has prepared the work, as he always had. He arrived at the studio in a beret always, and went straight to make-up, so we never saw him without his Dracula hair. We had quite a few dramatic scenes together, always very professional. To be honest, I can't remember much about actually being bitten by him, except, once bitten, I always had to have a big make-up job on my neck. I remember also going to a dentist to have fangs made—which any human bitten by Dracula always grew automatically—and my disappointment at not being allowed to keep them afterwards. I was really actually frightened when I was being chased by Dracula and six horses in the night through a forest of trees—the horses got nearer and nearer—but that was a Dracula double driving them, of course.

SM: *I really think you make Zena one of the most interesting female characters in Hammer's oeuvre (she's far sassier than the usual victim in billowing gown). Although Hammer were, I think, quite ahead of the game in employing female producers such as Aida Young, how did you feel about their representation of female characters, both then and now?*

BE: I can remember most trying to make Zena sound not too like an Antipodean! As I said, Aida was totally supportive, and, I think, respected me as an actress and just let me get on with it. As to how Hammer portrays women, you probably guess perfectly well what I now have to admit: I haven't ever seen another Hammer horror film! All I can say on that subject is, I *always*, in my own books, try to write good parts for older women.

SM: *Any other impressions of fellow cast or crew members?*

BE: All the cast were nice, and Christopher Lee was, of course, the *star* and the production revolved around him, but I got on best with Ewan Hooper, another stage actor. He was forever telling me of his dream of opening a theater in Greenwich (or no, maybe he had already started getting it built? I think I paid for a brick or a seat)—anyway, when it was built, I worked for him there several times, including in the play *Gymnasium* that was seen by a producer and casting director for Granada TV and from which I got my first TV lead in one of the *Country Matters* series: "The Little Farm," which was nominated for an Emmy. This led to me getting lots of leads in lots of Granada productions culminating in *Brass* [1983-1990; a popular mining sitcom, in which Barbara excels as revolutionary firebrand Agnes Fairchild], where I used the Hammer trick of emerging with a large bosom! So—although this has only occurred to me as I am writing this—you could say that, in a roundabout way, I owe my whole on-going acting career to Freddie Francis and Aida Young!

Regarding that bosom: When I was in *Brass*, I had quite a number of letters from women telling me their husbands said I was more sexy than their wives and other horrible things. So I *always* made it clear it was a false bosom. I always told them how to do it—but only after writing "Leave the bastard" first.

I also had my funniest film experience with Ewan. He was to burn me in the fire; we rehearsed and then did a take. *However*, in the rehearsals, the special effects guys hadn't turned up the fire, and nobody had warned me that they were going to, so, in the take, when Ewan put me into the fire, it blazed up (unexpectedly to me) and I said *SHIT* very loudly and we had to cut and start again! (It was gas, of course, not real flames, but I did get a fright!)

SM: *What was it like to act upon those fantastic sets at Pinewood?*

BE: I guess I just took them for granted, Stephen, although I remember being very impressed by the rooftops—Veronica and Christopher had to climb around them in the dark, which must have been very scary. The aforementioned chase through the trees at night (well, they were *real* trees, I think!) was, for me, the really frightening bit.

SM: *What can you recall of the Queen's Award to Industry ceremony?*

BE: All I can remember about the Queen's Award was that Peter Cushing came, too. He and Christopher accepted the award with Veronica Carlson and I standing on either side of them. Everybody at Hammer was very proud.

SM: *Finally, what are your feelings towards* Dracula Has Risen from the Grave, *both then and now?*

BE: So, as I've said, I was a bit snooty when I got the part, but I worked hard because I so admired Freddie and Aida and wanted to please them. And now—it just makes me smile. I'm glad I had that experience, and it amazes me that people still write to me about it.

Barbara Ewing and Christopher Lee

The Oblong Box
1968

Some things are better left buried.

The Oblong Box marks the first of Christopher Lee's films with Vincent Price (even though *The Masque of the Red Death* often turns up mistakenly in Lee filmographies, because John Westbrook's hooded "Man in Red" possesses a similar voice).

Described in the *House of Usher* trailer as "the screen's foremost delineator of the Draculean," Vincent Price (1911-1993) began his screen career with such borderline Universal horrors as *Tower of London* (1939), *The Invisible Man Returns* (1939) and *The House of the Seven Gables* (1940), before essaying meaty roles in 20th Century Fox classics like *The Song of Bernadette* (1943), *Laura* (1944) and *Leave Her to Heaven* (1945). While Fox offered him two movies, *Shock* and *Dragonwyck* (both 1945), which would prefigure his Gothic renown, Vincent's horror career proper didn't kick off until his marvelous performance as the disfigured sculptor in *House of Wax* (1953). This was swiftly followed by *The Mad Magician* (1953), *The Fly* (1958), *Return of the Fly* (1959) and two fun shockers for William Castle: *House on Haunted Hill* (1958) and *The Tingler* (1959). Price consolidated his fiendish screen persona at AIP, where frivolous appearances in *Master of the World* (1960), *Beach Party* (1963) and *Dr. Goldfoot and the Bikini Machine* (1965) were countered by his work on Roger Corman's Poe cycle. Beginning with *House of Usher* (1960), the Hollywood series took in *Pit and the Pendulum* (1961), *Tales of Terror* (1961) and *The Raven* (1962), before decamping to England for *The Masque of the Red Death* (1963) and *The Tomb of Ligeia* (1964). The latter title, in particular, benefits from its British locations, as does *Witchfinder General* (1967), which contains Price's most unsettling performance as real-life witch-hunter Matthew Hopkins.

Witchfinder director Michael Reeves was initially contracted to helm *The Oblong Box*, but frustrated with Laurence Huntington's script, he called in Christopher Wicking (1943-2008) to help rewrite it. (According to biographer Benjamin Halligan, one of Reeves' embellishments was to have the voodoo practitioners chant the name of Roger Corman backwards: "Namroc! Namroc!") Huntington, who had previously written, produced and directed *The Vulture* (1966)—one of the daftest films in horror history—would sadly die 11 days into *The Oblong Box*'s three-week shoot, making the film appear to be as cursed as its antagonists, especially when one considers Reeves' hospitalization, following a drug overdose, the Saturday before filming began. (The young filmmaker would die from an accidental barbiturates overdose on February 11, 1969.)

The very morning that *The Oblong Box* commenced shooting at Shepperton, on Monday, November 18, 1968, the unenviable task of replacing Reeves was accepted by German-born Gordon Hessler (1925-2014). A former associate producer of *The Alfred Hitchcock Hour*, Hessler came to England to helm *Catacombs* (1963), an interesting slice of Grand Guignol starring Jane Merrow, who tells me her director was: "Charming. A gentleman, I would say."

In 1989, Christopher Wicking told *Fangoria* #84 about his own contributions to *The Oblong Box*: "I made the theme of imperial exploitation of the natives the subtext, the cause of the curse. The film was banned in Texas for being too 'pro-Negro' at the time, a minor joy I didn't expect to get from a horror movie."

Wicking had certainly hit upon a valid political point, what with race riots, the assassination of Martin Luther King, Jr. and escalating warfare in Vietnam all taking place throughout 1968. But if *The Oblong Box* is really about the oppression of different races, then its message is lost in a mire of gratuitous violence and unsympathetic characters. (Wicking would tackle the subject more successfully with *Absolute Beginners* [1985].) Reflective of the aforementioned world events, such nihilistic qualities had already informed *Witchfinder General* and *Night of the Living Dead*. By comparison, though, *The Oblong Box* is pretty unengaging. It's doubtful that even Michael Reeves could have made a better film from such lackluster material. The movie benefits, nonetheless, from John Coquillon's rich cinematography, and a chilling finale that, alas, seems too long in coming.

Decked out in silver wig, "special guest star" Christopher Lee is the reluctant Dr. Newhartt, blackmailed into housing Vincent Price's voodoo-disfigured brother, Sir Edward Markham (Alister Williamson). Despite describing himself as "a man turned inside-out through sorcery," Edward's disfigurement, when finally unmasked, amounts to nothing more unsettling than a mild bout of acne. Although enjoying as much screen time as Price, Lee is confined to his laboratory set throughout, and the scenes that play out there largely fall flat. For instance, rather than being a thrilling showdown, the confrontation between Lee and Ivor Dean's police superintendent seems more like a competition to see which actor is wearing the worst hairpiece (Dean wins, *just*). Indeed, Lee made reference to Dr. Newhartt's Beatlesque rug when telling his fan club: "Both my wife and my secretary say I look like an old 'queen'!"

Christopher Lee appears as Dr. Newhartt

Dr. Newhartt may be a negligible role, but the real crime is that Lee doesn't get to share any scenes with Price, until his character lies dying and spattered in blood. "You're lying on my train," Lee recalled Price gurgling. To the same author, Lucy Chase Williams, Lee revealed that Vincent "had been told I was very remote and very reserved and very difficult to talk to …" Any apprehension was soon quashed when Price bounded over, shook Lee's hand and smiled: "Oh, I'm so happy that we're doing this picture together!"

In 1991, Price elaborated on the ensuing friendship (to Mark A. Miller): "We screamed with laughter from the minute we shook hands until now. We get along just like mad … write each other rude notes and funny letters … He's one of the few actors in my life that I have stayed in touch with … I think he's got a wonderful sense of humor, but I don't think everybody knows how to get at it. For some reason or other we strike each other as funny, and it's wonderful fun to be with him."

Hilary Dwyer (1945-2020), who had been assaulted by Price for her debut feature *Witchfinder General*, now found herself giving an excellent performance as the actor's wife. (She would next play his daughter in *Cry of the Banshee*, inspiring Vincent's comment: "If you ever play my mother, I'll marry you.") Dwyer went on to portray Isabella Linton in AIP's *Wuthering Heights* (1970), but after a 1976 appearance in *Space: 1999*, she retired from acting to become, under her married name of Heath, a successful producer. Her credits in this capacity include *The Worst Witch* (1986); two Gary Oldman vehicles, *Criminal Law* (1987) and *Nil by Mouth* (1996); and an episode of the paranormal reality series *The Dead Files* (2012).

Newhartt's maid is played by Sally Geeson (b. 1950; sister of Judy, Lee's mistress in *Diagnosis: Murder*). In a 2017 interview with *The Dark Side*'s John Martin, Sally remembered Christopher Lee: "He had a more serious personality [than Vincent Price], but he was very charming … and very handsome, such a nice man … At the time I thought, 'These are really great people.'" Sally would next attack Price with a meat fork in *Cry of the Banshee*.

Briefly glimpsed as one of Newhartt's patients is Barbara Kellerman (b. 1949), who, despite playing Michael Gough's ill-fated secretary in *Satan's Slave*, would later distinguish herself in *Quatermass*, *The Monster Club*, *Hammer House of Horror*: "Growing Pains" and, most notably, as the White Witch in *The Lion, the Witch, & the Wardrobe* (1988).

Elsewhere, Rupert Davies discovers a corpse while out walking his dog, and Peter Arne (b. 1918) gives a sly performance as a duplicitous lawyer. Arne, whose other credits include *The Pirates of Blood River*, *The Black Torment* and *Murders in the Rue Morgue* (1970), would be brutally murdered in 1983.

Christopher Lee and Vincent Price play chess between takes on *The Oblong Box*.

Also worthy of note is the music of Harry Robinson (1932-1996), who was fresh from penning the title theme for Hammer's *Journey to the Unknown* series. Robinson would succeed James Bernard as the company's most regular composer, notably for his excellent work on their Karnstein trilogy. His subsequent credits include *Countess Dracula*, *Demons of the Mind*, *The House in Nightmare Park* (1972) and *Hawk the Slayer* (1980, which he also co-scripted and produced under his real name, Robertson).

Paired with *The Dunwich Horror*, *The Oblong Box* grossed over a million dollars on its US release, from June 11, 1969 (when the Beatles were at No. 1 with "Get Back"). The movie was issued in the UK, almost a year later, on Sunday, July 19, 1970 (when Mungo Jerry topped the charts with "In the Summertime").

While *The Oblong Box* has nothing to do with the ship-bound tale of mystery from which it takes its title, this is nothing new: Classic Poe "adaptations" like *The Black Cat* (1934) and *The Raven* (1935) also stray far from their sources. The above-mentioned Karloff and Lugosi starrers may be more satisfying, but *The Oblong Box* does, at least, contain the germ of a good idea, as proven when the film's events were recycled, with superior handling, for a 1981 *Doctor Who* serial, "Black Orchid." Yet, for all its flaws, *The Oblong Box* looks like a masterpiece when compared to Christopher Lee's next venture.

The Loneliness of Evil

Eugenie ... The Story of Her Journey into Perversion 1969

Her body is bruised and embraced beyond her wildest dreams ...

I've never felt worse about appearing in a film ...—Christopher Lee, to Tom Johnson and Mark A. Miller.

While Christopher Lee had dabbled with Sadean horrors in *The Skull*, an outright adaptation of the Marquis de Sade's libertine writings would not have been dreamed of back then. In January 1969 Harry Alan Towers and Jess Franco followed their first interpretation of the 17th century author's work, *Justine* (1968), with a film provisionally titled *De Sade 70*, but more commonly known as *Eugenie ... The Story of Her Journey into Perversion*.

Based on de Sade's 1795 novel *Philosophy in the Boudoir*, Lee gave up a weekend's golf, at short notice, to fly into Barcelona and replace George Sanders as Dolmance, the film's narrator (Sanders, who, unlike Lee, had probably seen a full script, claimed to be ill). Lee was a great admirer of Sanders, so, naturally was quite happy to step into his shoes, but, as he always maintained, he had no inkling of what the results would entail, and nor would he, until over a year later, when a friend notified him that one of his films was playing at a Soho sex cinema.

"No scenes of [a sexual] nature were filmed in my presence," Lee insisted (to Johnson and Miller), "and there was no indication that any such scenes would be filmed at all. Through cutting, it was made to appear that I had done some very distasteful scenes. I can assure you that I *didn't* and *wouldn't*! I did request that my name be taken off the credits."

It wasn't. *Eugenie* opens with Lee using his best narrative tones to entice the viewer with "delicious promptings," seemingly oblivious to the nude Satanic sacrifice going on right behind him. While the actor looks awesome in his own red velvet smoking jacket (last seen in *Theatre of Death*), the rest of the movie is rather less resplendent.

Assets include Bruno Nicolai's Ennio Morricone-inspired soundtrack. Nicolai (1926-1991)—who had conducted Morricone's work on *The Bird with the Crystal Plumage*; *Lizard in a Woman's Skin*; *The Cat o' Nine Tails* and *Four Flies on Grey Velvet* [1971]—would also score *The Bloody Judge*, *Count Dracula*, *The Night Evelyn Came Out of the Grave* (1971), *The Case of the Bloody Iris* (1972) and *Caligula* (1976), among others.

Franco's compositions are slightly less annoying than usual; shots are actually framed, as opposed to zoomed at random. Despite this, and promise shown in his first horror offering, *The Awful Dr. Orlof* (1961; which he

Christopher Lee might be thinking, "I gave up a weekend of golf for this."

threatened to remake in 1996 with Christopher Lee), the majority of the director's output resembles creepy home movies from some disreputable uncle. This hasn't stopped him attaining admirers, though; a number of whom may have been influenced by Lee himself. When asked why he made so many films for the seemingly inept filmmaker, the actor told *Starlog* magazine: "I don't consider him to be a hack director; after all, he was Orson Welles' assistant on *Chimes at Midnight*."

While it's true that Franco shot the much-lauded second unit battle footage for the aforementioned epic, it was arguably Welles' creative editing which gave those scenes their power. After all, when Orson's widow Oja recruited Franco to assemble Welles' unfinished project *Don Quixote* (1957-1969) in 1992, she was "appalled" at the results (which included new scenes by Jess). As Chris Welles Feder reported in her memoir, *In My Father's Shadow* (Algonquin Books, 2009): "[Oja] had believed in Franco, who ... claimed to be Orson's admiring friend, never imagining he would prove himself so unworthy of the precious footage that had been entrusted to him."

To cap it all off, Franco himself stated (in Blue Underground's 2002 DVD documentary *Perversion Stories*): "I don't like my films in general," while admitting that *Eugenie* is "the one I hate the least."

Eugenie was granted a UK release as *Philosophy in the Boudoir* in March 1970, before emerging Stateside five months later. Other horror films to exert a Sadean influence include *De Sade* (1968), scripted by Richard Matheson; Anthony Hickox's *Waxwork* (dedicated, respectfully, to Hammer) and *House of Whipcord* (1973), wherein Robert Tayman plays a nefarious character called Mark E. Dessart. Harry Alan Towers was still peddling his Sadean fantasies as late as 1992 via *Night Terrors*; but even with Robert Englund as a marble-eyed de Sade and Tobe Hooper in place of Jess Franco, the results are just as tired.

Eugenie's premise of patriarchal figures corrupting the young and vulnerable is an uncomfortable one, as, depressingly, the same ethic often informs the creation of such exploitation projects. Marie Liljedahl—who went on to star as Sybil in *Dorian Gray* (1969)—was only 18 when she played Eugenie. In *Perversion Stories*, she describes her experience on the movie as "unpleasant." After admitting to having no knowledge of the source material, she states: "But when I met Christopher Lee, I thought maybe the film would be decent enough for me to be in it ..."

Lee (who, at least, got to keep his smoking jacket on) gave his own summation of *Eugenie* for the same documentary: "I suppose you could say I've been in nearly every kind of film, one way or another."

Scream and Scream Again
1969

> Triple distilled horror ... as powerful as a vat of boiling acid!

> I think in an odd sort of way we were trying to make a kind of warning movie. There was a sort of subversion we were trying to suggest existed. We were saying, 'Alright, it might be the swinging '60s, but the institutions are still in control ...—Gordon Hessler, *Eyeball* interview, 1998.

> The handcuff still dangled from the bumper of the police car. Attached to it was something which dripped blood.
> It was the killer's right hand.—from *The Disorientated Man*, Peter Saxon

In May 1969, Louis "Deke" Heyward had the brilliant and heretofore unexplored idea of teaming Christopher Lee with Vincent Price *and* Peter Cushing for *Scream and Scream Again*—AIP's first collaboration with Amicus Productions. The resultant film is stylishly put together by director Gordon Hessler, even as the director admitted to Lucy Chase Williams, "Nobody understood it." Christopher Lee confirmed this sense of befuddlement (to the same author): "We were all aliens if I remember rightly. I couldn't work it out at all."

Aliens were certainly involved in Peter Saxon's 1966 source novel *The Disorientated Man*, as well as Milton Subotsky's original script, but the latter was rejected by AIP, and Christopher Wicking was brought in for a complete rewrite. As he had done on *The Oblong Box*, Wicking ramped up the political aspects of the story, dropping the extra-terrestrial slant altogether. "We wanted to investigate science and politics," the writer told Philip Nutman, "so we used a lot of material from news headlines." (The much-criticized fragmentary approach to Wicking's screenplay is actually a flaw inherent from the novel, largely because "Peter Saxon" was a pseudonym for the swiftly cobbled-together work of several writers.)

An ex-film journalist, Wicking's script was also heavily influenced by the hard-hitting style of director Don Siegel—especially his conspiratorial *Invasion of the Body Snatchers* (1955). In addition, the screenwriter would call Price's character, Dr. Browning, after the director of Lugosi's *Dracula*. (Tod Browning is also the name Wicking would give his young male protagonist in *Blood from the Mummy's Tomb*.)

Despite such worthy inspiration, *Scream and Scream Again* is a wasted opportunity when it comes to its three top-billed stars. Lee, who completed his scenes in three days, is Fremont, a government official, whose contribution to the proceedings is never made entirely clear. Cushing, meanwhile, has one of the most negligible parts of his career as Major Benedek. (So insignificant is Cushing's participation that the compilers of the trailer run an image of 15th-billed Marshall Jones beneath his name.)

Price is given the most to do as the creator of vampire-like composites, but the movie's most impressive moment, a high-speed pursuit of one such creature, involves none of the horror trio. The composite in question, Keith (Michael Gothard), is a Mick Jagger lookalike in purple frilled shirt who stalks his prey in nightclubs. Unforgettably, he wrenches his own hand off to evade capture, before jumping in a vat of acid. (Gothard performed all of his own stunts—that's really him running up the steep face of the quarry, aided by a steel cable.)

A unique actor, Michael Gothard (1939-1992) put his talents to good use as the crazed exorcist of *The Devils* (1970), the jailer enraptured by Faye Dunaway in *The Four Musketeers* and the levitating Atmir in *Warlords of Atlantis* (1977). He was also a Bond villain in *For Your Eyes Only*, a psychopath in *Hammer House of Mystery and Suspense*: "The Sweet Scent of Death," the chain-smoking Dr. Bukovsky in *Lifeforce* (1984) and the Chairman of the Whitechapel Vigilance Committee in David Wickes' *Jack the Ripper* (1988). Gothard's final screen appearance was as a boatswain in Wickes' TV version of *Frankenstein* (1992), shortly after which he committed suicide by hanging. "I got to know [Michael] reasonably well," Christopher Matthews, who plays Dr. David Sorel in *Scream and Scream Again*, told Tim Greaves (in *LSoH* #13): "He was quite 'alone,' I think."

One of Keith's victims is played by Judy Huxtable (b. 1944), star of Amicus' *The Psychopath*, who would later be injected with porridge by Marty Feldman's Dracula in *Every Home Should Have One* (1969). Before her 1974 marriage to famed satirist (and screen Beelzebub) Peter Cook, Judy could be seen as a pop star-nabbing anarchist in *The Touchables* (1968), Leo Genn's incestuous daughter in *Die Screaming Marianne* (1970) and a rival to Ingrid Pitt in the backstage melodrama *Nobody Ordered Love* (1972).

Christopher Lee appears to be having fun on-set.

Scream and Scream Again also features Danish actress Yutte Stensgaard (b. 1946), who was then married to Amicus art director Tony Curtis. Immortalized as Carmilla Karnstein in *Lust for a Vampire*, Yutte was Robot No. 1 in *Some Girls Do* (1968), an alien poker enthusiast in *Zeta One* (1969) and a Scottish prostitute in Vernon Sewell's *Burke and Hare*. She made her final screen appearance in "Bedtime," a lost episode of the BBC horror anthology *Dead of Night* (1972), before retiring to America.

The best performance in *Scream and Scream Again*, however, belongs to Alfred Marks (1921-1996), whose Superintendent Bellaver is a dour delight, full of barbed asides, many of which were improvised by the actor himself. Marks, who fronted his own ITV comedy show, *Alfred Marks Time* (1956-1961), also brought his skills to such movies as *Penny Points to Paradise* (1950, with the Goons); Hammer's *A Weekend with Lulu* (1960, with Shirley Eaton) and the Ken Russell biopic *Valentino* (1976, as MGM executive Richard Rowland). The comedic connection continues with the casting of Julian Holloway (b. 1944), a member of the *Carry On* team, as Bellaver's aide, Detective Constable Griffin. The son of Stanley Holloway (the gravedigger of Olivier's *Hamlet*), Julian also appeared in a potent *Dead of Night* entry, "A Woman Sobbing" (1972), before providing the voice of *Captain Kronos: Vampire Hunter* and being menaced by Cheetah People for *Doctor Who*: "Survival" (1989).

In a nod to Subotsky's past in rock 'n' roll musicals, Welsh chart-toppers Amen Corner (whose hits include "Bend Me, Shape Me") can be glimpsed playing during the nightclub scenes. (Subotsky had previously featured Ronnie Wood's first group, the Birds, in *The Deadly Bees*, and would still be inserting musical acts into his horror films as late as 1980's *The Monster Club*—namely the Pretty Things and a pre-fame UB40.)

Although the non-pop score of David Whitaker (1931-2012) is inappropriately jazzy (the composer would redeem himself with excellent themes for *Vampire Circus* and *Dr. Jekyll and Sister Hyde*), a synthesized soundtrack by Kendall Schmidt, which actually suited the action better, was added when Orion acquired AIP's back catalogue in 1983. This was either a curious move to endear the movies to a 1980s audience, or simply and most likely, because they failed to secure the musical rights. (*Witchfinder General*, *Planet of the Vampires* and *Madhouse* were also rescored by Schmidt, in whole or in part, when first issued on video.)

Lee and Price celebrated their joint birthdays together during filming on Tuesday, May 27, 1969, at Madame Tussauds' Chamber of Horrors in the company of Uta Levka (b. 1942), who plays Dr. Browning's nurse. (Levka had earlier essayed a prostitute in *The Oblong Box*.). When production wrapped the following month, Terry Gilliam, of the soon-to-be-broadcast *Monty Python's Flying Circus*, prepared some animated titles which were sadly vetoed by AIP head James Nicholson. (Gilliam's opening credits artistry for *Cry of the Banshee* remains the best thing about that movie.)

Scream and Scream Again was released on Monday, February 2, 1970, in the US (when the Jackson 5 were at No. 1 with "I Want You Back") and six days later in the UK (where Edison Lighthouse topped the charts with "Love Grows [Where My Rosemary Goes].")

The deceitful lure of three top horror stars ensured that the movie was a huge success (especially when paired with *The Incredible 2-Headed Transplant* in 1971). Among its admirers, according to Christopher Wicking, was Fritz Lang, who had directed Vincent Price in the 1955 thriller *While the City Sleeps*, (In Germany, *Scream and Scream Again* was known as *Die lebenden Leichen des Dr. Mabuse*; Lang had, of course, introduced the titular villain to the screen with *Dr. Mabuse, the Gambler* [1922], *The Testament of Dr. Mabuse* [1932] and *The 1,000 Eyes of Dr. Mabuse* [1960].)

To publicize the film, Price appeared in a mad scientist sketch for *Frost on Sunday*; when Ronnie Corbett's hunchbacked assistant asks him to name his poison, Vincent replies: "Christopher Lee." Price next made a trio of British horrors (*The Abominable Dr. Phibes*, *Dr. Phibes Rises Again*, *Theatre of Blood*), in which the actor shines as inventive, charismatic murderers whose work is carried out with comic style (a motif which harks back to Ealing's *Kind Hearts and Coronets*).

As for Gordon Hessler, following the tawdry *Cry of the Banshee*, he went on to helm *Murders in the Rue Morgue* (1970, again with Wicking) and *The Golden Voyage of Sinbad* (1972), as well as episodes of *Kolchak: The Night Stalker* (1974-1975), *Tales of the Unexpected* (1979-1988) and *Wonder Woman* (1975-1979, one of which features John Carradine as a talking brain). Additional small-screen works include *Scream Pretty Peggy* (1973, with Bette Davis going mad in a Jimmy Sangster script); *The Strange Possession of Mrs. Oliver* (1977, written by Richard Matheson) and one of the highest-rated TV-movies of 1978, *KISS Meets the Phantom of the Park*.

While *Scream and Scream Again* fails as a vehicle for Lee, Price and Cushing, it is still an interesting, if confused, thriller in its own right.

Fremont, a government agent, is played by Christopher Lee shown here with Marshall Jones.

The Bloody Judge
1969

Horror will hold you helpless!

In August 1969, during a break in filming *The Private Life of Sherlock Holmes*, Christopher Lee flew into Portugal to be reunited with Harry Alan Towers and Jess Franco on *The Bloody Judge*. Although Lee saw the Holmes movie as a vital break from horror, his role as Judge Jeffreys in the Franco picture sees him sending suspected witches to their doom, while snarling: "Take this bitch away! See that she goes to London in chains!"

Welsh-born Baron George Jeffreys (1645-1689) was known as "the Hanging Judge" for the unjust severity of his sentences. "A real Jekyll and Hyde," is how Lee described him (to Tom Johnson and Mark A. Miller): "He'd behave like an animal then pass judgement on others." Today, Jeffreys' ghost is said to haunt various locations he frequented in life, including Dorset's White Hart Inn and London's Ilchester Arms. While an authentic biopic starring Lee as Jeffreys might have made for an interesting venture, *The Bloody Judge* is nothing more than a dull remake of *Witchfinder General*, with the Judge recast in the mold of Matthew Hopkins. Even Bruno Nicolai's score apes the music of the Michael Reeves classic. But, whereas *Witchfinder* is engaging and powerful, *The Bloody Judge* just plods along with little to recommend it save for some dodgy English accents for connoisseurs of badly dubbed films.

In a series of wigs and resplendent robes, Lee gives an imperial performance throughout, but his attempts to maintain historical accuracy, by showing that Jeffreys may have been driven to his actions through painful ill-health, are undercut by the same tactics Franco had deployed on *Eugenie*. At one stage, for instance, a hand purported to be Lee's, but clearly belonging to someone else, creeps into shot to caress the nude form of Maria Rohm. Such scenes were not mentioned in Lee's copy of the script, and were added, without his knowledge, once he'd moved on elsewhere.

Italian poster

Noteworthy support comes, nonetheless, from Swiss-American actor Howard Vernon (real name: Mario Lippert, 1914-1996), whose blood-streaked tortures as Jeffreys' club-footed executioner (patterned after Boris Karloff in *Tower of London*) were cut completely from US prints. Most notorious for starring as *The Awful Dr. Orlof*—a role he reprised, with an extra *f*, in *Only a Coffin* (1966), *Orloff Against the Invisible Man* (1970), *The Sinister Dr. Orloff* (1982) and *Faceless* (1987)—Vernon would essay a wild-eyed Dracula in *Dracula, Prisoner of Frankenstein* (1971) and *Daughter of Dracula* (1972, in which he is staked through the head). Other Franco credits include Professor Vicas in *The Diabolical Dr. Z* (1965), Cagliostro in *The Erotic Rites of Frankenstein* (1972), Count Zaroff in *The Perverse Countess* (1973), a witch's servant in *Lorna the Exorcist* (1974) and Dr. Usher in *Revenge in the House of Usher* (1983). He also worked for Jean-Luc Godard (*Alphaville* [1965] as Professor Nosferatu), Adrian Hoven (*Castle of the Creeping Flesh* [1967] as Count Saxon), Jean Rollin (*Zombie Lake* [1980] as the Mayor), Jeunet and Caro (*Delicatessen* [1990] as the Frog Man) and Walerian Borowczyk (*The Strange Case of Dr. Jekyll and Miss Osbourne* [1980] as Dr. Lanyon.)

Another Dr. Lanyon (to Jack Palance in *The Strange Case of Dr. Jekyll and Mr. Hyde* [1967]) was Leo Genn, who had last appeared with Christopher Lee in *Circus of Fear*. *The Bloody Judge* sees Genn deputizing for an ailing Dennis Price as Lord Wessex, a substitution that came so late in the day that Price's name actually appears on some publicity material.

An additional surprise is the casting of Maria Schell (1926-2005) as blind soothsayer Mother Rosa. The Austrian-Swiss actress, and sister of Maximilian Schell, enjoyed a long and varied career in such movies as *The Magic Box* (1951), Visconti's *White Nights* (1957), *The Hanging Tree* (1958, with Gary Cooper) and *Superman* (1977, as Krypton scientist Vond-Ah).

The Bloody Judge first saw European release in 1970. Two years later, Franco made a semi-sequel, *The Demons*, which featured Iranian actor Cihangir Gaffari as Jeffreys. As its title suggests, this was a rip-off of Ken Russell's *The Devils*. In May 1972, AIP paired *The Bloody Judge* with Hammer's *Blood from the Mummy's Tomb* in the US, where it was retitled *Night of the Blood Monster*. As Lee reflected to Johnson and Miller: "What sane person wants to see that?"

Christopher Lee portrays Baron George Jeffreys.

Count Dracula
1969

The Magic Christian (1969)
One More Time (1969)
Cuadecuc Vampir (1969)
Umbracle (1970)

Finally! The original version!

By 1969, the vampiric image of Christopher Lee was so ingrained in popular culture that the actor made a variety of fanged appearances that year—and not just in horror films.

Firstly, at the invitation of Peter Sellers, Lee joined the all-star cast of *The Magic Christian*. While interesting in its attempts to show how money corrupts, the film, directed by Joe McGrath, is one of those frothy, "anything goes" offerings of the mid-to-late 1960s, which—despite innocent beginnings via Richard Lester's zany Beatles outings—had since grown far too indulgent for audiences to make any sense of. (As best exemplified by another Sellers vehicle, the shambolic *Casino Royale*.)

Nevertheless, *The Magic Christian* remains eminently watchable, not only for some excellent Badfinger songs, but also for the surprising antics of its assembled guest stars: whether that be Laurence Harvey performing *Hamlet* as a striptease, Yul Brynner in drag or Raquel Welch as "Priestess of the Whip." Best of all, though, is Lee's turn as a vampire waiter aboard the titular vessel. Despite casting a reflection, the shots of him striding down the ship's corridors in slow motion as the camera tracks away are moodily effective, and any one of the actor's "serious" vampire movies could have benefited from such imaginative staging.

As a bonus, during filming, Lee got to meet the Beatles, whom he described to his fan club as "very pleasant young men," before adding, presciently: "It would seem that they are going through a very anxious time at the moment" (the band

was in the midst of recording their final album, *Abbey Road*). Several weeks later, the actor received a request from another admiring musician, Sammy Davis, Jr., to cameo as Dracula in *One More Time*. Directed by Jerry Lewis, the film is a silly caper that briefly shows Lee—alongside Peter Cushing as Frankenstein—in a smoky laboratory, complete with Monster, hunchback and manacled blonde. Lee raises a glass of blood and says, "Won't you join our little party" through a mouthful of fangs. Cushing's

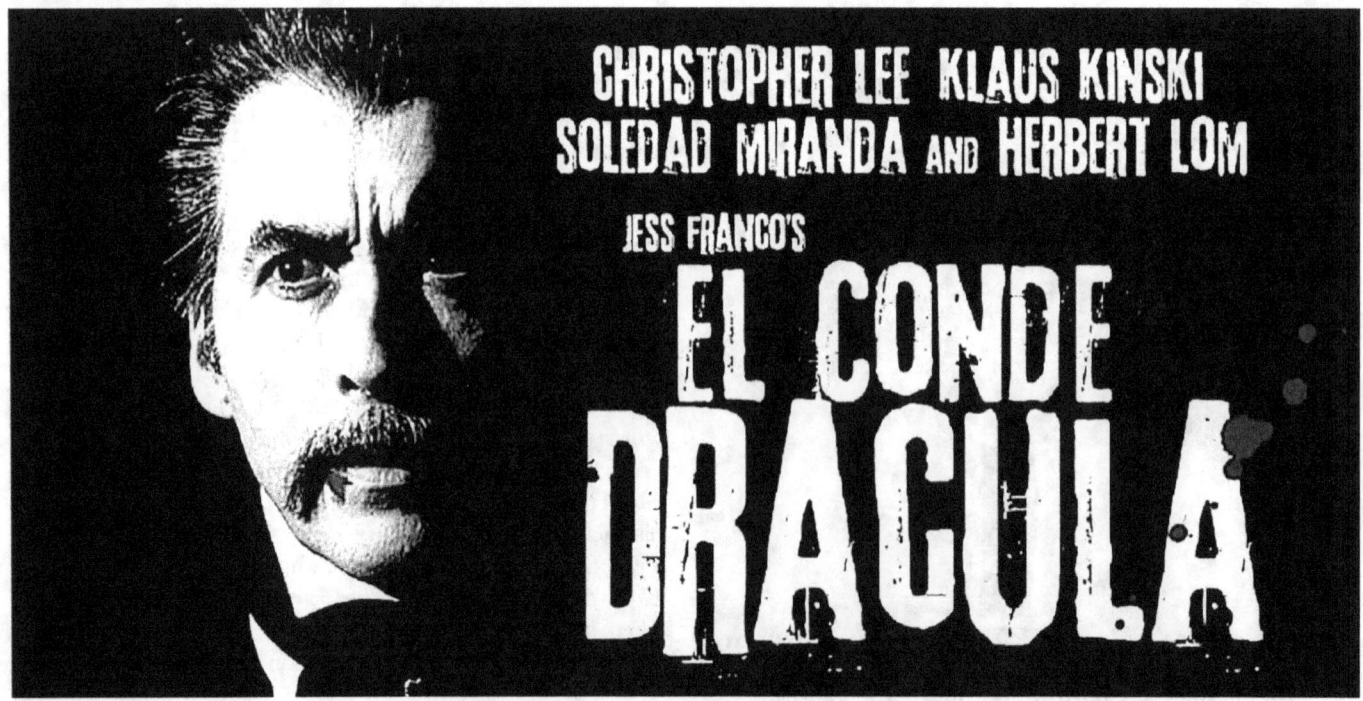

wife, Helen, accompanied her husband on-set and, sadly, this marked the last time that Lee would see her. Once their morning's work was complete, Davis feted the actors with champagne, and the Cushings even received a color TV set from the generous American star. Charmingly, a photo of Sammy flanked by the horror icons was captioned by Lee in his memoirs: "A rose between two thorns."

Next, Lee headed for Spain to play Dracula in what promised to be the first entirely faithful adaptation of Bram Stoker's novel. Originally announced, in a 1969 issue of *Today's Cinema* as a lavish vehicle from Pentagram Film Productions with Terence Fisher at the helm, *El Conde Dracula* (*Count Dracula*) eventually emerged as yet another low-budget collaboration between Harry Alan Towers and Jess Franco.

In his 1974 Introduction to Donald F. Glut's *The Dracula Book*, Lee wrote: "It is my earnest hope that one day I, or some other actor, will be permitted the golden opportunity of presenting Dracula on screen exactly as Bram Stoker would have wished. There have been some attempts at doing this, but they have fallen by the wayside through a lack of adequate production." There is no doubt that Lee was referring to *Count Dracula* in his final sentence as, ultimately, the film's sole loyalty to Stoker is the depiction of the Count as an old man with white hair and moustache who grows younger as he feeds on blood. (Prior to 1969, while owing much visually to *Nosferatu* and Lugosi's *Dracula*, the Turkish *Drakula Istanbul'da* [1952] had made a pretty good stab at working ideas from Stoker into its running time—and would remain more faithful to the novel than Franco's attempts.)

Although Lee had already been unwillingly committed by his agents to make a fourth Dracula film for Hammer (*Taste the Blood of Dracula*), the actor was more than happy to play the role for Franco at the time because, as he told his fan club, it was a chance "to recreate the original novel once and for all … when I have finally done this, that will be the end of it. This will mean that I have played the part of Dracula five times in all and only once as Stoker wrote it. And it will be with the latter that I will be content."

Unfortunately, there is little contentment to be found in Franco's movie, which Lee filmed over two weeks in Barcelona from mid-October 1969. (Hammer were apparently concerned about this rival Dracula venture, but, as it was taken from the original novel, which was now in the public domain, there was nothing they could do; Lee would go straight into *Taste the Blood of Dracula* on his return from Spain in November.)

The opening titles of *Count Dracula* promise much, with brooding shots of the vampire's castle set to Bruno Nicolai's blazing score. But, as soon as the credits end, we are treated to Franco's clumsy interpretation of Jonathan Harker's Transylvanian voyage. Once Harker has arrived at his destination, Lee's candelabra-clutching Count, complete with white hair and moustache, gives us the closest depiction of the novel's early chapters, but, visually, thanks to Franco's cack-handed camerawork, the scenes pale in comparison to both the Lugosi version and Hammer's first rendering.

In 2004, Lee told Marcus Hearn that it was he who insisted on inserting the long speech by the fireside ("This was a Dracula indeed!"), which he plucked directly from the book. It was a good idea, as the actor delivers this monologue with a bombast that soon betrays the vampire's weariness ("But now the wind

Count Dracula (Christopher Lee) grows younger each time he feeds on his victims. (See photo below)

blows coldly through the broken battlements …"). The castle location, incidentally, is the very hallway where Christopher Columbus announced his "discovery" of America to the King and Queen of Spain in 1492.

In another interesting touch, Franco presents the Count's brides as ghostly, transparent figures who solidify as they approach the sleeping Harker. Their attempts to take his blood, however, are broken by Lee's remarkable cry, almost like a wounded animal of: "Back! *Back!*" He then resolves his strength for a definitive reading of the line: "This man belongs to me!" As in the novel, Dracula gifts the women with a wailing baby on which to feast. A scene wherein the child's mother is shown crying outside the castle before being set upon by wolves is, puzzlingly, cut from some prints of *Count Dracula*, despite it being one of the movie's most effective moments. (Even if the "wolves" are clearly played by German Shepherds.)

Regrettably, any similarity with the book departs once we arrive at the sanitarium of Dr. Van Helsing, and the remainder descends into zoom-laden tedium.

thermore, the oval window that forms the backdrop of Dracula's vamping of Lucy is so uniquely Mediterranean in its design that it lends the scene a peculiar sense of Gothic exotica. But these moments are so fleeting, and set within such a stodgy framework, as to render the whole somewhat negligible.

Nevertheless, although there's no Arthur Holmwood in sight, we do witness Quincey Morris making his screen debut in the person of Jack Taylor. Born in Oregon, 1936, as George Brown Randall, Taylor had served as art director on *The Bloody Judge* (under the name George O. Brown) and would also provide a similar service to *Count Dracula*. In *The Dark Side* #38, Taylor told Cathal Tohill that he walked up to Lee, on one of his own upholstered sets, and said, "Christopher, do you remember me?" Referencing their last film together, *Eugenie*, Lee responded: "Oh yes. I think we first met under very disgusting circumstances."

"Christopher's very puritanical," Taylor added.

Not to be confused with a British thespian of the same name (who appeared in *The Trollenberg Terror* and *Paranoiac*), Jack Taylor made his genre debut as vampire slayer Igor for the 1959 Mexican serial *The Curse of Nostradamus* (the 12 parts of which were edited into four features for US release). After starring for Jess Franco in the controversial *Succubus* (1967) and as the title villain in *The Vengeance of Dr. Mabuse* (1971), the actor attended *The Vampires' Night Orgy* (1972), boarded *The Ghost Galleon* (1973), succumbed to Franco's *Female Vampire* (1973) and opposed Paul Naschy, in both *Dr. Jekyll vs. The Werewolf* (1971) and *The Mummy's Revenge* (1973). He next dubbed Naschy's voice for the English-language version of *Exorcism* (1974), before appearing, that same year, in another *Exorcist* knock-off, *Devil's Exorcist*, with special effects from *Horror Express*' Pablo Pérez. Gay characters in both *Conan the Barbarian* (1981) and *Pieces* (1982) were followed by a bit in *The Return of the Musketeers* (as "gentleman on horseback") and a slightly larger role, as a fiddle-playing book collector, opposite Johnny Depp in *The Ninth Gate* (1998). Taylor's last film to date is *Wax* (2014), wherein he plays the cannibalistic Dr. Knox.

Replacing Vincent Price in the role of Dr. Van Helsing is Herbert Lom (1917-2012). Despite having survived *The Face of Eve* with Lee, the two actors never actually met on *Count Dracula*. Their confrontation scenes were shot, not only on separate days, but also in different countries. (The sanitarium sequences were filmed in Italy, where Lom was concurrently starring as Henry Wotton for Harry Alan Towers' modern-day production of *Dorian Gray*.)

Although his greatest performance is as Hammer's *The Phantom of the Opera*, in which he perfectly captures the mental decay of a forgotten genius trapped underground, Lom is most renowned for his twitchy Chief Inspector Dreyfus in the *Pink Panther* comedies (*The Pink Panther Strikes Again* [1976] even sees him spoof his *Phantom*, while kidnapping a scientist and his daughter to create a death ray—just like Lee had done in *The Brides of Fu Manchu*). By contrast, Herbert is thoroughly vile as the sadistic prison governor of Franco's *99 Women* (1968), the witch-hunter in *Mark of the Devil* (1969) and the nefarious aristocrat of *And Now the Screaming Starts!*, whose villainy harks back to Lee's progenitors in *The Hound of the Baskervilles*.

Lom's other credits include Captain Nemo in *Mysterious Island* (1960), the acid-scarred killer of *Murders in the Rue Morgue* (1970) and the *Asylum* inmate who creates miniature robots in his own likeness. After reuniting with Lee for *Dark Places* (1972),

A cheapness pervades, not only in Franco's cost-cutting zooms, but in the big fake spiders and bats; the polystyrene bolder that bounces off the head of an unfazed horse, and an unbelievable sequence, improvised by the director, in which stuffed animals (including a badger, a swordfish, an owl and a fox) are turned and jiggled before the camera to induce the belief that they have somehow come to life. Presumably, this was meant to illustrate the dominion that Dracula holds over animals (including moths), but the moth-eaten taxidermy on display here is just downright daft, despite the cast doing their best to look terrified.

Other absurdities abound, such as Harker losing consciousness in Transylvania and waking up in London, or Van Helsing suffering, as he puts it airily, from "a slight stroke"—an inexplicable deviation from Stoker which, in other hands, might have been quite intriguing but, here, serves no dramatic purpose whatsoever. Additionally, the great spray of blood that hits Quincey Morris' face as he stakes one of the vampire brides is so unintentionally comic that it would later be parodied, with little alteration, by both Tom Holland for *Fright Night* (1985) and Mel Brooks in *Dracula: Dead and Loving It* (1995).

While *Count Dracula* is, overall, disappointing, throughout the mess of pans and zooms, a few diverting snapshots can be caught: The blue-tinted atmospherics of the Borgo Pass where a disguised Dracula first meets Harker, for example, or Harker's eye peering from a scratchy clearing in a misted window, or Lee's leather-gloved snatching of Maria Rohm from a theater. Fur-

Herbert made welcome appearances as Dr. Weizak in *The Dead Zone* (1983) and the head of *The Sect* (1990), whose plot, co-written by Dario Argento, echoes *To the Devil a Daughter*. Of further note is Lom's historical novel, *Dr. Guillotine* (1992), which reads, delightfully, like a Hammer *Frankenstein* movie.

Dr. Seward is played by Euro-horror regular Paul Muller (b. 1923), who has the character of Blind Pew in common with Lee (Muller plays him in John Hough's 1972 *Treasure Island* with Orson Welles). Paul's best genre role, however, is as Barbara Steele's sadistic husband in *Nightmare Castle*, while the sight of him gliding backwards through a forest with a noose round his neck, in *A Virgin Among the Living Dead* (1971), remains to my eyes at least the most arresting image in Jess Franco's oeuvre.

Seward's star patient is essayed by the notorious actor last seen with Lee in *Circus of Fear* and *Five Golden Dragons*. Harry Alan Towers told Allan Bryce in *The Dark Side* #2: "I wanted [Klaus] Kinski to play Renfield [but] ... He wouldn't do it, so I did the deal with his agents and persuaded them not to tell him the name of the picture he would be working on. He turned up for the first day's shooting and went straight into a scene where he had to strangle a girl, who was played by my wife. After the cameras stopped turning, he looked at me and said, 'Why do I feel I am in a *Dracula* picture?'"

According to Franco (in MPI's accompanying DVD feature *Beloved Count*), this wasn't true; but, in the same interview, the director did admit to the actor eating real flies for his role (when Kinski complained that he was filming on a set, Franco countered, perhaps only half-jokingly, that if they placed the actor in a real psychiatric hospital, he would never be let out). Indeed, Kinski gives an eerily convincing portrayal of one whose mind is shattered, throwing a bowl of blood-red soup at the white padded walls of his cell, then, with a wondering smile, smearing his fingers through the mess as if engaged in some Jackson Pollock-style art piece.

Fresh from working with Franco as the Marquis de Sade in *Justine* (1968) and as a perverted playboy in *Venus in Furs* (1968), Klaus would go on to portray *Jack the Ripper* for the director in 1976. By that time, the actor had made the first of his celebrated collaborations with Werner Herzog, *Aguirre, the Wrath of God* (1972). The pair continued their troubled but creative union with *Nosferatu the Vampyre* (1978), in which Kinski essays a world-weary Dracula (he reprised the role, less successfully, for an unofficial sequel, *Vampire in Venice* [1986]). His other genre films include *Slaughter Hotel* (1971), *Lifespan* (1974), *Schizoid* (1980), *Android* (1982), *Creature* (1984) and *Crawlspace* (1985), but 1980's *Venom* (started by Tobe Hooper, finished by Piers Haggard) is worth watching just to see Kinski and Oliver Reed trying desperately to upstage one another. (According to Haggard, the two actors shared a mutual hatred, with Reed going so far as to shake Kinski's trailer, while screaming: "Come out, you Nazi bastard!")

With Mrs. Harry Alan Towers, Maria Rohm, in the role of Mina, Lucy is essayed by actress/pop singer Soledad Miranda (1943-1970). Having appeared in the *House of Wax*-inspired *Pyro* (1963) and Ingrid Pitt's debut *Sound of Horror* (1965), Miranda would go on to star in Franco films like *She Killed in Ecstasy* (1970) before her untimely death in a car accident at the age of 27.

Rohm, on the other hand, went on to serve as associate producer on her husband's seedy version of Jekyll and Hyde, *Edge of Sanity* (1988), with Anthony Perkins (Perkins was set to star in Towers' *The Mummy Lives* [1992], but was replaced by Tony Curtis, in a performance that has to be seen to be believed). 1988 was a busy year for Towers, as he also produced three Poe-inspired outings (*Buried Alive*, *The House of Usher* and *The Masque of the Red Death*), which, between them, feature such luminaries as Robert Vaughn, John Carradine, Oliver Reed, Donald Pleasence and Herbert Lom. The following year, he delivered an underrated version of *The Phantom of the Opera* starring Robert Englund, an actor whom Harry went on to work with in the *Phantom* semi-sequel *Dance Macabre* (1991) and Stephen King's *The Mangler* (1993). Among Towers' last projects was a 2001 remake of *She* with French chanteuse Ophélie Winter.

Jess Franco, who turns up as Van Helsing's handyman, would next attempt a modern-day remake of *Dracula*, *Vampyros Lesbos* (1970), with Soledad Miranda's Countess Carody in place of the Count and Dennis Price as Van Helsing substitute, Dr. Eldon Seward. Besides a loose reworking of *Carmilla* (*Daughter of Dracula*, 1972), Franco took inspiration from 1940s Universal monster rallies and Spanish pop punk, respectively, for *Dracula, Prisoner of Frankenstein* (1971; which recycles Bruno Nicolai's *Count Dracula* score) and *Killer Barbys vs. Dracula* (2002). He reteamed with Christopher Lee for two execrable non-horror films, *Dark Mission: Flowers of Evil* (1987) and *Fall of the Eagles* (1989).

Because of its supposed fidelities to the book, a belief has grown up around *Count Dracula* that it was one of Lee's favorite movies. However, five years after making it, the actor told John Brosnan: "[*Count Dracula*] was a disappointment because it was done cheaply, without due attention to script, production or anything else." He then indicated that it was, in fact, the kind of picture that caused him to lose faith in horror subjects: "Put it on the screen, get it in focus and it will make money somewhere, if not a lot. But I don't accept this anymore." Lee's opinions of *Count Dracula* still hadn't changed 30 years later when he told Marcus Hearn in 2004: "The film was a disaster ... because it was shot on a shoestring budget and everything was a zoom ... the result was a mess, there's no other way of describing it."

Although a hit upon its 1970 Spanish release, *Count Dracula* didn't emerge in Britain until 1973, when it topped a double bill with the reissued *Dr. Terror's House of Horrors*. Despite being sold to late-night US television later that year, the movie does have a rather interesting addendum: Experimental filmmaker, and political activist, Pere Portabella (b. 1929), who had served as executive producer on Luis Bunuel's *Viridiana* (1961), shot 67 minutes' worth of behind-the-scenes footage on the set of *Count Dracula* and premiered the results at Cannes on Monday, May 17, 1971.

Even though its subject is erroneously described as a Hammer production, *Cuadecuc Vampir* has a strange, hypnotic quality.

Indeed, its grainy black-and-white visuals make for a more atmospheric piece than the film to which it is a "worm's tail" (literal translation of the word "cuadecuc"). To a soundtrack of doleful electronic notes from Carles Santos, intermingled with Burt Bacharach's "Here I Am," we are treated to scenes of the crew running around with smoke machines and bats on sticks, while Lee lies back in his coffin to be sprayed with fake cobwebs and Soledad Miranda smokes a fag in bed, as she waits for the actor to bite her. In his dressing room, Lee removes his fangs and false moustache, shows off his contact lenses with an impish grin, and closes the film with a windy discourse on the death of Dracula. After forgetting the name of Arthur Holmwood, he reads from Stoker's book as the camera closes in for a baleful glare.

The actor next collaborated with Portabella on *Umbracle*, another black-and-white experiment with pure cinema, which Lee described (to *ABC Film Review* in November 1970) as "a symbolic interpretation of me." The film shows Lee coolly walking the streets of Barcelona like a sinister Jacque Tati, to the aural accompaniment of some annoying vocal rhythms. This is interspersed with clips of comic giants like Laurel and Hardy (from *The Music Box* [1932]) and Buster Keaton (in *Neighbors* [1920]), and there's even some more Bacharach (a schmaltzy rendering of "Close to You") as Lee, in shades and tweeds, wanders along a cliff, before settling down to read. Elsewhere, alone on a stage, he belts out arias from *The Flying Dutchman* and *The Damnation of Faust* (taking off his jacket halfway through), then (removing his tie) treats us to a dramatic reading of Edgar Allan Poe's "The Raven." The final "Nevermore" is followed by a lengthy glower at the camera, with one half of his face in shadow, and the other brightly lit, giving the suggestion of a polarized figure. Despite flubbing a line while singing ("Damn!"), Lee looks absolutely delighted to showcase his fine operatic vocals and, if nothing else, *Umbracle* (which translates as *The Shady Place*) is a unique record of the actor's voice while in his prime.

Both of Lee's films with Portabella were screened together at New York's Museum of Modern Art and London's National Film Theatre in 1972.

While Christopher Lee longed to make a faithful version of Stoker's novel, *Count Dracula* isn't it. For the closest adaptation of Stoker, play Lee's audio recording of the novel from the mid-'90s and watch the movie that plays in your mind. In purely visual terms, however, it would be left to the BBC to craft the most faithful retelling to date with their 1977 *Count Dracula*—the only version that bothers to use authentic Whitby locations, which adds immensely to the atmosphere. In fact, all that is missing to make this TV-movie perfect is Christopher Lee as the Count.

Back in 1969, having appeared, in accordance with Stoker, *sans* cloak for the Franco film, Lee was ready to don the heavy black mantle of the vampire once more at Hammer House.

Taste the Blood of Dracula
1969

"Drink a pint of blood a day!"

We wanted to make a film about the decadence and hypocrisy of Victorian England much more than we wanted to do a Dracula, and it shows … We made a film with a story that said something.—Aida Young, *LSoH #13*

Reluctant to make another Dracula movie for Hammer, Christopher Lee told his fan club secretary, Gloria Lillibridge (in a personal letter dated August 27, 1969) that "there are loopholes by which I could escape if I decided, quite definitely, I would not do this picture for them."

These "loopholes" came about when, as a result of Lee's disinclination to reprise the character, Anthony Hinds was initially asked to write a Dracula film which didn't include Dracula. Thus, Hinds introduced the depraved character of Lord Courtley (to be played by Ralph Bates), who would return as a vampire after his murder at the hands of three Victorian thrill-seekers. (In the eventual film, Dracula is reborn through Courtley when the latter ingests the vampire's blood; Lee's subsequent complaint that Hammer would wedge Dracula into existing stories, rather than compose a script specifically for the character, stems solely from this instance.)

The basis for the story was an on-spec script, *Dracula's Feast of Blood*, from Freddie Francis' son Kevin (a runner on *Dracula Has Risen from the Grave*, and later the head of Tyburn Productions). On noticing similarities in the finished film to his original treatment, Kevin threatened to enforce a plagiarism suit against Hammer ("Don't mention the name 'Hammer' because it upsets me," the producer told John Brosnan some five years later). When Lee finally agreed to do the film (citing the precarious state of the British film industry and his status as a family man as his reasons), Hinds had to write the character in. "I have a feeling [Lee] found out," Hinds said of the actor's near replacement, in *LSoH #10/11*, "which did not improve our relationship!"

Lee's surviving shooting script discloses his frustration. The actor has stabbed at the pages with a black marker, writing such underscored objections as "Absurd"; "Ridiculous lines" and

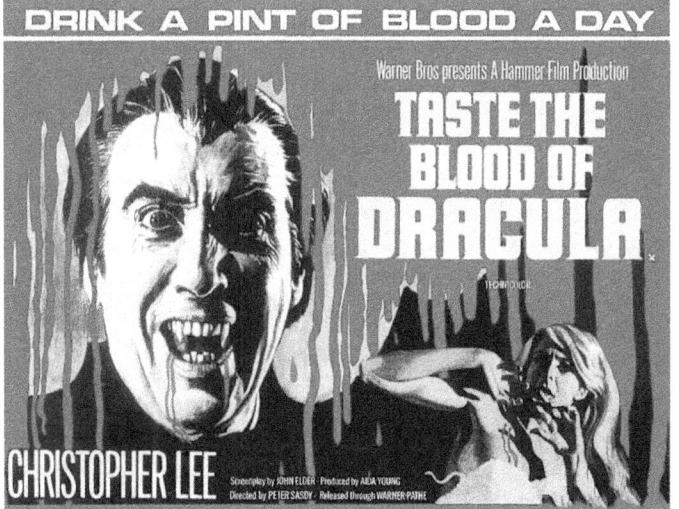

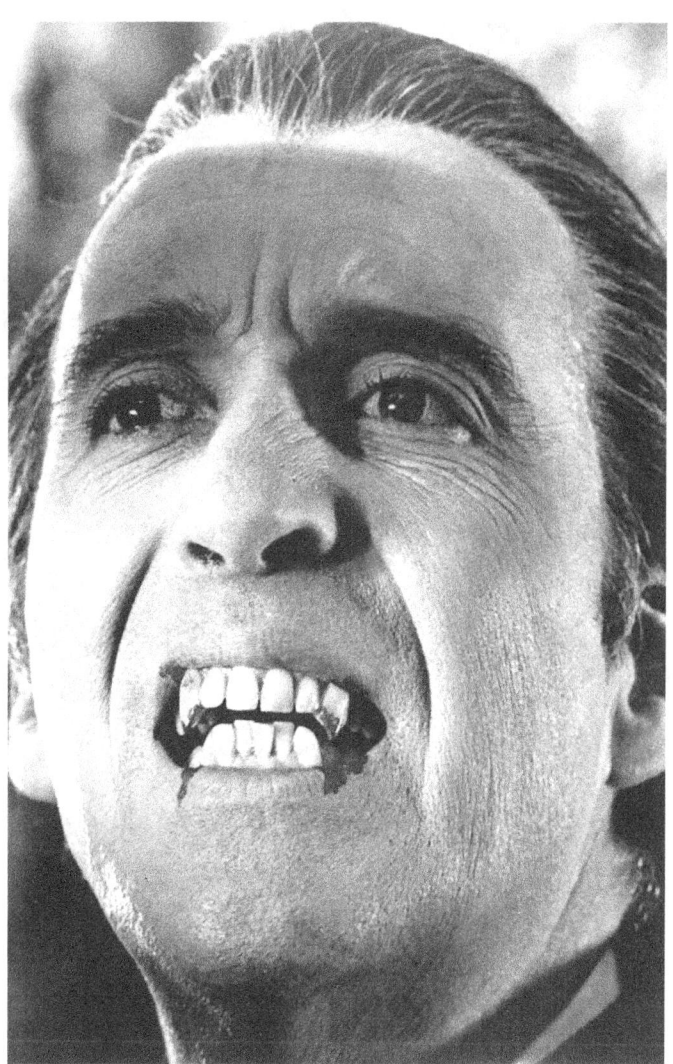

"No. These lines are silly" (most amusingly, beside Dracula's "half-witted" line of "Hello, Lucy," Lee references Hollywood's latest musical by suggesting: "Hello Dolly?"). It must be noted that Lee was not just being bad-tempered here; his proposal that actions speak louder than words was a sensible one that showed the respect and care he still harbored for Stoker's character.

Before Lee's first day of filming on Monday, November 10, 1969 (production had already begun at Elstree on October 27), there was one last note of hope in the actor's correspondence to his fan club secretary: "I am told there will be a completely new director and a 'fresh approach to the casting' … Anything to put an end to these monotonous chases of busty blondes in billowing nightdresses."

The "completely new director," Peter Sasdy, was born in Budapest ("at least he is the right nationality," quipped Lee) on May 27 (Lee's birthday), 1935. Arriving in Britain in 1956 (a refugee of the Hungarian Uprising, which he wrote about in his novel *Four Black Cars*), Sasdy began his career in television, where one of his early works was a 75-minute adaptation of Isaac Asimov's *The Caves of Steel* (1964) starring Peter Cushing as detective Elijah Baley and John Carson as his robot companion (sadly only a few brief clips of this BBC production survive). The director's other TV credits include "The Illustrious Client" for the Douglas Wilmer *Sherlock Holmes*, three episodes of *Out of the*

Dracula (Christopher Lee) with Linda Hayden (left) and Isla Blair

Unknown (1965-1971), a four-part adaptation of *Wuthering Heights* (1967) and two entries for Hammer's *Journey to the Unknown* ("Girl of my Dreams" and "The New People"). Following his sterling work on *Taste the Blood of Dracula* (his feature debut), Sasdy would draw out Ingrid Pitt's strongest performance for the underrated *Countess Dracula* and grace Hammer with a masterpiece in *Hands of the Ripper* (which was filmed on the Baker Street sets constructed at Pinewood for *The Private Life of Sherlock Holmes*). Jane Merrow, who stars in *Ripper*, remembers the Hungarian director for me as: "Wonderful, dynamic and enthusiastic. His energy would enthuse everyone on the set." Ralph Bates confirmed this view, in *LSoH*, where he said of Sasdy: "He's a Hungarian maniac. He's terrific."

When I met him at a London film fair in 2014, Sasdy told me that his intention was to infuse some "new blood" into Hammer. He also said that he wanted to bring Dracula "into the audience's back garden" by setting the film in Victorian England (surprisingly, the first of the Hammer *Dracula*s to take place there, rather than the middle-Europe of their earlier productions). Indeed, Sasdy's intelligent direction combines with an excellent cast, superbly lit by Arthur Grant, to make *Taste the Blood of Dracula* the best of Lee's vampire sequels.

The film begins with one of the finest pre-credits sequences of any horror movie: Traveling salesman Weller (Roy Kinnear) is hurled from his carriage (the very same one that took Jonathan Harker to the castle in Hammer's *Dracula*; it can also be seen in *The Brides of Dracula* and *Frankenstein Must Be Destroyed*). Awakening in the dark, Weller hears some gut-wrenching screams, before stumbling upon the finale of *Dracula Has Risen from the Grave*, with Lee writhing upon his golden cross and weeping tears of blood. As Weller goggles over Dracula's powdered remains, the credits roll and we are treated to James Bernard's melodious, romantic theme (the composer's greatest, in my opinion).

By direct contrast, the story then follows three seemingly respectable Victorian family men, Hargood (Geoffrey Keen), Paxton (Peter Sallis), and Secker (John Carson), who plunder London's underworld by night, in search of illicit thrills. (One of the prostitutes they cavort with is Madeline Smith [b. 1949], who, as well as being Roger Moore's first "Bond Girl," in *Live and Let Die*, would soon become a cult favorite for her performances in *The Vampire Lovers*, *Theatre of Blood* and *Frankenstein and the Monster from Hell*.)

By direct contrast again, the adolescent offspring of the middle-aged thrill-seekers are seen enjoying virtuous relationships, disapproved of by their hypocritical fathers. There's a charming sense of fairy tale romance as Hargood's daughter Alice (Linda Hayden) clambers down a tree that grows outside her window to make secret rendezvous with her lover Paul (Anthony Corlan), who also happens to be Paxton's son. Sasdy's background in television ensures that the scenes between the young paramours, never the strongest in this type of film, maintain the robust feel of BBC period dramas at their very best. Indeed, the production values on *Taste the Blood of Dracula* are evidently high, with a particularly pleasing sense of detail in Scott MacGregor's design: note the arcane symbols on the tapestries in the desanctified church, or the various bric-a-brac cluttering the Victorians' homes. (MacGregor's church set would be re-used by Hammer for *The Vampire Lovers*, *The Horror of Frankenstein* and *Scars of Dracula*.)

On the downside, the revolting beverage that results when Courtley adds his blood to Dracula's powder brings to mind one of those diet milkshakes. ("You drink the filth!" shouts an indignant Hargood; reportedly, the substance was mint-flavored, so as to make it more palatable for Ralph Bates). The consequent scene of the men savagely beating Courtley to death was cut for the film's US release (from which early UK video and television prints were struck), making it appear that the arrogant Lord had died merely from tasting Dracula's blood; current DVD and Blu-ray copies of *Taste the Blood of Dracula*, however, are uncut.

Looking like he has two tomatoes jammed into his eye sockets, Lee's Dracula emerges chrysalis-like from Courtley's dusted over corpse, before emitting the rather lame line: "They have destroyed my servant. They will be destroyed." Indeed, the actor is very ill-served by his dialogue here, but, as ever, proves himself more eloquent through sheer presence.

Dracula aside, Hinds' script is the best he ever turned in for Hammer. One of the story's most interesting aspects is Dracula's role as a kind of guru figure to his newfound enemies' offspring. This is especially pertinent when one considers the concurrent rise of cult leaders like Charles Manson, who similarly urged impressionable youth to murder. Indeed, the spiritual idealism of the late '60s came to a crashing close in the summer of 1969 with the spate of horrific killings in Los Angeles by Manson's followers. Among the victims was Roman Polanski's pregnant wife Sharon Tate, who was slain at home in a distorted echo of her onscreen attack from Count von Krolock in *Dance of the Vampires*. (Sharon's killer, Susan Atkins, told fellow prisoners that she actually tasted her victim's blood; in newsreel footage, the Manson women swoop down courthouse corridors like hippified brides of Dracula.) It would be a more sober and reflective populace that faced the dawning '70s. Ultimately, Hammer were extremely prescient, as testimony of Manson's antics didn't begin to reach the L.A. courts until Friday December 5, 1969—the very day that filming wrapped on *Taste the Blood of Dracula*. (The vampire figure as Manson-like guru would be explored, less effectively, but with more deliberation, by Robert Quarry's *Deathmaster* [1970].)

Another intriguingly prevalent strand, and one also reflected by the Manson case, is the disintegration of family values. By the late 1960s, the chasm between age and youth had grown ever wider, an alienation perfectly expressed through the 1967 Beatles' song "She's Leaving Home" from *Sgt. Pepper*. Both that album and Hammer's Dracula film explore their ideas through fantasy-fueled Victoriana; the era's hypocrisy was especially at the forefront of Peter Sasdy's mind as he'd just finished post-production on Henry James' *The Spoils of Poynton* for the BBC.

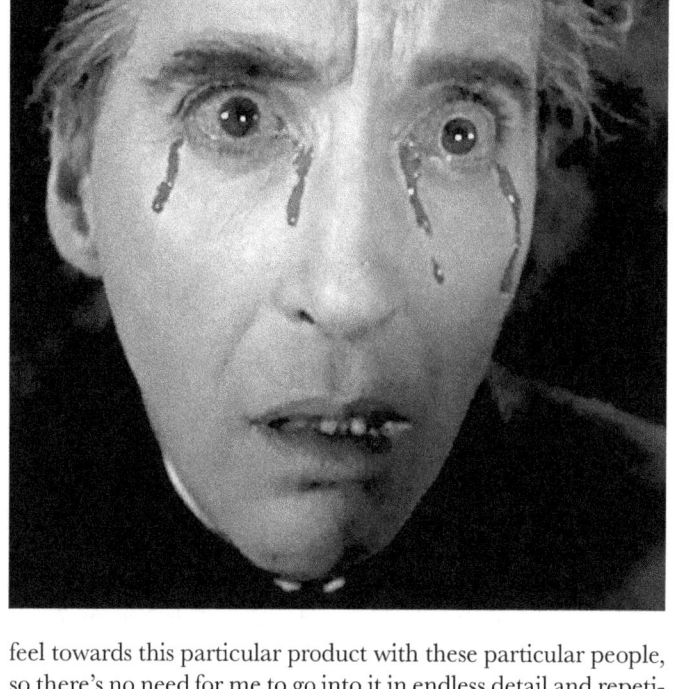

Sasdy's fresh approach extends to using an actual graveyard, London's Highgate Cemetery, as opposed to a stylized set. The supposed haunting ground of the undead Lucy in Stoker's novel, Highgate, makes for a superbly atmospheric location. It can also be seen in *The Abominable Dr. Phibes*, *Tales from the Crypt*, *Frankenstein and the Monster from Hell* and *From Beyond the Grave*. Bizarrely, throughout late 1969, while *Taste the Blood of Dracula* was in production, reports reached the British Psychic and Occult Society that "many local witnesses" had been "attacked" in the cemetery by "a tall dark figure" with "hypnotic red eyes"—"the Highgate Vampire"—to use the words of the Society's president David Farrant. When Farrant consequently investigated the graveyard, he was arrested for "vampire hunting" and appeared before a judge with the name of Christopher *Lea*. (According to Farrant's website, he [Farrant] would later serve as the model for Johnny Alucard in *Dracula A.D. 1972*—they certainly share an identical fashion sense.)

In *LSoH* #10/11, John Carson recalled the eerie atmosphere of Highgate: "We filmed there on a wet and misty day, and we needed no artificial help to create the atmosphere ... It was very spooky indeed. We all felt it, and we were very glad to get out of the place."

Following on from the spiritual conflicts explored in *Dracula Has Risen from the Grave*, at the climax of *Taste*, Dracula seems to be overcome, literally, by the power of God; a dispatch which, while admittedly lacking in the exciting visuals of the preceding film, lends itself to debate from the viewer.

Such notions aside, Christopher Lee was not happy throughout production, as he reported in the January/February 1970 edition of his *Club Bulletin*: "I'm speaking to you from my dressing room, where I'm at the present moment wading through this latest masterpiece from Hammer Films (*Taste the Blood of Dracula*). I know that you must realize by now how I

feel towards this particular product with these particular people, so there's no need for me to go into it in endless detail and repetition." Lee went on: "I am looming around in the dank undergrowth, as you can imagine, from time to time, burdened down by the cares of the role and an immensely heavy cape."

To his credit, however, Lee was on his best behavior when Jill Basten, a British member of his fan club, visited the actor on-set. Miss Basten wrote up her experience for a *Club Bulletin* article entitled "A Date with Dracula," wherein, on finding Mr. Lee "sinisterly garbed as the archfiend Dracula," she continues: "He was behaving in a decidedly unfiendish manner endeavoring to fulfill the wishes of a group of small boys who wanted him to frighten them! They remained resolutely unperturbed in spite of all his efforts, and the only indication of success was when one of them got the hiccupps ... 'Fans of the future,' said Christopher with a mischievous glint in his eye ..." After Lee kindly showed Jill around the studio, she concluded her report: "There's nothing false about Christopher Lee. None of this 'I'm a big film star' affectation, just a very talented actor, blessed with great integrity, and very grateful to his fans ..."

Indeed, producer Aida Young was quoted in *The Hammer Story* as saying: "I'm glad [Lee] agreed to do it [*Taste the Blood of Dracula*], because he was superb. And he loved it—I think he would have been so upset if somebody else had done it. Not that anybody else could have done it, of course."

Whatever misgivings the actor may have had, he eventually conceded, in his January/February 1970 *Club Bulletin*, that despite "a somewhat odd script ... we have got the best cast that I think they've ever had in a Hammer production."

The "busty blonde in the billowing nightdress," Linda Hayden

The Loneliness of Evil

(real name: Linda Higginson, b. 1953), came to Hammer's attention with her performance in the controversial *Baby Love* (1968). "All my movies seem to be played at [three o'clock] in the morning," she told *Funny Man* director Simon Sprackling for his 2003 documentary *Linda Hayden: An Angel for Satan*. "It was really great working for Hammer in those days," she went on, adding: "I was actually quite mesmerized by [Christopher Lee] when I first met him, because, on the screen, you know, with all the make-up and everything … and, actually, on the set, he was quite a chilling piece …But when you meet him, going out for lunch afterwards and seeing [him wearing] the woolly hat and singing his operatic arias—totally different."

Following *Taste the Blood of Dracula*, Linda came under the influence of Darkness once more as Angel Blake in *Blood on Satan's Claw*, before being bitten by Dracula again, this time in the person of David Niven, for *Vampira* (1973). After playing the overambitious actress who tries to seduce Vincent Price in *Madhouse*, Hayden made a handful of comedies (*Confessions of a Window Cleaner*; *Confessions from a Holiday Camp* [1977]; *Queen Kong* [1976]) with her then-boyfriend Robin Askwith, although she regretted starring alongside another screen Dracula, Udo Kier, in *Exposé* (1975)—a film she described, to *LSoH*, as "that ghastly thing." Linda's later appearances include *The Boys from Brazil* (1978), in which her corpse is discovered by Michael Gough, and *Hammer House of Mystery and Suspense*: "Black Carrion."

Linda Hayden with Christopher Lee … then

It has been rumored that Vincent Price was originally contracted to play a Victorian thrill-seeker, but, when he proved beyond Hammer's budget, his part was split into three. Unfortunately, I have been unable to find any evidence to support this and can't quite see how Hammer would have saved money by hiring three actors instead of one; it's possible that confusion has arisen over Price's rejection of Van Helsing in *Count Dracula*. (Nonetheless, Lee's *Taste the Blood of Dracula* stunt double, Peter Brace, would also double for Price in *Theatre of Blood*—and is clearly visible in both films.)

Whatever the rumors, the *Taste* antagonists are undeniably played by a trio of very fine actors: Geoffrey Keen (1916-2005), who had last worked for Hammer in the 1954 thriller *The Glass Cage*, is frighteningly convincing as the tyrannical Hargood. Having headed the murder investigations in both *Horrors of the Black Museum* and *Berserk*, he would reteam with Sasdy to play the manufacturer of dangerous chemicals in *Doomwatch* (1971), before essaying the Minister of Defence in every James Bond film from *The Spy Who Loved Me* (1976) to (Keen's last film) *The Living Daylights* (1986).

Fresh from a cameo in *Scream and Scream Again*, Peter Sallis (1921-2017) had also been the sly landowner in *The Curse of the Werewolf*, and would go on to play clerics in Robert Fuest's *Wuthering Heights* (1970), Roald Dahl's *The Night Digger* (1970) and *Frankenstein: The True Story*. He is best known to British TV viewers, however, as the sage old Cleggy in *Last of the Summer Wine* (1972-2010) and to international audiences as the voice of Wallace in the popular *Wallace & Gromit* animations from Nick Park. (One of which, the feature-length *Curse of the Were-Rabbit* [2005], is a tribute to Hammer.)

For the scene in which Paxton is staked, special effects assistant Mike Tilley told the *Sunday Mirror*: "Peter was wearing a false chest with 'blood' pumped in with a bicycle pump so that when the stake punctured it, the blood shot all over his shirt. Unfortunately, we pumped too much blood into the false chest with the result that Peter's shirt remained Persil white while the cameraman 10 yards away was drenched."

Also, during production, Christopher Lee sold his Armstrong Sibley car to the actor playing Secker, John Carson (1927-2016). In the back of the automobile, Carson revealed to *LSoH* that he found a red cushion embroidered with the word 'Dracula'—a gift from a fan.

Unforgettable as the villainous Squire Hamilton in *The Plague of the Zombies*, Carson's other credits include the army captain of *The Night Caller* (1965), a vampire who proves resistant to stakes in *Captain Kronos: Vampire Hunter* and the black magician of *Hammer House of Horror*: "Guardian of the Abyss." The Satanic rituals he performs in the latter are all genuine and, because of this, on subsequently gaining a firmer belief in such things, Carson told *LSoH* that he would not even allow a video of the show to enter his house. When I met John in November 2013, he had recently played a movie vampire in "Death and the Divas," a Hammer-inspired instalment of ITV's *Midsomer Murders*. After I complimented him on his performance, he replied with a mischievous twinkle to his eye: "It was terrible, dear fellow. But I had the best part, and they let me keep my fangs."

In his *LSoH* interview, Carson also recalled that the scene in which the men buy Dracula's blood and amulet from Weller had to be cut very carefully as each take dissolved into laughter, on account of the jocular Roy Kinnear (1934-1988). "We never got a complete take," said Carson, "Even Geoffrey Keen, who's pretty solemn, and the camera operator were having fits of laughter." The stalwart Kinnear was a much-loved face in character roles, including the cleaver-wielding Selden in *The Hound of the Baskervilles* (1977). He also starred with the Beatles as a mad scientist's assistant in *Help!* (1965) and reteamed with director Richard Lester (and John Lennon) as an inept soldier for *How I Won the War*. After playing the indulgent father of Veruca Salt in *Willy Wonka & the Chocolate Factory*, Lester cast Roy as the bumbling servant Planchet in the *Musketeers* films. Sadly, while filming the final entry in the series, *The Return of the Musketeers*, the actor died when he was thrown from his horse. "Roy's death spread such a pall of misery," Christopher Lee later wrote, "that it was surprising the film was ever finished and, in truth, the world would have lost nothing if it hadn't been."

On a happier note, Kinnear's son, Rory (b. 1978), is keeping the acting flame alive as Frankenstein's Creature in *Penny Dreadful* (2013-2016) and MI6's Chief of Staff in the Bond films *Quantum of Solace* (2008), *Skyfall* (2012), *Spectre* (2015) and *No Time to Die* (2019).

A descendent of Louis Pasteur, Ralph Bates (1940-1991) studied acting at Yale before catching the attention of Hammer as Caligula in ITV's *The Caesars* (1968). The awestruck young actor filmed his scenes as Lord Courtley over five days and, despite only encountering Christopher Lee for a brief greeting, did get to wear his cloak on-set ("Silly really as I'm five foot three and he's eight foot four," Bates quipped to *LSoH*). Nevertheless—in a quote reprinted in *The Dracula Book*—Michael Carreras told the press that Ralph could have been wearing the cloak on a more permanent basis: "We gave birth to Christopher Lee and Peter Cushing who play our monsters. Right now they're getting a little bit long in the tooth, so we're developing new talent. We're building up a boy called Ralph Bates who should make an excellent Dracula ..."

While Bates never fulfilled that role, he would go on to replace Cushing in both *The Horror of Frankenstein* and *Lust for a Vampire*, before working with the great man himself on *Fear in the Night* (1971). Giving his best genre performance as the first half of *Dr. Jekyll and Sister Hyde*, Ralph also starred as the son of Lana Turner—Jekyll's fiancée in the 1941 version—for *Persecution* (1973). The following year, he reunited with Peter Sasdy for *I Don't Want to Be Born* ("One of the biggest-grossing pictures in Chicago," according to the actor), then brought a lovely, nuanced quality to the title character of *Dear John* (1985-1987). Bates succumbed to pancreatic cancer at the age of 51.

Martin Jarvis (b. 1941), who would make three memorable contributions to *Doctor Who* (as a giant moth in "The Web Planet" [1965], a misguided scientist in "Invasion of the Dinosaurs" [1973] and the Varosian Governor in "Vengeance on Varos" [1984]) stars as Secker's son, Jeremy. Although originally offered the larger role of Paul, Jarvis was forced to turn it down due to stage commitments at Bernard Miles' Mermaid Theatre. Still, as the actor told Sinclair McKay: "Aida Young very kindly made sure that I was paid the same amount of money as I would have been for the lead." Jarvis also revealed to the same author that his fangs (which can only be seen in Japanese prints) were specially made by "a sinister dentist in Belsize Park," before going on to

The author with Linda Hayden ... now.

remember a wardrobe malfunction that meant, on Christopher Lee's days off, "the costume fitters let me wear Dracula's shirt." As a result: "You could tell when Christopher Lee was coming in because these male costume fitters were all much more tense than usual. 'No, Mr. Jarvis, you can't wear his shirt today.'" Jarvis further disclosed: "He [Lee] didn't have a lot of patience with us giggling youngsters. But ... he was a great Dracula." The cause of the hilarity was Isla Blair, as Paxton's daughter Lucy, struggling to say her dialogue through a mouthful of fangs: "It's very difficult without drooling and looking absurd," said Jarvis. "We were helpless with laughter. Christopher Lee was getting crosser and crosser ..." The elder actor eventually told the "youngsters" to leave the set until they had becalmed themselves.

Isla Blair elaborated to Oscar Martinez in *LSoH* #13: "Christopher Lee got *furious* at me for laughing. 'If you don't take it seriously, the audience won't take it seriously!' Of course he's right. But he was great. I liked him very much." She also recalled what it was like to be bitten by the horror star: "He did that ... He used to bite my neck, really." Nevertheless, when the two actors were reunited, 20 years later, for *Treasure Island*, they were able to laugh about their time on the Dracula film. (Blair also appeared in "The Tennis Court"—a rare supernatural entry for *Hammer House of Mystery and Suspense*.)

Blair's brother in *Taste the Blood of Dracula* is essayed by Anthony Corlan (b. 1947), who was fresh from an episode of *Journey to the Unknown* ("Stranger in the Family") and would later be near-unrecognizable as the feral, shapeshifting Emil of *Vampire Circus*. Under his real name of Anthony Higgins, he has enjoyed a successful career in such roles as Gobler, one of the Nazi villains in Steven Spielberg's *Raiders of the Lost Ark* (1980); the lead in Peter Greenaway's arthouse hit *The Draughtsman's Contract* (1981) and

Henry Clerval, alongside Sting's Baron Frankenstein, in Franc Roddam's stylish and underrated *The Bride* (1984). In addition, his Moriarty in Spielberg's *Young Sherlock Holmes* (1985) meets an icy dissolution that echoes Christopher Lee's in *Dracula: Prince of Darkness*. (Higgins would play the Great Detective himself for *Sherlock Holmes Returns* [1993].)

Higgins (Corlan) told David Taylor, in *LSoH* #30, that Lee "was very unhappy. He just felt that they'd torn the art out of him; taken him for granted." While being "terribly in awe of him," Higgins listened to Lee vent his spleen against Hammer between takes in Highgate Cemetery. The older actor expressed regret at not taking up Jussi Bjorling's offer of studying opera in Stockholm all those years ago. "Why did I not listen?" Lee raged. "Here I am in this drivel." Nevertheless, Higgins stayed in touch with Christopher. "Paradoxically, he is a very, very shy man. He is someone who has absolutely made the most of the hand of cards that life dealt him. I think what he overlooks is that it was the Hammer films that gave him his visibility and enabled him to do all kinds of other things."

It says much about *Taste the Blood of Dracula* that even the smaller roles are played by great actors. Gwen Watford (1927-1994), who had made her debut as Lady Madeline Usher in *The Fall of the House of Usher* (1947), plays Hargood's long-suffering wife, Martha, with restraint. In *Never Take Sweets from a Stranger*, 10 years earlier, she gave a powerful performance for Hammer as the mother of a child abuse victim, who bravely rails against ignorant authorities (her husband is played by *Night of the Big Heat*'s Patrick Allen). As well as portraying Calpurnia in *Cleopatra* (1962), Gwen appeared with Peter Cushing in both *The Winslow Boy* (BBC, 1958) and *The Ghoul*.

Russell Hunter (1925-2004), who features as fey brothel keeper Felix, was fresh from enjoying three roles apiece, alongside Peter Sallis, in *Mystery and Imagination*'s "Sweeney Todd" (1969), and would play very different characters, indeed, for both the spy series *Callan* (1967-1972) and *Doctor Who*: "The Robots of Death" (1976). His most extraordinary genre performance, however, is as the evil sorcerer Mr. Stabs on ITV's *Ace of Wands* (1970-1972) and *Shadows* (1975-1978).

Finally, Michael Ripper proves the adage that "there are no small parts, only small actors" with his wry police inspector. Witness the delightful way he heads straight for the brandy ...

Paired with *Crescendo* in the UK, *Taste the Blood of Dracula* premiered at London's New Victoria on Thursday May 7, 1970 (when Norman Greenbaum was at No. 1 with "Spirit in the Sky") and Stateside, the film went out supported by *Trog* from Wednesday, September 16, 1970 (when Edwin Starr topped the charts with "War").

Taste the Blood of Dracula was aided in its success by a great poster design from Tom Chantrell, which has found its way onto more merchandise than any other in the Hammer canon. I have it on a T-shirt, a fridge magnet, and Peter Sasdy was very impressed when I stood before him on one leg to show him my *Taste the Blood of Dracula* socks. In 2007, the UK National Lottery even placed the image on a "Count the Cash" scratch-card (with prizes of up to £6,666). Parenthetically, look out for a French *Taste the Blood of Dracula* poster upon the wall of Candy Clark's apartment in *Q: The Winged Serpent* (1981).

The "Drink a pint of blood a day" tagline was a pun on the Milk Marketing Board's then-current slogan "Drinka pinta milka day." Hammer had previously promoted the Board, during production of *The Mummy's Shroud*, by issuing shots of Eddie Powell clutching milk bottles in his bandaged hands. Later, the studio were involved in a 1974 advertisement for the Dairy Council which showed Peter Cushing and his fellow cast members from *Legend of the 7 Golden Vampires* chugging back glasses of milk on location in Hong Kong. ("Pick up a pinta—stay on top" was the slogan on this occasion.)

Taste the Blood of Dracula would inspire a nifty one-liner in itself—when Martin Jarvis took his mother to see the film, he revealed (to Sinclair McKay) that her sole line of opinion was: "I think I preferred you in *The Forsyte Saga*."

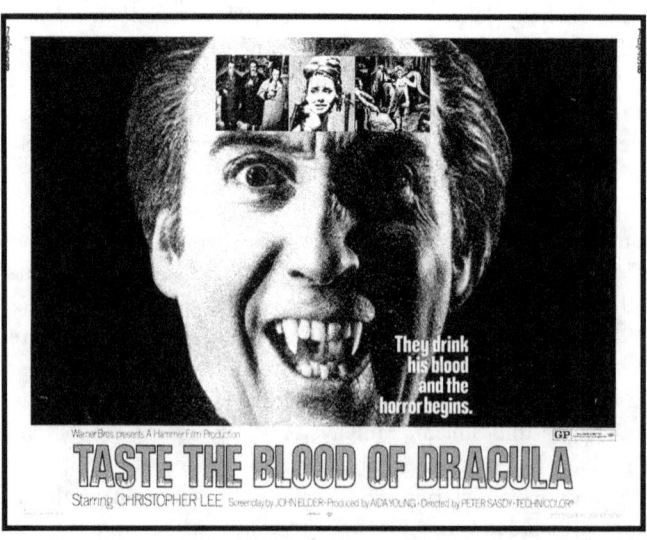

Scars of Dracula
1970

The most terrifying monster shock show of the year!

It was the beginning of the end and everybody knew it.—Aida Young (quoted in *A History of Horrors*)

Around 1970, an envelope arrived at Hammer House, 113 Wardour Street, addressed simply to: "Count Dracula Castle, Transylvania, Romania." The letter inside, written in a childish scrawl, read: "Dear Count Dracula, would you please vampirise my sister because she is a pest and always pinching my books and things. Yours sincerely, John. P.S. She doesn't leave her window open so you will have to find another way in."

This missive is telling in that it embodies the youthful appeal of Hammer's horrors, as does another letter, written in the spring of 1970 by Christopher Lee to his fan club president, Gloria Lillibridge: "You are probably aware of the fact that the next Frankenstein that they're making now is being made without Peter Cushing. I suppose they feel they can do without us now."

That last line strikes a sad, wistful note on the passing of time and the accent on youth; something already reflected by the diminishing ages of Dracula's victims: Melissa Stribling had just turned 31 when she played Mina in 1957, while Linda Hayden was a mere 16 when cast in *Taste the Blood of Dracula* 12 years later (Hammer would exploit the generation gap to its fullest extent with *Dracula A.D. 1972*). As Lee states above, the company had indeed cast a younger Baron, in the person of Ralph Bates, for *The Horror of Frankenstein*—a very light-hearted remake of *The Curse of Frankenstein*—which commenced filming in March 1970. Similarly, *Horror*'s stablemate, *Scars of Dracula*, opts to mine Hammer's Gothic origins by re-treading elements from their original *Dracula*, rather than following on from previous entries in the series.

In addition, the film's plot—which involves a young couple arriving at the Count's castle to investigate the murder of their friend—owes more than a little to *Psycho*, while the numerous bat attacks on display echo *The Birds*. The Alfred Hitchcock allusions are interesting, given that *Scars*' director, Roy Ward Baker (1916-2010), had begun his career as Hitch's assistant on *The Lady Vanishes* (1937). Since then, as well as guiding Marilyn Monroe through her most atypical, and arguably best, performance in *Don't Bother to Knock* (1952), Baker had been responsible for such classics as *The October Man* (1947), *A Night to Remember* (1958) and *The Singer Not the Song* (1960). His first Hammer film, *Quatermass and the Pit*, is one of the studio's most thought-provoking, and after Bette Davis herself requested him for *The Anniversary* (1967), he helmed *Moon Zero Two* and *The Vampire Lovers*. Although the latter is curiously unengaging, Baker redeemed himself with some unforgettable set-pieces in *Dr. Jekyll and Sister Hyde*, *Asylum*, and *And Now the Screaming Starts!* Rounding out his CV with *The Vault of Horror*, *The Legend of the 7 Golden Vampires*, *The Monster Club* and *The Masks of Death*, the director summed up *Scars of Dracula* (in *LSoH* #4): "I don't think it is a very good picture, but there are people in France who say, 'What a marvelous picture.' I keep on saying, you must be crazy."

Prior to production, Christopher Lee voiced his own misgivings to Gloria Lillibridge. "Think of it!" he wrote. "Another Dracula! This is titled *The Scars of Dracula*, another subtle and intelligent title." Feeling that the reason *Scars* held no continuity with previous sequels was because, as a stand-alone entry, it would be easier to recast the title role should he turn it down, Lee again cited the need for money as his reason for acceptance, admitting (understandably): "I've reached the end of my resourcefulness with this character. If you play a character four or five times like I have, you really don't know what more to do with it ... There are no more faces I can make and no more expressions ... The result is it's always going to have a sameness about it which I think is disastrous for an actor and rather boring for the audience." This didn't mean that Lee was tired of the genre, however: "I'm never going to turn my back on the horror field," he revealed in the same letter, "I'm just hoping and praying that the time will come when I shall be making these sort of films as well as they ought to be made ... like *Rosemary's Baby* ... with good scripts, good directors and good casts." Nevertheless, on reading the *Scars of Dracula* script, Lee had to confess: "It isn't bad at all [and is] considerably better than the last one ..."

Warner Bros., however, disagreed and rejected both *Scars of Dracula* and *The Horror of Frankenstein* outright. Hammer were forced to turn, instead, to EMI—marking the first time in 20 years that the company would be making a film with zero American finance.

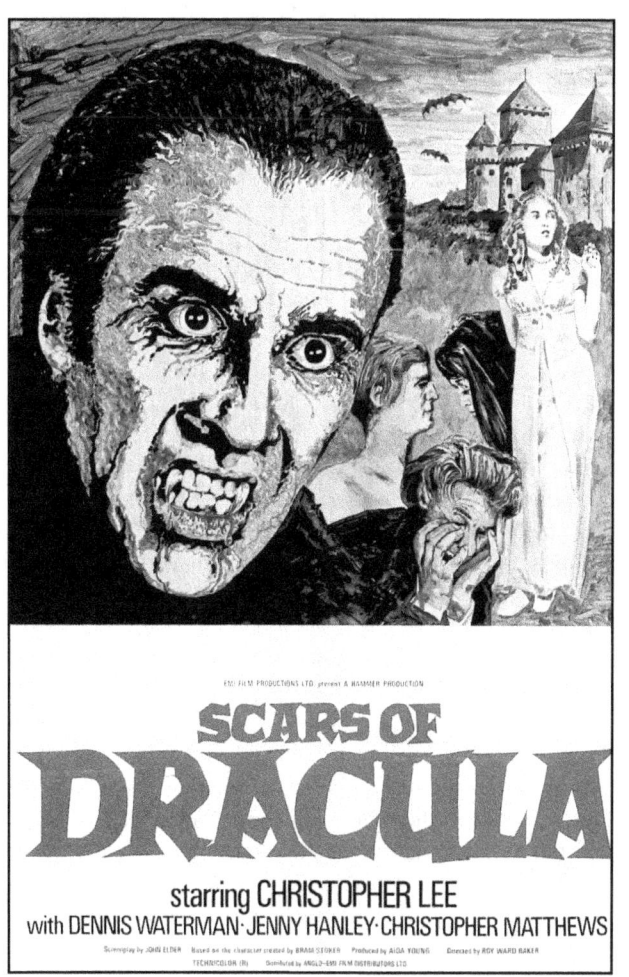

The throne beneath Jenny Hanley is the one Lee sat on in *Terror of the Tongs*. Dennis Waterman looks on.

Thus, equipped with a budget similar to that of Hammer's first *Dracula*, made 13 years previously, *Scars of Dracula* began filming at Elstree on Monday, May 11, 1970. In his autobiography, Lee wrote that the film "was truly feeble. It was a story with Dracula popped in almost as an afterthought. Even the Hammer make-up for once was tepid. It's one thing to look like death warmed up, quite another to look unhealthy." Despite appearances, Lee is in far livelier form than he was in *Taste the Blood of Dracula*—mostly because Hinds' script gives him more to do. (Which may account for his earlier approval of the screenplay.)

The actor also enjoyed the fact that Roy Ward Baker introduced elements from Bram Stoker's novel, which he believed had never been filmed before. The main instance of this is the scene of Dracula crawling upon the face of the castle (this had, in fact, already been done in *Drakula Istanbul'da* [1952], although it's doubtful that anyone outside of Turkey would have seen it). Despite the extra cost involved, a special set was built on which Lee could enact the effect. Just as in *Drakula Istanbul'da*, though, he scrabbles *up* the wall "in his lizard fashion," rather than *down* (we would have to wait until 1977's *Count Dracula* to see the feat as Stoker described).

Roy Ward Baker strove to include further magical effects, as he explained to John Brosnan: "One thing that I am keen about in horror films is that there should be a kind of supernatural element—an unexplained element." Thus, when Lee enquired of his director how he (or, rather, Eddie Powell) was supposed to open doors when he had his arms full of leading lady Jenny Hanley, Baker immediately responded "Magic," and had the doors open, seemingly of their own accord, as the actor strode towards them. "They've got them in all of the supermarkets now," Roy later quipped in *Flesh and Blood*.

But *Scars of Dracula* is not merely a magical fairy tale. Its depiction of graphic violence, enabled by relaxed censorship, takes quite a departure from the story's classic origins. Such moments include the gored remains of a bat attack and a startling, yet gratuitous, scene of Dracula stabbing his mistress Tania (Anouska Hempel). Cut from the film was a shot of Dracula lapping the blood from her wounded stomach. (Although a still of him doing so found its way onto a lobby card.)

Later on, the vampire punishes his servant Klove (Patrick Troughton) by applying a red-hot blade to the poor man's back ("If this scene was done today," Lee muses in Anchor Bay's DVD commentary for *Scars* [recorded in 2000], "it would be considerably more graphic and we'd all be dressed in black leather"; Troughton kept a still of the moment on his bathroom wall). Accounting for the more sadistic nature of the action, Roy Ward Baker told John Stoker (in *LSoH* #13): "If I was going to make a horror film, it was going to *be* a horror film. And I think I succeeded in that."

Although Lee was uncomfortable about filming such unnecessarily violent scenes, he got on with what he was asked to do in his usual professional manner. "He's a fusser, of course," Baker said of his star, to John Brosnan: "Everything has to be right. Both Chris and Peter Cushing are real perfectionists, though they are totally different. But I think Chris is marvelous the way he plays the part of Dracula … His whole interpretation ... was his own right down to the smallest detail. He played Dracula like no one ever did before, or will ever do again …"

Indeed, for all the problems surrounding *Scars*, Lee is uniformly good as the Count, tempering suavity and ferocity with the "loneliness of evil." Witness his look of drained remorse as he bites Wendy Hamilton, or the red-eyed expression of yearning he gives when faced with Jenny Hanley. Through his eyes alone, Lee illustrates the monster's angst far more effectively than subsequent attempts to convey this via dialogue. (For example, *Nosferatu the Vampyre*, *Bram Stoker's Dracula* and *Penny Dreadful* all give voice to subtext in a way that feels overly forced.) Nevertheless, Lee wrote of *Scars* in his autobiography: "I was a pantomime figure. Everything was over the top, especially the giant bat whose electronically motored wings flapped with slow deliberation as if it were doing morning exercises." (Throughout his DVD commentary, however, Lee enthuses about the movie's aesthetics, then concludes: "Do you know, I don't think I ever saw this film.")

It's true that the lack of American finance does show in *Scars of Dracula*: Scott MacGregor's chintzy sets (re-used in *Lust for a Vampire*) are over-lit in primal comic book colors, and the whole is peppered with some much-maligned special effects. The latter come courtesy of Roger Dicken (b. 1939), who had started out as a model maker on *Thunderbirds*, before working on *The Blood Beast Terror* and *2001: A Space Odyssey*. He also assisted Jim Danforth on the Oscar-nominated effects for *When Dinosaurs Ruled the Earth*. (The only Hammer film to be noted by the Academy.)

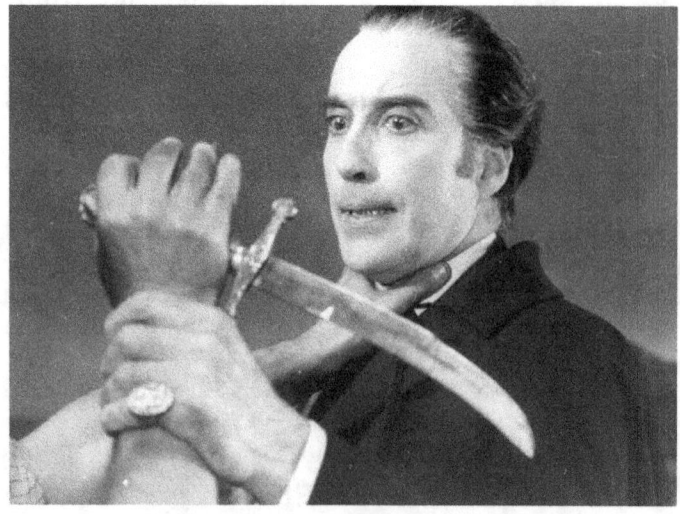

While the bat puppet Dicken created for *Scars of Dracula* would win neither Oscars, nor even plaudits from horror fans, it is still a lot of fun, especially when biting the priest's face (the resultant blood around the creature's maw gives the impression that it is wearing lipstick). The bat was also the subject of hilarity off-screen. During its attempts to snatch the crucifix from Jenny Hanley's throat, the puppet kept bouncing off the actress' bosom, causing the crew to collapse with laughter. As Jenny told Roger Moore (for his 2014 book *Last Man Standing*): "This prompted Sir Christopher Lee to walk on-set and tell everyone they ought to take the film more seriously …" Unfortunately, the frivolity continued when the two men operating the prop—who, according to Jenny, were "an item" who "dressed identically"—began to bicker "about how fast the wings should move versus how fast the mouth should snap." This gave rise to a riotous exchange: "That's too fast on the wings, dear … I'm not squirting *any* blood until you get the wings at the right speed."

"God, you're *such* a bloody diva!" came his partner's response.

Dracula (Christopher Lee) abruptly opens the curtains.

Still, the bat does contribute to a strikingly memorable opening, not included in the screenplay, whereby it revives Dracula (via reversed disintegration footage from *Taste the Blood of Dracula*) by drooling blood all over the vampire's remains. (Freddie Francis would later borrow the bat for his spoof *The Vampire Happening*, but when the prop returned to England, Dicken told *LSoH* that he was heartbroken by its dilapidated condition.)

For the climax of *Scars*—filmed on the last day of shooting, Friday, June 19, 1970—Dicken created an asbestos face mask, which is all too visible when Dracula is set on fire (the special effects man had used a similar mask to greater effect on *Witchfinder General*). Nevertheless, Lee contributes some very impressive retching as he expires (in burns make-up by Wally Schneiderman [b. 1922], who would later work on *The Elephant Man* [1980] and *Labyrinth* [1985]).

Hearing that Lee had made some important visual suggestions for the film's climactic action, Bill Kelley asked the actor whether this was true or not (in *LSoH* #13). "How does it look in the finished film?" Lee countered.

"Crummy," was Kelley's reply.

"Oh, well," said Lee, "then I had nothing to do with it."

One thing that is definitely not reflected by the diminished budget is *Scars*' first-rate cast. Aside from the comforting presence of Michael Ripper as the innkeeper, we welcome the return of an actor last seen with Lee in *The Gorgon*: Patrick Troughton (1920-1987) had made his professional debut in a 1939 production of the comic horror stage play *The Cat and the Canary*, before appearing as a robot in British TV's earliest sci-fi show *R.U.R.* (1948) and starring opposite Peter Cushing in *The Black Knight* (1953). Although his scenes as a grave-robber were cut from *The Curse of Frankenstein*, Troughton's name would still appear in the *Radio Times*' accompanying cast list whenever the film played on UK TV; ironically, he would play a grave-robber in Hammer's final nod to Mary Shelley, *Frankenstein and the Monster from Hell*.

Patrick's first visible role for Hammer, though, is as the Rat Catcher in *The Phantom of the Opera* ("They make a lovely pie, y'know"), in which he is stabbed through the eye by a homicidal dwarf. While filming *The Viking Queen* for the company, the actor learned he had been cast as TV's second *Doctor Who*, a role he essayed from 1966 to 1969, which saw him pit his wits against all manner of monsters, including Daleks, Cybermen, Abominable Snowmen and Ice Warriors.

Away from the TARDIS, Troughton would twice fall prey to the genius of Ray Harryhausen (*Jason and the Argonauts* [1961] and *Sinbad and the Eye of the Tiger* [1975]), while also making an impression as the impaled priest of *The Omen* (1975), Professor Wagstaff in *A Hitch in Time* (1978) and the mystical Punch and Judy man of *The Box of Delights* (1984). His *Scars* co-stars Jenny Hanley and Christopher Matthews both told me that Patrick was wonderful to work with ("a real giggler") and retain fond memories of the man. Jenny even treated me to her impression of Klove, complete with hunched shoulder and twitching eye (this took place at a London film convention in 2014; Jenny had around her neck the crucifix she wears in *Scars*—not for protection, I may add—which was her own from home). Just three days after his 67th birthday, Patrick Troughton suffered a fatal heart attack while attending a science fiction convention in Georgia.

The priest in *Scars of Dracula* is played by another Hammer stalwart, Michael Gwynn (1916-1976), who had previously been a prisoner on *The Camp on Blood Island*, the prosecuting attorney in *Never Take Sweets from a Stranger* and the sympathetic monster of *The Revenge of Frankenstein*. His other credits include the military leader in *Village of the Damned*, one of the "quite mad" denizens of *What a Carve Up!* and Hermes in *Jason and the Argonauts*.

Hammer Films are also something of a family tradition for Jenny Hanley (b. 1947): Her father, Jimmy, had been in *Room to Let* and *The Lost Continent*; while her mother, Dinah Sheridan, played the newspaper editor in *Hammer House of Horror*: "The Thirteenth Reunion." Jenny revealed, to Steve Green in *The Dark Side* #190, that Christopher Lee was a particular fan of Miss Sheridan: "His favorite day [on *Scars*] was when my mother was at the same studios, finishing off *The Railway Children*. So, mother and I were having a lovely time chatting, and Christopher came up,

The Loneliness of Evil

and immediately flirted—because he could flirt; boy, he could flirt, couldn't he? (laughs)—and had a lovely conversation with my mother. I'm out of the question now, you know, it's me in my nightdress and he couldn't give a damn! (laughs) It was lovely."

Speaking to Richard Klemensen, in *LSoH* #10/11, Jenny also remembered Christopher Lee as being "great fun." During production of *Scars*, her dressing room was next door to his and she could hear him belting out opera as she tried to listen to the band Bread on her tape player. Eventually, she plucked up the courage to knock on his door: "I'm sorry, but could you sing a bit softer?"

Lee asked her what music she was listening to, and he would try and sing it. Said Jenny: "He did listen to my tape with a great deal of interest, but I don't think it really was his sort of music. We had a good laugh … He was a very understanding man."

The two kept in contact after filming ended. Lee even agreed to open a fete that Jenny was helping to organize a few months later. Unfortunately, as Lee pulled up to the event in his Rolls Royce, wife and daughter in tow, the farmhand in charge of directing traffic caused the actor to scrape the side of his vehicle against a concrete post. "If Christopher could have struck this young man with lightning," Jenny recalled, "I'm sure he would have done so. His wife tried awfully hard not to cry, and only just succeeded; while his daughter tried awfully hard not to giggle, and didn't succeed. But Christopher was a gentleman throughout. He gave a lovely speech at the fete. He cut the ribbon and tried very hard not to wonder how they were going to get his car off that post. Believe it or not, he still spoke to me after all this."

Although Jenny had been cut from *The Private Life of Sherlock Holmes*, she would later play an imperiled starlet in Pete Walker's *The Flesh and Blood Show* (1972); a prostitute in *Soft Beds, Hard Battles* (1973, with Peter Sellers) and Miss Teenage Lust in *Percy's Progress* (1974, with Vincent Price).

Both Jenny and her romantic interest in *Scars*, Dennis Waterman (b. 1948), would go on to make guest appearances in the ITV sitcom *Man About the House* (1973-1976), one entry of which ("The Last Picture Show" [1975]) sees hapless landlord George Roper compare his wife, Mildred, to Christopher Lee's *Mummy* (Hammer made a spin-off movie from the series in 1974).

As a child actor, Waterman had witnessed his father being killed by Lee in *The Pirates of Blood River* (1961). Seven years later, Dennis returned to Hammer for *Journey to the Unknown*: "Eve" (in which he falls in love with a mannequin; the episode actually inspired a Carpenters song). After meeting a sticky end as Susan George's boyfriend in *Fright* (1971), Waterman became one of Britain's most popular TV stars via such series as *The Sweeney* (1974-1978) and *Minder* (1979-1994; the first episode of which was directed by Peter Sasdy), he can also be seen as the unfaithful husband in Philip Saville's *The Life and Loves of a She-Devil* (1986).

Waterman's brother in *Scars* is portrayed by Christopher Matthews. His character would be the third consecutive Dracula protagonist to be named Paul, because, as Anthony Hinds joked to Bruce Hallenbeck in *Fangoria*: "It's easy to type!" (Hinds would write his horror screenplays in three weeks, at a rate of five pages a day). For the memorable scene in which Paul is found impaled on Dracula's wall with a spike bursting through his chest, Matthews remembered (to Tim Greaves in *LSoH* #13) that, out of shot, Waterman "started pissing about," causing Matthews to laugh. The actor alleges that, in the finished film, you can see flickers of mirth start to form in his eyes just before the camera cuts away. Nevertheless, Christopher Lee thought enough of Matthews' performance to later invite the younger thespian to appear in one of his own Charlemagne productions. Although that would never be made, Matthews does feature in *Doctor Who*: "The Tenth Planet" (1966), Brian Clemens' *Blind Terror* (1970) and, of course, *Scream and Scream Again*. In 1974, he starred at the Savoy Theatre as Robert Morley's son in *A Ghost on Tiptoe*. Matthews' wife in the show was played by Delia Lindsay, with whom he also shares a bed in *Scars*. (In real life, Matthews became godfather to Delia's first child.)

Lindsay had earlier appeared in *The Devil's Widow* (1969)—a horror film directed by Roddy McDowall, which also features fellow Dracula starlets Jenny Hanley, Stephanie Beacham, Joanna Lumley and Madeline Smith. While filming *Scars*, Delia remembered (in *LSoH*) having lunches with Christopher Lee, at which he would produce "a beautiful little leather case," containing his fangs and red contact lenses. (Lee told Bill Kelley, in *LSoH* #13, that, although his wigs changed from film to film, the fangs were always the same—"the box would be produced, and there they'd be.")

Lindsay's father in *Scars*, the blustering Burgomaster, is portrayed by Bob Todd (1921-1992), a regular foil on *The Benny Hill Show*. Although Todd's presence is more in keeping with the kind of 1970s sex farce that Hammer would soon get into with their *On the Buses* trilogy (1971-1973), Lee called the actor (in Anchor Bay's DVD commentary): "The funniest man, I think, I've ever seen on the screen." (In *Confessions of a Pop Performer* [1975], Todd enacts a near-identical scenario to the one he plays in *Scars*; this time as an irate husband who arrives home while Robin Askwith is up to no good in his wife's bedroom). As well as essaying the firing squad officer who prepares Lee's Rochefort for execution at the outset of *The Four Musketeers*, Todd would appear in Vernon Sewell's *Burke and Hare*, Hammer's *Mutiny on the Buses* (1972), *Digby: The Biggest Dog in the World*, *Superman III* (1982) and *The Return of the Musketeers*. He also inspired the Half-Man/Half-Biscuit song "99% of Gargoyles Look Like Bob Todd."

Dracula's mistress, Anouska Hempel (b. 1941), who had been in *On Her Majesty's Secret Service* with Jenny Hanley, would be reunited with Bob Todd on *Go for a Take* (1972)—a comedy set in a movie studio which features Dennis Price as a disenchanted actor playing Dracula. After becoming a successful hotelier, Anouska was reportedly less than amused when colleagues began handing round videotapes of her performance in *Scars of Dracula*—a moment she preferred to forget.

Also appearing in *Scars*, as an ineffectual policeman, is David Leland (b. 1947), the future director of *Wish You Were Here* (1986). Leland would also play an officer in *The Pied Piper* (1971) and appeared for *I, Monster* director Stephen Weeks in both *1917* (1968) and *Gawain and the Green Knight* (1972).

Despite the aforementioned new talent involved, *Scars of Dracula* would, in many ways, mark the end of an era. It was, for example, the last Christopher Lee film to involve Anthony Hinds, who resigned from Hammer's board of directors during production on May 19, 1970. Retiring to the tranquil Warwickshire town of Stratford-upon-Avon—the birthplace of William Shakespeare—the ex-producer lived a quiet life, contentedly dabbling in amateur theatricals. Little did his fellow thespians know that the unassuming gentleman they shared the stage with was once the driving force behind Britain's most successful independent film company. Hinds broke his sabbatical to pen *Frankenstein and the Monster from Hell*, *The Ghoul* and *Legend of the Werewolf*, before concocting "Visitor from the Grave"—a grisly *Taste of Fear*-like scenario for *Hammer House of Horror*. His final screen credit would be on Tyburn's *The Masks of Death* (1984). He died on September 30, 2013, at the age of 91.

Scars of Dracula is also the last Christopher Lee film for composer James Bernard, whose score here is typically majestic. Bernard's remaining genre credits would consist of *Frankenstein and the Monster from Hell*, *The Legend of the 7 Golden Vampires* and two episodes of *Hammer House of Horror* ("Witching Time" and "The House That Bled to Death"). In the late '90s, he composed stirring new scores for both Murnau's *Nosferatu* and Kevin Brownlow's superlative documentary *Universal Horror*. With its fu-

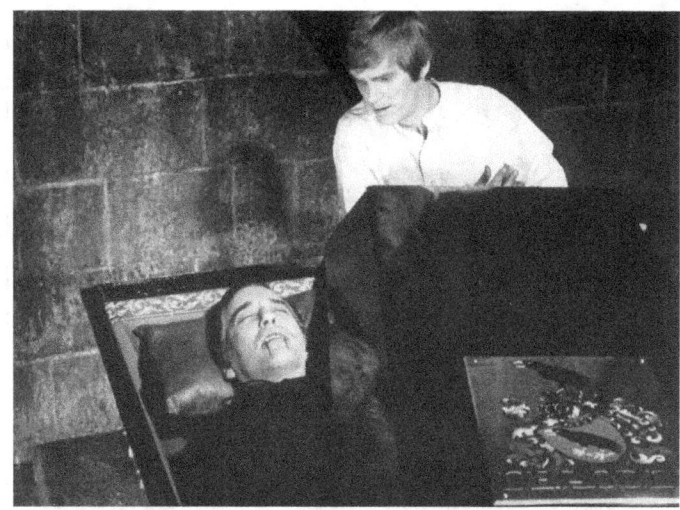

Christopher Lee and Christopher Matthews

sion of atonal and melodic themes, *Nosferatu*, in particular, recalls Bernard's *Dracula* triumphs with Lee.

Paired with *The Horror of Frankenstein*, *Scars of Dracula* premiered at London's New Victoria on Friday, October 23, 1970 (when Freda Payne was at No. 1 with "Band of Gold), before release in the US from Wednesday, December 23 (when Smokey Robinson and the Miracles topped the charts with "The Tears of a Clown").

While enjoying respectable business in the UK, *Scars of Dracula* showed the weakest overseas returns from any Hammer *Dracula* outing yet, thanks largely to sparse US distribution from Continental. Indeed, the *New York Times* dismissed the movie: "Avoid *Dracula* film like the plague; it's garish, gory junk."

Conversely, when the film reached the shores of Tunisia in 1974, it was advertised as "the masterwork of horror of the new English Cinema." While it hardly lives up to that bold claim, and

The sadistic side of Dracula is released as he burns his servant (Patrick Troughton) Klove's back.

Italian poster for *Scars of Dracula*

tial disdain on reading the screenplays very understandable. As such, the actor's efforts to preserve the vampire's dignity on-screen become all the more apparent and appreciable; whatever quality the later films maintain is largely due to him. *The Scars of Dracula* was reissued as a hardback by Severn House in 1987, with new artwork on the cover that bears no relation to Lee's vampiric visage.

Despite being widely regarded as Hammer's worst *Dracula* entry, clips from *Scars* are used to enhance "Dorabella"—a creepy episode of the BBC's *Supernatural* (1977), *My Stepmother Is an Alien* (1988, directed by *Love at First Bite*'s Richard Benjamin) and Tom Holland's *Fright Night* (1985). The latter features numerous affectionate echoes of Lee's *Dracula* films, such as the importance of faith in the destruction of the Undead—including a stake removal scene—à la *Dracula Has Risen from the Grave*, a near-restaging of the climax of *Dracula*; and a winsome heroine, played by Amanda Bearse, who is essentially a teenage Barbara Shelley from *Dracula: Prince of Darkness*. Among the movie's more original motifs is Chris Sarandon's vampire whistling "Strangers in the Night" as he goes about his business. This leads to one final note on *Scars of Dracula*: Production supervisor Roy Skeggs revealed, in *LSoH* #37, that, on the occasion of Hammer fan Frank Sinatra's 70th birthday, Skeggs sent the legendary crooner a card with a red-eyed still of Lee from *Scars* on its front. Sinatra responded that he loved the card, quipping: "Old blue eyes intends to live for a few years yet but he hopes old red eyes lives forever!"

lacks the artistry of its predecessors, *Scars of Dracula* is still, for all of its flaws, an enjoyably colorful entry in Hammer's vampire series, and never less than entertaining.

In early 1971, Sphere Books issued [*The*] *Scars of Dracula* as a novelization from Angus Hall (who had also written *Devilday*, the book on which Amicus' *Madhouse* was based). In addition to providing background on the private lives of Transylvanian farmers ("often ruled over by women of dark and chilly natures"), Hall's readable prose has Dracula turn into a bat and offers such vivid descriptions as Tania's censored death scene: "[Dracula] lowered his head to her breast and began to lap up the blood with a greed that was sickening to behold." What's more, we have all the dialogue from the script that Christopher Lee refused to say ("Sinners go down on their knees before me"; "Curiosity can kill more than cats"); a bit of naughtiness ("she had forced him inside her soft pink center…") and some interesting illumination to Dracula's reliance on Klove: "The relationship between them was weird and sick. Yet if one were to die or go away, it was doubtful if the other could survive alone. They needed each other, and this knowledge filled both of them with disgust."

What Hall's novelization really illustrates, though, is how far removed from Bram Stoker the character of Dracula had become in Anthony Hinds' original script (the source of Hall's adaptation): On paper, the Count is nothing more than a cruel and cackling pantomime villain, making Christopher Lee's ini-

French poster for *Scars of Dracula*

The House That Dripped Blood
1970

Terror waits for you in every room ...

Over six days in July 1970, Christopher Lee filmed his top-billed part in *The House That Dripped Blood*. For this Amicus anthology, Milton Subotsky hand-picked four Robert Bloch tales from his extensive collection and had the author adapt them. Milton connected the stories by having them related to Detective Inspector Holloway (John Bennett), who is investigating the disappearance of horror actor Paul Henderson (Jon Pertwee), former resident of the titular house. (In actuality, an old porter's lodge on the Shepperton backlot.)

The first tale sees horror writer Denholm Elliott (*To the Devil a Daughter*) fall prey to one of his own creations in a nicely jangled performance. The second has a lovelorn Peter Cushing lose his head over a mannequin. The third, and best, entitled "Sweets to the Sweet," features Lee succumbing to voodoo and the fourth is a light-hearted piece with Pertwee becoming a real vampire when he dons a magic cloak.

Stiff-backed in his tweed jacket, Lee does a marvelous job of conveying fright as widower John Reid, especially when the source of his fear comes in the unlikely form of Reid's cute little daughter Jane (Chloe Franks). To the eyes of her governess Ann (Nyree Dawn Porter), and, initially, the audience, Reid is a callous character, snatching a doll from his child's hand and hurling it on the fire, or declaiming gladness at his wife's death. Wild-eyed, he even slaps Jane on the house's staircase during a stormy night. But all, of course, is not as it seems.

The beauty of "Sweets to the Sweet" lies in its unfurling layers: Each different truth that rises to the surface is conveyed visually by director Peter Duffell through use of the stairway thereby showing that the story's varied perspectives operate on more than one level. For instance, when Reid nonchalantly telephones an acquaintance, we see Jane watching from above. Later, when the father points accusingly from his sickbed, the child flees downstairs, and the reversal of power is complete. Consequently, Franks steals the show from both of her elder co-stars; maintaining a childlike sense of glee, whether talking of "evil, magic trees" or stabbing a voodoo doll of Daddy. (The young actress would next be trampled on by Lee in *I, Monster*.)

For Anchor Bay's 2003 DVD featurette *A-Rated Horror Film*, Franks remembered: "It was interesting working with Christopher Lee ... He was quite a daunting person to be around. He kept his distance from me. I think that was partly because we weren't supposed to get on in the film, and so he didn't make a huge effort to establish a rapport with me and then that meant we could keep our distance on-set."

There was also another reason why Lee kept away from Franks, as he revealed to Tom Johnson and Mark A. Miller: "She, believe it or not, enjoyed pinching me whenever she got the chance." However, on reminding his young co-star of the upcoming scene in which he had to slap her: "She got the point, and the pinching stopped."

Slapped faces aside, Milton Subotsky had wanted *The House That Dripped Blood* to be a family-friendly film, so the casting of Franks, and then-current *Doctor Who* Jon Pertwee, could be seen as identification figures for his intended audience. At the insistence of the distributors, however, the movie eventually went out as an "X." (Subotsky's next attempt to aim horror at a family audience, 1980's *The Monster Club*, would be granted an "A" certificate.)

Having been kidnapped by both *Trog* and Shelley Winters (in *Whoever Slew Auntie Roo?* [1971]), Chloe Franks (b. 1963) can also be seen as Joan Collins' daughter in *Tales from the Crypt*, and as another noxious youth in Subotsky's *The Uncanny*. Diagnosed with

rheumatoid arthritis in 1994, Chloe is presently Director of Leadership Programs at the Disability Partnership and has served as government advisor on the Disability Discrimination Act.

Franks' governess in *The House That Dripped Blood* is played by New Zealand-born Nyree Dawn Porter (1936-2001), whose onscreen rape at the hands of Eric Porter in *The Forsyte Saga* (1967) became one of the most talked-about television moments of the era (and must surely have been the inspiration for Hammer to add an incongruous rape scene to *Frankenstein Must Be Destroyed*). Awarded an OBE in 1970, Nyree was possessed by an Elemental in *From Beyond the Grave* and appeared as Alice Hathaway in Subotsky's miniseries of *The Martian Chronicles* (1979).

John Reid snatches a doll from his daughter Jane.

The Loneliness of Evil

The doctor called in to examine John Reid is played by a fellow Sherlock Holmes, Carleton Hobbs (1898-1978), who essayed the Great Detective on radio from 1952 to 1969 (and would reappear with Lee in *Dark Places*).

Although the involvement of Lee, Cushing and Ingrid Pitt was a prerequisite for *The House That Dripped Blood* going ahead, the remainder of the cast was tastefully selected by its director: Like Nyree Dawn Porter's character in the film, Peter Duffell (1922-2017) had also worked as a private tutor—to Michael Gough's son, Simon—before honing his craft on episodes of *The Avengers* and *Journey to the Unknown*. To *The House That Dripped Blood*, his feature debut, he brings a classy reverence. "When I was a school kid, I had this affection for horror movies," Duffell told Mark A. Miller (citing Universal's *Frankenstein* series, *White Zombie* [1932] and *The Invisible Ray* [1935] as favorites), "and I just plowed back memories and feelings into this picture." Indeed, throughout the film, the director has shown his respect by carefully placing such genre-related tomes as Stoker's *Dracula*, Carlos Clarens' *An Illustrated History of the Horror Film* and Lotte Eisner's *The Haunted Screen* before the camera. Christopher Lee even brought in a favorite book of his own: One scene sees his character perusing *The Lord of the Rings* (which he claimed to read at least once every year).

Duffell told Mark A. Miller that Lee was "an extraordinary man. He's full of what you might think are Baron Munchausen stories about himself, but they all turn out to be true … He has a great passion for life …" After serving, uncredited, as second unit director of *Superman*, and helming two entries for *Tales of the Unexpected*, Duffell would be reunited with Lee on the Indian mini-series *The Far Pavilions* (1983).

In his Foreword to the director's 2010 memoir *Playing Piano in a Brothel*, Lee would write that "Duffell is the most underrated director we have had in Britain for a very long time." *The House That Dripped Blood* goes some way in proving this statement: Witness the improvised montage illustrating the lost nature of Peter Cushing's character (set to Schubert's "Death and the Maiden," which Duffell hoped would also be the name of the film). Nattily attired and forlorn, it's hard not to imagine Cushing was thinking of his own, terminally ill wife as he stands pensive by a river, strolls through a graveyard or watches two lovers entwined pass him by (to paraphrase the Smiths). *The House That Dripped Blood* would be released a month after Helen Cushing's death.

Elsewhere, Duffell has Cushing observe a Dracula waxwork bearing the likeness of Christopher Lee, and the latter's presence hangs more heavily over the story's fourth segment. After all, one can't help but feel that the script was referencing Lee's personal feelings toward Hammer when Paul Henderson states, on seeing a

The House That Dripped Blood **Blu-ray featured great art by Graham Humphreys.**

gaudily made-up hunchback: "If I go on working for this company, I shall finish up looking like him." Lee is more explicitly referenced when Henderson then soliloquizes: "That's what's wrong with these present-day horror films—there's no realism. Not like the old ones, no; the great ones: *Frankenstein*, *Phantom of the Opera* and *Dracula*—the one with Bela Lugosi, of course, not this new feller."

Pertwee's fine comic performance is well-matched by Lee's future *Wicker Man* co-star Ingrid Pitt (as Henderson's *Curse of the Bloodsuckers* co-star Carla), while the cloak itself is sold to Henderson in a ghoulishly stylized cameo, by one of Lee's fellow *Dracula* cast members, Geoffrey Bayldon. (Allegedly, Lee's soon-to-be leading lady from *The Satanic Rites of Dracula*, Joanna Lumley, can be seen lurking among the film crew, but it's difficult to ascertain whether the girl in question is really her or not.)

According to Philip Nutman, the part of Henderson was offered to Christopher Lee, as well as Vincent Price; but only the latter turned it down with any sense of regret. It seems likely that Robert Bloch tailored the character to suit the screen personas of either actor, as, in the author's original story, Henderson is not a horror star, but, rather, a Halloween reveler in fancy dress.

Interviewed about *The House That Dripped Blood* in 1992, for Liam-Michael Ruddens' documentary *Reverse the Polarity*, Jon Pertwee revealed: "I know Chris [Lee] very well and Chris came up to me and he said: 'I did like that … It was very funny … that character you played … you must have based that on somebody, but who did you base it on?'" Although refusing to give anything away to Lee, Pertwee told Ruddens: "Little did he know that, in fact, it *was* him that I based it on. It was exactly like Chris Lee. And people came up to me and said: 'You did that on Chris, didn't you?' And I said, 'Yes … the only person who doesn't know is him!'"

Paired with *The Honeymoon Killers* (1969), *The House That Dripped Blood* was released on Monday, February 22, 1971 in the UK (when George Harrison was at No. 1 with "My Sweet Lord"). The film received its first American screening in San Francisco on Wednesday, March 31 (when the late Janis Joplin topped the charts with "Me and Bobby McGee"). On both sides of the Atlantic, *The House That Dripped Blood* was greeted by some of the best reviews in Amicus' history—and deservedly so, as the film remains one of the company's finest.

For their next anthology, *Tales from the Crypt*, Amicus turned to the 1950s EC comic tales of Al Feldstein and William Gaines, but before that, they adapted a much earlier work, which finally allowed Christopher Lee to play the archetypal horror character(s) denied him by Hammer.

I, Monster
1970

The face of evil is ugly to look upon. And as the pleasures increase, the face becomes uglier!

Christopher Lee is quite a shy man in a funny way—you wouldn't believe it, and he was very nervous with one or two scenes where he had to be laughed at, for example. Fortunately, when he was doing that in the persona of the character called Blake, who is actually the Hyde character, then he didn't mind that because it wasn't 'him.' It was very strange, he turned out to have a sort of Jekyll and Hyde side as well …—*I, Monster* director Stephen Weeks (quoted in *Amicus: The Friendly Face of Fear*)

In November 1960, Milton Subotsky's first film with Christopher Lee, *The City of the Dead*, went out on the lower half of a UK double bill with Roger Corman's *I, Mobster* (1958). In October 1970, Milton kept that title in mind when naming his latest Lee project, wherein the actor plays, not Dr. Jekyll and Mr. Hyde, but Dr. Marlowe and Mr. Blake. Despite such variations, *I, Monster* is, in all other aspects, the closest screen adaptation of *Strange Case of Dr. Jekyll and Mr. Hyde*. Indeed, Subotsky's much criticized script features whole speeches lifted from Stevenson. So why alter the essential names?

In *LSoH* #2 (March 1973), the producer gave the closest thing to an explanation: "It was just a little game we played with the audience to see how many people would know what we had actually done." Subotsky's "little game" seems to have worked, as fans are still scratching their heads over the decision to this day—much to Milton's celestial amusement, I'm sure. My own belief is that Subotsky was eager to differentiate the film, not only from all previous versions, but also from Hammer's upcoming *Dr. Jekyll and Sister Hyde* (which had already been announced by his rivals in the June 13, 1970, issue of *Kinematograph Weekly*).

Subotsky offers further interesting twists by eschewing the Wildean influence of earlier movie versions, and moving the action forward to 1906, in order to add a healthy dose of Freudian thought to his script. Subotsky was inspired by the work of his psychologist wife, Fiona; Freudian philosophy would also infuse *Hands of the Ripper* and *The Creeping Flesh*. On his 2004 DVD commentary for the latter, Lee reveals that he actually met Freud, through a doctor friend, in 1937.

In addition, Subotsky elected to film *I, Monster* in a 3-D process, the Pulfrich effect (which requires a constantly moving camera). This was unusual for a 1970s movie, as the 3-D craze had reached its height back in 1953, when favorites like *House of Wax*, *The Maze* and *Creature from the Black Lagoon* were in production.

Unfortunately, most cinemas were not equipped to present *I, Monster* the way Subotsky intended, resulting in the 3-D effect being ridiculed as a hare-brained failure for the producer. Even Lee complained to his fan club in early 1971: "I've seen virtually every foot of the film and, to me, it doesn't look like 3-D even with the glasses on." Once we recover from the thought of an unimpressed Christopher Lee wearing 3-D glasses, it is worth considering the words of film historian Darrell Buxton, who tells me: "We've all heard for years and years that the 3-D process for *I, Monster* 'didn't work' and/or 'was abandoned during shooting.' Well, I've seen the film projected on (I think) 16mm, on what I'm pretty certain was a print from the collection of the late Harry Nadler. It was screened at Holborn's Gothique Film Society and also at Manchester's annual Festival of Fantastic Films (the event Harry co-created), the audience wore polarized glasses—and not only did the dimensional effects work, it might just be the most impressive 3-D I've ever witnessed. Haven't seen the movie in a while, but I seem to recall a scene with Christopher Lee lurking behind some wrought-iron railings in a park, about an hour in, which fairly popped off the screen."

Subotsky was certainly ahead of his time: 3-D would make a surprisingly successful comeback at the outset of the 21st century, with such crowd-pleasing releases as Tim Burton's *Alice in Wonderland* and Martin Scorsese's *Hugo* (both with Christopher Lee). To bring things full circle, in 2011, Dario Argento made *Dracula 3D*, which was acknowledged by its star, Asia Argento (in *The Dark Side* #185), as being inspired by Lee's Hammer films.

The perceived failure of Subotsky's 3-D process has undeservedly been blamed upon Stephen Weeks (b. 1948), who was hired to direct *I, Monster* only days before production began (Peter Duffell and Freddie Francis had both turned it down). Weeks was recommended to Subotsky by Christopher Lee himself, who'd been impressed with some atmospheric church-shot footage from the precocious filmmaker.

"Christopher Lee was slightly difficult to handle," Weeks told Derek Pykett (in *Amicus: House of Horrors*), "so one has to be quite sensitive to him and tolerate some little, minor foibles …" The director then gave an example: At the end of Lee's contractual period, the actor agreed to return, free of charge, to film some leftover close-ups of his hands; Weeks thought that he'd use the opportunity to get a few extra facial close-ups. However, Lee arrived on-set unshaven, which Weeks took to mean: "If you think you're going to do anything else on me, you can f-off!" Nevertheless, the director had to concede that Lee's performance in *I, Monster* is "among the best he's ever done. Without a doubt. It's an extraordinary performance. He's a very powerful and strong actor."

Weeks was less satisfied with other particulars of the production, however, as he told David Prothero (in *The Dark Side* #45): "It seemed to me most of *I, Monster*'s budget went on painting the Shepperton canteen. The equipment was out of the ark, the sets had been borrowed from *Oliver!* and *Anne of the Thousand Days*, and I was constantly trying to improvise." Indeed, Weeks' sense of style frequently overcomes the limitations dictated by the Pulfrich effect: Witness the tilted angles depicting Blake in his grime-speckled lodgings, or the vengeful, night-time pursuit of Marjie Lawrence's Anna upon the aforementioned *Oliver!* sets (which can also be seen to good advantage in *The Creeping Flesh*).

Weeks revealed further setbacks to Prothero: "The whole studio suffered from a lack of enthusiasm. When the camera operator discovered that his son was actually older than I was, he could hardly bring himself to speak to me." In fact, the director was so young that his parents had to append their names to his contract. "I wore long hair and sandals and carried a handbag, and everyone was outraged. Trying to finish a set reverse before lunch one day, an electrician up in the gallery deliberately swung a lamp into picture, so that I'd lose the whole afternoon."

Despite such hindrances, Weeks went on to direct *Gawain and the Green Knight* (1972), which marks the final screen appearance of Lee's *Face of Fu Manchu* co-star Nigel Green—the actor was found dead from a sleeping pill overdose during filming. "It was strange and painful to see Nigel's Green Knight commit suicide time after time on film," Weeks told Prothero. The director next made the M.R. James-inspired *Ghost Story* (1974) in India. Once obscure, *Ghost Story* is, today, a very well-regarded piece with notable appearances from Barbara Shelley and Vivian MacKerrell—the inspiration behind Richard E. Grant's character in *Withnail & I* (1986). After remaking his own *Gawain and the Green Knight* as *Sword of the Valiant* (1982), with Peter Cushing, Weeks returned to both India and Christopher Lee for *The Bengal Lancers* (1984), which, sadly, remains unfinished.

Blake, the Hyde character, is the ugly side of Dr. Jekyll (Christopher Lee).

In a 2001 interview with Mark Dawidziak (printed in *The Bedside, Bathtub & Armchair Companion to Dracula*), Lee gave his insight into playing monsters: "I go back to how John Barrymore played Mr. Hyde in the silent version of Stevenson's story. Barrymore still managed to maintain the human appearance, although it was evil … If you don't let people see the human part, no matter how evil, you miss the bigger meaning of the character."

Indeed, the actor gives two of his finest performances as Marlowe and Blake. He even manages to make Marlowe (Jekyll) an intriguing character, a feat achieved by none of his illustrious predecessors in the role, who saved their most dynamic theatrics for Hyde. Displaying a palpable sense of regret and sorrow when forced to destroy his cat, Lee skillfully conceals Marlowe's grief to consult a patient (Susan Jameson). This theme of hidden feelings courses throughout the movie, with the seemingly strait-laced doctor keeping pornography in his drawer and later confessing to Peter Cushing's Utterson that his much-respected father would use a golden-headed cane "for other things besides walking."

Ultimately, Lee's portrayal comes nearest of all in allaying the essence of Stevenson's story, i.e., Jekyll doesn't become a whole new being, but, rather, the bestial side of his character is merely an amplification of what already lies within. As well as showing us the darkness inside the man, Lee presents the humanity residing in the monster (something, again, which none of his predecessors had achieved). Whether wounded by the rejection of Anna or pleading pathetically with a child in an autumnal park, Lee brings a sympathy to Blake that, at times, approaches Karloff's work in *Frankenstein*. (Boris played only the doctor in 1953's *Abbott and Costello Meet Dr. Jekyll and Mr. Hyde*, leaving the more rigorous duties of Hyde to stuntman Eddie Parker.)

Lee is also careful to show the gradations of Blake's more violent urges, culminating in a ferocious cane-thrashing, but beginning with a jaunty, and ultimately playful confrontation with a youth in an alley (played by singer Michael Des Barres, who was married to *Scars of Dracula*'s Wendy Hamilton; *I, Monster* is lit in Rembrandt-like hues by *Scars*' cinematographer Moray Grant [1917-1977]).

Similarly, Marlowe's transformations become more monstrous with each successive intake of his serum (an allegory on the powers of addiction). Blake's various faces are the work of Harry Frampton (1915-1992), whose other creations include all nine of Alec Guinness' characters in *Kind Hearts and Coronets* and Peter Sellers' varied disguises for the *Pink Panther* series. Frampton also worked on *The House That Dripped Blood*, *Frenzy* and *Frankenstein: The True Story*. David Weston, who appeared in the latter, told Sam Irvin in *LSoH* #38: "Harry was one of the best makeup artists in the business, and he was quite a character, too. A red-hot Communist with a great sense of humor."

Note must also be made of Tony Curtis' Hogarthian art design, especially Marlowe's laboratory, which comes complete with a two-headed baby in a glass case. (Among those haunting the tavern set is Ian McCulloch [b. 1939], who, following appearances in *It!* [1966] and *The Ghoul* [1974], would become a cult figure for his starring roles in three Italian nasties: *Zombie Flesh Eaters* [1979], *Zombie Holocaust* [1979] and *Contamination* [1980].)

Another tremendous boon is the music of Carl Davis (b. 1936), who was appointed by Stephen Weeks himself. The composer would next provide loud, guitar-driven themes for Amicus' *What Became of Jack and Jill?* (1971), before scoring *Birth of the Bea-*

tles (1979), Ken Russell's *The Rainbow* (1988) and Roger Corman's *Frankenstein Unbound* (1989). In the 1990s, Davis collaborated with Paul McCartney on *Liverpool Oratorio*, and became well-known for composing new soundtracks to restored silent classics, including Lon Chaney's *The Phantom of the Opera*. In July 2005, he conducted the Royal Liverpool Philharmonic Orchestra for a re-recording of Benjamin Frankel's score for *The Curse of the Werewolf*, which was released on CD by Naxos (along with other Frankel themes, such as *So Long at the Fair*).

One downside to *I, Monster* is that Peter Cushing is slightly underused. But then, never has a performer looked so at one with his surroundings as when an exhausted, tearful Cushing descends the staircase at the climax; one has the feeling that we are watching a genuine Edwardian gentleman at home, and not an actor in costume on a film set.

Peter had every reason to look tired and emotional. Throughout the shoot, he was commuting 80-odd miles each day to and from Whitstable, where he cared for his ailing wife. (They had moved to the seaside town in 1958, because the air was good for Helen's emphysema.)

Lee and Cushing are joined by one of the most intriguing figures of the 1970s horror scene, Mike Raven (1924-1997), as Utterson's colleague, Enfield. Raven was a BBC Radio 1 disc jockey whose early forays into acting met with little success: "The difficulty was that I looked like Christopher Lee," he told Denis Meikle, while claiming to have worked as Lee's double on *Captain Horatio Hornblower R.N.*

In March 1971, Raven told Meikle: "I think it's probably true to say that I'm the only one of the actors at present working in horror films who would be there by choice." Indeed, with his gaunt features and pointy beard, Raven looked like the ideal horror star and was briefly considered to be the inheritor of Lee's Dracula mantle, an idea dispelled with the January 1971 release of *Lust for a Vampire*, wherein Raven's Count Karnstein speaks in the voice of Valentine Dyall and glares with the eyes of Lee. (Blood-shot close-ups were pilfered from *Dracula Has Risen From the Grave* and clumsily inserted.)

Nevertheless, Raven is a hoot as the demented artist in *Crucible of Terror* (1971) and the zombie sorcerer in *Disciple of Death* (1972), which he wrote and produced himself, under his real name of Austin Churton Fairman, after Hammer turned it down. The failure of these films saw that Raven's horror career was over before it really began. The budding actor retired to Cornwall's Bodmin Moor (home of a legendary Beast) to concentrate on sculpture. Offscreen, Raven always wore black (he owned several cloaks) and had a genuine interest in the occult. He revealed to Denis Meikle that the hand gestures he used as Count Karnstein were genuine invocations gleaned from his own magic books: "I mixed a few of them together, so that we wouldn't get any unwanted additions to the cast on the set!"

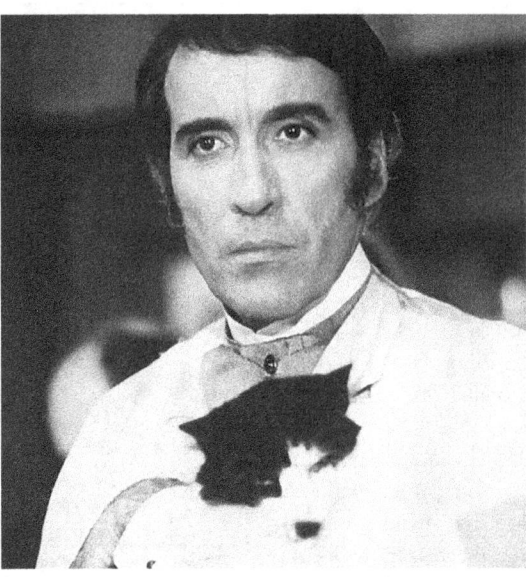

Marlowe, the Jekyll character, represents the handsome side of Christopher Lee.

Dr. Lanyon is enacted by Richard Hurndall (1910-1984), who joined Cushing and Vincent Price, in October 1976, for the BBC Radio sci-fi serial *Aliens in the Mind*. He would also make a very convincing replacement for deceased Time Lord William Hartnell in *Doctor Who*: "The Five Doctors" (1983).

Marlowe's butler Poole—a part essayed by Bela Lugosi in F.W. Murnau's sadly lost *Der Januskopf* (1920)—is veteran actor George Merritt (1890-1977), who, as well as playing the policeman in Lee's *Dracula*, had an uncredited part in *The Hands of Orlac*. Merritt's other credits include Hitchcock's *Young and Innocent*, *The Ghost Train*, *Quatermass 2* and *The Day the Earth Caught Fire*. His last film role was as the Old Knight in *Gawain and the Green Knight*.

Granted a UK release in November 1971—on the lower half of a double bill with Peter Collinson's *Fright*—*I, Monster* was not seen stateside until April 1973. That same year, it was announced Lee would star alongside Woody Strode in *Dr. Black, Mr. Hyde* (presumably Strode's Dr. Black would turn into Lee's Mr. Hyde). The film was eventually made in 1975 without Lee or Strode, but with *Gargoyles*' Bernie Casey playing both roles.

Lee would also not appear in Milton Subotsky's *The Monster Club* (1980), which the actor rejected without even reading the script—at that stage in his career, the title alone was enough to put him off. As such, *I, Monster* would be Lee's last film for Subotsky, although a remake of the Conrad Veidt classic *The Man Who Laughs* (1927) was mooted as an Amicus vehicle for the actor in the early 1970s.

By then, Subotsky was concentrating, instead, on more ambitious fantasies like *The Land That Time Forgot* (1974). Despite the latter being a great success, in-fighting between Milton and his partner Max J. Rosenberg saw that Amicus was dissolved shortly before the release of *The People That Time Forgot* in 1977. What's doubly unfortunate is that many of Subotsky's late 1970s ideas came to naught. These included a 3-D film of Marvel Comics' *Spiderman* and an adaptation of Lin Carter's Thongor fantasies (for which the producer approached a pre-fame Arnold Schwarzenegger). Nevertheless, Milton's finger was similarly on the pulse when he purchased the rights to six of Stephen King's *Night Shift* stories, which meant that, despite no hands-on involvement, he received a co-producer credit on *Cat's Eye* (1984), *Maximum Overdrive* (1985), *Sometimes They Come Back* (1990) and *The Lawnmower Man* (1991).

While many carp about the name changes in *I, Monster*, this is only a minor quibble. After all, no one ever complains that Dracula is renamed Orlok in *Nosferatu*, and even Lee's role model, Conrad Veidt, had played Dr. Warren and Mr. O'Connor for *Der Januskopf*. Moreover, at 77 minutes, *I, Monster* never outstays its welcome, packing some interesting musings on the nature of evil and the dangers of repression within that brisk running time. It is, in my opinion, the most underrated movie in Christopher Lee's entire canon.

In Search of Dracula
1971

Theatre Macabre (1971)

The bloodcurdling truth behind the legendary vampire.

The Dracula legend is based upon Vlad Tepes … he impaled some 100,000 people … oh boy.—
Vincent Price, *The Horror Hall of Fame* (1974)

Over two days in the spring of 1971, Christopher Lee found himself in the basement of Columbia's Wardour Street headquarters, not far from Hammer House, recording introductions for *Theatre Macabre*. This Polish TV series included 25-minute dramatizations of such literary classics as Poe's "The Tell-Tale Heart" and Oscar Wilde's "The Canterville Ghost." Lee's segments were directed by Ben Kadish—who'd worked as an assistant on *South Pacific* (1957) and Marilyn Monroe's *Bus Stop* (1956)—and the series' producer was Peter Marriott, with whom Lee had last worked on *One Step Beyond*. The incidental music was composed by Ron Grainer (1922-1981), who was also responsible for such legendary theme tunes as *Doctor Who* and *Tales of the Unexpected*. According to Jonathan Rigby, *Theatre Macabre* saw Lee "costumed in a fashion appropriate to each episode" and, for one entry, he even "used the very chair in which Oliver Reed's Father Grandier had recently been burned to death in *The Devils*."

While *Theatre Macabre* is frustratingly difficult to locate at the time of writing, Lee's next horror project is far more accessible: Originally an hour-long documentary for Swedish television, *In Search of Dracula* was augmented with scenes from *Scars of Dracula* for a May 1975 US theatrical release. Based on the best-selling book by Raymond T. McNally and Radu Florescu, the film takes a historical look at the vampire in folklore, literature and on the screen. Director Calvin Floyd (b. 1931), who also composed the dramatic music score, shot on authentic Romanian locations in September 1971. (The same year that a Romanian translation of Stoker's novel was first attempted, although it wouldn't officially see print until after the 1989 fall of the Communist regime.)

Christopher Lee lends his authoritative presence as narrator in both voice-over and two onscreen appearances, looking svelte in a black turtle-neck with bushy moustache. In addition, the actor appears as Count Dracula, imposing himself upon a female victim. These brief but atmospheric moments make one yearn for a full-length version of Stoker's novel directed by Floyd and starring Lee, which may have made up for the lost opportunity that was Jess Franco's *Count Dracula*. Floyd would go on to make the most faithful retelling of Mary Shelley's *Frankenstein* (*Victor Frankenstein*, a.k.a. *Terror of Frankenstein* [1975]), which is worth a look from all Gothic aficionados and gives further indication of what might have been. (The film, incidentally, is photographed by *The Skull*'s John Wilcox and features Harry Brogan, Professor Gaskell in *The Face of Fu Manchu*, as the blind hermit.)

In Search of Dracula begins with some fascinating footage of contemporary Transylvanians, for whom the belief in vampires is very real indeed. Lee tells us of a Gypsy named Tinka, for instance, whose father was staked by the villagers as one of the undead. This didn't happen in the Middle Ages, but as recently as 1932. On a lighter note, we are treated to a Romanian folk dance by members of the National Folklore Ballet (looking very much like Dick Van Dyke and friends performing "Me Ol' Bamboo" in *Chitty Chitty Bang Bang*), who beat the sticks they carry to ward off evil spirits.

In Search of Dracula is also worthwhile for providing odd facts which one rarely hears elsewhere. For example, did you know that the children of vampires are born without bones? Or that naked virgins on horseback are excellent at locating vampires' graves? Or that painting an extra pair of eyes on a large black dog acts as a useful vampire deterrent? It confuses them, apparently.

There is also some remarkable footage of a vampire bat going about its business (in this instance, sapping the blood from a guinea pig's cheek), along with accounts of "real-life vampires," such as Elizabeth Bathory, Peter Kurten ("the Vampire of Dusseldorf," who inspired the 1931 movie *M*) and a contemporary case study of a hapless soul named Bill, who is seen cutting his arms with a razor blade and drinking his own blood.

Screen vamps are represented by sequences from Murnau's *Noseferatu*, and some needlessly extended material from a Theda Bara showcase. In addition, Bela Lugosi can be seen menacing Lila Lee in *The Midnight Girl* (1925). As with the Bara clip, this is not entirely related to the documentary's subject matter, but it's a treat, nevertheless, to see the great Lugosi in what was then an obscure silent film appearance.

For its cinematic run, *In Search of Dracula* was distributed by Independent-International Pictures, who also released Al Adamson's *Dracula vs. Frankenstein* (1970). This is why clips from that trash classic are used to further pad out the original documentary when Lee narrates the origins of the literary vampire; a segment which also makes illustrative use of creepy automata—again causing one to wonder at the imagery Floyd may have conjured for a full-length Dracula movie.

The best scenes, however, involve Lee wandering the grounds of Romania's Castle Bran as the Wallachian prince Vlad Dracula (1431-1476), nicknamed "Tepes"—"the Impaler"—for his nasty little habit of impaling his enemies on giant stakes. Exploring the link between the historical figure and Bram Stoker's fictional Dracula, Lee relates the Impaler's exploits: From nailing turbans to peoples' heads, to enacting vile punishment on an ex-lover. (Incidentally, Vlad's latter-day descendants include Robert Pattinson—who plays vampire Edward Cullen in the *Twilight* saga—and Prince Charles, who knighted Christopher Lee in 2009. Lee also portrayed the Prince's father, Philip, in *Charles and Diana: A Royal Love Story* [1982].)

Debate still rages as to what extent Stoker took inspiration from Prince Vlad, but the author does have Van Helsing ponder: "He must indeed have been that Voivode Dracula who won his name against the Turk." Earlier in the novel, Dracula himself refers to his illustrious forebear: "Who was it but one of my own race, who as Voivode crossed the Danube and beat the Turk on his own ground? This was a Dracula indeed!"

Of course, Stoker never actually visited Transylvania, gleaning his (eerily accurate) descriptions of the place from books in Whitby Library, and most scholars agree that he took little more from the historical Dracula than the name and the "heavy moustache." Subconsciously or not, the grand Victorian actor Sir Henry Irving (1838-1905), of whom Stoker was manager, is said to have formed a more distinct model for Dracula's domineering character. Irving was the first in a long line of actors, including Christopher Lee, to be knighted; his roles also ran to the demonic in such offerings as *Faust* and *The Bells*. Indeed, noted essayist Max Beerbohm could have been describing Sir Christopher when he wrote of Sir Henry: "He had an incomparable power for eeriness, for stirring a dim sense of mystery ... a sharp sense of horror."

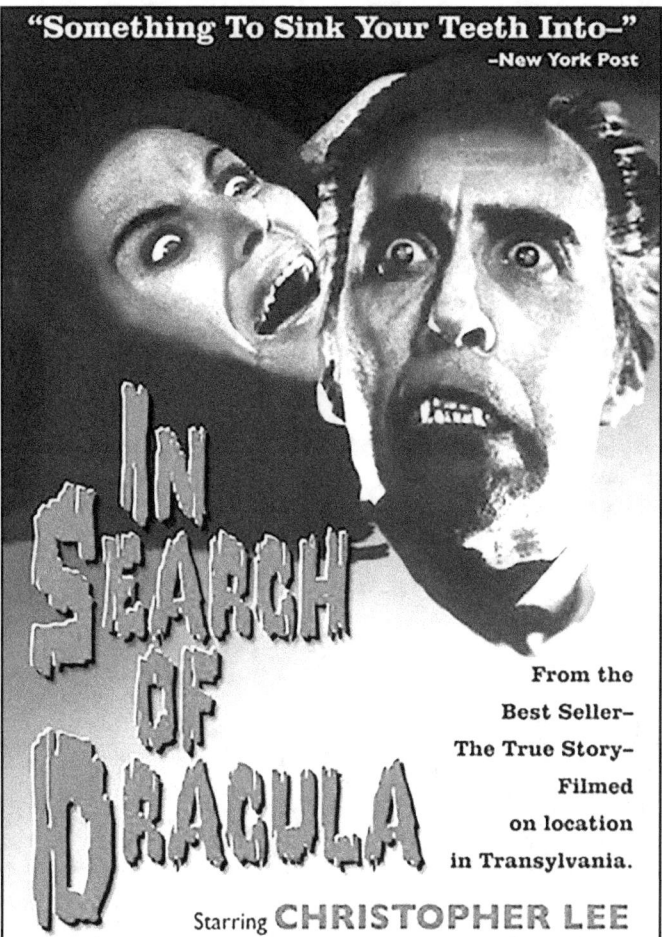

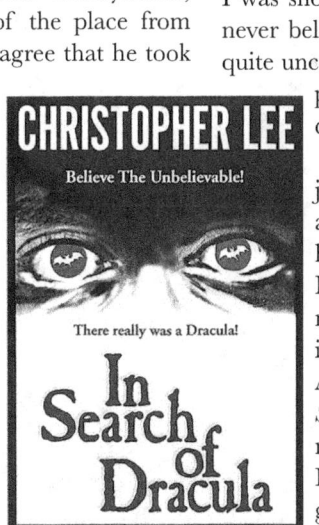

In January 1972, Hammer announced that Lee would star as Irving in *Victim of His Imagination*, a film which promised to investigate the actor's relationship with Stoker (to be played by Shanc Briant) and the creation of *Dracula*. Alas, this project was never made; a great shame, as Lee's saturnine features also bore a certain resemblance to Irving's, and he would surely have relished the chance to broaden his Dracula-related portrayals within such an intriguing premise.

But it wasn't just Irving with whom Lee shared a likeness. Recalling *In Search of Dracula* to Peter Haining (in *The Dracula Scrapbook*), Lee revealed: "The biggest surprise I got came when I was shown a wood engraving of Vlad Dracula's face. You'll never believe it ... but he looked exactly like *me*! It was really quite uncanny. And when someone suggested that maybe it was predetermined I should play Dracula. I could hardly disagree."

Unlike his later Hammer pictures, Lee clearly enjoyed working on *In Search of Dracula*, especially as it allowed him the opportunity to visit Transylvania, as he told Haining: "I was so fascinated by the place that I brought back some soil as a souvenir. And then in the next vampire picture I made, *Dracula A.D. 1972*, I threw it onto a grave as my tribute to Bram Stoker's memory." Although quite slow-paced by modern standards, *In Search of Dracula* is an invaluable record of Transylvanian life, as well as an excellent vehicle for Christopher Lee. Indeed, the final shot of the actor, as Dracula, glaring up from his victim's neck to warn the audience

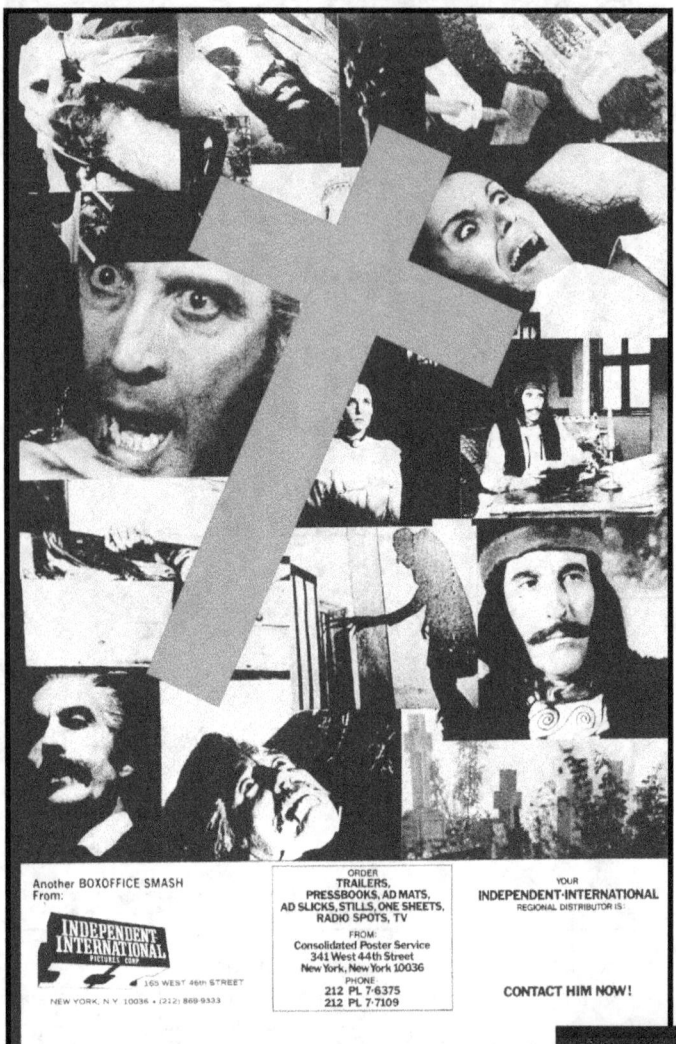

Helsing's given name was obvious: Both Stoker and his father were named Abraham. My literary conceit was to gradually tell the tale of Dracula parallel with the history of Stoker, using a combination of Hammer clips with Lee, with the rest of the cast in the novel's roles, wearing matching costumes, in recreated sets to intercut with Hammer clips. I knew that Hammer considered a similar project in its declining years, *Victim of His Imagination*, and called Michael Carreras about it. He had no interest in jumping back into production, and less interest in the old treatment. 'I'll just send it to you,' he said. When it arrived, I was delighted to find that: 1) The 12-page manuscript bore no similarity to mine and 2) it stunk. The Stoker bio parts came to a dead halt every 10 minutes or so to dramatize his short stories, potted mini-films of the giant in his fairy tale, the black cat on the castle ledge, the Judge's House and a desultory scene of Dracula biting a woman on yet another castle balcony. The prose itself was good, but the idea was just too diffuse as a biography or a portmanteau film like Amicus made.

"I sent my script to Lee, explaining he'd have to 'grow younger' as this Dracula, as well as grow older as Irving as the parallel stories progressed, and that he'd be required to play several Shakespearean characters. I brought up Ken Russell directing, since his early bio-films for the BBC were excellent, restrained of most of his later excess, and that since his career was in a slump, he'd be financially reasonable.

"'Of course, I would be delighted to play Henry Irving,' Lee responded. 'Who wouldn't? As for Ken Russell as director, well, I'm not so sure about that.' "Roy Skeggs of Hammer liked the idea—as long as I came up with all the money. And I had a two-scene cameo for Cushing—sedentary, for his benefit—as Vamberry, the scholar who puts Stoker hip to the historical impaler, and a short scene with Lee/Irving (Vamberry: 'I saw you do Macbeth many years ago.' Irving: 'How nice of you to remember.' Vamberry: 'Oh, don't distress yourself, I'm sure you're much better now.') "After we recorded the narration in Canterbury, I gave Cushing a copy of the script just before he left and said, 'There's work to be done.' He cackled happily and took the script. (I bought it off a dealer several years later. It had Cushing's penciled annotations.) I went inside and eyed Lee up and down as he was on the phone, nodded, and said, 'Yep. I think we can make you pass for 50.' It was Lee's turn to be nonplussed."In the end, no one seemed as keen on the project as I was. I dropped it."

Promotional materials for *In Search of dracula*

that "there *are* such things" is worth the price of admission alone.

Bram Stoker: A Nightmare of Dracula

Ted Newsom recalls an unfilmed Lee and Cushing project from 1994, which would have further explored the origins of *Dracula*.

"While editing *Flesh and Blood*, I read Daniel Farson's biography of Bram Stoker [*The Man Who Wrote Dracula*, 1975]. The complex interplay between him and Sir Henry Irving intrigued me. As I considered it, I could see other people in Stoker's sphere reflected in characters in the novel: Mina, the modern, determined yet entirely feminine Ellen Terry [Irving's leading lady at the Lyceum Theatre]; Jonathan Harker, the young Bram who ventures into an unknown world under the powerful thrall of Dracula (Henry Irving, obviously); Lucy, the lovely prize adored by all, who turns into a child-devouring monster, a dark riff on Florence Stoker [Bram's wife]. The significance of Dr. Van

Dracula A.D. 1972
1971

The Count is back with an eye for London's hotpants—and a taste for everything!

You're a 19th century man in the 20th! Perhaps you haven't yet collided with the complexities, the changes—but when you do … —Ilsa Strangway, *The Tomb of Dracula #4*, by Archie Goodwin (September 1972)

On Monday January 4, 1971, James Carreras passed over the management of Hammer Films to his son, Michael, who also inherited a slate of pre-sold productions, including two modern-day *Dracula* pictures requested by Warner Bros. Inspired by the success of AIP's *Count Yorga Vampire* (1970), the idea of placing the vampire in a contemporary setting, was, despite adverse criticism, not a bad one: With the advent of color television in 1969, over 90% of British households owned a set and Hammer had to transmogrify their horrors in order to entice people back into theaters.

Anthony Hinds turned down the offer of writing the latest vampire opus after his proposed script, *Dracula—High Priest of Vampires*, was rejected. (Although never made, this project would subsequently be reconsidered under the titles *Dracula in India* and *Kali … Devil Bride of Dracula*.) The job fell, instead, to Don Houghton (1930-1991), whose unfilmed treatments for Hammer included *The Day the Earth Cracked Open*, *Victim of His Imagination* and *The Savage Jackboot*. (For which Peter Cushing had gone so far as to design his character's Nazi costume.)

In 1970, Houghton had penned two *Doctor Who* adventures, which were extremely prescient, not only politically, but also in regard to the writer's future work at the House of Horror: While the noisy prison setting of "The Mind of Evil" is referred to as "Dracula's castle," the *Quatermass 2*-inspired "Inferno" depicts primordial monsters at a government drilling project. This fusion of ancient terrors in a modern world informs *Dracula A.D. 1972*.

Originally announced as *Dracula Chelsea '73*, filming began at Elstree, under the title *Dracula Today*, on Monday, September 27, 1971. The director was Canadian-born Alan Gibson (1938-1987), an ex-actor who had helmed three episodes of *Journey to the Unknown*, before Hammer offered him his first feature, *Crescendo* (1969). Despite a tired plot, Gibson brings considerable style to this thriller, as he does to the offbeat *Goodbye Gemini* (1969), which foreshadows *Dracula A.D. 1972* in that a dangerous outsider, this time in the person of Martin Potter, infiltrates the London party scene.

Resembling a slightly heftier version of the Doors' Jim Morrison, Gibson is Hammer's most underrated director, bringing both style and efficiency to his storytelling. On *Dracula A.D. 1972*, he contrasts the drabness of coffee bars and launderettes with the festering threat of vampires in midnight churchyards, bridging these disparate worlds with Satanic rituals and the gritty vérité of a police investigation.

The movie also benefits from its locations: At the outset of the 1970s, King's Road, Chelsea was the place to be for London's "swinging" youth, usurping Carnaby Street. (Deliciously

lampooned in the Kinks' 1966 hit "Dedicated Follower of Fashion," the capes and cloaks on sale there were inspired, in no small part, by Lee's Dracula.)

Another plus is the cinematography of Dick Bush (1931-1997), who had provided the crisp monochrome look of Jonathan Miller's *Alice in Wonderland* (1966) and *Whistle and I'll Come to You* (1968), the Devil-haunted landscape of *Blood on Satan's Claw* and the blue-lit atmospherics of Hammer's *Twins of Evil*. His other credits include *Phase IV* (1972), *The Fan* (1980) and Ken Russell's *Savage Messiah* (1972), *Mahler* (1973) and *Tommy* (1974, for which Christopher Lee was originally considered to play the doctor role eventually taken by Jack Nicholson; Russell next affixed a pair of Lee-like fangs to Paul Nicholas' Wagner in *Lisztomania* [1975]).

Having championed Aida Young, Hammer hired another female producer for *Dracula A.D. 1972*: Josephine Douglas (1926-

The Loneliness of Evil 163

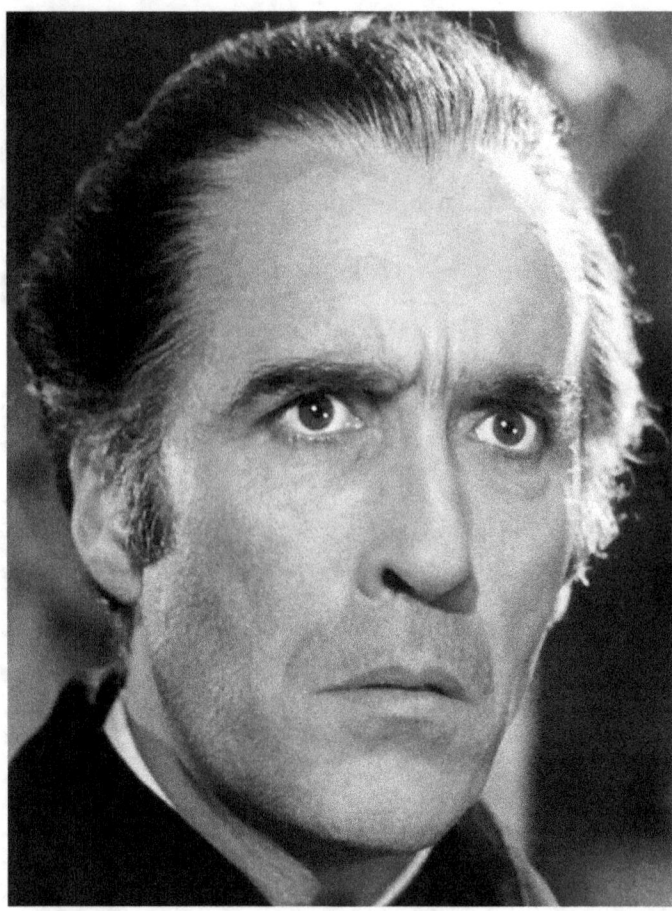

1988) had gone to drama school with Alfred Hitchcock's daughter Patricia, which led to both girls being cast as students in *Stage Fright* (1949). On learning that Josephine was keen to get into directing, Hitchcock kindly allowed her to remain on-set and observe him at work. "He taught me a very great deal," Josephine revealed to Richard Klemensen in *LSoH* #7, adding: "It was not easy for a woman to get into the film business because there was nowhere to start." Despite this sad truth, Josephine persevered as a television producer on *Six-Five Special* (a late '50s music show, which she also presented) and *Emergency-Ward 10* (the most popular soap opera of its day). When James Carreras invited her into the movie business with their modern *Dracula* entry, she described it as "the most interesting thing I'd ever done," and told Klemensen: "I certainly never met any prejudice against women when I worked for Hammer."

Remembering Don Houghton from his work on *Emergency-Ward 10*, Josephine hired him to write the script, and in all other aspects, she was "deeply involved on a day to day basis" with the film's production. Interviewed on-set by the *Daily Mirror*, Douglas complained: "I'm not happy with [Dracula's] face. It's not green enough." Nevertheless, she told Klemensen: "Christopher Lee is a great bouncing extrovert character but a very intelligent man, a delightful man to talk to." She also remembered him sprinkling genuine Transylvanian soil over a grave "because he said it would give the scene an authenticity that it might otherwise be lacking. I never could make out whether he was sending us all up or whether he really believed it. I know he did it with the utmost seriousness, which was a great day for all of us."

Lee gave further indication of the importance with which he held the part when, prior to filming, he was interviewed by scholar Leonard Wolf for *A Dream of Dracula* (Little, Brown, 1972). Seated in the actor's Cadogan Square flat, patiently waiting for him to finish watching the cricket match playing on TV, Wolf described the décor as seeming to have been "dipped into a tasteful sea-green dye" and also reported that Lee was wearing purple socks. Once the game was over, however, Wolf had Lee's full attention and reported: "It was at once evident that he took the role of Dracula with great seriousness and had read all about Stoker and the folklore of vampires." After admitting to being unimpressed by Lugosi's *Dracula*, which he had seen for the first time just 10 days prior to the interview, Lee got up to intercept yet another phone call from a persistent prank caller: "No. This is *not* Mr. Lee. Mr. Lee is not in. May I take a message?" (For more on these prank calls, see Ted Newsom's comments in the *Flesh and Blood* chapter.)

It would be a different group of youngsters causing trouble for Mr. Lee in *Dracula A.D. 1972*. Chief among them is Johnny Alucard, played by Christopher Neame (b. 1947). Not to be confused with Hammer's production manager of the same name, Neame had led the torch-wielding mob in *Lust for a Vampire* and would later earn the distinction of being the first male actor to appear nude on TV (for the 1973 fantasy *A Point in Time*). Recalling the scene where Dracula bites him, Neame revealed (in *Flesh and Blood*): "Christopher Lee sunk his fangs into me and he actually got a little carried away and drew blood, so I am a fully-fledged vampire." Indeed, it's rumored that the younger actor was momentarily considered by Hammer as a replacement for Lee's Dracula. While this didn't happen, Neame can be seen as the scarred villain of *Doctor Who*: "Shada" (1979), the secret agent tasked to arrest James Bond in *Licence to Kill* (1988) and the Maître D' of *Ghostbusters II* (1989).

Use of the name Alucard is a hoary plot device dating back to 1943's *Son of Dracula* (let's not forget the latter-day reincarnation of 17th century witch Elizabeth Selwyn disguising herself as Mrs. Newless in *The City of the Dead*). What's worse is that it seems to take Peter Cushing, as Van Helsing's grandson Lorrimer, most of the night, beside an overflowing ashtray, to work out the anagram.

Cushing fares better in his scenes with Stephanie Beacham (b. 1947), who plays Van Helsing's great-granddaughter, Jessica. Fresh from being tormented by Marlon Brando for *The Nightcomers* (1971), Beacham remembered (in the 1996 TV documentary *In Search of Dracula with Jonathan Ross*) that, when lying on Dracula's altar, her bosom was held up by gaffer tape. The noise of the tape rustling against her gown caused all kinds of problems for the sound men. She also recalled having the fillings in her teeth whitened so that they wouldn't show up on screen during her screaming scenes. Of her leading man, she told Jonathan Ross: "Christopher Lee said, 'This is one of the most difficult pieces of acting ever,' and I thought: Darling, you just put your teeth in, and put your cloak on, and you're away, aren't you? And I suppose it's because one just accepts him as Dracula and doesn't think it could be difficult, but he does bring enormous dignity to the part and brings the full presence of his personality."

Lee maintained his dignity, even when suffering another on-set mishap, as the actor explained to Al Taylor (in *LSoH* #24): For the scene where Dracula is burned by Beacham's crucifix, Les Bowie covered Lee's fingertips with raw acetic acid, then aimed a hair dryer at them to create a smoldering effect. Unfortunately, the skin on Lee's fingers was badly burned and "didn't grow back for several weeks. It was a sore point with me and became a running joke between me and Les whenever I met him. He did effectively destroy my fingerprints."

Beacham would be reunited with Peter Cushing on *And Now the Screaming Starts!* and returned to the *Hammer House of Mystery and Suspense* with "A Distant Scream." Her other genre credits include Pete Walker's *House of Mortal Sin* (1975) and *Schizo* (1976), and Richard Gordon's last production, *Inseminoid* (1980).

In a 1984 discussion with Greg Turnbull (first published in *LSoH* #12), Stephanie compared her Hammer co-stars: "Daddy Cushing, I'm so fond of him, I really am. I was cast as his daughter, and then he fell so ill after Helen died that we had to change it to his granddaughter. There was no other way. He was lovely, but a bit eccentric … Christopher Lee is an ambitious man, a totally different person. They were dear friends, but it was a strange friendship of complete opposites."

In the same interview, Beacham remembered another *Dracula A.D. 1972* cast member who "used to look disgustingly good at six o'clock in the morning!" Promoted as "the Hammer find of 1971," Caroline Munro (b. 1949) was one of the few Hammer artists to be put under contract (both Lee and Cushing were hired on a film-by-film basis) after James Carreras spotted her in a Lamb's Navy Rum advertisement (posters of which can be seen in both *Revenge* and *On the Buses* [1971]). Although she played only one more role for Hammer—her sweet Gypsy heroine is a highlight of *Captain Kronos: Vampire Hunter*—Caroline went on to gain the moniker "First Lady of Fantasy" for her appearances in *The Abominable Dr. Phibes*, *Dr. Phibes Rises Again*, *The Golden Voyage of Sinbad*, *I Don't Want to Be Born*, *At the Earth's Core* and *The Spy Who Loved Me*. Following a trio of films alongside Joe Spinell (*Starcrash* [1978], *Maniac* [1979] and *The Last Horror Film* [1981]), and a singing cameo in *Don't Open Till Christmas* (1984), the remainder of Munro's genre credits saw her cast as a former student at *Slaughter High* (1985), Paul Naschy's willful housekeeper in *Howl of the Devil* (1987), Telly Savalas' daughter in *Faceless* (1987), an ambitious actress in *The Black Cat* (1989) and herself in *Night Owl* (1992). Between 1983 and 1986, she became a gameshow hostess, alongside Dusty Bin, on *3-2-1*: The brainchild of Narciso Ibáñez Serrador—director of Spanish horror classic *The House That Screamed* and son of *Dracula Saga* star Narciso Ibáñez Menta—one episode of this baffling quiz features *The House That Dripped Blood*'s Jon Pertwee as a singing and dancing Dracula. (Munro finally got to play a vampire herself in Emma Dark's *Frankula* [2017].)

Having met Caroline a couple of times on the convention circuit, I have been treated to her reminiscences from *Dracula A.D. 1972*. Firstly, she revealed that the impressive sight of Lee as Dracula, and the very apparent seriousness with which he took the role, really inspired her to hone-in on her own performance. Consequently, Munro is at her most impressive in *Dracula A.D. 1972*, especially when her heart-wrenching cries dissolve into tearful fear, then wide-eyed awe as she faces the King Vampire. Caroline also told a funny story where, after filming the bite scene, she sped off in her Mini Cooper, late for a dinner party, without cleaning off the fake blood streaming down her neck. Unfortunately, she was stopped by a concerned policeman, who was only placated when Caroline pointed to her throat and said the magic words: "Christopher Lee," which seemed to make everything clear.

While Stephanie Beacham went on to acquire international fame in soap operas *Dynasty* (1981-1989) and *The Colbys* (1985-1987), another *A.D. 1972* alumnus would also make quite a splash in television: Following excellent performances alongside Patrick Magee in both *Orson Welles Great Mysteries*: "The Monkey's Paw" and *Beasts*: "What Big Eyes," Michael Kitchen (b. 1948) essayed Satan for Dennis Potter's controversial TV play *Brimstone and Treacle* (1976), before becoming familiar to cinemagoers as MI6's Chief of Staff in the James Bond films *GoldenEye* (1995) and *The World is Not Enough* (1999).

Dracula A.D. 1972 boasts another nascent talent in Marsha Hunt (b. 1946). Singer, novelist and Dracula's first black victim, the Pennsylvania-born Renaissance woman first came to England in 1966, where she appeared in the controversial zeitgeist musical, *Hair*. After having a child with Mick Jagger (who would write "Brown Sugar" for her), Marsha played Nurse Persil, infiltrator of *Britannia Hospital*, and was reunited with Christopher Lee on *Howling II*. Recalling *A.D. 1972*, Josephine Douglas told Richard Klemensen: "[Marsha] was really quite disturbed with the possibilities of what would happen if [Christopher Neame]

Christopher Lee, Stephanie Beacham, Marsha A. Hunt, Janet Key, and Caroline Munro in *Dracula A.D. 1972*

kept going in front of this terrible black altar thing and calling up the Devil and invoking him in all these right words and the right gestures. And she really got into quite a state. And we had to stop doing it …" This is not entirely surprising: Despite silly intonations from Neame, such as "Dig the music, kids," the aforementioned scene is genuinely unnerving, thanks largely to an electronic soundscape from White Noise ("Black Mass [Electric Storm in Hell]").

Among the "kids" digging such music is Philip Miller (b. 1947) and Janet Key (1945-1992). The son of singer Gary Miller (1924-1968)—who crooned the title themes for Gerry Anderson's *Stingray* (1964-1965)—Philip would fall afoul of vampirism once more in a creepy TV adaptation of E.F. Benson's *Mrs. Amworth* (1975). He can also be seen as Star Destroyer Captain #1 in *Return of the Jedi*. Janet Key, meanwhile, played the drowned babysitter in *I Don't Want to Be Born*, as well as housekeepers in both *And Now the Screaming Starts!* and *The Vampire Lovers*.

The Loneliness of Evil

Of the older actors in *A.D. 1972*, Michael Coles (1936-2005) brings a po-faced verisimilitude to the character of Inspector Murray (who returns in *The Satanic Rites of Dracula*). A veteran of such TV shows as *The Saint*, *The Avengers* and *Randall and Hopkirk (Deceased)*, Coles had previously worked alongside Peter Cushing as Ganatus, one of the crusading Thals in *Dr. Who and the Daleks*. Besides a great cast, *Dracula A.D. 1972* is a lot of fun. The opening party scene, for instance, not only recalls the musical interludes of 1950s favorites like *I Was a Teenage Werewolf*, *Attack of the Puppet People* and *How to Make a Monster*, but also allows some levity afore the ensuing darkness. Rod Stewart's group the Faces were initially contracted to appear, but Warner Bros. preferred San Francisco's Stoneground instead (led by former Beau Brummels vocalist Sal Valentino, the band would tour with the Beach Boys in December '71). Singer Annie Sampson remembered her stint on *A.D. 1972* to Bruce Hallenbeck (in *LSoH* #22): "It was wonderful, we had a great time! Christopher Lee came to the set, and he was a wonderful man. I talked to him and he was really gracious and kind …[He] thanked us for doing the movie; in fact, I was talking to him about it because I didn't know if I wanted to be in this movie about the Devil. Because I'm a Christian, you know what I mean? But I said to him, because the cross and the Bible win in the end, I think I can do it. And he goes, 'Yup, that's right!' But I was really concerned at first …"

The main score is provided by Michael Vickers (b. 1940), a former member of Manfred Mann (*A.D. 1972* marks Hammer's second connection with the band: Lead singer Paul Jones had just taken top billing in *Demons of the Mind*). In 1967, Vickers con-

ducted the orchestra for the Beatles' "All You Need is Love" on *Our World*—a live satellite broadcast which reached 700 million people worldwide—and he later programmed the Moog synthesizer heard on *Abbey Road*. The composer's work on *Dracula A.D. 1972*, though, is unjustly maligned, with critics concentrating on his jazzier themes, rather than the creepy tonalities he supplies elsewhere: The punchy brass is well-attuned to Lee's sleek, vampiric movements; the mournful horns increase suspense, and the result is a satisfyingly diverse soundtrack. (Vickers went on to score *At the Earth's Core* and *Warlords of Atlantis*.)

Bookended by two excellent confrontations between Dracula and Van Helsing, *A.D. 1972* sees Lee and Cushing give their all. Appearing in the aftermath of his wife's death (on Thursday January 14, 1971), Peter gallantly throws himself into his work, venting his grief. He even pays tribute to Helen by placing a picture of a departed lover on Lorrimer's desk. The actor would repeat this gesture in *Tales from the Crypt*, *The Creeping Flesh* and *The Ghoul* (but only in the latter does the photograph actually show Helen).

As for Lee, despite being confined to a desanctified church, he gives his most frightening portrayal of Dracula since the 1957 film; whether admonishing Johnny Alucard, or closely pursuing Van Helsing up a spiral staircase. He even manages to insert a cut-down line from Stoker: "You would play your brains against mine? Against me who has commanded nations?" As the actor told Peter Haining, in *The Dracula Scrapbook*: "It was a desperate cry from my heart to the author that at least I was trying to get something original into the film!"

Lee further opined, in his memoirs that, although *A.D. 1972* "had certain things in its favor," he was, "to begin with, aghast at the plan to bring the story into modern times, but a compromise was affected whereby at least [Dracula's] Gothic homestead and the church were retained." Sadly, it is Dracula's refusal to leave his Gothic dwelling that provides the film with its main weakness. Although *A.D. 1972* is better paced than *Count Yorga Vampire*, the latter title succeeds in its willingness to depict Robert Quarry's vampire merging with the modern world he inhabits. (This extends to him catching a late-night TV screening of *The Vampire Lovers* in *The Return of Count Yorga* [1971].)

The idea of placing the vampire legend in modern times, however, was not exclusive to the 1970s: Even Stoker's Dracula

Italian lobby cards

operated in the present, making the vampire, and his infiltration of the modern world, less of a distant fairy tale figure and more of an immediate (and hence more terrifying) threat. As *The British Review* wrote of *Dracula*, in July 1897: "The plot is ingenious, and the more interesting that it is laid chiefly in England at the present day." Another contemporary review of Stoker's novel, this time in *The Spectator*, would echo later criticisms of *Dracula A.D. 1972*: "The up-to-dateness of the book—the phonograph diaries, typewriters, and so on—hardly fits in with the medieval methods which secure the victory for Count Dracula's foes."

It's additionally easy to forget that Universal's *Dracula* (1930) and *Son of Dracula* (1943) are contemporaneous to the times in which they were made. Furthermore, one of Bela Lugosi's best, and most pleasingly atmospheric films, *The Return of the Vampire* (1943), plays out against the backdrop of World War II to no little effect, as author Barrie Pattison notes in *The Seal of Dracula* (Lorrimer, 1975): "Juxtaposing Lugosi's fog-wreathed, cloaked figure with the kitchen freezer gives the film its most memorable imagery." Similarly, *Drakula Istanbul'da* sees Atif Kaptan's bald-pated vampire being chased through the backstreets of 1950s Istanbul, while, in the same decade, *The Return of Dracula* (1957) transplants Francis Lederer's bequiffed Count into suburban small-town America.

Interestingly, production of *Dracula A.D. 1972* was sandwiched between two Dracula variants, of different races, who both haunted the present day. Firstly, Japanese filmmaker Michio Yamamoto's *Lake of Dracula* is a tasteful tribute to Hammer, with the vampire's terrifying disintegration being a near-identical restaging of Lee's in *Dracula*; while January 1972 saw filming commence on AIP's *Blacula*, in which William Marshall stalks downtown L.A. for his lost love.

As the year progressed, more successful attempts to integrate the vampire into a 1970s milieu followed: Marvel's *The Tomb of Dracula* first appeared in April 1972 (and was adapted into an anime TV-movie, *Dracula: Sovereign of the Damned*, in 1980; one of the comic's regular artists, Neal Adams, would later design the US poster for *The Satanic Rites of Dracula*). The stories in this 70-issue series, which also feature Van Helsing's great-granddaughter as an adversary, give some indication of the approach Hammer should have been taking, as does another 1972 release, *Grave of the Vampire*, which has Michael Pataki's titular bloodsucker teaching evening classes on occultism. Finally, on Tuesday, January 11, 1972, *The Night Stalker* premiered on ABC, with Barry Atwater's powerful bloodsucker at large in modern day Las Vegas. On the back of this TV triumph, Atwater was invited to promote *Dracula A.D. 1972*'s US release by donning a cobwebby, Lugosi-like disguise for *Horroritual*, a supporting featurette that shows him swearing viewers into the Count Dracula Society, ending his oath with the words, "So help me, Christopher Lee."

Another promotional supplement was *Prince of Terror*. This four-minute, behind-the-scenes piece treats us to such sights as Lee and Cushing sharing a laugh on the Stoneground party set, and Lee rolling his eyes as Alan Gibson demonstrates how best to look impaled on a carriage wheel. We also see a mustachioed Lee in his hounds-tooth jacket assuring us from his book-lined study that "Dracula *did* exist," while, on the soundtrack, an Orson Welles sound-a-like intones: "This genuinely scholarly and mild-mannered gentleman ... has been crowned 'Prince of Ter-

ror'," before adding: "He defers graciously to the late Boris Karloff as 'King.'"

Dracula A.D. 1972 wrapped on Friday, November 5, 1971. It premiered in the UK almost exactly a year after production began, on Thursday September 28, 1972 (when Slade were at No. 1 with "Mama Weer All Crazee Now"). The film went out with a reissued *Trog*, which had originally supported *Taste the Blood of Dracula* in the US.

Paired with *Taste*'s UK co-feature, *Crescendo*, *Dracula A.D. 1972* opened in America on Friday November 17, 1972 (when Johnny Nash topped the charts with "I Can See Clearly Now"). On later US screenings, it formed the lower half of a double bill with *Enter the Dragon* (1973), wherein Bruce Lee takes on a Fu Manchu-style villain in scenes that would prove influential to *The Man with the Golden Gun*.

Although *Dracula A.D. 1972* fared better at the box office than *Scars of Dracula*, Hammer were still disappointed by the film's financial takings. Nevertheless, it's a myth that the House of Horror had run out of steam by the early 1970s. Under Michael Carreras' headship, they were still producing interesting movies of superior quality: *Twins of Evil*, *Dr. Jekyll and Sister Hyde*, *Hands of the Ripper* and *Vampire Circus*, being just four examples made in 1971 (parenthetically, *On the Buses* was the biggest-grossing UK film of the year, out-performing *Diamonds Are Forever*). Even the studio's later blending of genres (*Captain Kronos: Vampire Hunter* and *The Legend of the 7 Golden Vampires*) shows daring invention.

While it's true that the tawdry, exploitative approach of *The Vampire Lovers* and *Lust for a Vampire* invites such witless parodies as *Lesbian Vampire Killers* (2009), Hammer, in all other aspects, took their horror ventures seriously, and their first modern-day vampire outing is no exception: Despite coming in for some very disparaging and sniffy remarks over the years, *Dracula A.D. 1972* is actually a well-made and engaging thriller, which deserves to be counted among the company's 1970s gems.

The Loneliness of Evil

Horror Express
1971

Your non-stop ride to Hell boards at 8pm.

I have letters saying, 'Please will you send me a photograph of yourself with Christopher Lee.' They think he and I live together in a cave down at Whitstable, which is sweet.—Peter Cushing, to Chris Knight and Peter Nicholson, *Cinefantastique* (summer 1972)

I found [Peter Cushing] in our so-called dressing room. "I can't stand this anymore," I said … Then I went into a tirade about the food. … This is a ghastly studio … A massive whinge. He looked at me and peeled his apple. He just said, "Well, there's no good belly-aching about it, you know." That was about as severe as he could be. Coming from him, it was shattering."—Christopher Lee recalls the filming of *Horror Express* (from his autobiography)

The end of 1971 saw Christopher Lee reteam with Peter Cushing for one of their most enjoyable pairings, *Panico en el Transiberiano*, better known as *Horror Express*. "I adored doing that," Cushing told John Brosnan. "We did that in Spain and Christopher was so kind because it was one of the first things I did after I had undergone a personal trauma. It was an enjoyable film to make, and Christopher was marvelous during it because he's so good with languages—he speaks about 10, bless him."

Lee had already started filming (on Monday, December 6, 1971) when Cushing arrived at Madrid's Estudios 70 a week later—solely with the intention of telling production outfit, Scotia International, that he was not up to the rigors of filming in another country so soon after the death of his wife. Lee persuaded him otherwise, taking Cushing under his wing and inviting him to spend Christmas with his family in Madrid. "Christopher was, as always, a tower of strength," Peter told Brosnan, concluding: "It was indeed a very happy film to make." The backstage camaraderie and genuine affection each man held for the other clearly fuels their performances here as rival scientists.

Snugly reminiscent of such train-bound mysteries as *The Lady Vanishes* and the Basil Rathbone *Sherlock Holmes* picture *Terror by Night* (1945)—but with the additional spectacle of boiled brains and blanched eyeballs—*Horror Express* kicks off with Lee's mustachioed Professor Saxton discovering a primordial ape in the frozen wastes of a Manchurian cave. Transporting the creature aboard the Trans-Siberian Express, it becomes apparent that the ape is really hosting an alien intelligence, which absorbs the essence of its victims, creating an army of zombies.

Saxton is at his best when railing against authority, something he is called upon to do at the station when a lazy official refuses to acknowledge his ticket. Looking on with simmering disinterest as Cushing's breezily cheerful Dr. Wells bribes his way on board, Saxton then proceeds to clear the official's desk with his umbrella. En route, the Professor's bluster melts in the presence of Silvia Tortosa's Countess Irina, particularly when she catches him dining alone. "I've eaten in worse circumstances," he admits, "and in worse company." She makes him aware of his own pomposity and Lee's performance softens in accordance: "You're right, Madame. I don't care as much as I should."

Lee is here essaying the archetypal, no-nonsense Brit abroad, something amplified by Cushing's celebrated line: "Monster? We're British, you know!" ("I worked on Peter very hard," Lee told an audience at L.A.'s first Science Fiction and Fantasy Film Convention in November, 1972, "and on the third take I managed to get him to say: 'British? We're monsters, you know!'") The script is peppered with such quotable dialogue, making good use of the contrasts between Lee and Cushing's characters. One particularly delightful exchange occurs when Saxton finds he has to share a compartment, not only with Wells, but also with Helga Liné's Russian spy "Natasha" and frostily settles into the upper berth.

This lightness of touch is juxtaposed with some real moments of horror. For instance, the truly frightening sight of the baggage man's corpse, bleeding-eyed and stuffed into a crate, is countered by Cushing's amazed pronouncement: "Are you telling me that an ape that lived two million years ago got out of that crate, killed the baggage man and put him in there, then locked everything up neat and tidy, and got away?"

"Yes, I am!" roars Lee. "It's alive!"

Another ingenious idea is the confined setting of a train: There's some real sharp intakes of breath to be had from such scenes as the ape watching over two sleeping children, its clawed hand hovering close to their faces. The monster itself is not just a marauding, mindless beast, but is, instead, presented in a thought-provoking manner, fulfilling Saxton's belief in evolution while, at the same time, proving the existence of Satan in the eyes of Alberto de Mendoza's Father Pujardov. Nevertheless, the introduction of Telly Savalas' overbearing Captain Kazan an hour into the movie, while a diverting cameo in itself, seems like

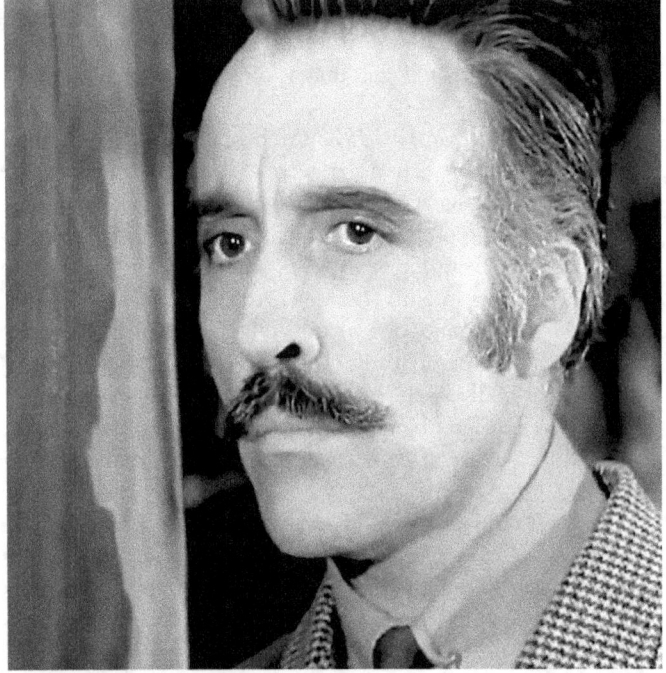

Mustachioed Professor Saxton (Christopher Lee) gets into trouble by discovering a primordial ape in the frozen wastes of a Manchurian cave.

an unnecessary intrusion, momentarily slowing down the carefully built-up action. Such minor quibbles aside, a suitably exciting and scary climax soon follows, with Lee in full heroic mode, saving his precious Countess from the blank-eyed zombies, who pounce from the shadows of the benighted train.

The notion of ghouls invading such a vehicle had just been put to eerily effective use in Amando de Ossorio's *Tombs of the Blind Dead* (1971), and further influence comes from John W. Campbell's 1938 novella "Who Goes There?"—the basis for *The Thing from Another World* (1951)—with which it shares the notion of an alien energy assuming the identity of its victims in an enclosed environment as desolate snows swirl outside.

Fresh from collaborating on *Psychomania*, the writers of *Horror Express*, Arnaud d'Usseau (1916-1990) and Julian Zimet (1919-2017) had been blacklisted from Hollywood in the 1950s—a fate they shared with the film's producer Bernard Gordon (1918-2007), screenwriter of *Earth vs. the Flying Saucers* (1955), *The Man Who Turned to Stone* (1956), *Zombies of Mora Tau* (1956) and *The Day of the Triffids* (1961).

Director Eugenio Martin (b. 1925) also had a background in fantasy. Having served as an assistant director on *The 7th Voyage of Sinbad* (1957) and *The 3 Worlds of Gulliver*, Martin made his first horror movie, *Dummy of Death*, in 1962. The Spanish filmmaker next worked in a variety of genres, including a Julio Iglesias musical (*La vida sigue igual* [1969]), a giallo-like thriller with Carroll Baker (*The Fourth Victim* [1970] and a comedy-Western starring Lee Van Cleef, Gina Lollobrigida and James Mason (*Bad Man's River* [1970]).

Shortly after the 28-day shoot of *Horror Express*, Martin married *Tombs of the Blind Dead* star Lone Fleming, then cast her in his next thriller, *A Candle for the Devil* (1973). Martin made one last horror film, *Supernatural* (1980), before dialogue from his 1966 Western *The Bounty Killer* was used on the soundtrack of Quentin Tarantino's Oscar-winning *Django Unchained* (2012).

Although Peter Cushing erroneously told John Brosnan that *Horror Express* came into being when the producer "bought the two model trains used in the film *Nicholas and Alexandra* ... and then wrote a script around them," the train set was actually a leftover from Eugenio Martin's previous production, *Pancho Villa* (1971). The star of that Western, Telly Savalas (1922-1994), had already been threatened by Talking Tina, the "Living Doll," of *The Twilight Zone*, before he found himself on board the *Horror Express*. After playing James Bond's arch-nemesis Blofeld in *On Her Majesty's Secret Service*, Savalas went on to essay the Devil in Mario Bava's *Lisa and the Devil*, displaying a penchant for lollipops that he reinstated for his most famous part as TV detective *Kojak* (1973-1978). Chief composer for that series was John Cacavas (1930-2014), who graces *Horror Express* with a haunting whistled theme. (The American musician would later score Christopher Lee starrers *The Satanic Rites of Dracula*, *Airport '77* and *Once Upon a Spy*.)

The remainder of the *Horror Express* players are just as impressive: Argentine actor Alberto de Mendoza (1923-2011) gives a standout performance as the superstitious monk. His other credits include Sgt. Brandon in the Lucio Fulci giallo *Lizard in a Woman's Skin* (1970), Professor Fulton in *The People Who Own the Dark* (1973) and the butler in Harry Alan Towers' *Ten Little Indians* remake, *And Then There Were None* (1974).

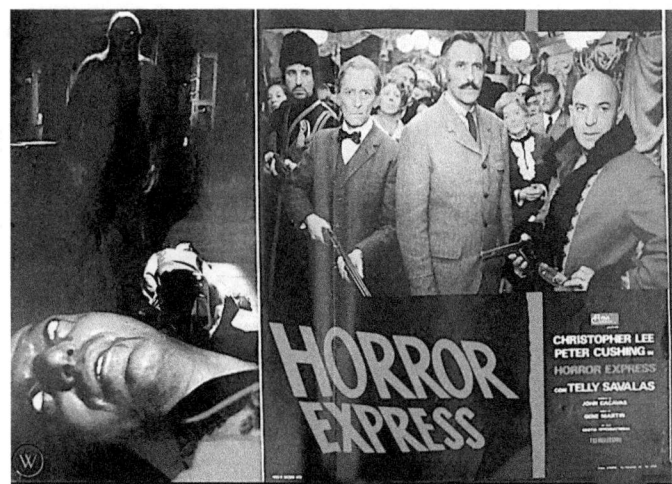

Leading ladies, Silvia Tortosa (b. 1947) and Helga Liné (b. 1932)—who both went on to Amando de Ossorio's *The Lorelei's Grasp* (1972)—are dubbed in *Horror Express*' English-language version by Olive Gregg (1925-2003), who also revoiced Ingrid Pitt's *Countess Dracula* and Valerie Leon in *Blood from the Mummy's Tomb*.

Haunted by Barbara Steele in *Nightmare Castle* (1965), Liné (a former circus acrobat) would proceed to *Horror Rises from the Tomb*, *The Vampires' Night Orgy*, *The Dracula Saga* (all 1972) and *The Mummy's Revenge* (1973). Tortosa, meanwhile, turns up in *El huerto del Francés* (1977), a serial killer thriller based on true events, which is widely regarded as one of Paul Naschy's finest.

Baggage man Victor Israel (1929-2009)—who appeared with Naschy in *The Man with the Severed Head* (1973) and *The Werewolf and the Yeti* (1975)—was also a veteran of such genre titles as *The Devil's Kiss* (1973, as Baron de Clanchart), *El jovencito Dracula* (1975, as Renfield) and *Zombie Creeping Flesh* (1980, as a zombie priest).

Making one of his last appearances before his death from a heart attack is Julio Peña (1912-1972), who plays the shifty Inspector Mirov (dubbed in the English-language print, according to IMDb, by *The Terror of the Tongs*' Roger Delgado). Having earlier joined Lee and Cushing as Arsites for *Alexander the Great* (1955), Peña would perform alongside Naschy in *Werewolf Shadow* (1970) and *Horror Rises from the Tomb*.

The red, lamp-lit contact lenses that make-up artist Julián Ruiz (1921-1983) plastered over the eyes of Peña and his fellow zombie actors rendered them sightless, adding a creepily fumbling style to their movements. Ruiz had worked on Luis

"Are you telling me that an ape that lived two million years ago got out of that crate?" Wells (Peter Cushing) says to Saxton (Christopher Lee).

The Loneliness of Evil

Spanish poster

contributed to John Gilling's last film, the Spanish-shot *Cross of the Devil* (1974), which Paul Naschy had originally written as a vehicle for Lee and Cushing (as Naschy revealed to Cathal Tohill in *The Dark Side* #41). In the November 3, 1971, edition of *Variety*, it was announced that Lee would star alongside Naschy in a project entitled *I, The Vampire*. Despite proposed involvement from *Werewolf Shadow* director Leon Klimovsky, this collaboration never happened, making Lee one of the few artists on *Horror Express* not to have worked with Spain's principal horrormeister (Cushing shared billing, if not screen time, with Paul for *Mystery on Monster Island* [1980]). Nevertheless, an image of Lee from *The Curse of Frankenstein* can be seen in the opening credits of *Buenas noches, señor monstruo* (1982), a musical comedy starring Naschy as "El Hombre Lobo," and melodies from *Hercules in the Haunted World* augment *The Beast and the Magic Sword* (1983). In a 2007 interview with Shade Rupe (reprinted in Troy Howarth's 2018 book *Human Beasts*), Naschy revealed that he was "writing a screenplay especially for Christopher Lee," which would see the older actor fulfill "one of the great dreams of his life" by playing Don Quixote. Sadly, neither this, nor a mooted appearance

Christopher Lee, Silvia Tortosa, Peter Cushing

Bunuel's *Tristana* (1969), as well as the Spanish horrors *The House That Screamed* (1969, with Victor Israel), *Horror Rises from the Tomb*, *The Hanging Woman* (1972, the latter two with Paul Naschy) and *The Bell of Hell* (1973, whose director, Claudio Guerin, fell to his death from the film's bell tower on the final day of shooting).

Ruiz is aided by special effects man Pablo Pérez, whose other credits include *The Vampires' Night Orgy*, and the Paul Naschy horrors *Hunchback of the Morgue*, *Count Dracula's Great Love* (both 1972), *Curse of the Devil* (1973), and *Inquisition* (1976). As well as supervising the effects for *The Three/Four Musketeers*, Pablo also

with Naschy in *The Valdemar Legacy* (2008) ever came to fruition, but Lee did provide the Foreword to Ángel Agudo and Ángel Gómez's 2009 tome *Paul Naschy: La Máscara de Jacinto Molina*.

Cinematographer Alejandro Ulloa (1926-2002), who brings an ochre sheen to *Horror Express*, would go on to light such Naschy ventures as *El caminante* (1978), *Human Beasts* (1980) and *The Night of the Werewolf* (1980). (As well as serving as second camera operator on Orson Welles' *Chimes at Midnight*, Ulloa photographed *The Blancheville Monster* [1963] and *The Diabolical Dr. Z* [1965].)

Despite faring well upon its initial Spanish release in June 1972, *Horror Express* wouldn't see issue in Britain and America for another two years. Nonetheless, the film was adapted as a comic book in Thailand and, in 2014, it inspired an exceptional *Doctor Who* adventure, "Mummy on the Orient Express." With its perfect balance of dread and humor, *Horror Express* is sublimely entertaining. The high standard it establishes would continue into Lee and Cushing's next collaboration.

The Creeping Flesh
1972

> The undisputed Masters of the Macabre … creating whole new heights in undiluted, flesh-creeping horror.

> Well, there are two basic horror stories. Where does the evil come from? It comes from out there, or it comes from in here—John Carpenter, to John Landis, *Monsters in the Movies* (DK, 2011)

Christopher Lee first returned to Tigon British Film Productions in January 1971 for *Hannie Caulder*. In his first Western, Lee gives a lovely performance as Bailey—a gunsmith who helps Raquel Welch exact revenge upon three lecherous bandits (played by Jack Elam, Strother Martin and Ernest Borgnine). Despite his character being a sympathetic family man, Lee's identification with the Prince of Darkness still haunted the Spanish shoot, as the actor recorded in his memoirs: "The people of Almeria recognized the demon beneath the hat, hauled the children off the street as I passed and made the sign of the evil eye."

And it is the personification of evil which concerns Lee's next film for Tigon. Since *Curse of the Crimson Altar* in 1968, the company had released numerous horror and science fiction pictures, including *The Body Stealers*, *Virgin Witch* and *The Beast in the Cellar*, but only *Blood on Satan's Claw* emerged as a production of quality. With their final venture, *The Creeping Flesh*, however, the studio delivered a sumptuous swansong that really gave Hammer a run for their money. (Before Michael Carreras took ownership, Tigon chief Tony Tenser had been on the verge of buying out his rivals; after serving as executive producer on Pete Walker's *Frightmare* [1974], Tenser retired to Southport on the North West coast of England.)

Filmed at Shepperton from Monday, January 31, 1972, under the auspices of Freddie Francis (taking over from Don Sharp, who exited at the pre-production stage), *The Creeping Flesh* sees Peter Cushing's Emmanuel Hildern bring home a monstrous skeleton from New Guinea, which turns out to be the "Evil One" of folklore: When its bones are touched by water, they miraculously grow flesh …

Lee plays Cushing's half-brother, James—a cold-hearted scientist who runs "the Hildern Institute for Mental Disorders" (the interiors of which are redressed sets from *The House That Dripped Blood*). Placing his ambitions above any human relationship, James is most at home among grotesquerie, peering into glass tanks containing disembodied body parts or ogling hairy blood cells beneath a microscope. (The look he gives Cushing's malformed skeleton is almost one of loving tenderness.) He thinks nothing of experimenting on his patients, or even shooting one in the back at point-blank range. (The slain internee is Dan Meaden [1935-2011], who, ironically enough, would next essay a *Nosferatu*-inspired Count in Francis' *Son of Dracula*, before haunting the asylum of the 1978 *Dracula*.)

Despite the forbidding nature of his character, Lee was his usual cheery self behind the scenes, although his constant singing would rile production manager Geoffrey Haine, whose office was below Lee's dressing room. As producer Michael Redbourn told John Hamilton (in *LSoH* #45), "[Haine] used to bang on the ceiling with a broom handle and shout 'shut up!'" Nevertheless, the actor was bolstered by the presence of his wife and daughter, who visited him on the asylum sets. In one charming production still, Lee shows eight-year-old Christina the workings of a movie camera. The family had reason to be happy: During a Christmas party in Spain, while shooting *Horror Express*, Christina had danced for the first time, an indication that the years of painful operations on the child's legs had come to an end.

Less cheerful sights at the Hildern Institute include Fred Wood (1922-2003), reaching through the bars of his cell. Wood's distinctive features haunt many a British horror film; he's a mourner in *Dracula: Prince of Darkness*, an audience member at the *Theatre of Death*, a roadie in *Circus of Fear*, an acolyte in *Curse of the Crimson Altar* and a bar patron in *I, Monster* (just to name those starring Lee).

Wood's fellow inmate, Lenny, is portrayed by Kenneth J. Warren (1929-1973). This burly Australian actor—who had been reduced to a blubbering wreck by Lee's serum in *I, Monster*—can also be seen as a young constable in the BBC's *Quatermass and the Pit* (1958), a perspiring sergeant in *Doctor Blood's Coffin* and Baron Zorn's frisky aide in *Demons of the Mind*. (He can be heard, on Vincent Price's radio show *The Price of Fear*, as a pushy horror movie director falling foul of the "Cat's Cradle" [1973].)

Hildern's institution is further populated by such familiar actors as Hedger Wallace (1927-2000) and Marianne Stone (1922-2009). Freddie Francis found room for Wallace in most of his films—notably as the resurrected Edgar Allan Poe in *Torture Garden*—while Stone can be glimpsed in everything from *The Quatermass Xperiment* to *Carry On Screaming!* (Though my personal favorite of her genre performances is as the mother of an alien abductee in *The Night Caller*.)

Another ubiquitous face is Duncan Lamont (1918-1978), who plays the police inspector investigating Lenny's disappearance. The Scottish actor also appears with Lee in *A Tale of Two Cities*, *The Devil-Ship Pirates* and *Nothing But the Night*. His other roles include Victor Caroon in the 1953 TV version of *The Quatermass Experiment*, the chief of police in *The Evil of Frankenstein*, the enthusiastic butcher in *The Witches*, the guillotined prisoner in *Frankenstein Created Woman* and the drill-toting Sladden in *Quatermass and the Pit*.

Also hailing from Scotland is the actress playing Emmanuel's inoculated daughter, Penelope: "Christopher Lee …

Christopher Lee plays James Hildern.

kept 'himself to himself'," Lorna Heilbron (b. 1948) remembered to Mark A. Miller. "He had a most wonderful singing voice, of which he was justly proud, and which would go ringing round the corridors of Shepperton. The crew called him 'Rabbity Lee' because he loved to talk, which he did very amusingly and at some length … He and Peter [Cushing] seemed close and distant at the same time. They probably didn't have that much in common apart from a very strong symbiotic working relationship."

Fresh from starring opposite Dudley Moore in a West End run of *Play It Again, Sam*, Heilbron went on to José Larraz's *Symptoms*, a British horror entry for the 1974 Cannes Film Festival. In a 2016 interview with Pete Tombs, included as a special feature on the *Symptoms* DVD, the actress recalled: "I loved doing [*The Creeping Flesh*] and I absolutely loved Peter Cushing … He treated me just like his daughter. He sort of felt, in some kind of strange way, because he was a spiritualist, that I was some sort of incarnation of his wife Helen who had died … He really took me under his wing and looked after me." In the same interview, she recalled one of her teenage daughters catching the film on television during a sleepover party and "being very embarrassed at me dancing around in my nightdress." Today, Lorna is a practicing psychotherapist—although she takes no inspiration from Lee's Dr. Hildern.

The other leading lady of *The Creeping Flesh* is Jenny Runacre (b. 1946), as Emmanuel's estranged wife, Marguerite. Bitten by Harry Nilsson's *Son of Dracula* (1972), Runacre went on to portray Miss Brunner in *The Final Programme* (1973), Queen Elizabeth I in *Jubilee* (1977), Mrs. Todhunter in *The Lady Vanishes* (1978) and Elsie, one of Roald Dahl's *The Witches* (1989).

The Creeping Flesh marks the final film appearances of both George Benson and Harry Locke (1913-1987). As Emmanuel's mild-mannered assistant, Benson is almost unrecognizable from the blundering official he plays in *Dracula*, while Locke—veteran of *The Devil-Ship Pirates* and *Tales from the Crypt*—enacts the rambunctious barman.

Hammer's usual innkeeper, Michael Ripper, can be seen as a harrumphing removal man in his last Christopher Lee horror movie. (Ripper's real-life wife, Catherine Finn, is also present as Cushing's maid.) During production, Ripper told *Photon* magazine: "Chris always makes me laugh. In fact, I don't think he likes working with me because we laugh so much. I think he's a very funny fellow." After playing a tramp in *Legend of the Werewolf*, Ripper made his final genre appearance—on the other side of the bar, for once—in *The Revenge of Billy the Kid* (1991). At the actor's memorial service in November 2000, Susan Cowie reported (in *LSoH* #15) that the vicar took one look at Christopher Lee, seated in the front row, and said: "I, for one, am glad to be this close to a crucifix today …"

Also making his final contribution to a Christopher Lee movie is make-up man Roy Ashton, but the impressive giant skeleton is the creation of Roger Dicken. (Watch closely when Cushing says, "And then the Sky Father will weep," the creature's foot moves to the left, seemingly of its own accord …) Here, the special effects man far surpasses his work on *Scars of Dracula*. After creating some engaging monsters for *The Land That Time Forgot* and *Warlords of Atlantis*, Dicken would be responsible for the "face-hugger" and "chest-burster" creatures in *Alien*.

The nerve-shredding music is composed and conducted by Paul Ferris (1941-1995), whose score here is in stark contrast to the pastoral themes he developed for *Witchfinder General*. (An ex-actor, Ferris, also plays the husband of the burned "witch" in that classic under the pseudonym Morris Jar—a pun on composer Maurice Jarre.) As well as scoring *The Blood Beast Terror*, Paul's background writing hits for Cliff Richard and The Shadows stood him in good stead for the swinging 1960s pop milieu of *The Sorcerers* (for which he also penned two songs). Following his work on *Persecution* (1973), Ferris left the movie business, joined the Merchant Navy, and, on his return, opened a fish and chip shop. A sufferer of Huntington's disease, he committed suicide by drug overdose at age 54.

Set in 1893—the same year that events in Bram Stoker's *Dracula* take place—*The Creeping Flesh* raises some profound questions on the essence of evil and its origins (does it come from within or without?). An open-ended conclusion is especially chilling, with the fully fleshed Evil One making its way into the world, where, no doubt, it is still at large. (How else does one explain such 21st century terrors as twerking, reality television and Donald Trump?)

Those closing moments, with the hooded creature silhouetted against the storm-lit sky, are handled with élan by Freddie

Francis and his cinematographer, Norman Warwick (1920-1994). (The two had just collaborated on Amicus' biggest money-spinner *Tales from the Crypt*; Warwick's other credits include *Torture Garden*, *The Abominable Dr. Phibes*, *Dr. Jekyll and Sister Hyde* and four episodes of *Hammer House of Horror*.) There's an additional visual delight, which recalls such silent horrors as *The Student of Prague* and *The Sorrows of Satan*, when the skeleton's elongated shadow rises against the edifice of Emmanuel's home. (The location is Thorpe House in Surrey, which also doubled as Edith Evans' habitat in *Craze* [1973.] Today, the building is an all-boys school). Other artful touches include the prism-smeared shot of Marguerite, which, as well as suggesting her fractured mind, also recalls Salvador Dali's portrait of Lady Macbeth. There's a further echo of Dali in the fantastic painting—which we see Emmanuel working on—that depicts the Evil One in all its colorful glory. Although the painter is uncredited, one assumes it to be the work of matte artist Doug Ferris (b. 1931), who would go on to enhance such fantasies as *The Dark Crystal* (1981), *The Princess Bride* (1986) and *Judge Dredd* (1994).

The Creeping Flesh exhibits the last burst of directorial brilliance from Francis, whose subsequent films seemed to lack heart. These include *Tales That Witness Madness*, *Son of Dracula* and the aforementioned *Craze*, a grubby, all-star voodoo shocker produced by Herman Cohen. In 1974, Francis redeemed himself slightly by making a pair of retrograde chillers, *The Ghoul* and *Legend of the Werewolf*, for his son Kevin's production company Tyburn. Although both films starred Peter Cushing, in the wake of *The Exorcist*, they were deemed too quaint for US theatrical distribution. Freddie later photographed the excellent Tyburn documentary *Peter Cushing: A One-Way Ticket to Hollywood* (1988), Martin Scorsese's *Cape Fear* (1991) and the David Lynch movies *The Elephant Man* (1980), *Dune* (1983) and *The Straight Story* (1999). Returning to direction with *The Doctor and the Devils* (1985)—a Burke and Hare fable from Dylan Thomas, Francis' last feature as a director, *Dark Tower* (1988), was so disagreeable that he was credited under the pseudonym "Ken Barnett." He did, however, helm "Last Respects," a 1996 episode of *Tales from the Crypt*, which owes much to "The Monkey's Paw."

With stalwarts Lee, Cushing and Francis on hand to ensure both quality and a cozy familiarity, *The Creeping Flesh* is additionally notable for being a film of refreshing originality. This can partly be explained via its use of fledgling talent: Peter Spenceley (b. 1943) and Jonathan Rumbold (who wrote the script expressly as a vehicle for Lee and Cushing) were not men who put pen to paper often; Spencely worked as an assistant editor on *What Became of Jack and Jill?* and *The Long Good Friday* (1979), while Rumbold would go on to write a Greek crime drama, *Order: Kill Makarios* (1975).

Producer Michael Redbourn (b. 1944) was also new to his role, having been a sound editor on *The Oblong Box*, *Scream and Scream Again*, *The House That Dripped Blood* and *I, Monster*. Following his stint on *The Creeping Flesh*, Redbourn returned to editing sound for such illustrious titles as *Fright Night*, *Teenage Mutant Ninja Turtles* (1989) and *Ghostbusters*.

Shooting concurrently with *The Creeping Flesh* at Shepperton was *The Asphyx*, an intriguing metaphysical shocker, which must have influenced *Ghostbusters*, what with its Slimer-like Spirit of Death being captured in beams of energy. *Asphyx* star Robert Stephens took the opportunity to visit Lee and Cushing on the neighboring set where all three enactors of Sherlock Holmes were photographed together. Referencing this, in his book *English Gothic*, Jonathan Rigby writes: "Sadly, the photo only makes one think how much better *The Asphyx* would have been if either Cushing or Lee had played the Stephens role … Though much fêted in the theatre, Stephens provides in *The Asphyx* a classic example of how a good actor can fail miserably in the unpredictable arena of the horror film … For that kind of magic, you need a specialist like Cushing or Lee."

Indeed, both actors are at their best in *The Creeping Flesh*. But though Lee gets top billing, it is Cushing who dominates the piece: In a *tour de force* performance, he provides a masterclass, not only in horror film acting, but in screen acting, period; by the time his dedicated man of science is reduced to a gibbering wreck, the viewer's heartbreak is as palpable as the one expressed onscreen. Unfortunately, that sense of sorrow also suffused the actor when away from the cameras.

Lee spoke of Cushing's mental state upon the death of his wife in an onstage interview at the 1999 Monster Rally (featured on the Midnight Marquee DVD *Christopher Lee: A Legacy of Horror and Terror*): "He was totally lost, absolutely lost, like a child, and he wouldn't see anybody, he wouldn't talk to anybody … he wanted to stay in the house." Commendably, Lee brought his friend out of his shell whenever he could.

Upon its March 1973 release, *The Creeping Flesh* was paired with *Psycho*-inspired thrillers on both sides of the Atlantic: Mario Bava's *Hatchet for the Honeymoon* (1969) in the UK and William A. Fraker's *A Reflection of Fear* (1971) in the US. Despite receiving warmer-than-usual reviews from the British press, the film received scant attention from audiences, limping along in support of Oliver Stone's debut feature *Seizure* (1972), for the latter's belated 1976 UK release before being sold to late-night TV in 1978.

While its storyline becomes a little busy at times, the abundance of good ideas on display is no bad thing, especially when one considers the dearth of originality that can all too often beset the film industry. As such, with its layers of invention emboldened by strong central performances, *The Creeping Flesh* emerges as a true masterpiece of 1970s Gothic cinema.

Death Line
1972

Mind the doors!

… we spend an inordinate time in the madman's dark, dank and bloody lair—peering through the murk at the most revolting sights imaginable and wondering how such a sick and sick-making film ever came to be made.— *The Daily Mail*

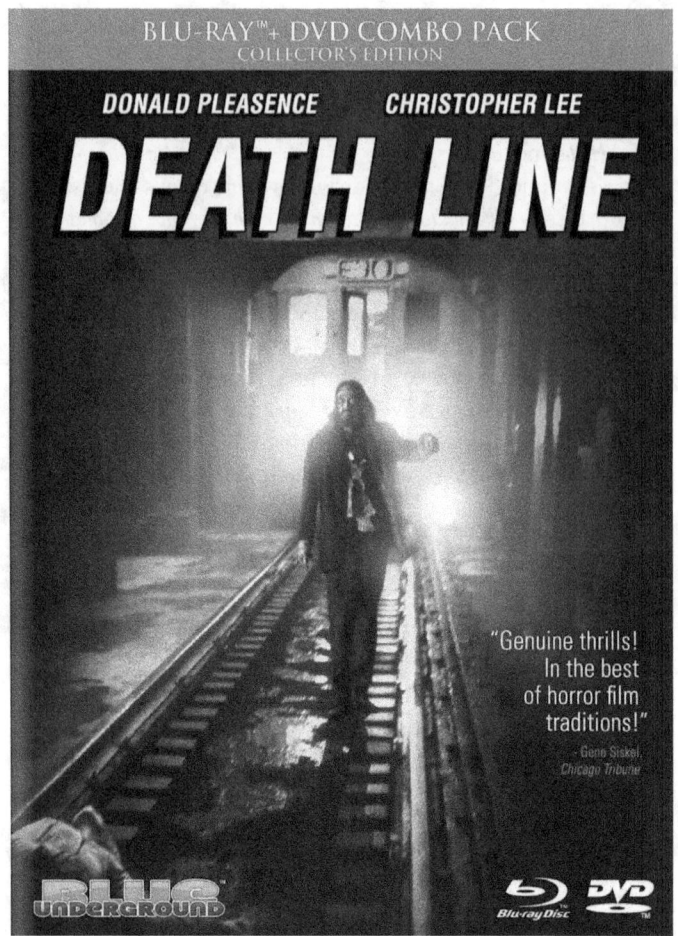

As filming closed on *The Creeping Flesh*, in March 1972, Christopher Lee took a Saturday off from his duties as Dr. Hildern to cameo in a contemporary horror classic involving cannibals on the London Underground. *Death Line* marks the feature debut of writer-director Gary Sherman (born in Chicago, 1945), whose background was in Coca-Cola commercials. Sherman told Chris Alexander (on *ComingSoon.net*, April 2017) that he wrote the part of Stratton-Villiers especially for Lee after the actor agreed to appear as a favor to his old friend, *The Castle of the Living Dead* producer Paul Maslansky: "If I don't have to wear the teeth [i.e., fangs] and I can do a scene with Donald Pleasence, I will do this for scale …" Sherman remembers Lee saying.

The London Underground had already served as an effective haunting ground for Martians in *Quatermass and the Pit* (1967) and the Yeti in *Doctor Who*: "The Web of Fear" (1968). Subsequently, *An American Werewolf in London* would claim one of its victims at Tottenham Court Road, a moment which finds a direct echo at the opening of *Death Line*, with the murder of seedy government official James Manfred O.B.E (James Cossins). In addition to appearing as MI6 ballistics expert Colthorpe in *The Man with the Golden Gun*, Cossins (1933-1997) gave memorable performances as the panty-snatching son of Bette Davis in *The Anniversary*, the Chief Engineer of *The Lost Continent*, the irate Dean in *The Horror of Frankenstein* and the sadistic male nurse of *Blood from the Mummy's Tomb*.

To the strains of Wil Malone's fantastically sleazy theme, with its farting synthesizer and strip-show brass, Cossins wanders neon-lit Soho in pursuit of cheap thrills. Arriving at Russell Square tube station, he accosts a lone woman and is kneed in the balls. Worse is to come: A young couple discover his body, only to find it has vanished when they return with help. The subsequent investigation of Inspector Calhoun (Donald Pleasence) and his accomplice Det. Sgt. Rogers (Norman Rossington) leads them to an altercation with Lee's Stratton-Villiers at the same Cheyne Walk residence where, four months later, Vincent Price would give Diana Dors the massage from Hell in *Theatre of Blood* (Bram Stoker had once lived just along the road). (One wonders if Lee's character was named after James Villiers—of *Repulsion*, *The Nanny* and *Blood from the Mummy's Tomb*—an actor so quintessentially British and upper class that Oliver Reed nicknamed him "Old Cocky Bollocks, 11th in line to the throne …"?)

Announced by Pleasence's mischievous line, "I might have known you'd turn up," Lee's sense of control as Stratton-Villiers is beautifully at odds with Donald's freewheeling style (his improvisational approach to Calhoun extended, as he admitted in *The Dark Side* #30, to actually getting pissed for his pub scene). There's a nice, amused quality to Lee's performance, a smile playing beneath the dark moustache throughout; he is comfortable in his superiority over Pleasence's uncouth inspector and advises: "Why don't you go back to planting pot on people, and

As Stratton-Villiers, Christopher Lee is shown with a "smile playing beneath a dark moustache throughout."

mind you don't become a missing person yourself." This is a topical allusion to Sgt. Norman Pilcher, who would be charged with perverting the course of justice in November 1972, after being found to have planted drugs on such luminaries as John Lennon, Mick Jagger and *Dr. Terror's House of Horrors*' Tubby Hayes. Corrupt officials are at the very heart of *Death Line*'s horrors.

The murderer of James Manfred turns out to be "The Man," a descendent of laborers entrapped by an 1892 cave-in (a consequence of cost-cutting indifference from a callous Establishment), who has survived through cannibalism and scrabbles the Underground in search of food. (Gary Sherman revealed to Chris Alexander that Marlon Brando had originally agreed to play this part, uncredited and buried under lots of make-up, because, "He loves doing that kind of stuff." Sadly, Brando had to pull out when his son contracted pneumonia.) By calling his cannibal "The Man," it's clear that Sherman meant him to represent the downtrodden working Man of society, exploited by the upper classes to monstrous ends, an extension of themes developed by Hammer in *The Hound of the Baskervilles*, *The Curse of the Werewolf* and *The Plague of the Zombies*.

Shuffling around his dwelling, and emitting the occasional tortured cry, "The Man" is as much victim as villain, especially when seen weeping over the corpse of his pregnant lover. The actor who plays him, Hugh Armstrong (1944-2016), had also been buried away, lost and confused within the confines of Oakley Court, for Freddie Francis' unique, offbeat *Mumsy, Nanny, Sonny & Girly* (1969); he would later play a Jun Priest in *The Beastmaster* (1981) and Filthy Harry in *How to Get Ahead in Advertising* (1988). For the August 1985 issue of *Fantasy Review*, eminent horror author Ramsey Campbell (whose first book, *The Inhabitant of the Lake* [1964], features characters named Sangster, Fisher, Leakey, and Lee) cited Armstrong's performance in *Death Line* as "one of the greatest and most moving in horror films."

Despite such plaudits, in the first edition of his memoirs, Christopher Lee called *Death Line* "a mistake, a stomach-churning satire on the excesses of espionage thrillers which somehow turned into an even greater excess than its targets." On the surface, Lee has a point; as in the film itself, there is far more going on beneath that surface: Not only does it play upon urban legends of spooky goings-on beneath the London streets, but, like most legends, it may have some basis in truth.

In his book *Cover-Ups & Secrets*, Nick Redfern cites his 2004 interview with British policeman Frank Wiley, who claimed to have investigated seven gruesome murders on the London Underground between 1967 and 1969. The victims were discovered in the tunnels late at night "with arms and/or legs viciously amputated—or possibly even *gnawed* off. Stomachs … ripped open, innards … torn out, and throats … violently slashed." The chief suspect was "a bearded, wild-haired man dressed in tattered filthy clothing," who had "uttered a low and threatening growl" at two workmen on the Bakerloo Line in 1968, before running away. This mysterious figure was never apprehended. According to Wiley: "It all got pushed under the rug when the Home Office said so." Referring to *Death Line*, the policeman added: "There's more to the film than people know. My thought then, and which it still is today, is someone making the film heard the stories, the deaths we investigated. They had to have; the film was too close to what happened."

Certainly, *Death Line* presents a wry study of humanity, wherein the "normal" civilians aboveground are just as unpleasant and disassociated as the "monster" lurking below. This sick society is reflected in the grey London skies that are drained of all life, the permanent catarrh that seems to cling to Calhoun, and the icy plops of water that provide the only sound in the cannibal's corpse-strewn dwelling (Gary Sherman brings a chilling verisimilitude to these shots, his camera languorously meandering through every blood-stained cranny for a full seven minutes); one almost feels the shivers and aches of flu just from watching. This unhealthy atmosphere is perfectly captured by the diseased browns of Alex Thomson's cinematography. Fresh from working on *Dr. Phibes Rises Again*, Thomson (1929-2007) would earn an Oscar-nomination for *Excalibur* (1980), before lighting *The Keep* (1982), *Legend*, *Labyrinth* and *Alien 3* (1991).

Wil Malone's soundtrack is just as inspired, mixing haunting oboe, broken-down electronic sounds and unearthly choral pieces to enhance the film's pervading feel of eerie desolation. Malone (b. 1952) would later contribute to such projects as *That'll Be the Day* (1972), *All This and World War II* (1976) and *Jubilee*, but is presently an extremely prolific musical arranger,

In the US *Death Line* was renamed *Raw Meat*.

having worked with such diverse artists as Black Sabbath, Iron Maiden, Peter Gabriel, Rod Stewart, Depeche Mode, Pavarotti, Take That, Kylie Minogue, the Spice Girls, the Verve, Oasis and Massive Attack.

While the thrills of *Death Line* stem from secular events, there was enough of the supernatural going on behind the scenes, as Donald Pleasence had just moved into a 17th century West London house: "We began hearing strange noises—thumping sounds," he told *Weekend* magazine at the time. "There was no explanation … Gradually, my wife, Meira, and I came to realize that the sounds were distinctly those of children running about …" The actor concluded: "When we'd knocked down the adjoining wall, we'd allowed the spirits of the children who'd once lived there to run through the house again as they'd probably done many years before … Now that we believe we know what the once-mysterious sounds are, we just treat them as sounds of joy. We can feel the happiness of the children; it seems they're

The Loneliness of Evil 175

happy to have a free run of the place after all those years, probably centuries. So what harm is that? A happy house is a haunted house!"

If so, then Donald must have been content with the extraordinary trappings of his career. Since appearing in *The Hands of Orlac*, he had headed the cast of George Lucas' *THX 1138* (1969) and portrayed the selfish Baron in *The Pied Piper*. Following *Death Line*, he was the bonkers botanist of *The Mutations* (1972), Fred Smudge in the musical version of *Doctor Jekyll and Mr. Hyde* (1973), Count Plasma in *Barry McKenzie Holds His Own* (1974) and, after delivering the Devil's baby in *I Don't Want to Be Born*, he pursued *The Devil's Men* (1975), *The Pumaman* (1979) and the *Phantom of Death* (1987). He also essayed crazed psychiatrists in *Tales That Witness Madness* and *Alone in the Dark* (1982), indulged in scene-stealing antics as Dr. Seward in *Dracula* (1978) and the fearful priest of *Vampire in Venice*, and lent his silken tones to the terrifying public information short *Lonely Water* (1973) and *The Dark Secret of Harvest Home* (1977). The actor's best genre roles, however, came in *From Beyond the Grave*—which paired him with his daughter Angela to creepy effect—and as Dr. Sam Loomis in John Carpenter's *Halloween* (1978; a role turned down by both Christopher Lee and Peter Cushing. "[Loomis] just shows up and says, 'This man's mad and he's dangerous,'" Lee told Denis Meikle. "I can't do anything with that"). Shortly after *Halloween*, Lee and Pleasence both guested in *Jaguar Lives!* (1978), a globe-hopping martial arts adventure which features several actors from James Bond films, as well as a plot twist that was later recycled for *GoldenEye*.

The 1980s saw Donald cited by *Variety* as the busiest actor in the world, a moniker he confirmed by starring in *The Monster Club* (as a vampire hunter), *The Devonsville Terror* (1982, as a maggot-riddled doctor), *Specters* (1986, as an archeologist), *Escape from New York* (1980, as the President of the United States) *Prince of Darkness* (1987, as Father Loomis) and *Halloween II* (1981), *4* (1988) and *5* (1989). While the latter titles saw him continue his association with John Carpenter, Pleasence also worked for two other legendary directors: Dario Argento, in *Phenomena* (1984) and Woody Allen in *Shadows and Fog* (1991). Succumbing to heart failure in February 1995, Donald's final film was *Halloween: The Curse of Michael Myers* (1994), which, upon release in September 1995, would be dedicated to his memory. (The part of Dr. Terence Wynn in this sequel had been written for Christopher Lee, but was eventually played by Mitchell Ryan.)

In 1977, Pleasence crooned "I Want You (She's So Heavy)" in Robert Stigwood's film of *Sgt. Pepper's Lonely Hearts Club Band*. But Donald's *Death Line* ally Norman Rossington (1928-1999) enjoyed an even closer association with the Beatles, having played the band's belligerent manager in *A Hard Day's Night*. Liverpool-born Rossington also portrays a jewel thief opposite Elvis Presley in *Double Trouble*, making him the only actor to have appeared onscreen with both rock 'n' roll icons. His other credits include Albert Finney's best mate in *Saturday Night and Sunday Morning*, a romancer of Lee's Dracula Bride Anouska Hempel in *Go for a Take*, another thief in *Digby: The Biggest Dog in the World* and the Station Master in *House of the Long Shadows* (1982).

Inspector Richardson is personified by Clive Swift (1936-2019), fresh from appearing in Hitchcock's *Frenzy*; he would become familiar in such TV terror shows as *A Ghost Story for Christmas*, *Beasts* and *Tales of the Unexpected*. Swift is particularly memorable as a snazzy Yuletide guest in *Dead of Night*: "The Exorcism" (1972), Lanyon in *Dr. Jekyll and Mr. Hyde* (1980)

and the embalmer of *Doctor Who*: "Revelation of the Daleks" (1985).

The youthful protagonists are David Ladd (b. 1947) and Sharon Gurney (b. 1950). The son of Alan Ladd, who had featured with Bela Lugosi in *Island of Lost Souls* (1932) and *The Black Cat* (1941), David debuted alongside his father in the classic Western *Shane* (1952, with another *Dracula*, Jack Palance). After appearing as William Castle's apprentice in *The Day of the Locust*, he was forced to eat heroin by Roger Moore in *The Wild Geese* (1977) and contacted aliens in *Beyond the Universe* (1980). In the late 1970s, he became a producer, specifically on Wes Craven's *The Serpent and the Rainbow* (1987)—a partially effective account of Haitian zombies, inspired by true events. (David's wife, Cheryl Ladd, would star opposite Christopher Lee in *Charlie's Angels*: "Angel in Hiding" [1980], and later gave a strong performance as the heroine of *Jekyll & Hyde* [1989]. Their daughter, Jordan Ladd [b. 1975], is a latter-day scream queen with starring roles in *Embrace of the Vampire* [1994], *Cabin Fever* [2001] and *Hostel: Part II* [2006], among others).

Sharon Gurney portrayed Oliver Reed's sister in *Women in Love* and Michael Gough's daughter for *The Corpse* (1969). Her brother in the latter is played by Gough's real-life son, Simon—who became Sharon's real-life husband.

As for Gary Sherman, he would next provide the story for *Phobia* (1979)—a psychological thriller directed by John Huston and co-scripted by Jimmy Sangster—before helming the gruesome *Dead & Buried* (1980) and the flawed-but-interesting *Poltergeist III* (1987). Despite citing the latter as the least favorite of his films—owing, in part, to the tragic death of its young star Heather O'Rourke—Sherman went on to serve as executive producer on the MGM/Showtime series *Poltergeist: The Legacy* (1996-1999). One of Sherman's most celebrated fans is Guillermo del Toro, who called *Death Line*, on *Trailers from Hell*, "a fantastic movie … which marred my childhood." Indeed, the influence of *Death Line* can be seen in del Toro's own work, particularly his grimly humorous debut *Cronos* (1992), which also showcases a deteriorating protagonist, forced into monstrous acts through no fault of his own, against the dark environs of an unforgiving urban landscape.

Double billed with *Night Hair Child* (1971), *Death Line*'s more modern approach to Gothic horror saw that it became a hit in the UK when released on Friday, October 13, 1972 (when David Cassidy was at No. 1 with "How Can I Be Sure"). Despite being paired with Ivan Reitman's *Cannibal Girls* (1972) under the sensationalized new title of *Raw Meat*, the film fared less well on its US release from Wednesday, October 3, 1973 (when Grand Funk topped the charts with "We're an American Band").

As *Death Line* so aptly appropriates the "loneliness of evil" to a contemporary milieu, it's a shame that Christopher Lee doesn't play a larger role in it. On a happier note, however, pregnant cinemagoer Christine Pugh reported in a 1974 edition of Lee's fan club newsletter that she was so frightened by the movie, an early labor was almost induced. When her baby did arrive on Lee's birthday, May 27, she named the child Christopher.

Forty-three years later, on a Dracula Society outing to Whitby in September 2017, I was fortunate to meet artist Arthur Payn, who worked as a make-up assistant on *Death Line*. Arthur recalls a wig made specially for Lee to wear in the film by "the

poor lace girls [who wove] each hair individually onto the lace." Unfortunately, as Arthur puts it, Lee "does not even doff his hat" in the movie, leaving the painstakingly created hairpiece unseen.

After confessing that his love of art and horror began as a child, when he saw an image of Lee's Creature outside a cinema showing *The Curse of Frankenstein*, Arthur was pleasantly surprised to come face to face with Christopher Lee not long after entering the film industry: "I was hurrying along through the corridors of Wig Creations, my place of work, proudly brandishing a newly created false moustache when, suddenly, my head collided into a breast pocket, obviously someone a foot taller than me. 'Sorry,' I blurted out, as I skipped and sidestepped out of his way. 'That's quite all right,' acknowledged a deep and cultured voice. I was instantly aware of the owner of those masterful tones. I had a delayed reaction, around two seconds I'd say, before spinning round to observe that oh-so tall figure gliding majestically down those corridors, unfortunately in the opposite direction to me."

After working on *Frankenstein: The True Story* and Stanley Kubrick's *Barry Lyndon* (both 1973), Arthur recalled attending, with Lee, an amateur theatrical performance of *Dracula* in London "around the early 1990s." Contrary to the actor's reported disinterest in the character by then, Lee went backstage after the show to warmly congratulate the cast. "Years later," says Arthur, "I was astonished at hearing the quality of his readings of 'The Fall of the House of Usher,' 'The Pit and the Pendulum' and more of Poe's tales. Scout them out if you can, it will be worth it. I also remember Lee at a fantasy art show, being taken aback by the work of Anne Sudworth, who he then became a lifelong admirer of." (It's easy to see the appeal of Miss Sudworth's moonlit visions.)

"My last dalliance with Mr. Lee," Arthur adds, "was at Covent Garden, in the Actor's Church. It was the memorial service for dear, departed Michael Ripper [November 2000]. There was a slight slip-up in the program and Mr. Lee, quite unfazed, and using his skill of words, turned it around to the service's advantage. He was like that. He could be abrupt; he could be charming; he didn't suffer fools but would be sensitive with friends. But, above all, as he once said of the Count himself, he was a human being. He will always be inspirational in my work as a sculptor, whether working on a piece of himself, or something more; he transcends."

Nothing But the Night
1972

Where science and the occult clash!

On *Nothing But the Night* ... we played [golf] at Thurlsdon. At least, I played. Peter [Cushing] carried my clubs and, great ornithologist that he is, constantly electrified me with cries of 'Look, there's a throstle-pated gurk!' or 'A blue-cheeked sandthruster!'—Christopher Lee (from his autobiography)

Once was enough!—Christopher Lee, on being a producer (to Marcus Hearn, 2004)

"One thing I adore about Vincent [Price] is that he does not mind in the least that his fame has been built up through his success in horror films. In fact, he revels in it! Unlike Christopher Lee, who practically has a seizure if one hints at his playing Dracula. I was making a film on location in Devon with Christopher and that other master of horror, Peter Cushing. One evening [my husband] Alan, Georgia Brown (who was also in the film), and several others, were dining at a restaurant down by Dartmouth harbor which was steeped in atmosphere with its old wine bottles and cobwebs all around the walls. Suddenly the doors opened and in walked Christopher and Peter, both looking grave. Alan's exuberance got the better of him and in a loud voice he cried, 'Look out, the sun's just gone down!' Had it been Vincent Price he would have roared with laughter, as did all the people at our table, but Christopher and Peter continued to glower, and passed on by."—Diana Dors, *For Adults Only* (Star Books, 1978)

Since persuading Hammer to make *The Devil Rides Out*, Christopher Lee had considered producing his own movies. In 1970, he set this dream into motion by forming Charlemagne Productions (named after Lee's illustrious ancestor) with Anthony Nelson Keys. While the company was spurred into being by the actor's growing disenchantment with what he perceived to be Hammer's fading production values and the tawdriness of their subjects, the House of Horror was certainly not bitter; as Keys revealed to *Cinefantastique*, the first telegram to arrive at Charlemagne's office at Pinewood was from Michael Carreras "wishing us very great success with our picture."

For this initial venture, Lee and Keys secured the rights to a number of supernatural literary works (including three by Dennis Wheatley), from which distributors Rank selected John Blackburn's 1968 novel *Nothing But the Night*. (Blackburn [1923-1993] was certainly a more critically respected author than Wheatley, having earned the soubriquet "today's master of horror" from the *Times Literary Supplement*.)

To adapt the novel, Charlemagne hired Brian Hayles (1931-1978), a writer new to feature films, who was best known for his work on *Doctor Who*, including such memorable creations as "The Celestial Toymaker" (1966) with Michael Gough, "The Ice Warriors" (1967) with Peter Sallis and "The

Christopher Lee and Diana Dors pose for publicity shots.

Curse of Peladon" (1972), with Geoffrey Toone. (On a DVD extra for the latter, the show's script editor, Terrance Dicks, described the tall, pale and bearded Brian as "mildly vampirish; like a sort of … nice vampire.") In 1974, Hammer bought the rights to Hayles' radio play *Lord Dracula*, which, as *Dracula the Beginning*, then *Vlad the Impaler*, he turned into a script for either Christopher Lee, Yul Brynner or Richard Burton. Ken Russell turned down directorial duties and the project languished at Hammer for decades. (They were still threatening to make it, with cameos from Lee and Cushing, into the 1990s.) After writing *Hour of the Werewolf* (1976, "the first horror play for children"), *Warlords of Atlantis*, and *Arabian Adventure*, Hayles passed away at the premature age of 47. (The novelization of *Arabian Adventure*, by Keith Miles, is dedicated to his memory.)

With Peter Sasdy as director, and Peter Cushing cast as second lead, *Nothing But the Night* sped into production on Monday, April 17, 1972. The 30-day shoot was hampered by a miniscule budget, with no second unit or special effects, and a somewhat convoluted script. (In a nutshell: orphanage trustees are being bumped off. Is it the work of Diana Dors, as a murderous prostitute fresh out of jail? Or are possessed orphans responsible? Lee's Colonel Bingham and Cushing's Sir Ashley investigate.)

During *Nothing But the Night*, Christopher Lee was not only Peter Cushing's co-star, but also his producer.

While it's certainly not as much fun as *Horror Express*, *The Creeping Flesh*, or even *Dracula A.D. 1972*, *Nothing But the Night* is a surprisingly gritty and naturalistic affair, with Lee and Cushing on dependable, if not exactly exciting form. Indeed, the film suffers by eliminating some of the novel's more intriguing characterizations, particularly when it comes to Lee's Colonel Bingham, who is called General Kirk in the book. (Presumably that sounded too close to *Star Trek*'s Captain Kirk.)

Responsible for sending "a hundred men to their deaths in cold blood," the general is missing three fingers from his left hand (described by Blackburn as a "torn talon") and reveals: "I had to be cold-blooded in my job or I would have gone insane very quickly." Having lost two children during the war, and being all too aware of his advancing age, Kirk also harbors a morbid preoccupation with death. Sadly, none of this psychological depth is present in the movie.

Brian Hayles does score points, however, for including a strong female protagonist in the person of investigative journalist, Joan Foster, who doesn't appear in the book. Furthermore, there are some particularly enjoyable shots of rain-strewn 1970s London, where a profusion of elderly passers-by notice the camera and peer at it, wondering what's going on. And the film does build to a genuinely chilling climax, which seems to have inspired Lee's next, and more celebrated, outing, *The Wicker Man*. (The writer of the latter, Anthony Shaffer, would certainly have been aware of *Nothing But the Night*, as he was already in cahoots with Lee and preparing his script at the time.)

The aforementioned climactic action takes place at *The Hound of the Baskervilles*' home of Dartmoor (doubling as Scotland). Present at the location during filming was Renée Glynne (b. 1926), who had provided continuity for Hammer since the late 1940s. Although, by her own choice, she steered clear of Dracula and Frankenstein—"I wasn't a fan of horror films," she tells me—Renée has since revised this opinion, citing *Twins of Evil*, *Vampire Circus* and *Dr. Jekyll and Sister Hyde* as favorites.

Renée's CV reads like a history of British cinema: Starting out as David Lean's production secretary on *Brief Encounter* (1945), her non-Hammer credits take in 1960s spy-fi (*Casino Royale*), 1970s sex comedies (*Confessions of a Window Cleaner*) and Merchant Ivory Productions (*A Room with a View*). She even worked with The Rolling Stones on *One Plus One* (1968), Led Zeppelin on *The Song Remains the Same* (1973) and The Beatles on *Yellow Submarine* (1968). "They kept teasing me!" Renée remembers of the Fab Four. "They stole the ribbon out of my typewriter!" But pranks aside: "They were teeny-weeny and very sweet." Invited by Anthony Nelson Keys to work on *Nothing But the Night* "for a few days when the script supervisor was sick," Renée remembers being out on those night shoots with Christopher Lee. Squinting her eyes, she says, "I can see him now sitting in a chair … he was a big presence. I found him respectfully professional and friendly to my role."

Renée recalls Peter Cushing being a stickler for continuity, keeping his own notes in a little book. "He looked after himself, for which I was grateful beyond belief. It made my job easier!" She was sympathetic, however, towards the recent loss of his wife. While filming *Shatter* in Hong Kong the following year, Renée recollects Cushing telling her that "he was looking forward to going home [on the plane], so that he could be in the sky and closer to Helen." Her *Nothing But the Night* stint led to Peter Sasdy wanting her to do continuity on *I Don't Want to Be Born*.

Nothing But the Night enjoys a further Hammer connection in its score, from *The Brides of Dracula* composer Malcolm Williamson (b. 1931), which features a slow, drawling saxophone and endless refrains of "Ten Green Bottles." Willamson, who also scored *Crescendo*, *The Horror of Frankenstein* and *The Masks of Death* was made Master of the Queen's Music from 1975 until his death in 2003.

With a clear desire to make his first production as classy as possible, Lee enlisted a first-rate cast, headed by Diana Dors. (It has often been reported that John Blackburn was unhappy with Dors' casting as Anna Harb, but she fits his character to a T.)

Born Diana Mary Fluck in Swindon, 1931, Dors was dubbed "Britain's answer to Marilyn Monroe" (by the tabloid press), a "junk shop Venus" (by her biographer Damon Wise) and a "wayward hussy" (by the Archbishop of Canterbury). Her notoriety took the form of racy books (*Diana Dors in 3-D* [1954]; *Behind Closed Dors* [1979]), a rather good swing album (*Swingin' Dors* [1960]) and bombshell roles in such fare as the Smell-O-Vision thriller *Scent of Mystery* (1959; a movie which literally stunk, with Peter Lorre) and *The Last Page* (1951)—Terence Fisher's first Hammer film. (Dors found herself further allied with the House of Horror when Peter Cook made reference to *When Diana Dors Ruled the Earth* in a *Not Only ... But Also* sketch.)

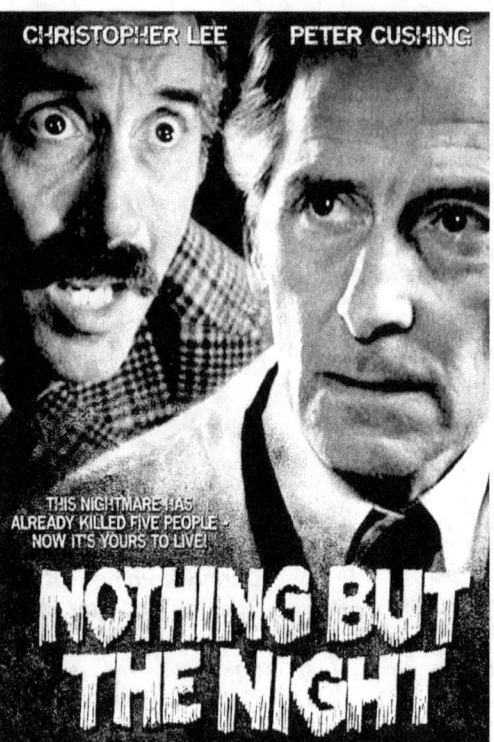

Proving her dramatic mettle with an exceptional performance in *Yield to the Night* (1955), Dors' status as a cultural icon was assured when the Beatles placed her wax likeness on the cover of *Sgt. Pepper*. Following this, she was Linda Hayden's mother in *Baby Love*, a child-hating housekeeper in *The Amazing Mr. Blunden*, Frau Poppendick in *The Pied Piper* and a brothel madam in *Hannie Caulder* (she had earlier appeared with Christopher Lee in 1947's *Penny and the Pownall Case*). As for her genre roles: Sawn in half for both *Alfred Hitchcock Presents* and *Berserk*, Diana was massaged by Vincent Price in *Theatre of Blood*, seduced by Jack Palance in *Craze* and starred as Ian Bannen's domineering wife in *From Beyond the Grave*, before impressing as the Satanic caregiver of *Thriller*: "Nurse Will Make it Better" (1974). While filming the latter (according to Damon Wise in *Come by Sunday*, Pan Books, 1998), Dors witnessed a fatal car crash on the way to the Elstree set (which subsequently flooded). When a prop crucifix "mysteriously snapped in two," Diana—a regular séance goer—was moved to report: "I believe in such things as black magic and the force of evil, and there were moments when I wished I had not taken part." Nevertheless, she went on to essay another brothel madam in the BBC's *Dr. Jekyll and Mr. Hyde* (1980) and Mrs. Ardoy, the matron of young werewolves, in *Hammer House of Horror*: "Children of the Full Moon." Five months after her death from ovarian cancer, Diana's grieving husband, Alan Lake—star of *Don't Open Till Christmas*—shot himself in the head on October 10, 1984. It was the 16th anniversary of the day they first met.

Other familiar faces in *Nothing But the Night* include Georgia Brown (1933-1992) as Joan Foster, and Keith Barron (1934-2017) as Dr. Haynes. An accomplished singer as well as an actress, Brown's vocal talents had been put to good use for *A Study in Terror*. Mauled by a tiger in *Tales That Witness Madness*, she later essayed Mrs. Sigmund Freud in *The Seven-Per-Cent Solution*, guested in *Cheers* and *Star Trek: The Next Generation*, and voiced the Headmistress of *Gravedale High* (1990).

Keith Barron had starred with Linda Hayden and Diana Dors in *Baby Love*, before going on to supporting roles in *The Land That Time Forgot* and *At the Earth's Core*. He subsequently became well-known to British viewers as the philandering lead of ITV comedy *Duty Free* (1983-1986), wherein he romances actress Joanna Van Gyseghem. (In real life, Joanna is a former wife of Ralph Bates and the niece of Christopher Lee's Dracula successor at Hammer, John Forbes-Robertson.)

Fresh from playing Peter Cushing's long-suffering wife in *Twins of Evil*, Kathleen Byron (1921-2009) turns up in *Nothing But the Night* as Dr. Rose. Byron, who had been a witch in *Night of the Eagle*, would later attend the "Night of the Marionettes" in *Supernatural* (1977) and appear as Lady Waddington in *The Elephant Man*. The highlight of her career, though, was her startling Gothic turn as the romantically tortured Sister Ruth in *Black Narcissus* (1946); the lowlight was being rolled up in a carpet by Jack Palance for *Craze*.

In addition, look out for Shelagh Fraser (1920-2000, Luke Skywalker's aunt in *Star Wars*); Fulton Mackay (1922-1987, the prison officer of BBC sitcom *Porridge* [1973-1977]) and Michael Gambon (b. 1940) in his first featured movie role as Inspector Grant. The following year, Gambon played a more prominent part in *The Beast Must Die*, before renown as *The Singing Detective* (1986), the violent gangster of *The Cook, the Thief, His Wife & Her Lover* (1988) and Dumbledore in the *Harry Potter* series. Gambon would next appear with Christopher Lee in Tim Burton's *Sleepy Hollow* (1999).

Also making her debut in *Nothing But the Night* is child actress Gwyneth Strong (b. 1959), who gives an impressive performance as the possessed Mary. After finding fame as Cassandra Trotter on one of Britain's best-loved comedy shows *Only Fools and Horses* (1981-2003), Gwyneth told the *Daily Record* in 2008, that making *Nothing But the Night* "was great fun." Of Lee and Cushing, she said: "I didn't really know who they were. As far as I was concerned, they were just friendly people working on the same film" (quoted in *A Celebration of Peter Cushing*, Buzzy Krotik Productions, 2017).

With Lee complaining (to Mark A. Miller) that Rank "didn't have any faith in it," *Nothing But the Night* was a poorly distributed bomb on its release in January 1973, despite a publicity tour from its two leads, and a promotional gimmick in the *Sunday Mercury*, which offered a cash prize to the most terrifying paranormal experience shared by their readers.

In his memoirs, Lee wrote that *Nothing But the Night* "failed because it was ahead of its time." In a sense, he is right: Although presaged by Lee's episode of *The House That Dripped Blood*, the vogue for "evil child" movies wouldn't flourish for another few years, with *The Omen*, Narciso Ibáñez Serrador's *Who Can Kill a Child?* and Jodie Foster's *The Little Girl Who Lives Down the Lane* all being made in 1975, the year of *Nothing But the Night*'s belated, and equally non-profitable, US release as *The Resurrection Syndicate*. (It later turned up as *The Devil's Undead* on American video.)

Unfortunately, it's not hard to see why *Nothing But the Night* flopped. The efforts of the cast are buried beneath a confused and unengaging storyline, and Peter Sasdy offers only the occasional interesting visual (a gunshot cuts into a fuming exhaust pipe, for example). In fact, after the masterful *Hands of the Ripper*, Sasdy seemed to lose his way with subsequent genre films *Doomwatch*, *I Don't Want to Be Born* and *Welcome to Blood City* (1976). It took a return to television, where his career began, for a resurgence of quality to emerge, firstly with Nigel Kneale's intelligent ghost story *The Stone Tape* (broadcast by BBC 2 on Christmas night 1972). Then, as well as guiding Christopher Lee through "Sherlock Holmes and the Leading Lady," Sasdy helmed a particularly good episode of *Supernatural* ("Viktoria," 1977), three entries apiece for *Hammer House of Horror* and *Hammer House of Mystery and Suspense*, and a modern-day tale of sorcery, *Witchcraft* (1992), which marks his final directorial credit.

Although the lack of finance engendered by *Nothing But the Night* ensured that Charlemagne bore no more fruit, the company would not be officially dissolved until Thursday, December 31, 1981. (The same day that Michael Carreras wound up his final Hammer subsidiary, the similarly fruitless Vulcan Film Productions Ltd.—no relation to Milton Subotsky's Vulcan Films of *The City of the Dead* fame.)

Nevertheless, three further Charlemagne projects reached the script stage, despite never being made by the company: Dennis Wheatley's *To the Devil a Daughter*, *The Haunting of Toby Jugg* and John Blackburn's *Bury Him Darkly*. While *To the Devil a Daughter* would, of course, be made at Hammer, and *The Haunting of Toby Jugg* was adapted by the BBC (as *The Haunted Airman*) in 2006, *Bury Him Darkly* remains unfilmed. (Though John Blackburn would dedicate his 1974 horror novel *Our Lady of Pain* to Lee "with gratitude," as the actor had actually suggested the book's subject—an updating of Elizabeth Bathory's antics, which he had recently recounted for *In Search of Dracula*.)

Portrait of Barbara, on the other hand, was an original screenplay by Robin Squire, a former BBC script editor, who'd played an Auton in *Doctor Who*: "Spearhead from Space" (1969). Lee worked closely with Squire on *Portrait of Barbara*'s development, which would have seen the actor in a very different role as John Blakemoor, a man so deranged by grief that he kidnaps the sister of his long-dead love. "Christopher was always charming and courteous," Robin tells me. "The image many retain of him is of the scary-eyed Count Dracula, but I always see him with a friendly, welcoming and encouraging smile. I once visited him at his flat on Cadogan Square in London and was privileged to meet there his wife Birgit and their daughter Christina, who was then a child full of mischief and fun … I met the great man several times while the script was in development, usually at Richmond Golf Club in Surrey.

Christopher Lee is all tied up.

He would have been memorably powerful in the role of Blakemoor."

I ask Robin if Lee had much creative involvement with the script's development. "The meetings with Christopher and Tony Nelson Keys were usually more functional than creative—they seemed happy enough with the story and didn't get too involved with the nuts and bolts of the script … Christopher did make one or two comments during the scripting, which I took heed of and incorporated. I remember when I'd written a rather tricky piece of dialogue for Blakemoor, he remarked, 'I have to make these words work on the screen, is there another way this could be said?' So, I rewrote that line with more focus and simplicity, and he was delighted."

So, what went wrong? "The project got to the point that a studio was booked at Pinewood, and we even had a meeting there, but when the full 100% of the funding didn't come through, Christopher moved on to make *The Wicker Man*—which I'm interested to note he saw as his favorite film. That being said, I can't help feeling his depiction of Blakemoor would have revealed him even more as a, literally, towering actor …

Fred Burnley [*Neither the Sea nor the Sand*] was to have directed, Anthony Nelson Keys was producer … While getting the script screenready, I worked mainly with Fred (who sadly died not all that long afterwards when filming for the BBC)." Burnley passed away in 1975, at the age of 42, from lung complications brought on by exposure to bat excrement during the making of a David Attenborough documentary.

Robin eventually published *Portrait of Barbara* as a novel in 1978 and is "still trying to interest film companies in [it], though who would play the Christopher Lee part is open to conjecture as he had such extraordinary presence … as you so rightly say, he was the last of the screen giants and it's tough to think of Blakemoor being portrayed by anyone else but him. If and when the film does eventually get made at long last, I'll make sure there's an onscreen dedication to the great man."

The Loneliness of Evil

The Wicker Man
1972

A Feast at Midnight (1994)
Strictly Supernatural (1996)
The Wicker Tree (2009)
Season of the Witch (2010)

Flesh to touch … flesh to burn! Don't keep the Wicker Man waiting!

Perhaps they had something, the way they lived here, living out their smutty fantasies. At least they were doing what they wanted. Which was more than he could say for himself.—David Pinner, *Ritual* (Arrow Books, 1967)

The role I'd like to be most remembered for is *The Wicker Man*. It was written for me, and it's almost the best film I've been in and the best performance I've ever given …—Christopher Lee (to Denis Meikle)

Belgian poster

Still wearing his producer's hat, in 1971, Christopher Lee approached Anthony Shaffer (1926-2001) with a view to filming the writer's *Play with a Gypsy* (eventually made with Richard Burton as *Absolution* [1978]). Instead, Shaffer—who was fresh from scripting the brutal but brilliant *Frenzy* for Alfred Hitchcock—convinced Lee and Peter Snell, the head of British Lion, to join him in investing £5,000 each for the rights to actor David Pinner's debut novel *Ritual*.

The book concerns London policeman Detective Inspector David Hanlin, who, on arriving at a "topsy-turvy" Cornish village to investigate the death of a young girl, Dian, discovers a conspiracy of witchcraft among the eccentric community. "I had, for quite an appreciable period of time, wanted to do a film in the, for want of a better word, horror movie genre without it actually following in the rather tired footsteps of Hammer Films," Shaffer explained (in Blue Underground's 2001 DVD documentary *The Wicker Man Enigma*). As it happens, *Ritual* makes blithe reference to Christopher Lee's former employers on a number of occasions. For example, when faced with the policeman's accusations, the Squire retorts: "Oh, come, come, Inspector, you've been over-reading Bram Stoker, what! Got Draculas on the brain!" Later on, after finding a photograph of Dian's twisted, bloodied corpse, another shady customer, ex-actor Cready, tells the inspector: "And to complete the ritual, I photographed the gory mess for Hammer Productions." (Among Pinner's other works was the lesbian vampire play *Fanghorn*, performed by Glenda Jackson at London's Fortune Theatre, 1968.)

Attempting to adapt Pinner's lyrical prose, Shaffer soon had second thoughts. "When I started to look at the thing closely," he told Allan Brown (for his book *Inside the Wicker Man*), "I realized it wasn't all that I had hoped. There were serious flaws in the construction; the philosophy of the piece was rather vague." In short, "the actual events of the novel weren't exciting enough," so, in early 1972, a new script was built upon Pinner's basic idea.

This clash of ideals forms a sturdy backbone to the plot, while raising some stimulating queries on attitudes of belief. Moreover, focus on the "old religion" allowed the writer to bring in the titular wicker man—a sacrificial effigy of the ancient Druids—which contributes to an astonishing finale, wholly different from the one presented by Pinner.

When Shaffer told Lee that his screenplay was finished, the actor responded immediately to the new title of *The Wicker Man*: "'Has that got anything to do with Druids and their sacrifices?'" he asked (in *The Wicker Man Enigma*), "And [Shaffer] said, 'I hate you!' Because," Lee laughed, "I was almost the only person who knew what the wicker man presented." He also believed in the project so much that he agreed to work without payment.

Renaming the policeman Sergeant Howie, Shaffer transformed him into a virutous Christian, who opposes an island of pagans, headed by Lord Summerisle (a part constructed specifically for Christopher Lee). Cast as Sergeant Howie, Edward Woodward told Allan Brown: "Christopher Lee was there most of the time to put [director] Robin Hardy right if necessary." Robin Hardy (1929-2016), who ran a TV commercial company with Shaffer, explained (in *The Wicker Man Enigma*) how his debut feature came into being: "[Anthony Shaffer and I] both liked horror films. We both crossed town to go see the latest Hammer, but we felt that horror films, as they were being done at the time, were missing something …"

Indeed, *The Wicker Man* would see Shaffer convert Hammer's tropes into a clever series of games (doing for the horror genre what his soon-to-be filmed play *Sleuth* had done for the crime thriller). While the premise of a community in compliance with human sacrifice, along with a flashy visual sense, can be found in J. Lee Thompson's *Eye of the Devil* (1965), Howie's arrival at the harbor bears a striking similarity to a scene in Peter Sasdy's *Doomwatch* (released March 1972), which sees Ian Bannen's ecologist faced by strange locals on a remote island.

The Wicker Man seems to owe its greatest debt, however, to Hammer's *The Witches* (1966). Scripted by Nigel Kneale, this underrated thriller stars Joan Fontaine as a Christian teacher, chosen to arrive amid a bizarre community by Kay Walsh's occult leader. (Her lair is Lee's castle from *Dracula: Prince of Darkness*.) As well as odd goings-on in the classroom and graveyard, other similarities include Fontaine awaking to find voodoo relics at her bedside, and a climactic sacrifice in which music plays a vital part (*The Witches* also features Edward Woodward's future wife Michele Dotrice in an early role).

Additional genre motifs at play in *The Wicker Man* include a raucous tavern, which falls silent on Howie's entrance, and the rattling carriage which subsequently transports him to Christopher Lee's castle (though, instead of a desolate Transylvanian backdrop, we are treated to sun-dappled views of phallic hedges and nude dancers).

Lee's Lord Summerisle also playfully twists the audience's expectations of his then-screen persona (what Anthony Shaffer glibly summarized, in Mark Kermode's 2001 documentary *Burnt Offering: The Cult of the Wicker Man*, as: "Chasing people like Ingrid Pitt and Barbara Windsor down papier-mâché corridors"). Throughout *The Wicker Man*, Lee is on sprightly form, clearly relishing the chance to play a different kind of character and organizing sacrifices to Nuada and Avenallau as if it were the most natural thing in the world. This singular sense of logic reaches its apex with a po-faced appearance in drag at the May Day festivities. Looking, in the words of critic Janet Maslin, "like Cher," Lee performs a jaunty dance (totally improvised by the actor himself), while wielding a sickle and rebuking a disguised Howie to "Cut some capers, man!" This, in turn, leads to one of the most devastating, powerful and inevitable conclusions in cinema history, with Lee on peak form, leading his people in a lustful sing-song beneath Howie's tortured cries.

Built on-site at Burrow Head (just one of 25 Scottish locations), the iconic 36-foot wicker man was the work of a six-man team, headed by art director Seamus Flannery (b. 1930)—whose other credits include *Repulsion*, *I'll Never Forget What's 'isname* (1967) and *The New Avengers*. (Lee kept the "last remaining piece of the wicker man" and shows if off in *The Many Faces of Christopher Lee*; the effigy's legs, left standing at Burrow Head, were stolen in November 2006. As of 2019, only two eroded stumps remain.)

Christopher Lee in Pagan dress

Howie's awe-struck expression on first seeing the wicker man is genuine: As Edward Woodward revealed in the movie's DVD commentary, he spared himself the sight of it until the scene was shot on Wednesday, October 25, 1972. (Filming had begun on Monday, October 9; to give the illusion of spring, the actors sucked on ice between takes, which prevented their breath from being visible in the cold air, and plastic blossoms were glued to the trees.)

In a uniform specially shortened to give the character a tense, restricted physicality, Woodward (1930-2009) gives an excellent performance as Howie. The actor—who had been far more informed on dark practices as an anthropology professor in *Incense for the Damned*—first came to prominence on television as secret agent *Callan* (1967-1972, a Don Sharp-directed film of which, initially mooted by Hammer, was produced by Magnum Films in 1973). As well as his Golden Globe-winning turn as *The Equalizer* (1985-1989), Woodward was Merlin in *Arthur the King* (1982), the Ghost of Christmas Present in *A Christmas Carol* (1984) and Sherlock Holmes in *Hands of a Murderer* (1989). He made his final appearance as Reverend Densham in *A Congregation of Ghosts* (2009).

Christopher Lee and the Wicker Man (with a captive inside)

The Loneliness of Evil

Christopher Lee oversees the arrival of a stranger to the island. Shown with Britt Ekland, Ingrid Pitt and Edward Woodward

One of Woodward's most memorable scenes in *The Wicker Man* comes when he is tempted by the seductive landlord's daughter, Willow (Britt Ekland). Here, Shaffer inverts a genre cliché that had not yet been commonly established, making *The Wicker Man* the one horror film where the protagonist dies from *not* having sex.

Born in Stockholm, 1942, Britt Ekland debuted with a walk-on in Elvis Presley's *G.I. Blues* (1960), before her short-lived marriage to Peter Sellers led to roles in *A Carol for Another Christmas* (1964), *After the Fox* (1965) and *The Bobo* (1966). Three months pregnant when she starred as Willow, it can now be ascertained, after much debate, that her Scottish accent in *The Wicker Man* is dubbed by Annie Ross (later to play a villain in *Superman III*), while her singing voice belongs to Rachel Verney. (A cover of "Willow's Song" can be heard in Eli Roth's *Hostel* [2005].) Reunited with Christopher Lee as James Bond's put-upon accomplice, Mary Goodnight, in *The Man with the Golden Gun*, Ekland was also stepmother to the *Night Hair Child*, Charlotte Rampling's mysterious associate in *Asylum*, a psychic in *Satan's Mistress* (1978), a vampire's mother in *The Monster Club* and Madame Cassandra in *Beverly Hills Vamp* (1988). Though none of the above won any awards, Charlize Theron earned a Golden Globe nomination for playing Britt in *The Life and Death of Peter Sellers* (2003).

Lord Summerisle's mistress, the schoolteacher Miss Rose, is portrayed by Diane Cilento (1933-2011), who, in her spare time, designed and marketed her own Tarot cards (one of which can be seen in the 99-minute print of *The Wicker Man*, on the ceiling of the Green Man Inn). The Australian-born Cilento made her screen debut in an early Hammer film, *Wings of Danger* (1951), before her skinny-dipping scene for the company's *The Full Treatment* (1960) was greeted by censor John Trevelyan with the warning: "We don't mind the topless bit, but we won't allow pubics." (Diane would don a black wig and white bikini to double, incognito, her then-husband Sean Connery's leading lady, Mie Hama, for a swimming scene in *You Only Live Twice*). After crooning to lions and winning the heart of "The World's Smallest Man" as *The Woman for Joe* (1954), Cilento could be seen with Gary Cooper and Peter Cushing in *The Naked Edge* (1960) and with Oliver Reed in the undeservedly obscure sci-fi outing *Z.P.G.* (1971). Oscar-nominated for her performance in *Tom Jones* (1962), Diane's 11-year marriage to Connery ended in 1973; after which, she took up with Anthony Schaffer (whom she met on *The Wicker Man*). The pair were married from 1985 until Schaffer's death in 2001.

"Christopher wanted me for the part that Edward Woodward played," Peter Cushing revealed to Mark A. Miller, "but I couldn't do it because I was involved in something else." (Peter was busy on *Frankenstein and the Monster from Hell* until October 24, 1972.) Nevertheless, *The Wicker Man* does find room for another Hammer alumna, Ingrid Pitt (1937-2010), as the island librarian. Although her acting is largely underrated elsewhere, Roy Ward Baker (in *Bizarre* #3) called Ingrid: "The most promising actress I have worked with since Marilyn Monroe ... She has got the talent of Bette Davis, the unique sex appeal of Marilyn Monroe and intelligence and wit to match."

A former member of Bertolt Brecht's Berliner Ensemble and fluent in five languages, Ingrid Pitt was born on a train, en route to the concentration camp where her parents were made prisoners of war. Fleeing war-torn Germany, one November night in 1962, by swimming the river Spree, Ingrid later found herself in Spain, fighting off invisible monsters for *Sound of Horror* (1965). After starring in her second horror film, the Philippines-shot *The Omegans* (1967), she played British agent, Heidi, in *Where Eagles Dare* with Clint Eastwood and Richard Burton. This led to her being cast as Carmilla Karnstein in *The Vampire Lovers*, which she followed with vampiric turns in *The House That Dripped Blood* and *Countess Dracula*; two guest spots on *Doctor Who*, and a slinky cameo in Clive Barker's *Underworld* (1985).

Pitt's experiences with Christopher Lee on *The Wicker Man* inspired her to write *Dracula Who ...?*, an un-filmed screenplay for Hammer, which became a comic novel about a vegetarian vampire (it was finally made available as an ebook in 2012). Ingrid's other books include: *Cuckoo Run* (1980), an action-packed spy thriller; *The Ingrid Pitt Bedside Companion for Vampire Lovers* (1998); *The Ingrid Pitt Bedside Companion for Ghosthunters* (1999); *The Ingrid Pitt Book of Murder, Torture and Depravity* (2000) and, for children, *Bertie the Bus* (1981). Although her performance as a drug dealer's mother was cut from Hammer's online serial *Beyond the Rave* (2007), she left a more poignant swansong by writing and narrating the animated short *Ingrid Pitt: Beyond the Forest* (2010), which details her real-life escape, aged eight, from a Nazi concentration camp. Ingrid passed away from congestive heart failure in November 2010.

Key among Summerisle's weird locals is the harbor master, played by Scottish actor Russell Waters (1908-1982). Last seen with Christopher Lee in *The Devil Rides Out*, Waters was also Detective Davis in *Seven Days to Noon*, the Brigadier in *Yesterday's Enemy* and a hospital attendant in Roy Boulting's *Twisted Nerve* (1968).

Russell is joined by one of Britain's foremost mime artists, Lindsay Kemp (1938-2018), who was cast as sly landlord Alder MacGregor after Robin Hardy had seen him in Ken Russell's *Savage Messiah* ("I was so drunk most of the time," Kemp remembered of *The Wicker Man*'s filming, to Allan Brown). In addition to being the man who taught Kate Bush how to dance, Lindsay was an ex-lover of, and major influence on, David Bowie, with whom he appeared in the promo for "John, I'm Only Dancing" (1972). "Kicked … off *2001: A Space Odyssey*, because" as he revealed to Brown, "[Stanley Kubrick] thought my arse was too big," Kemp can be seen in *The Vampire Lovers* (as Jester), *Valentino* (as the mortician) and *Velvet Goldmine* (1997, as an Old Mother Riley-style drag act).

The Summerisle graveyard is haunted by Aubrey Morris (1926-2015), an actor who brought a uniquely off-kilter flavor to every role he played, from the seedy bookstore owner in *The Night Caller*, a horror movie director in *Go for a Take* and Home Secretary, Sir Percy Heseltine, in *Lifeforce*, to the groin-grabbing Mr. Deltoid in *A Clockwork Orange* and Dr. Putnam in *Blood from the Mummy's Tomb*—a role he recreated in the 1997 remake *Bram Stoker's Legend of the Mummy*. (Morris' brother, Wolfe, also an actor, had been the mad waxworks proprietor in *The House That Dripped Blood*.)

The aforementioned talent is joined by a roster of local residents, whose wonderful faces add veracity to the island's peculiar activities. (Allan Brown was told by "Plockton resident Callum McKenzie" that "each one of the local extras who greet Howie on the quay died within a year of filming.")

What sets *The Wicker Man* aside is the poetic whimsy these characters and their settings share with Dylan Thomas' *Under Milk Wood* (filmed in 1971), while the casting of 21-year-old Lesley Mackie as a schoolgirl prefigures the adults-as-children innovation of Dennis Potter's *Blue Remembered Hills* (1978). Additionally, the often-surreal musical numbers, which blur the boundaries of fantasy and reality, foreshadow a similar device used by Potter on such works as *Pennies from Heaven* (1977) and *The Singing Detective*.

The remarkable music of *The Wicker Man*—which Christopher Lee called (in the sleeve notes of Silva Screen Records' 2010 soundtrack release): "Probably the best music I've ever heard in a film"—was the work of Paul Giovanni (1933-1990). The New York-born composer and stage director was the then-boyfriend of Anthony Shaffer's twin brother, Peter—the celebrated playwright of *Amadeus*—who helped, uncredited, to edit his partner's music sequences. Although *The Wicker Man* proved to be Giovanni's only film score, he would later write the Sherlock Holmes play, *The Crucifer of Blood* (filmed as a TV-movie with Charlton Heston in 1991) before his death from AIDS.

With filming complete on Saturday, November 25, 1972, *The Wicker Man* was assembled into a print running 102 minutes. This was then cut to 99 minutes by Robin Hardy and editor Eric Boyd-Perkins (1917-2014), before being sent to potential US distributor Roger Corman (the major scene excised at this stage, never to resurface, was one in which Lord Summerisle rhapsodizes over apples). Boyd-Perkins—whose résumé lists mainstream features (*The Bridge on the River Kwai*) alongside Hammer horrors like *Taste of Fear* and *The Gorgon*—told Allan Brown that he was then "handed … a letter from Roger Corman," which outlined further reductions, resulting in an 84-minute print. Blame for this shorter version is usually appended to British Lion, who apparently hated the film so much that they demanded it be cut down to fit the lower half of a double bill. As Shaffer remembered of the movie's UK distributors (in *The Wicker Man Enigma*): "Their reaction, of course, was sheer disbelief. They had been used to selling 'masterpieces' like *On the Buses* … this was altogether out of their league."

For the same documentary, a similarly dismayed Christopher Lee recalled *The Wicker Man*'s first screening in the basement of British Lion's offices in 1973: "I went upstairs afterwards, purely out of courtesy, to say 'thank you' to Michael Deeley, who had replaced Peter Snell as the managing director of British Lion. And he sat at his desk—he didn't get up when my wife walked in, which is always a pretty good guide towards somebody's character and behavior, and he said: 'Well, what do you think of the film?' And I said: 'Well, I think it's a marvelous film, Michael'… and he looked up at me and he said: 'I think it's one of the 10 worst films I've ever seen.'"

As such, *The Wicker Man* initially crept out in December 1973, beneath Nicolas Roeg's *Don't Look Now*. While the latter title got all the attention, mainly for its "realistic" sex scene, *The Wicker Man* was the superior feature—even if Lee had to encourage critics to go see it.

The actor was further influential in promoting the film on its October 1977 American reissue, going out of his way to appear on public-access talk shows and compiling press clippings to send back to Peter Snell in England. Lee's efforts were rewarded when *The Wicker Man* enjoyed a newfound critical respect, earning plaudits like "the *Citizen Kane* of horror movies" in *Cinefantastique*'s issue-length appreciation (Winter, 1977). Moreover, the re-release print had been restored to 91 minutes by Hardy and US distributor John Simon. This version, which incorporates the best of the missing footage without losing momentum, was is-

Is Ingrid Pitt about to be sacrificed on the island?

sued on DVD and to selected theaters in 2013 as *The Final Cut*. (It even enjoyed a "Scratch 'n' Sniff" screening in 2014. According to the publicity blurb, opportunities for releasing "10 encapsulated odors" from the viewer's scratch card included "whisky-sozzled pub patrons, fishy goings-on and the local chocolate shop … as for the infamous finale, shhh! Wait and sniff!")

It was while first preparing the 91-minute version in 1976 that the director learned, to his horror, that the film's original negative was missing, with rumors that it had been buried "accidentally" beneath the M3 motorway. Lee, however, was having none of that: "I am convinced that film does exist," he told Allan Brown. "And I am also convinced that certain people are responsible for keeping it hidden." Brown, however, was skeptical, writing: "Christopher Lee senses a conspiracy, clearly after viewing several of his Dennis Wheatley adaptations."

Conspiracies aside, Roger Corman was, thankfully, still in possession of his 99-minute print, which was used to splice-in footage absent from the original theatrical release. The missing scene of most interest (filmed on Thursday November 2, 1972) introduces Lord Summerisle beneath Willow's window, offering "another sacrifice for Aphrodite." Having done this, he quotes from section 32 of Walt Whitman's poem "Song of Myself," which pontificates on the superiority of animals over humans: "They do not lie awake in the dark and weep for their sins. They do not make me sick discussing their duty to God … Not one of them is respectable or unhappy, all over the earth." Lee was handed these words to learn by Robin Hardy at the very last minute. "He did it in one take," the director told Brown, "then walked off the set for dinner."

In 1978, Hardy did his bit to publicize the US re-release by converting Shaffer's screenplay into a novelization. Dedicated to Lee, this inevitably gives the fullest account of the authors' original story. Its closest onscreen equivalent, the 99-minute print, first emerged on US home video in 1981, before worldwide DVD release as *The Director's Cut* two decades later. While I personally think the film packs more of a punch in its 84-minute form, I will concur that *The Wicker Man* is essential viewing at any length.

Ignored in its time, now everyone loves the movie. (When Ingrid Pitt encountered Tom Hanks, he told her it was a personal favorite: "He particularly liked my naked dance," the actress reported in *Shivers* #87. "I didn't tell him that wasn't me, but it was a gallant effort …") For a brief period in the early '80s, *The Wicker Man* even had its own Appreciation Society, which published a newsletter, the *Summerisle News*. Since then, the film has gone on to inspire a stage production, a Scottish arts festival and a rollercoaster ride at Staffordshire's Alton Towers. In 2010, it even took the form of an amusing online comic by Paul O'Connell, *A Muppet Wicker Man*, with Kermit the Frog as Howie, Miss Piggy as Willow and Gonzo as Lord Summerisle.

Accounting for the movie's lasting appeal (in *Burnt Offering*), Lee broached the theological issues at its heart: "There is a touch of paganism in all of us, insofar as we do, all of us, depend on the elements, which have been there since the dawn of time, without which we couldn't exist." Certainly, *The Wicker Man*'s preoccupation with nature is more vital than ever in an age when people are too busy staring into smartphones to be aware of their environment. (Although I wouldn't go so far as to sacrifice such offenders.)

While Anthony Shaffer eventually fell out with Hardy, over what he perceived to be the latter's exaggerated claims to authorship of *The Wicker Man* (as related by Allan Brown), Lee remained on good terms with both men. In 1994, he waived his fee once more to star in the directorial debut of Robin Hardy's son, Justin: *A Feast at Midnight*. This beguiling comedy-drama, set in a boarding school, sees Lee give one of his best non-horror performances as Major 'Raptor' Longfellow. "We wanted the school to be the scariest school in the world," Justin told Alan Barnes, for

Hammer Horror #3, "and we wanted the Latin master to be the scariest master in the world, and we couldn't think of anything more scarier than having the Latin master played by Dracula."

In the same interview, Justin related a touching story of how Lee drew on his Hammer background to placate the young actor Stuart Hawley, who, as the schoolboy villain of the piece, became "quite distressed" by a scene in which he is pelted with food: "Christopher ... took the little boy away when he started to cry, and explained to him that for 230-odd films Christopher had had stakes rammed into his heart ... and that, ultimately, is the role that the baddie has to play." Later, after Stuart confided to the older actor that he wished, one day, to join the SAS, Lee gave the boy his own SAS tie "as a gift from one baddie to another." In 1996, Justin directed Lee once again on the three-part documentary series *Strictly Supernatural*, wherein the actor gives respectful discourse to the subjects of "Séance," "Tarot," and "Astrology."

But *The Wicker Man* legacy didn't end there. In July 2005, filming began on the long-threatened remake starring Nicolas Cage (who also co-produced). Unfortunately, whereas the original was vivacious and engaging, this was just plain dull. Scenes of Cage's policeman punching out women, while dressed as a bear, reach heights of inexplicable lunacy that the 1972 version, for all its eccentricities, never possessed (and, please, let's not mention those CGI bees). There had been whispers of Christopher Lee making an appearance, but as he bemoaned to interviewers at the time: "What on earth would I play? The wicker man?" The actor was best out of it and proves so irreplaceable that Lord Summerisle becomes Sister Summersisle in the person of Ellen Burstyn. *The Exorcist* star just looks embarrassed, though, and the gender switch is not enough to make the movie worthwhile.

Cage, who had produced *Shadow of the Vampire* and eaten real cockroaches for his role in *Vampire's Kiss* (1987), would actually star with the real Lord Summerisle five years later: In a disturbing make-up, Lee contributes a bizarre cameo to *Season of the Witch* (2010) as a plague-riddled Cardinal who believes his ailments to be the consequence of a witch's curse. Cage told MTV his motives for appearing in the latter: "I wanted to make movies that celebrated actors like Christopher Lee and Vincent Price, and the great Roger Corman classics that are unafraid to explore the paranormal and the supernatural." Pilloried upon release, *Season of the Witch* is actually more interesting than its reputation suggests. One contemporaneous film that deserved its bad reviews, however, is, alas, Robin Hardy's "spiritual successor" to *The Wicker Man*, *The Wicker Tree*.

Released on the festival circuit in the summer of 2011, the movie's road to fruition was a typically arduous one. In 1989, Anthony Shaffer had written a 30-page treatment for a *Wicker Man* sequel entitled *The Wonderful Legend of the Lambton Worm*. This would have seen an aged Lord Summerisle, now possessed of supernatural powers, pitting a rescued Sergeant Howie against the title creature (itself the inspiration for Bram Stoker's *The Lair of the White Worm*—filmed by Ken Russell in 1988, with rich cinematography from *Dracula A.D. 1972*'s Dick Bush and scenes which quote *Dracula* and *The Gorgon*). "I don't think Christopher particularly liked it," Robin Hardy said of *Lambton Worm*, to *The Huffington Post* in 2012. "And I don't think Tony was particularly satisfied with it ... I, personally, didn't like the idea ... so I was never involved." Hardy, instead, set to work on crafting

a sequel of his own. The director's initial screenplay, written in 2002 and entitled *The Riding of the Laddie*, eventually became a 2006 novel *Cowboys for Christ*. This, in turn, was adapted as *The Wicker Tree*. Lee was originally enlisted to play the Lord Summerisle equivalent, Sir Lachlan Morrison, but when filming began in July 2009, the actor was still incapacitated due to a back injury he'd suffered while filming Hammer's *The Resident*. Replaced by Graham McTavish—who would appear with Lee in the *Hobbit* movies and voice Dracula on *Castlevania* (2017-), Christopher, instead, settled for a cameo as the "Old Gentleman," who can be seen, briefly in flashback, mentoring the young Morrison on the nature of fate. There has been some speculation as to whether or not Lee's character is an aged Lord Summerisle, with Robin Hardy answering in the affirmative, and Lee insisting he was playing an altogether different person. But that is the least of *The Wicker Tree*'s problems: Although well-staged by Hardy and his cinematographer Jan Pester, the film offers few surprises, being mostly a retread of *The Wicker Man*, with none of the original's rustic charm and some attempts at humor which fall flat.

In 2015, Hardy set up a crowdfunding campaign to raise funds for the production of a second sequel, *The Wrath of the Gods*. Lesley Mackie told the *Evening Telegraph* that both she and Christopher Lee would have had roles in it, remembering: "I found Sir Christopher to be a really decent man. I have great memories of that time I had with him on *The Wicker Man* set."

Sadly, Robin Hardy passed away in July 2016. Whereas both *The Wicker Tree* and Hardy's only other film *The Fantasist* (1985) are disappointments, *The Wicker Man* stands alone as a truly lasting masterwork.

Poor Devil
1972

Directly after filming *The Wicker Man*, Christopher Lee set off for Hollywood on Wednesday November 15, 1972, to play the Devil for an old friend, Sammy Davis, Jr. (1925-1990), who overcame appalling racism and the loss of his left eye to become one of the world's biggest entertainers. He was also a big Hammer horror fan who first met Lee on *The Pirates of Blood River* set in August 1961. "He was absolutely blown away by it all," Lee recalled. "He couldn't believe that we created these pictures on such a small stage."

Eight years later, Davis invited Lee to cameo as Dracula in *One More Time*, after which, the pair were reunited at Paramount Studios for the three-week production of *Poor Devil*. While not a horror film, per se, Lee's casting as Lucifer comes as a direct result of his scary reputation, and he joins a pantheon of genre favorites who have also tackled the role, including Laird Cregar (*Heaven Can Wait* [1943]), Claude Rains (*Angel on My Shoulder* [1946]), Ray Milland (*Alias Nick Beal* [1948]), Vincent Price (*The Story of Mankind* [1956]), Lon Chaney, Jr. (*13 Demon Street* [1959]), John Carradine (*Autopsy of a Ghost* [1967]), Paul Naschy (*Vengeance of the Zombies* [1972]; *El caminante* [1978]) and Donald Pleasence (*The Greatest Story Ever Told* [1963]; *Paganini Horror* [1988]).

Although *Poor Devil* is very 1970s, with its hip score and groovy dialogue, the heart of this feature-length pilot harks back to such 1940s fantasies as *Here Comes Mr. Jordan* (1941) and *A Matter of Life and Death* (1945), which also present wonderfully imaginative visions of an afterlife. The Hell of *Poor Devil* looks very much like a *Star Trek* typing pool, where scarlet-clad workers are constantly busy with tiresome bureaucracy. (Everyone who enters has forms to fill out.)

The plot bears some relation to *It's A Wonderful Life* (1946), especially in its Yuletide setting, but rather than an angel helping out a lost soul on Earth, we have Davis' sharp-suited devil (also called Sammy) trying to capture the soul of bungling accountant Burnett J. Emerson (Jack Klugman).

As Lucifer, Lee is given a very impressive introductory shot—behind grand doors, he sits impassive at a desk in his flame-lapped dwelling, looking very glamorous in black wig, medallion and turtleneck sweater. Portals zap open and champagne corks pop with just a point of his finger; a large screen on the wall allows him to spy on the people of Earth. He even gets to expostulate on his loathing of Christmas in tones reminiscent of Boris Karloff's narration for *How the Grinch Stole Christmas!*

One of Lee's favorite actors was Walter Huston, father of John and grandfather of Anjelica, who had so memorably essayed the part of Old Scratch in the RKO classic *The Devil and Daniel Webster*. As in that film, *Poor Devil* introduces a panel of legendary criminals, including Al Capone and Blackbeard the pirate, from whom Sammy seeks counsel. The result is a night-time raid on the San Francisco department store where Emerson is employed. He and Sammy are aided by many respectable citizens who, in fact, owe their success to a pact with the Devil (including, predictably, lots of politicians).

Jack Klugman (1922-2012) delivers a sensitive performance as a man who feels lost and undervalued, a portrayal well-matched by Madlyn Rhue (1935-2003) as his loving wife and Adam West (1928-2017) as his younger, scheming boss. Emily Yancy (b. 1939) also scores as Lucifer's secretary (the actress had just been a victim of *Blacula* and would later play a reporter in James Cameron's *The Abyss* [1988]). Most of the actors are familiar television faces (Klugman as *Quincy M.E.*; West as *Batman*), and the crew are also veterans of the medium: Director Robert Scheerer (1928-2018) worked on everything from *The Love Boat* to *Star Trek: The Next Generation*; writer Richard Baer (1928-2008) scripted five episodes of *The Munsters*, as well as being a regular contributor to *Bewitched* (1964-1972) and composer Morton Stevens (1929-1991) is best known for his *Hawaii Five-O* theme and *Thriller* scores.

First aired by NBC on Wednesday, February 14, 1973, *Poor Devil* met with some indifference, as Lee recalled in *Christopher Lee's New Chamber of Horrors*: "Plans to turn it into a series have been squashed because the film company executives were afraid that as the Devil was shown as such an entertaining gentleman, and Hell as such an amusing place, the young people of America would never be afraid of doing anything wrong because that was where they would end up! Can you imagine?"

Paramount were not just being prudish: The film shows little of Hell's damnation, preferring to dwell on the material rewards accompanying Faustian pacts. While a series may not have been forthcoming—it's difficult to see how the premise would have sustained a multi-episode format—the combined charisma of Lee and Davis, Jr. is enough to make *Poor Devil* a charming and, at times, amusing diversion. One viewer impressed by Lee's performance was Anton LaVey (1930-1997), the founder of the Church of Satan. LaVey, who would serve as technical consultant on *The Devil's Rain* (1975), sent Lee two of his books, inscribed: "To Christopher Lee—a fine actor and a perfect devil!"

Davis, Jr. admitted in his autobiography *Why Me?* (Sphere, 1989) that he was a Church of Satan member at the time of *Poor Devil*'s production. "I wanted to have every human experience," he wrote, adding: "It was a turn-on. The chicks loved it." (It must be noted, however, that once Sammy learned there was a little more to Satanism than group sex, he soon reverted to Judaism.) Consequently, it's slightly unnerving to see a seemingly light, family-friendly film like *Poor Devil* peppered with genuine Satanic symbols, such as devil horn salutes and inverse pentagrams. Davis—who was Tim Burton's original choice to play *Beetlejuice* (1987)—died from throat cancer in May 1990. His tireless work for civil integration must never be forgotten.

A youthful-looking Christopher Lee and Sammy Davis, Jr.

While filming *Poor Devil*, on Friday, November 24, 1972, Christopher Lee gave a speech at L.A.'s Ambassador Hotel for the Count Dracula Society, advising his fellow fantasy stalwarts (including Robert Bloch, Forrest J Ackerman, Robert Quarry and Reginald Le Borg [director of *The Black Sleep*, *Voodoo Island* and *Diary of a Madman*]) that they should treat their genre work "with devotion, with taste, with style, with integrity and with belief." The following day, at the same venue, Lee answered questions for the first Science Fiction and Fantasy Film Convention. Around this time, he also filmed an introduction for an unnamed TV documentary on the occult, which was ultimately never made. Lee's footage was later purchased to bolster a movie lacking in either taste, style, or integrity ...

The Hollywood Meatcleaver Massacre 1972/1975

The Occult: Mysteries of the Supernatural (1977)
Tales of the Haunted: Evil Stalks this House (1981)

What you are about to see, you may find hard to believe.

So begins Christopher Lee's introduction to *Hollywood Meatcleaver Massacre* (a.k.a. *Evil Force*). In a wood-paneled study, full of arcane books and devilish visages, Lee speaks of the human soul, prophetic dreams and evil spirits ("dog-headed hags with bats' wings, bloodshot eyes and snakes for hair …"). This four-minute sequence is totally unrelated to the movie that follows, which was shot in 1975, but released to drive-ins in March 1977 (on the top half of a double bill with Charles Band's *Mansion of the Doomed* [1975]).

Tedious, flatly directed and underlit, *The Hollywood Meatcleaver Massacre* concerns a university anthropology professor (James Habif, "Sperm donor with mustache" in *Female Chauvinists* [1976]), whose family is killed in a brutal home invasion by four of his students. From the professor's hospital bed, he calls upon an ancient demon, Morak, to exact revenge. As the demon is conveniently invisible (until the very end, when we are treated to blurry flashes of a man with seaweed on his face), actors writhe about while under attack, as wild tom-toms pound offscreen. Lee pops up again at the climax to relate a story of two shamans, who engage in such "abracadabrical trick[s]" as producing monsoons from their ears. He also states that supernatural phenomena "has been tirelessly investigated and substantially verified," while questioning how much control we have over our futures.

The biggest mystery surrounding *The Hollywood Meatcleaver Massacre*, however, is the purported involvement of Ed Wood (1924-1978): The legendary director of *Plan 9 from Outer Space* (1956) can be seen briefly stepping into shot as a photographer about 20 minutes in. How he came to be involved is partly explained by writer Joe Blevins, who states on his online blog, *Dead 2 Rights*, that: "One reader, Lee Jones, has suggested to me via Facebook that Wood 'directed around 60% of *Meatcleaver Massacre*' because 'the original director was fired.' His source is Jim Bryan, the film's editor." (Bryan would later work on *Wolfen* [1980], *A Nightmare on Elm Street 4* [1988] and Stephen King's *The Dark Half* [1991]). While Blevins reasons that "the movie bears remarkable thematic and stylistic similarities to the Wood canon," this is, of course, open to debate. Certainly, no information is forthcoming about the film's credited director Evan Lee, whose first and only screen credit this was.

Indeed, few involved with *Massacre* had any industry experience: Paul Kelleher (Detective Shaye) would next play the Sheriff in *Night of the Demon* (1979), Maria Arnold (billed as Natasha) had been the star of Ed Wood's *Necromania* (1971), as well as one of Emperor Wang's cheerleaders in *Flesh Gordon* (1971), Guerdon Trueblood (who appears as "Boy in mask") would grow up to provide visual effects for such Lee starrers as *Alice in Wonderland* (2009) and *The Lord of the Rings*, and uncredited cinematographer Roy H. Wagner (b. 1947) went on to light *A Nightmare on Elm Street 3* (1986).

As for Christopher Lee: "I did not—*repeat*—did *not* appear in a film entitled *The Hollywood Meatcleaver Massacre*," he emphasized to Tom Johnson and Mark A. Miller, explaining that the first he knew of it was when "walking down a London street," he saw "a film poster advertising the above title—with my name prominently displayed!" On further investigation, though, Lee realized "there was nothing I could do, other than tear down every poster in London, New York and Los Angeles." To the same authors, the actor admitted never having seen the film. If he had, he would probably never have worked with *Massacre*'s writer and producer Ray Atherton (1949-1996), who officially hired Lee to host *The Many Faces of Sherlock Holmes* (1985). As well as producing documentaries on such American icons as John Wayne, Marilyn Monroe and Charles Manson, Atherton co-wrote a romantic comedy about flatulence, *F.A.R.T. The Movie* (1991), and he is the guy who has a TV smashed over his head in *Henry: Portrait of a Serial Killer* (1985).

Laid-back in tartan trousers and open-necked shirt, Lee is undoubtedly the best thing about *The Hollywood Meatcleaver Massacre*, bringing a languorous charm to his yarn-spinning, while

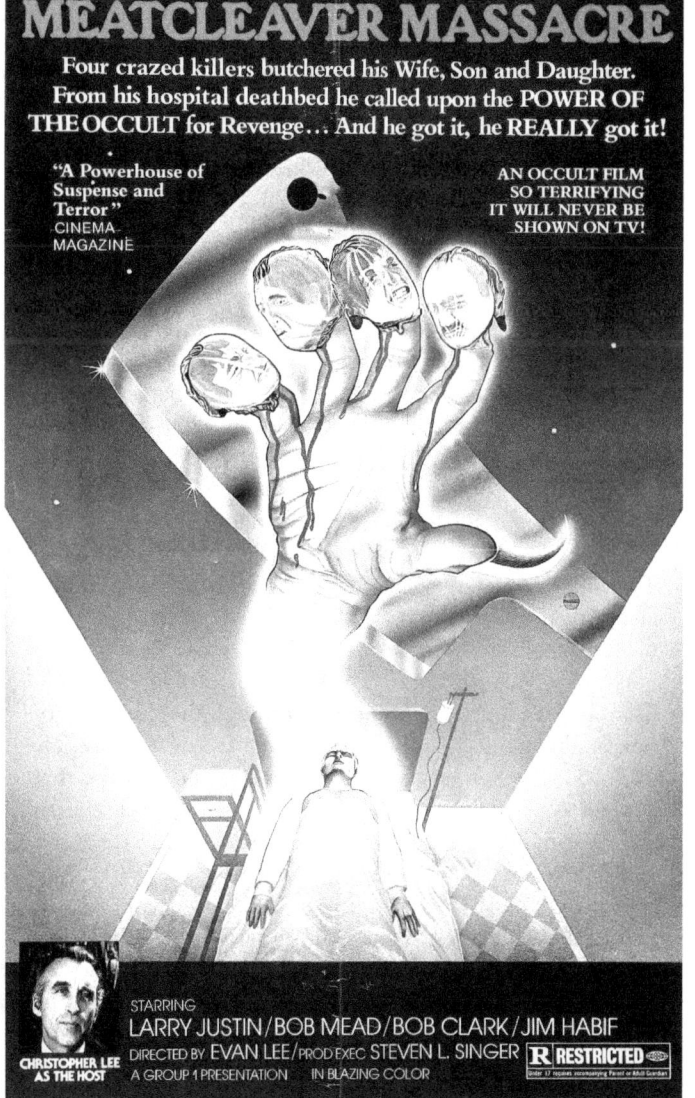

from *Race with the Devil*, *The Legend of Hell House*, *The Omen* and *Nosferatu*, Lee addresses ancient superstitions that have survived in contemporary society. He is aided along the way by footage of "the fascinating ritual of modern-day witches," a medium "channeling" spirits, pianist Maxine Bell, who claims that her musical talents are dictated to her by long-dead composers, including a new work by Tchaikovsky, and a scientific examination of a gentleman experiencing an out-of-body experience. "What seems incredible today," Lee concludes, "may be commonplace tomorrow."

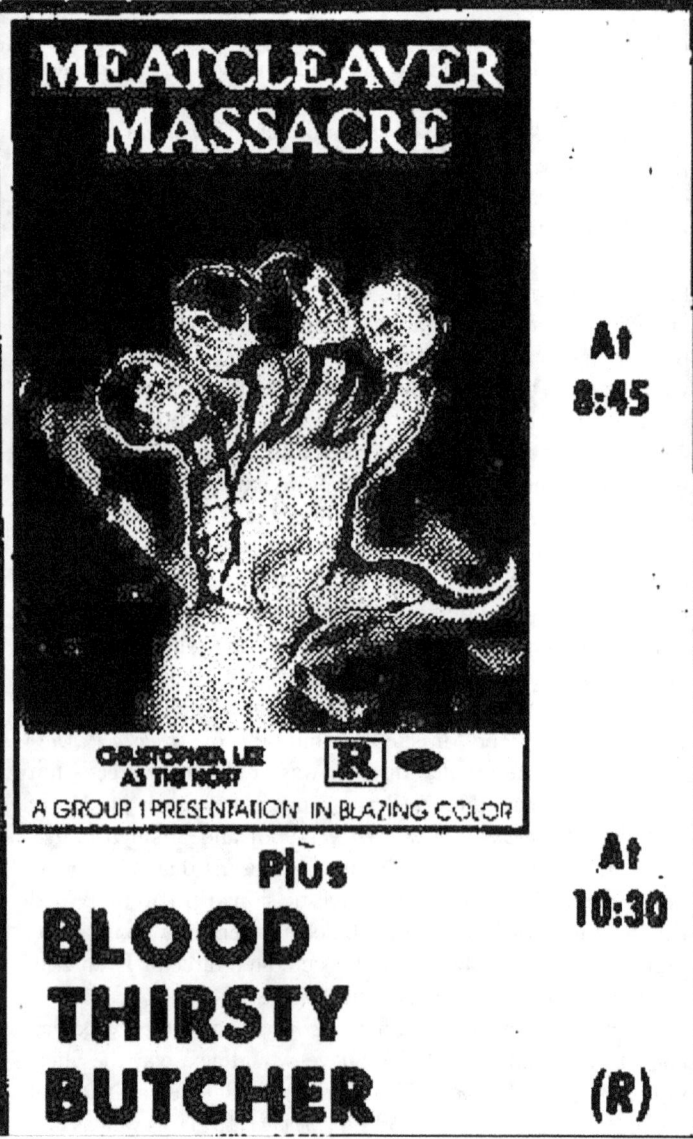

aligning himself with fellow Dracula actors who'd served as "horror hosts": During his British sojourn, Bela Lugosi compered an obscure compilation film entitled *Lock Up Your Daughters* (1951), which consists of scenes from the actor's Monogram horrors (including *Invisible Ghost*, *Spooks Run Wild* and *The Ape Man*). John Carradine followed suit via tacked-on footage to a Swedish sci-fier, *Invasion of the Animal People* (1958), then introduced trashy movie trailers, for producer Charles Band, in *The Best of Sex and Violence* (1981). That same year, Lee returned to horror hosting for a drama starring another screen *Dracula*, Jack Palance.

Advertised as "the unique late-night alternative," *Tales of the Haunted* consists of a five-part pilot, "Evil Stalks this House," for which Lee filmed his one-day introduction in Toronto. Directed by Gordon Hessler—whom the actor had last worked with on *Scream and Scream Again*—the stagy settings of "Evil Stalks this House" unfold like a 1960s *Dark Shadows* entry, with Palance as the unlikely father of two small children, huffing and panting his way through the titular weird house. The results, first broadcast in the US on Sunday, July 12, 1981, are not very stimulating and it's no surprise that a series never followed. To add insult to injury, subsequent showings pared all five episodes into a single hour, removing Lee's intro altogether.

Earlier in 1977, the actor had sat before a roaring fire, petting a black cat on his lap, as the host of *The Occult: Mysteries of the Supernatural*, a 25-minute documentary from the Encyclopedia Britannica Educational Corporation, directed by Victoria Hochberg (whose later TV work includes episodes of *Ally McBeal* and *Sex and the City*). Incorporating movie clips

Dark Places
1972

> I finished *Poor Devil* … on a Friday and started *Dark Places* the following Monday.—Christopher Lee, to Tom Johnson and Mark A. Miller

Immediately upon his return from Hollywood, Christopher Lee reunited with *Rasputin* and *Face of Fu Manchu* director Don Sharp for *Dark Places*. Compared to their previous collaborations, however, this was a thoroughly average affair.

Written by two American newcomers, Ed Brennan and Joseph Van Winkle, the film opens with Lee's Dr. Mandeville arriving at St. Columba's Mental Institution, announced by a thunderous burst of music (from composer Wilfred Josephs [1927-1997], who also scored *Cash on Demand*, *The Deadly Bees*, *Cry of the Banshee* and *The Uncanny*). Unfortunately, that's as exciting as the movie gets. What could have been a cozy supernatural chiller, in the tradition of *The Haunting* or *The Innocents*, becomes a rather tepid yarn involving greedy, unsympathetic protagonists coveting a fortune at a supposedly haunted house. ("A condemned house near Pinewood," Lee told Jonathan Rigby, "… extremely uncomfortable.")

What's more, it is revealed early on that the property's ghosts are merely a machination of Mandeville and his flirtatious sister Sarah (Joan Collins), who—in true *Scooby-Doo* fashion—wish to scare away the money's rightful inheritor, Edward Foster (Robert Hardy). While there's a subsequent hint that the hauntings may be real, this is not very convincing, and doesn't lead anywhere, rendering the "mystery" somewhat pointless (at least *Scooby-Doo* unmasks its phony phantoms in the end). Equally redundant are lengthy scenes of Hardy wandering around the house, patting the walls, as doors slam and a picture falls to the floor. He also suffers dull flashbacks involving Jane Birkin and Jean Marsh, which suggest he may be "possessed" by the murderous spirit of the building's former owner. Finally, in a mundane conclusion, he is arrested by the police, who also take the money. Although one longs to see a bony white face staring out from the window as Herbert Lom's duplicitous solicitor leaves the house empty-handed, no such thrill is forthcoming.

Despite winding up with a pickaxe in his chest, Lee is dependably good as the scheming doctor, and one of the few frissons displayed is provided by his onscreen relationship with Joan Collins. Engaged in frosty repartee at the dining table, one could be forgiven for mistaking them as husband and wife, rather than siblings. Indeed, Collins—who was fresh from playing Peter Cushing's spouse in *Fear in the Night*—was all set to play Lee's wife in *The Wicker Tree* (2009), but when Graham McTavish was cast as Sir Lachlan Morrison, a younger actress was selected instead.

Similar to Lee and Cushing, Collins (b. 1933) guested as an alien in *Space: 1999* (she even wears the same wig). A Golden Globe winner for *Dynasty*, Joan's other credits include the ill-fated love interest of Captain Kirk in *Star Trek*: "The City on the Edge of Forever" (1967), the inhabitant of a parallel universe in John Wyndham's *Quest for Love* (1970), an aggrieved stepmother in *Revenge* and the victim of a homicidal Santa Claus in *Tales from the Crypt*. After housing a monstrous tree in *Tales That Witness Madness*, she gave birth to a demonic baby in *I Don't Want to Be Born*, then cowered from the *Empire of the Ants* (1976). Her most recent performance is as Evie Gallant in *American Horror Story* (2011-).

"It's one of my small claims to fame that I transfixed Christopher Lee with a pickaxe," Robert Hardy (1925-2017) said of *Dark Places* (to David Taylor, in *LSoH* #31). Reteamed with Lee, as the school Headmaster, for *A Feast at Midnight*, one of Hardy's earliest roles was as the young man who has a "Vision of Crime" in Boris Karloff's *The Veil* (1958). Since then, he'd been Superintendent Brooks in *Berserk*, Baron Zorn in *Demons of the Mind*, the chief inspector of Don Sharp's *Psychomania*, the haunted archdeacon of *A Ghost Story for Christmas*: "The Stalls of Barchester" (1971), the Shakespearean actor who entertains the "Ghost of Venice" in *Supernatural* (1977) and Professor Krempe in *Mary Shelley's Frankenstein* (1993). A proverbial face on British TV as brash vet Siegfried Farnon in *All Creatures Great & Small* (1977-1990), Hardy won a whole new generation of fans when he became Cornelius Fudge, Minister of Magic, in the *Harry Potter* movies.

Hardy's mistress in *Dark Places* is played by Jane Birkin (b. 1946), who first gained notoriety with her nude scenes in *Blow-Up* (1966). After starring as a psychedelic mermaid in *Wonderwall* (1967), Birkin portrayed the imperiled heroine of *Seven Deaths in the Cat's Eye*, which also features her husband, Serge Gainsbourg (with whom she crooned and panted on the UK No. 1 hit "Je t'aime … moi non plus" [1969]). Jane had previously been married to Bond composer John Barry. The pair, who lived at the Thames-side penthouse building where Vincent Price takes a plunge in *Theatre of Blood*, were pictured with Christopher Lee and his wife at the 1966 Royal premiere of *Born Free*.

Jean Marsh (b. 1934), who plays Robert Hardy's wife in *Dark Places*, had just starred in Hitchcock's *Frenzy*. Submerged with Christopher Lee as the doctor on *Goliath Awaits* (1981), Jean's other roles include the tragic wife of George C. Scott in *The Changeling*, Mombi in *Return to Oz*, the evil Queen Bavmorda in *Willow* (1987) and Lady Constance de Momery in Mark Gatiss' supernatural mini-series *Crooked House* (2008). A former wife of *Doctor Who* star Jon Pertwee, Marsh made several contributions to that show, most notably as space agent Sara Kingdom in "The Daleks' Master Plan" (1965) and the villainous Morgaine in "Battlefield" (1989). (*Who* fans will further welcome the sight of John "Sergeant Benton" Levene as a doctor in *Dark Places*.)

Although some viewers might get a kick from the rare spectacle of Joan Collins doing the hoovering, there is little else to recommend about *Dark Places*, and the film would not see release in America until May 1974. Don Sharp would next direct Christopher Lee in the Alistair MacLean thriller *Bear Island* (1978), but back in 1972, the actor rounded out one of the busiest years of his career with a return to Hammer House—where he officially essayed his most famous character for a final time.

There's more than death waiting for you in dark places.

The Satanic Rites of Dracula
1972

> Vampire and vampire-hunter meet in one final, bloody conflict!

> From what inspirational abyss Hammer dredged up the script for their latest Dracula film one trembles to think ... Fortunately, Christopher Lee and Peter Cushing are on hand to lend the film what little dignity it has.—Nigel Andrews, *Financial Times*

> When I think about the films I made with Peter, the memories I have are not of what we achieved, but what we got away with, what we accomplished despite far from ideal conditions.—Christopher Lee, to Bill Kelley (*LSoH #13*, 1996)

> I think we all knew it was the last one, really. We all felt it was scraping the bottom of the barrel.—Assistant director Derek Whitehurst to Wayne Kinsey (*Hammer's Film Legacy*)

The second of the modern-day Hammer vampire films contracted by Warner Bros. began production at Elstree on Monday, November 13, 1972, before the disappointing box office returns from *Dracula A.D. 1972* had come in. Christopher Lee joined the sequel, for a guaranteed sum of £20,000, on Monday, December 18, once his work on *Dark Places* was complete. In an article by Don Glut, "Dracula's Last Stand" (*Monsters of the Movies #2*, August 1974), the actor brought his own unique approach to movie promotion: "I'm doing the next one under protest. I just think it's fatuous. I can think of 20 adjectives—fatuous, pointless, absurd. It's not a comedy. At least with me it's not a comedy. But it's a comic title. I don't see the point. I don't see what they hope to achieve. I think it's playing down to people."

While there is some justification to Lee's grumbling about its shooting title, *Dracula is Dead and Well and Living in London* (not altogether dissimilar to the moniker Mel Brooks appended to his farcical interpretation, *Dracula: Dead and Loving It*), the film that emerged as *The Satanic Rites of Dracula* is solid and entertaining, with screenwriter Don Houghton and director Alan Gibson actually improving on *Dracula A.D. 1972* in their efforts to blend the vampire into contemporary society. More significantly, Peter Cushing—wearing a natty brown Aquascutum overcoat from his own wardrobe—is paired with Lee for their final Hammer horror together.

Joining them, as jittery Professor Keeley, is Freddie Jones (1927-2019), an agreeably outlandish performer, who had not only been one of Cushing's most sympathetic "monsters" in *Frankenstein Must Be Destroyed* but was also fresh from essaying a bemonocled Baron Frankenstein in Freddie Francis' *Son of Dracula*. An ex-laboratory assistant, Jones started acting in his mid-20s, eventually becoming familiar through such television roles as Claudius in *The Caesars*, an eccentric, mind-swapping villain in *The Avengers* and a pop-eyed, BAFTA-nominated "Sweeney Todd" on *Mystery and Imagination*. His other credits include a camp lounge lizard in *Goodbye Gemini*, a Scottish psychiatrist in *The Man Who Haunted Himself* (1969), the scientist responsible for *Firestarter* (1983) and the desecrator of a mummy's tomb in *Young Sherlock Holmes*. After playing a blind man on radio alongside Vincent Price (in *The Price of Fear*: "Blind Man's Bluff" [1974]), Jones made three films with David Lynch (*The Elephant Man*; *Dune*; *Wild at Heart* [1989]), then guest-starred as an accursed veterinarian in *The League of Gentlemen*'s Amicus-inspired Christmas Special (2000). (Freddie's son, Toby [b. 1966], voices Dobby in *Harry Potter*, fights off monsters from *The Mist* [2007] and stars as Alfred Hitchcock in *The Girl* [2012].)

Replacing an otherwise engaged Stephanie Beacham, Jessica Van Helsing is a flame-haired Joanna Lumley (b. 1946). "I had seen Christopher Lee in *The Mummy* at the Hastings Roxy," Lumley wrote in her autobiography, *Stare Back and Smile* (Penguin, 1989), adding: "All his villains are somehow victims at the same time, and his victims as noble as kings." Lumley, too, succeeds in making the role of Jessica her own, despite being attacked by a basement full of vampires. Best known as Patsy Stone, the hilariously ramshackle fashion editor of *Absolutely Fabulous* (1992-2012), Joanna is also one of Blofeld's Angels of Death in *On Her Majesty's Secret Service*, Robot No. 2 in *Some Girls Do* and the ass-kicking Purdey of *The New Avengers* (1976-1977), the first episode of which, "The Eagle's Nest," stars Peter Cushing as a Frankenstein-like scientist. (Other guest spots in this borderline horror series are filled by John Carson and Caroline Munro.) Lumley's other roles include the first half of mysterious Time Agents *Sapphire & Steel* (1979-1982, the fifth season of which was co-written by Don Houghton), the reporter on the *Trail of the Pink Panther* (1982) and a couple of Tim Burton harridans in *James and the Giant Peach* (1995) and *Corpse Bride* (2004, with Lee).

Japanese poster.

Suave SI7 agent Torrence is essayed by actor William Franklyn (1925-2006), whose velvet tones could be heard on many a commercial for Schweppes tonic water between 1965 and 1973. Having last worked for Hammer in the late 1950s (as one of Brian Donlevy's fellow scientists in *Quatermass 2*, and the skeptical British Consulate in *The Snorkel*), Franklyn had previously starred with Peter Cushing as a highwayman in *Fury at Smugglers' Bay*. (A film which had originally been set to star Christopher Lee.)

Torrence's assistant, Matthews, is played by Richard Vernon (1925-1997), who was just as officious in *Village of the Damned*, *Goldfinger* and *A Hard Day's Night*, but played a far humbler character alongside Cushing in *Cash on Demand*. (Vernon had also been Professor Krempe to Ian Holm's "Frankenstein" on *Mystery and Imagination* [1968].)

SI7 secretary Jane is Valerie Van Ost (1944-2019), who had played in two earlier Cushing creepies, both directed by Robert Hartford-Davis: A small role in *Incense for the Damned* was preceded by *Corruption* (1967), in which Peter beheads her aboard a train. Valerie later became a casting director, pairing fellow Hammer alumni Barbara Ewing and Andrew Keir for *Haunters of the Deep* (1984), a typically charming supernatural effort from the Children's Film Foundation.

Dracula's disciple, Chin Yang, is portrayed by Barbara Yu Ling (1938-1997), who, credited as Barbara Lee, can be seen as one of the female prisoners in *The Camp on Blood Island*. After playing the recurring role of May in TV's *Tenko* (1981-1984), she made a second genre appearance in Richard Stanley's *Hardware* (1989).

The most striking of Lee's vampire brides in *Satanic Rites* is Pauline Peart (b. Halloween 1951). Having appeared with Ingrid Pitt in *Nobody Ordered Love*, Pauline later joined another Hammer heroine, Valerie Leon, for *Carry on Girls* (1973), before playing Arthur Lowe's secretary in *Man About the House* (1974) and the girlfriend of Jack Weston in *Cuba* (1978).

Christopher Lee often described Hammer's representation of Dracula in *Satanic Rites* as "a mixture of Dr. No and Howard Hughes," and this is perfectly encapsulated by the film's title credits: To the accompaniment of John Cacavas' sterling theme, the vampire's twisted shadow enlarges and envelops England's capital. We are then immediately present at a Black Mass, something which Anthony Hinds doubted "we'll ever be allowed to film" (in *She* magazine, 1966). Six years later this was more than possible, and the ceremony which opens *Satanic Rites* comes complete with a naked woman (Mia Martin) and a bleeding cockerel (unknown). The Mass is presided over by Chin Yang, and attended by such luminaries as a government official, an important landowner and the Nobel Prize-winning Keeley. One attendee, however, does not show up in the photographs surreptitiously taken by an SI7 spy ...

In his unpublished notes for *Dracula*, Bram Stoker alludes that the likeness of vampires cannot be photographed—an intriguing idea which is never mentioned in the finished novel, but is employed by Don Houghton here, along with some refreshing notions from European folklore. Slickly incorporated amid the film's more modern contrivances (the "chocka-chocka" soundtrack and *Avengers*-style action pieces), Van Helsing mentions such vampire deterrents as the purity of silver—although long associated with werewolves, this is also closely linked to vampiric superstition—and hawthorn, which derives from the shrub's sacred associations with Christ's crown of thorns.

Lee's misty materialization in *Dracula A.D. 1972* was an earlier nod from Houghton to folkloric descriptions of the Undead. In a similarly vaporous moment, Dracula first appears a good half hour into *Satanic Rites*, vamping his bruised captive, Valerie Van Ost, against the dirty yellow wallpaper of a sparse, cramped room—so at odds with the pristine maidens of old, reclining in ornately furnished chambers; only Lee's seductive pre-bite caresses remain the same.

Doubly different is the vampire's modern-day guise as property developer D.D. Denham—a rather apt thing for a vampire to be in 1970s London, given the proliferation of soulless skyscrapers blotting the city's horizon. From this position, he successfully inveigles a corrupt Establishment in his diabolical schemes. Residing in an office block (152 Grosvenor Road, Pimlico), Van Helsing finds him seated at a desk, sans cloak, silhouetted behind sliding doors (an image ostensibly borrowed from John Gilling's *The Night Caller*, whose alien invader adopts an identical camouflage on Earth). In what he described, to Mark A. Miller, as a "personal tribute" to Bela Lugosi, Lee speaks with a Hungarian accent—a nice touch!

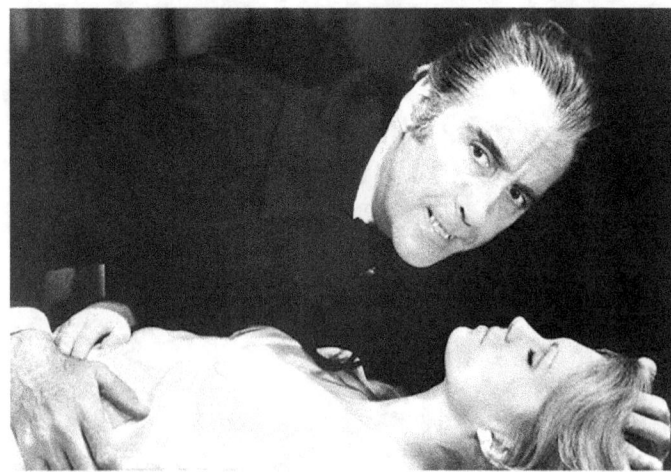

Jessica (Joanna Lumley) lies supine on the altar beneath the ravenous Dracula.

(Elsewhere, the script pays homage to another screen Dracula by naming one of the Count's acolytes Lord Carradine.) Once rumbled, the vampire has Van Helsing taken to his residence, Pelham House. (A jokey reference to James Carreras' home in Pelham Place; the exterior is High Canons, Hertfordshire, which also doubles as Mocata's lair in *The Devil Rides Out*.)

Here, Van Helsing is forced to look on as Jessica lies supine on an altar beneath the ravenous Count ("the King of the Undead marries the Queen of the Zombies," the film's US trailer cried misleadingly). In the ultimate expression of his "loneliness of evil," Dracula has a suicidal death wish to wipe out humanity via a specially created strand of bubonic plague. As Lee explains in *Flesh and Blood*: "You are living and yet you are dead—the Undead. You cannot die. You must *want* to."

Joanna Lumley recalled in her memoirs that Lee "always carried Bram Stoker's original *Dracula* with him and protected the reputation of the evil Count by refusing to sensationalize ..." Indeed, amid the subsequent climactic flames, Lee inserts a paraphrased line from Stoker, which he delivers with great relish: "My revenge has spread over centuries and has just begun!" (The actual line from the novel is: "My revenge is just begun. I spread it over centuries and time is on my side," which Lee culminates with a bloodcurdling laugh in his mid-1990s audiobook recording.)

Ultimately, Lee's feral portrayal of the Count remains the closest to Stoker's conception, and, despite allegations to the contrary, this is most apparent in *Satanic Rites*. As in the novel, Dracula is operating his Machiavellian schemes in the present-day, while the motorcycle thugs in his employ are the equivalent of the similarly sheepskin-clad Gypsies who aid him in the book. What's more, in accordance with Stoker, Lee presents a villain whose instincts are those of a wild animal—quite different from the dignified figure introduced to the world by Bela Lugosi. Indeed, Lee is at his most tigerish at the dissolution of *Satanic Rites*, where, confronting Cushing's formidable Van Helsing for a final time, he fights his way through a hawthorn bush in order to reach his prey.

Filming of this scene—which took place on the evening of Wednesday, December 27 (Lee's last day on-set) after a four-day break over Christmas—naturally, didn't pass without incident. "Dying as Dracula was usually worse than having a tooth out," Lee recorded in his memoirs, where he also remembered emerging from the hawthorn, "shedding genuine Lee blood like a garden sprinkler." As the actor reported to Mark A. Miller: "When I got to the set Alan Gibson said to me, 'We've got a bit of a problem, Mr. Lee.' I said, 'Tell me about it,' because these films were nothing else but problems from the first day to the last." Unfortunately, the prop bush that was supposed to have arrived for the scene was still in situ, so the actor had to make his way, painfully, through the real thing. "I got quite cut up," Lee told Miller. "A lot of that blood is real."

Shooting wrapped on Wednesday, January 3, 1973—exactly 15 years to the day that filming was finished on Lee's first Hammer *Dracula*. Still known as *Dracula is Dead*, etc. during post-production, Warner Bros. retitled the film *The Satanic Rites of Dracula* for issue in the UK from January 13, 1974, on a double bill with *Blacula*. The movie's British poster by Tom Chantrell—who painted the masterly cover of Denis Gifford's *A Pictorial History of Horror Movies*—depicts Dracula holding his arms aloft "as though he's scored a goal" (in Tom's words). Originally, the Count had been holding a sacrificial dagger in one hand, and a dead cockerel in the other, but Chantrell was told to remove the items due to their potentially offensive allusions to black magic.

Despite care in its promotion, the film flopped badly at the British box office, and an even worse fate awaited it in America: Sold to AIP by Warners, *Satanic Rites* sat on a shelf for four years, before being pawned off to Max J. Rosenberg's Dynamite Entertainment. The latter finally granted the movie US distribution as *Count Dracula and His Vampire Bride* in November 1978. (The following year, Dynamite released an edited version of *The Legend of the 7 Golden Vampires*.) This delayed release was prompted by the resounding success of Frank Langella's 1977 Broadway revival of the Hamilton Deane play, which Lee had turned down.

For all of its merits, a melancholy suffuses *Satanic Rites*: This is not only reflected in the gloomy hues of cinematographer Brian Probyn (1920-1982)—who also lit *Frankenstein and the Monster from Hell*—but also the inevitable credo that nothing lasts forever; one can't help but feel that the magic Lee and Cushing brought to Hammer horror (since *The Curse of Frankenstein* in 1956) reaches its natural close with *Satanic Rites*, something which would become even more apparent on the film's belated release in the wake of *The Exorcist*.

"I wasn't happy doing those films," Lee told Marcus Hearn, of his last two Dracula films, likening them to "taking the same train journey every day. Nothing is changing." To Lee's way of thinking, if the work no longer represented a challenge, then it wasn't worth doing. He had done everything he could with the

character. So, as he recorded in his memoirs, "At the age of 50, I took the firm decision to Draculate no more."

In the wake of Lee hanging up his cloak, we were treated to a glut of Draculas: Sunday, March 25, 1973, saw Canada's *Purple Playhouse* broadcast a concise yet faithful staging of Stoker's novel with Norman Welsh as a white-haired vampire who crawls down his castle wall and laughs a lot, until he is staked by Mina (Blair Brown). Just over a month later, on April 30, 1973, filming began at Shepperton on another TV adaptation, this time from *Dark Shadows* producer Dan Curtis and screenwriter Richard Matheson. With scenes inspired directly by Hammer's *Dracula*, this version benefits from some impressive locations and Jack Palance's surprisingly effective interpretation of the Count. Indeed, Lee himself was an admirer of Jack's performance, as he revealed on *In Search of Dracula with Jonathan Ross*: "The moment Palance appears on the screen, you can't take your eyes off him."

Less impressive was Clive Donner's *Vampira* (retitled *Old Dracula* on its November 1975 US release), which began filming at Elstree on July 30, 1973, with David Niven in the cape and fangs. Written by Joanna Lumley's ex-husband Jeremy Lloyd, this daft, politically incorrect comedy could not be further removed from Curtis' somber production. A bridge between the two styles was filmed in Italy from May 20, 1973: Paul Morrissey's *Blood for Dracula* stars Udo Kier as an oddly endearing, anemic Count who spews forth torrents of blood if it comes from an "impure" container.

In October 1973, London's Dracula Society was formed and Christopher Lee was made sole President, a position he still retains—as the Society's website states: "Who could possibly have followed him?!" Around the same time, Lee became an honorary president, along with Terence Fisher and TV comedian Bob Monkhouse, of the Gothique Film Society—a group of like-minded individuals who gathered to watch (what were then) hard-to-find fantasy movies in a screening room above Holborn Library. If his schedule permitted, Lee could be found among the audience, chatting to fans during the intervals, including, once, at a showing of *Nosferatu*.

From Monday, October 22 to Tuesday, December 11, 1973, Hammer were in Hong Kong making their first Dracula film without Lee in the role, *The Legend of the 7 Golden Vampires*. Screenwriter Don Houghton was influential in setting up Hammer's co-production deal with the Shaw Brothers, as his wife, Pik-Sen Lim—star of Don's *Doctor Who* entry "The Mind of Evil"—was an acquaintance of Run Run Shaw. Houghton's script had not originally included Dracula, but when Warner Bros. insisted that the character be featured, the writer simply bookended him into the action. While Michael Carreras kept telling the press that they needed "a younger, sexier Dracula"—even going so far as to propose a national talent contest to find one—the *Melody Maker* review of *7 Golden Vampires* eventually stated: "The part of Christopher Lee is played by a gent named John Forbes-Robertson, who … looks like an old queen whose make-up has run."

Forbes-Robertson (1928-2008) had previously played the sinister "Man in Black" for *The Vampire Lovers* and told Wayne Kinsey: "When it came to *Scars of Dracula*, Christopher Lee was being difficult and Roy [Ward Baker] offered the part to me. Then suddenly Christopher was back so that was the end of that. Roy must have remembered, because when he came to *The Legend of the 7 Golden Vampires*, he asked me again after Christopher had refused to play the part." (Forbes-Robertson would later feature with Lee in *The Far Pavilions*.)

Despite certain imperfections, *The Legend of the 7 Golden Vampires* is a bold and somewhat innovative melding of Kung Fu and horror, which offers the refreshing spectacle of Peter Cushing's Van Helsing battling moldy-faced vampires in a new locale.

February 1974 saw Cushing give an atypical performance as a bonkers horror star who dresses like Lugosi's Count in *Tender Dracula*—a French farce from director Pierre Grunstein, which had originally been offered to Lee (as revealed in a fan club newsletter). Although virtually plotless, the heroines' song in the old dark castle does have a bizarre *Rocky Horror Show* charm and the film's imagery causes one to wonder how Cushing would have tackled the role of Dracula in a serious adaptation.

That same year, Peter told John Brosnan: "[Christopher's] been such a dear friend. And it's taken tremendous courage on his part to break away from horror films and succeed in something different … But I think he will play Dracula again if and when a definitive version is done. He just doesn't want to keep on playing in the sort of Dracula film he has been playing—'Dracula in the Dark,' 'Dracula Meets Frankenstein,' 'Search the House for Dracula' and that sort of thing. As he said, the Van Helsing character, even though it's the same character, is more interesting; but all he has to do as Dracula is stand in a corner, show his fangs, and hiss. I do see his point, but if a good one comes along he'll do it, I know he will." Just as intriguing as Cushing's proposed film titles is his mention of Lee's desire to play Van Helsing. Aside from his audio reading of the novel, the closest Lee came to this was his stern, mustachioed vampire hunter, staking the memoirs of Richard Nixon for *Saturday Night Live* in 1978.

For the remainder of the '70s, Lee's vampiric image lived on through a series of Hammer bubble gum cards from Topps, as well as various television screenings (*The Curse of Frankenstein*, *Dracula*, and *The Mummy* had been sold to ITV for their first British small-screen outings in 1972). Towards the end of 1973, however—following his work on *The Three/Four Musketeers* and an experimental French comedy, *Le boucher, le star et l'orpheline*, alongside *Nosferatu the Vampyre*'s Roland Topor and *Daughters of Darkness*' Delphine Seyrig—the actor reunited with Alan Gibson for an all-new dip into TV terror.

Dracula is staked yet again by Van Helsing (Peter Cushing).

Orson Welles Great Mysteries: "The Leather Funnel," 1973

Space: 1999: "Earthbound" (1974)

> The charlatan is always the pioneer. From the astrologer came the astronomer, from the alchemist the chemist, from the mesmerist, the experimental psychologist. The quack of yesterday is the professor of tomorrow. Even such subtle and elusive things as dreams will in time be reduced to system and order …—Sir Arthur Conan Doyle, "The Leather Funnel" (1902)

The night before Halloween 1938, Orson Welles (1915-1985) brought panic to America with his ingenious radio adaptation of *The War of the Worlds*. Earlier that year, he had essayed both the Count and Dr. Seward in an efficient audio dramatization of *Dracula*, while also giving voice to *The Shadow*—a mysterious crime fighter, inspired by Stoker's vampire. But Welles' Gothic grandeur first graced the movies via *Citizen Kane* (1940)—the beginning of which mimics the opening shots from *Son of Frankenstein*. Indeed, the director's *Macbeth* (1947), with its Expressionistic settings, looks just like a Universal horror show.

When the over-budgeted *Kane* failed commercially, RKO deemed it necessary to create a low-budget horror unit as a sure-fire means of seeing profit. Thus, Orson became inadvertently responsible for masterworks like *Cat People* and *The Curse of the Cat People* (1943), which not only take place on grand sets from Welles' *The Magnificent Ambersons* (1941), but also employ that film's editors Mark Robson and Robert Wise.

By 1946, William Castle—future director of *13 Ghosts* and *Strait-Jacket*—brought *The Lady from Shanghai* to Orson's attention, and served as associate producer on the movie. "I've only met three geniuses in my lifetime," Castle told John Brosnan: "One was Orson Welles … the second was Charlie Chaplin … The third is the great Marcel Marceau [star of Castle's *Shanks*]."

While it's very unlikely that a chance encounter with Orson inspired Edward D. Wood, Jr. to complete *Plan 9 from Outer Space* (as depicted in Tim Burton's *Ed Wood* [1993]), Welles *did* influence one of the 1960s most seminal horror movies, as George Romero told *Fangoria*: "[*Night of the Living Dead*] probably borrows or steals more directly from Orson Welles than it does from anyone else. Just the lighting style and the angles call up a little of *Macbeth* or *Citizen Kane*. Not that it achieves it as well, but if I had anything in mind at the time, it was that."

Welles' own love for the bizarre manifested in a voodoo stage version of *Macbeth* (1936)—certain cast members of which stuck pins into a doll of critic Percy Hammond, who duly dropped dead—and a flair for conjuring, which left Peter Sellers fearful that Orson would sprinkle some bad juju on his performance in *Casino Royale* (1966). Hence, the actors were filmed separately, then, using cinema magic, their footage was spliced together to make it look as though they appeared in the same scene.

Other Gothic signifiers in the Welles filmography include his brooding portrayals of Rochester in *Jane Eyre* (1943, a moors-bound Kurt Menliff with a false nose); Cagliostro in *Black Magic* (1947, a hypnotic forerunner to *Rasputin: The Mad Monk*) and the Magician of *A Safe Place* (1970, a down-at-heels Saruman). Additionally, there's the "true" ghost story, *Return to Glennascaul* (1951); an amusing turn as Lord Mountdrago in *Three Cases of Murder* (1953), which prefigures the humiliation angle of Lee's *Dr. Terror's House of Horrors* segment; the grotesque masked revelers in the castle of *Mr. Arkadin* (1954); a wry half-hour take on John Collier's *The Fountain of Youth* (1956), which explores the same themes as *The Man Who Could Cheat Death*; the nightmare logic of *The Trial* (1962) and some exquisite narration for *Night Gallery*: "Silent Snow, Secret Snow" (1971).

Having also starred in such overt horror pictures as *Necromancy* (1970) and *Malpertuis* (1971), Welles became a natural choice to present his own late-night anthology series. Aired by Anglia TV between September 1973 and February 1974, *Orson Welles Great Mysteries* comprises 26 half-hour stories, including Balzac's "La Grande Bretèche" with Peter Cushing, and James Reach's "A Time to Remember," with Patrick Macnee and Charles Gray. Other guest stars throughout the series include Joan Collins, Donald Pleasence and Thorley Walters, while direction is supplied by such talents as Peter Sasdy, Peter Sykes and Alan Gibson. The latter guided Christopher Lee through "The Leather Funnel," which was first broadcast on Saturday, September 8, 1973.

Lee had introduced Sir Arthur Conan Doyle's original tale as "a favorite of mine" in *Christopher Lee's New Chamber of Horrors*, and screenwriter David Ambrose (whose future credits include *Amityville 3-D* [1983] and *D.A.R.Y.L.* [1985]) presents a reasonably faithful adaptation, adding only a romantic angle to an updated setting: Stephen Barrow (Simon Ward) visits the oak-paneled, skull-festooned study of Arnaud (Lee) with a desire to marry the latter's niece, Veronique (a simmering portrayal from Jane Seymour). The young suitor is frightened away, however, by Arnaud's dark insinuations and a nightmare-haunted sleep.

Lee brings a well-measured mixture of charm and chilliness to his bow-tie-sporting occultist, giving a good indication of how he would have tackled the role of Mocata in *The Devil Rides Out*.

The episode benefits from a creepy choral soundtrack and splendid cast: Simon Ward (1941-2012), who had already appeared with Jane Seymour in *Young Winston* (1971), was also fresh from playing the foppish Duke of Buckingham in *The Three Musketeers* and Arthur Holmwood in the Jack Palance *Dracula*. After

Christopher Lee, Jane Seymour and Simon Ward

making his film debut as an uncredited schoolboy in Lindsay Anderson's *If ...* (1968), he was Peter Cushing's beleaguered assistant in *Frankenstein Must Be Destroyed* and a murderous bus conductor in *I Start Counting* (1969). His other roles include the Antichrist in *Holocaust 2000* (1977), shifty sorts in Milton Subotsky's *Dominique* (1977) and *The Monster Club*, and Zor-El, father of *Supergirl* (1983). Simon's real-life daughter, Sophie Ward (b. 1964), is no stranger to the genre herself, having starred in *Return to Oz*, *Young Sherlock Holmes* and Clive Barker's *Book of Blood* (2009).

Following leads in *Live and Let Die*, *Sinbad and the Eye of the Tiger*, *Battlestar Galactica* (1978), the 1982 *Phantom of the Opera* and the 1988 *Jack the Ripper*, Jane Seymour (b. 1951) was reacquainted with Christopher Lee when he chopped off her head in *La Revolution Française* (1989; she'd also been decapitated as the female monster in *Frankenstein: The True Story*). "I adored working with Christopher again," Jane told Sam Irvin in *LSoH* #38. "He was such a character."

The theme tune of *Orson Welles Great Mysteries* is composed by John Barry (1933-2011). Most famous for his sterling work on the James Bond franchise, Barry's debut score was for *Beat Girl* (1959)—the first British movie to have an accompanying soundtrack album. Barry's other credits include *Séance on a Wet Afternoon*, a musical version of *Alice's Adventures in Wonderland* (1972), the 1976 *King Kong*, *Starcrash*, *The Black Hole* (1978) and *Somewhere in Time* (1979, with Jane Seymour).

Alan Gibson, who directed six other *Great Mysteries*—including "The Monkey's Paw" with Patrick Magee—would go on to helm two of Hammer's finest TV hours ("The Silent Scream" and "The Two Faces of Evil"), as well as two entries of Brian Clemens' *Thriller*, 10 *Tales of the Unexpected*, a TV-movie with Peter Cushing (*Helen Keller: The Miracle Continues* [1983]) and a video documentary entitled *The Best of All Time Horror Classics* (1985). He passed away from cancer at the age of 49 in July 1987.

Although Orson Welles only introduces "The Leather Funnel" (giving a brief preamble on the mysterious nature of dreams), Christopher Lee could at least take consolation from the fact that he had worked with the great director before—albeit on the abandoned *Moby Dick Rehearsed*. During filming of the latter at the Hackney Empire in 1955, it was Lee's job to ferry Orson to and from the theater in a tiny car that struggled to contain the two giants within. In 1974, both men would find their careers linked once more: Welles followed Lee by lending his voice to Harry Alan Towers' second version of *Ten Little Indians* (*And Then There Were None*), while the funhouse finale of *The Lady from Shanghai* informed the look of Lee's next feature film, *The Man with the Golden Gun*.

Before shooting that Bond epic, however, Lee reteamed with Charles Crichton (director of *The Avengers*: "The Interrogators") for another "special guest star" role at ITV. Filmed at Pinewood from Friday, March 15 to Monday, April 1, 1974, Lee donned a green robe, startling eye make-up and a long white wig to play extra-terrestrial Captain Zantor in "Earthbound"—the fifth episode of *Space: 1999*. Conceived as a follow-up to their first live-action series *UFO* (1969-1970), producers Gerry and Sylvia Anderson were determined that *Space: 1999* would be the sci-fi show to end all sci-fi shows, spending an estimated $300,000 on each episode and casting Martin Landau (1928-2017) as Moon traveler Commander Koenig.

Landau—whose other credits include the sinister henchman of *North by Northwest* (1958), the psychical investigator of

Christopher Lee in "Earthbound'

The Ghost of Sierra de Cobre (1964), a toxic waste expert in *The Being* (1980) and an Oscar-winning Bela Lugosi in *Ed Wood*—was joined by real-life wife Barbara Bain (b. 1931), whom he'd met while filming *Mission: Impossible*. (Their daughter, Juliet Landau [b. 1965], is the vampiric Drusilla on *Buffy the Vampire Slayer*.) Other series regulars included Barry Morse (1918-2008), who was fresh from grappling with Peter Cushing in *Asylum*, and Catherine Schell (b. 1944; *Moon Zero Two*, *The Prisoner of Zenda* [1978]).

Reactions to *Space: 1999* were mixed, but it did pick up some famous fans in Apollo 13 captain Jim Lovell and sci-fi writer Isaac Asimov. In addition, George Lucas was so impressed by Brian Johnson's special effects work that he hired him on *The Empire Strikes Back*. Johnson (b. 1939), whose previous credits include *Taste the Blood of Dracula*, would win Oscars for both the Lucas film and *Alien*.

"Earthbound" premiered on Thursday, December 4, 1975, in the UK (and Monday, January 19, 1976, in the US). First discovered lying atop a glowing sarcophagus like an intergalactic vampire, Lee's Zantor is a serene alien leader who moves with stately grace while extolling the virtues of suspended animation. When crew member Commissioner Simmonds (Roy Dotrice) goes berserk, zapping everyone in sight, Zantor calmly offers himself as a hostage, before outwitting the villain.

Roy Dotrice (1923-2017) would be reunited with Lee on the TV mini-series *Shaka Zulu* (1985), before playing a Dracula-like character in *Tales from the Darkside*: "My Ghostwriter, the Vampire" (1986) and guesting on *Buffy the Vampire Slayer* spin-off *Angel* (1999-2004). In real life, Dotrice was father-in-law to *The Wicker Man*'s Edward Woodward.

Despite such a fine cast, and the charm of Anderson's model spaceships, *Space: 1999* is curiously lifeless and never quite catches fire in the same way as *Star Trek*—which it emulates—or *Doctor Who*.

Future episodes saw Peter Cushing, Margaret Leighton, Leo McKern and Joan Collins inherit Lee's wig for their respective alien turns. Some fans recall that, in later years, Lee was reluctant to sign any stills of him as Zantor. Presumably that hand-me-down hairpiece had something to do with it.

To the Devil a Daughter
1975

… and suddenly the screams of a baby born in Hell!

Give me that look … You know, that look you give people on the screen, and it chills the very marrow in their bones.—Muhammad Ali, to Christopher Lee, March 1975.

Now that's a film you wanna burn! That's, like, so—so terrible!—Nastassja Kinski, on *To the Devil a Daughter* (to Nicolas Barbano, 1996)

In 1973, Hammer proposed a 13-part television series of Dennis Wheatley tales, entitled *The Devil and All His Works* (after Wheatley's factual book of that name), which would have seen Christopher Lee return as the Duc de Richleau. Unfortunately, this was never made. But the Devil would ride out once more for a disturbing classic, which—more than any movie since *The Curse of Frankenstein*—changed the look and feel of horror: When *The Exorcist* was released to American theaters on December 26, 1973, there were reports of mass hysteria; audience members fainted and threw up, while evangelist Billy Graham apparently declaimed: "The Devil is in every frame of the film."

Following its March 1974 British release, Christopher Lee offered his own views on *The Exorcist*, to John Brosnan: "I haven't seen it and I have no desire to see it. I don't say that I disapprove of it, it's just that I have no particular desire to see the possession of a very young child, with her using that kind of language and doing those sorts of things."

Michael Carreras, on the other hand, gave a very different take to the same author: "When I first saw *The Exorcist*, it really frightened me … To be perfectly honest, I wish I'd made that film."

In order to compete, Hammer again turned to the Satanic writings of Dennis Wheatley. As we have seen, the author's 1953 novel *To the Devil a Daughter* had originally been prepared for screen treatment by Christopher Lee's Charlemagne Productions. When *Nothing But the Night* bombed, the actor offered the rights to Hammer. After their own recent flops, including *The Satanic Rites of Dracula*, the company knew that their latest horror would have to be something very special. Thus, along with a top-notch cast, they engaged a slightly higher budget ($1 million) and longer shooting schedule (eight weeks, from Monday, September 1 to Friday, October 24, 1975). In short, the very future of Hammer horror rested on the success of *To the Devil a Daughter*.

Scripting duties fell initially to John Peacock (1945-2017), whose play *Children of the Wolf* had so impressed Michael Carreras that it inspired the plots of both *Twins of Evil* and *Demons of the Mind* (Carreras also put the star of the play, Shane Briant, under contract, casting him in the latter film). Hammer arranged a screening of *The Exorcist* for Peacock in March 1974 to help influence his adaptation of Wheatley's book. Somewhere along the line, though, Peacock's script was completely rewritten by *Scream and Scream Again*'s Christopher Wicking. Then, much to Wicking's chagrin, an uncredited Gerald Vaughan-Hughes—screenwriter of Dirk Bogarde's *Sebastian* (1968)—was hired by producer Roy Skeggs to provide further rewrites while the film was in production. Literally making it up as they went along, the results got further and further from Wheatley's original story, causing no end of confusion for cast and crew. (Wicking would go on to script *Lady Chatterley's Lover* [1981], with Shane Briant; the David Bowie musical *Absolute Beginners* [1985] and *Dream Demon* [1987], an interesting *Nightmare on Elm Street* variant.)

Following refusals from Don Sharp, Ken Russell and Alan Gibson, among others, Peter Sykes (1939-2006) was eventually selected to direct. A former TV director, with two episodes of *The Avengers* under his belt, Sykes made his feature debut with the experimental fantasy *The Committee* (1968), before wowing Michael Carreras with his second film *Venom* (1970)—a stylish but suspense-free rethink of *The Reptile*, this time concerning a Nazi-created "spider goddess." The Australian filmmaker next brought a visual grace to *Demons of the Mind*, before creating an enjoyable Gothic pastiche with *The House in Nightmare Park* (starring Frankie Howerd and Ray Milland).

With a reluctant EMI agreeing to provide 50% of the budget, a cash-strapped Hammer was forced to seek a co-production deal. When Universal, Warner Bros. and AIP all balked at the project, co-funding came, instead, from the German company Terra Filmkunst, whose one stipulation was that a native actor be cast in a leading role. This led to 14-year-old Nastassja Kinski winning the part of Devil's avatar Catherine Beddows, over the likes of Twiggy, Olivia Newton-John and Jane Seymour. Following global stardom as Roman Polanski's *Tess* (1978), Nastassja would lend her presence to remakes of *Cat People* (1981; a former Milton Subotsky project) and *The Day the World Ended* (2001).

In the role of occult author John Verney, Hammer had initially hoped to cast Nastassja's father Klaus—whom Lee had last starred with in *Count Dracula*. But, as the volatile thespian admitted to Peter Sykes that he couldn't promise to be on his best behavior for the duration of the shoot, Richard Widmark (1914-2008) was cast instead (Orson Welles, Richard Dreyfuss and Anthony Perkins were other considerations). Following an early radio role as Boris Karloff's murderous son-in-law on "The Corridor of Doom," a 1945 *Inner Sanctum Mystery*, Widmark made his Oscar-nominated screen debut as snickering hoodlum Tommy Udo in *Kiss of Death* (1947). One unforgettable moment in that classic film noir sees him push a lady in a wheelchair down some stairs and, by all accounts, the actor was just as much of a nuisance on the Hammer shoot; kicking over wind machines, being rude to the crew and calling the company "Mickey Mouse Productions" to anyone in earshot (the crew, in turn, nicknamed him "Skidmark"). "He was a difficult monkey, Richard," Honor Blackman confirmed in David Gregory's 2002 DVD documentary *To the Devil ... The Death of Hammer*.

Nevertheless, Widmark is very good in the finished film, bringing a no-nonsense candor to lines like: "98% of so-called Satanists are nothing but pathetic freaks ... I have a feeling we're dealing with that other 2%," and, later, unleashing a remarkable cry of "Damn you!" when faced with Lee's Satanic priest, Father Michael Raynor.

Widmark's other credits include Roy Ward Baker's *Don't Bother to Knock*, *Run for the Sun* (1955, a remake of *The Most Dangerous Game*), *A Talent for Loving* (1969, as Caroline Munro's father), *Coma* (1977, as Dr. Harris), *The Swarm* (1977, as General Slater) and *Bear Island*, with Christopher Lee. Indeed, Lee was one of the few people involved with *To the Devil a Daughter* who actually got along with the American star, as he told Bill Kelley in *LSoH* #12, 1994: "A couple of years ago, here in London, I was walking across the street and I saw Dick Widmark in front of me. I walked up from behind and said, 'Mr. Widmark'—[here Lee affects a nasally voice in the manner of an annoying fan asking for an autograph]—and when he turned around and saw it was me, we both broke out laughing."

While shooting *To the Devil a Daughter*, it was Widmark who suggested to Lee that a move to America would broaden his range of roles. The British actor—who had already made successful inroads into other genres with *The Private Life of Sherlock Holmes*, *Hannie Caulder* and *The Three/Four Musketeers*—was fresh from presenting a dark counterpart to Roger Moore's James Bond as *The Man with the Golden Gun*. In this international epic, Lee's Scaramanga operates a funhouse slay-ground on his island retreat, kitted out with *Caligari*-like structures and a Poe-esque stuffed raven. He also hunts Bond down, like Count Zaroff in *The Most Dangerous Game*, and has a death ray (like Bela Lugosi in *Chandu the Magician*) and a dwarf accomplice (*Seizure*'s Hervé Villechaize), like Lugosi in *Spooks Run Wild*, *The Corpse Vanishes* and *Scared to Death*. Still, Lee later told Tom Johnson and Mark A. Miller: "*The Man with the Golden Gun* was an important film for me [because it] proved ... that I was no longer thought of only as Dracula or as a horror star." This didn't stop O.J. Simpson from raising Lee's ire by calling him "Drac" throughout the May 1975 shoot of *The Diamond Mercenaries* in South Africa (as the film's director, Val Guest, revealed at the FANEX Baltimore film convention in 1997).

Further evidence of Lee bristling at his horror past came when Sam Irvin, editor of *Bizarre* magazine, interviewed the actor on the *Golden Gun* set. Irvin recalled (in *LSoH* #27): "It startled me how [Lee] said 'a Hammer film' with such disdain. His nostrils even flared, as if the words released the stench of excrement."

Nevertheless, just over a year later, the actor was back with the original Hammer for a final time. In *To the Devil ... The Death of Hammer*, Lee outlined his reasons for returning: "My argument was, this particular subject [black magic] is a subject about which the public knows very little. It is incredibly dangerous. It is obscenely powerful. It is literally soul-destroying. And if we make this film, we will show the dangers of this kind of worship and belief."

Armed with such intentions, Lee gives his most sinister performance as Father Michael. Witness his reptilian smile as he leers over the demonic childbirth, or the exaggerated look of sympathy as the mother, her legs bound, expires ("Margaret, you shall die now"). Elsewhere, his voice alone is enough to convince Catherine's father, Henry, that he is handling a dangerous snake. ("We're so close that I can hear your pulse beating ...")

Henry is essayed by *The House That Dripped Blood*'s Denholm Elliott (1922-1992), whose work here made him the very first recipient of the Dracula Society's Hamilton Deane Award. Elliott had himself played Dracula, with goatee beard and *horrible* teeth, for a very interesting 1968 instalment of *Mystery and Imagination*

Christopher Lee and Nastassja Kinski

(earlier in the same series, he seemed to be channeling the spirit of Lionel Barrymore as Roderick Usher). Denholm can also be seen reading a passage from Stoker's novel in Daniel Farson's 1974 documentary *The Dracula Business*; when Farson asks the actor if he enjoyed "devouring" women as the Count, Elliott chuckles, "That isn't really my scene."

Denholm's other TV credits include the fearful title role of "The Signalman" (1975), the downtrodden father in *Brimstone and Treacle* (1976), the lizard-loving doctor in *Supernatural*: "Lady Sybil" (1976) and the estate agent trapped inside his nightmares for *Hammer House of Horror*: "Rude Awakening." He was also the one-armed science correspondent in *Quest for Love*, the penis transplant surgeon of *Percy* (1970) and *Percy's Progress*, an aide to Bette Davis' *Madame Sin* (1971), the art collector who meets a voodoo death in *The Vault of Horror* and Stapleton, owner of a urinating Chihuahua, in the 1977 *Hound of the Baskervilles* (for the more serious 1983 version of the same tale, Elliott clutches a better-behaved pooch as Dr. Mortimer). After narrating an audio book of Dennis Wheatley's *The Haunting of Toby Jugg* in 1980, Denholm created mutants as Dr. Savary in *Underworld* (1985), then scored as Dr. Marcus Brody, mentor to Harrison Ford, in both *Raiders of the Lost Ark* and *Indiana Jones and the Last Crusade*. Diagnosed with HIV in 1987, Elliott passed away from AIDS-related tuberculosis in 1992. By the actor's own request, his ashes were scattered in Ibiza to the sound of Kermit the Frog singing "The Rainbow Connection."

To the Devil a Daughter is also graced by two very likeable turns from Honor Blackman (1925-2020), as Verney's agent, and Anthony Valentine (1939-2015), as her partner. Blackman, whose career stretched back to Terence Fisher's *So Long at the Fair* (1949), had last worked for Hammer in *The Glass Cage* (1954). Since then, she'd gained renown as Pussy Galore, the tough aviation expert of *Goldfinger*; Hera, Queen of the Gods, in *Jason and the Argonauts* and Cathy Gale, the crime-busting partner of Patrick Macnee in the early years of *The Avengers*. After playing the wife of a psychopath in *Fright*, Honor was the hunted huntress of Richard Gordon's *The Cat and the Canary* (1976) and Professor Sarah Lasky in *Doctor Who*: "Terror of the Vervoids" (1986, written by *Night of the Big Heat*'s Pip and Jane Baker). Reunited with Christopher Lee on *Talos the Mummy* (1997), Blackman next pursued "Lesbian Vampire Lovers of Lust" for *Dr. Terrible's House of Horrible* (2001) and is a hoot as the gun-toting Peggy in *Cockneys vs. Zombies* (2011): When her care home is invaded by the living dead, Peggy's fellow resident, Eric (Dudley Sutton), says: "We need crucifixes, garlic, silver, holy water and Christopher Lee!"

Anthony Valentine would return to the *Hammer House of Horror* as the policeman investigating the "Carpathian Eagle." He was also a psychiatrist in *Tower of Evil*, a vampire hunter in *The Monster Club* and, in 1995, did a beautiful job of recording Stoker's *Dracula* as an audiobook.

When Valentine's character in *To the Devil a Daughter* bursts into flames, Eddie Powell deputized. The result (filmed at St. Botolph's Church, Shenley) is most probably the first full-body fire stunt in a British film (the first American movie to feature this dangerous feat is *The Thing from Another World* [1951]). As Powell revealed to *LSoH*, he suffered some serious burns and, once extinguished, the vicar of the church quipped: "Now you know what it's like to be in Hell"—to which Eddie replied: "Piss off." (Powell also serves as Christopher Lee's nude double for the film's ceremonial orgy.)

The gloom of such depressing scenes is lightened by cameos from familiar character actors, Brian Wilde (1927-2008) and Frances de la Tour (b. 1944). Although best known for his work on TV sitcoms *Last of the Summer Wine* and *Porridge*, Wilde's genre credits have the distinction of appearing at the beginning, middle and end of the British horror boom. Following his memorably unhinged performance as the hypnotized Hobart in *Night of the Demon* (1956), he was a bar dweller in *Rasputin: The Mad Monk* (1965) and now, in Hammer's final 20th century horror film, he is the custodian of Satanic tomes.

De la Tour—who provides the film's sole note of cheer as a Salvation Army major—was immortalized as amorous Miss Jones in the classic British sitcom *Rising Damp* (the 1979 movie version of which was produced by Roy Skeggs and features Denholm Elliott). After Tim Burton cast her as Alice's eccentric Aunt Imogene in *Alice in Wonderland* (2009), Frances again appeared with Christopher Lee in Martin Scorsese's *Hugo* (2010).

This brilliant cast is aided by cinematographer David Watkin (1925-2008). A pioneer in his field, and inventor of the "Wendy-light," Watkin had worked on such Richard Lester pictures as *Help!*, *How I Won the War*, *The Bed Sitting Room* (1968) and *The Three/Four Musketeers*. He also lit *The Devils*, *Jesus of Nazareth* and *Return to Oz*, before winning an Oscar for *Out of Africa* (1985).

Another bonus is the genuinely frightening music score by Paul Glass (b. 1934). "We are looking for a very modern score for *To the Devil a Daughter*," Roy Skeggs outlined (on November

6, 1975), "containing considerable electronic effects." Glass certainly delivers, providing a sonic backdrop of unholy warbling and chilling stabs of noise. The Swiss-American composer had previously scored the thrillers *Lady in a Cage* (1963), *Nightmare in the Sun* (1963, with Ursula Andress and Sammy Davis, Jr.) and *Bunny Lake is Missing*, as well as 14 episodes of Rod Serling's *Night Gallery*. He would return to the *Hammer House of Mystery and Suspense* for "The Late Nancy Irving" (1984).

Less impressive is Les Bowie's demon baby puppet, complete with gelatinous tongue. Although the creature is endearingly cute, and the notion of his birth prefigures the chest-bursting antics of *Alien*, Christopher Lee was not amused, as he revealed to Bill Kelley (in *LSoH* #12): "That hideous, bloody puppet clawing its way out of the woman's belly should have never been shown … It's really uncalled for … It gets back to what I said about *Rosemary's Baby*, and not seeing the baby, and it being so much scarier."

Worse still, is the film's damp squib of an ending, in which Raynor's diabolical schemes are undone by Verney throwing a rock at him. Lee told Marcus Hearn that *To the Devil a Daughter* "was completely, utterly *ruined* in the last 10 minutes by some senseless and idiotic decisions made by some genius." The actor maintained that a suitably thrilling climax had been filmed, wherein divine retribution takes place and he is struck by lightning, but the powers that be decided this was too close to Lee's demise in *Scars of Dracula*. Still, the scenery is nice, what with the location being the Dashwood Estate, West Wycombe—previously the site of the nefarious Hellfire Club, but now home to Lee's *Hound of the Baskervilles* love interest Marla Landi. (Lee personally sought permission from Marla to film there; one wonders if they reminisced of happier times and happier films.) *To the Devil a Daughter* was released in the UK on Thursday, March 4, 1976 (when Tina Charles was at No. 1 with "I Love to Love [But My Baby Loves to Dance]"), and in the US four months later (when Wings had just spent the last of five non-consecutive weeks at the top of the *Billboard* charts with "Silly Love Songs").

While the world of horror had changed much since Christopher Lee's first triumphs in the genre, the sniffy reviews remained the same: "About as artistic as picking one's nose in public," was the opinion of *Films and Filming*. Perhaps the film's biggest critic, however, was Dennis Wheatley: Lee revealed to Marcus Hearn that the author was "incandescent with rage" on seeing the finished product. (His story would evolve into the big-budget Arnold Schwarzenegger actioner *End of Days* [1999]—not sure what Dennis would have made of *that*.)

While a tie-in edition of Wheatley's novel was issued in France, a more unusual tome emerged in Britain. Published in 1978, with text by Marjorie Bilbow, *The Facts about a Feature Film* is a brisk, nuts and bolts account of filming *To the Devil a Daughter*, which even mentions the kind of lavatories used: "They are, of course, of the chemical closet type." Complete with a brief Introduction from Christopher Lee, the book was part of a series aimed at young readers (*The Facts about a Pop Group*, for instance, focuses on Paul McCartney and Wings). Although a film about Satanism seems an odd choice for its target audience, there had been an earlier textbook, Edward Buscombe's *Making Legend of the Werewolf* (BFI, 1976), wherein schoolchildren could learn how to make movies about men in love with prostitutes who turn into blood-ravening beasts by night.

The Facts about a Feature Film ends on a promising note: "By the spring of 1977 … *To the Devil a Daughter* had been seen by at least one and a half million people in the United Kingdom. And it was still going strong … This is regarded as a very satisfactory return for a medium-budget production." Indeed, a myth has since grown up that *To the Devil a Daughter* was a complete flop at the box office, but, in fact, the film did good business, especially in the UK, with a gross of just under $3 million. The problem was that most of the profits went to EMI, not Hammer (according to David Taylor in *LSoH* #39, Lee himself received a 25% cut and Wheatley 5%). Such figures were as nothing, though, compared to the nearly $61 million grossed by a contemporaneous movie with an identical subject: As would happen with the remainder of Lee's 1970s genre output, *To the Devil a Daughter* was overshadowed by slicker product in a similar vein.

Filmed in London from October 1975 to January 1976, *The Omen* was released in the UK on June 6, 1976, just three months after *To the Devil a Daughter*. Both films dealt with the offspring of Satan and employed a top American star (Gregory Peck) supported by an excellent British cast (Patrick Troughton, Billie Whitelaw, David Warner, etc.). With such similarities, why did *The Omen* triumph so massively over Hammer's film? Clearly the subject matter was not at fault. In addition to the numerous *Exorcist* rip-offs emerging from every corner of the globe, Satanic

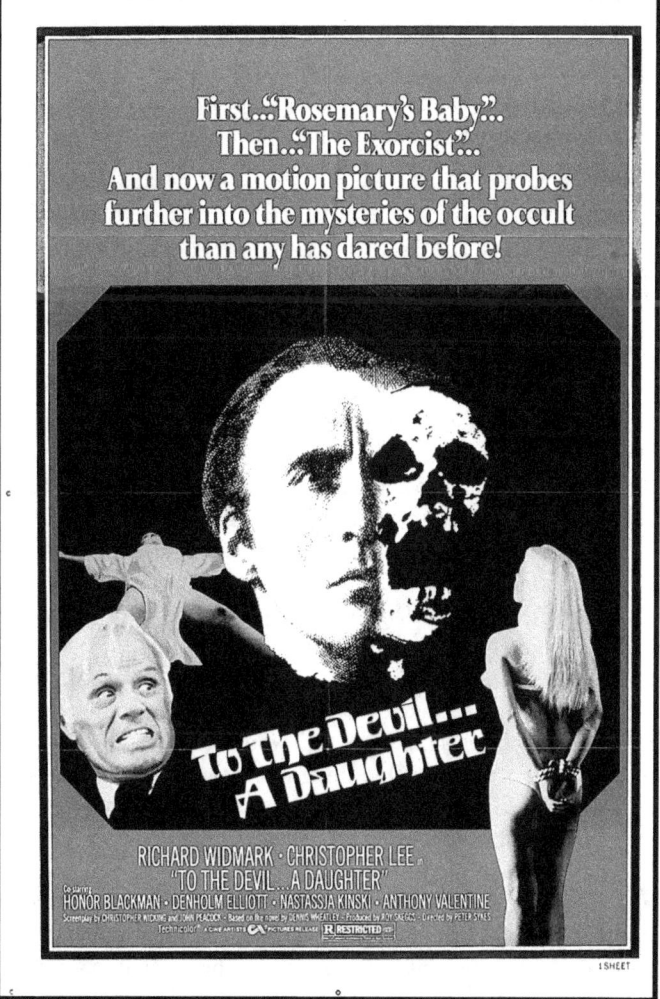

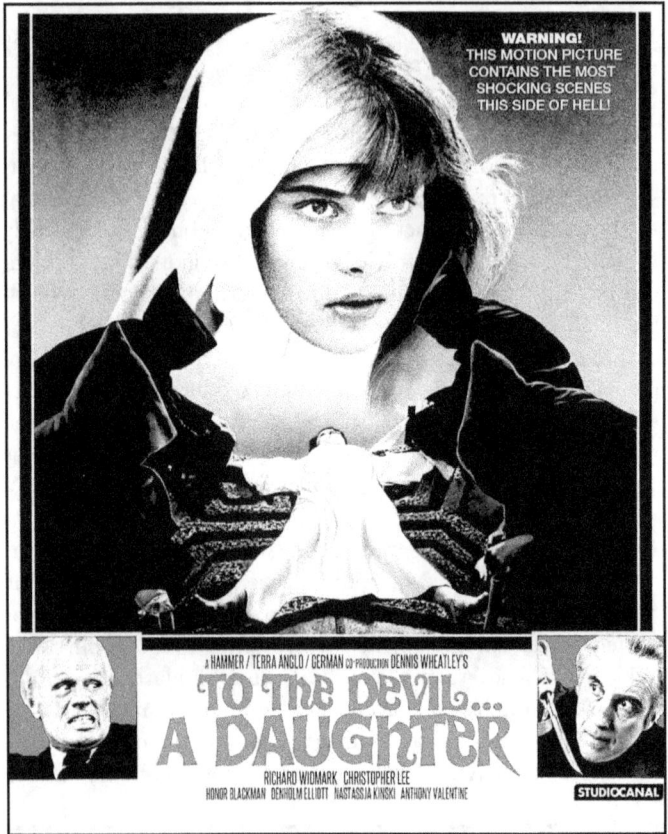

films flourished across the Atlantic, with *I Don't Want to Be Born*, *Race with the Devil*, *The Devil's Rain*, *The Devil's Men* and *Satan's Slave* all appearing within 12 months of *To the Devil a Daughter*. Nor did the public seem wearied of the topic, despite the glut of titles mentioned above.

Blame for Hammer's comparative floundering at this stage must lie with the execution of their product. For one thing, *The Omen*'s impressive set-pieces offered a new way of shocking audiences, just as Hammer's earliest horrors with Christopher Lee had done 20 years previously. While *The Omen* presented an imaginatively staged decapitation of graphic realism, *To the Devil a Daughter* could only muster a bloody hand puppet and a burning stuntman in obvious fireproof coverings. In addition, the clarity of David Seltzer's script was engaging and thought-provoking, whereas the muddle of writers engaged by Hammer delivered a plot as clear as mud. To cap it all off, Hammer's highly questionable idea of publicity at this time involved full frontal nude shots of an underage Natassja Kinski. Consequently, the success of *The Omen* would spell the final nail in Hammer's coffin.

After *To the Devil a Daughter*, the House of Horror promised various projects which never got made. A shame, as many of these titles were intriguing: *Nessie*; *Kali … Devil Bride of Dracula*, *Vlad the Impaler*, a remake of *Dead of Night* and a four-story portmanteau, *The Dracula Odyssey*, which would take the point of view of the Count's victims. One thing was clear, however: Christopher Lee would not be involved in the latter. The "younger, sexier" Dracula Michael Carreras kept promising never arrived. As had happened in the past, major distributors were wary about financing a Dracula film without Lee in the role, and the overriding consensus was that Hammer horror had had its day.

Indeed, Lee had invested so much into his revolutionary characterization of the vampire that the actor was ultimately irreplaceable. The only new Hammer film to make it to the studio floor, in September 1978, was a remake of Hitchcock's *The Lady Vanishes* with Elliot Gould and Cybil Shepherd. Against all odds, the finished film was not bad at all, but flopped dismally at the box office. Upon its failure, Hammer were forced to declare bankruptcy.

In a desperate wheeze to keep the company's name alive, Michael Carreras entertained notions of a new line in book publishing, as well as a leisure complex, "The Hammer House of Entertainment," wherein guests could dine while enjoying Grand Guignol-style plays, dance until dawn at "Dracula's Dungeon Discotheque" or watch a continuous stream of horror films at the "All-Night 'Shock' Cinema."

Sadly, the only idea that came to fruition was a waxwork exhibit in London's Palladium Cellars, which was opened by Yul Brynner on Thursday, May 15, 1980. Among the waxy horrors on show were animatronic likenesses of Christopher Lee's Dracula supping blood from a maiden's neck, Peter Cushing's Baron Frankenstein presiding over a Karloff-like monster (with mismatching feet) and Oliver Reed's Werewolf rattling his cell bars in fury. Alas, the operation was not a success and closed within a short time.

The following month, under the auspices of Roy Skeggs and Brian Lawrence, filming began on *Hammer House of Horror*—a better-than-average series which first graced ITV's Saturday night schedules in September 1980. The 13, hour-long episodes—filmed at Buckinghamshire's haunted Hampden House—include such memorably nightmarish images as the blood-drenched children's party in "The House That Bled to Death," Peter Cushing's "Silent Scream" and the toothsome voodoo idol "Charlie Boy."

Hammer next planned a "big-budget" *Dracula* thriller, but without Christopher Lee. "Already we are conducting a worldwide search for a suitable actor to portray our new Dracula," Brian Lawrence told *Screen International* in 1980, but aside from the feature-length entries for *Hammer House of Mystery and Suspense* (which were filmed from 1983 to 1984 when Lee's busy schedule precluded a mooted appearance), there were no further productions.

Perhaps there was nothing Hammer could do at that time to keep their brand alive. After all, it wasn't just them: The entire British film industry was in a slump. As Dennis Wheatley had written for the closing captions of *To the Devil a Daughter*: "In Light all things thrive and bear fruit. In Darkness they decay and die."

The Keeper
1975

Christopher Lee, master of the macabre, takes you and his patients to the brink of insanity.

It was supposed to be funny, by the way."— Christopher Lee, explaining *The Keeper* to Tom Johnson and Mark A. Miller

Filmed in Vancouver, Canada, from Monday, October 6 to Friday October 24, 1975, *The Keeper* is the sole directorial credit of writer T.Y. Drake (1936-2008). An ex-folk singer (who had written lyrics for the Kingston Trio in the early 1960s), Drake went on to script *Terror Train* (1979)—a mingling of *Halloween* with *Horror Express* that has gained quite a cult following. *The Keeper*, on the other hand, hasn't.

The film opens on a half-intriguing note with Christopher Lee, as "the Keeper" of Underwood Asylum, cooing to his writhing inmates, amid pulsating lights and swirling visuals: "Now is the time for us all to be happy ... *Love* the Keeper! *Obey* the Keeper!" These commands are accompanied by flashing images of Lee's grinning face. "The Keeper will keep you alive!"

Meanwhile, "two-bit snooper" Dick Driver (Tell Schreiber) investigates the mysterious deaths of potential heirs, whose wealthy relatives are all incarcerated at Lee's asylum—a plot strand reminiscent of Bela Lugosi's *The Dark Eyes of London*. In fact, *The Keeper* is kooky enough to merit comparison with such Lugosi potboilers as *The Devil Bat* (1940), *Bowery at Midnight* (1942) and *The Ape Man* (1942), all of which feature the actor as a mad authority figure, pursued by wiseacre protagonists. *The Keeper* is less entertaining, and an obviously low budget cannot quite sustain the illusion of its ambitious 1940s settings (although good use is made of Vancouver's historic Sylvia Hotel as a location).

Whereas the aforementioned Lugosi vehicles are each invested with knowing humor, the larkish tone of *The Keeper* never comes off. The film is further compounded by choppy editing, making the results akin to an amateur effort in which Christopher Lee has somehow been convinced to take the leading role.

Lurching round his asylum with a shortened cane, Lee's villain affects a lightly smiling visage, whether describing hypnotism as "quite a pleasant procedure, really," or referring playfully to his charges as "my dears." He also maintains an air of amusement while listening in on the patients, his head nodding almost to the rhythm of their woes.

Lee is able to balance this buoyant side with the more expected solemnity (a doom-laden look from a window, to the accompaniment of descending synthesizer notes; the torturing of transvestite Danny in an electric chair). At all times, Lee turns in a professional performance, affecting the slide from charm to menace with accustomed grace.

Although Ross Vezarian gives a spirited impression of a steam train, the film's next best performance, after Lee's, comes from 11-year-old Ian Tracey as a street urchin. Tracey would go on to play the title role in TV's *Huckleberry Finn and His Friends* (1979-1980) and continues to act with appearances in cult genre shows, *The X Files* (as embittered amputee Leonard "Rappo" Trimble, "The Walk" [1995]), *The Outer Limits* (1995-2002), *Poltergeist: The Legacy*, *Supernatural* (2005-) and *Bates Motel* (2013-2017, as Remo Wallace).

The remainder of *The Keeper*'s cast, including seven-foot twins Jack and Leo Leavy, barely acted again—though leading lady Sally Gray, who was married to the director, would co-write an episode of *MacGyver* with her husband in 1989.

Never released theatrically, *The Keeper* was eventually sold to television where it was first screened in the US as a "CBS Late Movie" on Thursday, December 19, 1985 (*Dracula Has Risen from the Grave* had received its small screen premiere in the same slot over a decade earlier). *The Keeper* was issued on video in 1987 with packaging that suggested its horror content was far higher than it is.

In a bid to escape the genre, Christopher Lee finally relented to the advice of colleagues like Richard Widmark and, in early 1976, moved to Los Angeles. En route, he stopped off in Paris to give his farewell performance as a vampire Count.

Dracula and Son
1976

Like father like son, it's in the blood.

> It is totally misleading. I do not play the part of Dracula in the picture ... The reason I did it was not to parody myself, which I do not do, but because by doing this I can close the door very firmly on the vampire.—Christopher Lee, in an article entitled "Christopher Lee plays Dracula for the last time...again!" *Cinefantastique* (Spring 1977)

Based on Claude Klotz's 1970 novel *Paris-Vampire*, the eight-week shoot of *Dracula Père et Fils* (Dracula Father and Son) began at the Studios de Billancourt on Tuesday, March 16, 1976. Although Christopher Lee insisted that the vampire Count he plays in this comedy is *not* Dracula, the character certainly announces himself as such in Klotz's book ("Je suis le comte Dracula, prince des vampires"). While this would mark a rare instance in which the actor didn't read his source material, Lee can be forgiven as the original script from first-time writer and director Edouard Molinaro (1928-2013)—who went on to helm *La Cage aux Folles* (1978)—only refers to the vampire figure as "the Count."

Perhaps Lee—who believed the film to be titled simply *Père et Fils*—was knowingly inveigled into the role? His co-star in the film, Bernard Menez (b. 1944), admitted in *Le Figaro* (June 12, 2015): "I was convinced that any adaptation [of *Paris-Vampire*] would only be interesting if the Dracula role was played, not by some French comic actor ... but by a specialist ... Naturally, Christopher Lee came to mind ... The problem—he didn't want to play Dracula. Molinaro persuaded him by saying it would be a high-class comedy like Polanski's *Dance of the Vampires*."

Indeed, the star of the latter, Lee's friend, Ferdy Mayne—who also played comic versions of Dracula in *The Vampire Happening*, *Frankenstein's Auntie* (1986) and *My Lovely Monster* (1988)—revealed in *100 Years of Horror*: "Christopher never liked my [Dracula] performances. He said, 'How *dare* you, how dare you make a funny character out of something that should be interpreted seriously.'"

This refusal to exploit the character—which many have mistaken for disdain—stems, instead, from respect. For instance, you would never see Lee's Dracula engaging in the sort of publicity which would later dilute the impact of Freddy Krueger (such as rapping with the Fat Boys or advertising a telephone hotline). Thus, to Lee's way of thinking, in *Père et Fils*, he was playing, if not *the* Count, then a Dracula-like figure—as he had in *Uncle Was a Vampire* and *The Magic Christian*. Therefore, his performance is not only much lighter, but also more talkative than the characterization he presented at Hammer.

First seen lurking behind a bronze likeness of himself, Lee's gray-wigged, brocaded vampire engages in romantic repartee with a visitor to his castle (Catherine Breillat). Sadly, she dies after bearing him a son, Ferdinand (Bernard Mendez, who had previously starred opposite Peter Cushing in another French horror spoof, *Tender Dracula*).

Comedy or not, Christopher Lee always took his portrayals of Count Dracula seriously.

When their castle is overtaken by Communists, father and son flee Transylvania. While Ferdinand winds up in Paris, a reluctant bloodsucker, the Count arrives in London, flopping from a net of fish. Looking suitably wearied, Lee is very funny indeed. After biting into an inflatable woman—and offering a priceless expression of consternation—he staggers into a pane of glass while pursuing another victim. In what is, perhaps, the film's best joke, he winds up as a Christopher Lee-like horror star (with a director who resembles Tim Burton).

Reunited with his offspring in Paris, when filming *Loves of a Vampire*, the Count falls for executive, Nicole, who resembles his late wife (this is because she is played by Catherine Breillat's sister, Marie-Hélène; both women had appeared with Marlon Brando in *Last Tango in Paris* [1971]). Ferdinand has eyes for Nicole and a Freudian rivalry fuels the remainder of the action.

Released in France on Wednesday, September 15, 1976, and in the US, as *Dracula and Son*, in May 1979, the film was clearly the blueprint for *Love at First Bite* (1978). In both movies, Dracula is forced to leave Transylvania by Communists, and, while adapting to foreign shores, he finds romance with women from the modern world of advertising. Unfortunately, in badly edited and redubbed form, *Dracula and Son* found itself competing, not just with the American film it inspired, but with a flood of Dracula releases. Brought on by Frank Langella's triumphal resurrection of the part onstage, *Nosferatu the Vampyre* premiered in January 1979, and, the following month, NBC aired a 10-part serial, *The Curse of Dracula*, with Michael Nouri prowling latter-day San Francisco as a seductive, Langella-like Count. April 1979 saw the release of *Love at First Bite*, while in June, John Carradine dusted off his *House of Dracula* outfit for *Nocturna*—an enjoyable blend of vampires, disco and bad acting. The following month, Frank Langella starred in the last cinematic *Dracula* adaptation issued until *Bram Stoker's Dracula* in November 1992.

French poster for *Dracula and Son*

Despite these varied interpretations, Christopher Lee never entirely turned his back on the character: "I would play him again," he revealed on *In Search of Dracula with Jonathan Ross* (1996), "but only on one condition: That it really *is* the book, in every respect, that Bram Stoker wrote; the physical description, the lines (not all of them, obviously), the names of the characters, the locations; that it is *exactly* what he wrote, because in all the years they've made films about this character, to this day, it's never been done."

Starship Invasions
1976

We know they are there—advanced beyond our imagination. Why have they come?

The question is not, "Is there intelligent life on other worlds?" No. The important question is, "Do they have ray guns?"—Christopher Lee, *100 Years of Horror*: "Aliens"

Shortly after decamping to Hollywood, Christopher Lee took part in the all-star disaster movie *Airport '77*, for which he was justly proud of his underwater stunt work. He would be less pleased, however, with his next professional outing, telling Tom Johnson and Mark A. Miller that, "I never looked or felt more ridiculous."

Filmed as *The Winged Serpent* at Toronto's Hal Roach Studios from Monday, October 18 to Sunday, December 5, 1976, *Starship Invasions* has attracted nothing but disparaging comments ever since. Typical is Janet Maslin's *New York Times* critique of October 1977: "*Starship Invasions* appears to have been made on a budget that might better have been used to supply hot dogs for a small picnic." Maslin ended her piece with a further wounding blow: "The Christopher Lee part isn't even properly played by Christopher Lee."

In fact, Lee's sincere performance as Captain Rameses, alien leader of the Legion of the Winged Serpent, actually lifts *Starship Invasions* from the mundane. Emoting to his own voice-over dialogue, much like Vincent Price as the mutilated Dr. Phibes, Rameses speaks only through his mind. "I thought it was a very interesting idea that people would communicate telepathically on the screen," Lee told David Del Valle (in *Films and Filming*, September 1985), before adding: "I didn't realize that I would be given a funny hat to wear and a rather ridiculous outfit." Lee's costume is indeed incredible: A tight black number with angular hood and dragon insignia, it's no wonder that the actor felt embarrassed. Commendably, though, he never once allows his performance to slip into camp, even when detailing the quality of an abductee's sperm cells.

Lee explained to Johnson and Miller that he willingly signed up on being told Robert Vaughn (1932-2016) would be playing UFO researcher Professor Allan Duncan. (Four years later, Vaughn enacted a character with a very different stance on the subject in *Hangar 18*.) The son of actress Marcella Gaudell (who starred as Lucy in a 1930 tour of *Dracula*), Vaughn made his debut (as an uncredited extra) alongside Vincent Price and John Carradine in *The Ten Commandments* (1955). After an early lead as Roger Corman's *Teenage Caveman* (1958), he found fame as one of *The Magnificent Seven* (1960, a part he would reprise in Corman's outer-space recreation *Battle Beyond the Stars* [1980].)

Further renowned for the cult spy series *The Man from U.N.C.L.E.* (1964-1968; on which Price and Carradine would guest), Vaughn parodied Lee's *Dracula* in *Transylvania Twist* (1989) and worked with Boris Karloff on *Thriller*, *The Girl from U.N.C.L.E.* and *The Venetian Affair* (1966). His other genre credits include the progressive Dr. Bergen in *The Mind of Mr. Soames* (1968), the voice of the evil computer in *Demon Seed* (1977), a latter-day Frankenstein in *Doctor Franken* (1979), the villain of *Superman III* (1982), the General who dreams of zombie armies in *C.H.U.D. II-Bud the Chud* (1988), the director of the Ravenscroft Institute in *Buried Alive* (1988, John Carradine's last film) and the Devil in Fred Olen Ray's *Witch Academy* (1991).

Vaughn's wife in *Starship Invasions* is touchingly played by Helen Shaver (b. 1951). Best known for starring as Paul Newman's girlfriend, Janelle, in *The Color of Money* (1986), Shaver is also clairvoyant Carolyn of *The Amityville Horror* (1978), geologist Kate Reilly in *Tremors 2: Aftershocks* (1994) and the voice of Littlefoot's mother in *The Land Before Time* (1987). As well as directing six episodes of *The Outer Limits* (1995-2002), she essayed the regular role of Dr. Rachel Corrigan on *Poltergeist: The Legacy*.

The writer and director of *Starship Invasions*, Ed Hunt, clearly knows his stuff when it comes to the UFO phenomenon: Details such as telepathic communication and the wand-like apparatus applied to abductees' bodies are in accordance with reports from those who claim to have had real-life alien encounters. Even the film's peculiar-looking androids are said to be based on actual accounts. Hunt would go on to make the 1979 documentary *UFO's Are Real*, which includes fascinating interviews with abductees Betty Hill and Travis Walton, as well as eyewitness testimony from retired military personnel. The director's later credits include *Plague* (1979), *Bloody Birthday* (1980) and *Alien Warrior* (1986), but his best work is undoubtedly *The Brain* (1988), whose astonishing imagery (bleeding teddy bears, *Re-Animator*'s David Gale as a mad TV psychologist and the unforgettable title monster) seizes us from the outset and never lets up. Hunt's most recent opus, *Halloween Hell* (2014), depicts a nightmarish reality show hosted by Dracula (Eric Roberts).

With *Starship Invasions*, Hunt appeals to, as one character puts it: "The same need religion used to fulfill … to know where we come from, where we're going"—a curiosity spurred by such books as Erich von Daniken's *Chariots of the Gods?* First published in 1968, Daniken's tome postulates that extra-terrestrials first visited Earth at the dawn of humanity, siring our civilization. Conversely, the aliens of Hunt's film discover that they are actually descended from

"I never looked or felt more ridiculous."

humans. As their own planet is dying, they must destroy their "parent race" in order to colonize the Earth. Thus, Rameses sets a death ray in motion, causing earthlings to commit suicide on the spot. Earth's military prove just as destructive, however: Blasting unidentified objects out of the sky without the least provocation, an underlying theme appears to be that an unwillingness to face the unknown is as dangerous as invasion itself.

The film's flying saucer effect is not as bad as critics make out; although inflatable, the prop does at least have some substance (unlike much of today's weightless CGI) and the opening shot of the craft zooming towards the viewer from a golden sunset is quite arresting. (Among the special effects crew is John Thomas [1947-1994], who progressed to *Superman*, *The Fly II* [1988] and Stephen King's *It* [1990] and Dennis Pike, who worked on *The Brood*, *Scanners* [1979] and *Return to Oz*.)

While a low-budget is betrayed by sparse sets, the aliens' red-lit base (within an underwater triangle structure) is passable—even if the UFO resembles a pie tray as it slides into port. The tin-pot robot that presides there, who describes Rameses as his "galactic brother," is pleasingly reminiscent of the droids in Terence Fisher's *The Earth Dies Screaming*. Less charming is a *Barbarella*-like moment which shows Rameses making telepathic love to a female alien called Gazeth in the "relaxation room." The lady in question is played by Victoria Johnson, who had just been mauled beneath a waterfall by *Grizzly* (1975) and would later be attacked under the shower as Angie Dickinson's body double in *Dressed to Kill* (1979).

Rameses' violent quest is opposed by a tribe of benign aliens, the League of Races, whose leaders are portrayed by Tiiu Leek (b. 1950) and Daniel Pilon (1940-2018). Although the joins of their prosthetic make-up are all too apparent on the brightly lit sets, both actors look salient with their pale, large-domed heads. Leek went on to specialize in news reporters and anchorwomen in everything from *Airheads* (1993) to *Honeymoon in Vegas* (1991), while Pilon had starred with Orson Welles in the obscure horror film *Malpertuis*.

Despite the action proving static at times, certain scenes stick in the mind: A small child observing dead bodies in the street, for instance, or Robert Vaughn scanning the countryside for evidence as a gentle snow drifts down. Also notable is the electronic score from celebrated jazz composer Gil Mellé (1931-2004), which blends the usual sci-fi sounds with cheesy 1970s funk. Fresh from scoring *The Sentinel* (1976), Mellé was quite a genre regular by this time, having worked on four *Night Gallery* entries, *Frankenstein: The True Story*, *The Questor Tapes* (1973) and the short-lived series *Kolchak: The Night Stalker*. Originally issued as a turntable-damaging hexagonal disc, his soundtrack album for *The Andromeda Strain* (1970) is now a collector's item. (The composer also designed striking record covers for fellow musicians Miles Davis and Thelonius Monk.)

Distributed by Warner Bros., *Starship Invasions* was released in the US on Friday, October 14, 1977 (when, appropriately, Meco's disco arrangement of John Williams' *Star Wars* theme was at No. 1). British viewers wouldn't see the film until it emerged belatedly on video in 1987, under the cheery title *Project Genocide*. With its original American release squeezed between the big-budget *Star Wars* (May 25, 1977) and *Close Encounters of the Third Kind* (which premiered November 15, 1977), *Starship Invasions* couldn't help but look shabby by comparison. Indeed, the film was originally set to be released as *War of the Aliens*, and then *Alien Encounter*, until the respective distributors of the aforementioned epics threatened to sue.

Lee told Johnson and Miller that *Starship Invasions* was "one of the few films I wish that I'd never made." But there are certainly far worse efforts in the actor's oeuvre (e.g., *Circus of Fear*, *The Castle of Fu Manchu*, *Eugenie*)—and, personally, I would much rather watch *Starship Invasions* than *Star Wars: Episode II* (2000) any day of the week. To those who disagree, the movie is still worth a look, if only to see Christopher Lee as you've never seen him before.

End of the World
1977

There is everything to look forward to …
except tomorrow.

I'm sorry to have made the film—what else can I say?—Christopher Lee to Tom Johnson and Mark A. Miller

End of the World begins with a man playing pinball in a diner. Stepping from the shadows is Christopher Lee. Looking much as he did as Father Rayner in *To the Devil a Daughter*, the actor's disconnected movements echo his Creature from *The Curse of Frankenstein*. The slow halting speech and shambling walk he employs are quite touching indications of a being adrift. After some mysterious explosions—which Lee reacts to like Dracula faced with a crucifix—he comes face to face with a shadowy doppelganger. Following this startling, pre-credits sequence, things go downhill rapidly: Stilted scenes are hampered, both by cheesy dialogue and the synthesized schmaltz of Andrew Belling's score. (Jerry Goldsmith's son Joel served as "electronic music programmer" for this one.)

Professor Andrew Boran (Kirk Scott) and his wife Sylvia (Sue Lyon) investigate signals from outer space, which seem to coincide with recent natural disasters on Earth. Their search leads them to Lee's Father Pergado, who is, in reality, an alien leader named Zindar. The extra-terrestrial has not only perfected the art of cloning, but he can also blow things up with his mind. Having taken over a convent and its six nuns, Zindar needs the scientist's help to return to his own planet. Unless the scientist cooperates, his wife will die. Although the alien claims to hail from a peaceful utopian world, he has no qualms in making such threats, or, indeed, exploding everything in sight. Regardless of the scientist's efforts, we later learn that Zindar must destroy the Earth anyway, as the wicked ways of humanity have made it a dangerous pollutant to other planets. Implementing the world's annihilation, via some useful stock footage, Zindar tells Boran: "On Earth, your talents are used for destruction; on our planet, we use them to build." We are then treated to a brief glimpse of the character's true face, as he beams himself back home.

When filming began in Los Angeles, April 1977, Lee was fresh from an altogether more lavish sci-fi affair: *Return from Witch Mountain* paired the actor with Bette Davis as misfits pursuing extra-terrestrial children across a rundown L.A. (shot through with Disney gloss by *Twins of Evil*'s John Hough). While some would question Lee's decision to star in such low-budget fare as *End of the World* so soon after working with the likes of Davis and Disney, one can see how the actor may have been attracted by the challenge of enacting an alien priest (a novel idea which Frank Ray Perilli's script fails to make the most of). An added bonus is that Lee receives sole top billing above the title—a feat even more impressive when one considers the caliber of his supporting players.

The Loneliness of Evil 207

Full Moon released a remastered version of *End of the World*.

Lew Ayres (1908-1996) first rose to fame as the star of Universal's powerful anti-war drama *All Quiet on the Western Front* (1929) but is best remembered by genre fans as the scientist possessed by *Donovan's Brain*, Mandemus in *Battle for the Planet of the Apes* (1972), Vaslovik in *The Questor Tapes*, the senior manager of Thorn Industries in *Damien: Omen II*, President Adar in *Battlestar Galactica* (1978) and the sympathetic English teacher of *Salem's Lot* (1979).

Macdonald Carey (1913-1994) had starred in Hitchcock's *Shadow of a Doubt* (1942) and Hammer's *The Damned*, while Dean Jagger (1903-1991) was Armand Louque in *Revolt of the Zombies* (1936), Dr. Adam Royston in *X the Unknown* and Elvis Presley's father in *King Creole* (1958). His last movie role was as the belligerent tycoon in *Alligator* (1980), co-written by *End of the World*'s Frank Ray Perilli.

Also making a final appearance in *Alligator* is Jagger's *End of the World* co-star Sue Lyon (b. 1946), who first found fame, aged 14, as *Lolita*. After losing out to Ursula Andress for *The Tenth Victim*, Lyon was cast as Elaine Harper in a 1969 TV version of *Arsenic and Old Lace* (directed by *Poor Devil*'s Robert Scheerer), with Helen Hayes, Lillian Gish and Herman Munster himself, Fred Gwynne as the Karloffian Jonathan Brewster.

Lyon's screen husband in *End of the World*, Kirk Scott (1936-2013), had made his debut in *Targets* with Karloff, and later appeared as Christian Slater's father in *Heathers* (1988).

Ironically, it's the aged veterans who add some much-needed energy to *End of the World* (the film's turgid pacing often leaves pauses large enough for a flying saucer to zoom through). Producer Charles Band (b. 1951) is to be commended for employing these venerable stars, despite the brevity of their appearances.

The son of director Albert Band (*I Bury the Living* [1957] and *Dracula's Dog* [1976]), Charles made *Mansion of the Doomed*, the X-rated fairy tale *The Other Cinderella* (1976) and *Crash!* (1976)—a killer car shocker with John Carradine and Sue Lyon—before embarking on *End of the World*. After the interesting *Tourist Trap* (1978), Band became the driving force behind production companies Empire and Full Moon Entertainment with cult titles like *Ghoulies* (*I* and *II*, 1984, 1986), *Re-Animator* (1984), *Troll* (1985) and the *Subspecies* quadrilogy (1990-1997). While Band's horror movies often show a penchant for tiny terrors (*Dolls* [1986], the *Puppet Master* series [1989-] and *Demonic Toys* [1991]), he also directed the first two entries in one of Empire's most popular franchises, *Trancers* (1984-2002), the super hero horror *Doctor Mordrid* (1991), the miniature monster rally *The Creeps* (1997) and *The Gingerdead Man* (2001), with Gary Busey as a killer cookie.

End of the World is directed by John Hayes (1930-2000), whose other works include *Grave of the Vampire* (1972), *Garden of the Dead* (1972) and a 1985 episode of *Tales from the Darkside* ("The Madness Room"). He was also responsible for numerous low-budget nudie features, including a pornographic remake of *Rosemary's Baby*.

Released in the US on Wednesday, October 12, 1977 to terrible reviews, *End of the World* later formed the lower half of a double bill with another of Band's sci-fi movies, *Laserblast* (1977).

A poster for *End of the World* can be glimpsed in the 1980 thriller *Fade to Black*, which also includes black-and-white moments of Christopher Lee from *Dracula* during a murder scene. (Look carefully and you'll see *Serial*—the 1979 comedy in which Lee plays a gay biker—advertised on a cinema marquee.)

Despite its downbeat climax lending pause for thought, *End of the World* is not entirely successful, either as a statement on world ecology, or as a wry comment on organized religion. Nevertheless, it's hard to dismiss outright a film which treats us to the surreal spectacle of nuns operating space machines.

House of the Long Shadows
1982

> The screen's masters of terror together for the first time ...

We filmed in this house which had several floors, and our make-up and dressing rooms were right on top of the building, needless to say, with four elderly gentlemen. I remember Vincent telling me, "My damn knees, my legs"—he was having problems going up stairs; well, we were all having them.—Christopher Lee, to Lucy Chase Williams, *The Complete Films of Vincent Price*

On Friday nights from February 9 to April 6, 1979, UK station ITV broadcast *Christopher Lee: Prince of Menace*, a season of the actor's terror films, comprising *Dracula*, *The Mummy*, *Dracula A.D. 1972*, *I, Monster*, *Scream and Scream Again*, *The Wicker Man*, *Theatre of Death*, *Dracula Has Risen from the Grave* and *Taste the Blood of Dracula*. Such showings already had more than a whiff of nostalgia about them as Lee, then living in Hollywood, had successfully left the genre behind and was busy starring in such varied fare as a Martial Arts picture (*The Silent Flute* [1977]), a *Thief of Bagdad*-meets-*Star Wars* homage (*Arabian Adventure* [1978]), a Steven Spielberg comedy (*1941* [1979]), an animated fairy tale (*Nutcracker Fantasy* [1979]) and a Chuck Norris actioner (*An Eye for an Eye* [1981]).

Indeed, since *End of the World* in '77, Lee had been wary of accepting other horror roles, a choice perhaps inspired by a review of the latter film in *Cinefantastique* which was more of an admonishment: "Another step down for Christopher Lee, who had better start watching his step." Unfortunately, in watching his step, Lee had turned down such promising offers as the Terence Stamp role in *Superman I* and *II* (shot concurrently throughout 1977), the Donald Pleasence role in *Halloween*, the Hal Holbrook role in *The Fog* (1979), the Louis Jourdan role in Wes Craven's *Swamp Thing* (1981) and the Leslie Nielsen role in *Airplane!* (1979). The latter, in particular, would not only have showcased Lee's deadpan comic gifts, but might also have transformed his entire screen persona: Nielsen, the stolid leading man of *Forbidden Planet* (1955) and *Dark Intruder* (1965), became a latter-day comedy god thanks to *Airplane!* If Lee had accepted the role, may

we have been further treated to his interpretation of Detective Frank Drebin in *Police Squad!* and *The Naked Gun* movies? As difficult as it is to imagine Christopher Lee making love to Priscilla Presley from inside a giant condom, or moonwalking across a baseball field, it's still an intriguing possibility. (I doubt, however, that we would have seen things come full circle, with Lee taking on Nielsen's humorous vampire in *Dracula: Dead and Loving It*.)

Nevertheless, 1982 saw Lee lured back to the genre with *House of the Long Shadows*, which not only gave him the opportunity to reunite with Peter Cushing, Vincent Price and John Carradine, but was also spookily old-fashioned enough to suit the actor's tastes. As he told presenter Ben Hunter, following a season of his films on US TV in 1980: "I never said I would not do another horror movie, because I'd be delighted to do one if somebody came up with a really good one, a really good story, a really good script and a really good part. I haven't seen many of the pictures today. Things have changed enormously. I don't think I'd want to. Not that they're badly made or badly acted. This graphic, realistic depiction of real violence to me is repellent. Quite nauseating. What I did was fantasy without risk."

Ironically, the man chosen to direct *House of the Long Shadows* was responsible for a number of graphic, violent shockers. An ex-stand-up comedian, Pete Walker (b. 1939) started out making squalid sexploitation items like *Cool It, Carol* (1970), before moving on to horror with *Die Screaming Marianne* (1970), *The Flesh and Blood Show* (1972), *House of Whipcord* (1973), *Frightmare* (1974), *House of Mortal Sin* (1975), *Schizo* (1976) and *The Comeback* (1977).

In February 1982, the director was approached by Cannon Films' Menahem Golan (1929-2014) and Yoram Globus (b. 1943), purveyors of such low-budget fun as *The Happy Hooker Goes Hollywood* (1980), with Martine Beswick; *Schizoid* (1980), with Klaus Kinski and *Hercules* (1982), with Lou Ferrigno (Cannon had also distributed *I, Monster* in the US; the company's later genre excursions include *King Solomon's Mines* [1985, with Her-

The British Quad for the movie

bert Lom], *Masters of the Universe* [1986, with Frank Langella as Skeletor], *Gor* [1986, with Oliver Reed], *Going Bananas* [1986, with a talking monkey] and three outlandish Tobe Hooper vehicles: *Lifeforce* [1984], *Invaders from Mars* [1985] and *The Texas Chainsaw Massacre 2* [1986]).

As Walker reported to Steve Gerrard, in *We Belong Dead* #17, the Israeli cousins said: "We want a horror picture with Boris Karloff or Bela Lugosi." Agreeing, instead, to an assignment that would unite the major *living* horror actors, Walker initially desired to remake *The Old Dark House*, but the rights proved too elusive (or expensive). In its place, he settled for a 1913 novel, *Seven Keys to Baldpate*, from Charlie Chan creator Earl Der Biggers. Already filmed six times between 1916 and 1947, the script for this latest version was dashed off by Michael Armstrong (b. 1944) in two weeks.

Armstrong began his career with *The Image* (1967)—a ghostly 13-minute short starring David Bowie—then went on to write and direct *The Haunted House of Horror* for Tigon and "the first film rated 'V' for Violence," *Mark of the Devil*. This *Witchfinder General*-inspired opus is notorious for the complimentary "vomit bags" that were handed out to audience members at its original theatrical showings. Once *Mark of the Devil Part II* was behind him, Armstrong directed Christopher Lee's three-and-a-half-minute intro to a 1990 video reissue of Lon Chaney's *The Phantom of the Opera* (with a new score by Rick Wakeman). While a tuxedo-clad, candle-bearing Lee claims to be introducing the re-tinted classic from the cellars of Le Palais Garnier, he is actually in the cellar of a London restaurant. Nevertheless, he provides an informative preamble to the film and its literary origins.

House of the Long Shadows began its five-week shoot on Monday, August 9, 1982, at Rotherfield Park—a 17th century estate in East Tisted (which would later house an episode of *Agatha Christie's Poirot*: "After the Funeral" [2005]). In November 1983, Peter Cushing revealed to James Kravaal, for *LSoH* #8: "I developed bronchitis while making [*House of the Long Shadows*]. We were working in a lovely house in Hampshire, but it was a section of the house that hadn't been used in many years. There was no heat, and it was very damp and very cold. I think the whole unit got colds of some sort. I think it looked all right for the film, but I didn't look my best, I must admit." (In the same interview, on spying a stray shadow behind him on the wall, Cushing quipped: "It might be Christopher.")

House of the Long Shadows concerns a writer (Desi Arnaz, Jr.) who bets his publisher (Richard Todd) that he can write a Gothic novel in 24 hours. Accepting the wager, Todd sends the young man to "Baldpate" Manor, Wales, where he encounters the eccentric Grisbane family, played by Lee, Carradine, Cushing, Price and Sheila Keith (1920-2004; standing in for Elsa Lanchester, who was too infirm to make the trip to England). Keith had appeared alongside Christopher Lee in his stage debut *The Constant Nymph* (1947), as well as several other Connaught Theatre productions. She remembered those days to Derek Pykett (as he revealed on the *House of the Long Shadows* DVD commentary): "In one of the plays ... [Christopher] had to kiss me quite passionately ... and he was wobbling like a jelly! I reminded him of it when we did *House of the Long Shadows*."

Since then, like Lee, Sheila had made quite a splash in horror films: She is truly frightening as the warden in *House of Whipcord*, the drill-wielding cannibal of *Frightmare*, "the one with the funny eye" at the *House of Mortal Sin* and the creepy Mrs. B in *The Comeback*. Incidentally, the red contact lenses she wore in *Frightmare* had originally been made for Lee, as Pete Walker explained in OEG's *House of Mortal Sin* DVD featurette *Interview with Director Pete Walker* (2010): "They were old Dracula contact lenses ... but they had never been worn by Christopher Lee," as "they were too small ... my make-up man, who had been doing *Taste the Blood of Dracula*, or one of those movies years before, had these contact lenses in his make-up box," and "said, 'How about these?'"

Keith would next work with Lee on *The Rainbow Thief* (1990), where she admonishes his mad Uncle Rudolf's choice of dinner party fodder with the line, "Bones are for cemeteries." Her final character—the mystic Grandma Lee in "And Now the Fearing" (one of the better episodes of *Dr. Terrible's House of Horrible*)—was named after her old co-star.

Despite being only slightly older than his fellow players, John Carradine (1906-1988) portrays Lord Grisbane, the family patriarch (camera operator John Simmonds told Derek Pykett that Carradine once nodded off in the middle of a take). While Lee had initially been attracted to *End of the World* by Carradine's mooted involvement, the pair wouldn't work together until *Goliath Awaits* (1981). This made-for-television fantasy mini-series was written by *The Return of Dracula*'s Pat Fielder and directed by Kevin Connor (b. 1937), whose credits include *From Beyond the Grave*, *Arabian Adventure* and *Motel Hell* (1980). Filmed aboard the haunted Queen Mary in Long Beach, California, Lee stars as the captain of the eponymous sunken ship, which he has transformed into a seemingly utopian society. Among the passengers, Carradine holds court as a famed actor, and Duncan Regehr (later to play Dracula in *The Monster Squad* [1986]) leads a rebel faction. With Lee in charge, nothing is as rosy as it appears ...

An ex-set designer for Cecil B. DeMille and noted Shakespearean, John Carradine began his film acting career with small spots in Universal horrors *The Invisible Man*, *The Black Cat* and *Bride of Frankenstein* before giving superlative performances for John Ford in *The Prisoner of Shark Island* (1935), *Stagecoach* (1938) and *The Grapes of Wrath* (1939). Having assisted Bela Lugosi in *Return of the Ape Man* (1943) and *Voodoo Man* (1943), Carradine replaced Lugosi as Dracula for Universal's *House of Frankenstein* (1944) and *House of Dracula* (1945). (Both films were directed by Erle C. Kenton, which is the name of John's werewolf character in *The Howling*.) Carradine was also the first actor to play the Count on TV, in

Christopher Lee, Vincent Price, John Carradine and Peter Cushing

a lost 1956 *Matinee Theatre* production. His other fang ventures include *The Face of Marble* (1945, in which he creates a vampire dog), *Billy the Kid vs. Dracula* (made over five days in 1965), *Blood of Dracula's Castle* (1966, as the Count's Moon-worshipping butler), *Las Vampiras* (1967, as Count Alucard), *Mary, Mary, Bloody Mary* (1974, as "The Man"), *Doctor Dracula* (1977, as the head of the Evil Ones), *Vampire Hookers* (1978, as a poetry-obsessed pimp) and *Evils of the Night* (1983, as an alien bloodsucker). Parenthetically, his son, David (1936-2009, star of *Death Race 2000*) plays a gun-toting Dracula in *Sundown: The Vampire in Retreat* (1988).

Away from vampires, John Carradine's genre roles comprise of gag cameos (*Munster, Go Home!* [1966], *Everything You Always Wanted to Know About Sex* [1972], *Monster in the Closet* [1983]), mad scientists (*Captive Wild Woman* [1942], *Revenge of the Zombies* [1943], *The Invisible Man's Revenge* [1944]), extra-terrestrials (*The Cosmic Man* [1958], *Invisible Invaders* [1958]), floating heads (*The Wizard of Mars* [1964], *Frankenstein Island* [1981]), Yeti enthusiasts (*Half Human* [1955], *Bigfoot* [1969]) and assorted weirdoes (*House of the Black Death* [1965], *Hillbillys in a Haunted House* [1967], *The Astro-Zombies* [1967]). His oeuvre also takes in Al Adamson schlock (*Horror of the Blood Monsters* [1966], *Blood of Ghastly Horror* [1969]), Jerry Warren junk (*The Incredible Petrified World* [1957], *Curse of the Stone Hand* [1959]), mainstream features (*The Secret of NIMH* [1980], *Peggy Sue Got Married* [1985]); vehicles for ageing actors (*Blood Legacy* [1970], *Terror in the Wax Museum* [1972]), TV terrors (*Daughter of the Mind* [1969], *Crowhaven Farm* [1970]),

The Loneliness of Evil

The titans of terror gather in Rotherfield Park to enjoy their legacy.

slasher pieces (*Silent Night, Bloody Night* [1970], *The Boogey Man* [1980]) and the occasional interesting project (*Shock Waves* [1975, with Peter Cushing], *The Nesting* [1979], *The Scarecrow* [1981]). Not long after making a brief, pajama-clad appearance as an entombed lunatic in Harry Alan Towers' *Buried Alive*, Carradine died of heart and kidney failure in Milan on Thanksgiving Day, 1988. His last, defiant act—before being rushed to hospital and dying in his son David's arms—was to climb the 328 steps of the Gothic Duomo Cathedral. With typical theatricality, his final words were: "Milan: What a beautiful place to die!" He was buried at sea.

Although Christopher Lee referred to *House of the Long Shadows* as "worse than nothing" (to Mark A. Miller and Tom Johnson), he also called it "one of my most enjoyable to work on." This was, of course, due to the camaraderie he shared with his screen companions. To Lucy Chase Williams, Lee recalled corpsing when attacking Vincent Price with an axe and told the same author: "One day, somebody said, 'Get Mr. Price down, we want to set up the scene,' and so we waited, and we waited." Price eventually "appeared … in front of everybody on the set, ready to do the setup—but he was *not* wearing his trousers. He was immaculately dressed, including his jockey shorts, but no trousers … He said, 'Yes, I'm ready when you are. What's the hold up?' … It was a marvelous experience for the four of us, we had a wonderful time …"

As well as sharing the same birthday, height and renown as horror stars, there were further parallels in the lives of Christopher Lee and Vincent Price: Both had been villains in versions of *The Three Musketeers* (Price in 1948 with Gene Kelly), both had fought onscreen against Errol Flynn (*The Adventures of Captain Fabian* [1950] for Price) and both would eventually appear in Disney movies (Price voiced Professor Ratigan in *Basil the Great Mouse Detective* [1986]). The two men were also professionals, often in films beneath their stature and intelligence, but finding reward in the challenge and learning of their beloved craft. *House of the Long Shadows* would prove a particular trial: "I hated it," Price told Mark A. Miller; when the same author asked Lee for "his memories of Pete Walker directing him," the actor "replied simply, 'He didn't.'"

First seen lit from beneath, like his entrance in *Dracula: Prince of Darkness*, Lee is, at least, able to broaden his sinister portrayal of Roderick Grisbane with a fine bit of subtle humor: Note his impatient winces throughout Keith's dreadful singing, or the way he twitches with discomfort at the flirtatious talk of ingénue Louise English (b. 1962; after making her debut in Alan Parker's *Bugsy Malone* [1975], Louise went on to join "Hill's Angels" on *The Benny Hill Show*). Price, too, is in particularly fruity form ("Please don't interrupt me while I am soliloquizing"), while Cushing's deadpan comic expressions are often evocative of Stan Laurel. (Cushing had, of course, worked with Laurel and Hardy in 1939's *A Chump at Oxford*.) Yet such elegant playing is not enough to save a hoary and all too obvious plot, which is neither horrific, nor bizarre enough to fulfil the promise of its advertising. (On the plus side, Richard Harvey's score is appropriately atmospheric—Harvey [b. 1953] also provided music for *Tales of the Unexpected* and Gerry Anderson's *Terrahawks* [1983-1986].)

Depressingly underlit throughout by Norman Langley (*Die Screaming Marianne*, *Jekyll & Hyde*), *House of the Long Shadows* never achieves the balance it requires: The incongruous acid soaking of Louise English's character, for example, is nasty rather than scary and the story's final "twist" is just as disagreeably outmoded as it was when presented in 1935's *Mark of the Vampire*. Despite the extended screen time allotted to its stars, the film as a whole comes across as a diluted imitation of *The Old Dark House* and is, ultimately, even less satisfying than *Scream and Scream Again*.

Given a simultaneous theatrical and video rental release in the UK on Thursday, June 16, 1983, *House of the Long Shadows* emerged in the US the following April. Met with withering critiques ("Christopher Lee [is] so wooden that it's hard to tell if he's in a coffin or not"—*Time Out*), the movie's lack of success is explained by Jonathan Rigby in *English Gothic*: "[*House of the Long Shadows*] found itself competing at one West End cinema with *Halloween III: Season of the Witch* and, at another, no less a cutting-edge gorefest than Dario Argento's *Tenebrae*."

As Vincent Price laments in the film itself: "The old order is gone forever, and now we too must crumble into dust."

Price would go on to *Bloodbath at the House of Death* (1983), *From a Whisper to a Scream* (1986) and *The Whales of August* (1986), before bowing out gracefully as the inventor of *Edward Scissorhands* (1989). He died of lung cancer on Monday, October 25, 1993. From the Russian location of *Police Academy: Mission to Moscow*, Christopher Lee told the press: "The world has lost a great actor and I have lost a wonderful friend."

Faerie Tale Theatre: The Boy Who Left Home to Find Out About the Shivers 1983

New Magic (1983)
Mio in the Land of Faraway (1986)

Sometimes people won't talk to me or approach me because they are frightened. Never children. They always see below the surface ...—Christopher Lee, quoted in *Christopher Lee and Peter Cushing and Horror Cinema*

Christopher was out somewhere, I was in the bathroom at the hotel with a face-pack on—looking like something out of one of Christopher's movies,... There was a knock on the door ... About a dozen little children ,,, with huge brown eyes stared in and said, 'We've come to see Christopher.' I explained that he was out and maybe they should come back later. They did and he sat talking to them. He could get about eight of their hands into his hand, and they stood there, looking adoringly up at him.—Gitte Lee recalls a family holiday in Panama to Susan d'Arcy, *Photoplay* (October 1972)

"Fairy tales suit me, as a witch does a black cat," Christopher Lee wrote in his memoirs. Indeed, Hammer scribe Jimmy Sangster often called his Gothic horror films with Lee "elaborate fairy tales" and described his starting point for writing them as: "Once upon a time, in a castle at the top of a mountain, there lived a wicked monster ..." Boris Karloff, too, was an aficionado of fairy tales, lending his voice to a 1964 Hans Christian Andersen animation, *The Daydreamer*, while Vincent Price maintained, in Alan Frank's *Horror Movies* (Octopus Books, 1974), that "*Snow White and the Seven Dwarfs* was one of the most frightening films I ever saw." (In his autobiography, Dario Argento states that *Snow White* was an inspiration for one of the most frightening films *anyone* ever saw: *Suspiria* [1976].)

What the above-mentioned Masters of Horror all understood is that fairy tales are not just exercises in wonder; they are often far grislier than your average terror movie. Especially dark are those 19th century parables collected by the Brothers Grimm, with their cannibalistic witches, baby-snatching elves and neurotic, talking animals. One such tale, "The Story of a Boy Who Went Forth to Learn Fear," would, with a slight retitling, provide a splendid showcase for Christopher Lee, as part of Shelley Duvall's *Faerie Tale Theatre*.

Named after Mary Shelley, Duvall (b. 1949) made her debut in Robert Altman's fantasy *Brewster McCloud* (1970), before giving standout performances as Millie Lammoreaux in *3 Women* (1976), Jack Nicholson's tormented wife in *The Shining* and Olive Oyle in *Popeye* (1980). It was while working on the latter that she had the idea of a fairy tale TV anthology, inspired by fond memories of *Shirley Temple's Storybook* (1958-1961; on which Boris Karloff had guested for "The Legend of Sleepy Hollow"). After forming her own company, Platypus Productions, Duvall convinced her *Popeye* co-star, Robin Williams, to star in the series' pilot "The Tale of the Frog Prince," which aired on Showtime in September 1982 (the second episode starred Lee's *Man with the Golden Gun* ally, Hervé Villechaize, as "Rumpelstiltskin"). Over the next five years, Shelley produced and hosted a total of 27 *Faerie Tale Theatre* entries, using her respected position in the industry to bag star names and even provide opportunities for up-and-coming talents: After playing the mother of young Victor Frankenstein in Tim Burton's original *Frankenweenie* (1983), Duvall invited Burton to direct "Aladdin & His Wonderful Lamp" (1984).

"The Boy Who Left Home to Find Out About the Shivers" was the seventh episode of a third season which had already treated viewers to Paul Reubens as "Pinocchio," Vincent Price as the Magic Mirror in "Snow White and the Seven Dwarfs" and Klaus Kinski and Susan Sarandon in Roger Vadim's "Beauty and the Beast." Lee's entry was videotaped at ABC Television Centre, Los Angeles, at the end of 1983, under the auspices of Australian-born director Graeme Clifford (b. 1942), who had recently put Malcolm McDowell through his paces as the Wolf in "Little Red Riding Hood."

Clifford began his career as an editor, bringing innovative cutting techniques to *Don't Look Now*, *The Rocky Horror Picture Show* and *The Man Who Fell to Earth* (1975), as well as four episodes of *The New Avengers*. After making his directorial debut on the latter series, he went on to helm the Oscar-nominated biopic *Frances* (1981), the skateboarding thriller *Gleaming the Cube* (1987) and the Emmy-nominated miniseries *The Last Don* (1997).

Broadcast on Monday, September 17, 1984, "The Boy Who Left Home to Find Out About the Shivers" is introduced by Duvall, in her sweet manner, from a windswept graveyard, complete with hanging corpse and howling wolves. Vincent Price's narration, like a beloved friend, first sets up the action "in the mysterious and forbidding land of Transylvania" where self-assured young Martin (Peter MacNicol) journeys from the garlic-festooned home of his superstitious family to rid a haunted castle of its evil spirits. The castle, of course, belongs to Christopher Lee, who, as King Vladimir, first meets Martin at the Stake & Brew Inn. A typical parody of Hammer taverns, where locals fall silent at the mention of certain castles, the place is run by David Warner's jovial innkeeper, Zandor.

Warner (b. 1941) would next play the heroine's father in the fairy tale inspired *The Company of Wolves* (1984), before giving a sensitive portrayal as the creation of *Frankenstein*. This Yorkshire TV production (broadcast on December 27, 1984) features a laboratory confrontation with Carrie Fisher's Elizabeth, which replicates, almost scene for scene, Lee's snaring of Valerie Gaunt in *The Curse of Frankenstein*. Since rising to fame as *King Kong* fan Morgan (1965), Warner had distinguished himself as the owner of a haunted mirror in *From Beyond the Grave*, the photographer who loses his head in *The Omen*, an

Christopher Lee (left), David Warner and young Peter MacNicol

obsessive bat hunter in *Nightwing* (1978), Jack the Ripper in *Time After Time* (1978); and the aptly named Evil in *Time Bandits* (1980, which also features Shelley Duvall). His subsequent genre credits include various mad scientists (*The Man with Two Brains* [1982], *My Best Friend is a Vampire* [1986], *Teenage Mutant Ninja Turtles II* [1990]), villains (*The Island* [1979], *Tron* [1981], *Waxwork* [1987]), Lovecraftian characters (*Cast a Deadly Spell* [1990], *The Unnamable Returns* [1992], *Necronomicon* [1993], *In the Mouth of Madness* [1993]) and star cameos (*Body Bags* [1993], *Scream 2* [1997] and *The League of Gentlemen's Apocalypse* [2004]).

Decked out in long silver wig, purple tunic and heavy black cloak, Vladimir is introduced, by Zandor, as "the son of Vlad the Impaler" ("Also known as 'Bad Vlad,'" Lee adds). The interplay between Vladimir and Zandor positively crackles, with Lee's well-timed corrections to the innkeeper's frequent errors in speech, and his look of mild disgust on sipping Zandor's wine, being especially amusing.

In fact, the film is full of such charming touches: Challenged to spend three nights in Vladimir's haunted castle ("No one has ever gone into that castle and come out ... alive," Lee warns with a faint smile), Martin is measured up for his coffin even as he signs the contract. If he survives, he will win the hand of Vladimir's daughter, Princess Amanda (Dana Hill), and their ensuing romance is sweetly played out.

Peter MacNicol (b. 1954) gives a puckishly deadpan performance in the title role. Before finding fame as offbeat lawyer John Cage on *Ally McBeal* (1997-2002), MacNicol was the young apprentice of *Dragonslayer* (1980), the possessed Dr. Janosz Poha in *Ghostbusters II*, the over-enthusiastic summer camp manager of *Addams Family Values* (1993) and a spirited Renfield in Mel Brooks' underrated *Dracula: Dead and Loving It*.

Dana Hill (1964-1996) would go on to play Audrey Griswold in *National Lampoon's European Vacation* (1984) and lent her voice to many cartoons, including *Tom and Jerry: The Movie* (1992, as Jerry) and Disney's *The Hunchback of Notre Dame* (1996). She passed away from diabetes at the age of 32.

Lee's mute, hunchbacked servant Attila, who breathes all over the food he serves, is played by musician Frank Zappa (1940-1993). As well as appearing with a talking bull in the Monkees' sublime fantasy *Head* (1968), Zappa created the amusingly inventive, if self-indulgent, *200 Motels* (1971). Among the zany cast of the latter is Theodore Bikel as Rance Muhammitz—a part originally intended for Christopher Lee.

With its creaking doors, swinging pendulum and living gargoyles, Vladimir's castle is a cobweb-smothered delight. Its ghosts, too, are superbly realized: Whether white-shrouded apparitions, scythe-wielding ghouls or a twisted face that floats from the fireplace (as MacNicol nonchalantly toasts marshmallows) these shambling phantoms are more enjoyably frightening than the stalk-and-slash bogeymen who were then haunting cinema screens (*Friday the 13th*'s Jason Voorhees, etc.).

Rising from a black coffin, delivered by the aforementioned ghouls, Vladimir disguises himself as an evil sorcerer in straight dark wig and wispy beard. "You are going to *die*," he snarls at Martin, but, despite an awesome display of hand gestures, he ends up rolled in a carpet, spitting out dust. When Martin tickles him with the fronds from the rug, Lee lets out an appealing giggle completely at odds with his imperious presence. Although Lee often admitted that, as an actor, he found it difficult to laugh convincingly onscreen, he successfully adds yet another unexpected endearment to his character. Indeed, Lee's skill at withering put-downs, his irritation barely concealed and his surprising bursts of bumbling fright, make King Vladimir one of the funniest, and most commendable, performances of the actor's career.

Just prior to his stint on *Faerie Tale Theatre*, Lee essayed another sorcerer for *New Magic* (1983)—a 22-minute short, released to theaters in February 1984. Accompanied by his bumbling apprentice, Gerrit Graham (*Phantom of the Paradise*, *TerrorVision*), Lee's Mr. Kellar (based on American magician Harry Kellar [1849-1922]) explains the virtues of a new cinematic process, Showscan. The brainchild of special effects legend Douglas Trumbull (*2001*, *Silent Running*, *Blade Runner*), Showscan gave the effect of "3-D without the glasses" by projecting 70mm footage at 60 frames per second (as opposed to the usual 24). Unfortunately, this innovation would swiftly be succeeded by the less expensive IMAX technology.

Comprehending the link between fairy tales and horror, Shelley Duvall next embarked upon *Nightmare Classics* (1989), which comprised four literary adaptations: "The Turn of the Screw" (again directed by Clifford), "Carmilla" (with Ione Skye), "The Strange Case of Dr. Jekyll and Mr. Hyde" (with Anthony Andrews) and Ambrose Bierce's "The Eyes of the Panther" (with C. Thomas Howell). Duvall would reappear with Lee in *Talos the Mummy*.

While the influence of the fairy tale had already been seen in such disparate efforts as Cocteau's *La Belle et La Bête* (1945), *Jack the Giant Killer* (1960) and *The Wonderful World of the Brothers Grimm* (1961), the advance of special effects eased the realization of fairy lands with such 1980s productions as *The Company of Wolves*, Ridley Scott's *Legend* and a wonderful Jim Henson series, *The Storyteller* (1986-1988)—the second episode of which, "Fearnot," was an adaptation of "The Boy Who Went Forth to Learn Fear." Lost among this influx was *Walhalla* (1986)—a Danish cartoon for which Christopher Lee provided the voices of Odin and Thor in its German-language version—and *Mio in the Land of Faraway* (1986), an exquisite Swedish fantasy filmed in Russia wherein Lee's steel-clawed ex-knight Kato captures children and transforms them into birds. Tracked to his castle lair by two brave youngsters (Nicholas Pickard and a pre-*Empire of the Sun* Christian Bale), Lee manages somehow to lend a sympathetic note to yet another evil character by the final reel. The results are recommended and make a fine companion piece to "The Boy Who Left Home to Find Out About the Shivers."

Howling II
1984

The rocking, shocking, new wave of horror!

> I impressed [Christopher Lee] when I got permission from the Vatican for him to desecrate the tomb of Good King Wenceslas by killing werewolves in it.—Philippe Mora to Calum Waddell, *The Dark Side*

In 1984, Hammer announced that Christopher Lee was to star in *Dracula: The Beginning*—Brian Hayles' old screenplay which merged Stoker's Count with Vlad the Impaler. While intriguing, it was never made. Unfortunately, *Howling II* was.

Joe Dante's *The Howling* had been a huge success upon its release in the spring of 1981. Three years later, with Dante busy on more personal projects (*Gremlins, Explorers*), the inevitable sequel was entrusted to director Philippe Mora (b. 1949)—for whom Lee had starred as Mr. Midnight in *The Return of Captain Invincible* (1981). Mora told Calum Waddell, in *The Dark Side* #168, that after filming this fun superhero musical in Australia, Lee said to him one evening: "You know what? It would be nice to add a werewolf film to this vampire résumé that I have." (In *Christopher Lee's New Chamber of Horrors* [1974], the actor had hinted at a similar desire when introducing Algernon Blackwood's "The Empty Sleeve": "Despite the variety of roles I have appeared in on the screen, I have yet to be asked to play a *Lycanthrope*—but if I were, here, in the role of the sinister Mr. Hyman, is one that I might enjoy …"; alas, *Howling II*, subtitled *Your Sister is a Werewolf* [US] and *Stirba—Werewolf Bitch* [UK], is a far cry from Algernon Blackwood.) As Mora put it to Waddell, "when *Howling II* came along there really was no one else to call …"

Described by Ferdy Mayne as "Very talented and quite daft," Philippe Mora was born in Paris, but raised in Australia. Entering the cinematic field with such documentaries as the Golden Globe-nominated *Brother, Can You Spare a Dime?* (1975, which incorporates clips from *King Kong*), Mora's dramatic debut, *Mad Dog Morgan* (1975, starring Dennis Hopper), was followed by an earlier exploration of metamorphosis, *The Beast Within* (1981): Written by *Fright Night*'s Tom Holland, this plays like a modern-day retelling of *The Curse of the Werewolf* with ickier special effects. Before putting Beverly D'Angelo through her paces as the *Pterodactyl Woman from Beverly Hills* (1997), Mora would direct *Howling III: The Marsupials* (1987) and *Communion* (1988). The latter is based upon the real-life extra-terrestrial encounters of Mora's friend, author Whitley Strieber, who would document the director's own experience with such beings in his 1988 book *Transformation*.

Howling II began filming on Monday, August 13, 1984, behind the Iron Curtain in Prague. This was a risky thing to do considering the political climate of the time, with the city occupied by Communist Soviet troops, who, according to Mora, forbid the use of "walkie-talkies, photocopiers or any sort of modern devices." The director further remembered, to Waddell, that he and his crew were "under constant watch," but, "We all got used to it—including Christopher."

The script was initiated by Gary Brandner (1930-2013), author of the original *Howling* books, as a straight adaptation of his 1979 novel *Return of the Howling*. Unfortunately, Brandner had a publishing deadline to meet and was replaced by first-time writer Robert Sarno. The resultant screenplay bears no relation to Brandner's work and often confuses its subject with vampires (garlic and stakes are introduced as werewolf deterrents, for example). Nevertheless, the film begins encouragingly enough with a pre-credit scene of Lee's occult investigator, Stefan Crosscoe, superimposed amid the stars, reading from the Book of Revelation, with a skeleton peeking over his shoulder. We then cut to the funeral of Karen White (the TV reporter played by Dee Wallace in the first movie), where Stefan introduces himself to Karen's brother Ben (Reb Brown) and Ben's girlfriend Jenny (Annie McEnroe). Together, they set off for Transylvania to destroy Stirba, Queen of the Werewolves (Sybil Danning).

As ever, Lee is to be commended for keeping a straight face, never once allowing his character's belief in the supernatural to slip. But his authenticity is surrounded and impaired by scenes of the utmost ludicrousness, such as when he has to chase an eyeless, chuckling dwarf, or when he glows with a red aura, as though he has just finished eating his Ready Brek.

One incredible moment sees Lee don shades, his own brown leather jacket and jeans in order to look inconspicuous at a punk club. Here, to the strains of a ridiculous song—performed ad infinitum throughout the film by a band named Babel—he spies upon werewolf Mariana (played by *Dracula A.D. 1972*'s Marsha Hunt). Among her obnoxious victims is Jimmy Nail (b. 1954), who was then familiar to British audiences from his role in the hit TV comedy-drama *Auf Wiedersehen, Pet* (1983-2004).

Also on hand is Ferdy Mayne (1916-1998), who had just portrayed an evil wizard in *Conan the Destroyer* (1983). "Christopher and I are old friends," Ferdy told David Del Valle (in *LSoH* #27), "and in fact share a secret joke about a glass eye that can still reduce us to giddy schoolgirls at the drop of a hat." Immor-

Christopher Lee and Sybil Danning

talized as Count von Krolock in *Dance of the Vampires*, the German-born Mayne fled the Nazis in 1932. Arriving in Britain, he made his debut, as a Prussian student, in Powell and Pressburger's *The Life and Death of Colonel Blimp* (1942), before establishing himself in such films as *Where Eagles Dare*, *The Magic Christian* and *The Vampire Lovers* ("It was rather delicious to be bitten by [Ingrid Pitt]," he enthused in *Flesh and Blood*). Prior to being stabbed by Christopher Lee for *Howling II* (near Franz Kafka's grave), he had starred as the resurrected horror star Conrad Ragzoff in *Frightmare* (1981)—a role turned down by Lee, who nevertheless features in the film via clips from *Uncle Was a Vampire*, which represent Ragzoff's early work.

Fresh from enacting *Yor, the Hunter from the Future* (1983, Antonio Margheriti's most financially successful movie), Reb Brown (b. 1948) had previously tussled with Christopher Lee in *Captain America II* (1979). This made-for-TV adventure sees Lee's villain unleash a chemical over Venice Beach that causes rapid aging (to the strains of an annoyingly cheesy 1970s soundtrack). Appropriately wholesome as the titular hero, Reb was given a cameo in *Captain America: The First Avenger* (2010). His other genre credits include *Sssssss* (1972), *Space Mutiny* (1988) and *Night Claws* (2012).

Annie McEnroe (born c. 1956), who had starred in Oliver Stone's horror film *The Hand* (1980) with Michael Caine, would later play interfering realtor, Jane Butterfield, in *Beetlejuice*.

Austrian actress Sybil Danning (b. 1952) had formerly co-starred with Christopher Lee as Eugenie in the first two *Musketeers* films, before rejoining him for *Whispering Death* (1975), a horrible rape-revenge drama, in which Lee excels as the Rhodesian Police Commissioner; the veracity of his performance stemming, no doubt, from his own wartime experiences. During filming in South Africa, Christopher proved just as heroic offscreen as on, by defying apartheid and insisting that an integrated crew be hired. (Sybil can also be seen with Lee in *The Salamander* [1980], an Italian thriller adapted by Rod Serling.)

Danning started out in a classic giallo, *The Red Queen Kills Seven Times* (1971), before falling victim to Richard Burton's *Bluebeard* (1971) and being imperiled by *Meteor* (1977). In between Golan and Globus outings as an international terrorist in *Operation Thunderbolt* (1976, with Klaus Kinski) and the evil Princess Adriana in *Hercules* (1982), she starred as intergalactic warrior Saint-Exmin of the Valkyrie in *Battle Beyond the Stars* and "The Dark Angel of Dallas" in *V* (1984). Her post-*Howling II* career includes *Amazon Women on the Moon* (1985, as Queen Lara), *The Tomb* (1985, in a pre-credits cameo totally unrelated to the female vampire-mummy movie that follows) and Rob Zombie's 2007 remake of *Halloween* (as Nurse Wynn).

Having recently seen his part excised from David Lynch's theatrical cut of *Dune*, Judd Omen (b. 1940) now faced the indignity of frolicking in a bestial *ménage à trois* as Stirba's werewolf aide, Vlad (this is even more embarrassing than when the actor was mauled by a zombie poodle in *C.H.U.D. II–Bud the Chud*). Judd would fare better as the escaped convict on *Pee-wee's Big Adventure* (1984), the Phantom in *Freddy's Nightmares*: "The Art of Death" (1988) and the Mayor in *Dollman* (1991).

Howling II was given limited theatrical release in the US, in December 1985. Just as *The Howling* had to compete with *An American Werewolf in London*, *Full Moon High* and *Wolfen* on its original release, *Howling II* had been preceded into American theaters by three other lycanthropic ventures: Paul Naschy's *The Night of the Werewolf* (its first US outing as *The Craving*), Stephen King's *Silver Bullet* and Michael J. Fox's *Teen Wolf*. Six further *Howling* sequels were issued straight-to-video, of which *Howling VI: The Freaks* (1990) is the most interesting. *Howling II* was a flop.

The film's camp tone is merely vulgar, not funny, and the whole is made even more depressing by being dingily lit. Indeed, the entire movie seems to hinge on the pathetic promise of seeing Sybil Danning in the nude. This intention is confirmed by the endless repetition of the actress ripping her top off throughout the final credits. To make matters worse, footage of Christopher Lee is intercut so it looks as though he is reacting to Sybil's breasts—in much the same way that Ed Wood made Bela Lugosi appear to be responding to writhing, scantily-clad women in *Glen or Glenda* (1953). Unlike the 1950s output of Ed Wood, however, *Howling II* lacks any sense of passion or sincerity. It is not even so-bad-it's-good. It is just simply bad.

Especially inane are the werewolf make-ups, which have no consistency whatsoever: A naked Marsha Hunt is given a lumpen visage that almost resembles rotting flesh, while a fully clothed Ferdy Mayne stumbles about in an ape-like rubber mask. In fact, most of the wolf costumes were refugees from the 1974 *Planet of the Apes* TV series. Their simian appearance gave rise to Lee's suggestion that Stefan should reference a monkey phase between human-to-wolf transformations, thus his improvised line: "The process of evolution is reversed."

Sadly, as Jonathan Rigby notes, Lee "looks unusually grey and ill" in *Howling II*. The problem turned out to be a leaking heart valve, for which the actor underwent open-heart surgery in June 1985. As he revealed on behind-the-scenes footage from *Flesh and Blood*, Lee suggested to his surgeon that Peter Cushing should perform the operation: "I said, 'As a matter of fact, I have a friend who'll do it for free … I don't know what I'll look like at the end of it …'" In the same clip, Lee further revealed that the first phone call he received on leaving hospital was from Vincent Price, who responded to Lee's weary groan of "Hello" with: "Is that the late Christopher Lee?"

Consequently, Lee made one more movie as a Los Angeles denizen, the fatuous comedy *Jocks* (1984), before returning to England permanently in April 1985. Here, he was rewarded with one of his best non-horror roles, as James I of Aragon, in the Channel 4 drama *The Disputation* (1985). As the actor told David Del Valle, in *Films and Filming* (September 1985): "I've made my point. I don't think the British casting directors, directors, or producers think of me now as they may conceivably have done before."

Panga
1989

Deep in the heart of darkness a nightmare is
about to begin ...

Shortly after *Howling II*, Christopher Lee starred as the chief of police in *Mask of Murder* (1985), alongside *The Time Machine*'s Rod Taylor. Despite spurious UK video packaging, the film is merely a thriller. Much better is the similarly titled *Murder Story* (1988), with Lee as a mystery writer, and *Treasure Island* (1989), wherein the actor's Blind Pew "makes Freddy Krueger look like Santa Claus" (in the words of the *Chicago Tribune*).

But Lee's true return to horror came with *Panga*, which began production on Sunday, June 4, 1989, in Southeast Africa. The film marked the directorial debut of Sean Barton (b. 1944), who edited such prestigious pictures as *Quadrophenia* (1978), *Eye of the Needle* and *Return of the Jedi*. Barton also contributed to the screenplay, which was based on an original story by South African actor Richard Haddon Haines (1948-1990).

This film would eventually be released straight-to-video in the US, on Friday, May 10, 1991, as *Curse III: Blood Sacrifice*—despite having nothing to do with the previous *Curse* movies.

Directed by *Firestarter* actor David Keith, *The Curse* (1986) is quite a faithful retelling of H.P. Lovecraft's "The Color Out of Space," with set-pieces that veer from the sublime (a creepy

The white-suited Dr. Pearson (Christopher Lee)

woman in the basement) to the ridiculous (Amy Wheaton being attacked by chickens). Sharing only the same Italian producer, Ovidio G. Assonitis, *Curse II: The Bite* (1988) is a more interesting piece, about a young man who gradually transforms into a snake, emboldened by good effects (courtesy of Screaming Mad George) and strong leads (Jill Schoelen and J. Eddie Peck).

Panga, on the other hand, is set in 1950 and concerns the voodoo curse laid upon an American visitor to Africa (Jenilee Harrison), when she interrupts an animal sacrifice. Aiding her is a top-billed Christopher Lee as the bearded, white-suited Dr. Pearson. Although suffering from a bad cold throughout filming (which he uses to good effect for Pearson's gruff voice), Lee gives a nicely relaxed performance, clearing his throat when he thinks he's alone and even wearing his own lucky elephant hair bracelet (which can also be seen in the famous publicity shot for *Dracula* with Melissa Stribling). In a refreshing change, he ends the film with the heroine clasped in his arms and brings a candor few other actors can reach to lines like, "I sacrificed a goat"; or "I've seen things that can't possibly be explained by modern science."

Unfortunately, though beautifully lit (by Philip Grosvenor, who had previously worked as a camera assistant on *The Spy Who Loved Me*, *Superman* [*I* and *II*] and *Moonraker*), *Panga* is a lumbering bore. Regardless of efforts to remain tasteful and atypical, the film's dull action ultimately gives way to too many 1980s horror clichés (gratuitous female nudity, point-of-view shots from an approaching threat). Furthermore, when the curse's machete-wielding monster finally does make an appearance, it is hardly worth waiting for, resembling nothing more than a stodgy second cousin to *The Monster of Piedras Blancas* (1958).

The fish-faced fiend was the work of Chris Walas (b. 1955), who provided superior effects on David Cronenberg's *The Fly* (1986). As well as directing *The Fly II* (edited by Sean Barton), Walas designed, created and operated the creatures who form the centerpiece of Christopher Lee's next genre movie.

The Loneliness of Evil

Gremlins 2: The New Batch 1989

The Rainbow Thief (1990)

It is often repeated that Lee considered Lord Summerisle the finest role he ever played. I recall asking him once which was the second best. He mulled for a moment, then said Doctor Catheter. In *Gremlins 2*.—Allan Brown, *Inside the Wicker Man*.

[Joe Dante] claims to have seen all of my films. I'm not sure whether I should congratulate him or apologize!—Christopher Lee to Tom Johnson and Mark A. Miller

Gremlins was America's fourth highest-grossing movie of 1984 (following *Beverly Hills Cop*, *Ghostbusters*, and *Indiana Jones and the Temple of Doom*). Naturally, its studio, Warner Bros. wanted a sequel. Unfortunately, the film's director, Joe Dante, wasn't interested in producing one … until he was promised complete creative control.

Having no desire to emulate the original, Dante and his screenwriter, Charles S. Haas (b. 1952; whose adaptation of Fredric Brown's humorous sci-fi novel, *Martians, Go Home*, had just been turned into a silly film), elected instead to create a manic,

anarchic in-joke of a movie, which breaks the fourth wall at every opportunity. As Dante told the *Telegraph* in 2003, this approach was very much influenced by Universal's 1941 comedy-musical *Hellzapoppin'*, which, akin to *Gremlins 2*, abandons narrative in favor of quick-fire gags, star cameos, and "film-within-a-film" innovations, such as the Frankenstein Monster (Dale Van Sickel) throwing Martha Raye onto the back of a pogoing bear. As Dante admits on his 2002 DVD commentary for *Gremlins 2*, he found further inspiration in William Castle's *The Tingler*, whose monster also invades a cinema, causing the film to break down.

Born in 1946, Dante outlined his own cinema-going habits in *Flesh and Blood*: "*(Horror of) Dracula* was a particularly big moment in my life and the life of a lot of kids my age." Among those "kids" were Joe's contemporaries, Steven Spielberg, George Lucas, and John Landis—a new wave of filmmakers, whose relative youthfulness was so at odds with the power they yielded that they were regarded as something of an '80s phenomenon. All of the above-named directors were inspired to make movies from an early love of horror, and all of them would consequently work with Christopher Lee.

As a youngster, Dante contributed articles to both *Famous Monsters of Filmland* and *Castle of Frankenstein*, before becoming a protégé of Roger Corman. The latter served as executive producer on Joe's genre debut, *Piranha* (1978). Despite an affectionate air, full of in-jokes and pop culture references, both *Piranha* and the director's next fantasy outing, *The Howling*, succeed as engaging thrillers. Indeed, Dante was responsible for the most interesting segment of *Twilight Zone: The Movie* (1982).

Prior to his *Fantastic Voyage*-inspired *Innerspace* (1986) and beautiful William Castle homage *Matinee* (1992), Joe paid tribute to Hammer's *Dracula* by partially restaging its climax for the first *Gremlins* movie (which took place on Christmas Eve, the same day the *Dracula* finale was filmed). Parenthetically, the writer of the first *Gremlins*, Chris Columbus, went on to helm the highly successful Harry Potter franchise. For the first film in the series, *Harry Potter and the Philosopher's Stone* (2000), Columbus again adapted *Dracula*'s closing moments: The disintegration of Ian Hart's villainous Voldemort was achieved with a little help from wardrobe mistress Rosemary Burrows—who had performed the same duties for Hammer since their first vampire film (Rosemary was also married to Lee's *Dracula* stunt double Eddie Powell).

Gremlins 2 began shooting on Friday May 26, 1989 (the day before Christopher Lee's 67th birthday). The film's cartoonish tone is set right from the outset with Bugs Bunny and Daffy Duck squabbling over the Warner Bros. logo, which then zooms and crashes into the screen. Following an aerial shot of New York (taken from *Superman IV: The Quest for Peace*), the proceeding action takes place at the high-tech skyscraper lorded over by Daniel Clamp (John Glover), a very thinly disguised Donald Trump-like tycoon. Here, we reunite with the amiable lovers of the first film, Billy Peltzer (Zach Galligan) and Kate Beringer (Phoebe Cates). (Galligan [b. 1964] is also the smart-ass hero of the *Waxwork* films, which reference Lee's earlier horror classics, while Cates [b. 1963] would snog Judge Reinhold [in *Fast Times at Ridgemont High*, 1981], marry Kevin Kline [in real life, 1989] and [try to] avoid *Drop Dead Fred* [1990].)

Another employee at the Clamp Centre is Christopher Lee's Dr. Catheter. Lee arrived at Warner Bros. Studios, Hollywood, to film his scenes in July 1989. As Dante remembered for the

Dr. Catheter vs. a Gremlin

DVD commentary: "When Chris came in the first day, to meet me in my office, one of the first things he did was apologize for being in *Howling II* ..." Dante further recalled that Lee had originally wanted to present Dr. Catheter as a wild-haired, Einsteinian figure, until the director steered him towards a more austere performance. Ultimately, as the actor told Johnson and Miller, "the doctor comes across as similar to Peter's Frankenstein—overly dedicated ... to the point of not recognizing the problems he's causing ..." Certainly, in the 1990 novelization of *Gremlins 2*, author David Bischoff gives Catheter's first name as Cushing and writes: "He was a tall man whose narrow features and crooked teeth made him look very much like the Dracula of Hammer horror films." (A *Gremlins 2* video game was also issued for Nintendo in October 1990, but this did not feature Dr. Catheter.)

Promoted as his 203rd film role, Lee brings a deft comic touch to his mad scientist ("Oh, splendid! This must be my malaria!" is his opening line). Among the oddities housed in Catheter's laboratory are a giant spider, an electric rat and a brain in a jar, belonging to W.H. Donovan; at one point, Lee is even seen clutching an *Invasion of the Body Snatchers* pod. A new addition is Gizmo, the adorable little Mogwai, who has been captured by the doctor's assistants, Martin and Lewis (played by real-life twins, Don and Dan Stanton [b. 1952], who reappear in *Terminator 2: Judgement Day* [1990] and Joe Dante's TV series *Eerie, Indiana* [1991-1992]).

"Cute. Isn't it," Catheter glowers, then looks on unimpressed as Gizmo dances across the table to Fats Domino's 1959 hit "I'm Ready." "He likes this music?" Lee utters with exquisite disgust, his tone lightening only at the thought of Gizmo's dissection. Catheter is less amused, however, when faced with the Mogwai's evil offspring: "All they have to do is to eat three or four children," he laments of the Gremlins, "and there'd be the most appalling publicity!" In a nod to Dracula, the actor then has to duck as a Bat Gremlin swoops around his head. This is just one of many imaginatively varied monsters, which also include a crazed Laurence Olivier-in-*Marathon Man* Gremlin ("Is it safe?"); a *Phantom of the Opera* Gremlin, complete with a shot-for-shot remake of Lon Chaney's unmasking scene; and a Wicked Witch of the West Gremlin ("I'm melting!"), while Gizmo himself eventually takes on the mantle of Sylvester Stallone's *Rambo*.

Referencing the above, Lee quipped to *Empire* magazine in July 1990: "After some of the people I've worked with, acting with lumps of inanimate fur was quite a refreshing change." The squeaks and burblings of that main lump of fur, Gizmo, are provided by Canadian comedian Howie Mandel (b. 1955)— who portrays a more obnoxious beastie in *Little Monsters* (1988). The Brain Gremlin, meanwhile, is voiced by Tony Randall (1920-2004). A familiar face from romantic comedies (*Pillow Talk* [1959]; *Let's Make Love* [1960]), Randall excelled as the *7 Faces of Dr. Lao* (1963), took part in Vincent Price's *Scavenger Hunt* (1979) and played a movie werewolf for an episode of *Happy Days* (1974-1984). He also brought his skills to NBC's *Arsenic & Old Lace* (1962), in which Boris Karloff reprised his original Broadway role of Jonathan Brewster.

The Loneliness of Evil

Christopher Lee with Dan Stanton, and Don Stanton

After having one of the monsters attach itself to his arm, Catheter is ultimately undone by an Electro-Gremlin. Despite reaching such an ignominious end, Lee told Jane Killick, in *Shivers* #13, that *Gremlins 2* was one of the "films where everything worked, where I had a very good script, a very good director, a good cast and crew and everything came together. It didn't happen all that often, you know …" (The other favorable movies cited by Lee in this piece are *The Wicker Man*, *A Tale of Two Cities*, *Dracula*, *The Man with the Golden Gun*, *The Three/Four Musketeers* and *Rasputin the Mad Monk*: "Then I have to start thinking …")

Gremlins 2 was also a favorite of its director, who states on the DVD commentary: "I don't think [Christopher] was prepared for how much the crew really loved him … When it came time for him to leave, they all … trooped up like they were going to church and shook his hand and wanted him to give autographs … I think it probably hadn't dawned on him how many people had grown up watching his movies and that he was actually …an icon."

As well as voicing the Witch Gremlin, Dante can be glimpsed briefly as the director of *Clamp Cable Network* horror host, Grandpa Fred, played by Robert Prosky (1930-2008). The Polish-American actor was also Father Fonescu in *The Keep* (1982), the grouchy garage owner of *Christine* (1983) and the magical cinema projectionist in *Last Action Hero* (1993). His Fred character is a tribute to Al Lewis' Grandpa from the legendary '60s show *The Munsters*. Between 1987 and 1989, Lewis could be seen in his vampire garb, introducing horror movies (including Lee's *The Mummy* and *Dracula Has Risen from the Grave*) for TBS' *Super Scary Saturday*. In *Gremlins 2*, Prosky has a nice exchange with Zach Galligan, which reflects both Dante's affection for classic genre cinema and the way those old myths sit within a modern world: "People that watch TV at three-thirty in the morning aren't scared of *The Wolf Man*. The only thing that scares those people is getting sober and finding work." While Billy urges Fred to "run some of the classic horror movies, like *Frankenstein* and *Dracula*," the dissatisfied host is, instead, forced by the network to screen the less-than-classic *Octaman* (1971), whose titular creature was the first to be designed by Rick Baker.

Born in 1950, Baker replaces an otherwise engaged Chris Walas as the special effects supervisor (and co-producer) of *Gremlins 2*. Especially adept at werewolves (*An American Werewolf in London* [for which Vincent Price presented him with the very first Academy Award for Best Makeup], *Werewolf* [1987-1988], *Wolf* [1993]) and primates (*Schlock* [1971], *King Kong* [1976, in which he also plays the eponymous ape], *Greystoke* [1983]), Baker's other amazing make-up and effects credits include *It's Alive* (1973), *The Funhouse* (1980), *Ghost Story* (1981), *Videodrome* (1981), Michael Jackson's *Thriller* (1983), *Harry and the Hendersons* (1986), the *Men in Black* trilogy (1996-2011) and *The Ring* (2002).

While Al Lewis may not have been on board to recreate his beloved Grandpa role, the star of *The Munsters*' rival show, *The Addams Family*, does appear in *Gremlins 2* as the Clamp Centre janitor: John Astin (b. 1930) was not only the exuberant Gomez Addams, but also Jodie Foster's father in *Freaky Friday* (1976), Dean Dunn in *Teen Wolf Too* (1987), Professor Gangreen in the *Killer Tomatoes* franchise (1987-1991) and the ghostly Judge of Peter Jackson's *The Frighteners* (1995). In addition, he essayed Van Helsing for the 1980s stage production *Dracula: The Story You Thought You Knew*; he can be seen discussing the finer points of *When Dinosaurs Ruled the Earth* with Vincent Price on the 1974 TV special *The Horror Hall of Fame*; and his 1972 marriage to actress Patty Duke made him the adoptive father of Christopher Lee's *Lord of the Rings* co-star Sean Astin.

Reprising his role as the avuncular Murray Futterman from the original *Gremlins*, is much-loved character actor Dick Miller (1928-2019). An ex-boxer from the Bronx, Miller began his screen career in such Roger Corman quickies as *It Conquered the World*, *Not of this Earth* and *The Undead* (all 1956). Following rare leads in Corman's *Rock All Night* (1956) and *War of the Satellites* (1957), Miller flourished as murderous sculptor Walter Paisley in *A Bucket of Blood* (1959), a character he reprised, in name only, for *Hollywood Boulevard* (1975), *The Howling*, *Twilight Zone: The Movie*, *Chopping Mall* (1985) and *Night of the Creeps* (1986). Other Corman credits include the flower-munching Fouch in *The Little Shop of Horrors* (1960), the fairground heckler of *X: The Man with the X-Ray Eyes* (1963) and Boris Karloff's butler in *The Terror* (1962; while paying tribute to Karloff in *100 Years of Horror*, Miller con-

fessed that the first two films he ever saw were *Frankenstein* and *King Kong*: "I knew, years later, that this was what caused it all …"). Having previously appeared with Christopher Lee in *1941*, Dick also made regular contributions to Joe Dante movies: He is the manager of the summer resort besieged by *Piranha*, the helicopter pilot in *Explorers* (1984), the cabbie who denudes Dennis Quaid in *Innerspace*, Vic the Garbage Man in *The 'Burbs* (1988), a B-movie actor in *Matinee*, Joe in *Small Soldiers* (1997)and a security guard in *Looney Tunes: Back in Action* (2002). Like Michael Ripper at Hammer, Miller possessed the gift of crafting fully fleshed characters with just a few moments' screen time, making him equally unforgettable as the pawn shop clerk blown away by *The Terminator*, the diner waiter of Martin Scorsese's *After Hours* (1985)or the possessed Uncle Willy in *Tales from the Crypt: Demon Knight* (1994). A documentary, *That Guy Dick Miller*, was produced in 2014.

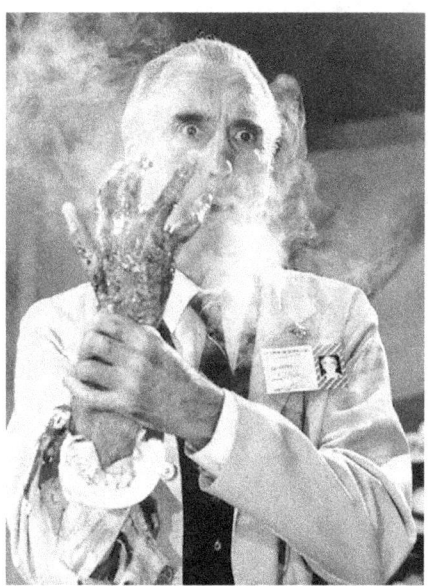

Also returning from the first film, as Gizmo's enigmatic owner Mr. Wing, is Keye Luke (1904-1991). Best known for his recurring role as Master Po in ABC's *Kung Fu* (1972-1975), the Chinese-American actor first found fame in the 1930s as Charlie Chan's "number one son." One such mystery, *Charlie Chan at the Opera* (1936), stars Boris Karloff as a deranged baritone. Luke would replace Karloff as Mr. Wong in Monogram's *Phantom of Chinatown* (1940) and the two men were both co-founders of the Screen Actors Guild. Following appearances opposite Peter Lorre in *Mad Love* (1935), *Mr. Moto's Gamble* (1938) and Universal's *Invisible Agent* (1942), Luke worked with William Castle (on *Project X* [1967]), John Carradine (on *The Cat Creature* [1973]) and Vincent Price (on *Dead Heat* [1987]). His voice can be heard in the English-language versions of *Godzilla Raids Again* (1955), *Rodan* (1956) and *Enter the Dragon* (as the villainous Han). A talented artist, Keye designed one of the most iconic posters for the original *King Kong* and sketched a fine Bela Lugosi profile for the March 31, 1932, edition of the *Los Angeles Times* (reproduced in Bill Kaffenberger and Gary D. Rhodes' book *Bela Lugosi In Person* [BearManor Media, 2015]).

Other notable cameos in *Gremlins 2* include the film's composer Jerry Goldsmith (*Planet of the Apes, Alien, Poltergeist*) as a concerned shopper; Gedde Watanabe (*Vamp*) as an unfortunately stereotyped Japanese camera fanatic; Paul Bartel (*Eating Raoul*) as the snooty theater manager; Kenneth Tobey (*The Thing from Another World*) as the ruffled projectionist and Hulk Hogan (*Suburban Commando*) as himself.

Gremlins 2 was released in the US on Friday June 15, 1990 (when Wilson Phillips were at No. 1 with "Hold On") and in the UK on Friday July 27, 1990 (when Partners in Kryme topped the charts with "Turtle Power"—from one of the year's highest-grossing movies *Teenage Mutant Ninja Turtles*). While *Gremlins 2* failed to recoup its $50 million budget, many critics continue to cite it as being superior to the original (although it is certainly an enjoyable watch, I wouldn't personally go that far; the anarchy and chaos sink the film before it ends—but then, that is presumably the intention).

While a mooted reunion with Dante—on Michel Parry's long-promised script, *Sweeney Todd*—never came to be, Christopher Lee, instead, entered the 1990s with a barmy turn as Uncle Rudolf in *The Rainbow Thief* (1990). Directed by Alejandro Jodorowsky (b. 1929)—the cult filmmaker behind *El Topo* (1969), *The Holy Mountain* (1972) and *Santa Sangre* (1988)—this surreal fantasy sees Lee clashing cymbals in time to Wagner, whilst gliding around on a wheeled Dalmatian. After feeding bones to his family, as his dogs feast on caviar and champagne, the pajama-clad Rudolf is tickled to death crooning operatic ballads to the bare-breasted "Rainbow Girls." All of the above takes place immediately after the opening credits, and the remainder is left to the less interesting misadventures of Rudolf's eccentric nephew (Peter O'Toole) and a thief (Omar Sharif) who live in the sewers, like a certain Opera Ghost.

First screened at the Venice Film Festival, *The Rainbow Thief* was granted a brief French release in January 1994. By that time, big-budget adaptations of Christopher Lee's foremost Gothic outings had been remade courtesy of *Bram Stoker's Dracula* (1991) and *Mary Shelley's Frankenstein* (1993). For all their lavish visuals, however, these new models couldn't hold a candle to the originals ("What do we see in Coppola's *Dracula*?" Lee enquired of Craig Cabell and Howard Maxford in *Shivers* #50: "A man with a strange kind of hairdo, a long red dress and no moustache. I thought, well, *that*'s odd…"). Meanwhile, Lee's next horror opus would straddle the boundary between his Hammer past and the more whimsical phantasmagoria of *The Rainbow Thief*. But while the latter movie is so individual as to seem lost in time, *Funny Man* is definitely a product of its era.

Christopher Lee seems to be enjoying himself in The Rainbow Thief

Funny Man
1993

He's cheeky and he's cruel!

On Halloween night 1991, Channel 4 in the UK broadcast *Fear in the Dark*—a documentary on the horror genre, narrated by Christopher Lee (which preceded a double bill of *The Hunger* and *The Vampire Bat* [1932]). Following a brief examination of vampirism and 1950s B-movies, *Fear in the Dark* devotes itself mainly to post-*Exorcist* cinematic terror: *The Texas Chain Saw Massacre*, *Halloween*, *A Nightmare on Elm Street* and *Hellraiser*. Despite serious beginnings, the bogeymen of the aforementioned films (Leatherface, Michael Myers, Freddy Krueger and Pinhead) would be portrayed as near-comical figures over a string of diminishing sequels. The wise-cracking antics of Krueger, in particular, would inform and be further exaggerated by Lee's first true horror film of the 1990s.

The brainchild of first-time writer and director Simon Sprackling, *Funny Man* began its five-week shoot on Friday, June 25, 1993 at Borough Court, a former psychiatric hospital in Henley-on-Thames. Christopher Lee, who shot his brief scenes as the ambiguous Callum Chance over the first two days of filming, is introduced in a pre-credits poker game, where he loses his ancestral home to record producer Max Taylor (Benny Young).

As we soon find out, the house contains the eponymous *Funny Man*, a wise-cracking, murderous demon with a penchant for surreal disguise.

White-suited with an overgrown moustache, Lee gives a solemn performance against the wisecracks of his fellow players (one of whom tells him to "Shit or get off the pot"). For the remainder of the movie, however, we experience him only briefly: smiling, wild-eyed, from behind a house of cards in a white room or reading from Lewis Carroll's "The Walrus and the Carpenter" on the soundtrack.

Elsewhere, a doll of Lee's recent *Gremlins 2* co-star, Gizmo, can be seen strapped to the grille of the protagonists' graffiti-sprayed van. Among those onboard are Scottish comedian Rhona Cameron (b. 1965) as Thelma Fudd—a character patterned after Velma of *Scooby-Doo*—and Pauline Black (b. 1953)—lead singer of influential ska outfit the Selecter—as "the Psychic Commando." Here, the tone is best vocalized by another passenger, who thinks the initials P.C. stand for "pure crap" and tells a more-New Age companion: "Sex and violence, mate—that's what the public wants." And, in *Funny Man*, that's what they get.

Well-directed and photographed, with impressive make-up and special effects from Neill Gorton (b. 1969)—whose credits include *Hellraiser II* (1988), *Nightbreed* (1989) and *Doctor Who* (2005-)—*Funny Man* is certainly an admirable achievement, especially when one considers its low-budget (approximately £50,000) and largely novice cast and crew. A former punk musician, Sprackling creates a film that plays fast and irreverent, like a blast of three-chord rock. Unfortunately, his script offers few surprises. Protagonists are killed off, one by one, in cartoonish segments, amid a surfeit of crude humor. On a more positive note, the *Funny Man* is a terrific showcase for Welsh actor Tim James, who in one of the movie's few unexpected touches, gives the character a Yorkshire accent (although his varied comic alter-egos—including real-life monster Jimmy Savile—do become a little wearing after a while). A slightly more consistent highlight is the song that plays over the closing credits, on which Lee gets to warble some of the lyrics (co-written by Stephen W. Parsons—lead vocalist of Babel, the band featured in *Howling II*).

Following its premiere at the Edinburgh Film Festival in August 1994, *Funny Man* was given a limited theatrical release in the UK from Friday, October 7, 1994. "People stayed away in droves!" as Lee remembered (to Tom Johnson and Mark A. Miller). The critics were also unimpressed: "This is a truly rubbishy little horror flick," opined the *Sunday Express*, "dignified only by the fleeting glimpses of the only surviving master of the genre."

Although the master himself said, in the film's publicity, that *Funny Man* possessed, "The most original screenplay I've read in 22 years" (by which, he presumably meant since *The Wicker Man*), Lee later distanced himself from the movie. As he told Johnson and Miller: "I simply don't agree with the gratuitous violence." For the actor's next genre project, he returned to the comparatively cozier environs of another past master.

Edgar Allan Poe's Tales of Mystery and Imagination 1994

While British audiences were busy avoiding *Funny Man*, Christopher Lee found himself engaged in Johannesburg, South Africa, where he hosted the 13-part TV anthology, *Edgar Allan Poe's Tales of Mystery and Imagination*. Despite attracting such talent as Susan George (*Straw Dogs*), Freddie Jones (*The Satanic Rites of Dracula*) and Fran Fullenwider (*The Rocky Horror Picture Show*), the project, much like Karloff's *The Veil*, was never broadcast at the time (although some episodes did sneak out onto the Horror Channel a decade later). The complete series has since been granted an Italian DVD release by Cult Media.

The adapted stories, some of which were filmed in Croatia, are "The Fall of the House of Usher," "The Oval Portrait," "Berenice," "The Black Cat," "Ligeia," "The Cask of Amontillado," "The Facts in the Case of M. Valdemar," "The Tell-Tale Heart," "Morella," "The Pit and the Pendulum" and "The Masque of the Red Death" (in two parts). The 13th episode is a "Biographical Portrait" of Poe directed by N. Hetherington, which shows the author falling over drunk in graveyards. Directorial duties for the remainder of the series are split between novice screenwriter Hugh Whysall, James Ryan (a martial artist who had starred with Reb Brown in *Space Mutiny* and also plays Poe in the aforementioned "Biographical Portrait") and Bill Hays (1938-2006), a British TV veteran who had previously helmed two entries of Brian Clemens' *Thriller*. Each half-hour episode of *Tales of Mystery and Imagination* begins with an atmospheric, lightning-infused title sequence, complete with a hooded figure, sinking slowly behind the raven-topped grave of Edgar Allan Poe.

The intentions of first-time producers Terry and Carrie Dempsey are certainly honorable, not only for staying relatively faithful to Poe's original stories, but also for including certain tales that are all too infrequently filmed ("Berenice," "The Oval Portrait"). The results, however, are only so-so, let down by cheap production values that are apparent in every shot-on-video frame: note the hazy visuals, synthesized music scores and sparse special effects. The green-eyes applied to the players of "The Black Cat" and the floating head of "Ligeia" are especially laughable, though I rather enjoyed the crude daubing of what looks like custard and ketchup on the decomposing, black-tongued "Mr. Valdemar," and the weird, enlarged eye of the old man in "The Tell Tail [sic] Heart." Meanwhile, "The Pit and the Pendulum" offers not only poorly integrated battle footage from another film, but also the spectacle of an actor playing a corpse who lifts his head when he thinks he's out of shot.

Less risible highlights include Freddie Jones' boozy jester Fortunato in "The Cask of Amontillado," and the mist-wreathed apparitions of "Ligeia" (here pronounced "Le-guy-a") and Madeline Usher. The latter embraces Jeremy Crutchley's Roderick, who expires with a Mr. Sardonicus-like rictus grin.

Best of all, Christopher Lee is a delight. Mustachioed in smoking jacket, he tops-and-tails each episode from the usual book-lined study, adding interesting, if appropriately melodramatic, insights into Poe's tortured mind. (In the first entry, "The Fall of the House of Usher," he interjects the action quite frequently with biographical asides of the author, but this approach was swiftly abandoned.) Particularly charming is Lee's intro for "The Black Cat" (in which he pets a kitty) and his usual final bidding of, "Good night. Sleep well."

Better still, for "The Masque of the Red Death," which the actor cites as "one of my personal favorites," he takes on the role of Prince Prospero with gusto. Unfortunately, although Lee attempts to present a character whose callous nature stems from an unhinged mind, Whysall's adaptation is anticlimactic and cannot help but compare unfavorably to Roger Corman's more full-blooded version starring Vincent Price.

Tales of Mystery and Imagination was not the only genre-related TV appearance made by Christopher Lee in the 1990s. Back on home soil, he caused all kinds of chaos as 4,000-year-old pharaoh Sam Rees in "The Rameses Connection" (1994), a five-part serial of *The Tomorrow People*. To Jane Killick (in *Shivers* #13), Lee described the show's titular teens: "They can ... what's the word ...? 'Beam up' and they do indeed teleport which is not as bizarre as it may sound, because telepathic thinking, telepathy, ESP definitely does exist."

Killick, who interviewed Lee on *The Tomorrow People* set, also reported in her article that, "During breaks in filming, he takes off his blue and gold Egyptian headdress and relaxes in a room adjacent to the set, puffing on a pipe. As his fellow cast members and crew walk past, they greet him with a 'Good morning, Mr. Lee.' He says hello to them all and treats them to stories from his distinguished filmmaking career. 'This is not the first time I wore this clothing because I wore it in *The Mummy* in 1958 [sic] as a high priest,' he reflects."

Along this theme, from Monday, October 4 to Friday, October 8, 1993, Lee kicked off the Sci-Fi Channel's "Classic Monsters Month" by providing informative introductions, amid decorative sarcophagi, for Universal's *Mummy* series. This was followed by similar intros for *Dracula* Week (10/11-10/15), *Frankenstein* Week (10/18-10/22) and *Wolf Man* Week (10/26- 10/29).

Then, in the spring of 1995, the actor hosted a season of his own films on satellite TV station Bravo. Beginning with *The Face of Fu Manchu*, which aired at 10 pm on Wednesday, May 3, 1995, the other movies shown were *Rasputin: The Mad Monk* (5/4/95), *The Brides of Fu Manchu* (5/10/95), *Theatre of Death* (5/11/95), *The Vengeance of Fu Manchu* (5/17/95), *Circus of Fear* (5/18/95), *The Blood of Fu Manchu* (5/24/95), *I, Monster* (5/25/95) and *The Castle of Fu Manchu* (5/31/95).

Also in 1995—thought not screened until autumn 1997—Lee was interviewed for *Clive Barker's A-Z of Horror* (BBC 2), one of the most fascinating documentary series ever produced on the genre. In the episode entitled "A Fate Worse than Death," the actor reads from Dennis Wheatley's *The Satanist* and *The Devil Rides Out*, whilst lamenting of his old friend: "In a way, it's a very good thing that [Dennis] is not alive [today] to see what has happened: The total, in my opinion, virtual breakdown of discipline in this country and in many others."

The previous year, Lee took part in a televised celebration of his horror past, which reunited him with another beloved acquaintance for what would, sadly, prove to be the final time.

Flesh and Blood
The Ted Newsom Productions
(1994-1996)

On Tuesday, May 17, 1994, Christopher Lee and Peter Cushing arrived at Talking Shop studios, Canterbury, to narrate Ted Newsom's *Flesh and Blood: The Hammer Heritage of Horror*. Born in Portland, Oregon, 1952, Newsom had previously written and directed such entertaining documentaries as *Dracula: A Cinematic Scrapbook* (1990), *Frankenstein: A Cinematic Scrapbook* (1990), *Wolfman Chronicles* (1991) and *Ed Wood: Look Back in Angora* (1994). His other credits include *Evil Spawn* (1987), with John Carradine, and *The Naked Monster* (2004)—an affectionate parody of 1950s B-movies starring John Agar (*The Brain from Planet Arous*), Kenneth Tobey (*It Came from Beneath the Sea*), Lori Nelson (*Revenge of the Creature*), Paul Marco (*Night of the Ghouls*), Robert Clarke (*The Hideous Sun Demon*), Gloria Talbott (*The Cyclops*), Robert Shayne (*Indestructible Man*) and Linnea Quigley (*The Return of the Living Dead*).

As well as being the last Lee and Cushing collaboration, *Flesh and Blood* remains the most in-depth Hammer documentary to date, with invaluable contributions from, among others, Michael Carreras, Hazel Court, Caroline Munro, Veronica Carlson, Jimmy Sangster, Roy Ward Baker, Freddie Francis and Lee himself.

The first part of the show was aired by BBC 1 on Saturday, August 6, 1994, at 11.35pm (followed by a screening of *The Curse of Frankenstein*). Too ill to watch the program, 81-year-old Peter Cushing died from cancer at Pilgrim's Hospice, Canterbury, on Thursday, August 11. Part two went out in his honor the following Saturday, along with a beautifully put-together montage and *The Hound of the Baskervilles*.

Here, Ted Newsom recounts the making of *Flesh and Blood*:

Misbehaving Schoolboys Together Again

"I jumped through complicated hoops to make sure Christopher Lee and Peter Cushing did the narration on my documentary *Flesh and Blood* ... Me, Hammer and the two actors agreed on $5,000 apiece for Cushing and Lee to narrate jointly. Hammer would pay Cushing; I'd be responsible for Lee.

"For once, his agent worked on Lee's behalf, albeit tentatively. After we'd all agreed, the John Redway Agency politely faxed me to confirm the engagement, adding, 'We would be much more interested if the rate was £5,000 rather than $5,000.' In other words, twice as much. I replied by fax, 'I'm sure you would, but it's still $5,000.'

"All well and good, but where was I going to get $5,000? I financed the whole project out of my own pocket bit by bit. I didn't have piles of cash laying around. There was only a brief window of availability for Lee and a tentative recording date. I had less than two weeks. Despite the vouching of his friends Bill Kelley and Joe Dante, Lee was adamant. 'I've been disappointed far too many times. It's not personal, but I've never worked with you. The money must be in the bank by the day we record, or I'm not showing up. That's that.'

"The clock was ticking at double speed. No one I knew could afford a loan, or was interested in charity. Would— could!—Cushing narrate alone? To hell with the whole idea? I had less than a week. Thank heaven my friend Arny Schorr at Rhino came through. He invented a fictitious video assignment for me, we contracted for it and I got an advance—$5,000. The Thursday before the Tuesday recording, I rushed to my bank to wire the funds to Lee's account ... They took the check, made out the transfer, hit 'Send,' and it was on its way. I sighed in relief ... for five seconds. 'The funds will be available in 10 working days,' the clerk said.

"'What?! No, no, not 10 days! Now! You pushed the button! It's electronic!'

"'Well, of course, it has to go to an international bank clearing house in New York, and they're already closed. They'll process it tomorrow, Friday, then probably relay it overseas. It's usually only a week to 10 days.'

"'You don't get it. If it's not there by Tuesday morning, I'm screwed. The only reason I wired this was to get it there on time.' The clerk nodded and said, 'Next customer.'

"I called Lee to explain payment was en route by wire, but that there might be a delay. 'Well, that's fine, but as I told you, if the money is not in the bank by the morning of the recording, I won't show up. Period. That's the end of it.'

"I packed, prepped and headed for the airport that Sunday with no guarantee that Lee would even be there on Tuesday morning. The eight-hour flight was nerve-wracking, the jet lag exhausting. I arrived in London at midday Monday, still unsure. From Jimmy Bernard's flat where I was staying, I called Lee. 'Oh, yes, the payment posted this morning,' he said casually. 'It's over and done with. See you tomorrow.' I fell asleep for 10 hours.

"To record the tandem narration, we arranged time at the Talking Shop studios in Canterbury, near Cushing's Whitstable home. He was too frail to do a two-hour ride to London. When I checked with Christopher Lee to make sure his payment cleared the bank, he said, 'I've spoken to Peter. He said, "I don't know if I'm up to this, old boy. You may have to do the whole thing yourself."' Lee added, 'Of course, if I have to do that, I should expect to be compensated.' The second part sounded like dry wit. The first didn't.

"Immediately I called Joyce Broughton, Mrs. Hudson to Cushing's Sherlock Holmes since 1959. Joyce just laughed. 'Oh, Sir's fine. He's looking forward to working,' she assured me. 'Sir' was her nickname for Cushing; 'Peter' seemed too familiar, 'Mr. Cushing' far too stuffy, so he suggested 'Sir Boss' after the character in A Connecticut Yankee in King Arthur's Court. That became simply: 'Sir.' 'He said Dr. Theater is just what he needed.' Meaning, of course, work as the antidote for depression.

"On the drizzling morning drive to Canterbury, Lee was exquisitely garrulous. I rode down from London with him, James Bernard and friend Matt Harrison. At one point, Lee pointed out at the long-stemmed yellow flowers covering a grassy field for miles, looking like yellow powdered sugar sprinkled across the green fields. 'It's called rape,' he said. 'Heaven knows why.'

"Nervousness lay beneath the charm. I knew that he never would have gone down to see Cushing in Whitstable, not because he didn't love him, but he would've been extremely uncomfortable about it being a last visit. He had confided that to Bill Kelley, who'd told me. I was glad to provide an excuse.

"Cushing beat us to the studio by a few minutes. He was sitting in a canvas-backed chair when Lee arrived, and cackled joyously, 'Ha-HAH-ha-ha-hah!' when he saw his old friend stride in, clasping Lee's hand in both of his. Cushing looked ill, wan, nearly skeletal. Sans toupée and with a scruffy two weeks' growth of beard, supporting himself with a cane, his fragility alarmed us all. The beard was ostensibly for the proposed Kevin Francis picture *A Heritage of Horror*.

"However, his joy at working, seeing Lee and being surrounded by fans clearly buoyed him. He and Lee regaled each other with half-anecdotes—often only the punch lines, since they both knew the stories by heart. The little studio was packed. There were two camera crews, one from *Entertainment Tonight*, the other from the BBC, and both of which wanted some interview time with the boys.

"'Look at all these people,' said Cushing, looking around. 'We ought to do a picture together.'

"'Yes, well, I think that's what we're doing.'

"'Huh! Are we getting paid?'

"'Well, we'll see about that!'

"Lee took the reins and regaled Cushing and everyone else with vocal impressions, funny stories and non-stop monologues designed to do exactly what they did—keep Cushing's spirits up. As happened with *Horror Express* years earlier, Lee verbally steamrolled over any doubts or stage fright Cushing might have. Cushing prodded Lee to tell a funny John Gielgud and Ralph Richardson story, a droll Noël Coward/Chuck Connors anecdote, plus assorted impressions of Jimmy Durante, Yosemite Sam, Miles Malleson, James Carreras, legendary radio host Long John Nebel and a dozen others, famous and obscure people.

"Lee also brought a gift that delighted the old gentleman—a Sylvester the Cat puppet. Actually, it was a golf club cover, but no matter. It sent Cushing into another round of hysterics. The two had decades before been ejected from a movie theater for laughing too much at Looney Tunes cartoons. Lee told the crowd that Cushing had said he didn't think he'd be able to do it—which sent Cushing into another laughing fit. Apparently, it was a gag all along. (And, apparently, the joke was on me.)

"'The last time we met ...,' said Cushing.

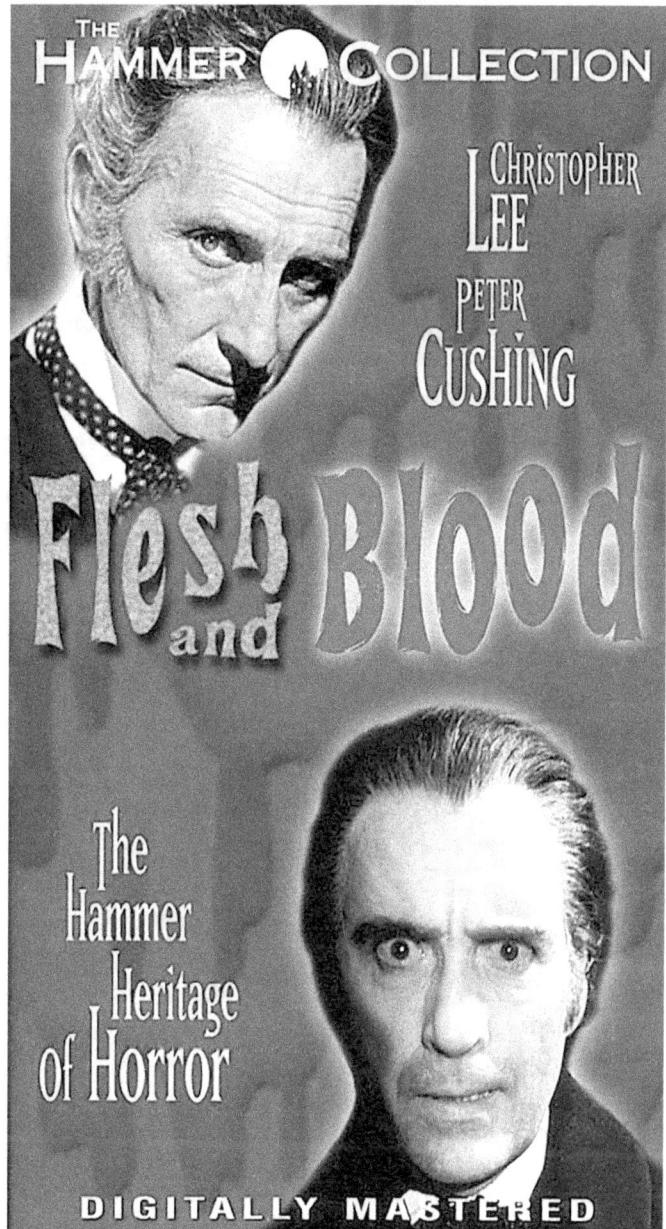

"'... when you disgraced yourself, me and everybody else on that Rank show. You remember the 50th anniversary of Rank, on TV?'

"'Oh, yes!'

"'And Stewart Granger was talking, without stopping. All of a sudden, I hear a voice from my left saying [in a Durante voice], "I could moider a cuppa tea." Well, that was it, I started to laugh, Virginia McKenna started to laugh, everybody started to laugh—and they didn't know why! We behaved disgracefully,' he grinned proudly, 'and I'm afraid Mr. Granger was not at all amused.'

"'And all seven foot of you started to slide down under the table.' Cushing adjusted his position, leaning forward, saying to us, 'I keep moving forward because he keeps getting in my light.'

"'That's quite deliberate,' said Lee.

"'New York!' Cushing insisted. 'Tell them, the interview ...'

"'Oh, yes, well. We'd gone over for the premiere of Dracula, and there was this large crowd: Television, radio. There was some disc jockey, quite famous, Long John Nebel. I told Peter, "I'm quite nervous. I've never done an interview like this." And he said, "Don't worry, I'll help out." So—this one—my friend...'

"Cushing chuckled.

The Loneliness of Evil

"'My help-meet!'

"Cushing laughed harder.

"'This man thrust a microphone up and said [in a grating American accent], "So, Misterr Cushing, how do ya like Amerrr- i-ca?" And Peter replied, "Oh, funny you should mention that. I was over here before the war actually, working in Hollywood ..." and he went on for an age. Then the chap turned to me and asked, "So, Missterr Lee, we've been watching this new Drack-you-lah pick-shure, tell us about it." I open my mouth, and this one butts in, "Well, it's quite interesting about that, because when we began ..." I never got a word in! That was the great mistake I made in saying, "Please help me out."'

"Cushing followed up. 'Oh, the other one was, when you got more used to it, we were with a lady interviewer on television. She supplied us with tea. And I said, "Would you like to be Mother?" And they didn't understand it a bit.'

"'No, no, not at all. In fact, that's when the stories started.' He leered at Cushing, who responded in his Jimmy Durante voice, 'Where's it gonna end?!'

"Throughout the interviews and jokes and reminiscences, they constantly touched each other, patting each other's hand. In one rare silent moment, sensing the stillness, Cushing leaned over and said to Lee, 'How are things?' Then added, 'In Glocca Morra.'

"For the only time that day, Christopher went silent. 'I'm speechless. I don't know what to say to that.' Cushing laughed his approval. Ha-HAH ha-ha-hah!

"They reminisced about their fellow actors, and Lee said, 'Oh, Miles Malleson, the Human Windmill!' Lee's arms waved crazy circles, and his voice duplicated the wheezing, aged character actor from *The Thief of Bagdad*, *The Brides of Dracula*, *Peeping Tom*, *First Men in the Moon* and dozens of others.

"'Oh, tell them, dear boy! Michael Gough—!'

"'Well, yes. On the first Dracula, poor Peter and Michael Gough were visiting the undertaker's. The place was filled with coffins, which had some vague relationship with me, I forget which. Miles Malleson says, "Now, where was he? Where are we, where are we?" And then he starts banging on the coffins like it's a song, like a conga drum and sings, "He was here a moment ago ..." And you and Michael Gough, standing there, trying to keep a straight face.'

"Cushing cackled again in delight. 'Impossible!'

"The script lines were clearly marked 'Lee' and 'Cushing,' but while they were setting up the microphones, Cushing began enthusiastically reading the opening. I started to interrupt, but Christopher beat me to it. 'No, I'm supposed to say that. That's my line.'

"'Oh! Sorry. I've stolen your line.'

"'Well, it's not the first time.' Another delighted cackle from 'Pete.'

"Christopher's delivery was perfect: Casual, authoritative, bemused. However, I could sense I was only getting 80% of his energy. That remaining energy was focused on Cushing, to make sure he was okay. Some psychic booster, a spiritual infusion to get him through. It was fine with me. Even 10% of Christopher Lee was worth 200% of anyone else. Eighty percent was golden.

"When we finally got through the session, we gave the boys time in the studio by themselves. My friend Bill Kelley had sent over a VHS tape of Warner Bros. cartoons. The Talking Shop guys set up a video player in the back, for a bit of privacy. From the control booth, we watched the old friends laugh and carry on watching Daffy Duck, Yosemite Sam, Bugs Bunny and Sylvester. "No one wanted it to end, but it was now after one pm. They posed for more pictures in the doorway, with a slight drizzle coming down. As Joyce Broughton helped Cushing into her car, I gave him a copy of my Bram Stoker script, and told him, 'There's work to do.' He laughed his approval and took the script. They left.

"Once Peter was gone, Christopher cooled to lower the room temperature. He took a phone call from a BBC reporter and I heard him be very terse and short with him ... understandably. He'd bottled his feelings for four hours and he'd just seen one of his best friends for the last time."

Lee read the Second Lesson for Cushing's memorial service at St. Paul's Church, Covent Garden, on Thursday, January 12, 1995. Other guests included Ingrid Pitt (*The House That Dripped Blood*), Dave Prowse (*Star Wars*), Ron Moody (*Legend of the Werewolf*), Patrick Allen and Sarah Lawson (*Night of the Big Heat*) and Joanna Lumley (*The Satanic Rites of Dracula*). Lumley told the assembled press, "Peter was the most-gentle man I have ever met, quite enchanting ..."

On a sunny afternoon in March 1995, Lee returned to his, and Cushing's, old stomping ground, Bray Studios, to host *100 Years of Horror*—26 half-hour episodes, written and produced by Ted Newsom, on such themes as "Dracula and His Disciples,"

"Frankenstein and Friends," "Mummies" and "Girl Ghouls." Among a multitude of clips and trailers, Lee dons 3-D glasses and gives a unique pronunciation of the word "ballyhoo"(in "Gory Gimmicks"), while at the end of "Sorcerers," he makes himself vanish: "As an actor, one must maintain that child-like faith that what we imagine is real ..."

Other highlights include Edward Van Sloan's original screen test for *Dracula*, snippets from Willis O'Brien's unfinished *Creation* (1931), color footage of Karloff on the *Son of Frankenstein* set, outtakes from *Abbott and Costello Meet Frankenstein* and Lon Chaney, Jr. discussing his father on a 1953 episode of *You Asked for It*. Previously unseen moments from Caroline Munro and Hazel Court's *Flesh and Blood* interviews are interspersed with new talking head pieces from, among others, Richard Matheson, Ray Bradbury, Sara Karloff, Bela Lugosi, Jr. and Jessica Rains (who recalls her dad reprising his *Phantom of the Opera* for Halloween). The result is a pleasingly nostalgic romp through horror history with Lee sometimes going off-script to deliver some personal anecdotes, such as the time he attended the premiere of *Mary Shelley's Frankenstein* with Francis Ford Coppola in 1994: "Somebody asked me what [I thought] the major difference was between [Coppola's] *Frankenstein* and mine. I answered only slightly tongue-in-cheek: 'Oh, 40 years and 40 million dollars.'" While the actor often repeated that story, he closes "The Evil Unseeable" with a family remembrance that can't be found elsewhere: "Some years ago, a certain Contessa Carandini ... lay on her deathbed. Her husband predeceased her by a number of years. She looked beyond those present, her children and grandchildren, in the room. Her expression softened. She said only one word: 'Frank.' And she closed her eyes. Now, some might say she was suffering from delusions. Others would explain it as an hallucination brought on by painkillers. Some might believe that, at the end, she saw the one man she had loved all her life, beckoning her to join him. I know what I believe. The lady was my grandmother, and her husband's name—and, indeed, I was named after him as well—was Frank Carandini." *100 Years of Horror* first aired in December 1996 on the Sci-Fi Channel and was also released as a 100-minute highlights DVD.

A home-video fate also awaited Newsom's next project, in which Lee invites us "on a cinematic time-trip through *A Century of Science Fiction*." Recorded in the summer of 1996, this 100-minute documentary follows the same pattern Newsom had established on *100 Years of Horror*, with a bearded and tuxedo-clad Lee—looking somewhat reminiscent of country crooner Kenny Rogers—introducing trailers and behind-the-scenes featurettes on such subjects as "Mad Doctors," "Sci-Fi Lunacy" and "Lost Worlds." Highlights include Charlie Sheen confirming his belief in extra-terrestrials, Burt Lancaster and Yul Brynner eloquently discussing *The Island of Dr. Moreau* (1977) and *Westworld* (1973) respectively, Vincent Price comparing his version of *The Fly* with David Cronenberg's 1986 remake, Robert Wise remembering *The Day the Earth Stood Still* (1951) and some enjoyable one-liners from Lee. Of *The Time Travelers* (1963), for instance, he says: "The strange, whirring sound you hear is H.G. Wells revolving in his grave," while some scientific gobbledygook from *Bela Lugosi Meets a Brooklyn Gorilla* is met with: "There you are. That should explain everything!" In addition, the actor supplies neat summations of both the 1976 *King Kong* ("This is what they call high-

concept. A 20-million-dollar remake of a film that was good in the first place") and *Eegah* (1962): "They don't make films like this anymore. They wouldn't dare."

An Interview with Ted Newsom:

SM: *It has been widely reported that Christopher Lee wished to distance himself from his horror portrayals in later years. Given that you were working together on projects that celebrated his horror legacy, what were his true feelings on being associated with the genre? Was he ashamed of being labeled "a horror star"?*

TN: So ... was Christopher Lee a pompous, humorless stiff who attained a level of stardom then scoffed at his prior association with horror films? Aw, hell, no. As someone who eventually worked with him four times and was on relatively good terms with him—through several projects which involved horror, sci-fi and mystery themes as well as his participation in the films—I can say plainly, "Bosh."

I first saw Christopher Lee at the first sci-fi convention I attended, in 1977. He spoke amusingly to a packed house, then later chatted with a clump of fans. I hung around, because it was awesome to be within shouting distance of a favorite actor. One fan gushed, "I really loved that make-up on you in *Horror Express*!" And he was serious. I said, "He didn't play the monster in that one." Lee met my eye and sighed subtly. It was an expression which said, "Thank you. You see what I put up with?"

That fan's comment points out not snootiness on Lee's part but the blinders that genre fans wear. If something falls out of our narrow range of interest, it has no importance. Even details of what should be obvious don't matter. Imagine getting to talk with Robert Mitchum, about 1975—then asking him only about Peter Cushing and Christopher Lee, together one last time.

Questions about Hopalong Cassidy movies. "What was it like to be Hoppy's sidekick?" "Was William Boyd a great guy?" "Did you do your own horseback riding?" "Was it neat to work with Andy Clyde?" "How come you don't play Hoppy's sidekick anymore?" "Do you think modern Westerns should be more like Hoppy Westerns?" "Was making a Western with John Wayne as cool as making a Hopalong Cassidy movie?" Now imagine this was the thousandth time Mitchum had heard the same damned questions. How long before he decks you?

Did Lee have reason to avoid or resent being categorized? You betcha. He knew what had happened to Lugosi and his Dracula association; the Hungarian actor had died only two years before Hammer filmed their remake.

Given the breadth of Lee's professional appearances even by the early 1960s, it was an unfair label, as it was when slapped on Basil Rathbone at the same time. My pal Mark McGee was lucky as a teen to visit the *Comedy of Terrors* set and meet the stars, but Rathbone stalked away in loud dudgeon after Mark dropped the phrase "horror star." Vincent Price calmed the old man down, coaxed him back and Mark exchanged a few nervous words, but Rathbone still seethed. Lee, to the contrary, was beginning his career arc, Rathbone, long past the apex and desirable only in genre films. Lee, at least, never stalked away in fury at a fan's mention of the word "horror." Most of the great screen heavies longed for respect out of their niche, few got it, once they were typed. Lugosi always wanted to do comedy or straight drama, as he had done for the first third of his career. Lorre had a background in improv and comedy, seldom seen after playing murderers. Of that bunch, only Karloff was happy just to keep working regardless of subject matter.

IMDb shows at least 25 credits with Lee in period costume pictures or TV episodes, with guys in doublets, hose and swords, yet Lee's not classified in the public mind as a guy who only plays villains in swashbucklers. Likewise spies and military types, which probably equal his number of sword-and-sandal movies.

My first genuinely substantial interaction with Lee was a long interview at his home in 1980, for the *L.A. Daily News*.

Sunday magazine. My then-wife Marsha accompanied me; Lee's wife Gitte stayed a few moments then went off on errands. Lee was charming, funny and knowledgeable about damned near everything from military history to literature to modern art. When my photographer asked him to smile, Lee lectured us amusingly on how awkward it is to pose smiling for a photographer if there's nothing that strikes you as funny. He managed an approximation. He had lived in L.A. for a couple of years at the time, in a spacious flat in Westwood overlooking UCLA and a golf course, which was handy for him. Some of his furniture and Oriental hangings I would recognize years later in London. He waxed enthusiastic about his recent Hollywood work, where he felt he was finally getting the recognition—and the salary—he'd earned in his 20-plus year career.

As the afternoon went on and he grew more at ease, he was joined by his cat, who apparently liked me. "His name is Renfield," Lee said. "And he really does eat flies! And when he sees a fly ..." Lee bent forward, his eyes on an imaginary fly, "... he'll go, 'Nnnaahhh-unhh! Nnnnahhhh-unhh! Nnyuhh!' And he'll get 'em." One does not expect a reserved English actor to imitate a cat, much less do it so well. It was absolutely funny.

The closest he came to bad-mouthing his early successes was a discussion of typecasting. "I haven't done that type of film in several years. People say, 'Oh, you're typecast,' but I've proven them wrong. I made *Serial*, playing a corporate headhunter who is a weekend leader of a homosexual biker gang. I had a line, 'My boys are not fairies!' A comedy for Steven Spielberg, *1941*. *Airport '77*, with Jack Lemmon and a cast of great stars. When I hosted *Saturday Night Live*, the show got the biggest rating—the biggest!—it received in its history. *Once Upon a Spy*, which I did for the Bond fans, and *Captain America II*, which I did for the kids. So, where's the typecasting?"

I did manage to bring up his singular iconic role, which he referred to as "that character," but he loosened. "I'd go back to playing Dracula again ... for 10 million dollars. Or five million, or whatever. Because what would happen is, they'd say, 'Oh, he's gone back to doing that, that's the only thing he can do,' and that would be the end of my career."

Did he dismiss his early work? No. Listen to his commentary tracks for *Scars of Dracula* with Roy Ward Baker, or the audio reunion I put together for *Dracula: Prince of Darkness* and *Rasputin: The Mad Monk*, with Lee, Barbara Shelley, Francis Matthews and Suzan Farmer. Yes, he takes center stage, putting Matthews and Farmer in the shade, but it was due to enthusiasm rather than egocentricity. The super-cool Matthews said after the recording, "Well, that's Christopher." On *Scars*, certainly the least beloved of the series, he's still enthusiastic and says, "I don't think I've ever seen that. It's pretty good!"

SM: *One movie producer famously said, "Christopher Lee has no sense of humor," but I gather you have memories that suggest otherwise?*

TN: In a preface to a Tom Weaver collection of genre interviews, producer Richard Gordon stated his dislike for Christopher Lee, whom he felt was self-important, un-humorous and generally a pain. This stemmed from making *Corridors of Blood* in 1958, in which Lee supported the star, Boris Karloff. Gordon overheard something Lee said and interpreted it as unforgivable egocentricity, an insult to Karloff and bloody cheeky. Lee evidently said something like, "Perhaps 30 years from now, they'll be talking about me playing the Monster like they do Boris now." The nerve.

Given Lee's adoration and respect for Karloff, I dismiss Gordon's sniping. Lee may well have said something like that, and, yes, Mr. Gordon, it's now 50 years later and we do talk about Lee's Frankenstein like we do Karloff's.

Thankfully, home video exists of Lee and Cushing together prior to recording the narration of my documentary *Flesh and Blood: The Hammer Heritage of Horror*. Home video clips of this event are now available on YouTube, and you can see for yourself how funny he was.

Yes, Christopher Lee had a sense of humor—when he was comfortable. Around strangers, he invariably kept his reserve in check. In 1995, as we were riding out to Bray to shoot *100 Years of Horror*, sitting in the rear of the hired car, eating our sandwiches. I was prattling on about some company giving me grief about acquiring footage, I think. Lee nodded, shrugged, and said, "Kill 'em," and continued munching his sandwich without missing a beat. I thought it was funny and would use that as my excuse in court ... Christopher Lee told me to kill 'em.

That first time I worked with him, I felt humbled and intimidated; two of my favorite stars—what was I going to do, second-guess them? So, I "directed" very little. This second time around a year later I felt more comfortable. So was Lee, possibly because I arranged to pay him five times what he received on my documentary. In any case, he enjoyed seeing Bray again. They gave us a tour—Lee, the video crew, and the gawking American director. The entryway had a half-dozen giant photos of actors mounted on the walls, including Lee's least favorite still from *Dracula A.D. 1972*: Fangs, wide mouth and a carriage spoke through the heart. I know, it wasn't shot at Bray. I expect he did, too. We all walked down a hallway decorated with posters from films shot there. He saw one for Kenneth Branagh's *Henry V* and grunted, "Hmf. Every poofter in England was in that one," and moved on. The crew—a cameraman and an assistant, lighting people, and a teleprompter operator—seemed awed and quiet, dealing with a legend. Me, I just got off on the idea that I was shooting a horror show with Christopher Lee at Bray Studios.

We shot exteriors first, in front of Oakley Court for the intro, and back to the riverside Bray lot for others, including Lee beneath the rooftop he'd walked as Frankenstein's creation, then standing beside the columned double doors which he crashed through as the Mummy. While we were doing these shots, planes constantly interrupted his dialogue. We'd start a take, hear yet another jet coming in or going out, wait for the sound to finally decay, and do it again.

"It was like that back then," Lee said to our small crowd. "Every time. Every time! We'd start a take and the sounds of aircraft would ruin it, and we'd start again. Heathrow's just over there. We're right beneath the flight path. And we'd do a scene, start some dialogue and they'd come again. Same as now. Just like this, back then."

I held for a beat, then said, "Back then? What were they? Biplanes?"

The English crew just went silent. Oh, bloody hell, this crazy Yank doesn't know who he's dealing with! Now he's gone and done it. We're all for it now.

Lee fixed me with his gaze and said deadpan: "No. They were bal-*looons*."

The video crew cracked up. We all had a good time the rest of the day.

I enjoyed taking the mick out of his defensive pomposity. Those who knew him, especially Cushing, understood that English reserve covered a caring, loyal, funny and extremely insecure man who used erudition to distance himself from being hurt. I knew that he was human and liked a good dirty joke; I also could sense when that defensive self-importance crept up. If he played the Grand Seigneur, then I'd respond with the crass American. The "balloons" gag was typical.

In 1996, when I went to his hotel in Santa Monica to record narration for *A Century of Science Fiction*, the silent *Hunchback of Notre Dame* was playing on the TV. Lee watched admiringly. "Chaney," he said. "Absolutely brilliant. A master." I glanced at the screen and mumbled, "Hm. Yeah. He was all right, I suppose." Lee sighed in exasperation and rolled his eyes.

In 1998, he was back in the States pushing his CD, *Devils, Rogues and Other Villains*. Since the bookstore hosting the signing was only two miles from my home, I went down with friends to say hi. I'd already bought the CD out of fan loyalty and curiosity. It was obvious why the concept appealed to his ego, to show his versatility. He got to sing Gilbert and Sullivan, "Man of La Mancha," Sondheim's *Sweeney Todd*, two Western songs in a peculiar "American" accent, Kurt Weill's "Mack the Knife," opera arias by Mozart, Wagner, Verdi and Gounod in a rainbow of languages. It sounded lush and precise, he was in good voice no matter what the style or language, but despite all this, the Samuel Johnson quote came to mind: "A woman's preaching is like a dog's walking on his hind legs. It is not done well, but you are surprised to find it done at all." This was done well, and it was the most godawful and uncommercial thing I'd ever heard.

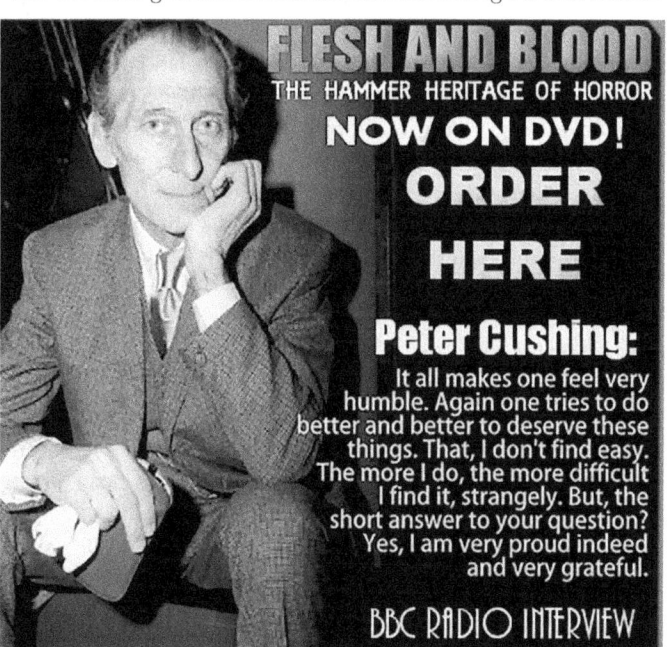

Peter and Helen Cushing, an appreciation posted by the Peter Cushing Society.

The queue was long, several hundred people, and once out of the heat and into the store, you could hear Lee speaking to fans, frequently rhapsodizing: "I sing them all in the original languages. English, French, German. I'm fluent in all these languages. Opera in the original Italian. 'Ghost Riders in the Sky' in a genuine American Western dialect. It's never been done before, in the history of recorded music. It's never been done before!"

A half hour later, I made it to his table, exchanged greetings and jokes, and offered him my CD. He announced yet again, "And you realize I sing them all in their original languages. In English, in French, in German. I speak all these languages, of course. I sing Verdi in the original Italian. I did 'Streets of Laredo' and 'Ghost Riders in the Sky' in a genuine Western American dialect, with a proper Texas twang. It's never been done before, in the history of music. Opera, and operetta, and country-western standards and Sondheim. It's never been done before!"

"Christopher," I said, "you think there might have been a reason for that?"

He grunted and signed my CD.

Prior to my first interview with Lee in 1980, I'd heard on the grapevine that he was terribly angry with Forrest J Ackerman, beloved editor of *Famous Monsters* magazine. The magazine often featured Lee's face, and pushed the assorted Hammer and other horror films Lee was in. I knew Forry had presented him with a copy of Bela Lugosi's *Dracula* signet ring, which Lee dutifully wore in every film from *Dracula Has Risen from the Grave* onward. I asked him about the contretemps. "I've had phone calls here, incessantly," he groused. "Hang-ups sometimes, fans. It's all quite annoying. And I know where it's from. I gave my number to Forrest Ackerman and he gave it out. I'm convinced that's what happened."

I countered that this didn't sound like Ackerman, but that "Dr." Donald Reed [founder of the Los Angeles *Count Dracula Society*] was a likely suspect, as were any of the fanboy acolytes who roamed the Ackerman home. Lee was not swayed.

I'm assuming they at least got back to a casual friendship over the next 15 years, based on the next conversation in which Ackerman's name came up. I was ferrying Lee in my little Toyota across Mulholland Drive and over into the San Fernando Valley to shoot the *Century of Science Fiction* bridges and intros, as well as his stuff for our *Devil Rides Out* promo. I mentioned our mutual friend Bernard Gordon, who produced *Horror Express*. Lee chuckled. "Bernie Gordon! Every sentence he said was prefaced by 'Welllll ...' Every sentence!" Not only was his observation correct after 25 years, he did a spot-on impression of Bernie's nasal Brooklyn dialect, with only one syllable. Then the subject of Ackerman came up.

"We were at John Landis' house for dinner last night," he said, staring out at the curl of traffic. "Several people there. Forry Ackerman was one of them. I went up to him and said hello. He just looked at me ... blankly. I said, 'Forry! It's me!' But there was no response. 'Forry? Don't you know me?' He looked at Gitte and said, 'Well ... I know your wife ...' I didn't know what to make of it. He was serious. Not rude, just ... not ... there ... "

Fans who knew Ackerman in his later years usually resist considering the idea that Forry was slowly losing his memory over a far longer period than just his last few months. He lived for another 12 years.

The last Forry/Chris incident I became aware of was when *The City of the Dead* was released on DVD. Lee had appeared in new video footage to talk about the film, and when he was told the camera was off, someone mentioned Ackerman. He smiled wryly, and said, "Oh, I know him. Nice man. But weird. You know what it says on his mailbox? 'Holly-weird, Karloffornia.' So, yes, nice. But weird!" That outtake clip was put on the disc as an "Easter egg," accessible only when you know the secret place to touch the screen. The content was innocuous enough and he certainly said nothing scandalous about Forry, but it was grossly bad form to use the material without Lee's permission. I called and brought up the subject. I faced the Wrath of Dracula.

He went off on the unprofessional nature of the people who made the video, the absolute betrayal of confidence. Without one obscene word, he tore them up and spit them out. When I suggested legal action, he ignored that and continued his furious tirade against them and all the lying producers he'd ever known. I knew consciously that he was not angry at me—I didn't do anything!—but I was the surrogate target. Blistering, it was.

His vehemence surprised me. As outtakes go, it was scarcely embarrassing. His opinion was not unique. There were a lot of things about Forry, which were genuinely even disturbingly weird. My guess: He was angry because something he said, however innocent it might be to most, would hurt someone's feelings unnecessarily. Plus, of course, it was bad form, dear boy. The other time I faced the fury of Christopher Lee was the day after the *Flesh and Blood* recording. I had invited two professional news crews to be there (from BBC and *Entertainment Tonight*) and sent word to my friend Harry Nadler in Manchester. He and his pals had an annual sci-fi horror convention there, and I knew he'd love to see the reunion. Harry and friends came down by train with an S-VHS camera and recorded nearly the entire morning, from Christopher Lee's arrival and first embrace of Cushing, through the last moments before Sir drove off forever.

After two days of sightseeing and on the verge of returning home, I checked back with Lee. He boiled over with betrayed anger. "I've no idea who those people were. Why were they there? It was absolutely unprofessional! I want that tape destroyed. I know what'll happen, they'll copy it, sell it and make a lot of money. Well, I'll sue them, and I'll have Hammer sue and they have a lot more money for lawyers than I have! I'll withdraw my permission to use the narration. I'll absolutely revoke my permission, and Peter will, too, and Hammer. I want the original and every copy of that thing destroyed or my participation in this is at an end!" Jeez. I saw my three years of work evaporating. I managed to get Harry and his friends to quickly send me the original by train and promise never to copy it and dropped it off at Lee's home. He and Gitte were out, so I left it in the basement landlord's hands with instructions. I called a couple hours later, and Lee went off again. "I've seen nothing of this and consider this an absolute betrayal! You promised something and did not deliver! I'm going to withdraw my agreement for the use of my voice, I'll ..." I managed to get a word in between the fiery blasts from Hell, telling him that it was downstairs with the landlord. I added that I trusted him with the original, because obviously someone with a background in military intelligence is a man to

trust. I called a few minutes later, and he said, "Fine. Over and done with."

His reaction, I felt, went far beyond reasonable. Both he and Cushing were quite aware of the cameras—there were three crews, and they played to all of them. Harry Nadler had a presentation where he gave each of them a statuette from the Manchester fan club, all played to their S-VHS camera. Chris has raised not a finger that day to complain. Now the recording of the historic, sweet morning was gone. Yes, I'd gotten my narration recorded, which is what I needed, but that morning became ephemeral, knowable only to those who experienced it. (As it turned out, the Manchester boys lied to me. They had indeed copied the tape, which I learned later. Thank God.)

Lee's rage puzzled me until I thought about his curt, impatient telephone interview I overheard that afternoon with a BBC radio reporter. This, I knew, was an extension of that bottled-up sadness and anger at his coming loss. It was not so much that the Manchester boys were unprofessional; they were polite and unobtrusive, just like the BBC and *Entertainment Tonight* video crews. Lee was upset about Cushing. He did not want the world to see how ill he was. He did not want him to die.

The footage is now seen worldwide on YouTube, for free, only after Sir Christopher's passing.

SM: *Did Lee enjoy a close personal friendship with Cushing and his wife Helen?*

TN: That would be 50% true, probably believed by Peter Cushing. Everybody seemed to like—no, everyone loved Peter.

On the other hand, nobody I've ever met who knew Peter Cushing during the time Helen was alive, including Christopher Lee, liked her. None ever said this publicly (including Lee) for the obvious reason: They never wanted to hurt Peter. His devotion to her more than made up for the distaste of everyone else in the world. We fans have all heard his repeated, forlorn and wistful comments after her passing, that he only wished to be reunited with her, that he bided his time until God decided to reunite them forever if he's a good boy and that such eternal bliss is the only thing which lets all our earthly suffering make any sense.

She was by all accounts his biggest fan, his soulmate, his rock. She wore the pants in the family. It was Helen who kept

The Loneliness of Evil

Peter on the acting path when work was spare in the late 1940s. Helen who insisted he go into television (with great success), Helen who advised him, cajoled him and reminded him he was talented beyond any other actor.

But all this was at the expense of the fragile egos of other actors, even friends. One anecdote will do. Sometime in the 1960s, at the premiere of a film which co-starred Cushing and Lee, miraculously Lee was billed above Cushing for a change.

Helen sniffed at Lee and said, "I don't know why they billed you above Peter. Peter is much bigger than you." Lee had a quick comeback: "Well, Helen, that's not exactly true, is it? Since Peter is five-foot-11 and a half, and I'm six-foot-four." Riposte aside, it was apparently typical for Helen Cushing. And horribly hurtful at that!

Okay, another anecdote. Vincent Price was friends and colleagues with both Cushing and Lee. As many fans know, all three nearly shared the same birthday in different years, Price and Lee on May 27th, Cushing on the 26th. In birthday season, some years after Helen died, Lee phoned Price in Hollywood. After the joshing, and family catching up, the subject changed. (You really need to imagine their voices.)

Price: "So how is Peter?"

Lee: "Oh, you know. The same. He only talks about joining Helen again. Waiting for that wonderful day when they'll be together. Reunited for eternity. All the time. Just biding his time here, waiting to see her once again. All he ever talks about."

Price: "Hmm. What if ... when Peter dies and goes to Heaven ... she's not there?"

They had a naughty schoolboy laugh over that. A couple of days later, Lee called Cushing. Once again, cartoon impressions, family news, gossip. Along the way:

Lee: "Oh, I spoke to Vincent. He sends his love."

Cushing: "How marvelous. Such a lovely man."

Lee: "Yes. He talked about Helen a bit."

Cushing: "How lovely. Just what did he say?"

Lee (uh-oh.): "Well, uh ... we, er ... we were just talking, and ... ummm ... "

Cushing: "What did he say?"

Lee: "Oh. Well, Vincent ... he said ... umm ... what if—that is, what if Peter ... when Peter dies and ... he goes to Heaven ... what if ... uh ... what if Helen is ... out?"

Lee heard a clunk on the end of the line, then silence. His heart sank, his stomach opened into an empty pit. He knew he had crossed the line, broken the absolute taboo. He heard only the silence of an empty room in Whitstable, for long seconds which felt like hours. Peter will never speak to him again. It's over. He will never, ever forgive me.

At length, after several years which were probably only 10 seconds, Cushing got back on the line and said, "Dreadfully sorry, old darling! I was laughing so hard, me teeth fell out!"

SM: Lee's war years are somewhat shrouded in mystery. Was this a part of his life that he ever discussed?

Lee never spoke of his war years to me, and I never asked. I've met enough veterans to know that if they've "seen action" they seldom want to be specific. They'll talk of old mates, officers they hated, practical jokes, bawdy adventures but avoid the real horrors, the death and torture, cold fear and animal rage.

Most men, if they want to remain sane, try to forget about that, intentionally. He did collect military ribbons, though. He had an impressive array, and not just from his own time in service. Not knowing what to get for the man who has everything, I sent him a couple of American ribbons, one Christmas. And elsewhere in his collection, he prized a letter written by H.P. Lovecraft to a friend. The author's precise scrawl was cramped and nearly microscopic, indicating to me (with my insignificant knowledge of graphology) a man for whom Freud coined the term "anal-retentive." I asked Lee to bring this along when we shot *100 Years of Horror*, but he demurred, bringing a Xerox copy instead. "There's a reason for that," he confided. "I bought it in good faith out of interest in the subject. The writing but especially his hand tell a great deal. Later I was informed the letter had been stolen from some other collector, then sold. So, I'd rather not show the real thing on camera."

SM: Finally, do you have any favorite or lasting memories of Christopher Lee?

TN: The first half of *Flesh and Blood* went out barely on schedule, having gotten a cover story in the *Radio Times*, the UK equivalent of *TV Guide*. I got a call from Roy Ward Baker the next day complimenting me on it. (The director of *A Night to Remember* thought I did okay? Whoa!) I wanted to know if Peter Cushing got to see it. I called the Broughtons, who took care of him. Joyce told me, no, it was broadcast too late for him, but he asked them to tape it for later. Her husband Bernard got on to chat and mentioned Cushing was in hospital. "What kind of hospital?" I asked, knowing the answer.

"I don't think I should say," he replied.

It was, of course, a hospice. He died a day later. I called several friends and we commiserated, then I called Lee. It was already afternoon there. He had been getting calls all day. His voice was somber. "He looked so dreadful that last time. Full of life, but so shrunken. Couldn't have been more than seven stone. He was six foot tall in his prime. Then ... tiny ... bent over." Lee went quiet.

"I'm the last one," he said.

There was no egoism, no grandiosity, no false pride. It was a straightforward declarative sentence. He repeated it, in an equally offhand statement of fact. "I'm the last one."

Ted Newsom passed away on July 4th, 2020.

Talos The Mummy 1997

The curse is legend. The terror is real.

I don't believe I know what a horror movie is nowadays … It seems to consist of two extremes, and they are special effects and make-up, and the actor is in the middle trying to keep his head above water.—Christopher Lee to Craig Cabell and Howard Maxford, *Shivers #50* (February 1998).

With *Talos* I've made a Mummy film starring my idol Christopher Lee and I've cut him in half in what will be a show-stopping death scene. It doesn't get any better than this.—Russell Mulcahy to Alan Jones, *Shivers #50*

Throughout August 1996, London's Barbican Centre hosted a Hammer retrospective, which opened with a showing of *Dracula* introduced by Christopher Lee. Reporting on the event in *Shivers #34*, Anthony Tomlinson wrote that "guest of honor" Lee was "the focus of much attention, like a king holding court" and that the actor "seemed genuinely happy to be present." As well as being reunited with such old friends as Jimmy Sangster, Ingrid Pitt and Michael Ripper, among others, Lee even took the time to chat with, and sign autographs for fans. Before the film began, Lee paid tribute to his late friend Peter Cushing, later telling Craig Cabell and Howard Maxford in *Shivers #50*: "I was kind of upset that evening, talking about Peter. I became a little choked up. It became a little too much for me …" Among the 51 films screened by the Barbican that summer were *The Curse of Frankenstein*, *The Devil Rides Out* and *The Mummy*. Presciently, the latter movie would inspire Lee's next horror outing, *Talos the Mummy*, filmed over 37 days in Luxembourg, from Wednesday, September 3, 1997, under the direction of Russell Mulcahy.

Born in Australia, 1953, Mulcahy had previously been responsible for *Highlander*. This 1985 fantasy adventure has the feel of a lavish music video, thanks to its fluid action, neon-lit atmospherics and Queen rock score. Indeed, Mulcahy started out creating era-defining 1980s pop promos for the likes of Bonnie Tyler ("Total Eclipse of the Heart"), Ultravox ("Vienna"), Spandau Ballet ("True"), the Buggles ("Video Killed the Radio Star"), Duran Duran ("Rio") and Elton John ("I'm Still Standing"), before making his first feature, *Razorback* (1983)—which Kim Newman calls (in *Nightmare Movies*), "one of the most gripping, stylish and imaginative horror debuts in recent years."

Mulcahy's collaborator on many of the above music videos, Keith Williams, revealed to Alan Jones, in *Shivers #50* that *Talos the Mummy* came into being over Christmas 1995, when Mulcahy had broken his leg in a skiing accident. "Russell in a wheelchair is not a pleasant thing to deal with," Williams told the magazine: "So to stop him tormenting everyone through boredom I suggested we write something together as a kind of therapy. He said, 'What?' I said, 'Well, what's your favorite fantasy film ever?' And he said 'Hammer's *The Mummy* from 1959'…"

Mulcahy confirmed this in the same article: "Hammer's *The Mummy* made a huge impact on me. I can remember when I was a kid in Australia looking up at the poster in awe. That and the Ray Harryhausen pictures made me want to make movies … However, the one thing that really annoyed me when I actually saw *The Mummy* is you never get any scene where a ray of light goes through its torso as depicted on the poster … *Talos the Mummy* is being made so we can put right what we felt cheated by nearly 40 years ago!"

Before shooting began, Williams' original screenplay received a rewrite from New Yorker John Esposito, who had scripted Stephen King's *Graveyard Shift* (1990) and produced *From Dusk Till Dawn* (1995) with Quentin Tarantino. "There's stuff in the script that audiences expect from a *Mummy* movie," Esposito told Alan Jones: "The opening, for example, is the classic architectural dig scene in which Christopher Lee appears and the audience says, 'Okay! This is what I paid to see!'"

Indeed, Lee—who was only required for three days' shooting—finds himself eviscerated in the first 10 minutes as Sir Richard Turkel, desecrator of the Mummy's tomb. With reference to *Dracula*, once caught in the beams emitting from the opened crypt, he crumbles to dust in an early, and none too convincing display of CGI. Despite his short screen-time, the actor, at least, endeavors to present a fully fleshed character, whose determination to explore the Egyptian catacombs is contrasted by a tender exhibition of respect and affection for a local child.

Sadly, the remainder more resembles dreary efforts like *The Awakening* and *Bram Stoker's Legend of the Mummy*, than it does the slick, well-paced output of Hammer. Fifty years after Turkel first unleashes it, the Mummy's trailing bandages pursue the archeologist's granddaughter Sam (Louise Lombard) and her team, including Brad (Sean Pertwee), Claire (Lysette Anthony) and Professor Marcus (Michael Lerner). Bearing an unfortunate resemblance to soiled toilet paper, the vengeful coverings are rendered in non-suspenseful CGI action shots, which—although pointing the way forward to Universal's 1999 hit, *The Mummy*—would have been rather more effective if presented with shadowy style. While they creep up on Lysette Anthony in a recreation of the *Psycho* shower scene, a more typical attack shows them being pulled from a towel dispenser, before flushing their poor victim down a toilet—a nod, no doubt, to Danny Boyle's 1995 smash *Trainspotting*, in which Ewan McGregor's heroin-addicted hero slides head-first into a commode.

The 1990s *Trainspotting* vibe is also apparent in *Talos'* neon-lit rave club, shots of rain-strewn London with damp posters peeling from the walls and a shaven-headed Sean Pertwee running amok through

Talos the Mummy was released in the USA as *Tale of the Mummy*.

Christopher Lee as Sir Richard Turkel

the city. In a nod to the less recent past, Talos itself is named after the bronze giant of *Jason and the Argonauts*, while Stefano Mainetti's musical themes owe much to Wojciech Kilar's work on *Bram Stoker's Dracula*. (Born in 1957, Mainetti would also score the 1987 Italian horrors *Rat Man* and *Zombie 3*.)

On the plus side, a great oil painting of Christopher Lee can be seen in the Richard Turkel Foundation and the film is well-photographed by Gabriel Beristain (b. 1955). The Mexican cinematographer—whose previous credits include Aerosmith's 1993 music video "Amazing" and Stephen King's *Dolores Claiborne* (1994)—would go on to light *Blade II* (2001), *Blade: Trinity* (2003) and *The Ring 2* (2004), as well as providing additional photography for *The Green Mile* (1998), *Iron Man* (2007) and *Guardians of the Galaxy* (2013).

Talos is most notable, however, for its cast: Louise Lombard (b. 1970) had been a sensation in the BBC period drama *The House of Eliott* (1991-1994), while Lysette Anthony (b. 1963) was already something of a genre regular thanks to her starring roles in *Krull* (1983, as Princess Lyssa), *Jack the Ripper* (1988, as Mary Jane Kelly), the 1990 revival of *Dark Shadows* (as Angelique), *Dr. Jekyll and Ms. Hyde* (1995, as the doctor's long-suffering girlfriend), *Dracula: Dead and Loving It* (as Lucy) and *Trilogy of Terror II* (1996, as three different characters).

Sean Pertwee (b. 1964)—the son of Lee's friend and *House That Dripped Blood* co-star, Jon—had made his debut in *Prick Up Your Ears* (1986) with Gary Oldman, before enduring Hell-in-space for *Event Horizon* (1997) and wobble-cam werewolves in *Dog Soldiers* (2001).

Michael Lerner (b. 1941)—veteran of *Strange Invaders* (1982), *Maniac Cop 2* (1990), and *Omen IV: The Awakening* (1990)—is most familiar for his fiery turns in *Barton Fink* (1990, for which he was Oscar-nominated); *Godzilla* (1997, for which he wasn't) and *Elf* (2003).

Top-billed as Detective Riley is American actor and martial artist Jason Scott Lee (b. 1966), who began his career with small roles in *Back to the Future Part II* and *Ghoulies Go to College* (1990). Following his powerhouse performance as Bruce Lee, in *Dragon: The Bruce Lee Story* (1992), Jason went on to decapitate vampires as the *Blade*-inspired Father Uffizi in *Dracula II: Ascension* and *Dracula III: Legacy* (both 2001). The first film in this series, *Dracula 2000* (2000), features Gerard Butler as a bare-chested Count, who romances the staff of the Virgin Megastore before being outed as Judas Iscariot. Butler (b. 1969) can also be seen briefly in *Talos the Mummy* as a doomed archeologist. Fresh from an even briefer appearance in the James Bond extravaganza *Tomorrow Never Dies* (1997), the Scottish actor would earn fame as *The Phantom of the Opera* (2003, with Oscar-nominated production design from Boris Karloff's great-nephew, Anthony Pratt).

Detective Riley's assistant, Barton, is enacted by Jack Davenport (b. 1973), who would next essay a vampire-hunting police detective in the TV mini-series *Ultraviolet* (1998), as well as Norrington in the *Pirates of the Caribbean* franchise.

There are welcome appearances, too, from Shelley Duvall (as a psychic) and *To the Devil a Daughter*'s Honor Blackman (as a police captain), while British TV fans will be pleasantly surprised to see *EastEnders*' Bill Treacher (b. 1930) firing a gun at the reconfigured Mummy in one of the few scenes to quote Lee's original.

Granted a limited release in February 1999, *Talos* was very much overshadowed by the aforementioned big budget, effects-laden remake of *The Mummy* from Universal, which came out in May of that year. Director Stephen Sommers' melding of Universal horror with *Indiana Jones*-style heroics was more in line with the tastes of the public, even if the title monster lacked any of the sympathetic qualities that Lee had brought to the role 40 years earlier. In a final twist, Russell Mulcahy wound up directing a prequel to the prequel of Sommers' blockbuster, *The Scorpion King 2: Rise of a Warrior*, which went straight-to-DVD in 2008.

Returning to the undead theme with *The Curse of King Tut's Tomb* (2006) and *Resident Evil: Extinction* (2006), Mulcahy's other genre work includes *Highlander II: The Quickening* (1990), *The Shadow* (1993) and TV episodes of *Tales from the Crypt* (1989-1996), *The Hunger* (1997-2000) and *Teen Wolf* (2011-2017).

Just prior to *Talos*, in March 1997, Christopher Lee gave what he felt to be his greatest performance as *Jinnah*, the founder of Pakistan. Written, produced and directed by Jamil Dehlavi, this biopic's grueling 10-week shoot was dogged by controversy, especially when Karachi journalists expressed outrage at Lee's casting. "I was accused of playing 'lethal' characters in horror and sex films," the actor told the *Guardian* in September 1998, adding: "The sex bit was news to me, I have to say …" Nevertheless, Lee proved that he could induce shivers of a very different sort in a powerfully moving climax, which shows him fighting back real tears. Unfortunately, *Jinnah* failed to gain UK or US distribution and wouldn't see a decent DVD release until 2016—a year after the actor's death.

The non-emergence of *Jinnah* only seemed to compound a growing sense of disappointment in Lee, who gave his views on contemporary cinema to *Shivers* #50 (February 1998): "Everything today seems to have nothing but sex and violence and bad language in it. Sometimes it's valid, in a picture like *Goodfellas*, because people do act like that. But to see—*again*—another couple wrestling in a bed, you might as well go to a farmyard."

Lee rounded out the 1990s with his cameo in Tim Burton's *Sleepy Hollow* (discussed later) and a melancholy turn as Flay, the cat-hurling servant of *Gormenghast* (1999). Exquisitely realized by an all-star ensemble—including Steve Pemberton (*The League of Gentlemen, Inside No. 9*) and future TV Dracula Jonathan Rhys Meyers—Mervyn Peake's eccentric fantasy was first aired on BBC 2 from January 17 to February 7, 2000. At the latter end of the year, the same station would broadcast Lee's next venture into the world of horror.

Ghost Stories for Chrismas 2000

Since the 1843 publication of Charles Dickens' *A Christmas Carol*, the seemingly conflicting pleasures of Yuletide and ghosts have been paired as a British tradition. One notable upholder of this custom was Montague Rhodes James (1862-1936), the Provost of Eton College, who wrote ghostly tales as a Christmas entertainment to be read aloud to his students.

Christopher Lee was almost one of those students. "The first thing I saw was a mummy in a glass case," he wrote of his 1936 Eton interview. "The second was a little old man in glasses with a skin like parchment." This was M.R. James, and the young Lee was familiar with the author's work. By the light of a roaring fire, on dark evenings, his Summer Fields schoolmaster would read James' stories to the pupils, who thrilled to "the weird inventions of the pussyfooting old scholar."

In *Christopher Lee's New Chamber of Horrors*, Lee called James "the greatest of all ghost story writers" and described himself as "a devoted student of his work," citing "Count Magnus" as his personal favorite among the writer's tales. In Clive Dunn's 1995 TV documentary *A Pleasant Terror: The Life and Ghosts of M.R. James*, Lee elaborated further: "The frightening thing about James' stories [is that] they were so brilliantly and learnedly written that you actually *believed* them … they, literally, like a great wall of darkness, begin to *envelop* you." The actor even revealed James as an inspiration to his work in horror cinema: "I've always tried to *suggest* things which would surprise the audience … that's where, I'm sure, I was greatly influenced by James."

Few cinematic interpretations have been made of James' work, with the classic exception of Jacques Tourneur's *Night of the Demon* (1956), based on "Casting the Runes." Then, inspired by Jonathan Miller's superlative TV-film of *Whistle and I'll Come to You* (1968), documentarist Lawrence Gordon Clark turned his hand to adapting a series of M.R. James stories for the BBC under the banner *A Ghost Story for Christmas*.

The first of these, "The Stalls of Barchester," was screened on Christmas Eve 1971, and was followed by "A Warning to the Curious" (Christmas Eve, 1972), "Lost Hearts" (Christmas Day, 1973), "The Treasure of Abbott Thomas" (December 23, 1974) and "The Ash Tree" (December 23, 1975). For his December 22, 1976, offering, Clark strayed from James and directed Dickens' "The Signalman" to great effect. The remainder of the series consisted of original stories, "Stigma" (Christmas Day, 1977) and "The Ice House" (December 28, 1978), the latter of which was helmed by Derek Lister. Despite a tailing off in quality with these last two films, the series continues to leave disquieting impressions, and remains, in my opinion, the finest representation of the paranormal onscreen. But, after this, seasonal ghost stories and the BBC parted ways until the new millennium, when producer Richard Downes decided that the time was right to resurrect the formula.

Downes aptly describes *Ghost Stories for Christmas* to me as "*Jackanory* for grown-ups" and says that Lee was "the obvious choice" to bring the words of M.R. James to life. "He was really into doing it and was genuinely interested in M.R. James and ghost stories. Christopher Lee was the perfect person to articulate that world." However, Richard also describes the three-day shoot as "fraught" and "not a pleasant experience." The budget, which came from the BBC's Arts (as opposed to Drama) department, wouldn't stretch to dramatizations of the tales, so a reading was the next best thing.

By this time, while Britain itself was producing little in the way of spooky television shows, BBC 2 was screening Joss Whedon's US import *Buffy the Vampire Slayer*—the best genre series to emerge since those halcyon days of the 1970s, and itself responsible for a new boom in fantasy TV. When asked if he watched the series, however, Lee's response was an unequivocal "No." Nevertheless, *Buffy* took the vampiric lore developed by Hammer and added an element that was never the company's forte: Strongly written roles for women. And, for the first time in Lee's career, it was a woman who directed his primary genre outing of the 21st century.

Eleanor Yule was a young, BAFTA-nominated documentarian when she got the job of directing *Ghost Stories for Christmas*. "Christopher was a challenging actor to work with," she tells me, but: "We had a great crew and a lot of talented people working on it even if the budget was tiny." Eleanor went on to write and direct the award-winning thriller *Blinded* (2004), as well as producing various documentaries on serial killers and artists.

Filmed by BBC Scotland in October 2000, with Elton Hall, near Peterborough, standing in for King's College, Cambridge, each 30-minute episode of *Ghost Stories for Christmas* shows Lee as James, telling his latest supernatural tale to a rapt audience of students in the half-hour before midnight on Christmas Eve.

That fine blend of austerity and coziness which typifies the appeal of ghost stories suffuses the program, just as the glow of a flickering fire and various candles pervade the mustiness of the Provost's book-lined study.

Lee relates the stories with such veracity that one believes he is describing events that actually happened (indeed, his performance earned him a Hamilton Deane Award from the Dracula Society). As his voice is enough to bring the tales to life in our minds, Yule wisely elects to keep her camera trained on the actor, with only the occasional cutaway to a grainy illustrative visual.

Tellingly, the *Radio Times* listed the series as *Christopher Lee's Ghost Stories for Christmas*. The four episodes, screened after 11pm by BBC 2 over Christmas 2000, were: "The Stalls of Barchester"

An almost unregonizable Christopher Lee

(December 23); "The Ash Tree" (December 26); "Number 13" (December 29); and "A Warning to the Curious" (December 31).

Richard Downes, whose subsequent credits include *The Strange Case of Sherlock Holmes & Arthur Conan Doyle* (2005), kindly took time from his latest editing assignment in October 2016 to discuss Christopher Lee with me. Remembering that the actor "didn't command a massive fee," Richard first arranged to discuss the project with Lee at The Gay Hussar, a renowned Hungarian restaurant in London.

Arriving early, the producer was approached by the left-wing politician Michael Foot, who mistook him for someone else and struck up a conversation. "Then Lee walked in, came over to us and stood there." Richard introduced Lee to Foot.

"I know who he is," said Lee, frostily.

Richard then remembered that Lee was a staunch Conservative ("a big *Daily Telegraph* reader," as he puts it), who had little time for Foot's socialist politics. "It was an inauspicious, weird start. Things never really recovered from the awkwardness ..."

The problems started with Lee's accommodation for the shoot. "It was an awful motel in the middle of a big, busy roundabout," Richard tells me. Although it had been decked out with flowers and chocolates, Lee was not happy with the room (it had no windows) and demanded to be accommodated elsewhere. Thus, Richard drove the grumbling actor around Peterborough that night in search of a better hotel. They eventually found one "which perversely overlooked a graveyard." Owing to this, the girl who showed Lee to his new room quipped, "You'll be right at home here."

"He wasn't impressed," says Richard. "He just gave her a withering look."

Filming began the next morning. "It was an overambitious schedule," Richard tells me, "and Lee was quite demanding. He never liked the food." As such, oysters were ordered in specially. "He liked to eat his meals alone at night at the hotel." Richard remembers that Lee took the young extras playing the students under his wing. "They came in from Ellesmere Port, near Liverpool, and spoke in broad Liverpudlian accents. Lee liked them and held court, telling stories. They were in awe of the great man."

Nevertheless, Lee was "difficult to direct." Unaware that Richard and Eleanor were then-married, Lee voiced his suspicions to co-workers that they were having an affair, a misunderstanding which was never resolved. "He had worked with lots of great directors," says Richard. "He felt he didn't need direction." However, "due to the sheer volume of material," it was important that the readings didn't appear as though they were simply being reeled off from an autocue. Direction was needed to add nuance to the actor's delivery. Richard also recalls the impressive crane shot which opens each episode: "[Lee] didn't like that at all. He didn't feel M.R. James would stand by a window and didn't understand why this was necessary. He got quite angry."

Unfortunately, Richard remembers Lee as "bad tempered" and "not the most gracious of people. He would pick on small things and inflate them, making them more difficult than they were." Matters were not helped when Lee insisted that he leave the four-day shoot a day ahead of schedule in order to appear in (what Richard remembers to be) a music video directed by John Landis. This meant the crew had to work even longer hours in order to finish everything within just three days. "But we got through it."

Richard recalls that on the last day, when Lee's limousine arrived, he gathered his team and said: "I know this hasn't been the easiest of shoots, but let's all go outside and say farewell to Christopher." As they left the building, Richard and his crew saw Lee storming towards them, still dressed in his cloak-like gown. "Who's locked the toilets?" he demanded. "I need to do a piss!" When no answer was forthcoming, Lee turned his back and muttered, "I'll just do it here." As the actor relieved himself against a brick wall, he was caught in the glare of the limousine's headlights, which caused a great cloud of steam to rise all around him. "He looked every inch the vampire," Richard remembers.

(I'm fairly certain the music video that Lee had to leave the shoot early for is "She'll Fall for Me" with Gary Curtis. In this bizarre yet strangely enjoyable slice of countrified pop, Lee rolls up in the white limousine remembered by Richard and competes with Curtis for the affections of a lady who is far too young for either of them. It's definitely not directed by John Landis, though. Perhaps Richard misheard or misremembered the name Gary Curtis as John Landis?)

One director who worked with Lee around this time called him "a disappointed man" in terms of his career. Was there any truth to this statement? "I think he was a disappointed man," Richard explains. "He compared himself to other actors of his age and thought his abilities and range went further than Dracula—although he was always extremely proud of *The Wicker Man*.

"*Star Wars* and *Lord of the Rings* [yet to be released] gave him the profile he felt he deserved. Unlike Vincent Price, who was a brilliant actor, Lee had a more limited range, but he alienated everybody by telling them what a great actor he was. He wasn't in the least interested in what anybody else had to say. While I'm glad that we did it, it's a shame. He had the potential but was stuck being locked into the horror world."

I ask Richard if he has any happy memories of Christopher Lee. "When he was sitting there, once everything was in place and ready for recording, he fitted into his role so well. The man had such presence and charisma. He was electrifying to watch. No one else could have done it like him. At the end of the day, I thought, 'That's Christopher Lee sitting there. This is quite a special thing.'"

Multi-Media Macabre: Books, Audio Recordings and Video Games

Christopher Lee's association with the horror genre was so widespread that it incorporated more than just movies. In fact, the actor was lending his name to other forms of media from a relatively early stage of his career. When *Dracula* and *The Curse of Frankenstein* enjoyed a successful US reissue in December 1964, both films were featured in a photo-story magazine, Warren Publishing's *Famous Films #2* (*Famous Films #1* [November '64] was devoted to *The Horror of Party Beach*; #3 [January '65] was *The Mole People*). The stories were adapted, with lots of YAAAAAAAs and some rare images (such as Jonathan Harker's corpse and Lee's half-disintegrated face), by Russ Jones (b. 1942), who also provided the striking cover art.

The founder of *Creepy* magazine, Jones painted some memorable covers for *Famous Monsters of Filmland* and, with less success, wrote *Dr. Terror's Gallery of Horrors*. The last segment of this 1966 portmanteau movie is a potted version of *Dracula*, which closes on the comic book-style surprise of Harker becoming a werewolf. That same year, Jones produced a graphic novel adaptation of *Dracula*, introduced by Christopher Lee, for Ballantine Books (which predates by 12 years what most historians agree is the first graphic novel, Will Eisner's *A Contract with God*). The artwork was by Alden McWilliams, who had previously drawn strips for *Creepy*, *Boris Karloff Tales of Mystery* and *Twilight Zone*, before co-creating the comic world's first African American hero, Danny Raven, for *Dateline: Danger!* (1968-1974). In his well-written and informative Introduction, Lee discusses the loneliness of evil: "Despite his actions, there is to me a sadness about Dracula, a brooding, withdrawn unhappiness. He is in this world, but he is not of this world …" The actor also expounds: "It is an accepted historical and medical fact that vampirism has existed throughout the centuries." He even goes so far as to reveal: "I have also been contacted in a personal letter from France by one who claims to be the lineal descendent of Count Dracula." More significantly, after citing the various actors who have played the Count over the years, Lee ends his piece by stating: "I am proud to be of that number."

The *Dracula* graphic novel also sired a two-disc spin-off album from Stamford, in which Lee's narration follows, more or less word for word, the condensed action of Otto Binder and Craig Tennis' adaptation. After his silent performance in *Dracula: Prince of Darkness*, it's refreshing to hear Lee give full voice to the character: Accompanied by booming bursts of brass, the cold, clipped tones, familiar from Hammer's first vampire film, rise to a throaty roar during moments of fury: "A mirror? They aren't allowed in my castle!" It's doubly refreshing to hear Lee weep and wail as a Transylvanian peasant woman ("Monster! Monster! Give me back my child!"), until his frenzied reading brings apt excitement to the climax. (Although Donald F. Glut mentions, in *The Dracula Book*, a private 1964 recording that the actor had made of "Dracula's Guest," the 1966 *Dracula* record marks Lee's first official audio release; Lee also refers to the "Dracula's Guest" recording in his Afterword for *The Ghouls*, claiming that the occasion allowed him to meet Stoker's granddaughter and great-grandson.)

Russ Jones next issued *Christopher Lee's Treasury of Terror* (Pyramid Books, September 1966), which comprises comic-strip adaptations of Rudyard Kipling's "The Mark of the Beast," H.P. Lovecraft and August Derleth's "Wentworth's Day," Robert Bloch's "The Past Master," Ambrose Bierce's "The Death of Halpin Frayser" and Stoker's "Dracula's Guest." The stories were, according to the blurb: "Selected by Christopher Lee—the movies' most sensational portrayer of arch-fiends …" Dubbed within the paperback as "Mr. Terror" and "the screen's new 'man of a thousand faces'," Lee provides an intelligent Introduction, which explores humanity's "rapt fascination with the Prince of Darkness and all his works," while negating the "harmful" effects of such literature and movies, "except to those poor souls who already suffer, through no fault of their own, from twisted and unbalanced minds." The book is topped by a charming cover illustration, from *Mad* magazine artist Mort Drucker (1929-2020), depicting an avuncular-looking Lee, surrounded by a menagerie of fiends (including a werewolf, a Frankenstein-like creation and a Lovecraftian tentacle).

Ted Newsom offers this Russ Jones-related anecdote: "I had bought a Fu Manchu portrait print at convention from the artist, Russ Jones. It had originally appeared as the back cover of an issue of *Castle of Frankenstein* magazine … and I wanted Lee's autograph on it, along with the artist's. When Lee was in town, I showed him the picture. He approved, then saw the artist's name. 'Rus-s-s-s Jo-o-o-nes?' He said, 'I haven't heard that name in 20 years.' He did the second verse with increased bafflement and surprise, with an edge that said there's something here I don't want to know. 'R-u-u-s-s-s-*s-s-s* Jo-o-*o-o-n-n-*nes-s-*ssss*?!' I didn't ask for an elaboration. He did sign it though, with his name, and added beneath, 'A bit of Chinese.' Figuring there was a joke I was missing, I asked what that meant. He explained unhelpfully, 'Well, you know. A bit of Chinese.'

"Ah. That clears that up."

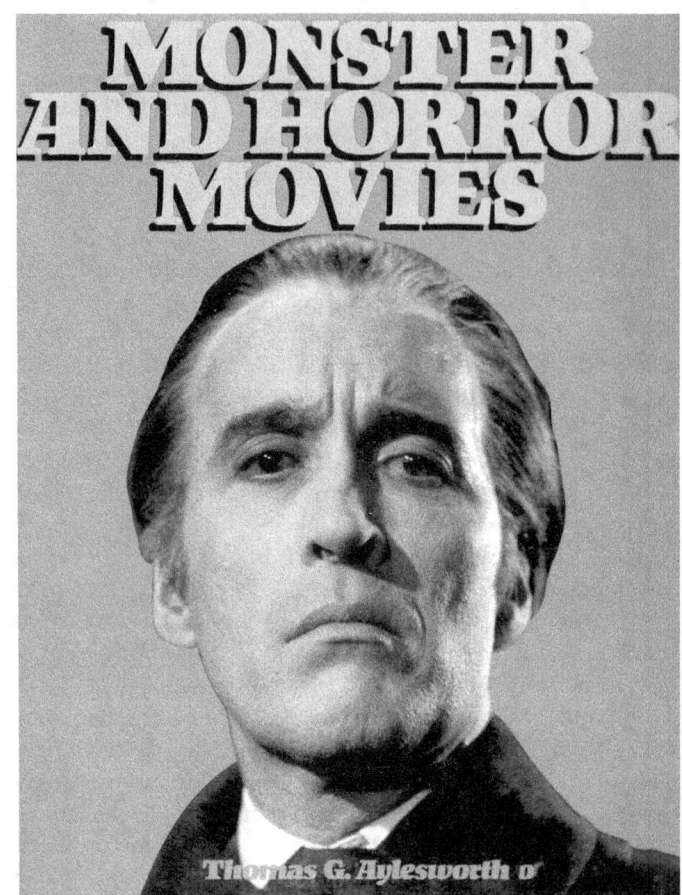

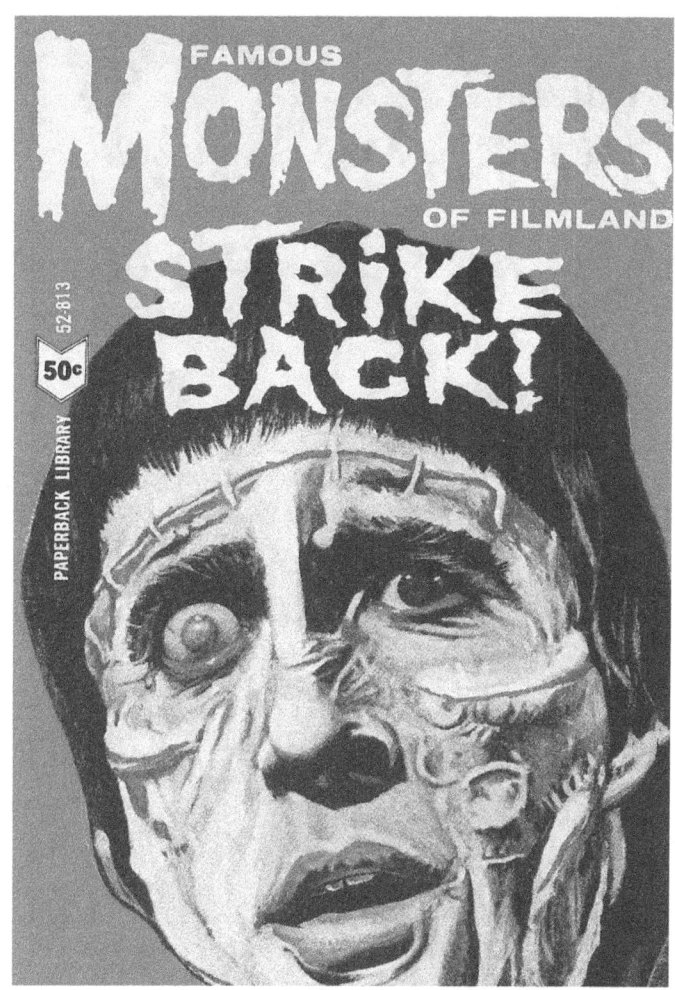

The Loneliness of Evil

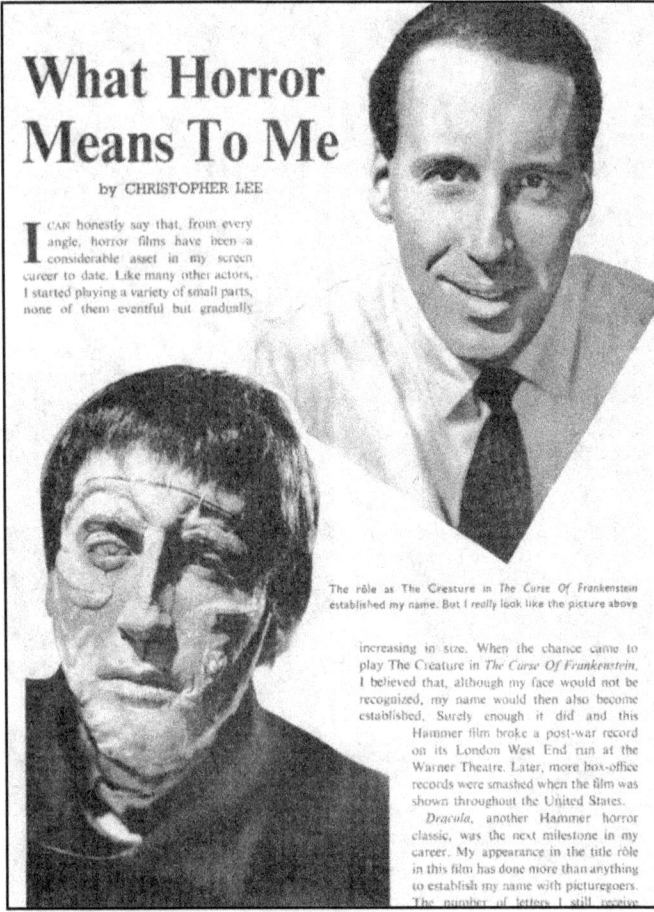

An article Lee wrote for *Picturegoer Film Annual*.

The notion of an actor co-editing and introducing a book of genre stories had begun with three tasteful selections from Boris Karloff: *Tales of Terror* (World, 1943), *And the Darkness Falls* (World, 1946) and *The Boris Karloff Horror Anthology* (Souvenir Press, 1965). Vincent Price followed suit with *18 Best Stories by Edgar Allan Poe* (Dell, 1965), while Orson Welles lent his name to a science fiction collection, *Invasion from Mars: Interplanetary Stories* (Dell, 1949), off the back of his *War of the Worlds* controversy.

Christopher Lee first joined the world of anthologies in 1970, by penning an Afterword to *The Ghouls*, a collection of "18 classic stories that inspired great horror films" (including *Freaks* [1931], *The Beast from 20,000 Fathoms* [1953] and *Black Sunday* [1960]). Here, Lee calls Karloff's performance in *Frankenstein*, "probably the finest piece of individual acting we have ever seen on the screen," but cites Lon Chaney as "the greatest of them all, a genius in fact."

Originally published by W.H. Allen in February 1971, with an equally illuminating Foreword from Vincent Price, *The Ghouls* marked Lee's debut collaboration with Peter Haining (1940-2007). One of the finest anthologists in the field, Haining was proud to live in a haunted house and also wrote excellent reference works on *Doctor Who*, Sherlock Holmes and James Bond.

Lee and Haining continued their association with *Christopher Lee's New Chamber of Horrors* (Souvenir Press, 1974; this book was later chopped in half to be issued as two 1976 Mayflower paperbacks: *Christopher Lee's New Chamber of Horrors* and *More of Christopher Lee's New Chamber of Horrors*). For this more involved compendium, Lee expounds on his lifelong love of fantasy fiction, naming Lord Dunsany and Ray Bradbury as particular favorites. Indeed, he admits to owning a copy of Bradbury's landmark 1962 novel *Something Wicked This Way Comes* inscribed: "To Christopher Lee who is Mr. Dark, with the admiration of his Fan, Ray Bradbury." (When the book was eventually filmed by Disney in 1981, the part was essayed by Jonathan Pryce; Lee had previously enacted Bradbury's *Leviathan '99* on BBC Radio 3 in May 1968.)

Also for Haining, Lee discussed the rigors of playing monsters ("Frankenstein, Dracula and Me") for *The Frankenstein File* (New English Library, 1977), provided a brief introductory essay, "The Midnight Side," to *Bram Stoker's Midnight Tales* (Peter Owen Publishers, 1990) and wrote the Foreword to *Vampires at Midnight* (Warner Books, 1993). The latter, in particular, is typical of Haining's devoted approach: Neglected gems and lesser-known authors are placed alongside old favorites, making for a read that is both cozy and enlightening.

Lee's second-most frequent collaborator in the anthology field was Michel Parry (1947-2014), whose 1975 interview with the actor for *Castle of Frankenstein* magazine led to four W.H. Allen publications: *Christopher Lee's 'X' Certificate* (1975), *Christopher Lee's Archives of Evil* (1976), *The Great Villains* (1978) and *Lurking Shadows* (1979). "I have to admit a fatal attraction to weird stories with a humorous slant," Michel once wrote to me: "Saki, John Collier and Fredric Brown being particular favorites." The first two of those authors would be showcased within the pages of the aforementioned books, which also gave Lee the opportunity to express his own worthwhile thoughts on the genre, while providing fascinating insights into his friends Robert Bloch, Ray Bradbury and Boris Karloff. (Parry went on to script "Rouse Him Not," a Manly Wade Wellman adaptation for *Monsters* [1988-1990], *Xtro* [1982], a weird alien shocker with some unique imagery and *The Uncanny* [1976], wherein a very nervous Peter Cushing sets out to prove that cats are evil—both Lee and Vincent Price were offered parts in this movie but turned them down.)

In 1975, along with fellow judges Kingsley Amis and Patricia Highsmith, Lee selected the 13 tales which make up *The Times Anthology of Ghost Stories* (Jonathan Cape). The result of a ghost story competition held in the London *Times* newspaper, this collection is notable for publishing the earliest fiction from two future winners of the Booker Prize, Julian Barnes and Penelope Fitzgerald.

Elsewhere, Lee introduced *Realms of Darkness* (Octopus Books, 1985), a bumper collection of 73 "nightmarish tales of the supernatural and macabre" from such wide-ranging authors as Roald Dahl, Stephen King, H.G. Wells and Dennis Wheatley. Edited by Mary Danby (b. 1941)—who, as well as being the great-great-granddaughter of Charles Dickens, had long been responsible for the *Fontana Book(s) of Great Horror Stories*—*Realms of Darkness* features a whip-wielding still of Lee from *The Return of Captain Invincible* on its cover. Within, the actor admits to "an enthusiasm for macabre stories that began in boyhood and is still with me," while stating the superiority of the written word over cinematic effects. He also relates an amusing anecdote dating from Gitte's pregnancy: Following a tire blow-up in Italy, Lee "tottered through fields of turnips ... covered in mud and sand ... to fetch help." Arriving at "a solitary building," the occupant took one look at the bedraggled actor on his doorstep, "uttered a piercing shriek, cried '*E lui*' ('It's him.')—and fainted. It turned out that he had confused me with the dreaded Count and thought it would not be long before he joined the ranks of the undead."

Lee also provided similarly enlightening Forewords to the second volume of Walt Lee's exhaustive *Reference Guide to Fantastic Films* (Chelsea-Lee Books, 1973: "I myself have been involved to some degree in this 'Secret, black, and midnight' world and I feel most strongly that there is still a great deal of work to be done …"); Al Taylor and Sue Roy's chronicle of movie make-up artists *Making a Monster* (Crown Publishers, 1980: "It is always with a slight tingle of anticipation that we settle into our chairs in front of the mirror in the theater dressing room, and apply the first touches of Five and Nine …") and Richard Dalby's *The Mammoth Book of Ghost Stories 2* (Robinson, 1991: "When we read a story, there is no limit whatever to our own imagination …"). Finally, in May 2010, Lee remembered his "very dear friend" Boris Karloff for the fifth volume of Dark Horse Books' *Boris Karloff Tales of Mystery Archives* ("I think of him often … I will never forget him"). One of the comicstrip stories in this handsome collection—John Celardo and Sal Trapini's "Creature of the Sargasso Sea" (from March 1970)—concerns an alien intellect which, after arrival on Earth, possesses the planet's lifeforms, then assembles materials in order to build a spaceship and return home—just as in *Horror Express*.

But Lee's talents extended into more than just the occasional writing assignment. Beneath the headline "Mr. Ghoul in the Groove," the September 20, 1970, edition of *Sunday Mirror* announced: "Christopher Lee, high priest of horror films, has stepped from the grave to the groove to become a pop singer. Due out next month is the single 'I Am Yours,' with Mr. Lee, minus fangs and batwings, emerging as a stylish ballad singer." Unfortunately, this EMI record (b/w "The Seasons") was never issued at the actor's own request. According to *LSoH #4*, Lee felt that the orchestral backing was too loud and obscured his vocal performance. This didn't stop the actor from appearing on the cover of EMI's biggest-selling album of 1973, *Band on the Run*, at the invitation of Paul McCartney. ("He and the other Beatles were fans," Lee explained to Tom Johnson and Mark A. Miller.)

That same year, Lee hooked up with another rock legend, David Bowie, as he reported in the August 1973 edition of his International Club Journal: "We both got on very well together and after David had played a bit on his guitar and I had sung, he asked me if I would like to make records with him. I said that I would be delighted to do so, providing we could find the right material and this is where the whole idea came to a dead stop." Alas, according to Lee, someone at Bowie's management decided that: "We simply wouldn't know how to start for a voice such as yours. None of our clients have real voices, our styles of writing are totally different from anything we could think of for you. And indeed, to be frank, your voice is too powerful and good." Regardless of whether this record company representative was merely being diplomatic, a photo of Lee with Bowie was among the actor's effects, inscribed by the musician: "For Christopher. With my regards, Bowie '78."

One record that did get released was *Hammer Presents Dracula* (Hammer City Records, 1974). "Invite Christopher Lee inside your living room!" ran the ads in *The House of Hammer* magazine.

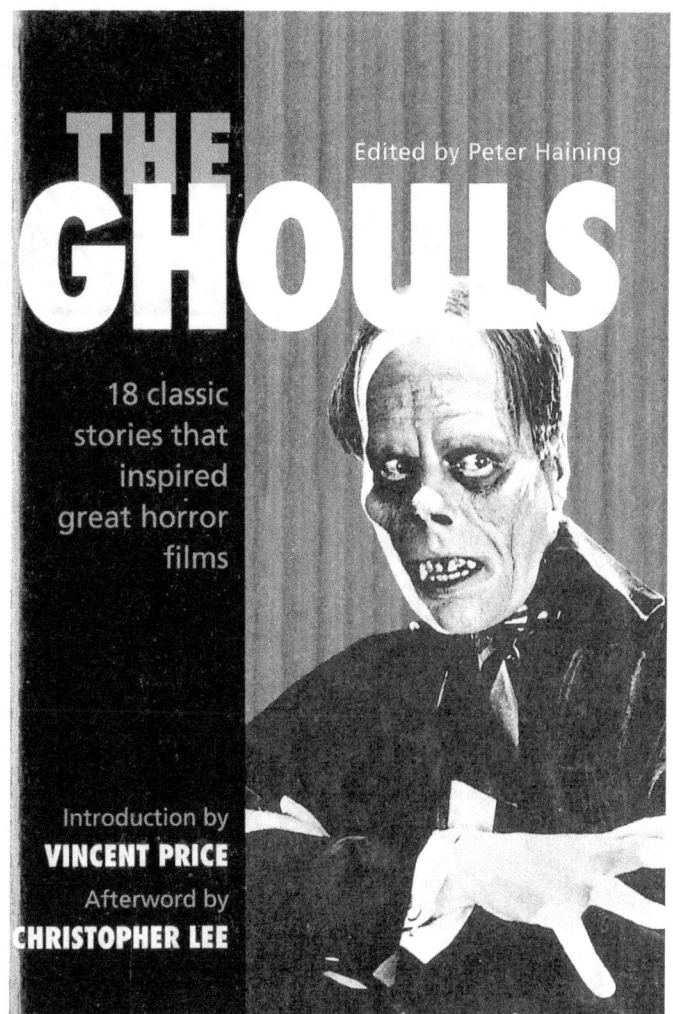

To a carefully arranged backing of James Bernard's Dracula scores, Lee narrates a Don Houghton-scripted tale of a couple ensnared at Castle Dracula. The slight story is of little interest, as the record is really an exercise in audio atmospherics. Screams, squeaking bats, crackling tempests, howling wolves and throbbing hearts assail us at every opportunity, with Houghton's script offering some particularly descriptive passages for Lee to get his teeth round, while building uneasy pictures in the listener's mind.

The record is introduced by Canadian actor Bill Mitchell (1934-1997), whose graven purr could also be heard alongside Lee's in *Ten Little Indians*. As well as voicing the prologue to *The Little Shop of Horrors* (1986), Mitchell appeared in *Night of the Eagle*, *You Only Live Twice* (as an astronaut) and *Doctor Who*: "Frontier in Space" (1972, as a newscaster). Not long after the Dracula album, he would replace Orson Welles as the voice of Carlsberg beer.

The second half of *Hammer Presents Dracula* includes welcome suites from *Fear in the Night*, *She*, *The Vampire Lovers* and *Dr. Jekyll and Sister Hyde*, newly recorded by the Hammer City Orchestra. The original British release had a gatefold sleeve, denied American buyers, boasting an essay by horror writer Basil Copper on the vampire in fact and fiction. With a fantastic cover image of Lee and Caroline Munro from *Dracula A.D. 1972*, the record previewed exclusively on London's Capital Radio, during their first annual "night of horror," in March 1974. That year,

Dracula was adapted brilliantly by comic artist Paul Neary.

Michael Carreras could be seen languidly promoting the disc ("our latest diversification") in an interview with Bram Stoker's grand-nephew Daniel Farson for the fascinating BBC documentary *The Dracula Business*.

After releasing a Peter Cushing-narrated record of *The Legend of the 7 Golden Vampires*, Hammer next prepared a Frankenstein-related audio drama, again with Cushing. Sadly, this never emerged, as Michael Carreras revealed (in *LSoH* #4), the man with whom Hammer set up their record division made off with the master tapes, as well as all the profits from the first two releases. And that was the end of Hammer's delve into the record industry—until June 1990, when they purchased the publishing and release rights of Warfare's rock tribute *Hammer Horror*, an album for which Lee and Cushing penned sleeve notes. The band's lead singer and drummer, Evo, told *Hammer Horror* #4 that one of his songs, "Scream of the Vampire," sympathized with Lee's desire to play Dracula in accordance with Stoker: "Lee does not think Dracula has been done authentically, and I reflected that through the lyrics as a loathing for the unfaithful storylines."

In 1977, Lee narrated and sang on *The King of Elfland's Daughter* (Chrysalis), a folk-rock concept album from Steeleye Span's Bob Johnson and Peter Knight. Based on the 1924 novel by Lord Dunsany, the record sold poorly, being a perfect example of the over-earnest fantasy warbling later parodied by *This Is Spinal Tap*.

More successful was a double cassette offering, *Christopher Lee Reads Edgar Allan Poe Tales of Horror*, which appeared in 1979 on the Listen for Pleasure label. The stories read by Lee are "The Fall of the House of Usher," "The Pit and the Pendulum," "The Cask of Amontillado" and "The Black Cat." The cover illustration shows a vein-streaked hand being gnawed on by rats. A companion set, *Christopher Lee Reads Tales of Mystery and Horror* (which features a nice cover painting of a raven on a graveyard wall), has Lee intone Poe's "Hop Frog," "The Raven," "The Masque of the Red Death," "The Tell-Tale Heart" and "Murders in the Rue Morgue."

"The Black Cat" was also the first story to be recited by Lee for *Christopher Lee's Fireside Tales*, a BBC Radio 4 Extra series, broadcast over five nights from Christmas Eve to Saturday, December 28, 2013. The other tales were Jerome K. Jerome's "The Man of Science," E. Nesbit's "John Charrington's Wedding," Ambrose Bierce's "The Man and the Snake" and W.W. Jacobs' "The Monkey's Paw." Redolent of a slightly crazed grandfather ("It's getting late. Time for your story, I think"), Lee's readings are a delight.

With its affectionate references to classic horror and science fiction cinema, it seemed inevitable that Lee would one day be involved with *The Rocky Horror Show*. Indeed, Richard O'Brien's liberating musical enjoys several links with Hammer horror. The program for the show's opening night, on Tuesday, June 19, 1973, ends with the telling acknowledgement: "Special thanks to Hammer Films without whom …" (among the gleeful audience members that stormy evening was Vincent Price). As we have already seen, *The Rocky Horror Picture Show* was made at Bray Studios at the tail-end of 1974, with Oakley Court standing in for the aliens' castle; Lee's bandaged dummy prop from *The Curse of Frankenstein* being put to good use and Mocata himself, Charles Gray, narrating the strange events. In 1981, *Rocky Horror* was remade as an Egyptian Dracula movie, *Fangs*, in which Lee's Count, seen as a portrait on the castle wall, is described as "a dropout from school" who "became an actor" (the film also pilfers music from *The Man with the Golden Gun*). That same year, O'Brien, in collaboration with *Rocky Horror* musical arranger Richard Hartley, wrote three numbers for *The Return of Captain Invincible*, most memorably the delectable "Name Your Poison," which Lee belts out in style. In

October 2016, I was present at a *Rocky Horror* event at London's BFI where Hartley recalled Lee as being "game for anything. He took [the song] extremely seriously" with "no sense of irony. When it got to the Springsteen bit, the engineers were rolling on the floor, laughing." This lack of irony was, perhaps, Lee's greatest strength as a horror performer. It meant that he treated every role, no matter how ridiculous, with the utmost seriousness—making the incredible credible.

Lee finally got to play *Rocky Horror*'s narrator for a National Symphony Orchestra Ensemble CD of the show's songs, recorded at Abbey Road Studios at the beginning of 1995. While the musical arrangements are close to the rough-and-ready sound of the original 1973 cast album, the addition of Dolby Digital Surround adds a modern and noisy touch (lots of thunder rumbles and lightning crackles). Lee is joined by Anita Dobson—ex-star of the popular British TV soap opera *EastEnders*—as Magenta, and her husband, Queen guitarist Brian May, as the reanimated delivery boy Eddie. Around the same time, Lee also contributed to the NSO Ensemble recordings of *The King and I* (as the King, the musical's historical heroine, Anna Leonowens, was the grand aunt of Boris Karloff) and *Annie Get Your Gun* as Chief Sitting Bull. (*The Rocky Horror Picture Show*'s Barry Bostwick took the lead role of Frank Butler.)

Four years later, in 1999, Lee lent his talents to *The Rocky Interactive Horror Show*. The aim of this video game is to wander around Frank N. Furter's castle and find the components of the De-Medusa machine that will free either Brad or Janet from their statue-like form. Lee, in requisite smoking jacket, pops up seated on a wooden throne to remind players how to do "The Time Warp," reading the lyrics in a hilariously po-faced fashion ("Let's do the Time Warp again—let's *do* the Time Warp again"). He is just as weirdly humorous when explaining the virtues of KY jelly: "Protection for those really *sticky* moments." Unfortunately, lines like this, and the game itself, only indicate how far the show had descended into pantomime vulgarity by this time. Aside from Lee, the only other bonus is Richard O'Brien himself, who turns up now and again to taunt the player—and can even be heard playing new recordings of the *Rocky Horror* songs on his acoustic guitar.

Another interactive effort was *Ghosts*, released in late 1994 for CD-ROM and PC Mac. This sees Lee, in smoking jacket and bow tie, as Dr. Marcus Grimalkin, who has "devoted [his] life to the study of the paranormal." (Lee is wearing the same smoking jacket he'd worn in *Sherlock Holmes and the Deadly Necklace*, *Theatre of Death* and *Eugenie*.) As the character explains, against a stuffy library backdrop, the purpose of the game is to help him "decide, once and for all, whether ghosts are reality or fiction." As Lee tells ghost stories from the left-hand corner of the screen, the player investigates the fictional Hobbs Manor. Each significant item in the house's 3-D-rendered rooms inspires a wry comment from Lee ("I couldn't help but notice that you were admiring this splendid carpet ..."). Along with 1,500 images of alleged spirit activity, a number of real-life experts show up to relate their paranormal experiences, including Maurice Grosse—the investigator of the disturbing "Enfield Poltergeist" case—and Robin Furman, the psychologist founder of Ghostbusters UK, who shows off his ghostbusting device (which looks like a big gun made of torches). "We used it once in a deserted church," Robin explains. "We fired the beam of light into a swirling green ominous mist which exploded into trillions of glistening lights ..."

"Christopher Lee was the obvious choice," the game's art director Dave Hornsby told Marcus Hearn (in *Hammer Horror* #1). "He'd previously recorded a pilot for another CD-ROM about the history of comics. He knew the score, so when he came in for his one day's filming everything went smoothly. Obviously, he's been doing this sort of thing for a lot longer than we have!"

In the mid-1990s, Lee read five classic novels of horror (*Dracula*, *Frankenstein*, *Dr. Jekyll and Mr. Hyde*, *The Phantom of the Opera* and *The Hunchback of Notre Dame*) for the Music Collection International label. These audio recordings made full use of the actor's expressive voice, something that films didn't always do (although, early on in his career, he provided all the varied comic mutterings for the English-language version of *Monsieur Hulot's Holiday* [1951]; "I even did the old lady!"—*Shivers* #50). Lee's tonal modulations really bring the words to life, proving, beyond doubt, what a versatile actor he was. The listener gets to hear him show off an array of accents—from Russian to Scottish to Irish to Swiss, by way of Paris via Transylvania—as he takes on characters both young and old, male and female.

For *Dracula*, Lee has the Count speak in a low baritone, when not snarling in demonic fury. This is truly the sound of a being "not attuned to mirth," who loves "the shade and the shadow." Indeed, Lee's vampiric voice, like the doors to Dracula's castle, creaks from long disuse and seems to be formed of shadows itself. The actor's dramatic reading makes a great work seem greater still, and he brings particular relish to Stoker's key moments of horror. By subtly modulating his voice, Lee conveys the different characters, adding the appropriate notes of terror for Jonathan Harker, a present and correct Texan twang for Quincey Morris and a Dutch accent for Van Helsing that is not too far removed from Frank Finlay's interpretation in *Count*

The Loneliness of Evil

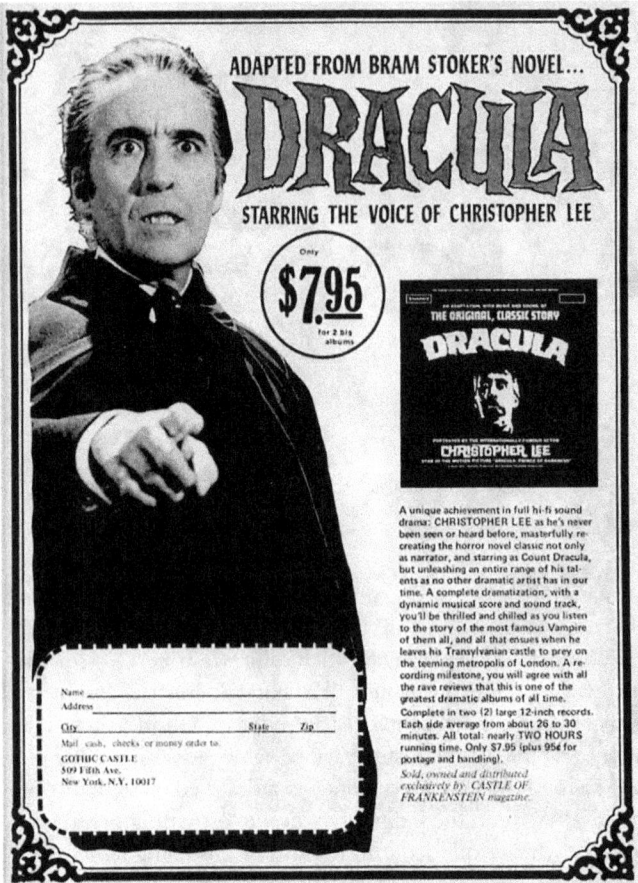

Castle of Frankenstein's ad for Christopher Lee's two-LP recording of *Dracula*.

Dracula (1977). For the female voices, Lee appears to heed the advice of Lon Chaney, who stated in the press book for his only talkie *The Unholy Three* (1930) that, for feminine imitation, a falsetto is to be avoided, and the best results are yielded through a quiet softening of the voice to give a lighter tone. Employing this technique, Lee communicates both Lucy Westenra's blood-drained weariness and the chilling grace of her vampiric form.

Amazingly, Lee recorded *Frankenstein* on the same day in March 1995 that he also filmed his introductions for Ted Newsom's *100 Years of Horror* (the audio book was done in the morning, the TV show in the afternoon). Particularly effective is the voice Lee gives to the Creature, a hoarse wheeze which sounds as though it issues from the grave. The disjointed manner in which the living corpse first grapples with words is an aural equivalent to Lee's physical presentation in *The Curse of Frankenstein*. With voice alone, Lee affects a fine balance between the Creature's solitary yearning and its embittered fury and is careful to show the character's depredation; by the story's end, its voice has descended to a fractured growl. Lee employs a similar voice for the blind old peasant, which only serves to illuminate the bond between these two outcasts.

On *Dr. Jekyll and Mr. Hyde*, we have the hoarse, broken voice of Hyde scraping from Lee's throat, as well as a pernickety Utterson, various Cockneys and a Scottish Dr. Lanyon, who sounds, at times, not dissimilar to Lee's sometime golfing partner Sean Connery.

Gaston Leroux's *The Phantom of the Opera* also gives Lee a satisfyingly broad range of characters to enact, which he achieves with beautiful shades of vocal texture: From the wittering cries of frightened spectators, to the gruff pomposity of the opera managers, from the Eastern brogue of the Persian, to the airy tones of Christine Daae. The mellifluous baritone Lee affects for Erik, the Phantom, makes one regret that he never essayed this role on film.

Finally, Victor Hugo's *The Hunchback of Notre Dame* allows Lee to provide the "raucous, guttural voice" of Quasimodo—another archetypal character that eluded him on film—but it is the story's real villain, the icy Archdeacon Claude Frollo, who would have made an ideal screen role for the actor.

Other audiobooks recorded by Lee include Dennis Wheatley's *The Devil Rides Out* and *Strange Conflict*, Agatha Christie's *The Hound of Death* ("Spine-chilling stories of the macabre and occult from the Queen of Crime, read by the Prince of Darkness ..."), James Herbert's *The Fog* and William Peter Blatty's *The Exorcist* (of which there is an amusing video on YouTube comprised of just "the naughty bits").

Lee also used his voice to express more than the spoken word. "Come, enter into my imagination," he invites the listener on the second track of his *Revelation* LP. Indeed, the actor's song selection here, from "The Impossible Dream" to "Wand'rin' Star," does reveal something of his inner life that cannot be found elsewhere. The overriding feeling given by Lee's singing is one of great passion; he truly believes every word, despite the odd bum note (he was 84 years old). Critics were unkind to the album on its release in June 2006, however, even though the results are far more heartfelt and sincere than anything conjured by the twerking terrors of the contemporaneous music world.

Revelation was followed by two symphonic metal albums, *Charlemagne: By the Sword and the Cross* (2010) and *Charlemagne: The Omens of Death* (2013), which charted the history of Lee's ancestor "via the medium of an unholy racket" (in Darrell Buxton's words, *We Belong Dead* #17). Then, in December 2013, at the age of 91, Lee released "Jingle Hell"—a heavy metal version of "Jingle Bells," with lyrics that traded on his horror reputation. When the single entered the Billboard charts at #22, it made Lee the oldest living musician to have a Top 40 hit. Incidentally, the oldest person to perform on a #1 record is Vincent Price, when he provided the ghoulish rap for Michael Jackson's "Thriller" at the age of 71.

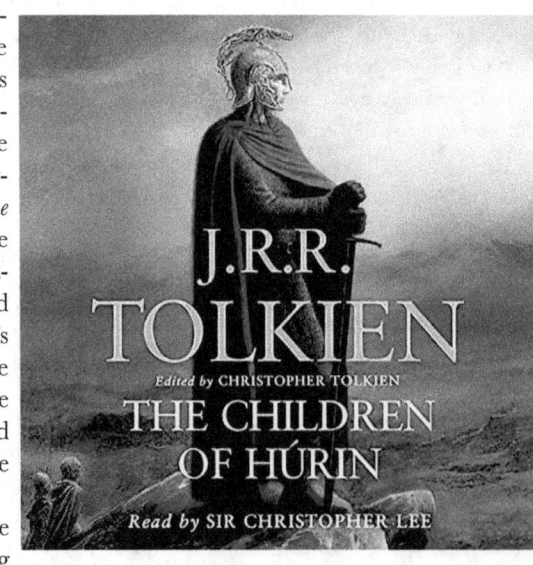

"Acting is survival," Price had once said. As a survivor, Christopher Lee outrode any career disappointments of the late 20th century and earned, within the next millennium, a beloved status of living legend. The first step came at the bequest of a filmmaker, whose imagination had been shaped by Lee's past.

The Tim Burton Films

Sleepy Hollow (1999)
Charlie and the Chocolate Factory (2004)
Corpse Bride (2004)
Alice in Wonderland (2009)
Dark Shadows (2011)

Born in Burbank, California, on August 25, 1958, Tim Burton began his career as an animator at Disney, where he wrote, designed and directed *Vincent* (1982)—a charming, animated tribute to Vincent Price. "I've always loved monsters and monster movies," Burton told Mark Salisbury. "For a while I wanted to be the actor who played *Godzilla* … Because I was quiet, because I was not demonstrative in any way, those films were my form of release."

The filmmaker's subsequent fantasies, *Pee-wee's Big Adventure* (1984), *Beetlejuice* (1987), *Batman* (1988), *Edward Scissorhands* (1989) and *The Nightmare Before Christmas* (1991) are all splendidly imaginative, personal treatises on the plight of the outsider. Their success saw Burton integrate his singular visions into the mainstream, while consolidating his reputation as a vital creative talent; at the 2011 BAFTA ceremony, Christopher Lee would call him: "One of the great directors of our age."

Burton first cast Lee in *Sleepy Hollow* (1999), whose executive producer Francis Ford Coppola (b. 1939) had, earlier in the decade, brought his own retellings of *Bram Stoker's Dracula* and *Mary Shelley's Frankenstein* to the big screen. The screenwriters of *Sleepy Hollow*, however, were the perpetrators of less remote thrillers: Andrew Kevin Walker (b. 1964) had penned the acclaimed *Se7en* (1995), while Kevin Yagher (b. 1962) is the special effects maestro behind *A Nightmare on Elm Street 2* to *4*, *The Phantom of the Opera* (1989) and *Child's Play* (1987). Having designed the iconic Chucky doll for the latter, Yagher serves additionally as *Sleepy Hollow*'s "creature effects co-ordinator," and his grotesque set-pieces help to ensure that the film remains ideal Halloween viewing.

"The Legend of Sleepy Hollow"—Washington Irving's 1820 source story—had previously been infused into *The Curse of the Cat People* (1943), Disney's *The Adventures of Ichabod and Mr. Toad* (1949) and Vincent Price's TV anthology *Once Upon a Midnight Scary* (1979). But in Tim Burton's hands, the tale plays out as an affectionate tribute to Terence Fisher, Roger Corman and Mario Bava, with blatant visual nods to *The Brides of Dracula*, *Pit and the Pendulum*, and *Black Sunday*, to name just three examples.

While the washed-out tones of Emmanuel Labezki's photography came as a result of Burton's initial desire to shoot the film in black-and-white, the Oscar-winning production design of Rick Heinrichs (b. 1954) mimics the parochial villages of Bernard Robinson, albeit with an Expressionistic twist. Especially stunning is the Tree of the Dead: Constructed upon Shepperton's Stage H—where Lee had filmed *The City of the Dead* 40 years previously—this twisted gateway between worlds spirals towards the whitewashed skies and houses the decapitated heads of the Horseman's victims.

Aided by such remarkable visuals, Burton clearly sets his action in the European netherworld established by Hammer: Although Sleepy Hollow is a village in upstate New York, even the film's American stars, Johnny Depp and Christina Ricci (*The Addams Family* [1991]; *Casper* [1994]), speak with English accents among an all-star British cast, including Michael Gough, Michael Gambon and Alun Armstrong (who starred as a snooker-playing faux-Dracula in Alan Clarke's singular musical *Billy the Kid and the Green Baize Vampire* [1985]).

The Hammer feel is truly enforced by Christopher Lee's brief but impressive pre-credits appearance as the Burgomaster, who dispatches Ichabod Crane (Depp) to the titular village in order to investigate the mystery of the Headless Horseman (Christopher Walken, who'd contributed an arresting vampire vignette to *The Addiction* [1994]).

Lee filmed his cameo on Thursday, March 18, 1999, at Leavesden Studios, a former Rolls-Royce factory in Hertfordshire, which would later house the *Harry Potter* franchise. "It was an amazing experience watching this person work, this person who has inspired you," Burton said of Lee on *Sleepy Hollow*'s DVD commentary. "I remember when I first met him that I felt like I had been hypnotized by Dracula. There's such a power to him. He *is* Dracula." Indeed, Burton was so mesmerized that he inscribed the actor's copy of the script with the words: "You're the reason I became a filmmaker."

Johnny Depp was similarly effusive, as Lee revealed to Tom Johnson and Mark A. Miller, he was surprised to enter the younger actor's dressing room and find the walls plastered with pictures from his Hammer horror days; Depp admitted (to Jean Cummings in *Shivers #73*) that he perfected the English accent he employs in *Sleepy Hollow* by studying the diction of Lee and Peter Cushing. (Having made his debut as a fresh-faced victim of Freddy Krueger in *A Nightmare on Elm Street* [1984], Depp [b. 1963] became Burton's most frequent collaborator, with career-best performances as *Edward Scissorhands* and *Ed Wood*. Other horror credits include *Tusk* [2013], *From Hell* [2000] and *The Ninth Gate* [1998], in which his mercenary "book detective" could almost be a younger version of Lee's Duc de Richleau from *The Devil Rides Out*.) Surrounded by such adulation, Lee admitted to Johnson and Miller that he began to enjoy himself so much that he actually forgot his lines. With the ease of a professional, however, he slickly substituted a worthy paraphrase from his own mind. "I know you didn't say the line correctly," Lee recalled Burton telling him after the take, "but you covered it up so fast that it made perfect sense. I've never known an actor to do that like you."

Christopher Lee in *Sleepy Hollow*

Christopher Lee and director Tim Burton

When the director first suggested Lee for the film he was told by a producer, "But he's dead!" This echoes a scene in *Ed Wood*, when the eponymous filmmaker tries to cast Bela Lugosi in *Glen or Glenda*. "The line between success and failure is a very thin one," Burton admitted to Mark Salisbury. "That's why I responded so much to him [Wood]." Indeed, as Burton is also an impassioned filmmaker working with a boyhood hero, it could be argued that Lee was something of a Lugosi figure to Burton's Ed Wood. The two next worked together in June 2004, when Burton, fresh from remaking *Planet of the Apes*, began production on an equally redundant updating of *Willy Wonka & the Chocolate Factory* (1970).

Although it adheres more closely to Roald Dahl's book, every frame of Burton's *Charlie and the Chocolate Factory* only serves to remind the viewer of the original's superiority. Abandoning the stop-motion effects of his earlier Dahl production *James and the Giant Peach*, Burton, instead, chooses to slather everything in CGI, which not only lends a ghastly, unnatural sheen to the child actors' faces, but also fails to compete with the more solid and believable world of the 1970 version. Bright spots include some melting automatons inspired by *House of Wax*, and the film's one original addition: Wonka's dentist father in the person of Christopher Lee. Through oversized dentures, he disparages young Willy's Halloween treats—and it's something of a treat in itself

Christopher Lee in *Charlie and the Chocolate Factory*

to hear Lee draw out the words "choc-o-late" and "loll-i-pops," while decrying the latter as "cavities on a stick." There is also a great shot of Lee inspecting Johnny Depp's bicuspids from *inside* the mouth, and their subsequent reunion, although a long way from Dahl, *is* quite touching. Screenwriter John August (b. 1970), who had recently completed work on *Big Fish* (2003) for Burton, also scripted a project made concurrently with *Charlie* for which the director seems to have reserved most of his creativity.

Corpse Bride is a wonderful, stop-motion animated phantasmagoria to which Lee lends his quavering tones as the irascible Pastor Galswells. Reminiscent of *Mad Monster Party?*, with its dancing skeletons and old movie references (both films feature characters influenced by Peter Lorre), *Corpse Bride* incorporates Burton's fascination with fairy tales, while offering the interesting proposition that, once freed of the illusory shackles imposed by "civilized" society, the dead are, conversely, more vibrant than the living. The whole is enlivened by the songs of Danny Elfman (b. 1953), whose music, from *Pee-wee's Big Adventure* to *Dumbo* (2017), plays such an important part in evoking Burton's world. A former frontman for Oingo Boingo (with whom he performed the title track of *Weird Science* [1984]), the composer's other credits include *Scrooged* (1988), *Big Top Pee-wee* (1988), *Dick Tracy* (1989), *Darkman* (1989), *Mars Attacks!* (1996), *The Wolfman* (2008) and *Goosebumps* (2014), as well as episodes of *Amazing Sto-*

Christopher Lee provided the voice of the Jabberwocky

ries (1985-1987) and *Pee-wee's Playhouse* (1986-1990), themes for *Tales from the Crypt* (1989-1996) and *The Simpsons* (1989-), and onscreen appearances in *Forbidden Zone* (1978, as Satan) and *The Gift* (2000, as a ghostly fiddler).

Though it's a shame that *Corpse Bride* doesn't apportion Lee a share of Elfman's compositions, the actor would be even more bereft when, owing to time constraints, his ghostly narrator was cut at the last minute from Burton's grisly adaptation of the Stephen Sondheim musical, *Sweeney Todd: The Demon Barber of Fleet Street* (2007). The director made amends in the summer of 2009 by giving Lee a couple of lines in the first of a two-picture deal he had struck with Disney.

Rather than being a direct adaptation of Lewis Carroll, Burton's *Alice in Wonderland* is actually an original sequel from *Beauty and the Beast* screenwriter Linda Woolverton (b. 1952). Johnny Depp and Helena Bonham Carter (b. 1966) are ideally, if predictably, cast as the Mad Hatter and Red Queen respectively,

Christopher Lee with Johnny Depp, along with director Tim Burton, on the set of *Dark Shadows*

while Christopher Lee voices the fearsome Jabberwocky (until his tongue is cut out by Mia Wasikowska's Alice). Although Lee originally attempted a "burbled" voice, as described by Carroll's poem, Burton insisted that the actor's natural tones were far scarier (Michael Gough can also be heard briefly, in his final role, as the Dodo Bird). While the film does have its points of interest, such as the occasional striking visual and Crispin Glover (*Back to the Future*, *Willard*) as the Knave of Hearts, these merits are outweighed by an over-reliance on CGI and an overly blanched look that puts one in mind of a vampire's victim. Which is apt, as Burton next put Lee into his "reimagining" of Dan Curtis' Gothic soap opera *Dark Shadows* (filmed at Pinewood—and Black Park—from May 18, 2011).

As "king of the fishermen" Silas Clarney, Lee is hypnotized by Depp's Barnabas Collins—an 18th century vampire resurrected in 1972 (Burton has often cited *Dracula A.D. 1972* as one of his favorite films). Depp's physical performance, which references Klaus Kinski's *Nosferatu the Vampyre* and Vincent Price in *The Tomb of Ligeia*, is complemented by Eva Green (b. 1980) as the witchy Angelique. The star of *Casino Royale* (2006) and *Penny Dreadful*, Green would excel in the title role of *Miss Peregrine's Home for Peculiar Children* (2015)—a return to form for Burton.

Duncan Casey, who plays a policeman in *Dark Shadows*, was extremely impressed by his director's working methods, telling me: "He is very good at what he does and is very involved. He doesn't just sit behind the monitors the whole time. He jumped in a big muddy hole on the first day to show an extra how he wanted a body covered." Despite such devotion, the movie is let down by a larkish tone and aimless plot (the script was courtesy of Seth Grahame-Smith [b. 1976], best-selling author of *Pride and Prejudice and Zombies* and *Abraham Lincoln: Vampire Hunter*—both subsequently filmed, the latter produced by Burton).

Dark Shadows also features a musical cameo from Alice Cooper (b. 1948), who, on receiving a "Legend" award shortly after Lee's death in 2015, told *Kerrang!* magazine: "This [award] goes out … to Christopher Lee [who] was an inspiration to every horror rock guy out there. He was the best …" (Lee lent his voice to "The Last Vampire," the opening track of *Hollywood Vampires*, a 2015 tribute album to dead rock stars put together by Cooper, Johnny Depp and Aerosmith's Joe Perry. It marked Lee's final appearance on record; his last words being, appropriately: "Listen to them: The children of the night. What music they make.")

On Sunday February 13, 2011, at the 64th British Academy Film Awards, Lee became the recipient of a special award himself, a BAFTA Fellowship, in recognition of "outstanding achievement in the art forms of the moving image." The award was presented to him by Tim Burton, who told the star-studded audience that "the range of his performances is truly amazing," before being embraced by the emotional actor.

Burton paid further tribute the following year, with the second picture of his Disney contract, *Frankenweenie* (a feature-length animated remake, with added monsters, of his own 1983 short). Rendered in gorgeous black-and-white, *Frankenweenie* is a vast improvement over *Alice in Wonderland*, and tells the story of young Victor Frankenstein, who revives his dead dog, Sparky, in an attic laboratory. Aptly, the boy's parents fail to notice him drag the animal's corpse upstairs, because they are so engrossed with what's on TV—*Dracula*, starring Christopher Lee.

Released for Halloween 2012, *Frankenweenie* ensured that Lee and Burton could end their collaborations on a high.

The Loneliness of Evil

Final Fantasies 2000-2015

In the 2003 edition of his autobiography, retitled *Lord of Misrule*, Christopher Lee outlined the importance of *Sleepy Hollow* to his later career: "Those five minutes, right at the beginning of the story, were enough in some strange way to prefigure a roll of luck that has lasted me through until the time of writing. When people in the business said, 'He's back,' they didn't mean that they'd seen me in London, but that I was getting work. A perception like that tends to lead to your getting more."

Indeed, such was the slew of offers coming in that Lee could once again afford to turn down work. In 2000, director Sam Irvin offered him the Poe-esque role of Lord Vladimere Hellsubus in *Elvira's Haunted Hills* but was told by the actor's agent: "He doesn't play those kinds of roles anymore. That's all behind him." (*LSoH* #27). The part went to Richard O'Brien.

Parenthetically, O'Brien's *Rocky Horror Picture Show* co-star Patricia Quinn recalled—during an onstage interview at the BFI in October 2016 at which I was present—that, at some point in the late 1990s, White Zombie singer Rob Zombie met with her to discuss a role in what he hoped would be his directorial debut: A futuristic sequel to Brandon Lee's 1993 horror hit *The Crow*, in which Quinn would be joined by Richard O'Brien and Christopher Lee. Quite how they would have fit into the action remains a mystery, as the project was never realized. (Zombie would start shooting his first movie, *House of 1000 Corpses*, in May 2000 and would eventually cast Quinn in *The Lords of Salem* [2011].)

One project that did see fruition—despite the many who said it could never be done—was New Line Cinema's adaptation of *The Lord of the Rings*. Although Lee had long desired to play Gandalf, he was instead cast as the evil wizard Saruman when all three parts of Tolkien's fantasy were filmed simultaneously in New Zealand (from October 1999 to December 2000) by director Peter Jackson (b. 1961). Having begun his career with amusing splatter-fests (*Bad Taste* [1987], *Meet the Feebles* [1989] and *Braindead* [1991]), Jackson's taste for horror ensures that the *Rings* trilogy impresses most at its darkest moments. What's more, Saruman's treacherous agent, Grima Wormtongue, is essayed by one of the best genre actors of a new generation: Brad Dourif (b. 1950) is not only the voice of Chucky in the *Child's Play* franchise (1987-2017), but he also brings distinctive characterizations to *Eyes of Laura Mars* (1977), *The Exorcist III* (1989), *Trauma* (1992) and *Alien Resurrection* (1996).

Christopher Lee plays Count Dooku in the second *Star Wars* trilogy.

Christopher Lee as Saruman in *Lord of the Rings, The Return of the King*

Whether dueling with Ian McKellen's Gandalf, or overseeing his army of orcs, Lee's Saruman remains a salient figure amid *The Lord of the Rings'* myriad special effects. Further bells and whistles awaited the actor when he played the villainous Count Dooku in George Lucas' *Star Wars* prequels *Attack of the Clones* (2000) and *Revenge of the Sith* (2003). The former, which was the first movie to be shot with digital cameras, includes a lightsaber duel between Dooku and Yoda that earned Lee a 2002 MTV Movie Award. As can be seen in a behind-the-scenes DVD documentary, *Star Wars: From Puppets to Pixels,*

Revenge of the Sith

a larkish George Lucas (b. 1944) appended some vampire fangs to the Yoda model used during rehearsals. Lee responds wearily, but with a smile: "I didn't think you'd do that to me, George …"

Lucas and Jackson have both cited numerous times that they were inspired to cast Lee because they had grown up loving his work in Hammer films, and Lee's old employers had long been threatening to return. In the early-to-mid 1990s, big-budget Hollywood remakes of Hammer's earlier successes were mooted, but, despite *Alien* screenwriter Dan O'Bannon actually completing a script for a new version of *The Quatermass Xperiment*, nothing ever came of this. (Following the death of Vincent Price, Roy Skeggs said of these remakes [in the *Times*, October 27, 1993]: "I have arranged with Peter Cushing and Christopher Lee to play cameos. I wanted Vincent to do the same.")

Over a decade later, on February 27, 2005, the *Sunday Telegraph* revealed that a new line of Gothic fashionwear inspired by Hammer was ready to hit the catwalks via a company called Coolabi, whose chief executive Janet Woodward told the paper: "Christopher Lee as Dracula has become the ultimate in cool …" This news coincided with the issue of a 12-inch likeness of Lee's vampire as a fully posable, collectible action figure. In addition, late-night television revivals and DVD releases of Hammer's old horrors continued to draw in a new generation of fans. The time was ripe for the House of Horror to return.

After years of empty promise, the company finally resumed active production in 2007, beneath the headship of new chairman Simon Oakes. Initially, they explored the innovation of online serials by issuing 20, four-minute instalments of *Beyond the Rave* through social networking website MySpace. The first feature film of the new Hammer, however, was *Wake Wood* (2008), which at times resembles a low-rent *Wicker Man*, with Timothy Spall as a rustic Lord Summerisle-type presiding over revivifying community rituals. The real Lord Summerisle, however, made a welcome return to Hammer in June 2009.

Filmed in NYC with some New Mexico interiors, *The Resident* marks the debut feature of director Antti Jokinen (b. 1968) and shows Dr. Juliet Deverau (Hilary Swank, who also served as

Christopher Lee as grandfather August from *The Resident*

executive producer) being terrorized by her new landlord (Jeffrey Dean Morgan, of *The Walking Dead* fame). Lee is on hand to peer from doorways and contribute to Morgan's psychological breakdown as the latter's infirm grandfather. A good-looking but claustrophobic thriller, *The Resident* unfortunately favors gross-out moments over suspense, with not even a uniformly excellent star turn from Swank being enough to redeem it. While filming in New York, Lee suffered an on-set injury, tempered somewhat by the news of his incipient knighthood. Nevertheless, despite his relatively small screen time, he featured prominently in *The Resident*'s advertising upon its release in March 2011. The new Hammer would hit their stride one year later, when *The Woman in Black* broke box-office records on both sides of the Atlantic.

Another famed British studio also rose from the grave at the beginning of the new millennium. In 2010, *An American Werewolf in London* director John Landis (b. 1950) took over a revitalized Ealing Studios to make an enjoyably coarse comedy of *Burke and Hare*. While its pallid hues evoke *Corridors of Blood*, the film also benefits from real Edinburgh locations and some of Britain's finest character actors, including Jessica Hynes (*Spaced*, *The Royle Family*) as Hare's conniving mistress, Reece Shearsmith (*The League of Gentlemen*, *Psychoville*) as a bungling police sergeant and the great Tim Curry, who saws gleefully at his specimens' legs as Dr. Monro. Best of all is a supine performance from Christopher Lee as Old Joseph (named after Lugosi's character in *The Body Snatcher*). Rudely awoken from his reveries of war, Lee's grizzled veteran growls, "You bleedin' Irish bastards" in a perfect Edin-

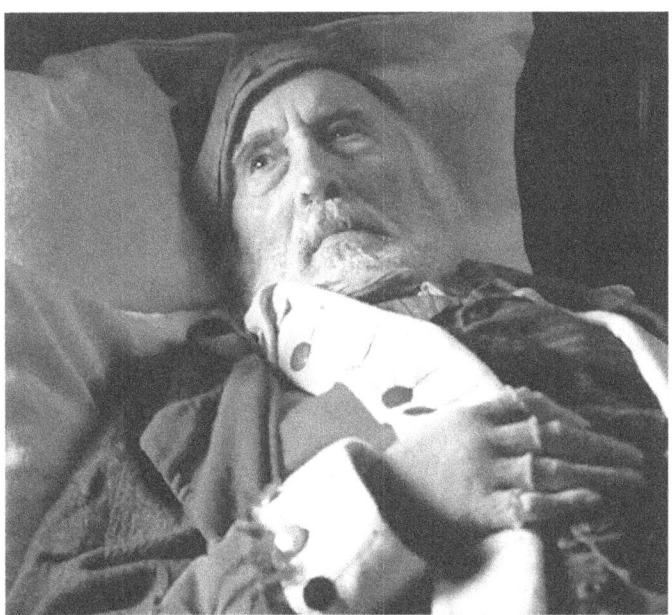

As Old Joseph in *Burke and Hare*

The Loneliness of Evil

burgh accent, before wheezing out reminiscences of his military past. Proudly clad in his soldier's jacket and mittens, Joseph is snuffed out by Burke (Simon Pegg, whose *Shaun of the Dead* is widely regarded as the best of 21st century horror spoofs) and Andy Serkis as Hare (looking frighteningly like Robert Helpmann's Childcatcher gone to seed). (Lee had performed a similarly amusing cameo for Landis as the Evil Sender in *The Stupids* [1995]. Three years earlier, the director inserted *Dracula*'s finale into his vampire actioner *Innocent Blood*, earning both Lee and Peter Cushing a special mention in the credits.)

As well as reuniting *American Werewolf*'s Jenny Agutter, John Woodvine and David Schofield, *Burke and Hare* features cameos from cinematographer Robert Paynter, *Death Wish* director Michael Winner and stop-motion legend Ray Harryhausen. In the summer of 2010, Lee paid homage to another fantasy film pioneer, Georges Méliès, at Shepperton, with his appearance in *Hugo*—an adaptation of Brian Selznick's illustrated book *The Invention of Hugo Cabret*. Directed by Martin Scorsese (who acknowledges *Frankenstein Created Woman* as one of his favorite films), produced by Johnny Depp and scripted by John Logan (creator of *Penny Dreadful*), *Hugo* tells the story of an orphan (Asa Butterfield) who lives behind the clocks at Paris' Montparnasse railway station, where he makes the acquaintance of a forgotten Méliès (Ben Kingsley). Lee plays Monsieur Labisse, the owner of the station's musty old bookshop described by Méliès' goddaughter Isabelle (Chloë Grace Moretz, the young vampire star of Hammer's *Let Me In* [2009]) as "the most wonderful place on Earth. It's Neverland and Oz and Treasure Island all wrapped into one." Last seen discussing the possible merits of "canine socialization" with his *To the Devil a Daughter* co-star Frances de la Tour, Lee's Labisse switches from charming codger to frosty patrician with the merest flicker of a smile. Released in 3-D on Wednesday, November 23, 2011, *Hugo* is an often beautiful movie marred only by some needless comic padding.

Too ill to travel to New Zealand, Lee's revival of Saruman for *The Hobbit* trilogy was shot over four days in July 2011 at Pinewood Studios. *The Hobbit* was scripted by Guillermo del Toro (b. 1964)—creator of elegant fantasies *The Devil's Backbone*

Christopher Lee as Saruman from *The Hobbit*

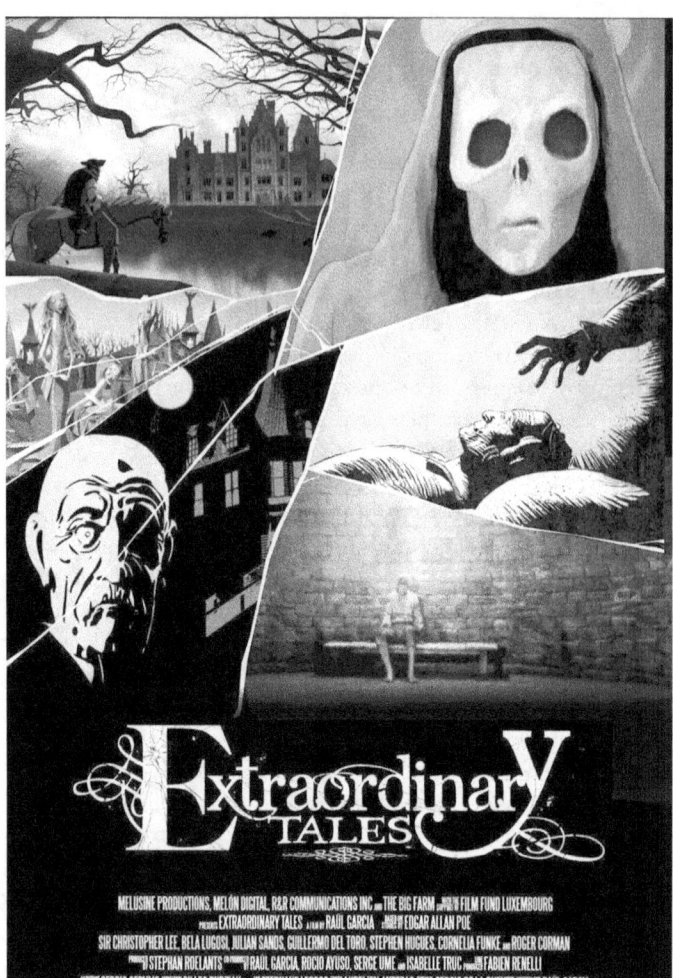

(2000), *Pan's Labyrinth* (2005) and *The Shape of Water* (2016)—who also had a hand in Lee's next, and final, horror project.

Adapted and directed by Raul Garcia—an animator who'd worked on such Disney efforts as *Who Framed Roger Rabbit* (1987) and *The Hunchback of Notre Dame* (1996)—*Extraordinary Tales* collates five Edgar Allan Poe stories, animated in varied styles. The film kicks off with Lee's sublime reading of "The Fall of the House of Usher" (2012), which owes much, visually, to the oeuvre of Tim Burton. The other stories are "The Tell-Tale Heart," from a newly discovered audio recording of Bela Lugosi (the screen's two greatest Draculas in the same movie at last), "The Facts in the Case of M. Valdemar" narrated by Julian Sands (*Gothic*, *Tale of a Vampire* and Argento's *Phantom of the Opera*), "The Pit and the Pendulum" narrated by del Toro and a purely visual rendering of "The Masque of the Red Death," which grants a single line to Roger Corman as Prince Prospero.

Extraordinary Tales may have been Lee's final horror movie, but the actor's last film has, at the time of writing, yet to be released: *Angels in Notting Hill* (2015) is a visual poem to life, love and London, and a fittingly poignant swansong for Christopher Lee, who supplies both the voice of God and the male lead's charming toy dog, Mr. President (as whom, his final line of dialogue is: "I'll haunt your dreams …"). The film's writer and director, Michael Pakleppa (b. 1950)—whose other credits include an intriguing documentary on psychic artist Coral Polge, *Your Life Will Never End* (1982)—kindly shares his memories with me:

"I knew Christopher since 1980 when he did the German (and English) voice of King Haggard [in the animated fantasy

The Last Unicorn]. As it happens, I 'saved' *The Last Unicorn* from being lost. What you see today is my version. I picked it up from a bankrupt former British media giant, Lord Grade's ITC … The film was cut into pieces, the music mix was lost in a warehouse fire, nobody wanted it and the only distributor was a bankrupt Salt Lake City distributor, Jensen-Farley … I contracted the film, collected the pieces and found the original music tracks. Then we reconstructed and remixed the film in the original version from scratch in Munich and Berlin. I made the campaign that is in use until today and we gave the film with Christopher a glorious premiere in one of the biggest cinemas and promoted it as big as *E.T.* in Germany. Christopher raced through all major cities and TV shows in Germany, and it became a huge success. Then, slowly, the rest of the world woke up and showed the film. Author Peter Beagle and creative producer Michael Walker came from the US. Christopher even became godfather for Michael's son.

Christopher Lee pre-records his voice for *Angels in Notting Hill*. Courtesy of Michael Pakleppa.

Christopher Lee provided the voice of King Haggard in *The Last Unicorn*.

"Christopher loved the film so much that he suggested to do all that and he dubbed it twice in English and German. This is when we became friends forever. We traveled together with him and his wife and had lots of fun. I was speechless about his energy.

"One day we had dinner at the Berlin Intercontinental and the seven desserts on the desert trolley looked so delicious that I ordered them all. I had just bought a pair of crazy red shoes and was wearing them at dinner. Christopher laughed his head off. From then on, he opened every phone call with: 'Have you had your seven desserts already in your red shoes?' It became a running joke for the next 30 years.

"After *The Last Unicorn*, we did another voice role: Odin, the king of the Gods in the Danish animation film, *Walhalla*. We always wanted to make a live-action movie out of *The Last Unicorn*, one of Christopher's absolute favorites, but it didn't work out in time."

As a stepping-stone towards that live-action remake, the two men, instead, embarked upon a more affordable original feature, as Michael explains. "*Angels in Notting Hill* was a pure labor

Christopher Lee is the voice of Mr. President in *Angels in Notting Hill*

of love and Christopher did it for free like everything we did together because we were friends. In all these years we saw each other whenever possible and spent many hours talking on the phone about simply everything. He was really one of my very best friends. So, of course, there are many fond memories.

"I invented the two voice roles for Christopher on the fly and we created an animatronics character for his voice. Marc Jefferis, one of the best character puppeteers, played to Christopher's pre-recorded voice. It surely wasn't meant as a farewell, but as a funny little intermezzo between his next big jobs. But I always wanted to see or, at least, hear him in roles that were not the usual villain horror stuff, but as ironical, sarcastic, warm-hearted, philosophical, and in many ways deep and wise as he really was. So, I took the chance to have him in the film, since he was incredibly wide and open for experiments.

The Loneliness of Evil

Christopher Lee in The Far Pavilions

"The recording was done in Redwood Studios, the recording engineer Andre Jacquemin had done all the Terry Gilliam films, most Monty Pythons, and the last Robin Williams film. Christopher enjoyed it like every role. He was always so good in the first takes that many directors wanted to just leave it as it was, but he always insisted on variations and often we didn't

Christopher Lee and Jeff Cooper in The Silent Flute

know what to choose, because they were all perfect. He was incredibly versatile, so we got used to getting quickly finished and used the rest of the day listening to his memories, his jokes or drinking his favorite Linie Aquavit. I have never seen any actor so easy to work with. We met on festivals, the set of Scorsese's *Hugo* in Shepperton Studios, where also Pauline Fowler, the creature designer, worked. Sometimes my co-producer Stefanie Wallis was there too, sometimes my son, who Christopher called 'der kindische Alb,' a Wagnerian character; translated it means something like 'the childish nightmare.' Sometimes he called me the same on the beginning of our long phone calls. He was always joking and teasing. I used to be a distributor and we loved Christopher because we had actually nothing to do. Just get 100 journalists together with him into a room and let him do what he likes, then come an hour later and watch all journalists listening with open mouth. It was wonderful and I was always speechless that this was the man I met first in a film that frightened me most as a child, *Dracula: Prince of Darkness*. But he hated to be typecast as a vampire, he was more interested in serious roles like *The Far Pavilions*. In *The Silent Flute*, he played a kind of Zen monk, who keeps the book of truth that had only one page, a mirror.

"All this motivated me to write his two voice roles in *Angels in Notting Hill*. But mostly I just couldn't wait for the next bigger film that we had planned to do together. Big films take years and sometimes decades to come together. I wanted to do something now out of the mood of the moment.

"We had a small camera that automatically filmed his recording. When we spoke about it, I said, 'It runs by itself forever, don't worry.' And he said: 'Okay. Well, I don't.' And we all burst into laughter. Working with Christopher was, besides all his perfection, almost like a party. He was one of the most wonderful people to spend time with and very uplifting. He gave me lots of advice and treated my friends like his friends. He had no star ambition; he stood far above that and was always politically engaged for peace and freedom. During the Iraq war, when many actors and pop stars kept their mouth shut in fear of losing jobs, three brave big actors held public speeches and loudly protested together: Christopher Lee, Roger Moore, and Dustin Hoffman.

"*Angels in Notting Hill* was like a personal homage to Christopher's humor, kindness and genius. I wanted him to be an invisible anchor of the story like a good spirit. Because that is what he was for me in my life. Now it has sadly become his swansong, but at least we did it and I am happy and proud about it. *Angels in Notting Hill* deals on many levels with loss, death, love and rebirth, with the angels and demons within ourselves, and the improvised film story, which strangely reflects now in real life. The new *Last Unicorn* has still not been made; I still have the remake rights but without Christopher I wonder if it will ever be made.

"Christopher worked hard to get it [*The Last Unicorn* remake] off the ground; he spoke with [Peter] Jackson, Spielberg, Burton, Johnny Depp and many more—he knew simply everybody. In arts, politics, society, science, even the military. One day I had to call a general for him. I didn't expect to get connected, but just mentioning Christopher's name opened every door. He was reading thousands of books and was informed about everything that mattered. And he could see through people, sense their true intentions or hidden agendas, very important in the world of stardom. He wasn't interested in false glitter; he was real, but experienced enough to play his part on all levels and situations in life, not only in films and surely not only in *Dracula*.

"By the way, I am still distributing some of his old movies—yet not *Dracula*—for occasional TV reruns in Germany."

I ask Michael if Christopher ever got a chance to view his final screen work. "Christopher saw the finished film in a rough cut and thought it was charming. It's a poetic, partially improvised experiment. A kind of eccentric spiritual comedy ... No horror whatsoever. And that is one reason why Christopher loved it. He especially liked [the character] Miss Maple and said of the actress Tina Gray, 'she is an old circus horse like me.' I absolutely loved him; he was almost like a father to me."

Christopher Lee was a man who refused to be categorized. At times, he could appear as intimidating as some of the characters he played, but in the autumn 1973 issue of *Cinefantastique*, his frequent co-star Peter Cushing, who knew him better than most, made the telling observation: "Christopher has a delicious sense of humor and wit, plus a deep personal kindness ... beneath his

outward aloofness and dignity lies a very *human* being: sensitive, warm and oft-times suffering from nerves which he goes to great length to conceal."

An abundance of creative work was one way of channeling those nerves in a positive direction. By his own admission, Lee never stopped learning and would stress the importance of this within any profession. "I'm an enormous enthusiast," he told *Shivers* #50. "I still retain that enthusiasm, though sometimes I wonder why! Sometimes I wonder *how*, dealing with the sort of people one has to deal with!"

Nonetheless, Lee was always active, especially during his old age. "I wonder what people do when they retire at 65 or less," he mused to Jane Killick (in *Shivers* #13), "what do they do with their lives?" It was as if the constant flurry of work was what kept him together, his ever-alert mind constantly in search of fresh challenges. I recall him being interviewed by broadcaster Richard Madeley around the time of *Star Wars* and *Lord of the Rings*. On being asked about the secret of his success, Lee simply replied: "Hard work." When Madeley suggested that Lee's career had been a "lucky" one, the actor responded along the lines of: "It's funny. The harder I work, the luckier I get."

On Thursday, December 12, 2013, the actor's annual Christmas message was uploaded onto YouTube. Dressed in a snazzy hat—"which was left to me, in his will, by my dear, dear friend, the late Vincent Price"—Lee looked frail, and, despite his optimistic updates, we all knew in our hearts that this would be the last one.

When asked by Craig Cabell and Howard Maxford, in *Shivers* #50, if he feared death, Lee replied: "Oh, no. What is there to be afraid of?" He went on to quote Woody Allen ("I don't mind dying. I just don't want to be there when it happens"), before revealing, "I've been close to death on several occasions. Twice during the Second World War and once during a heart operation ... But I didn't see or experience anything during that time, so I have no fear of dying."

Christopher Lee passed away on the morning of Sunday, June 7, 2015, at the Chelsea and Westminster Hospital. The news was made public four days later, once friends and family had been informed.

Asked to sum up his life in 1997, on the BBC News show *HARDtalk*, Lee responded: "As a person, I suppose, he did his best ... As an actor, he proved them wrong. Because so many people said: 'He's too tall, he's too foreign looking, he doesn't play comedy, he can't do Westerns ... he can't become a stuntman, he can't do this, he can't do that.' I've done it all. I've proved them wrong. And that, I must say, gives me a considerable degree of satisfaction."

What Lee perfectly encapsulated onscreen was the Byronic hero, a type described by Elizabeth Miller, in her "documentary journey" *Bram Stoker's Dracula* (Pegasus Books, 2009), as "a complex, aloof aristocrat whose past is shrouded in secrecy; who, driven by some inner force, travels far and wide in search of oblivion." Elaborating further, Jim Steinmeyer, in *Who Was Dracula?* (Penguin, 2013), depicts Byonic heroes as "dark, haunted characters—combinations of charm and cruelty ... They were nobles who might find themselves cast as rebels, in exile or seeking revenge." What better fits those images than the screen persona of Christopher Lee? From Dracula to the Marquis St. Evrémonde, from Scaramanga to Saruman, Lee's performances, in the words of his beloved Don Quixote, helped to "add some measure of grace to the world."

The legacy he leaves behind is as rich as any actor could wish for.

Christopher Lee passed away on June 7, 2015.

The Loneliness of Evil 253

Sources and Acknowledgments

Special thanks to Gary and Susan Svehla for believing in this project from the start. For taking the time to share their memories with me, I would like to thank: Duncan Casey, Richard Downes, Barbara Ewing, Renée Glynne, Melvyn Hayes, Jane Merrow, the late Ted Newsom, Michael Pakleppa, the late Michel Parry, Arthur Payn, Pauline Peart, Robin Squire and Eleanor Yule. I would also like to thank the following, not only for sharing first-hand experiences through previous encounters, but for the hours of enchantment their work has provided: Martine Beswick, Veronica Carlson, the late John Carson, Jenny Hanley, Richard Hartley, Linda Hayden, Christopher Matthews, Caroline Munro, Patricia Quinn, Yvonne Romain, Peter Sasdy and the late Barbara Shelley. I am also grateful to Eric McNaughton at *We Belong Dead* for printing my first articles, and to Charles Heppenstall for friendship, photos and admonition.

Select Bibliography

Many books and articles were consulted during the writing of this volume, but those listed below are especially recommended. Special mention must also be made of Richard Klemensen's superior magazine *Little Shoppe of Horrors* (1972-). The doyen of Hammer research, no work on British horror films should be attempted without it.

Ackerman, Forrest J (ed.). *The Frankenscience Monster* (Ace Publishing Corporation, 1969).
Baker, Phil. *The Devil is a Gentleman: The Life and Times of Dennis Wheatley* (Dedalus, 2009).
Bloch, Robert. *Once Around the Bloch: An Unauthorized Autobiography* (Tor, 1993).
Brosnan, John. *The Horror People* (Macdonald & Jane's, 1976).
Brown, Allan. *Inside the Wicker Man* (Polygon, 2010).
Bryce, Allan. *Amicus: The Friendly Face of Fear* (Ghoulish Publishing Ltd, 2016).
Butler, Ivan. *Horror in the Cinema* (A.S. Barnes and Company, Inc., 1970. Revised edition: 1979).
Court, Hazel. *Horror Queen-An Autobiography* (Tomahawk Press, 2008).
Cushing, Peter. *An Autobiography and Past Forgetting* (Midnight Marquee Press, 1999).
Del Vecchio, Deborah, and Tom Johnson. *Peter Cushing: The Gentle Man of Horror and His 91 Films* (McFarland, 1992).
—. *Hammer Films: An Exhaustive Filmography* (McFarland, 1996).
Eyles, Allen (ed.). *House of Horror: The Complete Hammer Films Story* (Creation Books, 1994).
Frank, Alan. *Horror Films* (Hamlyn, 1977).
Frayling, Christopher. *Nightmare: The Birth of Horror* (BBC Books, 1996).
Gifford, Denis. *A Pictorial History of Horror Movies* (Hamlyn, 1973).
Glut, Donald F. *The Dracula Book* (Scarecrow Press, 1975).
Haining, Peter. *The Dracula Scrapbook* (Souvenir Press, 1987).
Halligan, Benjamin. *Michael Reeves* (Manchester University Press, 2003).
Halliwell, Leslie. *The Dead that Walk* (Paladin Books, 1986).
Hearn, Marcus, and Alan Barnes. *The Hammer Story* (Titan Books, Revised Edition: 2007).
Jacobs, Stephen. *Boris Karloff: More Than a Monster* (Tomahawk Press, 2011).
Johnson, Tom, and Mark A. Miller. *The Christopher Lee Filmography* (McFarland, 2004).
Kinsey, Wayne. *Hammer's Film Legacy* (Peveril Publishing, 2014).
Lee, Christopher. *Tall, Dark and Gruesome* (Midnight Marquee Press, 1999).
Lucas, Tim. *All the Colors of the Dark* (Video Watchdog, 2007).
McKay, Sinclair. *A Thing of Unspeakable Horror* (Aurum Press, 2007).
McNaughton, Eric (ed.). *70s Monster Memories* (Buzzy Krotik Productions, 2016).
Meikle, Denis. *Vincent Price: The Art of Fear* (Reynolds & Hearn, 2003).
—. *A History of Horrors* (Scarecrow Press, 2009).
Miller, David. *The Peter Cushing Companion* (Reynolds & Hearn, 2000).
Miller, Mark A. *Christopher Lee and Peter Cushing and Horror Cinema* (McFarland, 1995).
Minney, R.J. *Rasputin* (Cassell & Company Ltd, 1972).
Neame, Christopher. *Rungs on a Ladder: Hammer Films Seen Through a Soft Gauze* (Scarecrow Press, 2003).
Nutman, Philip. *Scream and Scream Again: The Uncensored History of Amicus Productions* (published as *Little Shoppe of Horrors* #20, June 2008).
Pirie, David. *A New Heritage of Horror* (I.B. Tauris, 2008).
Pitts, Michael R. *Horror Film Stars* (McFarland, 2002).
Rigby, Jonathan. *English Gothic* (Reynolds & Hearn, 2000).
—. *Christopher Lee: The Authorised Screen History* (Reynolds & Hearn, 2001).
—. *Euro Gothic* (Signum Books, 2016).
Sachs, Bruce, and Russell Wall. *Greasepaint and Gore: The Hammer Monsters of Roy Ashton* (Tomahawk Press, 1999).
Salisbury, Mark (ed.). *Burton on Burton* (Faber and Faber, 1995).
Sangster, Jimmy. *Do You Want It Good or Tuesday?* (Midnight Marquee Press, 1997).
— *Inside Hammer* (Reynolds & Hearn, 2001).
Sellers, Robert. *What Fresh Lunacy Is This?* (Constable, 2013).
Skal, David J. *Hollywood Gothic* (Faber and Faber, 2004).
Weaver, Tom. *I Talked with a Zombie* (McFarland, 2014).
Weldon, Michael. *The Psychotronic Encyclopedia of Film* (Plexus, 1983).
Williams, Lucy Chase. *The Complete Films of Vincent Price* (Citadel Press, 1995).

Author's Biography

A lifelong lover of movies and monsters, Stephen Mosley played the monster in the movie *Kenneth*. His other acting credits include the eponymous paranormal investigator of *Kestrel Investigates*; the shady farmer, James in *Contradiction*, the crazed Alcoholics Anonymous leader in *Elevator Gods* and a blink-and-you'll-miss-it appearance opposite Sam Neill in *Peaky Blinders*. As well as being the author of *Klawseye: The Imagination Snatcher of Phantom Island*, *The Lives & Deaths of Morbius Mozella* and *The Boy Who Loved Simone Simon* (selected by *Entertainment Focus* as one of the 10 Best Books of 2011), Stephen is one half of the music duo Collinson Twin and has contributed to the books *Masters of Terror, Mistresses of the Macabre, Dead or Alive: British Horror Films 1980-1989, 70s Monster Memories; Unsung Horrors, A Celebration of Peter Cushing* and *Son of Unsung Horrors*. His articles have appeared in magazines *Midnight Marquee, We Belong Dead, Multitude of Movies* and *The Dark Side*, while his short stories have been included in such anthologies as *Dracula's Midnight Snacks* and *Zombie Bites*.

Stephen Mosley and Harry Hutchinson in *Kestrel Investigates*

Index of Film and Television Titles

A-Rated Horror Film (2003), 154
Abbott and Costello Meet Dr. Jekyll and Mr. Hyde (1953), 82, 158
Abbott and Costello Meet Frankenstein (1948), 16, 52, 82, 128, 205, 226
Abominable Dr. Phibes, The (1970), 108, 109, 111, 137, 145, 165, 173
Abominable Snowman, The (1957), 25, 45, 62, 68, 95
Abraham Lincoln: Vampire Hunter (2011), 248
Absolute Beginners (1985), 132, 199
Absolutely Fabulous (1992-2012), 192
Absolution (1978), 182
Abyss, The (1988), 188
Accident, The (1963), 63
Ace of Wands (1970-1972), 148
Across the Bridge (1957), 41
Addams Family, The (1964-1966), 220
Addams Family, The (1991), 246
Addams Family Values (1993), 213
Addiction, The (1994), 246
Adventures of Baron Munchausen, The (1987), 59
Adventures of Captain Fabian, The (1950), 211
Adventures of Dr. Fu Manchu, The (1952, 1956), 94
Adventures of Ichabod and Mr. Toad, The (1949), 245
Adventures of Sherlock Holmes, The (1921), 39
Adventures of Sherlock Holmes' Smarter Brother, The (1975), 43
Adventures of Superman (1951-1957), 89
African Queen, The (1951), 96
After Hours (1985), 221
After the Fox (1965), 184
Agatha Christie's Poirot (1988-2013), 210
Aguirre, the Wrath of God (1972), 141
Airheads (1993), 206
Airplane! (1979), 209
Airport '77 (1976), 170, 205, 228
Alexander the Great (1955), 17, 170
Alfred Hitchcock Hour, The (1962-1965), 81-82, 132
Alfred Hitchcock Presents (1955-1962, 1985-1989), 46, 55, 68, 81, 82, 110, 180
Alfred Marks Time (1956-1961), 136
Alias John Preston (1955), 18-20, 29, 39, 45, 54, 55, 91, 112
Alias Nick Beal (1948), 188
Alice in Wonderland (1949), 32, 48
Alice in Wonderland (1966), 93, 164
Alice in Wonderland (2009), 157, 189, 201, 245, 247, 248
Alice's Adventures in Wonderland (1972), 197
Alien (1978), 49, 71, 110, 172, 198, 201, 221, 249
Alien Resurrection (1996), 248
Alien 3 (1991), 175
Alien Warrior (1986), 206
Aliens (1985), 50
All Creatures Great & Small (1977-1990), 191
All Quiet on the Western Front (1929), 208
All the Colors of the Dark (1971), 73
All This and World War II (1976), 176
Alligator (1980), 208
Ally McBeal (1997-2002), 190, 213
Alone in the Dark (1982), 176
Alphaville (1965), 138
Amadeus (1983), 46, 185
Amazing Mr. Blunden, The (1971), 118, 180
Amazing Stories (1985-1987), 247
Amazon Women on the Moon (1985), 216
American Haunting, An (2005), 84

American Horror Story (2011-), 191
American Werewolf in London, An (1981), 52, 54, 113, 174, 216, 220, 249
Amicus: House of Horrors (2012), 54, 157
Amityville Horror, The (1978), 206
Amityville 3-D (1983), 197
And Now the Screaming Starts! (1972), 87, 93, 140, 149, 165, 166
And Soon the Darkness (1969), 111
And Then There Were None (1974), 170, 197
Android (1982), 141
Andromeda Strain, The (1970), 207
Angel (1999-2004), 198
Angel for Satan, An (1966), 76, 124
Angel on My Shoulder (1946), 188
Angels in Notting Hill (2015), 250-251
Anne of the Thousand Days (1968), 157
Anniversary, The (1967), 149, 174
Antichrist, The (1974), 64
Ape Man, The (1942), 190, 203
Ape Woman, The (1963), 84
Appointment, The (1981), 113
Arabian Adventure (1978), 11, 55, 62, 179, 209, 211
Armstrong Circle Theatre (1950-1963), 18
Around the World in 80 Days (1988), 112
Arsenic and Old Lace (1941), 96
Arsenic & Old Lace (1962), 219
Arsenic and Old Lace (1969), 208
Arthur? Arthur! (1969), 107
Arthur the King (1982), 118, 183
Asphyx, The (1972), 173-174
Assassination Bureau, The (1968), 61, 110
Assignment Outer Space (1960), 75
Assignment Terror (1969), 115
Astro-Zombies, The (1967), 211
Asylum (1972), 33, 56, 93, 140, 149, 184, 198
At the Earth's Core (1976), 165, 166, 180
Atom Age Vampire (1960), 52
Attack of the Crab Monsters (1956), 16
Attack of the Killer Tomatoes! (film series, 1978-1991), 220
Attack of the Puppet People (1957), 166
Auf Wiedersehen, Pet (1983-2004), 215
Austin Powers (film series, 1996-2002), 65
Autopsy of a Ghost (1967), 188
Avenger, The (1960), 109
Avengers, The (1961-1969), 11, 89, 91, 110-111, 118, 155, 166, 192, 193, 197, 199, 200
Avengers: Age of Ultron (2014), 56
Awakening, The (1979), 65, 234
Awful Dr. Orlof, The (1961), 134, 137
Babes in Bagdad (1951), 16
Babes in Toyland (1934), 94
Baby Love (1968), 145, 180
Bachelor of Hearts (1958), 89
Back to the Future (1985), 247
Back to the Future Part II (1989), 234
Bad Man's River (1970), 169
Bad Taste (1987), 248
Banana Splits Adventure Hour, The (1968-1969), 107
Barbarella (1967), 206
Baron Blood (1971), 73, 129
Barry Lyndon (1973), 177
Barry McKenzie Holds His Own (1974), 176

Barton Fink (1990), 234
Basil the Great Mouse Detective (1986), 211
Bat, The (1959), 50
Bat Whispers, The (1930), 88
Bates Motel (2013-2017), 204
Batman (1966-1968), 56, 109, 111, 188
Batman (1988), 125, 127, 245
Batman & Robin (1996), 125
Batman Forever (1994), 125
Batman Returns (1991), 88, 125
Battle Beyond the Stars (1980), 206, 216
Battle for the Planet of the Apes (1972), 208
Battle of the River Plate, The (1955), 20, 61, 80, 93, 110
Battle of the V-1 (1957), 123
Battle of the Worlds (1960), 75
Battlestar Galactica (1978), 197, 208
Bay of Blood, A (1971), 71
Beach Party (1963), 132
Bear Island (1978), 191, 199
Beast and the Magic Sword, The (1983), 170
Beast from 20,000 Fathoms, The (1953), 240
Beast in the Cellar, The (1970), 171
Beast Must Die, The (1973), 45, 55, 56, 63, 119, 180
Beast with Five Fingers, The (1945), 15-16
Beast Within, The (1981), 215
Beastmaster, The (1981), 175
Beasts (1976), 93, 98, 166, 176
Beat Girl (1959), 39, 45, 59, 63, 197
Beatles Anthology, The (1995), 72
Beauty and the Beast (1991), 247
Bed Sitting Room, The (1968), 201
Bedazzled (1967), 55, 116, 136
Bedknobs and Broomsticks (1970), 55
Bedlam (1945), 54
Beetlejuice (1987), 188, 216, 245
Behemoth the Sea Monster (1959), 19, 41
Being, The (1980), 197
Bela Lugosi Meets a Brooklyn Gorilla (1952), 16, 227
Bell of Hell, The (1973), 170
Belle et la Bête, La (1945), 214
Bells, The (1926), 88
Beloved Count (2007), 141
Bengal Lancers, The (1984) [unfinished], 158
Benny Hill Show, The (1969-1989), 152, 211
Berserk (1966), 56, 61, 109, 125, 146, 180, 191
Bespoke Overcoat, The (1955), 59-60
Best of All Time Horror Classics, The (1985), 197
Best of Sex and Violence, The (1981), 190
Beverly Hills Cop (1984), 218
Beverly Hills Vamp (1988), 184
Bewitched (1964-1972), 188
Beyond the Rave (2007), 184, 249
Beyond the Universe (1980), 177
Big Fish (2003), 247
Big Night, The (1958), 54
Big Top Pee-wee (1988), 247
Bigfoot (1969), 211
Bikini Beach (1964), 86
Billy the Kid and the Green Baize Vampire (1985), 246
Billy the Kid vs. Dracula (1965), 211
Bird with the Crystal Plumage, The (1969), 109, 134
Birds, The (1962), 149
Birth of the Beatles (1979), 158
Birthday Party, The (1968), 54, 93
Bitter Victory (1957), 39, 61

Black Castle, The (1952), 97
Black Cat, The (1934), 16, 116, 133, 211
Black Cat, The (1941), 177
Black Cat, The (1980), 75, 93
Black Cat, The (1989), 165
Black Christmas (1974), 33, 91
Black Hole, The (1978), 197
Black Knight, The (1953), 61, 151
Black Magic (1947), 196
Black Narcissus (1946), 180
Black Sabbath (1963), 70, 71, 73, 85
Black Sleep, The (1956), 188
Black Sunday (1960), 36, 55, 70, 71, 76, 89, 114, 124, 240, 245
Black Torment, The (1964), 48, 122, 133
Black Widow, The (1950), 86, 123
Black Zoo (1962), 32
Blackmail (1929), 20
Blacula (1972), 167, 188, 194
Blade (1997), 234
Blade II (2001), 234
Blade Runner (1981), 214
Blade: Trinity (2003), 234
Blair Witch Project, The (1997), 56
Blanche Fury (1947), 32
Blancheville Monster, The (1963), 72, 170
Blind Terror (1970), 152
Blinded (2004), 236
Blithe Spirit (1944), 16
Blob, The (1957), 112
Blood and Black Lace (1963), 16, 71, 73, 74
Blood and Roses (1960), 35, 64, 76
Blood Beast Terror, The (1967), 42, 122, 123, 150, 172
Blood Demon (1967), 75, 94, 102, 114-115
Blood Feast (1963), 106
Blood for Dracula (1973), 32, 75, 146, 195
Blood from the Mummy's Tomb (1971), 51, 68, 93, 99, 135, 138, 170, 174, 185
Blood Legacy (1970), 211
Blood of Dracula (1957), 29
Blood of Dracula's Castle (1966), 211
Blood of Fu Manchu, The (1967), 62, 93, 95, 97, 114, 123, 223
Blood of Ghastly Horror (1969), 211
Blood of the Vampire (1957), 29, 41, 61, 65, 79, 108
Blood on Satan's Claw (1970), 61, 88, 92, 129, 145, 164, 171
Bloodbath at the House of Death (1983), 212
Bloody Birthday (1980), 206
Bloody Judge, The (1969), 109, 134, 137, 140
Blow-Up (1966), 191
Blue Blood (1973), 89
Blue Eyes of the Broken Doll (1973), 97
Blue Remembered Hills (1978), 185
Bluebeard (1944), 16
Bluebeard (1971), 216
Bobbikins (1959), 37
Bobo, The (1966), 184
Body Bags (1993), 213
Body Snatcher, The (1944), 38, 249
Body Stealers, The (1968), 113, 123, 171
Boneyard Collection, The (2008), 125
Boogey Man, The (1980), 211
Book of Blood (2009), 197
Born Free (1965), 89, 191
Boucher, le star et l'orpheline, Le (1973), 196
Bounty Killer, The (1966), 169
Bowery at Midnight (1942), 203

Box of Delights, The (1984), 151
Boys from Brazil, The (1978), 146
Brain, The (1988), 206
Brain from Planet Arous, The (1957), 223
Braindead (1991), 248
Bram Stoker's Dracula (1991), 34, 121, 150, 205, 221, 234, 245
Bram Stoker's Legend of the Mummy (1997), 185, 234
Brass (1983-1990), 131
Brewster McCloud (1970), 213
Bride, The (1984), 54, 83, 147
Bride of Frankenstein (1935), 21, 23, 29, 32, 47, 52, 100, 119, 211
Bride of the Monster (1954), 29, 36
Brides of Dracula, The (1960), 32, 42, 53, 60, 62, 64, 68, 73, 99, 144, 179, 226, 245
Brides of Fu Manchu, The (1966), 62, 93, 95-96, 97, 108, 124, 140, 223
Bridge on the River Kwai, The (1957), 41, 185
Brief Encounter (1945), 179
Brigand of Kandahar, The (1964), 39, 69
Brighton Rock (1947), 32, 89
Brimstone and Treacle (1976), 166, 200
Britannia Hospital (1981), 92, 166
Brood, The (1978), 59, 206
Brother, Can You Spare a Dime? (1975), 215
Bucket of Blood, A (1959), 220
Buenas noches, señor monstruo (1982), 170
Buffy the Vampire Slayer (1992), 84
Buffy the Vampire Slayer (1996-2003), 56, 102, 197, 236
Bugsy Malone (1975), 211
Bullet for the General, A (1966), 109
Bunny Lake is Missing (1965), 38, 92, 201
'Burbs, The (1988), 220
Burial Ground (1980), 75
Buried Alive (1988), 141, 206, 211
Burke and Hare (1970), 123, 136, 152
Burke and Hare (2010), 249
Burnt Offering: The Cult of the Wicker Man (2001), 183, 186
Burnt Offerings (1975), 59
Bus Stop (1956), 160
Cabin Fever (2001), 177
Cabinet of Dr. Caligari, The (1919), 14, 63, 114, 129, 199
Caesars, The (1968), 147, 192
Cage aux Folles, La (1978), 204
Caged Heat (1974), 124
Caligula (1976), 134
Call of Cthulhu, The (2005), 126
Callan (1967-1972; film: 1973), 148, 183
Caltiki, the Immortal Monster (1959), 70
Caminante, El (1978), 170, 188
Camp on Blood Island, The (1957), 41, 61, 62, 79, 80, 151, 193
Campbell's Kingdom (1957), 97
Candle for the Devil, A (1973), 169
Cannibal Apocalypse (1980), 75
Cannibal Girls (1972), 177
Cannibal Holocaust (1979), 75
Cape Fear (1991), 173
Captain America II (1979), 216, 228
Captain America: The First Avenger (2010), 216
Captain Clegg (1961), 39, 61, 66, 89, 105, 113, 117
Captain Horatio Hornblower R.N. (1950), 16, 80, 159
Captain Kronos: Vampire Hunter (1972), 111, 136, 146, 165, 168
Captain Scarlet and the Mysterons (1967), 98
Captain Sinbad (1962), 62
Captive Wild Woman (1942), 211
Care of Time, The (1989), 49
Carnival of Souls (1961), 56, 122

Carol for Another Christmas, A (1964), 184
Carrie (1976), 54, 100
Carry On film series (1958-1992), 23, 87, 89, 108, 136, 172, 193
Casablanca (1942), 14
Case of the Bloody Iris, The (1972), 134
Cash on Demand (1961), 41, 89, 190, 193
Casino Royale (1966), 55, 60, 62, 73, 89, 90, 129, 138, 179, 196
Casino Royale (2006), 94, 248
Casper (1994), 246
Cast a Deadly Spell (1990), 213
Castle Freak (1994), 126
Castle of Blood (1963), 71, 75, 76, 124
Castle of Fu Manchu, The (1968), 62, 70, 93, 95, 97, 111, 207, 223
Castle of the Creeping Flesh (1967), 138
Castle of the Living Dead, The (1964), 52, 70, 73, 83-84, 86, 114, 121, 124, 174
Castlevania (2017-), 187
Cat and the Canary, The (1976), 200
Cat Creature, The (1973), 221
Cat Girl (1957), 48, 79
Cat o' Nine Tails, The (1970), 96, 134
Cat People (1942), 51, 79, 82, 100, 196
Cat People (1981), 199
Catacombs (1963), 132
Catch-22 (1969), 68
Cat's Eye (1984), 159
Catweazle (1969-1970), 32
Cauldron of Blood (1967), 90
Caves of Steel, The (1964), 143
Century of Science Fiction, A (1996), 121, 227, 229, 230
Challenge for Robin Hood, A (1967), 108
Chandu the Magician (1932), 200
Changeling, The (1979), 123, 191
Chariots of the Gods (1970), 114
Charles and Diana: A Royal Love Story (1982), 161
Charlie and the Chocolate Factory (2004), 245, 246-247
Charlie Chan at the Opera (1936), 221
Charlie's Angels: "Angel in Hiding" (1980), 177
Cheers (1982-1993), 180
Children of the Damned (1963), 92
Child's Play (film series, 1987-2017), 245, 248
Chiller (1994), 130
Chimes at Midnight (1965), 84, 134, 170
Chitty Chitty Bang Bang (1967), 95, 115, 118, 160, 249
Chopping Mall (1985), 220
Christine (1983), 220
Christmas Carol, A (1984), 183
Christmas That Almost Wasn't, The (1966), 83
Christopher Lee: A Legacy of Horror and Terror (1999), 108, 174
Christopher Lee: Prince of Menace (ITV film season, 1979), 209
C.H.U.D. II-Bud the Chud (1988), 206, 216
Chump at Oxford, A (1939), 23, 212
Church, The (1988), 89
Circus of Fear (1965), 54, 95, 96, 108-109, 111, 138, 141, 171, 207, 223
Circus of Horrors (1959), 39, 45, 48, 53, 62, 65, 68, 108
Citizen Kane (1940), 93, 185, 196
City of the Dead, The (1959), 20, 52, 54-56, 68, 82, 84, 108, 156, 164, 181, 231, 246
City of the Walking Dead (1980), 64, 75
City Under the Sea, The (1964), 41
Clash of the Titans (1979), 90
Cleopatra (1962), 89, 99, 148
Climax, The (1944), 27
Clive Barker's A-Z of Horror (1995), 223
Clockwork Orange, A (1971), 38, 93, 125, 185

Close Encounters of the Third Kind (1976), 207
Cobra Woman (1943), 16
Cockneys vs. Zombies (2011), 200
Colbys, The (1985-1987), 165
Colonel Bogey (1947), 23, 63
Colonel March of Scotland Yard (1952-1953), 17, 23, 37
Color Me Blood Red (1964), 106
Color of Money, The (1986), 206
Coma (1977), 199
Comeback, The (1977), 54, 200, 210
Comedy of Terrors, The (1963), 117, 228
Committee, The (1968), 199
Communion (1988), 215
Company of Wolves, The (1984), 213, 214
Conan the Barbarian (1981), 140
Conan the Destroyer (1983), 215
Condorman (1980), 59
Cone of Silence (1960), 45, 98
Confessions from a Holiday Camp (1977), 146
Confessions of a Pop Performer (1975), 20, 152
Confessions of a Window Cleaner (1974), 32, 146, 179
Congregation of Ghosts, A (2009), 183
Connecticut Yankee in King Arthur's Court, A (1947), 224
Contamination (1980), 158
Cook, the Thief, His Wife & Her Lover, The (1988), 180
Cool It, Carol (1970), 209
Coronation Street (1960-), 125
Corpse, The (1969), 125, 177
Corpse Bride (2004), 192, 245, 247
Corpse Vanishes, The (1942), 200
Corridor of Mirrors (1947), 15
Corridors of Blood (1958), 11, 35, 37-39, 55, 56, 64, 72, 89, 98, 109, 110, 122, 229, 249
Corruption (1967), 193
Cosmic Man, The (1958), 211
Count Dracula (1969), 94, 109, 134, 138-142, 146, 160, 199
Count Dracula (1977), 17, 142, 149, 244
Count Dracula's Great Love (1972), 102, 170
Count Yorga Vampire (1970), 126, 163, 167
Countess Dracula (1970), 39, 119, 133, 143, 170, 184
Country Matters (1972), 131
Crash! (1976), 208
Crawlspace (1971), 66
Crawlspace (1985), 141
Craze (1973), 173, 180
Creation (1931), 226
Creature (1984), 141
Creature from the Black Lagoon (1953), 82, 156
Creature Walks Among Us, The (1955), 44
Creature Wasn't Nice, The (1981), 110
Creature with the Blue Hand (1967), 109
Creeping Flesh, The (1972), 32, 91, 156, 157, 166, 171-174, 179
Creeps, The (1997), 208
Crescendo (1969), 83, 148, 163, 168, 179
Crimes at the Dark House (1939), 18, 27
Crimes of Stephen Hawke, The (1936), 15, 27
Criminal Law (1987), 133
Crimson Pirate, The (1951), 16
Cronos (1992), 177
Crooked House (2008), 191
Cross of the Devil (1974), 170
Cross-Roads (1954), 18
Crow, The (1993), 248
Crowhaven Farm (1970), 211
Crucible of Terror (1971), 32, 159

Crucifer of Blood, The (1991), 185
Cry of the Banshee (1969), 119, 123, 133, 136, 190
Crypt of Horror (1963), 72-73, 76-77
Cuadecuc Vampir (1969), 138, 142
Cuba (1978), 36, 193
Cul-De-Sac (1965), 122
Curse, The (1986), 217
Curse II: The Bite (1988), 217
Curse of Dracula, The (1978), 205
Curse of Frankenstein, The (1956), 10, 15, 16, 17, 20-28, 29, 30, 31, 36, 37, 38, 40, 44, 45, 46, 49, 51, 53, 57, 68, 70, 80, 84, 87, 98, 99, 108, 110, 149, 151, 170, 177, 194, 195, 198, 207, 213, 224, 227, 229, 233, 237, 240, 243, 244
Curse of King Tut's Tomb, The (2006), 235
Curse of Nostradamus, The (1959), 140
Curse of the Blair Witch (1999), 56
Curse of the Cat People, The (1943), 196, 245
Curse of the Crimson Altar (1968), 122-126, 171
Curse of the Devil (1973), 170
Curse of the Fly (1964), 62, 95, 105
Curse of the Mummy's Tomb, The (1964), 16, 33, 51, 80
Curse of the Stone Hand (1959), 211
Curse of the Undead (1959), 50
Curse of the Vampire, The (1971), 84
Curse of the Were-Rabbit, The (2005), 146
Curse of the Werewolf, The (1960), 31, 32, 39, 41, 49, 59, 62, 80, 105, 146, 158, 175, 203, 215
Cyclops, The (1955), 223
Dad's Army (1968-1977), 41, 110
Daleks Invasion Earth 2150 A.D. (1966), 89, 99
Damien: Omen II (1977), 46, 208
Damned, The (1961), 20, 59, 74, 113, 208
Dance Macabre (1991), 141
Dance of the Vampires (1966), 18, 68, 113, 127, 144, 204, 215
Danger: Diabolik (1967), 68, 71
Danger Man (1960-1966), 19
Danger Route (1967), 68
Dangerous Mission (1953), 20
Danse du Feu, La (1899), 88
Dark Avenger, The (1954), 18, 47
Dark Crystal, The (1981), 173
Dark Eyes of London, The (1939), 14, 31, 96, 203
Dark Half, The (1991), 189
Dark Intruder (1965), 209
Dark Light, The (1950), 123
Dark Mission: Flowers of Evil (1987), 141
Dark Places (1972), 95, 140, 155, 191, 192
Dark Secret of Harvest Home, The (1977), 176
Dark Shadows (1966-1971, 1990), 190, 195, 234, 247
Dark Shadows (2011), 245, 247-248
Dark Tower (1988), 173
Darkman (1989), 247
Darling (1964), 91
D.A.R.Y.L. (1985), 197
Daughter of Dracula (1972), 137-138, 141
Daughter of Dr. Jekyll (1956), 16
Daughter of Fu Manchu, The (1990), 97
Daughter of the Dragon (1931), 94
Daughter of the Mind (1969), 211
Daughters of Darkness (1970), 114, 196
Dawn of the Dead (1977), 52
Day of the Locust, The (1974), 84, 107, 177
Day of the Outlaw (1958), 54
Day of the Triffids, The (1961), 33, 62, 85, 169
Day the Earth Caught Fire, The (1961), 60, 80, 89, 159

Day the Earth Stood Still, The (1951), 227
Day the World Ended, The (2001), 199
Daydreamer, The (1964), 212
De Sade (1968), 134
Dead & Buried (1980), 177
Dead Eyes of London (1961), 109
Dead Files, The (2011-), 133
Dead Heat (1987), 221
Dead of Night (1945), 15, 32, 63, 67, 68, 84, 85, 111, 202
Dead of Night (1972), 136, 177
Dead of Night (1976), 110, 117
Dead Zone, The (1983), 140
Deadlier than the Male (1966), 39, 52, 61
Deadly Bees, The (1965), 92, 108, 136, 190
Dear John (1985-1987), 147
Death Drums Along the River (1962), 94
Death Line (1972), 65, 82, 174-178
Death Race 2000 (1974), 211
Death Smiles on a Murderer (1972), 75
Death Trap (1976), 64
Death Wish (1974), 249
Deathmaster (1970), 144
Deep Red (1974), 71
Delicatessen (1990), 138
Dementia 13 (1963), 68
Demon, The (1963), 73
Demon Seed (1977), 206
Demonic Toys (1991), 208
Demons (1985), 73
Demons 2 (1986), 73
Demons, The (1972), 138
Demons of the Mind (1971), 54, 93, 125, 133, 166, 171, 191, 199
Devil and Daniel Webster, The (1941), 56, 188
Devil Bat, The (1940), 203
Devil-Doll, The (1936), 106
Devil Doll (1963), 19, 39, 97
Devil Girl from Mars (1954), 18, 19, 26, 38, 112
Devil Inside, The (2011), 107
Devil Rides Out, The (1967), 10, 103, 113, 116-121, 178, 184, 193, 197, 230, 233, 243, 246
Devil-Ship Pirates, The (1963), 11, 76, 80, 95, 99, 105, 172
Devils, The (1970), 59, 136, 138, 160, 201
Devil's Agent, The (1961), 72, 79
Devil's Backbone, The (2000), 250
Devil's Daffodil, The (1961), 53, 109
Devil's Exorcist (1974), 140
Devil's Kiss, The (1973), 170
Devil's Lover, The (1971), 70
Devil's Men, The (1975), 176, 202
Devils of Darkness (1964), 95, 108, 112
Devil's Rain, The (1975), 188, 202
Devil's Wedding Night, The (1972), 70
Devil's Widow, The (1969), 152
Devonsville Terror, The (1982), 176
Diabolical Dr. Z, The (1965), 138, 170
Diaboliques, Les (1954), 67, 68
Diagnosis: Murder (1974), 110, 113, 133
Dial M for Murder (1953), 113
Diamond Mercenaries, The (1975), 200
Diamonds Are Forever (1971), 58, 119, 168
Diary of a Madman (1962), 188
Dick Barton at Bay (1948), 110
Dick Tracy (1989), 247
Dick Tracy Meets Gruesome (1947), 115
Die, Monster, Die! (1965), 37, 49, 93, 98, 122

Die Screaming Marianne (1970), 136, 209, 212
Digby: The Biggest Dog in the World (1972), 105, 152, 176
Disciple of Death (1972), 125, 159
Disputation, The (1985), 216
Django Unchained (2012), 169
Doctor and the Devils, The (1985), 86, 173
Dr. Black, Mr. Hyde (1975), 159
Doctor Blood's Coffin (1960), 46, 68, 171
Dr. Crippen (1962), 56, 62, 65
Dr. Cyclops (1939), 27
Doctor Dolittle (1966), 39
Doctor Dracula (1977), 211
Doctor Faustus (1966), 116
Doctor Franken (1979), 206
Dr. Goldfoot and the Bikini Machine (1965), 132
Dr. Goldfoot and the Girl Bombs (1966), 73
Dr. Heckyl and Mr. Hype (1980), 59
Doctor in the House (1953), 28
Dr. Jekyll and Mr. Hyde (1919), 57, 158
Dr. Jekyll and Mr. Hyde (1931), 17, 23, 57, 107
Dr. Jekyll and Mr. Hyde (1941), 57, 141
Dr. Jekyll and Mr. Hyde (1956), 17
Doctor Jekyll and Mr. Hyde (1973), 176
Dr. Jekyll and Mr. Hyde (1980), 60, 177, 180
Dr. Jekyll and Ms. Hyde (1995), 234
Dr. Jekyll and Sister Hyde (1971), 60, 78, 108, 111, 125, 136, 147, 149, 156, 168, 173, 179, 242
Dr. Jekyll Likes Them Hot (1978), 53
Dr. Jekyll vs. The Werewolf (1971), 140
Dr. Mabuse, the Gambler (1922), 137
Doctor Mordrid (1991), 208
Dr. Morelle (1948), 55
Dr. No (1962), 15, 34, 61, 63, 86, 88, 89, 90, 94, 193
Dr. Phibes Rises Again (1971), 62, 137, 165, 175, 205
Doctor Strange (2016), 61
Dr. Strangelove (1963), 11, 107, 111
Doctor Syn (1937), 19
Dr. Terrible's House of Horrible (2001), 63, 65, 200, 210
Dr. Terror's Gallery of Horrors (1966), 87, 237
Dr. Terror's House of Horrors (1964), 16, 82, 85-87, 88, 90, 124, 142, 175, 196
Dr. Terror's Vault of Horror (1992-1996), 87
Doctor Who (1963-), 20, 33, 38, 45, 48, 50-51, 55, 61, 63, 66, 79, 90, 93, 98, 99, 105, 107, 109, 110, 112, 123-124, 125, 129, 133, 136, 148, 151, 152, 154, 159, 160, 163, 164, 170, 174, 177, 178, 181, 184, 191, 195, 198, 200, 222, 241, 242
Dr. Who and the Daleks (1965), 62, 86, 91, 112, 166
Doctor X (1932), 27
Doctor Zhivago (1965), 109
Dog Soldiers (2001), 234
Dolce Vita, La (1959), 47, 70
Dollman (1991), 216
Dolls (1986), 208
Dolores Claiborne (1994), 234
Dominique (1977), 197
Don Quixote (1957-1969, 1992) [unfinished], 134
Donovan's Brain (1953), 69, 85, 208, 219
Don't Be Afraid of the Dark (1973), 66
Don't Bother to Knock (1952), 149, 199
Don't Look Now (1972), 84, 185, 213
Don't Open Till Christmas (1984), 165, 180
Don't Raise the Bridge, Lower the River (1967), 119
Doomwatch (1971), 32, 146, 181, 183
Dorian Gray (1969), 135, 140
Double Face (1969), 109

Double Trouble (1966), 39, 176
Douglas Fairbanks Presents (1952-1956), 17
Dracula (1930), 10, 14, 28, 29, 30, 34, 44, 48, 99, 135, 139, 155, 164, 167, 220, 223, 226
Dracula (1957), 10, 12, 13, 15, 16, 23, 29-36, 37, 38, 39, 40, 44, 45, 46, 47, 49, 50, 51, 53, 55, 56, 57, 59, 64, 65, 67, 69, 70, 72, 75, 80, 82, 90, 98, 99, 100, 102, 107, 112, 116, 118, 124, 127, 139, 144, 149, 154, 155, 159, 166, 167, 172, 187, 194, 196, 206, 208, 209, 217, 218, 219, 225, 226, 233, 234, 237, 240, 242, 248, 249, 251
Dracula (1973), 92, 101, 117, 125, 177, 190, 195, 197
Dracula (1978), 9, 26, 50, 101, 107, 171, 176, 205
Dracula (2013), 235
Dracula (2019), 63
Dracula: A Cinematic Scrapbook (1990), 223
Dracula A.D. 1972 (1971), 100, 145, 149, 161, 163-168, 179, 187, 192, 193, 209, 215, 229, 242, 247
Dracula and Son (1976), 204
Dracula Business, The (1974), 200, 242
Dracula by Northern Ballet (2019), 34
Dracula: Dead and Loving It (1995), 140, 192, 209, 213, 234
Dracula Has Risen from the Grave (1968), 10, 123, 126-132, 143, 144, 145, 154, 159, 204, 209, 220, 230
Dracula in the Provinces (1975), 52
Dracula: Pages from a Virgin's Diary (2001), 34
Dracula: Prince of Darkness (1965), 5, 10, 13, 33, 37, 79, 80, 83, 98-103, 104, 108, 110, 114, 127, 147, 154, 171, 183, 211, 228, 240, 251, 252
Dracula, Prisoner of Frankenstein (1971), 137, 141
Dracula Saga, The (1972), 165, 170
Dracula: Sovereign of the Damned (1980), 167
Dracula 2000 (2000), 234
Dracula II: Ascension (2001), 234
Dracula III: Legacy (2001), 234
Dracula 3D (2011), 157
Dracula vs. Frankenstein (1970), 161
Dracula's Daughter (1936), 88, 99
Dracula's Dog (1976), 208
Dragon: The Bruce Lee Story (1992), 234
Dragonslayer (1980), 213
Dragonwyck (1945), 132
Drakula Istanbul'da (1952), 30, 139, 149, 167
Draughtsman's Contract, The (1981), 147
Dream Demon (1987), 199
Dream of Home (1954), 18
Dressed to Kill (1979), 206
Dresser, The (1983), 65
Drop Dead Fred (1990), 219
Drums of Fu Manchu (1940), 94
Duel (1971), 117
Dumbo (2017), 247
Dummy of Death (1962), 169
Dune (1983), 173, 192, 216
Dunwich Horror, The (1969), 122, 133
Duty Free (1983-1986), 180
Dynasty (1981-1989), 165, 191
E.T. the Extra-Terrestrial (1981), 250
Earth Dies Screaming, The (1964), 87, 93, 98, 112, 206
Earth vs. the Flying Saucers (1955), 169
EastEnders (1985-), 235, 243
Eating Raoul (1981), 221
Ed Wood (1993), 196, 197, 246
Ed Wood: Look Back in Angora (1994), 223
Edgar Allan Poe's Tales of Mystery and Imagination (1994) 223
Edge of Sanity (1988), 141
Edward Scissorhands (1989), 212, 245, 246

Eegah! (1962), 227
Eerie, Indiana (1991-1992), 219
8 ½ (1962), 124
Elephant Man, The (1980), 151, 173, 180, 192
Elf (2003), 234
Elvira's Haunted Hills (2000), 248
Embalmer, The (1965), 74
Embrace of the Vampire (1994), 177
Emergency-Ward 10 (1957-1967), 37, 164
Empire of Dracula, The (1966), 102
Empire of the Ants (1976), 191
Empire of the Sun (1987), 214
End of Days (1999), 121, 201
End of the Affair, The (1954), 80
End of the World (1977), 207-208, 209, 210
Enter the Dragon (1973), 168, 221
Entertainer, The (1959), 80
Entertainment Tonight (1981-), 225, 231
Equalizer, The (1985-1989), 183
Erotic Rites of Frankenstein, The (1972), 138
Errol Flynn Theatre, The (1956), 31
Escape from New York (1980), 176
Escape from the Planet of the Apes (1970), 46
Eugenie…The Story of Her Journey into Perversion (1969), 134-135, 137, 140, 207, 244
Event Horizon (1997), 234
Every Home Should Have One (1969), 136
Everything You Always Wanted to Know About Sex (1972), 211
Evil Dead (film series, 1979-1991), 52
Evil of Frankenstein, The (1963), 42, 78, 85, 91, 92, 105, 172
Evil Spawn (1987), 223
Evil That Is Eve, The (1957), 46
Evils of the Night (1983), 211
Excalibur (1980), 175
Exorcism (1974), 97, 140
Exorcist, The (1973), 42, 72, 93, 140, 173, 187, 194, 198, 199, 202, 222
Exorcist III, The (1989), 248
Explorers (1984), 120, 215, 220
Exposé (1975), 146
Expresso Bongo (1959), 57
Extraordinary Tales (2012), 250
Eye for an Eye, An (1981), 209
Eye of the Devil (1965), 41, 65, 183
Eye of the Needle (1981), 121, 130, 217
Eyeball (1974), 89
Eyes of Laura Mars (1977), 248
Face at the Window, The (1939), 14, 27
Face of Eve, The (1967), 90, 97, 140
Face of Fu Manchu, The (1965), 36, 39, 62, 94-96, 105, 108, 115, 157, 160, 190, 223
Face of Marble, The (1945), 211
Face the Music (1953), 45
Faceless (1987), 137, 165
Fade to Black (1980), 208
Faerie Tale Theatre (1982-1987), 213-214
Fahrenheit 451 (1966), 45
Fährmann Maria (1935), 114
Fall of the Eagles (1989), 141
Fall of the House of Usher, The (1947), 148
Fan, The (1980), 164
Fanatic (1964), 84, 109, 117
Fangs (1981), 243
Fangs of the Living Dead (a.k.a. *Malenka, the Vampire*, 1968), 76
Fantasist, The (1985), 187
Fantastic Voyage (1965), 65, 218

Far Pavilions, The (1983), 155, 195, 251
F.A.R.T. The Movie (1991), 189
Fast Times at Ridgemont High (1981), 219
Fatal Attraction (1986), 32
Fawlty Towers (1975-1979), 89
Fear Chamber, The (1968), 122
Fear in the Dark (1991), 221-222
Fear in the Night (1971), 62, 147, 191, 242
Feast at Midnight, A (1994), 182, 186, 191
Fellini's Casanova (1976), 84
Female Chauvinists (1976), 189
Female Vampire (1973), 140
Ferry Cross the Mersey (1964), 96
Ferry to Hong Kong (1958), 61
Fiend, The (1970), 69, 93
Fiend Without a Face (1957), 36
Fiendish Plot of Dr. Fu Manchu, The (1980), 62, 97
Final Column (1954), 18
Final Programme, The (1973), 172
Fire Maidens from Outer Space (1956), 31
Firestarter (1983), 192, 217
First Man into Space (1958), 39, 41, 61
First Men in the Moon (1963), 55, 111, 226
Fistful of Dynamite (1971), 75
Five Golden Dragons (1966), 96, 141
Five Star Final (1931), 61
5,000 Fingers of Dr. T, The (1952), 11
Flaming Star (1960), 124
Flash Gordon (1979), 119
Flesh and Blood Show, The (1972), 152, 209
Flesh and Blood: The Hammer Heritage of Horror (1994), 26, 36, 56, 67, 120, 121, 150, 161, 164, 194, 215, 216, 218, 224-232
Flesh and the Fiends, The (1959), 25, 38, 46, 65, 77
Flesh for Frankenstein (1973), 75
Flesh Gordon (1971), 189
Fly, The (1958), 15, 23, 32, 132, 227
Fly, The (1986), 217, 227
Fly II, The (1988), 206, 217
Flying Serpent, The (1945), 15
Fog, The (1979), 209
For a Few Dollars More (1965), 109
For Your Eyes Only (1980), 71, 87, 92, 107, 136
Forbidden Planet (1955), 209
Forbidden Territory (1934), 61
Forbidden Zone (1978), 247
Forsyte Saga, The (1967), 148, 155
Fortune is a Woman (1956), 14, 80
Fountain of Youth, The (1956), 196
Four Flies on Grey Velvet (1971), 134
4 for Texas (1963), 90
Four Musketeers, The (1973), 59, 119, 136, 146, 152, 170, 196, 199, 201, 216, 219
Four Sided Triangle (1952), 17, 19, 23, 112
Fourth Victim, The (1970), 169
Frances (1981), 213
Frankenstein (1931), 10, 13, 14, 16, 21, 23, 28, 38, 44, 119, 155, 158, 220, 223, 240
Frankenstein (1984), 213
Frankenstein (1992), 136
Frankenstein: A Cinematic Scrapbook (1990), 223
Frankenstein and the Monster from Hell (1972), 33, 46, 86, 101, 120, 144, 145, 151, 153, 184, 194
Frankenstein Created Woman (1966), 51, 90, 98, 99, 172, 250
Frankenstein '80 (1972), 89
Frankenstein Island (1981), 211

Frankenstein Meets the Wolf Man (1942), 28
Frankenstein Must Be Destroyed (1969), 33, 38, 49, 55, 98, 120, 128, 144, 155, 192, 197
Frankenstein 1970 (1958), 28
Frankenstein: The True Story (1973), 81, 146, 158, 177, 197, 207
Frankenstein Unbound (1989), 158
Frankenstein's Auntie (1986), 204
Frankenstein's Castle of Freaks (1973), 73
Frankenstein's Daughter (1958), 28
Frankenstein's Great-Aunt Tillie (1983), 47
Frankenweenie (1983), 213, 248
Frankenweenie (2012), 248
Frankula (2017), 165
Freaks (1931), 240
Freaky Friday (1976), 220
Freddy's Nightmares (1988-1990), 216
Frenzy (1971), 89, 107, 158, 176, 182, 191
Freud (1961), 60
Friday the 13th (film series, 1979-2008), 12, 71, 214
Fright (1971), 152, 159, 200
Fright Night (1985), 140, 154, 173, 215
Frighteners, The (1995), 220
Frightmare (1974), 171, 209, 210
Frightmare (1981), 216
From a Whisper to a Scream (1986), 212
From Beyond (1986), 126
From Beyond the Grave (1973), 56, 87, 145, 155, 176, 180, 210-211, 213
From Dusk Till Dawn (1995), 233-234
From Hell (2000), 246
From Russia with Love (1963), 15, 39, 48, 108
Frost on Sunday (1968-1970), 137
Frozen Dead, The (1966), 93
Full Circle (1976), 92
Full Moon High (1981), 216
Full Treatment, The (1960), 69, 184
Fun in Acapulco (1963), 90
Funhouse, The (1980), 220
Funny Man (1993), 145, 222
Funny Thing Happened on the Way to the Forum, A (1965), 55, 119
Further Mysteries of Dr. Fu Manchu, The (1924), 94
Fury at Smugglers' Bay (1961), 78, 93, 192
G.I. Blues (1960), 184
Game of Thrones (2011-2019), 110
Gamma People, The (1955), 16, 94
Garden of the Dead (1972), 208
Gargoyles (1972), 159
Gawain and the Green Knight (1972), 153, 157-158, 159
Gay Cavalier, The (1957), 28
Ghost, The (1962), 124
Ghost Galleon, The (1973), 140
Ghost in the Shell (2016), 61
Ghost of Frankenstein, The (1941), 21, 119
Ghost of Rashmon Hall, The (1947), 55
Ghost of Sierra de Cobre, The (1964), 197
Ghost Ship (1952), 26, 32, 123
Ghost Stories for Christmas (2000), 235-237
Ghost Story (1972), 54
Ghost Story (1974), 157
Ghost Story (1981), 220
Ghost Story for Christmas, A (1971-1978), 32, 130, 176, 191, 200, 235-236
Ghost Train, The (1931), 68, 110
Ghost Train, The (1941), 19, 48, 110, 159
Ghostbusters (1983), 126, 173, 218
Ghostbusters II (1989), 164, 213
Ghosts of Berkeley Square, The (1947), 48, 123

Ghoul, The (1933), 61
Ghoul, The (1974), 129, 148, 153, 158, 166, 173
Ghoulies (1984), 208
Ghoulies II (1986), 208
Ghoulies Go to College (1990), 234
Giants of Thessaly, The (1960), 71
Gift, The (2000), 247
Gilbert Harding Speaking of Murder (1953), 19
Gingerdead Man, The (2001), 208
Girl, The (2012), 192
Girl from Rio, The (1967), 97
Girl from the Red Cabaret, The (1973), 64
Girl from U.N.C.L.E., The (1966-1967), 206
Girl Who Knew Too Much, The (1962), 71, 73
Gladiator (1999), 59
Glass Cage, The (1954), 146, 200
Gleaming the Cube (1987), 213
Glen or Glenda (1953), 68, 216, 246
Glory (1989), 85
Gnome-Mobile, The (1966), 107
Go for a Take (1972), 152, 176, 185
Godzilla (film series, 1954-), 114, 221, 234, 245
Going Bananas (1986), 209
Golden Voyage of Sinbad, The (1972), 95, 137, 165
GoldenEye (1995), 166, 176
Goldfinger (1964), 62, 66, 95, 97, 110, 193, 200
Golem, The (1920), 16, 107, 114
Golem, The (1936), 85
Goliath and the Dragon (1960), 70
Goliath and the Vampires (1961), 70, 84
Goliath Awaits (1981), 191, 210-211
Gonks Go Beat (1965), 62
Good Against Evil (1977), 107
Good, the Bad and the Ugly, The (1966), 129
Goodbye Gemini (1969), 163, 192
Goodfellas (1989), 235
Goosebumps (2014), 247
Gor (1986), 209
Gorgo (1959), 39, 50, 66, 84, 109
Gorgon, The (1963), 77-80, 87, 98, 103, 104, 151, 185, 187
Gorilla at Large (1954), 27
Gormenghast (1999), 45, 235
Gothic (1986), 250
Gourmet, The (1986), 119
Grapes of Wrath, The (1939), 211
Grave of the Vampire (1972), 167, 208
Gravedale High (1990), 180
Graveyard Shift (1990), 233
Great Alligator, The (1979), 64
Great Escape, The (1962), 65
Great Expectations (1946), 16, 38
Great Houdini, The (1976), 41
Great Muppet Caper, The (1980), 110
Great Silence, The (1967), 109
Greatest Story Ever Told, The (1963), 188
Greed of William Hart, The (1947), 77
Green Mare's Nest, The (1959), 60
Green Mile, The (1998), 234
Gremlins (1983), 215, 218, 220
Gremlins 2: The New Batch (1989), 218-221, 222
Greystoke: The Legend of Tarzan, Lord of the Apes (1983), 220
Grindhouse (2006), 97
Grip of the Strangler (1957), 36, 37
Grizzly (1975), 206
Guardians of the Galaxy (2013), 234

Half a Sixpence (1967), 57
Half Human (1955), 211
Halloween (film series, 1978-), 91, 105, 176, 203, 209, 212, 216, 222
Halloween Hell (2014), 206
Hamlet (1947), 15, 16, 39, 48, 51, 56, 61, 64, 110, 136
Hammer House of Horror (1980), 25, 98, 118, 130, 133, 146, 151, 153, 173, 180, 181, 197, 200, 201, 203
Hammer House of Mystery and Suspense (1983-1984), 62, 111, 119, 136, 146, 147, 165, 181, 201, 203
Hammer: The Studio That Dripped Blood! (1987), 10, 29, 119
Hand, The (1980), 216
Hands of a Murderer (1989), 183
Hands of Orlac, The (1960), 53, 56, 65-66, 75, 159, 176
Hands of the Ripper (1971), 113, 143, 156, 168, 181
Hangar 18 (1980), 206
Hanging Tree, The (1958), 138
Hanging Woman, The (1972), 170
Hangover Square (1944), 45
Hannibal (2000), 67
Hannie Caulder (1971), 170-171, 180, 199
Happy Days (1974-1984), 219
Happy Hooker Goes Hollywood, The (1980), 209
Hard Day's Night, A (1964), 80, 86, 107, 110, 139, 176, 193
HARDtalk (1997-), 252
Hardware (1989), 193
Harry and the Hendersons (1986), 220
Harry Potter (film series, 2000-2010), 85, 180, 191, 192, 218, 246
Hatchet for the Honeymoon (1969), 174
Haunted (1967-1968), 119
Haunted Airman, The (2006), 181
Haunted House of Horror, The (1968), 54, 126, 210
Haunted Palace, The (1963), 122
Haunters of the Deep (1984), 130, 193
Haunting, The (1962), 15, 55, 191
Hauser's Memory (1970), 69
Hawaii Five-O (1968-1980), 188
Hawk the Slayer (1980), 133
Head (1968), 214
Head, The (1959), 56
Heart of a Man, The (1959), 89
Heathers (1988), 208
Heaven Can Wait (1943), 188
Helen Keller: The Miracle Continues (1983), 197
Helen of Troy (1955), 75
Hell is a City (1959), 65
Hellfire Club, The (1960), 39, 41, 52, 68
Hello, Dolly! (1968), 143
Hellraiser (film series, 1986-2016), 87, 102, 222
Hellzapoppin' (1941), 218
Help! (1965), 108, 139, 146, 201
Henry V (1988), 229
Henry: Portrait of a Serial Killer (1985), 189
Hercules (1957), 52, 69
Hercules (1982), 75, 209, 216
Hercules and the Captive Women (1961), 70
Hercules in New York (1969), 71
Hercules in the Haunted World (1961), 70-71, 72, 73, 83, 170
Hercules, Prisoner of Evil (1964), 70
Hercules the Avenger (1965), 70, 76
Hercules Unchained (1958), 52, 69
Here Comes Mr. Jordan (1941), 188
Hideous Sun Demon, The (1957), 223
Highlander (1985), 233
Highlander II: The Quickening (1990), 235
Hillbillys in a Haunted House (1967), 211

History of Horror with Mark Gatiss, A (2010), 63
Hitch in Time, A (1978), 151
Hitler's Madman (1942), 66
Hitler's Son (1977), 42
Hobbit, The (film series, 2011), 187, 248, 250
Hollywood Boulevard (1975), 220
Hollywood Ghost Stories (1986), 69
Hollywood Meatcleaver Massacre, The (1972/75), 189-191
Holocaust 2000 (1977), 197
Holy Mountain, The (1972), 221
Homicidal (1961), 62
Honeymoon in Vegas (1991), 206
Honeymoon Killers, The (1969), 156
Horrible Dr. Hichcock, The (1962), 73, 102, 124
Horror at 37,000 Feet, The (1972), 113
Horror Express (1971), 64, 87, 102, 118, 140, 168-170, 171, 179, 203, 225, 227, 230, 241
Horror Hall of Fame, The (1974), 160, 220
Horror Hospital (1972), 109, 125
Horror of Frankenstein, The (1970), 129, 144, 147, 148-149, 153, 174, 179
Horror of it All, The (1963), 54, 55, 85
Horror of Party Beach, The (1963), 237
Horror of the Blood Monsters (1966), 211
Horror Rises from the Tomb (1972), 170
Horroritual (1972), 167
Horrors of the Black Museum (1958), 32, 45, 56, 146
Hostel (film series, 2005-2011), 12, 177, 184
Hot Enough for June (1963), 52
Hound of the Baskervilles, The (1939), 40, 97
Hound of the Baskervilles, The (1958), 19, 39-44, 99, 110, 140, 175, 179, 201, 224
Hound of the Baskervilles, The (1972), 41, 113
Hound of the Baskervilles, The (1977), 42, 146, 200
Hound of the Baskervilles, The (1983), 200
Hour of Mystery (1957), 45, 65
House by the Cemetery, The (1981), 52
House in Marsh Road, The (1960), 19
House in Nightmare Park, The (1972), 133, 199
House of 1000 Corpses (2000), 248
House of a Thousand Dolls (1967), 96
House of Dark Shadows (1970), 46
House of Dracula (1945), 205, 211
House of Eliott, The (1991-1994), 234
House of Evil (1968), 122
House of Frankenstein (1944), 211
House of Mortal Sin (1975), 165, 209, 210
House of Mystery (1960), 123
House of the Black Death (1965), 211
House of the Living Dead (1973), 40
House of the Long Shadows (1982), 176, 209-212
House of the Seven Gables, The (1940), 132
House of Usher (1960), 69, 72, 75, 115, 117, 132
House of Usher, The (1988), 141
House of Wax (1953), 16, 27, 132, 141, 156, 246
House of Whipcord (1973), 134, 209, 210
House on Haunted Hill (1958), 132
House That Dripped Blood, The (1970), 33, 155-156, 158, 165, 171, 173, 181, 184, 185, 200, 226, 234
House That Screamed, The (1969), 165, 170
House That Would Not Die, The (1970), 54
How I Won the War (1966), 110, 127, 146, 201
How the Grinch Stole Christmas! (1966), 122, 188
How to Get Ahead in Advertising (1988), 175
How to Make a Monster (1958), 166

Howl of the Devil (1987), 97, 165
Howling, The (1980), 110, 120, 211, 215-216, 218, 220
Howling II (1984), 66, 166, 214-216, 219, 222
Howling III: The Marsupials (1987), 215
Howling VI: The Freaks (1990), 216
Huckleberry Finn and His Friends (1979-1980), 204
Huerto del Francés, El (1977), 170
Hugo (2010), 157, 201, 249-250, 251
Human Beasts (1980), 97, 170
Humanoid, The (1979), 75
Hunchback of Notre Dame, The (1923), 10, 229
Hunchback of Notre Dame, The (1966), 92
Hunchback of Notre Dame, The (1981), 87
Hunchback of Notre Dame, The (1996), 214, 250
Hunchback of the Morgue (1972), 97, 170
Hunger, The (1982), 46, 54, 80, 221
Hunger, The (1997-2000), 235
Hysteria (1964), 69, 85, 86, 91, 92, 107
I Bought a Vampire Motorcycle (1989), 62
I Bury the Living (1957), 208
I, Desire (1982), 54
I Don't Want to Be Born (1974), 147, 165, 166, 176, 179, 181, 191, 202
I, Mobster (1958), 156
I, Monster (1970), 57, 76, 90, 153, 154, 157-159, 171, 173, 209, 223
I Start Counting (1969), 197
I Walked with a Zombie (1942), 43
I Was a Teenage Frankenstein (1957), 28, 32
I Was a Teenage Werewolf (1957), 166
Idol, The (1966), 92
If.... (1968), 197
Ill Met by Moonlight (1956), 20, 40
I'll Never Forget What's'isname (1967), 183
I'm All Right Jack (1959), 108
Image, The (1967), 210
Imitation Game, The (2013), 31
In Search of Dracula (1971), 160-162, 181
In Search of Dracula with Jonathan Ross (1996), 164-165, 195, 205
In the Mouth of Madness (1993), 213
Incense for the Damned (1969), 20, 56, 110, 119, 183, 193
Incredible Invasion, The (1968), 122
Incredible Melting Man, The (1977), 82
Incredible Petrified World, The (1957), 211
Incredible Shrinking Man, The (1956), 117
Incredible 2-Headed Transplant, The (1970), 137
Indecent Proposal (1992), 71
Indestructible Man (1954), 223
Indiana Jones (film series, 1980-), 68, 107, 121, 147, 200, 218, 235
Inferno (1979), 71
Ingrid Pitt: Beyond the Forest (2010), 184
Innerspace (1986), 218, 220
Innocent Blood (1992), 249
Innocents, The (1961), 85, 127, 191
Inquisition (1976), 170
Inseminoid (1980), 165
Inside No. 9 (2014-), 235
Interview with Director Pete Walker (2010), 210
Interview with the Vampire (1993), 106
Invaders from Mars (1952), 27
Invaders from Mars (1985), 210
Invasion (1965), 95
Invasion of the Animal People (1958), 190
Invasion of the Body Snatchers (1955), 124, 135, 219
Invasion of the Body Snatchers (1978), 84, 107
Invasion of the Saucer Men (1957), 107
Invisible Agent (1942), 221

Invisible Dr. Mabuse, The (1961), 115
Invisible Ghost (1941), 190
Invisible Invaders (1958), 211
Invisible Man, The (1933), 52, 112, 211
Invisible Man Returns, The (1939), 132
Invisible Man's Revenge, The (1944), 211
Invisible Ray, The (1935), 155
Ipcress File, The (1964), 39
Iron Man (2007), 234
Island, The (1979), 213
Island of Dr. Moreau, The (1977), 46, 227
Island of Lost Souls (1932), 177
Island of Lost Women (1958), 54
Island of Terror (1965), 50, 95, 112, 113
Isle of the Dead (1944), 51
It! (1966), 158
It (1990), 206
It Came from Beneath the Sea (1954), 223
It Came from Outer Space (1953), 82
It Conquered the World (1956), 220
It's Alive (1973), 220
It's a Wonderful Life (1946), 188
It's Never Too Late to Mend (1937), 18, 29
It's Trad, Dad! (1961), 54, 84, 86
ITV Play of the Week (1955-1974), 112
Jack the Giant Killer (1960), 214
Jack the Ripper (1958), 41, 46, 49, 50
Jack the Ripper (1976), 141
Jack the Ripper (1988), 136, 197, 234
Jackanory (1965-1996), 236
Jaguar Lives! (1978), 176
Jamaica Inn (1938), 20
Jamboree (1957), 53
James and the Giant Peach (1995), 192, 246
Jane Eyre (1943), 196
Januskopf, Der (1920), 159
Jason and the Argonauts (1961), 39, 95, 151, 200, 234
Jaws (1974), 68, 118
Jekyll & Hyde (1989), 177, 212
Jesus of Nazareth (1975), 52, 201
Jinnah (1997), 235
Jocks (1984), 216
Journey to the Unknown (1968), 32, 38, 81, 93, 110, 133, 143, 147, 152, 155, 163
Journey's End (1929), 61
Jovencito Dracula, El (1975), 170
Jubilee (1977), 172, 176
Judex (1963), 52
Judge Dredd (1994), 173
Juke Box Jury (1959-1990), 54
Jules Verne's Rocket to the Moon (1967), 73
Juliet of the Spirits (1964), 52, 70
Julius Caesar (1969), 92, 110, 127
Juno and the Paycock (1929), 20
Just for Fun (1963), 84
Justine (1968), 52, 96, 134, 141
Katarsis (1963), 52, 70, 74-75, 76, 83
Keep, The (1982), 175, 220
Keeper, The (1975), 203
Kentucky Fried Movie, The (1977), 97
Kill, Baby…Kill! (1966), 71, 72, 73
Killer Barbys vs. Dracula (2002), 141
Kind Hearts and Coronets (1949), 32, 68, 137, 158
King and I, The (1955), 62, 66, 243
King Creole (1958), 208

King Kong (1932), 88, 213, 215, 220, 221
King Kong (1976), 197, 220, 227
King Lear (1983), 9
King of Kong Island (1968), 76
King of the Zombies (1941), 15
King Solomon's Mines (1985), 209
KISS Meets the Phantom of the Park (1978), 137
Kiss of Death (1947), 199
Kiss of the Vampire, The (1962), 33, 56, 80, 84, 87, 99, 101, 105
Kojak (1973-1978), 170
Kolchak: The Night Stalker (1974-1975), 137, 207
Kong: Skull Island (2015), 126
Konga (1960), 32, 48, 54
Krull (1983), 234
Kung Fu (1972-1975), 221
Kwaidan (1963), 85
Labyrinth (1985), 151, 175
Lady Chatterley's Lover (1981), 199
Lady Craved Excitement, The (1950), 99
Lady Frankenstein (1971), 70, 76, 84, 97
Lady from Shanghai, The (1946), 196, 197
Lady in a Cage (1963), 201
Lady Vanishes, The (1937), 19, 109, 149, 168
Lady Vanishes, The (1978), 68, 172, 202
Lair of the White Worm, The (1988), 187
Lake of Dracula (1971), 167
Land Before Time, The (1987), 206
Land That Time Forgot, The (1974), 159, 172, 180
Las Vegas Story, The (1951), 55
Laserblast (1977), 208
Last Action Hero (1993), 220
Last Don, The (1997), 213
Last Horror Film, The (1981), 82, 165
Last Judgement, The (1961), 52
Last Man on Earth, The (1963), 117
Last Mile, The (1958), 53
Last of the Summer Wine (1972-2010), 62, 146, 201
Last Page, The (1951), 48, 180
Last Performance, The (1927), 14
Last Tango in Paris (1971), 205
Last Temptation of Christ, The (1987), 71
Last Unicorn, The (1980), 250, 251
Latin Quarter (1945), 123
Laura (1944), 132
Lavender Hill Mob, The (1951), 67
Lawnmower Man, The (1991), 159
League of Gentlemen, The (1999-2002, 2017), 63, 65, 192, 235, 249
League of Gentlemen's Apocalypse, The (2004), 213
Leave Her to Heaven (1945), 132
Legacy, The (1978), 119
Legend (1984), 49, 50, 175, 214
Legend of Hammer Mummies (2013), 50
Legend of Hammer Vampires (2008), 78
Legend of Hell House, The (1972), 87, 117, 125, 190
Legend of the 7 Golden Vampires, The (1973), 31, 148, 149, 153, 168, 180, 194, 195, 242
Legend of the Werewolf (1974), 19, 91, 153, 172, 173, 202, 226
Lesbian Vampire Killers (2009), 168
Let Me In (2009), 250
Let's Kill Uncle (1966), 39, 95
Let's Make Love (1960), 219
Licence to Kill (1988), 164
Life and Death of Colonel Blimp, The (1942), 215
Life and Death of Peter Sellers, The (2003), 184
Life and Loves of a She-Devil, The (1986), 152

Lifeforce (1984), 136, 185, 210
Lifespan (1974), 141
Linda Hayden: An Angel for Satan (2003), 145
Lion in Winter, The (1967), 113
Lion, the Witch, & the Wardrobe, The (1988), 133
Lisa and the Devil (1972), 52, 73, 170
Lisztomania (1975), 164
Little Big Man (1969), 46
Little Girl Who Lives Down the Lane, The (1975), 181
Little Monsters (1988), 219
Little Shop of Horrors, The (1960), 84, 220
Little Shop of Horrors, The (1986), 242
Little Vampire, The (1985), 125
Live and Let Die (1972), 49, 90, 144, 197
Living Daylights, The (1986), 146
Living Dead, The (1932), 85
Lizard in a Woman's Skin (1970), 134, 170
Lobster Man from Mars (1988), 110
Lock Up Your Daughters (1951), 189-190
Lodger, The (1943), 45
Lolita (1960), 25, 208
Lonely Water (1973), 176
Long Good Friday, The (1979), 173
Long Hair of Death, The (1964), 70, 73, 75, 76, 124
Look Back in Anger (1958), 78
Looney Tunes (animation series, 1930-1969), 225, 226
Looney Tunes: Back in Action (2002), 221
Lord of Illusions (1994), 63
Lord of the Rings, The (1977), 92
Lord of the Rings, The (film series, 2000), 11, 14-15, 44, 88, 128, 189, 196, 220, 237, 248-249, 252
Lords of Salem, The (2011), 248
Lorelei's Grasp, The (1972), 73, 170
Lorna the Exorcist (1974), 138
Lost Boys, The (1986), 84
Lost Continent, The (1967), 45, 85, 118, 151, 174
Lost in Space (1965-1968), 81
Lost Weekend, The (1944), 43
Love at First Bite (1978), 154, 205
Love Boat, The (1977-1987), 188
Love Bug, The (1968), 55
Lust for a Vampire (1970), 55, 76, 133, 136, 147, 150, 159, 164, 168
M (1931), 69, 160
Macabre (1980), 73
Macbeth (1947), 196
MacGyver (1985-1992), 204
Mad Dog Morgan (1975), 215
Mad Love (1935), 63, 64, 106, 107, 221
Mad Magician, The (1953), 132
Mad Monster Party? (1966), 122, 247
Madame Sin (1971), 200
Madhouse (1973), 38, 82, 136, 146, 153
Madhouse (1980), 75
Magic Box, The (1951), 138
Magic Christian, The (1969), 138, 204, 215
Magician, The (1926), 116
Magnificent Ambersons, The (1941), 196
Magnificent Seven, The (1960), 90, 206
Mahler (1973), 164
Malpertuis (1971), 196, 206
Maltese Falcon, The (1941), 108
Man About the House (1973-1976; film: 1974), 152, 193
Man at the Top (1973), 57
Man Dies, A (1969), 127
Man from Planet X, The (1950), 16

Man from U.N.C.L.E., The (1964-1968), 66, 206
Man in Black, The (1949), 55, 68, 77, 80
Man in Grey, The (1943), 34
Man in Half Moon Street, The (1943), 44, 81
Man in the Iron Mask, The (1939), 23
Man in the White Suit, The (1951), 32
Man of a Thousand Faces (1956), 82
Man Who Changed His Mind, The (1936), 19, 31, 54, 109
Man Who Could Cheat Death, The (1958), 9, 43-47, 48, 49, 50, 67, 99, 196
Man Who Disappeared, The (1951), 20
Man Who Fell to Earth, The (1975), 213
Man Who Finally Died, The (1962), 93
Man Who Haunted Himself, The (1969), 192
Man Who Laughs, The (1927), 159
Man with the Golden Gun, The (1974), 10, 15, 62, 63, 65, 80, 168, 174, 184, 197, 199-200, 213, 219, 243, 252
Man Who Turned to Stone, The (1956), 169
Man with the Severed Head, The (1973), 170
Man with Two Brains, The (1982), 213
Man Without a Body, The (1957), 93
Mangler, The (1993), 141
Maniac (1962), 48, 69
Maniac (1979), 165
Maniac Cop 2 (1990), 234
Manimal (1983), 90
Manitou, The (1977), 69
Mansion of the Doomed (1975), 189, 208
Mantrap (1952), 79
Many Faces of Christopher Lee, The (1995), 94, 95, 100, 103, 104, 116, 120, 183
Many Faces of Sherlock Holmes, The (1985), 96, 189
Marat/Sade (1967), 93
Marathon Man (1975), 219
Maria Marten (1935), 15, 27
Mark of the Devil (1969), 140, 210
Mark of the Devil Part II (1972), 45, 210
Mark of the Vampire (1935), 29, 36, 212
Mark of the Wolfman, The (1968), 86
Marriage (1954), 52
Mars Attacks! (1996), 247
Martian Chronicles, The (1979), 155
Martians Go Home (1989), 218
Martin (1976), 52
Mary, Mary, Bloody Mary (1974), 211
Mary Poppins (1963), 55
Mary Shelley's Frankenstein (1993), 9, 191, 221, 227, 245
Mask of Fu Manchu, The (1932), 61, 94
Mask of Murder (1985), 216
Masks of Death, The (1984), 45, 149, 153, 179
Masque of the Red Death, The (1963), 39, 46, 93, 108, 109, 132, 223
Masque of the Red Death, The (1988), 141
Masque of the Red Death (1989), 110
Master of the World (1960), 132
Masters of the Universe (1986), 209
Matinee (1992), 218, 221
Matinee Theatre: "Dracula" (1956), 211
Matter of Life and Death, A (1945), 188
Maximum Overdrive (1985), 159
Maze, The (1953), 156
McCloud: "McCloud Meets Dracula" (1976), 82
Medium, The (1934), 123
Meet Me Tonight (1952), 47
Meet the Feebles (1989), 248
Men in Black (film series, 1996-2011), 220

Men of Sherwood Forest (1954), 31, 46
Menaces (1938), 63
Mephisto (1981), 121
Meteor (1977), 216
Metropolis (1926), 23
Michael Jackson's Thriller (1983), 220, 245
Midnight Girl, The (1925), 161
Midsomer Murders: "Death and the Divas" (2012), 146
Midsummer Night's Dream, A (1968), 110
Mill of the Stone Women (1960), 64
Million Eyes of Sumuru, The (1966), 97
Millionairess, The (1960), 60
Mind of Mr. Soames, The (1968), 206
Minder (1979-1994), 152
Minotaur, The (1960), 52
Minutes Past Midnight (2016), 125
Mio in the Land of Faraway (1986), 212, 214
Mirror and Markheim, The (1953), 17
Misery (1990), 100
Miss Marple (film series, 1961-1964), 98
Miss Peregrine's Home for Peculiar Children (2015), 248
Mission: Impossible (1966-1973), 197
Mist, The (2007), 192
Mr. Arkadin (1954), 31, 196
Mr. Holmes (2014), 44
Mr. Moto (film series, 1937-1938), 61, 221
Mr. Sardonicus (1961), 69, 223
Mr. Wong (film series, 1938-1940), 61, 221
Mr. Wu (1927), 61
Mrs. Amworth (1975), 166
Moby Dick Rehearsed (1955) [unfinished], 197
Mole People, The (1956), 82, 237
Monkey (1978-1979), 62, 92
Monsieur Hulot's Holiday (1951), 244
Monster Club, The (1980), 86, 93, 133, 136, 149, 155, 159, 176, 184, 197, 200
Monster Dog (1984), 97
Monster in the Closet (1983), 211
Monster of Highgate Ponds, The (1960), 98
Monster of Piedras Blancas, The (1958), 217
Monster on the Campus (1958), 82
Monster Squad, The (1986), 211
Monster That Challenged the World, The (1956), 37
Monsters (1988-1990), 241
Monte Carlo Story, The (1956), 52
Monty Python's Flying Circus (1969-1974), 136
Monty Python's Life of Brian (1978), 89
Moon Zero Two (1969), 38, 149, 198
Moonraker (1978), 86, 217
Morgan: A Suitable Case for Treatment (1965), 213
Morgenrot (1932), 123
Morons from Outer Space (1984), 105
Most Dangerous Game, The (1932), 44, 200
Mostro di Frankenstein, Il (1920), 51
Motel Hell (1980), 211
Mother Riley Meets the Vampire (1951), 16, 27, 30, 33, 41, 78
Moulin Rouge (1952), 17, 48, 57
Mountain of the Cannibal God, The (1978), 90
Mouse on the Moon, The (1962), 60
Mouse That Roared, The (1958), 60
Mummy, The (1932), 10, 38, 47, 49, 50, 223
Mummy, The (1959), 10, 13, 28, 45, 46, 48-51, 53, 57, 58, 64, 66, 79, 84, 88, 90, 95, 101, 102, 152, 192, 196, 209, 220, 223, 229, 233, 235
Mummy, The (1998), 234, 235

Mummy Lives, The (1992), 141
Mummy's Curse, The (1944), 47
Mummy's Ghost, The (1943), 47
Mummy's Hand, The (1940), 47
Mummy's Revenge, The (1973), 72, 140, 170
Mummy's Shroud, The (1966), 41, 51, 61, 148
Mummy's Tomb, The (1942), 47
Mumsy, Nanny, Sonny & Girly (1969), 86, 175
Munster, Go Home! (1966), 211
Munsters, The (1964-1966), 81, 82, 188, 208, 220
Murder! (1930), 19
Murder by Decree (1978), 43, 84
Murder Story (1988), 216
Murders in the Rue Morgue (1931), 17
Murders in the Rue Morgue (1970), 106, 133, 137, 140
Music Box, The (1932), 142
Mutations, The (1972), 176
My Best Friend is a Vampire (1986), 213
My Lovely Monster (1988), 204
My Stepmother Is an Alien (1988), 154
Myra Breckinridge (1969), 32
Mysterious Dr. Fu Manchu, The (1929), 94
Mysterious Island (1960), 72, 140
Mysterious Mr. Wong, The (1934), 61
Mystery and Imagination (1966-1970), 113, 119, 148, 192, 193, 200
Mystery of Dr. Fu Manchu, The (1923), 94
Mystery of the Mary Celeste, The (1935), 29, 77
Mystery of the Wax Museum (1932), 27, 75
Mystery on Monster Island (1980), 170
Naked as Nature Intended (1961), 122
Naked Edge, The (1960), 63, 67, 184
Naked Gun, The (film series, 1988-1993), 209
Naked Monster, The (2004), 223
Name of the Game is Kill!, The (1968), 69
Nanny, The (1965), 45, 67, 89, 92, 174
Napoleon (1951), 52
National Lampoon's European Vacation (1984), 214
Nazarin (1959), 90
Necromancy (1970), 196
Necromania (1971), 189
Necronomicon: Book of the Dead (1993), 213
Neighbors (1920), 142
Neither the Sea Nor the Sand (1971), 181
Nesting, The (1979), 211
NeverEnding Story, The (1983), 113, 115
Never Say Never Again (1982), 34, 68
Never Takes Sweets from a Stranger (1959), 33, 48, 85, 87, 148, 151
New Avengers, The (1976-1977), 183, 192, 213
New Chilling Tales (2010-), 113
New Magic (1983), 212, 214
Next Step Beyond, The (1978), 66
Nibelungen, Die (1922, 1966), 114
Nicholas and Alexandra (1971), 106, 169
Night Caller, The (1965), 146, 172, 185, 193
Night Claws (2012), 216
Night Digger, The (1970), 146
Night Evelyn Came Out of the Grave, The (1971), 134
Night Gallery (1969-1973), 66, 115, 196, 201, 207
Night Hair Child (1971), 177, 184
Night of the Big Heat (1967), 11, 109, 111, 112-114, 119, 148, 200, 226
Night of the Creeps (1986), 220
Night of the Demon (1956), 23, 33, 68, 116, 120, 201, 236
Night of the Demon (1979), 189
Night of the Eagle (1961), 53, 113, 117, 180, 242
Night of the Generals, The (1966), 121

Night of the Ghouls (1957), 223
Night of the Hunter, The (1954), 12, 68
Night of the Living Dead (1967), 115, 117, 132, 196
Night of the Werewolf, The (1980), 97, 170, 216
Night Owl (1992), 165
Night Stalker, The (1971), 54, 117, 167
Night Strangler, The (1972), 117
Night Terrors (1992), 134
Night to Remember, A (1958), 97, 149, 232
Night Visitor, The (1970), 64
Nightbreed (1989), 222
Nightcomers, The (1971), 164
Nightmare (1962), 69, 85
Nightmare Before Christmas, The (1991), 245
Nightmare Castle (1965), 115, 124, 140, 170
Nightmare Classics (1989), 214
Nightmare in the Sun (1963), 201
Nightmare on Elm Street, A (film series, 1984-2009), 10, 82, 189, 199, 204, 216, 222, 245, 246
Nights of Cabiria, The (1957), 84
Nights of Rasputin, The (1960), 39
Nightwing (1978), 213
Nil by Mouth (1996), 133
Nineteen Eighty-Four (1954), 15, 23, 41
1941 (1979), 209, 220, 228
1917 (1968), 153
99 Women (1968), 140
Ninth Gate, The (1998), 121, 140, 246
No Place to Hide (1981), 54
No Time to Die (2019), 147
Nobody Ordered Love (1972), 136, 193
Nocturna (1978), 205
North by Northwest (1958), 197
North Sea Hijack (1979), 129
Nosferatu (1921), 13, 25, 30, 35, 85, 114, 116, 139, 153, 159, 161, 171, 190, 195
Nosferatu the Vampyre (1978), 141, 150, 196, 205, 247
Not of this Earth (1956), 220
Not Only…But Also (1964-1970), 180
Nothing But the Night (1972), 12, 15, 124, 172, 178-181, 198
Notting Hill (1998), 55
Nowhere to Go (1958), 67
Nutcracker Fantasy (1979), 209
Nutty Professor, The (1962), 57
Oblong Box, The (1968), 108, 111, 123, 132-134, 135, 136, 173
Occult: Mysteries of the Supernatural, The (1977), 189, 190
Octaman (1971), 220
October Man, The (1947), 149
Octopussy (1982), 50, 87, 95
Odyssey, The (1996), 71, 92
Old Dark House, The (1932), 52, 75, 210, 212
Old Dark House, The (1962), 122
Oliver! (1967), 59, 157
Omegans, The (1967), 184
Omen, The (1975), 56, 65, 66, 107, 151, 181, 190, 202, 213
Omen III: The Final Conflict (1980), 46
Omen IV: The Awakening (1990), 234
On Her Majesty's Secret Service (1968), 80, 110, 152, 169, 192
On the Buses (film series, 1971-1973), 152, 165, 168, 185
Once Upon a Midnight Scary (1979), 245
Once Upon a Spy (1980), 100, 170, 228
100 Greatest Scary Moments, The (2003), 102
100 Years of Horror (1995), 47, 122, 204, 205, 220, 226-227, 229, 232, 244
One Million Years B.C. (1965), 89, 90, 129

One More Time (1969), 138, 188
One Night with You (1947), 15
One Plus One (1968), 116, 179
One Step Beyond (1959-1961), 66, 160
Only a Coffin (1966), 137
Only Fools and Horses (1981-2003), 180
Operation Thunderbolt (1976), 216
Order: Kill Makarios (1975), 173
Orderly, The (1961), 52, 70
Orders to Kill (1958), 57
Orlacs Hände (1924), 63
Orloff Against the Invisible Man (1970), 137
Orson Welles Great Mysteries (1973-1974), 165, 196-198
Ossessione (1943), 84
Othello (1951), 84
Other Cinderella, The (1976), 208
Other Side of Paradise, The (1953), 63
Our Town (1939), 69
Our World (1967), 166
Out of Africa (1985), 201
Out of the Unknown (1965-1971), 143
Outer Limits, The (1963-1965, 1995-2002), 65, 204, 206
Outside the Law (1920), 61
Overcoat, The (1952), 52
Paganini Horror (1988), 188
Pancho Villa (1971), 169
Panga (1989), 217
Pan's Labyrinth (2005), 250
Paradine Case, The (1947), 68
Paranoiac (1962), 59, 69, 85, 87, 91, 140
Patrick Macnee's Ghost Stories (1997), 110
Paul Temple Returns (1952), 25, 55
Peeping Tom (1959), 16, 45, 57, 80, 226
Pee-wee's Big Adventure (1984), 216, 245, 247
Pee-wee's Playhouse (1986-1990), 247
Peggy Sue Got Married (1985), 211
Pennies from Heaven (1977), 185
Penny and the Pownall Case (1947), 16, 17, 87, 180
Penny Dreadful (2013-2016), 147, 150, 248, 250
Penny Points to Paradise (1950), 136
Penthouse, The (1967), 109
People That Time Forgot, The (1977), 62, 98, 159
People Who Own the Dark, The (1973), 73, 97, 170
Percy (1970), 200
Percy's Progress (1974), 152, 200
Perfect Woman, The (1949), 32
Persecution (1973), 98, 147, 173
Perverse Countess, The (1973), 138
Perversion Stories (2002), 134, 135
Peter Cushing: A One-Way Ticket to Hollywood (1988), 173
Phantom of Death (1987), 176
Phantom of the Opera, The (1924), 27, 155, 158, 210, 219, 241
Phantom of the Opera (1943), 27, 227
Phantom of the Opera, The (1961), 19, 31, 32, 57, 62, 63, 80, 98, 113, 140, 151
Phantom of the Opera (1982), 197
Phantom of the Opera, The (1989), 141, 245
Phantom of the Opera, The (1998), 250
Phantom of the Opera, The (2003), 234
Phantom of the Paradise (1974), 214
Phantom of the Rue Morgue (1953), 27
Phase IV (1972), 164
Phenomena (1984), 176
Phobia (1979), 177
Piccadilly (1929), 63

Picture of Dorian Gray, The (1944), 27
Pieces (1982), 140
Pied Piper, The (1971), 153, 176, 180
Pillow Talk (1959), 219
Pink Panther, The (film series, 1963-1993), 62, 140, 158, 192
Piranha (1978), 124, 218, 220
Pirates of Blood River, The (1961), 11, 39, 41, 59, 72, 78, 99, 133, 152, 187
Pirates of the Caribbean (film series, 2002-), 235
Pit and the Pendulum (1961), 68, 73, 75, 114, 115, 117, 124, 132, 245
Pit and the Pendulum, The (1990), 59
Plague (1979), 206
Plague of the Zombies, The (1965), 41, 42, 62, 78, 98, 103, 146, 175
Plan 9 from Outer Space (1956), 189, 196
Planet of the Apes (1967), 221, 246
Planet of the Apes (1974), 216
Planet of the Apes (2001), 246
Planet of the Vampires (1965), 71, 135
Playgirls and the Vampire, The (1960), 52
Pleasant Terror: The Life and Ghosts of M.R. James, A (1995), 235
Point in Time, A (1973), 164
Police Academy (film series, 1983-1993), 83, 121, 212
Police Dog (1954), 19
Police Squad! (1982), 209
Poltergeist (1981), 221
Poltergeist III (1987), 177
Poltergeist: The Legacy (1996-1999), 177, 204, 206
Poor Devil (1972), 188, 190, 208
Pop Gear (1965), 90
Popeye (1980), 213
Porridge (1973-1977), 180, 201
Port Afrique (1955), 76
Premature Burial (1961), 46
Price of Vanity, The (1954), 18
Prick Up Your Ears (1986), 234
Pride and Prejudice and Zombies (2014), 248
Prince of Darkness (1987), 176
Prince of Terror (1972), 167
Princess Bride, The (1986), 173
Prisoner, The (1966-1967), 91, 113
Prisoner of Shark Island, The (1935), 211
Prisoner of Zenda, The (1978), 198
Private Life of Sherlock Holmes, The (1969), 39, 43-44, 137, 143, 152, 199
Private's Progress (1955), 20, 41
Project X (1967), 221
Projected Man, The (1965), 42, 122
Psych-Out (1967), 69
Psycho (1959), 11, 55, 63, 68, 69, 81, 102, 149, 174, 234
Psychomania (1971), 19, 169, 191
Psychopath, The (1965), 20, 87, 91, 92, 98, 136
Psychoville (2008-2010), 249
Pterodactyl Woman from Beverly Hills (1997), 215
Pumaman, The (1979), 176
Pumping Iron (1975), 71
Punch and Judy Man, The (1962), 96
Puppet Master (film series, 1989-), 208
Puppet Masters, The (1994), 84
Purple Playhouse: "Dracula" (1973), 195
Pyro (1963), 141
Q: The Winged Serpent (1981), 148
Quadrophenia (1978), 217
Quantum of Solace (2008), 147
Quatermass (1978), 88, 133
Quatermass and the Pit (1958), 15, 41, 61, 125, 171
Quatermass and the Pit (1967), 16, 78, 99, 107, 109, 149, 172, 174

Quatermass Experiment, The (1953), 15, 17, 172
Quatermass Xperiment, The (1954), 16, 17, 23-24, 27, 31, 39, 70, 102, 129, 171-172, 249
Quatermass II (1955), 15, 25
Quatermass 2 (1956), 16, 20, 31, 33, 70, 159, 163, 192
Queen Kong (1976), 146
Queen of Spades, The (1948), 16, 31
Queens of Evil (1970), 84
Quest for Love (1970), 191, 200
Questor Tapes, The (1973), 207, 208
Quincy M.E. (1976-1983), 188
Quo Vadis (1951), 108
R.U.R. (1948), 151
Race with the Devil (1975), 83, 121, 190, 202
Railway Children, The (1970), 89, 151
Rainbow, The (1988), 158
Rainbow Thief, The (1990), 210, 218, 221
Rambo (film series, 1981-2018), 219
Randall and Hopkirk (Deceased) (1968-1969), 19, 108, 113, 166
Rasputin (1995), 106
Rasputin and the Empress (1932), 104, 105
Rasputin, Dämon dur Frauen (1931), 104
Rasputin: The Mad Monk (1965), 10, 63, 80, 98, 104-106, 107, 111, 190, 196, 201, 219, 223, 228
Rat Man (1987), 234
Raven, The (1935), 133
Raven, The (1962), 46, 117, 132
Razorback (1983), 233
Re-Animator (1984), 126, 206, 208
Rebel, The (1960), 59
Red Dragon (2002), 67
Red Queen Kills Seven Times, The (1971), 216
Reflection of Fear, A (1971), 174
Reflections in a Golden Eye (1967), 84
Reptile, The (1965), 31, 33, 50, 62, 78, 98, 103, 105, 199
Repulsion (1964), 47, 92, 107, 122, 174, 183
Requiem for a Vampire (1971), 36
Reservoir Dogs (1991), 25
Resident, The (2009), 187, 249, 250
Resident Evil: Extinction (2006), 235
Return from Witch Mountain (1977), 10, 208
Return of Captain Invincible, The (1981), 215, 241, 243
Return of Chandu, The (1934), 85
Return of Count Yorga, The (1971), 167
Return of Dracula, The (1957), 29, 37, 56, 167, 210
Return of Dr. Fu Manchu, The (1930), 94
Return of Dr. Mabuse, The (1961), 73
Return of the Ape Man (1943), 211
Return of the Blind Dead (1973), 73
Return of the Fly (1959), 132
Return of the Living Dead, The (1984), 223
Return of the Musketeers, The (1988), 59, 97, 140, 146-147, 152
Return of the Vampire, The (1943), 167
Return to Glennascaul (1951), 196
Return to Oz (1984), 83, 191, 197, 201, 206
Revenge (1971), 129, 165, 191
Revenge in the House of Usher (1983), 138
Revenge of Billy the Kid, The (1991), 172
Revenge of Frankenstein, The (1958), 28, 35, 39, 42, 53, 80, 151
Revenge of the Blood Beast (1965), 83, 124
Revenge of the Creature (1954), 223
Revenge of the Dead (1982), 75
Revenge of the Zombies (1943), 211
Reverse the Polarity (1999), 155
Revolt of the Zombies (1936), 208

Revolution Française, La (1989), 197
Rich and Strange (1931), 19
Richard III (1954), 32, 61
Ring, The (2002), 220
Ring 2, The (2004), 234
Rising Damp (1974-1978; film: 1979), 201
Road to St. Tropez (1966), 32
Rock All Night (1956), 220
Rock Rock Rock! (1956), 53
Rocketship X-M (1950), 17
Rocky Horror Picture Show, The (1974), 26, 118, 119, 195, 213, 222, 243-244, 248
Rodan (1956), 221
Rojo sangre (2003), 82
Room at the Top (1958), 34, 57
Room to Let (1949), 55, 77, 151
Room with a View, A (1985), 179
Rosemary's Baby (1967), 12, 113, 115, 149, 201, 208
Royle Family, The (1998-2012), 249
Ruling Class, The (1971), 39
Run for the Sun (1955), 199
Safe Place, A (1970), 196
Saint, The (1962-1969), 19, 108, 129, 166
Salamander, The (1980), 216
Salem's Lot (1979), 208
Samson in King Solomon's Mines (1964), 70
Santa Sangre (1988), 221
Sapphire (1959), 89
Sapphire & Steele (1979-1982), 192
Saraband for Dead Lovers (1947), 16
Satanic Rites of Dracula, The (1972), 111, 155, 166, 167, 170, 192-195, 198, 222, 226
Satan's Mistress (1978), 184
Satan's Slave (1976), 125, 133, 202
Saturday Night and Sunday Morning (1960), 67, 176
Saturday Night Live (1975-), 44, 195, 228
Savage Messiah (1972), 164, 184
Saw (film series, 2003-2019), 12
Scanners (1979), 206
Scarecrow, The (1981), 211
Scared to Death (1946), 27, 29, 200
Scarlet Blade, The (1963), 78, 98
Scars of Dracula (1970), 49, 69, 90, 98, 103, 144, 149-154, 158, 160, 168, 172, 195, 201, 228
Scavenger Hunt (1979), 219
Scent of Mystery (1959), 180
Schalcken the Painter (1979), 119
Schizo (1976), 165, 209
Schizoid (1980), 141, 209
Schlock (1971), 220
Scooby-Doo (animation series, 1969-), 191, 222
Scorpion King 2: Rise of a Warrior, The (2007), 235
Scream (1996), 33
Scream 2 (1997), 213
Scream and Scream Again (1969), 17, 123, 135-137, 146, 152, 173, 190, 199, 209, 212
Scream of the Wolf (1973), 117
Scream Pretty Peggy (1973), 137
Scrooge (1951), 16, 32, 39, 110
Scrooge (1970), 39
Scrooged (1988), 247
Séance on a Wet Afternoon (1964), 93, 125, 197
Season of the Witch (2010), 97, 182, 187
Sebastian (1968), 199
Seconds (1966), 96

Secret Man, The (1958), 39
Secret of Blood Island, The (1964), 79, 89, 90, 92, 98
Secret of Dr. Mabuse, The (1963), 47
Secret of NIMH, The (1980), 211
Secret of the Red Orchid, The (1961), 109
Secrets of Sex (1969), 55
Sect, The (1990), 140
Seizure (1972), 174, 200
Sentinel, The (1976), 207
Sgt. Pepper's Lonely Hearts Club Band (1977), 176
Serial (1979), 208, 228
Serpent and the Rainbow, The (1987), 177
Servants of Twilight (1990), 55
Se7en (1995), 245
Seven Days to Noon (1949), 31, 41, 184
Seven Deaths in the Cat's Eye (1972), 45, 73, 75, 191
7 Faces of Dr. Lao (1963), 219
Seven Keys to Baldpate (1916, 1917, 1925, 1929, 1935, 1947), 210
Seven-Per-Cent Solution, The (1975), 119, 180
Seven Year Itch, The (1954), 43
Seventh Seal, The (1956), 56
Seventh Veil, The (1945), 34, 67, 68
Seventh Victim, The (1943), 51
7th Voyage of Sinbad, The (1957), 169
Sex and the City (1998-2004), 190
Shadow, The (1993), 235
Shadow of a Doubt (1942), 208
Shadow of the Cat, The (1960), 41, 53, 77, 79
Shadow of the Vampire (1999), 82, 187
Shadows (1922), 61
Shadows (1975-1978), 148
Shadows and Fog (1991), 176
Shaka Zulu (1985), 198
Shane (1952), 177
Shanks (1973), 196
Shape of Water, The (2016), 250
Shatter (1973), 45, 179
Shaun of the Dead (2003), 112, 249
She (1925), 88
She (1935), 88
She (1964), 37, 48, 79, 88-90, 99, 108, 110, 112, 129, 242
She (2001), 141
She Killed in Ecstasy (1970), 141
Sherlock (2009-2016), 63
Sherlock Holmes (film series, 1939-1946), 40, 97, 168
Sherlock Holmes (1954-1955), 96
Sherlock Holmes (1964-1965, 1968), 41, 66, 92, 95, 143
Sherlock Holmes (1984-1994), 119
Sherlock Holmes and the Deadly Necklace (1962), 39, 43, 72, 244
Sherlock Holmes in New York (1975), 110
Sherlock Holmes Returns (1993), 147
Sherlock Holmes: The Golden Years (1990), 39, 44, 110, 181
Shining, The (1979), 56, 90, 102, 213
Shirley Temple's Storybook (1958-1961), 213
Shivers (1974), 124
Shock (1945), 132
Shock (1977), 173
Shock Treatment (1980), 119
Shock Waves (1975), 211
Shuttered Room, The (1966), 122
Silence of the Lambs, The (1990), 67
Silencers, The (1965), 73
Silent Flute, The (1977), 209, 251
Silent Night, Bloody Night (1970), 211
Silent Running (1971), 214

Silent Scream (1979), 124
Silver Bullet (1984), 216
Simpsons, The (1989-), 247
Sinbad and the Eye of the Tiger (1975), 151, 197
Singer Not the Song, The (1960), 149
Singing Detective, The (1986), 180, 185
Sinister Dr. Orloff, The (1982), 137
Six-Five Special (1957-1958), 164
Skin Game, The (1930), 20
Skull, The (1965), 16, 68, 91-93, 108, 112, 124, 134, 160
Skyfall (2012), 147
Slaughter High (1985), 165
Slaughter Hotel (1971), 141
Slave Girls (1966), 80, 89, 119, 129
Sleepy Hollow (1999), 180, 235, 245-246, 248
Sleuth (1972), 183
Small Soldiers (1997), 221
Smell of Reeves and Mortimer, The (1993-1995), 113
Snake People (1968), 122
Snake Pit, The (1948), 108, 114
Snake Woman, The (1960), 45
Snorkel, The (1957), 20, 192
Snow White (1987), 110
Snow White and the Seven Dwarfs (1937), 83, 115, 212
So Long at the Fair (1949), 41, 48, 158, 200
Soft Beds, Hard Battles (1973), 152
Some Girls Do (1968), 73, 136, 192
Some Like It Hot (1958), 43
Some May Live (1966), 89, 123
Some Mothers Do 'Ave 'Em (1973-1978), 103
Something Wicked This Way Comes (1981), 240
Sometimes They Come Back (1990), 159
Somewhere in Time (1979), 197
Son of Dracula (1943), 16, 164, 167
Son of Dracula (1972), 86, 171, 172, 173, 192
Son of Dr. Jekyll, The (1951), 20
Son of Frankenstein (1938), 14, 75, 196, 226
Song for Tomorrow, A (1948), 16, 23
Song of Bernadette, The (1943), 132
Song Remains the Same, The (1973), 179
Sons and Lovers (1959), 85
Sorcerers, The (1967), 80, 83, 108, 122, 173
Sorrelina (1995), 73, 76
Sorrows of Satan, The (1926), 173
Sound of Horror (1965), 141, 184
South Pacific (1957), 160
Space Mutiny (1988), 216, 222
Space: 1999 (1974-1977), 133, 191, 196, 197-198
Spaced (1999-2000), 249
Spaceways (1952), 16, 17, 19, 112
Sparrows (1926), 88
Spartacus (1959), 60
Spasms (1981), 59
Specters (1986), 176
Spectre (2015), 147
Spiral Staircase, The (1945), 16
Spirits of the Dead (1967), 71
Spoils of Poynton, The (1969), 145
Spooks Run Wild (1941), 190, 200
Spy in Black, The (1938), 14
Spy Who Loved Me, The (1976), 61, 81, 129, 146, 165, 217
Squadron Leader X (1943), 64
Sssssss (1972), 216
Stage Fright (1949), 41, 164
Stagecoach (1938), 211

Stand by Me (1985), 84
Star Knight (1985), 97
Star Trek (1966-1969), 53, 66, 81, 117, 179, 188, 191, 198
Star Trek: The Next Generation (1987-1994), 118, 180, 188
Star Wars film series (1976-), 13, 31, 50, 60, 87, 107, 110, 166, 180, 198, 207, 209, 217, 226, 237, 249, 252
Starcrash (1978), 70, 165, 197
Starship Invasions (1976), 205-207
Steel Bayonet, The (1956), 108
Stingray (1964-1965), 166
Stolen Face (1951), 23, 41
Stone Tape, The (1972), 181
Story of Mankind, The (1956), 188
Storyteller, The (1986-1988), 214
Straight Story, The (1999), 173
Strait-Jacket (1963), 196
Strange and Deadly Occurrence, The (1974), 54
Strange Case of Dr. Jekyll and Miss Osbourne, The (1980), 93, 138
Strange Case of Dr. Jekyll and Mr. Hyde, The (1967), 138
Strange Case of Sherlock Holmes & Arthur Conan Doyle, The (2005), 236
Strange Invaders (1982), 234
Strange Possession of Mrs. Oliver, The (1977), 137
Strange World of Planet X, The (1957), 66
Stranger from Venus (1954), 39
Stranger on the Third Floor (1940), 108
Stranger Within, The (1974), 117
Strangler of the Swamp (1945), 15
Stranglers of Bombay, The (1959), 41, 49, 60, 61
Straw Dogs (1970), 123, 222
Strictly Supernatural (1996), 182, 186
Student of Prague, The (1926), 14, 173
Student of Prague, The (1935), 114
Study in Terror, A (1965), 38, 43, 109, 122, 180
Stupids, The (1995), 249
Subspecies (film series, 1990-1997), 121, 208
Suburban Commando (1990), 221
Succubus (1967), 140
Sugar Hill (1974), 83
Sundown: The Vampire in Retreat (1988), 211
Sunset Blvd. (1949), 43, 51
Super Scary Saturday (1987-1989), 220
Supergirl (1983), 93, 197
Superman (1977), 26, 138, 155, 206, 209, 217
Superman II (1977), 209, 217
Superman III (1982), 152, 184, 206
Superman IV: The Quest for Peace (1986), 219
Supernatural (1976-1977), 154, 180, 181, 191, 200
Supernatural (1980), 169
Supernatural (2005-), 204
Suspect (1959), 48
Suspense (1949-1954), 104
Suspiria (1976), 212
Svengali (1931), 105
Svengali (1954), 60, 65
Swamp Thing (1981), 209
Swarm, The (1977), 199
Sweeney, The (1974-1978), 152
Sweeney Todd (1935), 27
Sweeney Todd: The Demon Barber of Fleet Street (2007), 247
Sword of Sherwood Forest (1960), 54, 59, 80, 93, 97
Sword of the Valiant (1982), 158
Symptoms (1973), 48, 172
System, The (1963), 113
Tale of a Vampire (1991), 250
Tale of Two Cities, A (1957), 34, 172, 219, 252

Tale of Two Cities, A (1980), 25
Talent for Loving, A (1969), 199
Tales from the Crypt (1971), 31, 33, 56, 87, 93, 97, 145, 155, 156, 166, 172, 173, 191
Tales from the Crypt (1989-1996), 173, 235, 247
Tales from the Crypt: Demon Knight (1994), 221
Tales from the Darkside (1983-1988), 111, 198, 208
Tales of Frankenstein (1958), 42, 44-45, 65
Tales of Hans Andersen (1953), 17-18
Tales of Hoffmann, The (1950), 16
Tales of Terror (1961), 85, 117, 132
Tales of the Haunted: Evil Stalks this House (1981), 189, 190
Tales of the Unexpected (1979-1988), 137, 155, 160, 176, 197, 212
Tales of Tomorrow (1951-1953), 66
Tales That Witness Madness (1972), 86, 119, 173, 176, 180, 191
Talos the Mummy (1997), 121, 200, 214, 233-234
Tarantula (1955), 82
Targets (1967), 82, 122, 208
Tarzan and the She-Devil (1952), 115
Tarzan, the Ape Man (1959), 82
Tarzan the Magnificent (1960), 37, 56
Tarzan's Magic Fountain (1948), 115
Taste of Blood, A (1967), 106
Taste of Evil, A (1971), 54
Taste of Fear (1960), 68-69, 75, 153, 185
Taste of Honey, A (1961), 78
Taste the Blood of Dracula (1969), 32, 83, 86, 92, 94, 107, 128, 139, 142, 143-148, 149, 150, 167, 198, 209, 210
Teen Wolf (1984), 216
Teen Wolf (2011-2017), 235
Teen Wolf Too (1987), 220
Teenage Cave Man (1958), 206
Teenage Mutant Ninja Turtles (1989), 173, 221
Teenage Mutant Ninja Turtles II: The Secret of the Ooze (1990), 213
Tell-Tale Heart, The (1960), 20, 38
Ten Commandments, The (1955), 206
Ten Little Indians (1965), 62, 73, 108, 170, 197, 242
Tender Dracula (1974), 82, 195, 204
Tenebrae (1982), 212
Tenko (1981-1984), 193
Tenth Victim, The (1965), 90, 114, 208
Terminator, The (1984), 105, 221
Terminator 2: Judgement Day (1990), 219
Terrahawks (1983-1986), 212
Terrified (1962), 76
Terror, The (1962), 220
Terror (1978), 62
Terror-Creatures from the Grave (1965), 73, 124
Terror in the Haunted House (1958), 60
Terror in the Wax Museum (1972), 211
Terror of the Tongs, The (1960), 33, 62-64, 94, 149, 170
Terror Train (1979), 203
Terrornauts, The (1966), 87
TerrorVision (1985), 214
Tess (1978), 199
Testament of Dr. Mabuse, The (1932), 137
Texas Chainsaw Massacre, The (film series, 1973-), 102, 127, 210, 222
That Guy Dick Miller (2014), 221
That'll Be the Day (1972), 176
That's Your Funeral (1972), 20, 48
Theatre Macabre (1971), 160
Theatre of Blood (1972), 52, 87, 110, 111, 119, 137, 144, 146, 174, 180, 191
Theatre of Death (1965), 16, 87, 92, 106-107, 109, 134, 171, 209, 223, 244

Them! (1953), 27
They Came from Beyond Space (1966), 86, 93
They Dare Not Love (1940), 23
Thief of Bagdad, The (1940), 32, 209, 226
Thing, The (1981), 126
Thing from Another World, The (1951), 169, 201, 221
Thing That Couldn't Die, The (1958), 36
Things to Come (1935), 68
Third Man, The (1948), 94, 96
13 Demon Street (1959), 188
13 Ghosts (1960), 196
39 Steps, The (1958), 89
This Is Horror (1989), 115
This Is Spinal Tap (1983), 110, 243
This Is Your Life (1955-2003), 90, 129
This Island Earth (1954), 82
1,000 Eyes of Dr. Mabuse, The (1960), 137
Three Cases of Murder (1953), 196
Three Musketeers, The (1948), 211
Three Musketeers, The (1973), 10, 39, 59, 146, 170, 196, 197, 199, 201, 211, 216, 219
3-2-1 (1978-1988), 165
3 Women (1976), 213
3 Worlds of Gulliver, The (1959), 33, 64, 169
Thriller (1960-1962), 66, 68, 81, 90, 188, 206
Thriller (1973-1976), 111, 180, 197, 222
Thunderball (1965), 15, 53, 62
Thunderbirds (1964-1966), 98, 128, 150
THX 1138 (1969), 176
Time After Time (1978), 213
Time Bandits (1980), 213
Time Machine, The (1959), 216
Time Travelers, The (1963), 227
Time Without Pity (1956), 68
Tingler, The (1959), 132, 218
To the Devil a Daughter (1975), 80, 103, 109, 120, 140, 154, 181, 198-202, 207, 235, 250
To the Devil...The Death of Hammer (2002), 199, 200
Tom and Jerry: The Movie (1992), 214
Tom Jones (1962), 184
Tom Thumb (1957), 56
Tomb, The (1985), 216
Tomb of Ligeia, The (1964), 62, 132, 248
Tomb of the Werewolf (2003), 86
Tombs of the Blind Dead (1971), 169
Tommy (1974), 164
Tomorrow Never Dies (1997), 234
Tomorrow People, The: "The Rameses Connection" (1994), 223
Too Hot to Handle (1959), 52, 109
Top Secret! (1982), 125
Topaz (1969), 115
Topo, El (1969), 221
Torso (1972), 109
Torture Garden (1966), 92, 124, 130, 171, 173
Toto in the Moon (1958), 70
Toto, Peppino e i fuorilegge (1956), 76
Touch of the Sun, A (1978), 25
Touchables, The (1968), 136
Tourist Trap (1978), 208
Tower of Evil (1971), 53, 56, 93, 200
Tower of London (1939), 93, 132, 137
Tower of London (1962), 122
Trailers from Hell (2007-), 177
Trainspotting (1995), 234
Traitor, The (1956), 20, 45, 65, 96

Trancers (film series, 1984-2002), 208
Transylvania Twist (1989), 206
Trauma (1992), 248
Treasure Island (1949), 68
Treasure Island (1972), 140
Treasure Island (1989), 59, 147, 216
Treasure of San Teresa, The (1959), 58, 94
Tremors 2: Aftershocks (1994), 206
Trial, The (1962), 91, 196
Trilogy of Terror (1975), 117
Trilogy of Terror II (1996), 234
Trip, The (1967), 69, 91
Tripods, The (1984-1985), 111
Tristana (1969), 170
Trog (1969), 42, 56, 98, 125, 148, 155, 167
Troll (1985), 208
Trollenberg Terror, The (1957), 29, 86, 140
Tron (1981), 213
Trottie True (1948), 37
Tudor Rose (1936), 21, 31, 119
Tusk (2013), 246
28 Days Later (2001), 49
20,000 Leagues Under the Sea (1954), 118
Twice-Told Tales (1962), 85
Twilight film series (2008-2011), 161
Twilight Zone, The (1959-1964, 1985-1989), 46, 65, 66, 81, 82, 110, 117, 169, 237
Twilight Zone: The Movie (1982), 218, 220
Twins of Evil (1971), 49, 76, 133, 164, 168, 179, 180, 199, 208
Twisted Nerve (1968), 184
Two Faces of Dr. Jekyll, The (1959), 33, 45, 48, 58-61, 64, 80, 99, 108
200 Motels (1971), 214
Two of a Kind (1983), 59
2001: A Space Odyssey (1967), 150, 184, 214
Two Way Stretch (1959), 56, 89
Two Weeks in Another Town (1962), 53
UFO (1969-1970), 197
UFO's Are Real (1979), 206
Ugly Duckling, The (1959), 56, 57, 60
Ulysses (1954), 75
Ultraviolet (1998), 235
Umbracle (1970), 138, 142
Uncanny, The (1976), 82, 155, 190, 241
Uncle Silas (1947), 76
Uncle Was a Vampire (1959), 50, 52-53, 70, 74, 83, 204, 216
Unconquered (1947), 115
Undead, The (1956), 220
Under Milk Wood (1971), 185
Under Secret Orders (1937), 63
Underworld (1985), 184, 200
Unearthly, The (1956), 82
Unearthly Stranger (1963), 66
Unholy Three, The (1930), 244
Universal Horror (1998), 153
Unknown, The (1927), 109
Unnamable Returns, The (1992), 213
Unseen, The (1980), 107
Up the Creek (1957), 80
V (1982-1985), 216
Valdemar Legacy, The (film series, 2008), 170
Valentino (1976), 136, 184-185
Vamp (1986), 221
Vampira (1973), 129, 146, 195
Vampira Show, The (1954-1955), 15, 81
Vampiras, Las (1967), 211

Vampire, The (1956), 37
Vampire and the Ballerina, The (1959), 72, 74
Vampire Bat, The (1932), 222
Vampire Circus (1971), 38, 53, 98, 109, 115, 136, 147, 168, 179
Vampire Happening, The (1970), 129, 150, 204
Vampire Hookers (1978), 211
Vampire in Venice (1986), 141, 176
Vampire Lovers, The (1970), 58, 76, 95, 133, 144, 149, 166, 167,168, 184, 195, 215, 242
Vampire of the Opera, The (1961), 72
Vampires (1978), 103
Vampire's Kiss (1987), 187
Vampires' Night Orgy, The (1972), 140, 170
Vampiri, I (1956), 51, 70
Vampyr (1930), 76, 85, 90
Vampyres (1974), 89
Vampyros Lesbos (1970), 141
Van Helsing (2003), 9
Varan the Unbelievable (1958), 82
Vault of Horror, The (1972), 56, 58, 149, 200
Veil, The (1958), 18, 110, 191, 222
Velvet Goldmine (1997), 185
Velvet Vampire, The (1970), 97
Venetian Affair, The (1966), 206
Vengeance (1962), 85
Vengeance of Dr. Mabuse, The (1971), 140
Vengeance of Fu Manchu, The (1966), 50, 62, 91, 93, 97, 109, 223
Vengeance of She, The (1967), 89, 119, 129
Vengeance of the Zombies (1972), 188
Venom (1970), 199
Venom (1980), 141
Venus in Furs (1968), 141
Vertigo (1957), 36
Victor Frankenstein (a.k.a. *Terror of Frankenstein*, 1975), 160
Vida sigue igual, La (1969), 169
Videodrome (1981), 220
View to a Kill, A (1984), 71, 87, 110
Viking Queen, The (1966), 38, 89, 90, 99, 113, 119, 151
Village of the Damned (1959), 38, 79, 95, 151, 192
Vincent (1982), 245
Violent Playground (1957), 25, 94
Virdiana (1961), 142
Virgin Among the Living Dead, A (1971), 141
Virgin of Nuremberg, The (1963), 63, 64, 75-77, 83
Virgin Witch (1970), 171
Visa to Canton (1960), 60, 89
Voodoo Island (1956), 188
Voodoo Man (1943), 211
Vulture, The (1966), 19, 132
Wait Until Dark (1967), 15
Wake Wood (2008), 249
Walhalla (1986), 214, 250
Walking Dead, The (2010-), 249
Wallace & Gromit (animation series, 1989-), 146
War of the Planets (1965), 75
War of the Planets (1977), 89
War of the Satellites (1957), 220
War of the Worlds, The (1952), 27, 112
Warlords of Atlantis (1977), 136, 166, 172, 179
Watch It, Sailor! (1961), 56
Watcher in the Woods, The (1979), 87
Water Babies, The (1976), 89
Water Margin, The (1976-1978), 62
Wax (2014), 140
Waxwork (1988), 110, 134, 213, 219

Waxwork II: Lost in Time (1991), 110, 219
Waxworks (1923), 14
We Dive at Dawn (1942), 64
Web of the Spider (1970), 75
Weekend with Lulu, A (1960), 136
Weird Science (1984), 247
Welcome to Arrow Beach (1973), 57
Welcome to Blood City (1976), 181
Werewolf (1987-1988), 220
Werewolf and the Yeti, The (1975), 170
Werewolf in a Girls' Dormitory (1961), 39, 72, 73
Werewolf of London (1935), 94
Werewolf Shadow (1970), 170
West of Shanghai (1937), 61
West Side Story (1960), 63
Westworld (1973), 227
Whales of August, The (1986), 212
What a Carve Up! (1961), 54, 65, 151
What a Crazy World (1963), 25
What Became of Jack and Jill? (1971), 32, 158, 173
What's New, Pussycat? (1965), 90
When a Stranger Calls (1978), 33
When Dinosaurs Ruled the Earth (1968), 20, 55, 113, 150, 180, 220
Where Eagles Dare (1968), 45, 184, 215
Whicker's World: "I Don't Like My Monsters to Have Oedipus Complexes" (1968), 122, 124
While the City Sleeps (1955), 137
Whip and the Body, The (1963), 19, 53, 72-73, 74, 76, 83, 91, 196
Whisky Galore! (1948), 55
Whisperer in Darkness, The (2011), 126
Whispering Death (1975), 96, 216
Whistle and I'll Come to You (1968), 164, 236
White Nights (1957), 138
White Zombie (1932), 85, 155
Who Can Kill a Child? (1975), 181
Who Framed Roger Rabbit (1987), 250
Whoever Slew Auntie Roo? (1971), 155
Wicked Lady, The (1945), 34
Wicker Man, The (1972), 10, 89, 102, 113, 124, 155, 179, 181-187, 198, 209, 217, 219, 222, 237, 249
Wicker Man, The (2005), 187
Wicker Man Enigma, The (2001), 182, 183, 185
Wicker Tree, The (2009), 182, 187, 191
Wild at Heart (1989), 192
Wild Bunch, The (1968), 25
Wild Geese, The (1977), 177
Wild, Wild Planet (1965), 75
Willard (2002), 247
Willow (1987), 191
Willy Wonka & the Chocolate Factory (1970), 39, 146, 246
Wilson (1944), 20
Win a Mink (1959), 45
Wings of Danger (1951), 184
Winslow Boy, The (1958), 148
Wish You Were Here (1986), 153
Witch Academy (1991), 206
Witchcraft (1964), 105
Witchcraft (1992), 181
Witches, The (1966), 45, 79, 119, 172, 183
Witches, The (1989), 172
Witchfinder General (1967), 83, 92, 115, 122, 123, 132, 133, 136, 137, 151, 172, 210
Withnail & I (1986), 157
Wizard of Mars, The (1964), 211
Wizard of Oz, The (1939), 11, 219

Wolf (1993), 220
Wolf Man, The (1941), 10, 43, 66, 220, 223
Wolfen (1980), 189, 216
Wolfman, The (2008), 247
Wolfman Chronicles (1991), 223
Woman for Joe, The (1954), 60, 184
Woman in Black, The (2010), 249
Womaneater (1957), 19, 93
Wombles, The (1973-1975), 89
Women in Love (1968), 59, 119, 177
Women in War (1940), 23
Wonder Woman (1975-1979), 137
Wonderful World of the Brothers Grimm, The (1961), 214
Wonderwall (1967), 191
World is Not Enough, The (1999), 39, 166
World of Hammer, The (1990), 59
Worst Witch, The (1986), 110, 133
Worzel Gummidge (1979-1981), 33, 55
Wrong Arm of the Law, The (1962), 89
Wrong Box, The (1965), 41
Wuthering Heights (1967), 143
Wuthering Heights (1970), 133, 146
X Files, The (1993-), 204
X-Men (1999), 44
X: The Man with the X-Ray Eyes (1963), 220
X the Unknown (1956), 21, 23, 25, 27, 55, 67, 113, 208
Xtro (1982), 241
Yellow Submarine (1968), 179
Yes, Minister/Yes, Prime Minister (1980-1988), 119
Yesterday's Enemy (1959), 46, 62, 184
Yield to the Night (1955), 180
Yor, the Hunter from the Future (1983), 216
You Asked for It (1950-1959), 226
You Only Live Twice (1966), 20, 62, 65, 68, 95, 115, 184, 242
Young and Innocent (1937), 20, 159
Young Frankenstein (1974), 76
Young Ones, The (1961), 95
Young Sherlock Holmes (1985), 147, 192, 197
Young Winston (1971), 197
Your Hidden Master (1940), 23
Your Life Will Never End (1982), 250
Z.P.G. (1971), 184
Zeta One (1969), 136
Zombie Creeping Flesh (1980), 170
Zombie Flesh Eaters (1979), 158
Zombie Holocaust (1979), 158
Zombie Lake (1980), 138
Zombie 3 (1987), 75, 234
Zombies of Mora Tau (1956), 169
Zulu (1963), 39

To see all
Midnight Marquee Press titles
visit our website at
http://www.midmar.com

Midnight Marquee Press, Inc.
9721 Britinay Lane
Baltimore, MD 21234
410-665-1198
mmarquee@aol.com

www.ingramcontent.com/pod-product-compliance
Lightning Source LLC
Chambersburg PA
CBHW081354070526
44583CB00020B/2548